18th International Conference on Cognition and Exploratory Learning in Digital Age (CELDA 2021)

Online
13-15 October 2021

Editors:

Demetrios G. Sampson
Dirk Ifenthaler
Pedro Isaías

ISBN: 978-1-7138-3939-2

Printed from e-media with permission by:

Curran Associates, Inc.
57 Morehouse Lane
Red Hook, NY 12571

Some format issues inherent in the e-media version may also appear in this print version.

Printed with permission by Curran Associates, Inc. (2022)

For permission requests, please contact International Association for Development of the Information Society (IADIS) at the address below.

International Association for Development of the Information Society (IADIS)
Rua Sao Sebastiao Da Pedreira
No. 100, 30, 1050-209
Lisbon, Portugal

Phone: 351 21 3151373
Fax: 351 21 3151244

secretariat@iadis.org

Additional copies of this publication are available from:

Curran Associates, Inc.
57 Morehouse Lane
Red Hook, NY 12571 USA
Phone: 845-758-0400
Fax: 845-758-2633
Email: curran@proceedings.com
Web: www.proceedings.com

TABLE OF CONTENTS

18th International Conference on Cognition and Exploratory Learning in Digital Age (CELDA 2021)

13-15 October 2021

Virtual Meeting

POSTSYNAPTIC SIMULATOR: AN OPEN-SOURCE VISUAL INTERACTIVE SIMULATION FOR TEACHING ACTION POTENTIALS

Alexander Salgo[1], Galen O'Shea[2], Kim Hellemans[3, 4] and Jim Davies[2, 4]
[1]Queen's University, School of Computing, Canada
[2]Carleton University, Dept. of Cognitive Science, Canada
[3]Carleton University, Dept. of Neuroscience, Canada
[4]Dr.

ABSTRACT

We introduce an open-source game-like educational software that teaches users about how action potentials work. The Postsynaptic Simulator requires users to demonstrate understanding of neural mechanisms to progress through levels, each of which teaches a different aspect of neuron activity.

KEYWORDS

Edutainment, Education, Neuroscience, Serious Games, Action Potentials

1. INTRODUCTION

Neuroscience undergraduates have a relatively hard time understanding the chain of events leading up to neuron firing, known in neuroscience as an "action potential." In introductory textbooks, the role that post-synaptic potentials play in causing an action potential is often unclear. For example, a 2011 textbook reads: "A neuron with thousands of inputs responds no differently from one with only a few inputs. It democratically sums up all inputs that are close together in time and space. The cell-body membrane, therefore, always indicates the summed influences of multiple inputs" (Kolb & Whishaw, 2011). While descriptions like this are technically correct, they paint a misleading picture of the cell membrane as a homogenously charged surface that sums inputs instantly.

Explanations like these miss out on much of the detail and complexity involved with the process of action potential generation. The rate at which a neuron fires depends on the integration of thousands of inhibitory and excitatory post-synaptic potentials, as well as the shape and electrophysiology of the neuron receiving these potentials (Etherington et al., 2001). People commonly, but mistakenly, believe that any activation at dendrites contributes to charge at the axon hillock, which is the part just before the axon—the charge at this point determines whether the neuron will fire or not. But in truth, the activation has to exceed the decay rate, or the signal will vanish before it reaches the hillock. While a linear explanation of this process is easy for students to digest, it can also cause them to form an incorrect mental model of how electrochemical charge is transferred across the surface of a neuron. Misleading mental models make it difficult for students to learn more complex concepts such as temporal summation, spatial summation, inhibitory post-synaptic potentials, and how individual neurons integrate information.

The mental models that exclude these crucial details are reinforced by current methods of teaching neuroanatomy and electrophysiology. At present, most educators use static diagrams (either from textbooks or drawn manually) when teaching these topics. While diagrams are useful, they fail to capture the dynamic nature of electrophysiology and potentially contribute to misunderstandings. An example of such a diagram is the extremely popular action potential voltage graph, a representation of which is shown in Figure 1: the sharp and near-instantaneous changes in voltage suggest that the action potential is caused by a single large post-synaptic potential. The "failed initiations" shown in the diagram add to this misconception.

Many educators attempt to supplement this with animated videos that show the process unfolding (Korey, 2009). The nature of video-based education is also limiting, however, and most videos present the same type of linear sequence that the diagrams do.

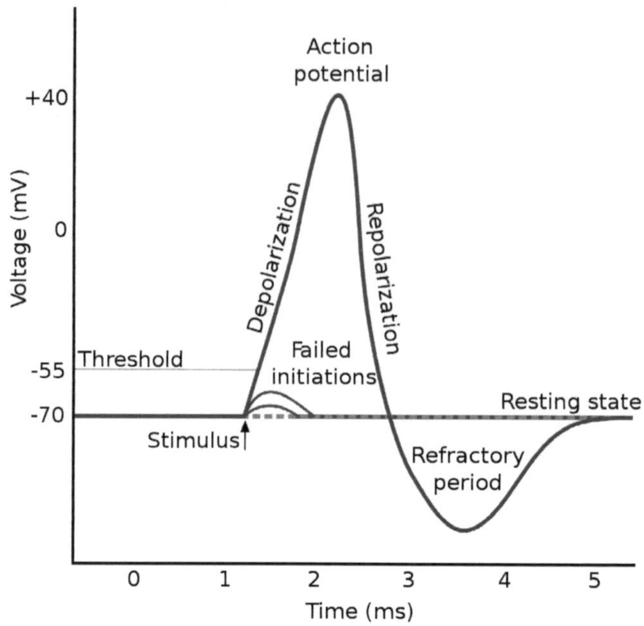

Figure 1. An example commonly used diagram that teaches students about action potentials (tiZom, 2007)

Neither diagrams nor videos allow students to experiment with neural activity in an interactive way. Interactive simulations have been a popular tool for teaching both basic and advanced physics for years (Wieman, Perkins, & Adams, 2008), and have been shown to aid education in other fields. These simulations are often game-like, with students being given goals to accomplish in order to complete pre-designed scenarios. Stieff and Wilensky (2003) showed that students who used interactive simulations demonstrated a better ability to reason about chemistry problems and relied less on memorized answers. This is indicative of the type of deep understanding that is needed when learning about complex dynamic processes.

It is likely that analogous methods could be employed in neuroscience courses to achieve a similar level of understanding of neural function. In this paper we describe such an interactive learning system for teaching students about how action potentials work.

1.1 Goals of the System

The goal of this paper is to present a new interactive simulation program, the Postsynaptic Simulator, that harnesses the benefits of interactivity in a way that has yet to be done in neuroscience. While educational neuroscientific simulations exist (as will be discussed below), they tend to lack some of the core features that make simulation such a useful tool for teaching. The core goals of this new program are as follows:

1. Provide a game-like interactive environment to motivate students to use it (i.e., make it fun).
2. To teach students about basic neuroanatomy, temporal and spatial summation of post-synaptic potentials, and the sequence of events leading up to an action potential in a neuron.
3. To provide an easy-to-customize, open-source framework upon which educators can build additional exercises, with significantly less programming experience than existing programs would require.

The third goal of this program is perhaps its most unique aspect. This program is designed such that additional levels, complete with customized goals and layouts, can be added using an entry-level programming language. This should also allow for the addition of features that are not present in the base program. The open-source nature of this program will also allow educators to share their levels and add-ons with others, meaning that they can access new supplementary material without having to buy new software.

The way in which these goals will be met is discussed in the section titled *Postsynaptic Simulator*. First, an overview of some existing programs will help demonstrate why this program is a useful addition to existing computer-based educational tools.

1.2 Existing Simulations in Neuroscience Education

This section is an overview (and evaluation) of three simulation programs currently used by educators.

g-PRIME (Lott et al., 2009) is a software tool designed to allow for investigation of various aspects of neurophysiology. It is a multi-purpose program, in that it facilitates both simulation and real data-acquisition. This flexibility makes it useful in lab settings, but the extra functionality is not as useful for early-year undergraduates (who are unlikely to be performing experiments using live neurons). It does not appear to be particularly designed to help teach students how neurons work, but rather how to analyze physiological data.

In terms of simulation, g-PRIME does not directly simulate readings from instruments. Instead, because it allows for both real-time and offline data analysis, educators are able to provide a data file that students can view and analyze using the program. This allows them to perform analyses on data as though they had gathered it themselves. The visual outputs of the program are a series of graphs which correspond to the readings taken. This is useful for teaching students about the types of readings they will encounter in a lab setting but does little to provide an in-depth understanding of why it is that the readings occur.

Because the interface allows for real data analysis, it has a level of complexity that is greater than a program designed purely for increasing conceptual knowledge. This is not a weakness of the program but it makes it difficult to teach new concepts with it. Instead, this program is ideal for students who are already familiar with the basic concepts of neuroanatomy and physiology.

A benefit of this program is that it allows for some customization. By giving students different data to analyze, educators can teach students about diverse neurophysiological phenomena. Unfortunately, this is limited to the those that are easily detected by lab instruments, so fundamental aspects of neuroanatomy are beyond the scope of the program.

Meta-Neuron (Newman & Newman, 2013) is a simulation designed specifically for educational purposes, and comes with six built-in exercises. These exercises cover similar topics to our program, with simulations that teach students about resting membrane and action potentials. Rather than analysing existing data for a lab exercise (as would g-PRIME), Meta-Neuron generates simulated readings.

Simulating readings allows students to view the responses that they would see if they were stimulating a neuron themselves. The visual outputs of Meta-Neuron are similar to those in g-PRIME, presented in graph-form, with aspects of the process (such as ion levels) presented as an updating line on the graph. While this is useful for students who already understand what is occurring at a molecular level, it does not help students understand the fundamental nature of the electrochemical changes that lead to action potentials.

The simulation environment is also complex. Students interact with the simulation by manipulating parameters that adjust variables involved in the process. This is a complex process for new users and does not intuitively aid students in figuring out the best course of action to achieve their goal.

In terms of customizability, Meta-Neuron is not designed for custom exercises. While educators can give different instructions to students in order to achieve different results, students will always be working with the same interface and the same built-in exercises.

NeuroLab (Schettino, 2014) is designed to teach a variety of neurophysiological concepts to students. It does so in a way that is more conducive to a deep understanding of the phenomena involved. NeuroLab is a set of differently designed simulations. Each of these simulations is short and designed to teach a particular concept such as the temporal integration of inputs or principles of axonal guidance. Simulations are visually straightforward and allow students to explore the physical processes behind neuronal activity.

Because of the short nature of the exercises, the interface is not overly complicated. Unfortunately, interaction often takes the form of parameter adjustment. This limits users' direct involvement in the on-screen visual simulation. Although this does not stop it from being a useful tool, this is a key aspect that could be improved upon to increase student comprehension.

Neuro-lab is quite flexible: The open-ended nature of simulations allows professors to design their own goals for the students to achieve. Unfortunately, these cannot be built into the program, and as such there are limitations on the complexity of goals that can be assigned. It also may make it difficult for a student to know when they have achieved a desired outcome.

2. POSTSYNAPTIC SIMULATOR: SYSTEM DESCRIPTION

Core Functionality: The Postsynaptic Simulator is currently available, free, in the iOS store (for iPhones and iPads). The game is designed to simulate the complex intracellular electrochemical activity that leads to an action potential. It allows students to control the inputs a neuron receives in a more realistic way than those provided by other simulations to date. Rather than showing students graphs representing the ion gradients or electric charge levels at the axon hillock, the Postsynaptic Simulator allows students to see how post-synaptic potentials progress from the synapse to create a graded potential across the membrane.

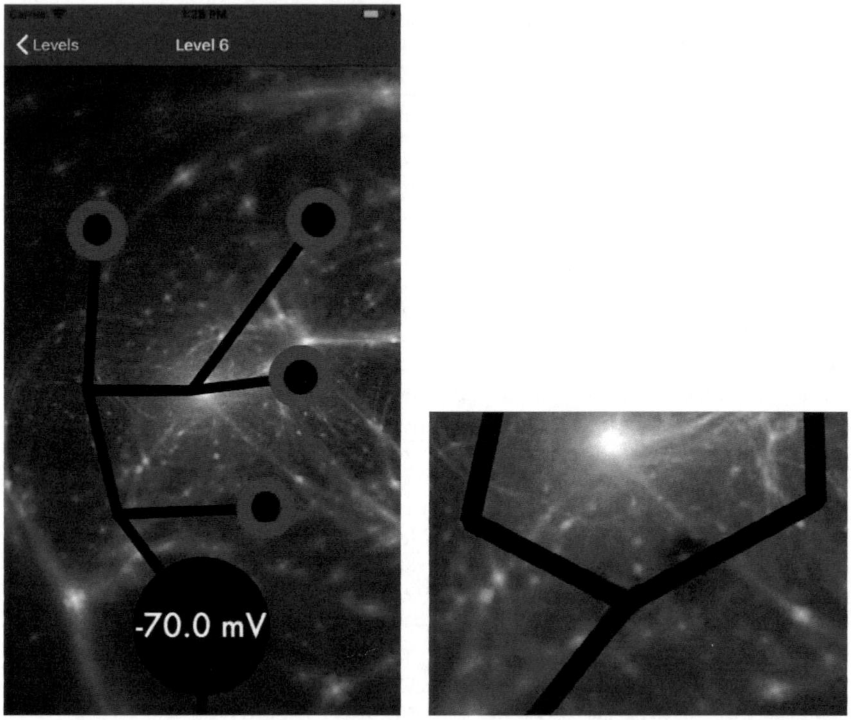

Figure 2. Left: Screenshot of a basic level layout, with dendritic branches (black lines), four synapses (excitatory shown as blue circles and inhibitory shown as red circles), a cell body (black circle with a voltage meter measure in millivolts), and an axon hillock (stemming from the bottom of the cell body). Right: Excitattory and Inhibitory graded potentials that travel toward the hillock (blue and red, respectively)

The graded potential that this program simulates demonstrates the basic principles of electrochemistry in a neuron. It propagates along the cell membrane (that is, the outside of the neuron), degrading with both time and distance; critically, the interface allows for a student to observe how the activation of a synapse causes a degrading wave of electrical activity. This allows students to see why temporal and spatial summation are required for charge to accumulate at the axon hillock.

Charge gradients within the cell are represented by the colour of cell walls. Red represents more positive charge, blue represents more negative charge, and black represents resting-state charge levels. These colours were chosen because they align with popular depictions of charge. More intense colours (further from black) as well as increased size are used to show the accumulation of charge, which further reinforces the "summation" aspect of neuronal activity.

Interface: The interface of the program has an abstract design, as shown in Figure 2. Students will be able to select a level from the level menu. From there it will take them to the Objective screen, which explains how they can beat the level. Once they press "continue" the game will begin. At any point they can go back to the level menu by clicking the "Levels" button on the top left of the screen. Levels are designed individually in a Level Builder. Each level can have a different layout, different goals, and specific features to design a wide range of levels.

Users interact with levels by touching synapses on the iOS device's touch screen. The synapses are colour coded to whether they are excitatory or inhibitory and are located on dendrites or the cell body (as in the case with real neurons; although a synapse can occur anywhere on the cell membrane, we opted for the two more common regions). A level is won by touching the right combination of synapses at the right times to cause the neuron to fire. Each level is designed like a puzzle, and solving each puzzle teaches something about neuronal activity. That is, they need to understand a concept to be able to progress past the level.

Level Layout: Each level contains one or more neurons, represented by abstract neuron diagrams. These diagrams depict the cell body (as a black circle), one or more dendrites (represented by lines), and an axon (another line extending downwards from the cell body). These diagrams also depict synapses, which are the primary points of interaction that users have with the simulation. Synapses are represented as circles with black central dots. Neuron layouts are customized for each level. Different levels can have different numbers of dendrites located at different points on the cell and can have branches connected in any arrangement.

Levels have "victory conditions." The victory conditions for a level dictate when a student has accomplished the goals of that particular level. These can be simple (e.g., "cause an action potential" or "block an action potential") or they can be extremely complex (e.g., "cause three action potentials in a row without clicking on the same synapse twice.")

Simulation: The simulation of intracellular electrical activity is the core function of this program. The algorithms behind the simulation are designed to strike a balance between realism and clarity. For example, exact simulations of voltage levels are not used, as they would greatly increase the complexity and computational requirements of the program without adding additional clarity. Rough estimates generate depictions on screen similar enough to reality to teach the intended concepts.

Synapses are represented by blue or red circles, identifying excitatory or inhibitory graded potentials, respectively. Dendrites are represented by black paths which extend from the synapses to the cell body. Synapses can be pressed to simulate activation, thereby changing the local membrane potential on the dendrite or cell body. These electrochemical signals (graded potentials) travel along the cell membrane.

The graded potential is represented by red and blue particles that travel from the synapses down through the dendrite. These particles help visualize the nature of graded potentials as they propagate along the cell walls. The charge gradients are represented by the colour blue to signify positive charge from excitatory graded potentials and the colour red to represent negative charge from inhibitory graded potentials.

To help visualize presynaptic spatial summation, each graded potential's size is directly proportional to its strength, with larger glows representing more accumulated charge. There is also a non-linear function, known as synaptic coincidence detection, added into the spatial summation equation. This acts as a multiplier as more charge accumulates. That is, if two excitatory graded potentials meet, they sum to a single, greater graded potential. Inversely to the spatial summation of like charges, the summation of *opposite* charges is represented by a size decrease, or even disappearance, if the opposite charges are equivalent.

Another key feature is the decay of graded potentials along the path to the cell body. This concept is represented by the graded potential visually fading along with the strength of its charge as it propagates along the dendrite. The decay can be seen in Figure 3.

The cell body is represented by a larger black circle at the bottom of the screen. In it is a voltage meter (see Figure 4), which depicts the state of intracellular activity, and provides feedback to the student's actions in the level. The cell body will begin to glow blue to represent that it is being mostly stimulated by excitatory graded potentials leading to an action potential. In contrast, the cell body will glow red to represent the stimulation of inhibitory graded potentials. The size and intensity of the glow represents the strength to which the cell body is being affected. Stemming from the bottom of the cell body to the bottom of the screen is the axon, which is represented by a black line (see the bottom of Figure 2). When the threshold has been achieved, and an action potential is triggered, the axon hillock will fire a wave of charge. Depending on how much the threshold is surpassed, the wave will pulse faster, simulating the way a real action potential would fire (i.e., greater depolarization, increased rate of firing).

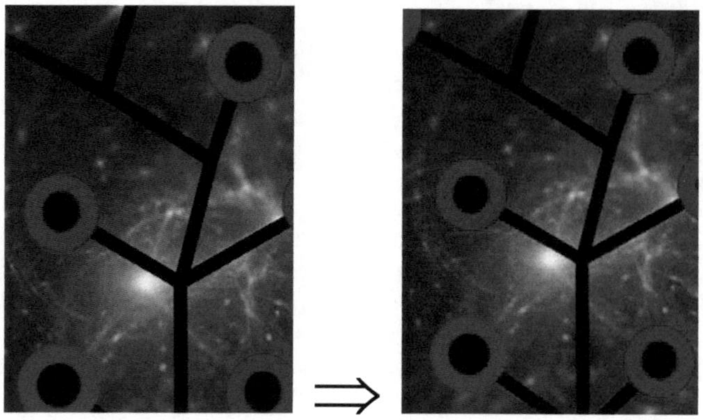

Figure 3. The decay of a graded potentials stength as it propogates through the denfdrite. At time 1, left, the potential (the fuzzy blue glow ¼ from the top) is brighter and less decayed than at time 2, right (near the bottom)

Customizability: The program currently has several levels, each designed to teach users about some aspect of neuron function. But new levels can be created with a Level Builder, allowing several ways for custom levels to be programmed. As with similar programs, customizing levels or creating new features requires a certain level of programming knowledge. In order to minimize the amount of knowledge needed to create content for this program, we used the swift programming language.

Figure 4. The label indicates the default threshold of -55mV has been surpassed. The Cell Body shows a blue halo along the outside, identifying it as being stimulated by excitatory graded potentials. An action potential appears different from a graded potential. It moves in a self-propagating wave along the axon

Swift is a high-level programming language designed to facilitate the creation of mobile applications. Swift is programmed using Xcode which is a free development software built by Apple, Inc. Xcode offers a variety of resources including storyboard functionality (a visual editor) which connects code to the user interface, Spritekit (a game building framework), and a simulator (to test the application on multiple devices). All of these resources, in conjunction with the custom level builder, are beneficial to developers looking to add additional content with little programming experience and minimal lines of code. Swift also increases the application's accessibility as it can also be posted directly to the Apple Appstore. Students will be able to quickly and easily download the app to their mobile devices and access the app wherever they go. They can find the source code and a tutorial to get started at: https://github.com/galenoshea/Postsynaptic-Simulator. The built-in variables that allow for customization are listed in Table 1.

Table 1. A list of features that can be customized using either a single variable or a new instance of a preprogrammed type of object

Feature	Variables	Notes
Cell Body	Shape	circle and straight lines currently programmed
	Size	-
	Layout	Can be connected in any desired format using connection points
	Thickness	-
	Colour	-
Synapses	Location	Can be placed at any point along a charge surface
	Size	Can make synapses easier to click for levels requiring sequential firing
	Inhibitory or excitatory effect	-
	Strength of effect	-
	Duration	How long the synapse remains active for after activating
	Count	How many times the synapse can fire.
Synapses (cont.)	Refractory period	Customizable to any interval.
	Automatic firing	Synapses trigger automatically instead of requiring user input
Axons	Activation threshold	Defaults to -55mV. customizable
	Refractory period	-
	Action potential speed	How fast an action potential moves along the axon. Proportional to the rate at which the threshold was surpassed.
Postsynaptic Potential	Rate of diffusion	The rate at which charge spreads along charge surfaces
	Decay rate	The rate at which charge gradually returns to neutral
Game	Background colour	Custom image or colour. Defaults to neuron background.
	Window size	Adaptive to all iphones/ipods.
	Game timer	Can create custom count down to win/loss
	Level objective	Can write custom instructions to play level.

3. CONCLUSION

The Postsynaptic Simulator provides an excellent framework with which to create supplementary material for introductory neuroscience courses. It provides an intuitive interface for students to explore basic electrophysiology. It allows students to see the ways in which graded potentials propagate and how they can be summed to cause action potentials. Our contribution is the software itself, currently available in the App Store and ready for use in classrooms.

The Postsynaptic Simulator also provides a foundation for further simulations of both individual and connected neurons. By creating a generalizable foundation for this, the program allows for both new and experienced programmers to add features that suit their curriculum. Because it has a Level Builder, new educational modules can be created using it. Instructors who are not comfortable with programming can assign level design as class assignments for groups of students that include some that are comfortable with software.

This program hopes to serve as a valuable addition to introductory neuroscience material, and to help newcomers to the field understand the processes behind causing an action potential. Future work will evaluate the benefits of using the Postsynaptic Simulator, in terms of enjoyment and learning outcomes.

REFERENCES

Kolb, B., Whishaw, I.Q. and Teskey, G.C., 2011. *An introduction to brain and behavior.* (3rd Ed.) New York: Worth.

Korey, C.A., 2009. Teaching undergraduate neuroscience in the digital age. *Journal of Undergraduate Neuroscience Education*, *8*(1), p.A55.

Lott, G.K., Johnson, B.R., Bonow, R.H., Land, B.R. and Hoy, R.R., 2009. g-PRIME: a free, Windows based data acquisition and event analysis software package for physiology in classrooms and research labs. *Journal of Undergraduate Neuroscience Education*, *8*(1), p.A50.

Newman, M.H. and Newman, E.A., 2013. MetaNeuron: a free neuron simulation program for teaching cellular neurophysiology. *Journal of Undergraduate Neuroscience Education*, *12*(1), p.A11.

Reas, C. and Fry, B., 2007. *Processing: a programming handbook for visual designers and artists*. Cambridge: MA: MIT Press.

Schettino, L.F., 2014. NeuroLab: a set of graphical computer simulations to support neuroscience instruction at the high school and undergraduate level. *Journal of Undergraduate Neuroscience Education*, *12*(2), p.A123.

Stieff, M. and Wilensky, U., 2003. Connected chemistry—incorporating interactive simulations into the chemistry classroom. *Journal of Science Education and Technology*, *12*(3), pp.285-302.

tiZom, O. by en:User:Chris 73 updated by en:User:Diberri converted to SVG by (2007). Schmatic of an action potential without labels. Retrieved from https://commons.wikimedia.org/wiki/File:Action_potential_(no_labels).svg

Wallis, J.D., Anderson, K.C. and Miller, E.K., 2001. Single neurons in prefrontal cortex encode abstract rules. *Nature*, *411*(6840), pp.953-956.

Wieman, C.E., 2006, December. Interactive Simulations for Teaching Physics; What Works, What Doesn't, and Why. In *American Astronomical Society Meeting Abstracts* (Vol. 209, pp. 249-01).

DESIGN OF AN EASY-TO-USE MOBILE AUGMENTED REALITY LEARNING SETTING BY MEANS OF A CONJECTURE MAP

Luca Moser
University of St.Gallen, Switzerland
St. Jakob-Strasse 21, CH-9000 St.Gallen, Switzerland

ABSTRACT

Despite the positive effects of mobile augmented reality (MAR)-tools for learning, MAR-tools are not commonly used in classrooms. The scientific discourse identified a lack of concepts that guide the practical application of mobile augmented reality (MAR)-tools in education. Teachers often feel insecure when designing and applying digital learning settings and therefore need tools and concepts to support them. The present contribution outlines how to develop an easy-to-use mobile augmented reality learning setting (MARLS). Thus, a MARLS to foster artificial intelligence (AI)-literacy is developed and studied to explore what makes MARLS easy-to-use. AI-literacy serves as an exemplary topic. It appears to be suiting because MAR-technology is based on AI-systems and hence allows students to experience a positive form of human-AI-interaction first headedly. The educational design research is conducted by means of a conjecture map to enable the concurrent investigation of learning, teaching and its interdependence. Derived from the high-level conjectures, (I): AI-literacy is a set of competences, (II): a digital learning environment is crucial to foster it, (III): a good MARLS considers usability, user centeredness, conscious application, basic learning theories and cognitive load, the MARLS is developed. The MARLS and its conjecture map lay ground for the yet to follow measure and improvement of the learning design.

KEYWORDS

Marker Based Augmented Reality, Mobile Augmented Reality, AI-literacy, Conjecture Map, Education, Educational Design Research

1. INTRODUCTION

Mobile augmented reality (MAR)-applications are increasingly discussed in the field of education (Akçayır and Akçayır, 2017; Pedaste et al., 2020). Like other augmented reality (AR)-tools, they are designed to "supplement the reality" with virtual elements (Azuma, 1997) and create an augmented environment where physical and digital features complement each other (Davies, 2004; Milgram and Kishino, 1994). Distinct about MAR-tools is that they can be applied with any mobile device (smartphone or tablet computer). Most upper secondary students own a smartphone (Cano and Sevillano-Garcia, 2018; Suter et al., 2018), what makes MAR-tools particularly cost-effective, as no further hardware has to be acquired. Hence, MAR-tools are potentially easier to distribute on a big scale than other AR-tools (Akçayır and Akçayır, 2017). Furthermore, the most comprehensive meta-studies on the subject identified significant potential for MAR-learning settings (MARLS) to increase learner engagement, motivation, learning effects, and the quality and quantity of interaction (Akçayır and Akçayır, 2017; Altinpulluk, 2019). MARLS enable authentic, interactive, and learner-centred learning experiences (Bacca et al., 2014), deeper knowledge acquisition, and better application of acquired knowledge in different contexts (Radu, 2014).

Despite the potential scalability and the considerable positive effects, MAR-tools are not regularly used in classrooms (Wang et al., 2018). A possible reason for the scarce practical use might be that many teachers still feel insecure when it comes to developing or applying digital learning settings in classroom (Fraillon et al., 2019; Seufert et al., 2019). Although several design principles for creating MAR-tools exist, a lack of principles illustrating how MAR-tools can be effectively used to design complete learning settings has been noted in scholarly discourse (Kerr and Lawson, 2020; Kourouthanassis et al., 2015). While little

MAR-research has been conducted for the primary and tertiary levels of education, there are even less concepts and empirical data for the secondary level of education (Hedberg et al., 2018).

Consequently, a MARLS is designed that enables teachers to foster Artificial Intelligence (AI)-literacy in upper secondary practice and contribute to the research on design principles of easy-to-use MARLS. AI-literacy, the competence to use smart machines effectively and consciously (Davenport and Kirby, 2016; Long and Magerko, 2020), serves as an exemplary topic. It appears to be suiting because, even if there is consensus that the effective and conscious handling of AI should be fostered at school (Pedro et al., 2019; UNESCO, 2019), in educational practice AI-literacy is still insufficiently addressed (Holmes et al., 2019; Luckin et al., 2016). Additionally, MAR-technology is based on AI-systems such as image recognition (Sahu et al., 2021) and hence allows students to experience a positive form of human-AI interaction whilst using the application.

Two project goals are pursued: 1) the development of a MARLS that enables teachers to foster AI-literacy in practice; 2) the contribution to the scientific discourse on the effective design of easy-to-use MARLS. The Main research Question derives from these goals:

How to design an easy-to-use mobile augmented reality learning setting (MARLS) for upper secondary education by means of conjecture mapping?

The content of the paper is structured as follows: the next section elaborates why the conjecture map is a favourable tool to design the MARLS and explains the applied educational design research method; the third section provides an overview of the findings: 1) the MARLS design principles 2) the conjecture map and the created learning design; and the last section concludes the paper by discussing the results and providing recommendations for future research.

2. METHOD

Design Research allows to pursue the two goals at hand: the development of innovative practical solutions and the advance of theoretical insight on how to do so (Dunning, 2011; Seufert, 2014). The applied educational design research (EDR) developed by McKenney and Reeves, consists of three phases that are conducted iteratively (McKenney and Reeves, 2018; Wozniak, 2015):

1. Analysis and exploration (phase 1): In order to be able to plan and design suitable measures for teachers, the required skills initially have to be discussed and formulated (Sandoval, 2014). The most extensive literature review to conceptualize the competences related to AI-literacy was conducted by Long and Magerko (2020). Their four dimensions "What is AI?", "What can AI do?", "How does AI work?", and "How should AI be used?" and the 16 related competences are therefore applied in the outlined EDR-project. Furthermore, a systematic literature analysis on the construction and application of MAR-tools for educational purpose is conducted to condense the scientific findings to MARLS-design principles. The results of the literature analysis and development of the design principles are presented in detail in (Moser, 2020). However, the most important results are outlined in this contribution to clarify the design principles that build the foundation of the designed AI-literacy MARLS.

2. Design and construction of the learning setting (phase 2): To develop the MARLS, conjecture mapping is used. Conjecture mapping is a proven method to design digital learning settings (Wozniak, 2015). It forces the designers to explicate the main set of assumed relationships (conjectures) and thereby helps to render the applied rationale transparent. The main advantage of the conjecture map is that it puts the focus on the different levels of conjectures that require studying (Sandoval, 2014; Wozniak, 2015) and hence guides phase 3 of the EDR. The conjecture map illustrates three different types of conjectures of the created learning design. The *high level conjectures* (1) are the basic assumptions – concept of learning goals and understanding of learning and teaching processes. Derived from the high level conjectures, the materials, tasks, and participant structure – the embodiment – is developed. *Design conjectures* (2) reveal how the embodiment is supposed to induce the observable mediating processes – student artefacts and interactions – which should help to achieve the learning goals. The *theoretical conjectures* (3) illustrate how the mediating processes are supposed to lead to the desired outcomes (Sandoval, 2016). The research of teaching and learning as isolated processes cannot grasp the complexity of the subject (Deng et al., 2019).

The Conjecture map allows to conduct research that includes the learning and the teaching dimension and its interdependence in a given learning design (Prensky, 2011) and is therefore a valuable tool for the purpose at hand. The second phase of the EDR process constitutes the main part of this contribution.

3. Evaluation and reflection (phase 3): The conjectures, have to be evaluated and, if necessary, to be adjusted in order to increase the maturity of the design knowledge (Gregor and Hevner, 2013). Additionally, the evaluation of the conjectures allows to improve the MARLS-design. A mixed method-approach will be applied to study what factors contribute to the acceptance and easiness to use a MARLS. To capture the acceptance and willingness of students to use MARLS, a questionnaire that follows the unified theory of technology acceptance and use (Venkatesh et al., 2012) is deployed. Qualitative data contextualizing and enhancing the evaluation is captured in the same survey, to make up for the limited number of participants. In addition, user data from the platform will be included in the analysis. This paper does not address the third step of the EDR process, for the necessary data has yet to be collected. In October 2021 the data of the first 100 students that will have worked with the AI-literacy MARLS, should be available. This will allow to refine the MARLS, the conjectures, and thereby enhance the theoretical understanding of MARLS-development.

3. RESULTS

3.1 Identifying MARLS design principles (phase 1)

The literature review, presented in Moser (2020), focused on the pedagogical and technical aspects of MAR for education. 77 articles entered the analysis but only twelve studies proposed design principles or frameworks for the construction or application of MAR-tools for educational purposes (Table 1) that also consider pedagogical aspects. The 54 proposed design principles were clustered to five design categories that summarize the main pedagogical and technical challenges when designing easy-to-use MARLS (Figure 1).

MARLS Design Principles	
	Usability (techn.) – easy and appealing to use for teachers and students (Cuendet et al., 2013) – interface containing only relevant information and functions (Ko et al., 2013)
	User/learner centeredness (pedag.) – focus on the needs and requirements of the targeted learners (Stefan and Moldoveanu, 2013) – easy classroom management and efficient use of the scarce learning time (Cuendet et al., 2013) – motivational design and a context relevant to the learners (Dunleavy, 2014; Kerr and Lawson, 2020)
	Basic learning theories – classical learning theories still apply for MARLS (Messuti et al., 2015) – create motivational and learner-centered MARLS (Bucher et al., 2020)
	Conscious application of MAR – organize and scaffold the activities to use the learning time effectively (Stefan and Moldoveanu, 2013) – restrict MAR use to the activities where it supports the learning process effectively (Tuli and Mantri, 2020)
	Cognitive (over)load – special attention to the cognitive load of students (Garzón et al., 2019) and teachers (Cuendet et al., 2013)

Figure 1. MARLS Design Principles. Moser, 2020

Fundamentally, it seems to be important to design learning settings that fulfil the needs of students and teachers alike. By not only respecting technological design principles and basic learning theories but also including possibilities for a lean classroom-management it seems possible to reduce the cognitive load of both students and teachers (Cuendet et al., 2013).

3.2 Design and Conjecture Map of the AI-literacy MARLS (Phase 2)

To ensure a save digital learning environment, the Xtend platform and the associated application Xpanda (https://www.augmentedreality.ch) will be used for implementing the MARLS. The company has successfully supported several educational projects in Switzerland and guarantees data protection. Furthermore, the mobile application supports iOS and Android and can be downloaded by the students for free. A registration or identification in the application is not necessary. The developed MARLS and the rationale behind it, is outlined along the conjecture map, displayed in Figure 2.

Desired Outcomes: The desired outcome of the learning setting regarding the students equals their learning in the realm of AI-literacy as described by Long and Magerko (2020). The effectiveness of the MARLS regarding the learning effect is a prerequisite for the teachers' acceptance and further use, as it effects the perceived usefulness that has repeatedly shown to be relevant for technology acceptance (Venkatesh et al., 2012). However, the focus of this research project lies on the question of how to design a MARLS that is easy-to-use and accepted by students and teachers alike. Therefore, an objective measurement of AI-literacy is not part of the MARLS.

High level conjectures: Combined with the applied notion of *AI-literacy* (I.) (Long and Magerko, 2020) and the awareness that a *digital learning environment* (II.) is necessary, the five design principles outlined in chapter 3.1 embody the high-level-conjectures that guide the development of the MARLS. To ensure a decent *usability* (III.) and reduce the *cognitive load* (VII.) of students and teachers alike, the easy-to-use application Xpanda will be used for implementing a marker-based MARLS. *User-centeredness* (IV.) regarding the teachers' needs is further ensured by developing a complete learning setting that includes a slide set and a booklet entailing all the necessary information to use the MARLS in class. *User-centeredness* (IV.) regarding the students and *conscious application* (V.) is implemented through an inquiry-learning approach (Pedaste et al., 2015) where students work in groups of 3-4 on a AI-Map. Marker-based-MAR has shown positive effects in combination with *inquiry- or exploration-based learning* (VI.) in multiple studies (Billinghurst and Duenser, 2012; Bower et al., 2015; Puja and Parsons, 2011). Also, MAR-enhanced learning appears to be valuable for intensifying interaction with the learning material and between members of learning groups (Akçayır and Akçayır, 2017; Altinpulluk, 2019).

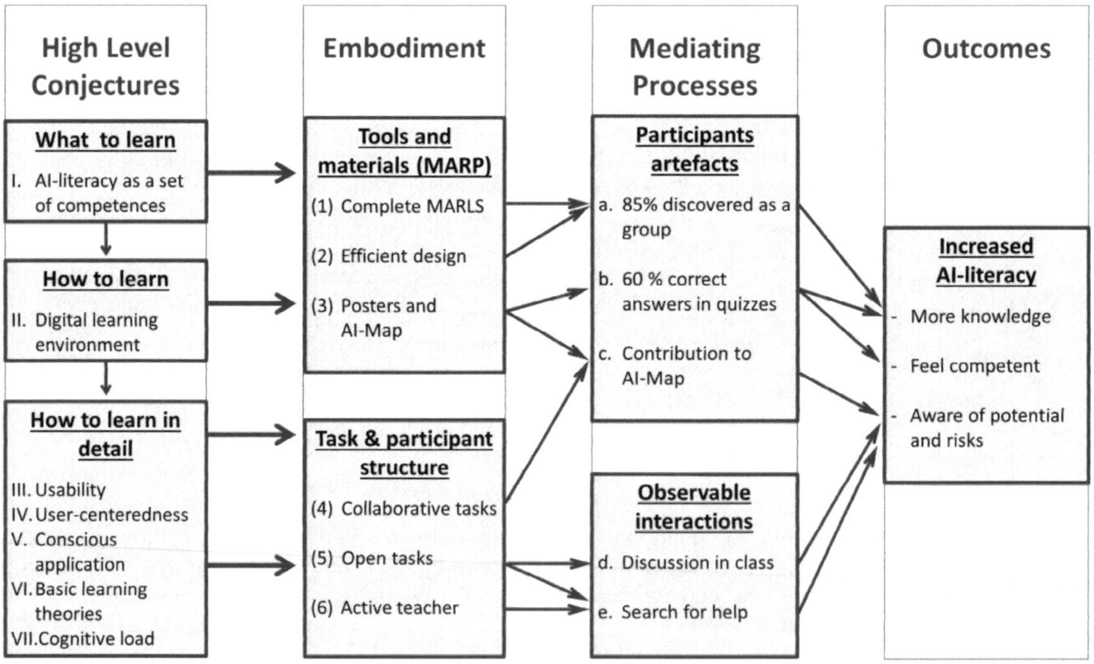

Figure 2. MARLS Conjecture Map

Embodiment: Because of the teachers' insecurities (Fraillon et al., 2019) a *complete MARLS* (1) is provided and additional material for an easy implementation in class is provided. To ensure an *efficient design* (2), after a brief introduction to AI and the MAR-app, the students start to work with the *posters* to complete their *AI-Map* (3). In addition to basic theories and applications about smart machines and AI, they explore which AI-systems are necessary for social robot 'Lexi' to work properly. To enable the students to learn in an inquiry- and exploration-based setting, *open and collaborative tasks* (4)(5) are formulated. When scanning the picture-based markers on the AI-Map and the posters (see Figure 3), students activate quizzes, videos, readings and visualizations experiencing the underlying relationships in the field of smart machines, to enhance their AI-literacy. In groups of 3-4, the students enhance their knowledge and awareness about smart machine applications – e.g. the topic of natural language processing and translation is explored by actively deploying "DeepL" and "Google Translate". Earlier projects with digital learning settings (Moser et al., 2020; Moser et al., 2021) indicate that students and teachers might both appreciate and profit from an *active involvement* (6) and support of the teacher in the students' digitally supported learning process.

Mediating processes: Students collect the physical markers provided as stickers on the posters and *contribute to the groups AI-Map* (c.) by *discussing* (d.) the potentials and possible dangers of the respective applications, they should engage intensively with the learning materials. By building basic knowledge and gaining practical insights, the students are enabled to build a reflected opinion and shape their attitudes (Ingram, 2015; Zan and Di Martino, 2007). Furthermore, the Xpanda platform allows the teacher to monitor the students' activity and interaction with the learning materials and thereby to monitor the *rate of discovery* (a.) and the *rate of correct responses* (b.). This information facilitates the teacher to take an active role and support the learning processes of the students when they are *looking for help* (e.) or need help but do not approach the teacher on their own.

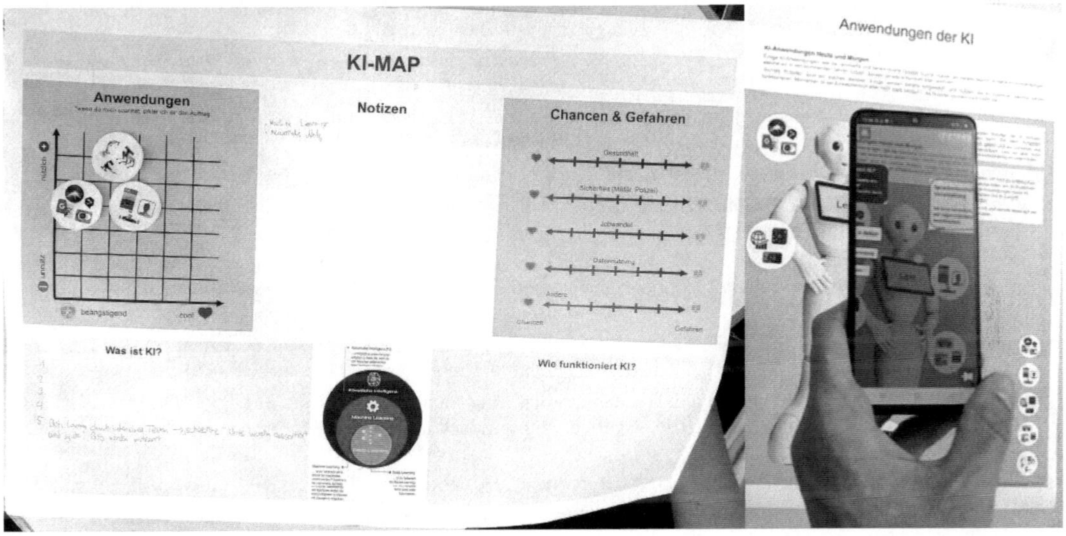

Figure 3. AI-Map and Lexi-poster with AI-supported applications

4. CONCLUSION

Limitations: The outlined EDR-cycle is still in its first iteration. The MARLS-evaluation is yet to follow. Furthermore, in order to increase the overarching validity, compromises in terms of reliability and validity of isolated effects are made and have to be respected when interpreting and discussing the results. Previous projects studying digitally enhanced learning processes (Moser et al., 2020; Moser et al., 2021) indicate that considerable novelty-effects are a further challenge for the validity of studies regarding innovative learning settings. Only the repeated use of MARLS really allows to control for these novelty effects. Further investigations have to clarify which findings can be transferred to other MARLS and other educational levels.

Another important limitation is the fast evolvement of MAR-technology (Cuendet et al., 2013) and the increasing capacities of the smartphones the average students possess and use to learn with MARLS. The technical possibilities are likely to change, how a conscious application (Tuli and Mantri, 2020) can be achieved. Despite these numerous limitations, the present project may contribute to the further exploration on how to facilitate the transfer of scientific innovation into practical learning environments.

Theoretical and Practical Implications: The MARLS is designed as an open educational resource and can therefore be used in classrooms by any interested teacher and student. Feedbacks from and interviews with further participants may produce more theoretical insight and practical improvement of the work with MARLS in the second and third EDR-cycle. The need to empirically study the perceptions and competence levels of students, concerning AI-literacy, identified by Long and Magerko (2020) could also be addressed in future research using the developed AI-MARLS.

For the practical application and dissemination of MARLS, the availability of simple development tools will probably be a relevant factor. Considering the amount of new digital learning solutions and approaches that are developed (Brooks et al., 2020), it appears crucial to intensify the scientific discourse about how to allow educational innovations to enter the classrooms more easily. The ongoing research on MARLS might contribute to do so.

REFERENCES

Akçayır, M. and Akçayır, G., 2017. Advantages and challenges associated with augmented reality for education: A systematic review of the literature. *Educational Research Review*, Vol. 20, pp. 1–11.

Altinpulluk, H., 2019. Determining the trends of using augmented reality in education between 2006-2016. *Education and Information Technologies*, Vol. 24 No. 2, pp. 1089–1114.

Azuma, R.T., 1997. A survey of augmented reality. *Presence: Teleoperators & Virtual Environments*, Vol. 6 No. 4, pp. 355-385.

Bacca, J., et al., 2014. Augmented Reality Trends in Education: A Systematic Review of Research and Applications. *Educational Technology & Society*, Vol. 17 No. 4, pp. 133–149.

Billinghurst, M., and Duenser, A., 2012. Augmented reality in the classroom. *Computer*, Vol. 4 No. 7, pp. 56-63.

Bower, M., et al., 2014. Augmented Reality in education–cases, places and potentials. *Educational Media International*, Vol. 51 No. 1, pp. 1-15.

Brooks, D. C., et al., 2020. *Higher Education's 2020 trend watch and top 10 strategic technologies.* EDUCAUSE. Retrieved 2020/09/01 from: https://library.educause.edu/resources/2020/1/higher-educations-2020-trend-watch-and-top-10-strategic-technologies

Bucher, K., et al., 2020. Von Medienbeiträgen und Applikationen–ein interdisziplinäres Konzept zum Lehren und Lernen mit Augmented und Virtual Reality für die Hochschullehre. Preprint, pp. 225–238.

Cano, E.V. and Sevillano-García, M.L., 2018. Ubiquitous Educational Use of Mobile Digital Devices. A General and Comparative Study in Spanish and Latin America Higher Education. *New Approaches Educational Research*, Vol. 7, pp. 105–115.

Cuendet, S., et al., 2013. Designing augmented reality for the classroom. *Computers & Education*, Vol. 68, pp. 557–569.

Davenport, T. H. and Kirby, J., 2016. Just how smart are smart machines?. *MIT Sloan Management Review*, Vol. 57 No. 3, pp. 21-25.

Davies, E. R., 2004. *Machine vision: theory, algorithms, practicalities*, (3rd ed.). Academic Press, New York, USA.

Deng, R., et al., 2019. Progress and new directions for teaching and learning in MOOCs. *Computers & Education*, Vol. 129, pp. 48-60.

Dunleavy, M., 2014. Design principles for augmented reality learning. *TechTrends*, Vol. 58 No. 1, pp. 28–34.

Dunning, D., 2011. Chapter five - The Dunning–Kruger Effect: On Being Ignorant of One's Own Ignorance. *Advances in Experimental Social Psychology*, Vol. 44, pp. 247-296.

Fraillon, J., et al., 2019. *Preparing for life in a digital world: the IEA International Computer and Information Literacy Study 2018 International Report*. IEA, Amsterdam, Netherlands.

Garzón, J., et al., 2019. Systematic review and meta-analysis of augmented reality in educational settings. *Virtual Reality*, Vol. 23 No. 4, pp. 447–459.

Gregor, S. and Hevner, A. R., 2013. Positioning and presenting design science research for maximum impact. *MIS quarterly*, Vol 39 No. 2, pp. 337-355.

Hedberg, et al., 2018. A Systematic Review of Learning through Mobile Augmented Reality. *International Journal of Interactive Mobile Technologies (iJIM)*, Vol. 12 no. 3, pp. 75-85.

Holmes, W., et al., 2019. *Artificial intelligence in education.* Center for Curriculum Redesign, Boston, USA.

Ingram, N., 2015. Students' relationships with mathematics: Affect and identity. In M. Marshman, et al. (Eds.), *Mathematics education in the margins. Proceedings of the 38th annual conference of the Mathematics Education Research Group of Australasia, MERGA*, Sunshine Coast, Australia, pp. 301-308.

Kerr, J. and Lawson, G., 2020. Augmented Reality in Design Education: Landscape Architecture Studies as AR Experience. *International Journal of Art & Design Education*, Vol. 39 No. 1, pp. 6–21.

Ko, S.M., Chang, W.S. and Ji, Y.G., 2013. Usability Principles for Augmented Reality Applications in a Smartphone Environment. International Journal of Human-Computer Interaction, Vol. 29 No. 8, pp. 501–515.

Kourouthanassis, P.E., et al., 2015. Demystifying the design of mobile augmented reality applications. *Multimedia Tools and Applications*, Vol. 74 No. 3, pp. 1045–1066.

Long, D. and Magerko, B., 2020. What is AI literacy? Competencies and design considerations. *Proceedings of the 2020 CHI Conference on Human Factors in Computing Systems*, April, 2020, pp. 1-16.

Luckin, R., et al., 2016. *Intelligence unleashed: An argument for AI in education.* Pearson Education, London, UK.

McKenney, S. and Reeves, T. C., 2014. *Educational design research. Handbook of research on educational communications and technology*. pp. 131-140, Springer, New York, USA.

Messuti, A., et al., 2015. Usability principles to design mobile workplace learning content. *Open Journal per la formazione in rete*, Vol. 15 No. 1, pp. 118-128.

Milgram, P., and Kishino, F., 1994. A taxonomy of mixed reality visual displays. *IEICE TRANSACTIONS on Information and Systems*, Vol. 77 No. 12, pp. 1321-1329.

Moser, L., 2020. Mobile Augmented Reality: Design Principles for the Use in Educational Settings. Proceedings of the *17th International Conference on Cognition and Exploratory Learning in Digital Age, CELDA 2020*. Lisbon, Portugal, pp. 335-339.

Moser, L., et al., 2020. Lehrer*innenbildung von digitalen Kompetenzen in einer forschungsbasierten Lerngemeinschaft. Fallbeispiel i-MOOC zur Förderung von Informationskompetenzen auf der Sekundarstufe II. In Kaspar, K., et al., (Eds.), *Bildung, Schule, Digitalisierung.* Waxmann, Münster, Germany, pp. 203-209.

Moser, L., et al., 2021. Improving a MOOC to foster information literacy by means of a conjecture map. *International Journal of Learning Technology*, Vol. 16 No. 1, pp. 65-86.

Pedaste, M., et al., 2015. Phases of inquiry-based learning: Definitions and the inquiry cycle. *Educational research review*, Vol. 14, pp. 47-61.

Pedro, F., et al., 2019. *Artificial intelligence in education: Challenges and opportunities for sustainable development.* UNESCO.

Prensky, M., 2011. Digital natives, digital immigrants Part 1. *On the Horizon*, Vol. 9 No. 5, pp. 1-6.

Puja, J. C., and Parsons, D., 2011,. A location-based mobile game for business education. *2011 IEEE 11th International Conference on Advanced Learning Technologies*, Washington DC, USA, pp. 42-44.

Radu, I., 2012. Why should my students use AR? A comparative review of the educational impacts of augmented-reality. 2012 *IEEE International Symposium on Mixed and Augmented Reality (ISMAR)*, Atlanta, USA, pp. 313–314.

Sahu, C. K., et al., 2021. Artificial intelligence (AI) in augmented reality (AR)-assisted manufacturing applications: A review. *International Journal of Production Research*, Vol. 59 No. 16, pp. 4903-4959.

Sandoval, W., 2014. Conjecture Mapping: An Approach to Systematic Educational Design Research. *Journal of the Learning Sciences*, Vol. 23 No. 1, pp. 18–36.

Seufert, S., 2014. Potenziale von Design Research aus der Perspektive der Innovationsforschung. *Zeitschrift für Berufs- und Wirtschaftspädagogik*, Beiheft Vol. 2 No. 27, pp. 79-96.

Seufert, S., et al., 2019. Professionelle Kompetenzen von Lehrpersonen im Kontext des digitalen Wandels. *Zeitschrift für Berufs-und Wirtschaftspädagogik*, Vol. 115 No. 2, pp. 312-339.

Stefan, L. and Moldoveanu, F., 2013. Game-based learning with Augmented Reality-from technology's affordances to game design and educational scenarios. *The International Scientific Conference eLearning and Software for Education*, 2, 105–114.

Suter, L., et al., 2018. *JAMES – Jugend, Aktivitäten, Medien – Erhebung Schweiz.* Zürcher Hochschule für Angewandte Wissenschaften, Zurich, CH.

Tuli, N. and Mantri, A., 2020. Usability Principles for Augmented Reality based Kindergarten Applications. *Procedia Computer Science*, Vol. 172, pp. 679–687.

UNESCO, 2019. beijing consensus on artifcial intelligence and education. *Outcome document of the International Conference on Artificial Intelligence and Education 'Planning education in the AI era: Lead the leap'*, May 2019, Beijing, People's Republic of China.

Venkatesh, V., et al., 2012. Consumer acceptance and use of information technology: extending the unified theory of acceptance and use of technology. *MIS quarterly*, Vol. 36 No. 1, pp. 157-178.

Wang, M., et al., 2018. Augmented reality in education and training: pedagogical approaches and illustrative case studies. *Journal of ambient intelligence and humanized computing*, Vol. 9 No. 5, pp. 1391-1402.

Wozniak, H., 2015. Conjecture mapping to optimize the educational design research process. *Australasian Journal of Educational Technology*, Vol. 31 No. 5, pp. 597-612.

Zan, R. and Di Martino, P., 2007. Attitude toward mathematics: Overcoming the positive/negative dichotomy. *The Montana Mathematics Enthusiast*, Vol. 3 No. 1, pp. 157-168.

360°-VIDEO REFLECTION IN TEACHER EDUCATION: A CASE STUDY

Eric Tarantini
Institute for Educational Management and Technologies at the University of St.Gallen (IBB-HSG)
St.Jakobstr. 21, 9000 St.Gallen, Switzerland

ABSTRACT

360°(degree-)-videos inherit interesting potentials for teaching competence development. Reflecting on personal teaching performance from multiple perspectives potentially increases the depth in situated reflection and provides new learning insights for pre-service teachers. In this light, this paper describes a case study conducted at the University of St.Gallen where 360°-videos were used for reflection on personal performance of pre-service teachers in order to clarify, whether they add value to reflective observations compared to classical video recordings. Key findings are that (I): 360°-videos can add value to reflection processes in teacher education when combined with feedback and situated learning processes in a learning design and (II): 360°-videos offer advantages to follow teacher-student-interactions and to reflect upon personal teaching performance from multiple perspectives.

KEYWORDS

360°-video, Immersion, Social Video Learning, Teacher Education, Situated Learning, Experiential Learning

1. INTRODUCTION

The use of 360°-videos in education is still in its infancy. Nevertheless, the technology is enjoying steadily growing interest and relevance (Yildirim et al., 2020, p. 241; Schmoelz, 2018; Parker et al., 2016; Radianti et al., 2020, p. 26). Prior research shows, that participants pointed out elevated levels of interest, engagement and enjoyment when experiencing learning with 360°-videos (Snelson & Hsu, 2020). Sato and Kageto (2018, p. 267) affirm that 360°-videos watched with HMDs (Head Mounted Displays) support learners to remember how they felt when they were engaged in an activity. Future research efforts should therefore aim to deepen understanding of how and under what conditions 360°-videos effectively support learning (Snelson & Hsu, 2020, p. 411; Nissim & Weissblueth, 2017, p. 52; Kalliopi-Evangelia, 2020, p. 31). In addition, Wohlgenannt et al. (2019, p. 4) and Radianti et al. (2020, p. 26) affirm that researchers should aim to identify adequate learning theories to ground didactic designs using 360°-videos.

To contribute to the closure of this knowledge gap, the purpose of this research is to describe a case study conducted in the teacher education programme at the University of St.Gallen. The programme is designed for students who aim to be educated as teachers in the subjects of business, law and economics for high school and vocational education. The purpose of this study was to test, wheter reflection processes with self-recorded 360°-videos of teaching performances could add value to the learning process of pre-service teachers. Accordingly, the following research question has been defined:

RQ. Can 360°-videos of personal teaching performance watched with an HMD effectively extend learning and reflection processes of pre-service teachers?

To answer this question, we worked with a small group of pre-service teachers and recorded their microteachings (teaching units in front of a simulated class) with a 360°-video camera. Additionally, we used live-video annotation (Social Video Learning (SVL)) to visually explicate important teaching situations by using a smartphone-based SVL-application. This procedure should assure a goal-oriented reflection using the 360°-video technology. Therefore, the paper is structured in four parts: the first chapter focuses on the rationale of the research project. In the second chapter, the study design and the methodology are described. In the third chapter, the case study, the corresponding learning design as well as the data analysis and collection process are themathized. Finally, the fourth chapter concludes and discusses the key findings of this research.

2. RATIONALE OF THE RESEARCH PROJECT

What distinguishes 360°-videos from VR (Virtual Reality)? First of all, it is essential to bring the heterogeneous definition landscape around the terms 360°-videos and VR to a common denominator that makes sense for the context. According to Feurstein (2018, p. 3), VR can be defined as an "environment in which the participant is fully immersed into a computer simulated reality or a stereoscopic perspective". Schmoelz (2018, p. 8) developed a classification of immersive density showing, how different forms of engagement in an immersive environment can be classified:

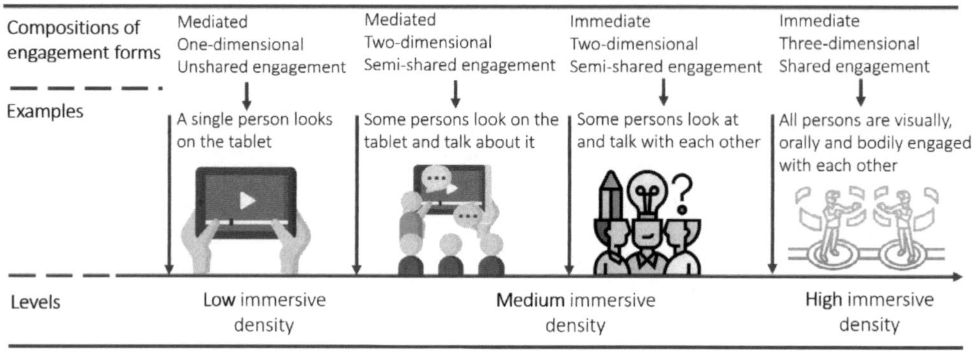

Figure 1. Immersive density
Own illustration based on Schmoelz (2018)

Nevertheless, 360°-videos make use of vital elements that characterize VR. From a personal perspective, they can be classified as medium/high immersive according to Schmoelz (2018), as they allow immersive experiences but without a motion free, virtual and shared engagement (see Figure 1). Although they are generated with real-world footage and not by using computer software, 360°-videos are characterized by self-directed control and multi-perspectivity. In consequence a sense of immersion is generated and results in an enhanced feeling of presence within the specific environment (Snelson & Hsu, 2020, p. 1; Feurstein, 2018, p. 2). It is important to underline that 360°-videos are immersive experiences which are limited to the viewer looking around statically in a 360°-space. In case of usage with a projection device (e.g. HMD), they can be classified as a VR application due to the generated perception of being virtually present in a specific environment, according to Milgram et al. (1994) and Zobel et al. (2018). 360°-videos can also be used browser-based supported by video-platforms like YouTube VR, which is interesting from a cost-saving perspective as HMDs are not necessairily needed to watch them. The present research limits its experimental efforts to self-recorded 360°-videos used with an *OculusGo* HMD for reflection processes.

Why do we think that 360°-videos can represent an added value for teacher education? The immersive experience provided by 360°-videos watched on an HMD allows pre-service teachers to re-experience their teaching performance from different angles (also depending on where the camera is positioned in the room). According to recent studies, the 360°-view allows the *analysis of behavior and reactions* in the complete classroom-surrounding resulting in an improved understanding regarding the conduction of constructive and fruitful teacher-student interactions (Luo et al., 2020, p. 11; Stavroulia & Lanitis, 2017; Feurstein, 2018, p. 5). As a consequence of previous research efforts, we assumed that the immersive experience of teaching performances by watching 360°-videos with an HMD could positively affect the subsequent reflective activity as it disconnects the user from distracting factors of the "real world" (Theelen et al., 2019, p. 584; Zobel et al., 2018). Teachers can take on the students' position and emphasize with their problems. Furthermore, it is assumed that 360°-videos can facilitate *situated learning*, i.e. social collaborative knowledge construction (Gaudin & Chaliès, 2015, p. 58; Greeno, Collins & Resnick, 1996, p. 40). Key components of situated learning are storytelling, reflection (video-based and peer-based reflections about one's own and others' practices), collaboration, coaching and real-life experience. Immersive technological support (e.g. 360°-videos) can expand the intensity and flexibility regarding key components of situated learning and promote the development of reflective practice (McLellan, 1996, p. 48; Gaudin & Chaliès, 2015, p. 58). Focusing on the field of teacher education, 360°-videos can be used to experience classroom situations up close with HMDs.

3. STUDY DESIGN AND METHODOLOGY

The participants were pre-service teachers at Bachelors` level from the University of St.Gallen. 60% of the participating students were female, aged 21-30 with a mean age of 21.9. The students could participate in the study on a voluntary basis given that it was not a mandatory element to successfully complete the course. The study was conducted within an obligatory course in teacher education called *Didactic Transfer*. The course runs during a whole semester. Students teach their fellow colleagues (simulated class) to gain their very first teaching experiences in a protected setting. They plan their microteachings of 45 minutes in tandems and are simultaneously coached by a lecturer. The course is split up in two rounds of microteachings, i.e. every student tandem teaches twice during the semester. The microteachings of the first round are purely for practice, whereas those of the second round are graded by the lecturer (see Figure 2):

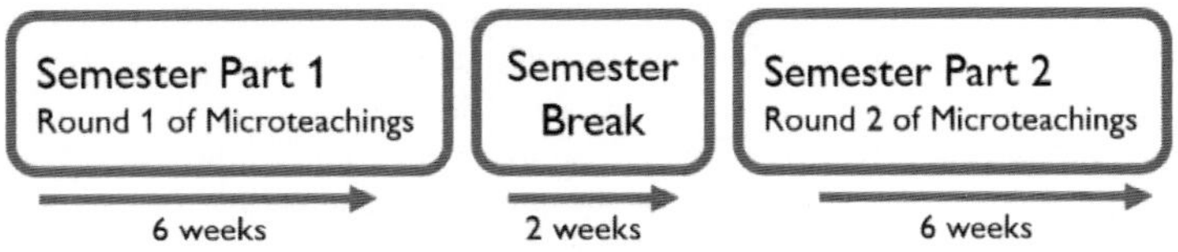

Figure 2. Semester structure
Own illustration

The small size of the group resulted in practical advantages. The course was attended by 40 students split up in grous of 10. From a lecturer`s point of view this was highly beneficial to create a positive and trustful group culture resulting in critical, honest and constructive feedback processes. Especially since reflecting on one's individual teaching practice can be shameful and therefore challenging for some students, we have experienced many times that a positive group culture is essential for learning success. Practically speaking, we have tried to estaböish this culture by using elements like a kick-off meet-and-greet or joint coffee breaks.

4. RESULTS

4.1 Development and Implementation of the Learning Design

The creation of a meaningful learning design integrating the 360°-video reflection represented a particular challenge. We already worked with Social Video Learning (SVL) in our course (Tarantini, 2020). SVL means an interactive annotation of videos (Vohle & Reinmann, 2012, p. 416; Meixner, Siegel, Hölbling, Kosch & Lehner, 2009; Krüger et al., 2012, p. 200). The learner visually specifies the reference point for his or her interpretation of a specific teaching situation (annotation) (Tarantini, 2020; Chatti et al., 2016). Explaining personal observations, insights or critical remarks within this learning process represents an effective way to develop a precise and constructive feedback competence (Vohle & Reinmann, 2012, p. 416). The idea is, that the students representing the simulated class explicate their observations after a microteaching on a SVL-platform for a very specific situation (video annotation). To sum up, SVL represents a form of situated learning.

The video annotation process is split up in two steps: Firstly, students (simulated class) can annotate a live- video by using the *edubreak App* (visual tags) while the lecturer records the microteaching via smartphone (see Figure 3). They can add time stamps accurate to the second (so-called "visual tags") and immediately "save" observed critical or positive teaching situations. Secondly, after recording the video, it is uploaded to the SVL-platform (edubreak CAMPUS, edubreak.de) including all annotations made during the microteaching. Participants can now explicate their annotations with specific text-based comments on their computer (see Figure 3).

Figure 3. Live-video in the microteaching (left), user interface on the edubreak App (centre) and SVL-platform (right)
Own illustration

The importance of this well-established design element for the current research lies in the thought, that the concrete explication of observations sensibilizes the simulated class and the teaching students for important situations during a microteaching. In consequence, this situated learning approach could lead to a deeper learning and reflection process (Tarantini, 2020). With these annotated situations from the single-perspective video in mind, the complementary 360°-video of the microteachings could potentially support the teaching students in exploring these "critical situations" form different perspectives in a more immersive environment. One could justifiably claim that it doesn`t make sense to record two videos in order to reflect on one microteaching but 1) unfortunately the SVL-platform does not yet support the annotation of 360°-videos and 2) the live-annotation process requires a live-recording via the smartphone-based *edubreak App*, which in consequence represents a classical video. To sensefully combine the explained elements, we followed the logic of an **experiential learning process** to create an adequate learning design which fitted very well with the course structure:

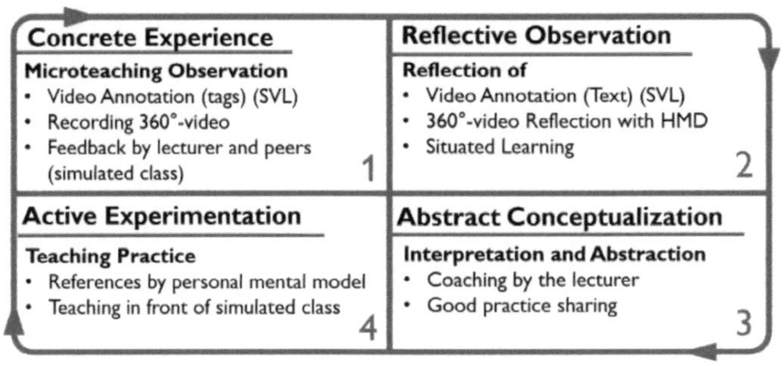

Figure 4. Learning Design
Own illustration adapted from Kolb (1984)

The micorteaching was conducted by the student tandem in front of the simulated class (*concrete experience*) (1). Meanwhile, the 360°-video is recorded by using a laptop, a 360°-camera (in our case a RICOH THETA Z model) and a tripod. We opted for this type of camera as it was quite lean and easy to use. The camera was set up in the middle of the room, in order to provide the teaching students the "class perspective", when watching the video with the HMD:

Figure 5. 360°-video recording (left) and 360°-video in YouTube VR (right)
Own illustration

Furthermore, the simulated class annotated live-situations with the *edubreak app* (see Figure 3). The SVL was followed up by an oral peer feedback to identify and discuss the crucial situations highlighted in this process (Kleinknecht & Gröschner, 2016, p. 47; Prilop et al., 2020). The lecturer moderated the feedback session. Subsequently, the 360°-video was uploaded to YouTube VR for the *reflective observation* of the students with an *OculusGo* model (HMD) (2). We decided to use YouTube VR, because 1) the platform was supported by the *OculusGo* and 2) it is very easy and intuitive in use. The reflection process supported by the 360°-video took place at another day and was combined with a coaching session (3). This decision had practical reasons, as uploading the videos to YouTube VR took several hours due to the huge data size of the 360°-video files in 4K-quality. Lower video quality (1080p) resulted in enormous blurriness due to the scaling of the viewing field in the YouTube VR environment. The supervising lecturer provided feedback regarding ciritical situations to sensibilize the students by showing them selected 360°-video sequences. Again, the selection process of those situations was facilitated by the preceding SVL process. Furthermore, theoretical implications of good teaching practice could be *abstracted from the concrete teaching situation*, resulting in a learning process in the sense of situated and experiential learning. In conclusion, it seems that the students have effectively developed their mental teaching models in order to provide them concrete references during their future teaching practices as a consequence of the combined, situated SVL and 360°-video-reflection approach (*active experimentation*) (4).

4.2 Data Collection and Analysis

During the course we recorded five 360°-microteaching-videos, i.e. one per tandem. Due to the COVID-19 pandemic it was not possible to record more videos for the second half of the semester in fall 2020 because the University of St.Gallen completely shifted to online lecturing via ZOOM (see comparison in chapter 5). Data was collected by 1) personally interviewing the participants after the coaching sessions and, 2) with an online-questionnaire (via surveymonkey.com) to be filled out right after the reflection on personal teaching performance with the HMD-based 360°-video. Excel was used to analyze the collected data. The students evaluated the 360°-video environment as experienced in YouTube VR based on seven items: 1) *Intention to use*, 2) *Attitude*, 3) *Awareness*, 4) *Presence*, 5) *Ease of use*, 6) *Playfulness* and 7) *Usefulness*. The items were defined by considering findings from Fang et al. (2014), Tcha-Tokey et al. (2014) as well as Venkatesh et al. (2003) and operationalized with specific questions. Figure 5 shows an overview of the average values of the student responses to the questions regarding an item. A 5-point likert scale was used to classify the questions within the survey (1 = Not at all true; 5 = Strongly agree).

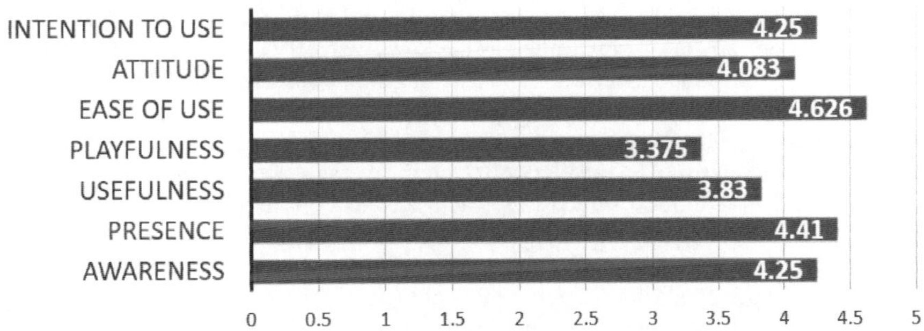

Figure 6. Means questionnaire 360°-video reflection (n = 10)
Own illustration

The results showed that the 360°-environment in YouTube VR was perceived as highly user-friendly and intuitive (*ease of use*). Furthermore, it was emphasized in the evaluation as well as in the interviews that interactions between teacher and students can be better followed and perceived (*presence and awareness*). The participants positively assessed the *usefulness* of 360°-videos for reflection processes in teacher education (3.83), especially due to multi-perceptivity and the sensibilization for ciritcal teaching situations via SVL. In the interview, a participant mentioned that he was able to notice details in the classroom (student`s attitude), which were not visible to the viewers eyes when watching the classical video on the SVL-platform. Two items that can be considered as interdependent are *intention to use* and *attitude*. The positive attitude of the participants towards new technologies, which is probably due to the young average age of the participants (around 21.9 years), could be an indicator for the high intention of further wanting to use of 360°-videos for reflection processes. Finally, it is noted that the item *playfulness* scored somewhat lower in the evaluation. On the one hand, this could be due to the fact that the immersion through the HMD takes some familiarization time and can lead to visual and physical discomfort. However, this has not been the case for our students as they stated in the interview. On the other hand, it is an experience that does not allow any playful actions compared to a virtual simulation, but focuses on observation by rotating statically around one's own body axis.

5. CONCLUSION AND DISCUSSION

This paper sheds light on the valuable use of 360°-videos for reflection processes in teacher education. Referring to the research question, results of this research imply that 360°-videos are promising and fruitful for the reflection on teaching performance when 1) embedded in a learning design which provides feedback from peers or/and experts and 2) combined with a situated learning method (e.g. SVL) to sensibilize for critical situations in order to enable a goal-oriented watching of the 360°-video in YouTube VR.

From a practical point of view, we experienced 360°-videos as a very interesting technology for education. They are easy to produce, cameras are affordable and the upload to and use via YouTube VR is relatively easy.

From a theoretical standpoint it shall be highlighted that situated learning can be embedded in or combined with an experiential learning procedure. In our case, it was important to abstract concrete situations in order to discuss about concepts and methods of effective and good teaching, such as asking the right questions at the right time or how to provide constructive feedback to the learners.

From a methodological point of view the personal interviews with the pre-service teachers in the study revealed interesting findings, such as the possibility to perceive environmental factors of the classroom by using the 360°-video reflection. Furthermore, this method helped to establish a trustworthy and deeper dialogue with the participants, which also became noticeable during the semester in a positive working and discussion culture in the group but also with the lecturer.

As mentioned in chapter 4.2, we had to switch to ZOOM teaching for the second half of the semester. However, since there was no longer any face-to-face teaching, it must be said that it is difficult to compare the two scenarios because too many variables were changed by the ZOOM teaching compared to the face-to-face teaching. It was no longer possible to record microteachings camera-based (neither classic nor 360°-videos) and as a consequence only the ZOOM recordings were used as reflection tools. In addition, SVL by practicing live-annotation was not possible anymore. Nevertheless, at the end of the semester the participants mentioned that the pandemic-related changed circumstances in the second half of the semester had positive side effects. It made them even more aware of how valuable the work with SVL in combination with the 360°-video environment was in terms of concrete reflection on teaching situations. Especially the observation with multiple perspectives helped them to gain new insights regarding their own teaching style.

However, there are other limitations to this research. The learning design could only be tested with a small sample of students characterized by a relatively young average age. Despite the positive reactions, the pedagogically valuable use of 360°-videos in teacher education requires further validation due to this circumstance. From the author's point of view, this factor had an impact on the results with regard to the attitude towards technology but also the handling of the video platforms (SVL and YouTube VR). Secondly, there is the restriction to framework conditions of our context at the University of St.Gallen and our teacher education programme in business and law. It would be insightful to test the technology in other contexts as well.

Regarding future work, it would be interesting to further investigate the enrichment of 360°-teaching performance videos with hotspots (interactive elements within the video) or follow-up activities. This would allow to virtually take action in the video, which influence the further course of the scene. Thus, an effective learning medium for teacher training could be created. Secondly, experimenting with different 360°-camera positions and perspectives in the classroom would provide exciting insights. For example, the static camera position could be replaced by an action camera carried by the teacher in order to be able to follow the action situation closely in the video. Furthermore, several 360°-cameras could be used to capture new perspectives. In our case, we decided to position the camera in the middle of the classroom to provide the viewer with a complete view of the classroom from the student's perspective.

To sum up briefly, the case study at hand aims to motivate for follow-up experiments with 360°-videos in the context of teacher education. The results and the reactions of the participants are encouraging. In particular, the use of new perspective observation possibilities in a spatial 360°-setting allows to further enrich the development process of teaching competencies.

REFERENCES

Chatti, M. A., Marinov, M., Sabov, O., Laksono, R., Sofyan, Z., Yousef, A. & Schroeder, U. (2016). *Video annotation and analytics in course mapper. Smart Learning Environments, Vol. 3,* No. 10. Aachen: Springer.

Fang, T. W., Wang, P., Liu, C., Su, M. & Yeh, S. (2014). Evaluation of a haptics-based virtual reality temporal bone simulator for anatomy and surgery training. *Computer Methods and Programs in Biomedicine,* No. 113, pp. 674–681.

Feurstein, M. S. (2018). *Towards an Integration of 360-degree Video in Higher Education. Workflow, challenges and scenarios*. Proceedings of DeLFI Workshops 2018. Germany: Frankfurt.

Gaudin, C. & Chaliès, S. (2015). Video viewing in teacher education and professional development: A literature review. *Educational Research Review, Vol. 16*, pp. 41–67.

Greeno, J. G., Collins, A. M. & Resnick, L. B. (1996). Cognition and learning. In Berliner, D. & Calfee, R. C. (Eds.), *Handbook of educational psychology*. New York: Macmillan.

Kalliopi-Evangelia, S. (2020). *Assessing the potential of using Virtual Reality based approaches for enhancing the professional development of teachers*. Doctoral Dissertation. Cyprus: University of Technology.

Kleinknecht, M. & Gröschner, A. (2016). Fostering preservice teachers' noticing with structured video feedback: Results of an online- and video-based intervention study. *Teaching and Teacher Education, Vol. 59*, pp. 45–56.

Kolb, D. (1984). *Experiential Learning. Experience as the source of learning and development.* Englewood Cliffs, NJ: Prentice-Hall.

Krüger, M., Steffen, R. & Vohle, F. (2012). Videos in der Lehre durch Annotation reflektieren und aktiv diskutieren. In: Csanyi, G., Reichl, F. & Steiner, A. (Hrsg.). *Digitale Medien – Werkzeuge für exzellente Forschung und Lehre, pp. 198–210*. Münster: Waxmann Verlag GmbH.

Luo, H., Li, G., Feng, Q., Yang, Y. & Zuo, M. (2020). Virtual reality in K-12 and higher education. A systematic review of the literature from 2000 to 2019. *Journal of Computer Assisted Learning (WILEY).* Central China Normal University: Faculty of Artificial Intelligence in Education.

McLellan, H. (1996). Situated Learning Perspectives. *Educational Technology Publications*. New Jersey: Englewood Cliffs.

Meixner, B., Siegel, B., Hölbling, G., Kosch, H. & Lehner, F. (2009). SIVA Suite – Konzeption eines Frameworks zur Erstellung von interaktiven Videos. In Eibl, M. (Hrsg.), *Workshop Audiovisuelle Medien WAM 2009. Aus der Reihe Chemnitzer Informatik–Berichte, pp. 13–20*. Chemnitz: Technische Universität.

Milgram, P., Takemura, H., Utsumi, A. & Kishino, F. (1994). Augmented Reality. A class of displays on the reality-virtuality continuum. In: *Proc. SPIE, Vol. 2351, Telemanipulator and Telepresence Technologies*.

Nissim, Y. & Weissblueth, E. (2017). Virtual Reality (VR) as a Source for Self-Efficacy in Teacher Training. *International Education Studies, Vol. 10*, No. 8.

Parker, M., Patton, K. & O'Sullivan, M. (2016). Signature pedagogies in support of teachers' professional learning. *Irish Educational Studies, Vol. 35*, No. 2, pp. 137–153. DOI: 10.1080/03323315.2016.1141700

Prilop, C. N., Weber K. E. & Kleinknecht, M. (2020). Effects of digital video-based feedback environments on pre-service teachers` feedback competence. *Computers in Human Behavior, Vol. 102*, pp. 120–131.

Radianti, J., Majchrzak, T. A., Fromm, J. & Wohlgenannt, I. (2020). A systematic review of immersive virtual reality applications for higher education: Design elements, lessons learned, and research agenda. *Computers & Education, No. 147.*

Sato, S. & Kageto, M. (2018). *The Use of 360-degree Movies to Facilitate Students' Reflection on Learning Experiences*. International Symposium on Educational Technology (ISET), Hong Kong. DOI: 10.1109/ISET.2018.00066

Schmoelz, A. (2018). Enabling co-creativity through digital storytelling in education. *Thinking skills and creativity, Vol. 28*, pp. 1–13.

Snelson, C. & Hsu, Y. (2020). Educational 360-Degree Videos in Virtual Reality. A Scoping Review of the Emerging Research. *TechTrends, Vol. 64*, pp. 404–412.

Stavroulia, K.E. & Lanitis, A. (2017). On the Potential of Using Virtual Reality for Teacher Education. In: Zaphiris P. & Ioannou A. (Eds.). *Learning and Collaboration Technologies. Novel Learning Ecosystems.* LCT 2017. *Lecture Notes in Computer Science, Vol. 10295.* Cham: Springer Verlag GmbH. Verfügbar unter https://doi.org/10.1007/978-3-319-58509-3_15

Tarantini, E. (2020). Social Video Learning – Creation of a Reflection-Based Course Design in Teacher Education. In: Vittorini, P., Di Mascio, T., Tarantino, L., Temperini, M., Gennari, R. & De la Prieta, F. (Eds.). Methodologies and Intelligent Systems for Technology Enhanced Learning, 10th International Conference. MIS4TEL 2020. *Advances in Intelligent Systems and Computing, Vol. 1241*. Springer: Cham. DOI: 10.1007/978-3-030-52538-5_3

Tarantini, E. (2021). *Immersives Lernen in der Lehrerbildung. Reflexionsprozesse mit Virtual Reality-Technologie gestalten*. Arbeitsbericht. Universität St.Gallen: Institut für Bildungsmanagement und Bildungstechnologien (IBB-HSG). Retrieved from ibb.unisg.ch

Tcha-Tokey, K., Loup-Excande, E., Christmann, O. & Richir, S. (2016). *A Questionnaire to Measure the User Experience in Immersive Virtual Environments.* International Virtual Reality Conference 2016, Laval (France).

Theelen, H., van den Beemt, A. & den Brok, P. (2019). Using 360-degree videos in teacher education to improve preservice teachers' professional interpersonal vision. *Journal of Compuer Assisted Learning, Vol. 35*, pp. 582–594. DOI: 10.1111/jcal.12361

Venkatesh, V., Morris, M. G., Davis, G. B., & Davis, F. D. (2003). User acceptance of information technology: toward a unified view. *MIS Quarterly, Vol. 27*, No. 3, pp. 425–478.

Vohle, F. & Reinmann, G. (2012). Förderung professioneller Unterrichtskompetenz mit digitalen Medien: Lehren lernen durch Videoannotation. *In Schulz–Zander, R., Eickelmann, B., Moser, H. Niesyto, H. & Grell, P. (Hrsg.), Jahrbuch Medienpädagogik 9,* pp. 413–429. Wiesbaden: Springer VS.

Wohlgenannt, I., Fromm, J., Stieglitz, S. & Radianti, J. (2019). *Virtual Reality in Higher Education. Preliminary Results from a Design-Science-Research Project*. Retrieved from https://www.researchgate.net/publication/335490099

Yildirim, B., Sahin-Topalcengiz, E., Arikan, G. & Timur, S. (2020). Using virtual reality in the classroom. Reflections of STEM teachers on the use of teaching and learning tools. *Journal of Education in Science, Environment and Health (JESEH), Vol. 6*, No. 3, pp. 231–245. DOI: 10.21891/jeseh.711779

Zobel, B., Werning, S., Berkemeier L. & Thomas, O. (2018). Augmented- und Virtual-Reality Technologien zur Digitalisierung der Aus- und Weiterbildung – Überblick, Klassifikation und Vergleich. In: Thomas, O., Metzger, D. & Niegemann, H. *Digitalisierung in der Aus- und Weiterbildung*, pp. 20–34. Heidelberg / Berlin: Springer Gabler.

THE EFFECT OF SOCIAL CLOSENESS ON PERCEIVED SATISFACTION OF COLLABORATIVE LEARNING

Shihui Feng[1], Shuming Qiu[1], David Gibson[2] and Dirk Ifenthaler[3]
[1]*University Of Hong Kong*
[2]*Curtin University, Australia*
[3]*University of Mannheim, Germany; Curtin University, Australia*

ABSTRACT

Effective communication and coordination supported by well-established patterns of interactions are vital to collaborative learning. The quality of social relationships among group members can affect group dynamics and communication, as well as further influence students' learning experiences and perceived learning outcomes. In this study, we employ an ego network approach to measure an individual's social closeness with group members and examine effects on the individual's collaborative learning experience. The data was collected through a survey of 120 university students. Our findings indicate that social closeness among group members has a positive effect on the perceived satisfaction of collaborative learning, as students with stronger social closeness with group members tend to be more satisfied with their collaborative learning experience. These results provide advanced theoretical insights for understanding the factors associated with the success of collaborative learning. Based on our findings, appropriate activities for strengthening social closeness among group members are suggested. Implications include pedagogical approaches for facilitating students' collaborative learning experience and outcomes.

KEYWORDS

Collaborative Learning, Group Collaboration, Social Closeness, Tie Strength, Social Network Analysis

1. INTRODUCTION

Collaborative learning can be understood as a system-level social activity, in which a group works together to achieve a common goal. The complexity and context of collaboration drives important changes of social ecologies in a group as well as influences the processes of learning (Ifenthaler, 2014; Zuike et al., 2016). Collaboration serves as a mechanism for eliciting a social learning process in which an individual observes and learns from the shared information within a group (Dillenbourg, 1999; Ifenthaler, 2014). The shared space of sense-making within a group forms through active information sharing and inquiring. Social skills are therefore needed for interactions such as coordinating among group members, solving conflicts, negotiating, providing support, and driving group cohesiveness. The importance of social interactions in collaborative learning has been well recognized in previous studies (Miller et al., 1994; Oliver et al., 1998; Rimor et al., 2010; Isohätälä et al., 2017). Through social interactions, individuals' knowledge and perceptions towards a learning task can be enhanced or reshaped (Oliver et al., 1998) so interactions are considered a primary mechanism for individuals to gain new knowledge and improve social skills. Social closeness, defined in detail below, is one measure of social interaction. With the advancement of information technology, blended learning environments supported by various learning analytic tools can enrich the methods for facilitating social interactions in collaborative learning (Chen et al., 2018; Lin et al., 2016). The design of an effective collaborative situation (e.g., who should work together and the duration of the activity) and the social relationships among group members, including social closeness, may thus have a significant influence on group dynamics, as well as the perceived success of a collaborative learning experience (Kerrigan et al., 2021).

Social network analysis, a method focusing on analyzing social connections among individuals, offers an effective approach to analyze social ties in group collaboration (De Laat et al., 2007). In this study, we employ an ego network approach to explore the effect of social relations among group members on students' perceived satisfaction of collaborative learning, which has been a rather neglected aspect of previous studies on collaborative learning. The research question guiding this study is: Does the strength of a student's social ties have an effect on their perception of collaborative learning?

2. THEORETICAL BASIS AND HYPOTHESES DEVELOPMENT

Social closeness represents the extent of connections an individual has with others in a community or group (Nardi, 2005), and has been regarded as a core component of individuals' perceived social support (Sarason et al., 1987). Consequently, social closeness has been a long-standing research interest in psychology and sociology. The level of closeness children and young adults have with family members is suggested to be associated with their psychological development and behavioral preferences (Euler et al., 2001; Murray et al., 2005; Roberts et al., 2001; Ledbetter, 2009). In this study, the operational definition of social closeness in collaborative learning refers to an individual's perceived strength of relationships with group members. Social closeness among group members can be built on time spent together, mutual benefits, and social friendship. According to social interdependence theory, social structure largely influences the types of interactions in a group setting (Johnson & Johnson, 2009). Cohesive social relations, for example, have a positive influence on the intensity of interactions (Kawachi & Berkman, 2000; Lin et al., 2016). The social closeness among group members in collaborative learning could be positively associated with the perceived social support of individuals, and therefore close social relationships within a group could lead to a trusting and cohesive learning environment and further improve active engagement of individuals in the learning process, which can further enhance learning outcomes and levels of satisfaction.

Various psychometric instruments for measuring social closeness have been proposed in previous studies based on context and study population (Aron et al., 1992; Burnett & Demnar, 1996; Ifenthaler, 2014; Popovic et al., 2003). Unlike psychometric approaches, social network analysis offers a theory-based method to assess social ties based on the structural characteristics of captured social connections (Wasserman & Faust, 1994). In a network, social closeness can be measured based on the strength of ties between the connected actors (Ifenthaler, 2010). Granovetter (1977) developed weak tie theory, which suggests that tie strength in a network plays a critical role in determining the effectiveness and novelty of information sharing and acquisition. Weak ties exist in more casual relationships with less time or emotional exchange and input, and are effective for acquiring new information and making progress, for instance in job seeking or status attainment (Granovetter, 1977). By contrast, strong ties indicate a high level of perceived closeness, intimacy, and high frequency of interactions, and are more effective in maintaining stable relations and increasing social affinity. In this study, we adopt an ego network approach to construct the collaboration network of each participant, based on which the social closeness of the individual is gauged by the average strength of ties in the constructed ego networks.

Ego networks are the networks revealing the social connections of an individual rather than the social relationships among a group of people (Wasserman & Faust, 1994; Borgatti et al., 2009). In an ego network, the ego (focal) node represents the individual that is the focus of interest, and edges represent the social ties that the individual has with others (alters). The links between ego and the alters are characterized by the strength of ties between them. The ego network approach is widely adopted in anthropology to model and analyze individuals' social connections. In this study, an ego network approach is used to capture the social relationships of individual students with their group members in small-team collaborative learning, and the average strength of social ties in an individual's ego network is used to measure their perceived social closeness with group members in a collaborative learning process. A higher value of average strength indicates a stronger social closeness with group members. Following previous research findings, the hypothesis of this study is:

H_0: There is no correlation between students' average social tie strength in their ego networks and their satisfaction with collaborative learning experiences.

H_1: Students with higher average social tie strength in their ego networks are more satisfied with their collaborative learning experiences.

3. METHODS

3.1 Participants and Procedures

In this study, a web-based questionnaire including 19 items was administered in October 2018. The questionnaire was distributed to university students who had participated in any kind of group project in their study program. They completed the survey based on their most recent experience of collaborative learning. The informed consent form – which included the information about research purpose, procedures, data management, and approved ethics for the study – was attached in the first page of the questionnaire. The questionnaire includes three parts: 1) demographic information (including age, gender, academic year, major); 2) items for constructing an individual's ego-network and tie strength; 3) items focusing on the perceived satisfaction of the collaborative learning experience. The items for measuring social closeness and perceived satisfaction of collaborative learning are provided in the subsection below. 120 students from a university in Hong Kong were randomly invited to participate in this study. After screening out the incomplete responses, 109 valid responses (out of 115 responses in total) were received. The average age of participants in the sample was 23 (*SD* = 1.491). Among the participants, 70 students were female (64.2%) and 39 were male (35.7%). There were 67 students (61.5%) who majored within science and engineering and 42 students (38.5%) who majored within arts, social sciences, or humanities. The beginning of the questionnaire asked about the frequency of the student's participation in group-based collaborative projects, to ensure that each valid responder had experienced collaborative learning in their study program. Respondents were asked to answer questions about their perceived closeness to group members and satisfaction level based on their latest experience in group-based collaborative projects.

3.2 Measures

3.2.1 Social Closeness

The average tie strength of ego networks was used to measure the social closeness of participants towards other members in a collaboration group. In the questionnaire, responders (egos) were asked to recall the latest experience of group work in his/her academic program and answer questions such as "Who were your group members (alters)?", and "How close did you feel to each of listed group member?". Social closeness with each group member was measured using a five-point Likert scale (1 = not close at all, 5 = very close). Ego networks for all respondents were constructed based on the collected information. Figure 1 below shows an example of an ego network of one responder in this study. This responder ('R1') had five group members in a group project and the perceived closeness or strength of relationships with the five group members is illustrated through the thickness of the links. The social closeness of this student to their other group members is measured by the mean value of the sum of weights of all links in the ego network. The social closeness of each participant with their group members is acquired using this approach.

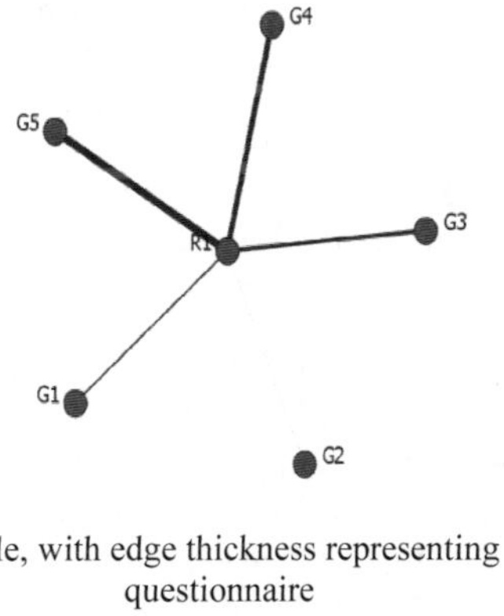

Figure 1. Participant ego network example, with edge thickness representing tie strength as measured through the questionnaire

3.2.2 Perceived Satisfaction of Collaborative Learning

In the questionnaire, responders were also invited to answer questions about their satisfaction towards the same collaborative learning experience. The items for measuring the perceived satisfaction of collaborative learning are presented in Table 1. These items were created based on the characteristics of successful collaborative learning proposed by Dillenbourg (1999), which include: (1) average division of labor; (2) effectiveness of communication and negotiation; (3) shared understanding among group members; (4) acquisition of new knowledge through the learning process. All items were measured using five-point Likert-type scales (1=strongly disagree, 5=strongly agree). The factor loadings of each item were all above 0.5 (see Table 1 below) and the Cronbach's α of all items was .837, indicating that this scale for measuring the perceived satisfaction of collaborative learning shows a high level of reliability.

Table 1. Factor loadings of individual items

Items	*Factor loading*
The division of the workload was reasonable in my group.	.754
Group members actively exchanged ideas with each other.	.704
There were no difficulties in communicating with my group members.	.592
It was easy to achieve consensus in my group.	.658
I could get help from my group members when I encountered difficulties in group work.	.542
By discussing with my group members, I developed new skills and knowledge.	.789
Overall, I was satisfied with my collaborative learning this time.	.811

4. RESULTS

4.1 The Impact of Demographic Factors on Social Closeness and CL

The examined demographic information of participants includes age, gender, and study major. An independent samples t-test was performed to test whether responders with different demographic characteristics had differences in their perceived social closeness to their group members and their perceived satisfaction of collaborative learning. First, we tested the influence of gender on perceived social closeness and satisfaction in collaborative learning. According to the collected data, there was no significant difference, as female (M = 4.09, SD = 0.70) and male students (M = 4.14, SD = .56) did not differ significantly in their perceived closeness with their group members, $t(107)$ = .380, p = .7047. Male students (M = 3.66, SD = .33) had a significant higher satisfaction level with their collaborative learning experience than female students (M= 3.43, SD = .61), $t(107)$ = 2.545, p <.05. Second, we tested whether or not students from different majors behave differently regarding their perceived social closeness and satisfaction in their collaborative learning experience. Students were classified into two groups based on their majors, with responders studying science and engineering classified into one group and students in social sciences, arts and humanities classified into the other group. We find there was no significant difference in the perceived satisfaction of collaborative learning of students majoring in science (M = 3.48, SD = .43) and students majoring in social sciences (M = 3.63, SD = .47), $t(107)$= -1.604, p = .112. There was also no significant difference in social closeness with group members of students majoring in science (M = 4.19, SD = .62) and students majoring in social sciences (M = 4.02, SD = .60), $t(107)$= -1.376, p = .172. Third, the influence of age on the perceived social closeness and satisfaction in CL was also tested. According to the results of a Pearson correlation analysis, there was no significant correlation between age and the two studied variables, $r(107)$ = .110, p=.344. In summary, individuals' social closeness to their group members and perceived satisfaction with collaborative learning were not influenced by their age or academic discipline, but there was a significant difference between male and female students in their satisfaction with collaborative learning.

4.2 The Impact of Social Closeness on CL

Correlation analysis was conducted to test the relationship between individuals' social closeness to their group members and their perceived satisfaction with their collaborative learning experience. Based on Pearson correlation analysis, we found a significant correlation between perceived social closeness and perceived satisfaction with collaborative learning ($r = .210$, $p < .05$), which allows us to reject H_0, indicating that individuals' social closeness with group members is significantly associated with their perceived satisfaction with collaborative learning. The individuals with a close social relationship with their group members tended to be more satisfied with their collaborative learning experience. A linear regression analysis was further conducted to test the predictability of social closeness and gender on collaborative learning. It was verified that social closeness was a significant predictor of perceived satisfaction of collaborative learning ($\beta = .151$, $p < .05$). The variables of social closeness together with gender explained 9.8% of the variance of the perceived satisfaction of collaborative learning. While the explanatory capacity of one independent variable on perceived satisfaction of collaborative learning is limited, it provides a significant explanation of individuals' perceived satisfaction of collaborative learning, and so this result provides a theoretical contribution to our understanding of this process. Accordingly, the hypothesis is accepted, students with higher average social tie strength in their ego networks are more satisfied with their collaborative learning experiences.

5. DISCUSSION

This research examines the relationship between social closeness within a collaboration group and students' perceived satisfaction with collaborative learning. Findings indicate that an individual's perceived social closeness to their group members has a positive association with their satisfaction with collaborative learning. Students who had a closer social relationship with their group members tended to be more satisfied with the collaborative learning experience. This study contributes empirical evidence of the importance of social ties in collaborative learning. Based on this finding, we provide advanced evidence-based insights into instructional design of collaborative learning in educational practice in the paragraphs below.

The rationale for understanding the positive influence of social closeness on perceived satisfaction with collaborative learning can be considered from two perspectives. First, social closeness can increase trust among group members, which can facilitate information sharing and individual engagement in the collaborative learning process (Lin et al., 2016). Second, social closeness can create an inclusive social environment, which can enhance participation by facilitating negotiations and conflict solving among group members. Wilson (2010) highlighted that trust has a positive influence on the willingness of information sharing and also plays an intermediating role in adjusting the competing effects of risk and reward on information sharing. A close social relationship may indicate a level of interpersonal trust, and may have an impact on the willingness of information sharing among group members. Previous studies have highlighted that information sharing and interactions among group members are key to the success of collaborative learning (Dillenbourg, 1999; Ifenthaler, 2014; Vuopala et al., 2016). Beyond that, close social relationships among group members also facilitates an inclusive social environment in which open communication and effective negotiation can be achieved on the basis of mutual understanding and tolerance. Wang (2009) found that forming groups based on friendship can enhance the effectiveness of collaborative learning by creating a harmonious social atmosphere and allowing members to reach agreement about regulations of the collaboration. Close social relationships among group members can promote trust and an inclusive social environment, which can further facilitate information sharing, individual engagement, and consensus driving, as well as create a pleasant social space for collaborative learning processes. In addition to the effect of social closeness on perceived satisfaction of collaborative learning, this study also found that there is a gender difference in the perceived satisfaction of collaborative learning. Male students had an overall higher level of satisfaction of their collaborative learning experience than female students. This result can be interpreted based on Eagly's social role theory (1987) that gender differentiated skills could affect feelings associated with activities. However, the previous study by González-Gómez et al. (2012) found that female students tended to be more satisfied than male students in online learning. Here, we suggest future studies further examine the gender difference in perceived satisfaction of collaboration learning with a larger sample size.

Based on our findings, practical strategies can be applied in instructional design and group management in order to build social closeness among group members in collaborative learning. First, empower students to organize their own collaborative learning groups based on their own social connections and preferences. Ramírez-Correa and Fuentes-Vega (2015) put forward three factors affecting the formation of collaborative learning groups which include homophily, academic performance, and level of happiness. Students like to work with peers who are similar to themselves and have similar academic performance (Ramírez-Correa & Fuentes-Vega, 2015). It is thus easier for students to develop close social relationships with group members selected by themselves rather than arranged by instructors. Freedom to organize their own groups can facilitate the development of a shared sense-making space among group members, as well as effectively aid in achieving consensus in group discussions. Instructional design should also provide time and support for group members to build or strengthen closeness among the members of a team to facilitate a positive perception of the group experience.

Second, incorporating activities for developing group members' social closeness in collaborative learning. Multiple techniques have been proposed with an aim to facilitate social interactions in computer-supported collaborative learning (Bluemink et al., 2010; Johnson et al., 2009; Kobbe et al., 2007). In offline collaborative learning, in addition to the required learning tasks for achieving collaborative learning objectives, group building activities can be introduced at the beginning to help students know their prospective group members better, build social connections, as well as create a more active and relaxing atmosphere for students to conduct collaborative activities. The group building activities should not be complicated but require strong cooperation and coordination among group members. Incorporating group building activities in collaborative learning is important, in particular for the individuals who are new to a study program and have no prior collaboration experience with peers in the program. Group building activities can then help them gain familiarity and develop social connections with each other, which could effectively facilitate the development of social closeness and allow them to achieve more satisfaction with their collaborative learning.

6. CONCLUSION

Engaging students in collaborative learning has always been an important consideration for instructors, and the findings of this study provide advanced theoretical and practical insights for understanding collaborative learning from a social perspective. The success of collaborative learning is partially determined by an effective social learning environment that supports intensive engagement and interactions among group members. In addition to instructional methods for facilitating students' engagement in the learning process, appropriate guidance and intervention should also be integrated to help students develop social closeness with their group members, as this can further enhance the effectiveness of collaborative learning. Future studies are recommended to further test the effect of social closeness with a larger sample size as well as in both online and offline settings. Mixed methods are recommended to further elaborate the theoretical underpinnings for understanding these effects, are suggested for future research.

ACKNOWLEDGMENT

We would like to thank Dr Van Aalst, Jan C. W for valuable discussions and comments on the manuscript. This research is supported by Curtin University's UNESCO Chair of Data Science in Higher Education Learning and Teaching (https://research.curtin.edu.au/unesco/).

REFERENCES

Aron, A., Aron, E. N., & Smollan, D. (1992). Inclusion of other in the self scale and the structure of interpersonal closeness. *Journal of personality and social psychology*, 63(4), 596.

Bluemink, J., Hämäläinen, R., Manninen, T., & Järvelä, S. (2010). Group-level analysis on multiplayer game collaboration: how do the individuals shape the group interaction?. *Interactive Learning Environments*, *18*(4), 365-383.

Borgatti, S. P., Mehra, A., Brass, D. J., & Labianca, G. (2009). Network analysis in the social sciences. *science*, 323(5916), 892-895.

Burnett, P. C., & Demnar, W. J. (1996). The relationship between closeness to significant others and self-esteem. *Journal of Family Studies*, 2(2), 121-129.

Chen, B., Chang, Y. H., Ouyang, F., & Zhou, W. (2018). Fostering student engagement in online discussion through social learning analytics. *The Internet and Higher Education*, *37*, 21-30.

De Laat, M., Lally, V., Lipponen, L., & Simons, R. J. (2007). Investigating patterns of interaction in networked learning and computer-supported collaborative learning: A role for Social Network Analysis. *International Journal of Computer-Supported Collaborative Learning*, 2(1), 87-103.

Dillenbourg, P. (1999). *Collaborative-learning: Cognitive and Computational Approaches.,* Oxford: Elsevier, pp.1-19,

Eagly, A. H. (1987). *Sex differences in social behavior: A social-role interpretation*. Earlbaum, Hillsdale, NJ

Euler, H. A., Hoier, S., & Rohde, P. A. (2001). Relationship-specific closeness of intergenerational family ties: Findings from evolutionary psychology and implications for models of cultural transmission. *Journal of Cross-Cultural Psychology*, 32(2), 147-158.

González-Gómez, F., Guardiola, J., Rodríguez, Ó. M., & Alonso, M. Á. M. (2012). Gender differences in e-learning satisfaction. *Computers & Education*, *58*(1), 283-290.

Granovetter, M. S. (1977). *The strength of weak ties*. In Social networks (pp. 347-367).

Ifenthaler, D. (2010). Scope of graphical indices in educational diagnostics. In D. Ifenthaler, P. Pirnay-Dummer, & N. M. Seel (Eds.), *Computer-based diagnostics and systematic analysis of knowledge* (pp. 213–234). Springer.

Ifenthaler, D. (2014). Toward automated computer-based visualization and assessment of team-based performance. *Journal of Educational Psychology, 106*(3), 651-665. https://doi.org/10.1037/a0035505

Isohätälä, J., Järvenoja, H., & Järvelä, S. (2017). Socially shared regulation of learning and participation in social interaction in collaborative learning. *International Journal of Educational Research*, *81*, 11-24.

Johnson, D. W., & Johnson, R. T. (2009). An educational psychology success story: Social interdependence theory and cooperative learning. *Educational researcher*, *38*(5), 365-379.

Johnson, T. E., Ifenthaler, D., Pirnay-Dummer, P., & Spector, J. M. (2009). Using concept maps to assess individuals and team in collaborative learning environments. In P. L. Torres & R. C. V. Marriott (Eds.), *Handbook of research on collaborative learning using concept mapping* (pp. 358–381). Information Science Publishing.

Kawachi, I., & Berkman, L. (2000). Social cohesion, social capital, and health. *Social epidemiology*, *174*(7).

Kerrigan, S., Feng, S., Vathaluru, R., Ifenthaler, D., & Gibson, D. C. (2021). Network analytics of collaborative problem-solving. In D. Ifenthaler, D. G. Sampson, & P. Isaias (Eds.), *Balancing the tension between digital technologies and learning sciences.* (pp. 53–76). Springer.

Kobbe, L., Weinberger, A., Dillenbourg, P., Harrer, A., Hämäläinen, R., Häkkinen, P., & Fischer, F. (2007). Specifying computer-supported collaboration scripts. *International Journal of Computer-Supported Collaborative Learning*, *2*(2-3), 211-224.

Ledbetter, A. M. (2009). Family communication patterns and relational maintenance behavior: Direct and mediated associations with friendship closeness. *Human Communication Research*, 35(1), 130-147.

Lin, L., Mills, L., & Ifenthaler, D. (2016). Collaboration, multi-tasking and problem solving performance in shared virtual spaces. *Journal of Computing in Higher Education, 28*(3), 344–357. https://doi.org/10.1007/s12528-016-9117-x

Miller, J. E., Trimbur, J., & Wilkes, J. M. (1994). Group dynamics: Understanding group success and failure in collaborative learning. *New directions for teaching and learning*, 1994(59), 33-44.

Murray, S. L. (2005). Regulating the risks of closeness: A relationship-specific sense of felt security. *Current Directions in Psychological Science*, 14(2), 74-78.

Nardi, B. A. (2005). Beyond bandwidth: Dimensions of connection in interpersonal communication. *Computer Supported Cooperative Work (CSCW)*, 14(2), 91-130.

Oliver, R., Omari, A., & Herrington, J. (1998). Exploring student interactions in collaborative World Wide Web learning environments. *Journal of Educational multimedia and Hypermedia*, 7(2/3), 263-287.

Popovic, M., Milne, D., & Barrett, P. (2003). The scale of perceived interpersonal closeness (PICS). *Clinical Psychology & Psychotherapy: An International Journal of Theory & Practice*, 10(5), 286-301.

Ramírez-Correa, P., & Fuentes-Vega, C. (2015). Factors that affect the formation of networks for collaborative learning: an empirical study conducted at a Chilean university. Ingeniare. *Revista chilena de ingeniería*, 23(3), 341-347.

Rimor, R., Rosen, Y., & Naser, K. (2010). Complexity of social interactions in collaborative learning: The case of online database environment. *Interdisciplinary Journal of E-Learning and Learning Objects*, 6(1), 355-365.

Roberts, B. W., Caspi, A., & Moffitt, T. E. (2001). The kids are alright: growth and stability in personality development from adolescence to adulthood. *Journal of personality and social psychology*, 81(4), 670.

Sarason, I. G., Sarason, B. R., Shearin, E. N., & Pierce, G. R. (1987). A brief measure of social support: Practical and theoretical implications. *Journal of social and personal relationships*, 4(4), 497-510

Vuopala, E., Hyvönen, P., & Järvelä, S. (2016). Interaction forms in successful collaborative learning in virtual learning environments. *Active Learning in Higher Education*, 17(1), 25-38.

Wang, Q. (2009). Design and evaluation of a collaborative learning environment. *Computers & Education*, 53(4), 1138-1146.

Wasserman, S., & Faust, K. (1994). *Social network analysis: Methods and applications* (Vol. 8). Cambridge university press.

Wilson, T. D. (2010). Information sharing: an exploration of the literature and some propositions. *Information Research: an International Electronic Journal*, 15(4), n4.

Zuiker, S. J., Anderson, K. T., Jordan, M. E., & Stewart, O. G. (2016). Complementary lenses: Using theories of situativity and complexity to understand collaborative learning as systems-level social activity. *Learning, Culture and Social Interaction*, 9, 80-94.

STUDYING DESIGN ATTRIBUTES OF VIRTUAL CHARACTERS TO SUPPORT STUDENTS' PERCEIVED EXPERIENCES IN VIRTUAL REALITY LECTURES

Brittany Garcia[1], Soo Chun[1], Caleb Kicklighter[1], Bin Mai[2], Marco Palma[3] and Jinsil Hwaryoung Seo[1]

[1]Department of Visualization Texas A&M University, College Station, TX, USA

[2]Department of Educational Administration & Human Resource Development, College Station, TX, USA

[3]Department of Agriculture and Economics, College Station, TX, USA

ABSTRACT

Virtual reality recently expanded to collaborative and social networking environments where users interact with virtual characters (VCs) of various appearances and behaviors, often impacting the quality of experience. In this paper, we present preliminary survey results of perceptions about characteristics of VCs and a user study of a VR lecture app with different styles of virtual instructors. VCs were collected from existing collaborative and social VR applications and categorized by body types and design style. Survey results coupled with prior works guided the development of design styles, which we briefly present. In the user study, 12 users experienced two different VR lectures with randomly assigned character styles. Results show participants found the stylized VC familiar and human while the realistic VC was engaging and trustworthy. Results also show feelings of learning more about the lecture topic with the stylized VC.

KEYWORDS

Virtual Reality, Virtual Character Design, 3D Avatar Design, Perception, Virtual Reality Lecture, Immersive Learning

1. INTRODUCTION

Virtual Reality (VR) environments support a wide range of activities like activities in real environments (Sung, Moon, and Lin, 2011). They are rapidly becoming popular in training, education, and entertainment (Yee, Bailenson, and Rickertsen, 2007), due to VR's interactive and embodied experiences which cannot be easily accessible or possible in the real world (Erolin, Reid, and McDougall, 2019). In addition, the recent expansion of VR technology during the COVID-19 pandemic allows users to meet and work together in a collaborative or social VR environment. In these virtual environments, users often interact with virtual characters (VCs) or avatars: a user plays with another player's avatar in a VR game; a user follows an instruction from a VC in a training application. Users select avatar designs from a list of options or design their own avatar with detailed parts. Different brands or applications provide unique styles on VCs' appearances and behaviors.

Research shows that visual styles of VCs have subsequent impacts on performance in virtual environments (Erolin, Reid, and McDougall, 2019). Yee and Bailenson (2007) found that appearance cues of a VC led users to experience attitudinal and behavioral changes in a manner stereotypically consistent with these cues (Yee and Bailenson, 2007). In educational VR applications, the appearance cues of VCs for instructors, experts, and colleagues are important to create positive impacts on students' learning and learning related experiences. However, there is no strong body of research guiding the design of VCs for VR learning environments. Therefore, we address the following research question in this paper: How do different visual types of VCs impact users' perception and support learning?In this paper, we present preliminary survey results of perceptions on characteristics of VCs, which were collected from existing collaborative and social VR applications and categorized by body types and design style. Then we present a user study of a VR lecture app that we created. This application includes different design styles of virtual instructors. Finally, we discuss meaningful insights of designing virtual instructor characters for educational VR applications.

2. BACKGROUND

2.1 Perception of Virtual Characters

VCs exist within computer simulations and have a perceptible digital character whose behavior is executed by self, others or generated by an intelligent system (Yee and Bailenson, 2007). The visual style of VCs varies; appearance can be influenced by genre, target-audience, or cultural differences. Various design features of VCs' appearances impact participants' emotions, behaviors, interactions and so on. Steptoe et al. (2010) assessed the impact of the addition of realistic eye motion in avatar-mediated communication and found realistic eye movement increases participant accuracy in detecting truth and deception when interacting with virtual avatars (Steptoe et al, 2010).

The domain of VR aims to design characters to foster immersion in the virtual world. Sometimes highly realistic characters create negative reactions and break immersion. This was first observed in the 1970s by Masahiro Mori, a roboticist who noticed humans' negative response to robots or prosthetics that are not quite human-like (Mori, MacDorman, and Kageki, 2012). Mori called this the uncanny valley, which is a serious challenge for designers when creating VCs. Guidelines to avoid the uncanny valley to enhance the quality of experience are needed to design successful products.

2.2 VCs in Educational VR

VCs have been used to deliver educational content as part of a vision that virtual instructors can advantageously influence learning (Krämer and Bente, 2010). These characters have an identifiable body and communicate using voice, gesture, or facial expression for instructional purposes. They embody instructional objectives and goals (Paiva and Machado, 1998; Johnson, Rickel, and Lester, 2000) to support face-to-face interaction in learning environments and have been extensively applied to Virtual Learning Environments that utilize immersive head-mounted displays (HMDs) or virtual reality rooms (Dede, 2009).

Prior research suggests the presence of a human-like animated character can have a positive influence on students' learning experience. For example, people experience more positive emotions when interacting with a VC that gives positive feedback (Pour et al, 2010). Other work has found that people who viewed a human-voiced character with facial expression and body movements performed better on a test of knowledge transfer compared to either a nonmoving character or no character (Mayer and DaPra, 2012; Wagner, Billinghurst, and Schmalstieg, 2006). Further, it has been proposed that in terms of VCs, it is not the presence of the VC itself, but its behavior and the instructional method embedded in its use that impacts positively on learning (Krämer and Bente, 2010). Therefore, the design of VCs focusing on appearance and behavior matters in educational VR environments.

3. PRELIMINARY STUDY IN VC PERCEPTION

To obtain users' general perception of VCs in virtual environments, we developed a survey by collecting 89 VC images with different body types (e.g., full body, half body, torso), styles (e.g., stylized, realistic, non-human) and skin tone (e.g., light, medium, dark) from existing collaborative and social VR applications. Researchers collected images from the following applications: Vspatial (Platt and Tucker, n.d.), Mozillahub (Mozilla Mixed Reality Team, 2018), Rumii (Doghead Simulations, 2017), Spatial (Agarwala, A. and Lee, J. 2016), AltSpace (Microsoft, 2015), Engage (Immersive VR Education Ltd, 2016), VIVE Sync (HTC Vive, 2018), Virbela (Howland, 2012) and VrChat (VRChat Inc., 2014). Researchers took the following steps in selecting the VC images: i.) select VC gender; ii.) select the skin tone, if applicable; iii.) select business casual clothing option for VC if this option was not available researchers went with attire the application automatically generated for the VC; and iv.) researchers took a screenshot of the VC. In the survey a total of 10 representative VC images were presented to participants (Figure 1). These 10 avatars were chosen based on a discrete choice experiment (DCE) which we also used to determine participants preferences. In a DCE preference for a product or service, in our case VCs, are decomposed as preferences for the attributes of a

VC. In essence, a product is viewed as a bundle of attributes and we evaluate the customer, or participant, response to each attribute. The first step in designing the experiment is to select the most relevant attributes and attribute levels for a VC (e.g., gender, body type, skin tone and style). Given the number of attributes and attribute levels, there are a total of 54 possible combinations of attributes. Since it is not feasible to ask respondents to evaluate all possible combinations, we used a fractional factorial design using the %ChoiceEff macro in SAS 9.4 with a modified Fedorov algorithm to optimize the VC combinations (Kuhfeld, 2013). In particular, the design is optimized for orthogonality (independence of the attributes) and balance (the attributes appearing the same number of times). The final design consisted of 9 choice sets of two VC alternatives with a D-efficiency measure of 95.68%. Researchers chose ten combinations of the VCs based on the SAS results. Researchers tested this first draft of the survey, asking about 20 VCs, with six individuals and found that the participants found the survey to be too long lasting 1.5 to 2 hours, therefore researchers chose ten VCs of the for the final survey (Figure 1).

Figure 1. Representative virtual characters for survey

Likert scales were used to rate characters on familiarity (Hiroi, Ito, and Nakano, 2009), engagement (IJsselsteijn, de Kort, and Poels 2013), trust (Chae, Lee, and Seo, 2016) and humanness (Ho and MacDorman, 2010), which are critical perceptive aspects when users interact with VCs. We asked participants to imagine the style (e.g., robot, stylized, realistic, other, unsure) they preferred for a VC instructor. Researchers were interested in investigating preference, to do so a discrete choice experiment (DCE) was implemented to assess participant's preferences for VCs. Participants choose the option they prefer, and their choice provides a measure of their preference. This experimental design has two main advantages. First, it provides more realistic VC environments by providing actual VCs instead of asking participants to simply rate their liking for individual design features. Second, it is easier and more intuitive for participants to choose the VC character that they would prefer in an educational context. The survey was distributed via university bulk email, word of mouth and social media.

3.1 Results

A total of 105 responses were collected, 36 males, 68 females and 1 prefer not to say aged 18-24 (54.29%), 25-34 (19.05%), 35-44 (11.43%), 45-54 (8.57%), 55-64 (5.71%) and 65+ (.95%). 64.76% of participants reported experience with VR using head mounted displays and mobile VR. 39.81% reported experience with VCs in VR with the most common style being stylistic in gaming applications. Participants reported preferences for stylized and realistic VCs as educational instructors. Analysis of variance results are reported in the sections below along with the results for a mixed logit model to determine participants' VC preference.

3.1.1 Familiarity

An independent one-way ANOVA showed a significant effect of VC body (full body, half body and torso) on familiarity ($F(2, 1057) = 16.78$, $p<.001$). Post hoc testing revealed full bodies resulted in greater familiarity than half bodies ($p<.001$). There were also significant differences in familiarity between half and torso bodies ($p<.001$), with torso being more familiar. There were no significant differences in familiarity between full and torso bodies ($p=.588$). An independent one-way ANOVA showed a significant effect of VC style (stylized, realistic, and non-human) on familiarity (F (2, 1056) =19.231, p<.001). Post hoc testing revealed that stylized VCs were significantly more familiar than realistic style (p<.001) and non-human styles were significantly more familiar than realistic styles (p=.025). There were no significant differences in familiarity between stylized and non-human styles (p=.515).

3.1.2 Engagement

An independent one-way ANOVA showed a significant effect of body type on engagement (F (2, 1057) =6.120, p=.002). Post hoc testing revealed torso bodies resulted in greater engagement than half bodies (p=.002). There were no significant differences in engagement between full and half bodies (p=.089) nor between full and torso bodies (p=.743). An independent one-way ANOVA showed a significant effect of style on engagement (F (2, 1057) =10.776, p<.001). Post hoc testing revealed stylized VCs were significantly more engaging than realistic styles (p<.001). There were no significant differences in engagement between stylized and non-human styles (p=.517) nor realistic and non-human styles (p=.202).

3.1.3 Trust

An independent one-way ANOVA showed a significant effect of body type on trust (F (2, 1057) =6.834, p=.001). Post hoc testing revealed torso bodies were significantly more trustworthy than half bodies (p<.001). There were no significant differences in trust between full and half bodies (p=.150) nor full and torso bodies (p=.458). An independent one-way ANOVA showed a significant effect of style on trust (F (2, 1057) =9.554, p<.001). Post hoc testing revealed stylized VCs were significantly more trustworthy than realistic style (p<.001). There were no significant differences in trust between stylized and non-human styles (p=.750) nor realistic and non-human styles (p=.139).

3.1.4 Humanness

An independent one-way ANOVA showed a significant effect of body type on familiarity (F (2, 1057) =14.072, p<.001). Post hoc testing revealed full bodies were significantly more human than half bodies (p=001). There were also significant differences in humanness between half and torso bodies (p<.001), with torso being greater. There were no significant differences in humanness between full and torso bodies (p=.742). An independent one-way ANOVA showed a significant effect of style on humanness (F (2, 1057) =11.383, p<.001). Post hoc testing revealed stylized VCs were significantly more human than realistic style (p<.001) and non-human styles were more human than realistic (p=.002). There were no significant differences in humanness between stylized and non-human style (p=.708).

3.1.5 Mixed Logit Model

Since in our experimental design participants are choosing between two products (VCs), we estimate a mixed logit model. Authors will first explain the purpose of a mixed logit model and then report the model's results. A mixed logit model allows for the estimation of mean preference parameters and standard deviations to provide measures of preference heterogeneity. The mean parameters represent the average preference of the entire sample. A positive parameter indicates that the specified attribute increases the probability of the VC being chosen. Hence, a positive coefficient is interpreted as a most preferred design feature. Similarly, a negative mean parameter indicates a lower likelihood of choosing the VC for that attribute and therefore a lower preference for that attribute. A statistically significant Standard Deviation parameter provides indication of preference heterogeneity. That is that some respondents may prefer an attribute while other respondents dislike it. The MEAN parameters show the likelihood of choosing an avatar with those characteristics. Each attribute is relative to the baseline, which is Male, Half-body, Medium skin color, Non-Human. A positive and significant variable means a preference for that variable. A negative and significant parameter is a negative preference. The mean results show the aggregate effects. The standard deviation results show how heterogeneous the responses are.

Results from the mixed logit model indicate that there were no significant differences in the mean preferences for VCs gender. The standard deviation coefficient for females is significant showing heterogeneous effects for gender. Figure 2 Graph A shows that the mean response is symmetrical and around zero, with about half of participants preferring a female VC (positive coefficient) and half preferring a male VC (negative coefficients); therefore, there is no statistical significance of the mean parameter for gender. With regards to body type torso was less preferred to half body, but full body was preferred to half-body.

There were also heterogeneous effects for torso. In Figure 2 Graph B the distribution of torso is negative, meaning everybody disliked it. Full bodied VCs had a positive distribution indicating that all participants liked it (Figure 2 Graph C). For style of VC realistic was preferred to non-human while stylized was no different than non-human. Realistic and stylized VCs also had heterogeneous effects. The distribution for realistic VCs shows that although a group of participants disliked them the mass concentration of the distribution was positive (Figure 2 Graph D). Stylized VCs were almost evenly distributed among positive and negative coefficients, meaning some people liked it while others didn't (Figure 2 Graph E).

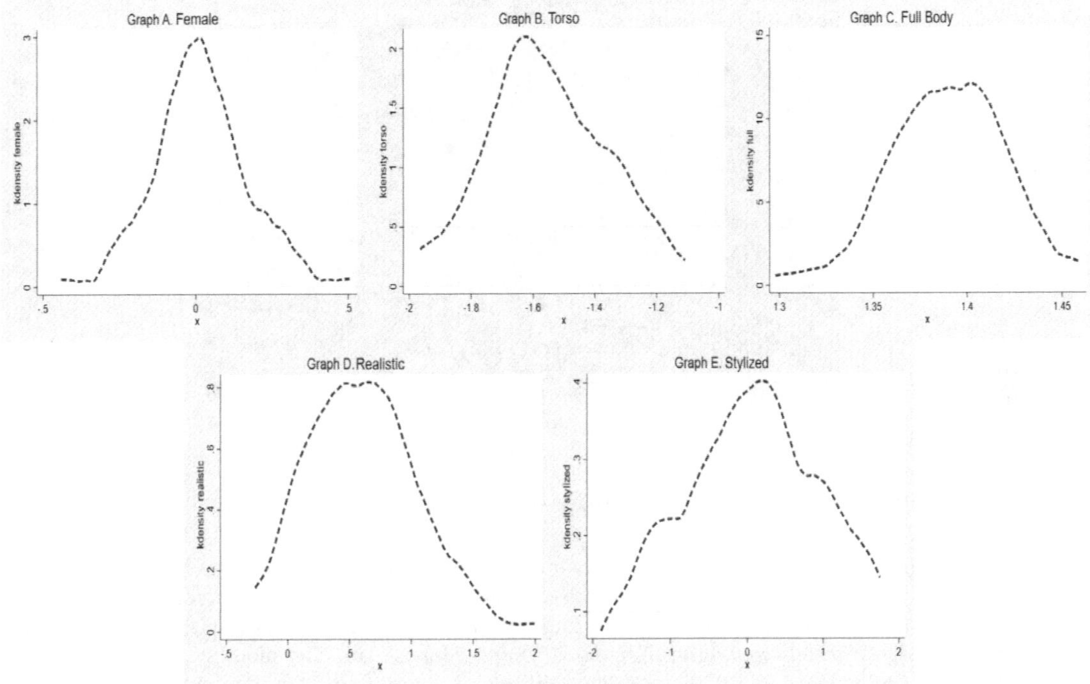

Figure 2. Mixed logit model graphs

4. DESIGNING THE VR LECTURE APPLICATION

In this section we discuss shortly the findings from the survey obtaining perceptions of VCs followed by a description of how we designed the VR Lecture application. For VC style we found stylized characters were engaging, familiar, human, and trustworthy, while non-human style characters were more human and familiar. Results of instructor preferences indicated that female was preferred over male, torso is less preferred to half-body while full body is preferred to half body, and realistic VCs were preferred to non-human while stylized VCs were no different than non-human. Based on these results, we designed a lecture VR application with a virtual instructor in a simulated classroom that was female and full bodied. Researchers were interested in comparing realistic VCs to stylized VCs and therefore decided to make both a realistic and stylized VC instructor. In the developed virtual reality application, the instructor stands on a stage behind a lectern, and faces the VR user, who sits in a seat in front of the stage. The instructor then gives a 10-minute psychology lecture, speaking directly to the user while supplementary visuals and text appear on a projection screen (Figure 3).

Figure 3. VR lecture user view

4.1 Design of the Virtual Instruction

We began the design of our VCs by creating two female personas (Maria and Amanda). We then used a software package, Fuse (Adobe, 2020), to create a photo-realistic character model for each VC based on personas and concept art. Once we had the two realistic models, we were then able to create stylized versions of each. The stylized models were built from an existing base mesh and later modified in a digital sculpting program, Zbrush (Pixologic, 2020). This resulted in four total instructors for our experiment: two realistic characters built in Fuse, and two stylized models based on the realistic characters (Figure 4).

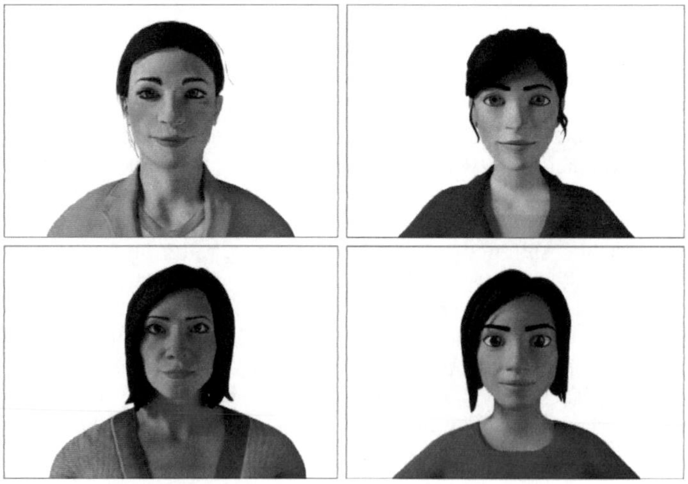

Figure 4. 3D Virtual Instructors: Amanda (Top) and Maria (Bottom)

4.1.1 Character Appearance

Character Stylization: There are numerous ways that a VC can be abstracted or stylized. For this project, we focused primarily on four processes: exaggerate the body's proportions; simplify the shape or profile of features; eliminate non-expressive anatomical details; and create a less-detailed skin texture. In this process of stylizing our realistic VCs many different aspects of their design were impacted. However, specific features like skin color, nose width, jaw size, hair style, and eye shape were preserved to maintain an identifiable relationship between the realistic models and their stylized versions.

Body Shape: We established a design target to use as reference for effective 3D character stylization. We went with female characters from Disney's animated film "Big Hero 6" (Hall and Williams, 2014). Working from screenshots and artwork, the team's 3D artists used Zbrush (Pixologic, 2020) to morph our character's body shapes. For a female character in a modern Disney film, that means the head is larger than real life while the torso, hands, and feet remain small. The silhouette of the body is simplified to resemble more geometric shapes (like triangles and ovals) and lines, markers become streamlined.

Facial Proportion: The face was treated the same way: shapes were simplified, proportions were exaggerated, features that were unique to the character were accentuated. Special attention was given to the most expressive parts of the face: eyes, mouth, and eyebrows. These regions are integral to reading information in the face and are cornerstones for facial recognition algorithms (Sadr, Jarudi, and Sinha, 2003) and taxonomy systems like the Facial Action Coding System (Ekman, Rosenberg, 1997). Large eyes are a common feature in animated films and have the added benefit of making the subject appear more trustworthy (Zebrowitz, Voinescu, and Collins, 1996).

4.1.2 Character Motion

We had access to a motion-capture stage with a VICON Motion Capture Unit System. A university professor donned the suit to act out the lecture, movements were later mapped to a 3D skeleton and cleaned in Motionbuilder (Autodesk, 2020). The same motion and skeleton were applied to all four VCs. Mouth animation was generated procedurally with SALSA LipSync (Crazy Minnow Studio, 2019). A script was fed into the software, which translated the text into visemes that matched the words.

4.1.3 Interactions

In this version of the application user interactions are minimal. In the application users are greeted with a start menu. After pressing the start button users enter the virtual classroom which consists of four interaction options: pausing and resuming the lesson, a summary of the lesson and the instructor, and an exit option.

4.1.4 Lesson Development

The research team decided to cover two topics in psychology: Stress, Lifestyle and Health and Introduction to Personality Psychology. We utilized open educational resources to create initial outlines and created slides covering the two topics, based on which transcripts for the presentation were created. We worked with a professional voice actress to create supplemental audio for the lectures.

5. VR LECTURE PILOT STUDY

We conducted a between-subjects pilot study with 12 participants (7 male and 5 female) whose ages ranged from 18-24 (5) and 25-34 (7). Participants were recruited through word of mouth. Participants were randomly assigned to two of eight possible conditions which consisted of the learning topic (Personality Psychology or Stress, Health and Wellbeing), VC (Maria or Amanda) and VC style (realistic or stylized), which were then counterbalanced for session order. Participants were greeted by a researcher and then debriefed and given a consent form. During the first session, participants were given a pre-survey addressing demographic questions, experience with VR, experience with VCs in VR, prior knowledge on the learning topics and what style of educational VC they would want (e.g., robot, stylized or realistic) as an instructor. After the pre-survey participants used an Oculus Quest 2 headset to experience the VR Lecture, each lasting 10 minutes. After the lesson the participant was given a post-survey which included a short quiz and Likert scale items addressing overall experience, perception of VCs (e.g., familiarity (Hiroi, Ito, and Nakano, 2009), engagement (IJsselsteijn, de Kort, and Poels 2013), trust (Chae, Lee, and Seo, 2016) and humanness (Ho and MacDorman, 2010) and learning experience. Participants were then offered a five-to-ten-minute break if needed, if not the study continued. In the second session participants answered a short pre-survey addressing prior knowledge of the second learning topic and then experienced the second lesson. After completing the session, the participant was given a post-survey which contained the same constructs as the first. Once the post survey was completed a short semi-structured interview was conducted, participants were debriefed and thanked for their time.

5.1 Results of the VR Lecture Study

Of these participants 11 had experience with VR using predominantly head mounted displays (HMDs) followed by mobile VR. 6 participants had experience with VCs in VR specifically those that are stylized followed by realistic in gaming applications. When asked what style VC they would like to see in an educational setting 8 participants wanted stylized and 4 wanted realistic VCs. Independent samples t-tests were conducted to see if there were any differences in the perceptions participants had on the VC's style (e.g., realistic or stylized) with regards to familiarity, engagement, trust, humanness, and learning. There were no significant differences found for any of the constructs (Table 1).

Table 1. Independent samples t-test results

Construct	Group	M	SD	*t*	df	*p*
Familiarity	Realistic	4	.95	-.516	22	.068
	Stylized	4.17	.39			
Engagement	Realistic	3.31	.96	.286	22	.917
	Stylized	3.2	.95			
Trust	Realistic	3.96	.75	.722	22	.935
	Stylized	3.75	.66			
Humanness	Realistic	3.38	.74	-1.15	22	.115
	Stylized	3.79	.52			
Learning	Realistic	3.75	.62	-1.149	22	.157
	Stylized	4	.43			

6. DISCUSSION AND CONCLUSION

We investigated how different types of VCs impact users' perception and support learning. Despite there not being any significant differences in t-tests, like the survey results, we found that stylized characters were more familiar and human. This finding is like previous findings in VR research where stylized characters are more appealing than realistic (McDonnell, Breidt, and Bülthoff, 2012). This preference can be related to the uncanny valley where users are comfortable with VCs that appear realistic but still have robotic aspects and tendencies to them. Unlike the survey we found that realistic characters were more engaging and trustworthy. This could be because participants in the survey were looking at a 2D image of a 3D character while participants in the pilot study were in an immersed environment and able to see the 3D character in front of them. Another possibility to this finding can be attributed to the behavior of instructing, as previous research has found that behavior of a realistic character impacts user's affinity towards that character (Zibrek, Kokkinara, and McDonnell, 2018). Cui et al (2021) conducted a study investigating the realism of a VC in their Japanese language learning application, Daigaku Life, and found that users were more immersed and found the VC more realistic based on the conversational and instructional behavior exhibited (Cui et al, 2021). With regards to learning, participants felt as if they learned more about the lesson topics with stylized characters, this is interesting because participants rated the realistic style character as being more engaging. This finding aligns with research done by Vicneas and Zamzuri (2019) who found cartoon styled characters resulted in greater perceptions of learning than realistic (Vicneas and Zamzuri, 2019). Implications from this work include information on how to design VC instructors for lecture purposes. By developing trustworthy and engaging VCs we can provide students with a more immersive remote learning experience, which is greatly needed in the current times. In future research we aim to design and compare male VCs to the female in a larger study. Limitations of this study include i.) for the survey, participants rated 2D images of 3D VCs without interaction; ii.) for the pilot study there was a small sample size and the users had minimal interaction in the learning environment.

ACKNOWLEDGEMENT

T3 Grant Program at Texas A&M University; the Visualization Undergraduate Research Students who participated in this project.

REFERENCES

Adobe. 2020. Fuse [Computer Software]. Retrieved from https://www.adobe.com/wam/fuse.html.

Agarwala, A. and Lee, J. 2016. Spatial. [online] Available at: https://spatial.io/ (Accessed 11 June 2020).

Autodesk. 2020. Motionbuilder [Computer Software]. Retrieved from https://www.autodesk.com/products/motionbuilder/overview?.

Chae, S.W., Lee, K.C. and Seo, Y.W., 2016. Exploring the effect of avatar trust on learners' perceived participation intentions in an e-learning environment. International Journal of Human–Computer Interaction, 32(5), pp.373-393.

Crazy Minnow Studio. 2019. SALSA LipSync [Computer Software]. Retrieved from https://crazyminnowstudio.com/unity-3d/lip-sync-salsa/.

Cui, D., Whittinghill, D., Fukada, A., Mousas, C., and Adamo, N., 2021. Interacting with virtual instructors: The effect of gender and years of study on the perception of in-game instructors. Computer Animation and Virtual Worlds., 32(3-4), p.e2026.

Dede, C., 2009. Immersive interfaces for engagement and learning. science, 323(5910), pp.66-69.

Doghead Simulations. 2017. rumii. [online] Available at: https://www.dogheadsimulations.com/rumii (Accessed 9 June 2020).

Ekman, P., and Rosenberg, E.L. eds., 1997. What the face reveals: Basic and applied studies of spontaneous expression using the Facial Action Coding System (FACS). Oxford University Press, USA.

Erolin, C., Reid, L. and McDougall, S., 2019. Using virtual reality to complement and enhance anatomy education. Journal of visual communication in medicine, 42(3), pp.93-101.

Big Hero 6 (2014) Directed by Don Hall and Chris Williams [Film]. Walt Disney Animation.

Hiroi, Y., Ito, A. and Nakano, E., 2009. Evaluation of robot-avatar-based user-familiarity improvement for elderly people. KANSEI Engineering International, 8(1), pp.59-66.

Ho, C.C. and MacDorman, K.F., 2010. Revisiting the uncanny valley theory: Developing and validating an alternative to the Godspeed indices. Computers in Human Behavior, 26(6), pp.1508-1518.

Howland, A. 2012. Virbela. [online] Available at: https://www.virbela.com/ (Accessed 11 June 2020).

HTC Vive. 2018. VIVE Sync. [online] Available at: https://sync.vive.com/ (Accessed 5 June 2020).

IJsselsteijn, W.A., de Kort, Y.A. and Poels, K., 2013. The Game Experience Questionnaire. Eindhoven: Technische Universiteit Eindhoven.

Immersive VR Education Ltd. 2016, March. Engage. [online] Available at: https://engagevr.io/ (Accessed 9 June 2020).

Johnson, W.L., Rickel, J.W. and Lester, J.C., 2000. Animated pedagogical agents: Face-to-face interaction in interactive learning environments. International Journal of Artificial intelligence in education, 11(1), pp.47-78.

Krämer, N.C. and Bente, G., 2010. Personalizing e-learning. The social effects of pedagogical agents. Educational Psychology Review, 22(1), pp.71-87.

Kuhfeld, W. and Cai, W., 2013. Introducing the new ADAPTIVEREG procedure for adaptive regression. In Proceedings of the SAS Global Forum 2013 Conference, Cary, NC: SAS Institute Inc. Available at http:/support. sas. com/resources/papers/proceedings13/457-2013. pdf.

Mayer, R.E. and DaPra, C.S., 2012. An embodiment effect in computer-based learning with animated pedagogical agents. Journal of Experimental Psychology: Applied, 18(3), p.239.

McDonnell, R., Breidt, M. and Bülthoff, H.H., 2012. Render me real? Investigating the effect of render style on the perception of animated virtual humans. ACM Transactions on Graphics (TOG), 31(4), pp.1-11.

Microsoft. 2015, May. AltspaceVR. [online] Available at: https://altvr.com/ (Accessed 9 June 2020).

Mori, M., MacDorman, K.F. and Kageki, N., 2012. The uncanny valley [from the field]. IEEE Robotics & Automation Magazine, 19(2), pp.98-100.

Mozilla Mixed Reality Team. 2018. Mozilla Hubs. [online] Available at: https://hubs.mozilla.com/ (Accessed 1 June 2020).

Paiva, A. and Machado, I., 1998, August. Vincent, an autonomous pedagogical agent for on-the-job training. In International Conference on Intelligent Tutoring Systems (pp. 584-593). Springer, Berlin, Heidelberg.

Pixologic. 2020. Zbrush [Computer Software]. Retrieved from https://store.pixologic.com/.

Platt, R. and Tucker, D. n.d. vSpatial. [online] Available at: https://www.vspatial.com/about#Team (Accessed 5 June 2020).

Pour, P.A., Hussain, M.S., AlZoubi, O., D'Mello, S. and Calvo, R.A., 2010, June. The impact of system feedback on learners' affective and physiological states. In International Conference on Intelligent Tutoring Systems (pp. 264-273). Springer, Berlin, Heidelberg.

Sadr, J., Jarudi, I. and Sinha, P., 2003. The role of eyebrows in face recognition. Perception, 32(3), pp.285-293.

Steptoe, W., Steed, A., Rovira, A. and Rae, J., 2010, April. Lie tracking: social presence, truth and deception in avatar-mediated telecommunication. In Proceedings of the SIGCHI Conference on Human Factors in Computing Systems (pp. 1039-1048).

Sung, Y., Moon, J. and Lin, J.S., 2011. Actual self vs. avatar self: The effect of online social situation on self-expression. Journal of Virtual Worlds Research, 4(1).

Vicneas, M. and Zamzuri, A., 2019. Different Realism Designs of 2D Virtual Agents and its' Arousal Effect on Students' Emotions in Learning.

VRChat Inc. 2014, January. VRChat. [online] Available at: https://hello.vrchat.com/ (Accessed 11 June 2020).

Wagner, D., Billinghurst, M. and Schmalstieg, D., 2006, June. How real should virtual characters be?. In Proceedings of the 2006 ACM SIGCHI international conference on Advances in computer entertainment technology (pp. 57-es).

Yee, N. and Bailenson, J.N., 2006. Walk a mile in digital shoes: The impact of embodied perspective-taking on the reduction of negative stereotyping in immersive virtual environments. Proceedings of PRESENCE, 24, p.26.

Yee, N., Bailenson, J.N. and Rickertsen, K., 2007, April. A meta-analysis of the impact of the inclusion and realism of human-like faces on user experiences in interfaces. In Proceedings of the SIGCHI conference on Human factors in computing systems (pp. 1-10).

Zebrowitz, L.A., Voinescu, L. and Collins, M.A., 1996. " Wide-eyed" and" crooked-faced": Determinants of perceived and real honesty across the life span. Personality and social psychology bulletin, 22(12), pp.1258-1269.

Zibrek, K., Kokkinara, E. and McDonnell, R., 2018. The effect of realistic appearance of virtual characters in immersive environments-does the character's personality play a role?. IEEE transactions on visualization and computer graphics, 24(4), pp.1681-1690.

TOWARDS A USER FOCUSED DEVELOPMENT OF A DIGITAL STUDY ASSISTANT THROUGH A MIXED METHODS DESIGN

Katharina Schurz[1], Johannes Schrumpf[1], Felix Weber[1], Maren Lübcke[2], Funda Seyfeli[2] and Klaus Wannemacher[2]
[1]*Osnabrück University, Germany*
[2]*HIS Institute for Higher Education Development, Germany*

ABSTRACT

Digital Study Assistants (DSA) aim to support individual learning processes by designing them appropriately and efficiently based on recommendations. In this paper we present a prototype of a DSA for students in higher education of three German universities. The digital data driven DSA is integrated into the local learning management system and consists of recommender modules with a certain kind of recommendation for a specific purpose, e.g., recommending Academic Contacts that fit an expressed academic interest. The modules implemented so far use a wide range of methods: Classic rule-based Artificial Intelligence (AI) or Neural Networks, that can detect complex features and patterns in large data sets. To evaluate the current prototype of the DSA we used a mixed methods design approach with concurrently collected user data and qualitative data. A first insight in the user data suggests that recommender modules providing personalized recommendations are more likely to be used by students. A focus group discussion with students confirmed these findings with the suggestion to make the DSA more personal, individual, interactive, supportive, and user-friendly. In conclusion we present ideas for the further development of the prototype based on these findings.

KEYWORDS

AI in Education, Digital Study Assistant (DSA), Higher Education, Individual Learning Process, Innovative Learning Management Systems (LMS), Mixed Methods Design, Recommender Systems

1. INTRODUCTION

In the digital age learners are confronted with an overwhelmingly rich supply of educational resources of various qualities (Atenas *et al.*, 2014), but limited temporal and attentional processing capabilities (Sweller, 1988). In contrast to former times, when access to information and education was a privilege, nowadays the choice of the right learning resource at the right time has become a key aspect of successful education.

Digital Study Assistants (DSA) have the potential to support individual learning processes by designing them appropriately and efficiently. They can preprocess large databases containing educational resources and recommend those fitting the individual needs of the user by leveraging AI technology (Alexander *et al.*, 2019).

Although self-regulated learning (Zimmerman, 1990) in higher education plays an important role in the demand for lifelong learning, studies show mixed results when it comes to integrating technology into the learning process (Broadbent and Poon, 2015). Students can benefit from elaborating on and developing personal educational goals (Morisano, 2013; Schippers *et al.*, 2020) and it has been argued that self-regulated learning relies on goals (Zimmerman, 1990; Virtanen et al., 2013) Digital assistants can remind and nudge learners to keep them on track towards their self-set educational goals, even in face of distractions.

Learning partnerships or learning groups of students can amplify learning processes (Okita, 2012). Digital assistants can find peers with similar educational interests, based on data patterns, and provide contact recommendations to students. In the context of higher education, digital assistants can guide students to plan, follow their plan and reflect upon learning behaviors and potential improvements. In these ways digital assistants can serve as amplifiers of learning processes.

1.1 Study Assistant Software Prototype used in our Field Study

We have developed a digital data-driven study-assistant, which is integrated into the local learning management system (LMS) Stud.IP of three German universities. Connecting the DSA software to an established LMS provides students with easy access to the assistant and its features. Simultaneously, attaching the DSA to the LMS allows for an aggregation of information of a university's educational resources such as courses, study programs and user relations, by obtaining information from its LMS database.

Students interact with the service through the learning management system *Stud.IP* (Stockmann and Berg, 2005). The main frontend of our study assistant is implemented as a plugin for the LMS. The job of the frontend is exclusively to visualize data provided by the backend and to react to user-inputs. The frontend can interact with services of the user's university, such as collecting data from the Stud.IP database to and send it to the backend. As the Stud.IP system allows to regularly execute jobs on its servers, the frontend can additionally serve as a data collection interface for courses, dates of scientific talks, and other information added by lecturers and students. Backend and frontend communicate via a RESTful interface using textual representations with a stateless protocol which allows to *receive, transfer, update* or *delete* data through *requests* formatted following the JSON-API standard. Especially when web services dealing with personal data are concerned, adhering to high security standards is mandatory. The data we transfer over the internet is pseudonymized, transferred over encrypted channels, and *salted* (Morris and Thompson, 1979). Furthermore, the backend does not communicate with requests other than the respective instance of the frontend. The core of our architecture resides on the backend server, written in *python3* and based on the Django ("Django", 2020) framework and runs a PostgreSQL database (Stonebraker and Kemnitz, 1991).

1.2 Modular Software Architecture with Recommender Modules

The current software prototype is the third version in a row of annual releases with a growing set of functionalities. These functionalities are encapsulated into so-called *recommender modules*, each presenting contextual information for a specific topic.

Recommender modules are always defined from the user perspective: They provide a certain kind of recommendation for a specific topic, e.g., recommending academic contacts that fit to an expressed academic interest. The modules implemented so far use a wide range of methods: Classic rule-based Artificial Intelligence, often used in expert systems, combines known facts about the world with rules about these facts to derive new potentially useful knowledge, while modern approaches of AI, such as Neural Networks, can detect complex features and patterns in large data sets.

Following object-oriented software design patterns, this design allows to develop separate functionalities and to test, evaluate and improve them independently. The designed recommender modules offer recommendations to optimize their study organization (e.g., information on studying abroad, information on funding). But also, students can learn more about the role of the memory function in learning processes and receive personalized recommendations for optimizing their learning behavior or can inform themselves about techniques for self-regulated learning. Currently the following recommender modules have been implemented, used, and tested by university students in an ongoing field study:

Academic Interests: An AI-based semantic search engine relating natural language inputs with a knowledge domain and suggesting educational resources, e.g., suggestions for courses, based on their content.

To-do: A list of tasks the user formulates in natural language.

Scientific Career: This module gives hints towards funding, external sources of information in the web and events, institutions, and courses within the local university, directed towards a scientific career.

Data Ethics: This module provides learning content about data-ethical questions related to digital assistants.

Personality Module: Long-term memory, short-term memory and the ability for task-switching are measured with psychometric measures. Based on the results students get recommendations for their learning behavior.

Learning Organization: A list of methods to inform about techniques for self-regulated learning.

Open Educational Resources: A general introduction in the field of open educational resources (OER) and a list of OER depositories.

Funding: A step by step guide giving tips for multiple approaches towards financing oneself during one's studies.

Evaluation: A questionnaire asking the users to rate their experience with the DSA.

Academic contacts: This recommender module offers students the possibility to find other learners at the three partner universities that share adjustable properties, such as common interests, study program, degree or a common destination country for a semester abroad.

The goal of this study is to derive requirements for enhancement for a current DSA system through quantitative and qualitative methods. These requirements ought to cover suggestions for individual recommender modules as well as general aspects of the DSA.

2. METHODS

To evaluate the current prototype of the DSA we used a mixed methods design approach (Schoonenboom and Johnson, 2017) with concurrently collected quantitative and qualitative data from the current field study, running since December 2020 at three universities in Northern Germany.

2.1 Quantitative: Data Collection, Data Set and Data Analysis

To evaluate the user interactions with the DSA we used data from the PostgreSQL database of the backend server, generated between December 2020 and May 2021. The resulting adjusted data set includes information about interaction of users with recommender modules, the evaluation of the single activities in the recommender modules, the university of origin, the user target degrees, the subjects of study and the current semester of the enrollment. We use descriptive statistics to give a first insight in the interaction of the users with the recommender modules. It is important to note that albeit originating from the same data, our analyzing methods highlight different perspectives on this data. These perspectives are dependent on how much data users donated. This means that while some, more general statistics can be generated from the entire data set, other statistics rely on more specific data that not all or only few participants shared with the DSA.

2.2 Qualitative: Design Thinking Workshop

For the purpose of iteratively evaluating the prototype, a total of four virtual focus group discussions were held in March 2021 in a design thinking workshop format (Plattner et al., 2010) with seven to nine students from each of the three university locations involved. The primary compilation criterion of the groups was the study phases, which were subdivided into introductory phase, middle study phase, and study completion phase.

The overall goal of these discussions was to evaluate the status of the prototype for the purpose of gathering suggestions for optimization.

To evaluate the current state of the prototype, the students were divided into small groups in which they selected two to three recommender modules and tested them together. Finally, the group was asked to complete an online questionnaire, tailored to the respective recommender module. The entire group then collected suggestions for optimizing the individual recommender module and the DSA in general.

3. RESULTS

We present the results from the quantitative method based on data from the DSA's backend followed by the results from the qualitative method based on a design thinking workshop.

3.1 Quantitative Data Analysis Results

The latest developed prototype is used by Bachelor and Master students of various study programs of three German universities. From December 2020 till the mid of May 2021 the DSA had 688 active users from all three partner universities with more than 40.000 single interactions with different recommender modules.

When a student interacts with the DSA the first time, all recommender modules are presented with a short teaser prompt. Students can then choose which recommender modules they want to explore and use further. Students can either choose to activate recommender modules, to deactivate them or to not interact with them at all. Figure 1 shows the usage decisions per recommender module. The *OER*-module is activated by the most users, followed by the *Academic Interests*, *Personality* and *Learning Organization Modules*.

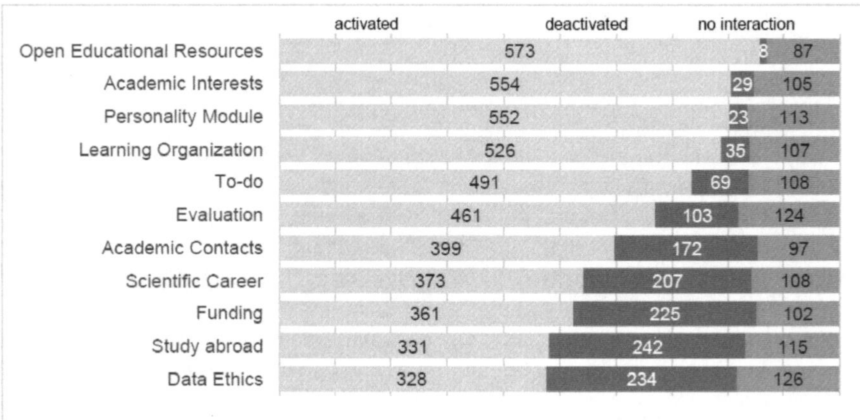

Figure 1. Usage per recommender module for N = 688 users. The numbers in the colored areas represent the amount of interaction decisions made by users where the first number represents recommender module activation, the second number deactivation and the third number inaction

Conversely, the deactivation rate follows a trend inverting activation rate per recommender: While the *OER* recommender module was seldomly deactivated, 34% of users deactivated the *Data Ethics* recom-mender module. With an average of 108, non-interactions stay relatively uniform between recommenders.

User data, such as their semester of enrollment and their degree are visualized in figure 2. As a comparison, we also included the number of PhD students ("Promotion") and an excerpt of students with enrollment in non-Bachelor and non-Master studies ("Magister"). The data presented in figure 2 shows that most users study in a Bachelor's program. When it comes to the semester of enrollment, most users within a Bachelor's or Master's program are first semester students. This is followed by students in their third semester.

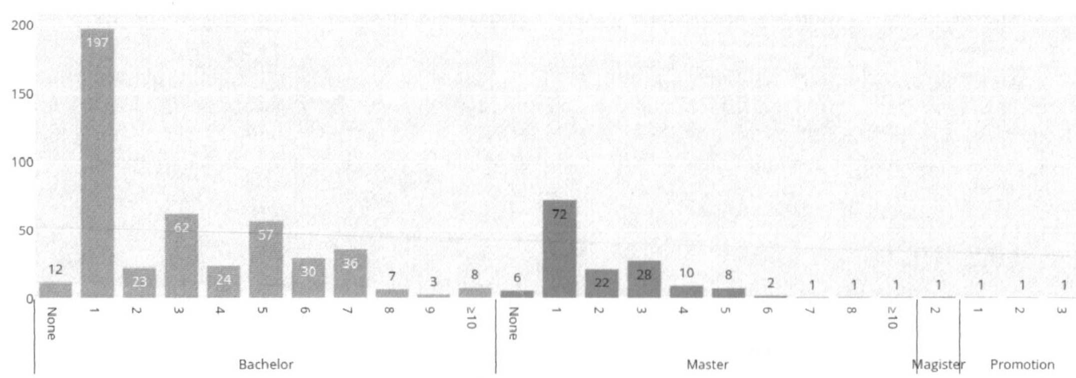

Figure 2. User target degrees and usage of recommender modules (N = 614)

To further analyze the recommender usage in relation to degree, we analyze the recommender interaction frequency of 458 Bachelor and 151 Master students. This leads to a total of 609 users. We investigate whether there are differences in recommender module usage frequency between users enrolled in their Bachelor and Master studies respectively. We present the results in table 1.

Table 1. Comparison of relative usage between Bachelor and Master degree

Recommender Module	Relative usage Bachelor	Relative usage Master	Difference in relative usage frequency
Academic Interests	82.3	80.8	1.5
To-do	75.9	63.6	12.3
Scientific Career	55.5	54.3	1.2
Data Ethics	48.3	45.0	3.3
Personality Module	82.9	76.8	6.1
Learning Organization	80.3	72.8	7.5
Open Educational Resources	87.1	85.5	1.6
Funding	64.2	44.4	19.8
Evaluation	71.4	60.9	10.5
Academic Contacts	60.9	58.2	2.7
Study Abroad	53.0	35.7	14.3

Investigating the difference between relative usage by Bachelor and Master students, there is a >10% difference between relative recommender usage in the *To-do, Funding, Evaluation* and *Study Abroad* recommenders. All these recommenders are used relatively more frequently by Bachelor students than by Master students.

3.2 Qualitative Results: Design Thinking Workshop

During the *design thinking workshops*, students were asked to select two to three recommender modules and test them, as indicated above. Table 2 illustrates which recommender modules were tested to what extent.

Table 2. Recommender module-Ranking of the Design Thinking Workshops

Recommender Module	*n*
Personality Module	7
Academic Contacts	7
Academic Interests	4
Learning Organization	4
Study Abroad	3
To-do	2
Scientific Career	2
Data Ethics	1

To assess the current state of each tested recommender module, following the group work, students were asked to rank their impressions for each recommender module in a four-dimension matrix with the attributes very/not helpful and very/not comprehensible. The results show that the recommender modules *Personality Module* and *Academic Contacts* were used most frequently.

With regard to the latter, it was suggested that more transparency of the assigned matches should be established so that more information on each match is shown in advance.

The students also recognize great potential in the *Personality Module*. In particular, students in the introductory phase expressed great interest in this recommender module. In order to optimize this module, it was suggested that individual input be taken into account and to shape the recommender module in a more personal way.

The students also see great potential in the AI-supported module *Academic Interests*. The most common feedback in this area was that it is unclear how to formulate academic interests. Specific suggestions from the students were to raise students' awareness of how to formulate and pursue individual educational goals. In keeping with one of the DSA's goal dimensions of initiating student self-reflection, questions should help students reflect on various aspects of their own studies to derive specific learning goals. This reflection process should be stimulated by reflective questions.

In this sense, students should receive sample input for the formulation of study interests. For this purpose, examples could appear that have been entered by other students.

These results can be linked to the general suggestions for improvement: Within the framework of a structuring qualitative content analysis according to Kuckartz, (2018), five categories were developed inductively, from which the following attributes students ask from a DSA, result: *personal*, *individual interactive*, *supportive* and *user-friendly*.

4. DISCUSSION

In this section, we interpret the results presented in section three and derive future development requirements from them.

4.1 Interpretation of the Results

Investigating the usage decisions per recommender, a clear hierarchy in recommender preference can be derived. Generally, the number of non-interactions with recommender modules is relatively uniform across recommenders. This indicates that recommenders were explored evenly across users.

The *OER* recommender was used almost universally among all users. This is followed by the *Academic Interests*, *Personality Module* and *To-Do* recommenders with less than one hundred deactivations. The high number of activations of these recommenders suggests that students were particularly interested in the domain of service these recommenders reside in. For the Personality Module recommender, this is reflected in the number of selections of recommenders students were interested in during the design thinking workshop, with seven students selecting this recommender for exploration. The low number of deactivations of these recommenders conversely indicates that students did at least deem these recommenders useful enough to keep them in their activated recommenders list. In contrast, the *Academic Contacts*, *Scientific Career*, *Funding*, *Study Abroad* and *Data Ethics* recommenders all were activated by less than 400 users and, save of *Academic Contacts*, were deactivated by over 200 users. This indicates that these recommenders were not deemed to be as useful or relevant as the aforementioned recommender modules. Even though the *evaluation* recommender was deactivated by 103 users, a non-trivial number of 461 users activated this recommender module. Because this recommender module serves the sole purpose to collect more detailed feedback from users, it can be assumed that the general level of readiness of users to help improve the DSA through feedback is elevated. In the light of the data presented here being collected from users that agree for a data donation, this result is to be expected.

When it comes to DSA use per degree and semester, our results show that there is a higher number of users in their Bachelor studies compared to users in their Master studies. Again, this mismatch is to be expected assuming a distribution of users in terms of degree as there are more Bachelor students enrolled at German universities compared to Master students. Additionally, our data shows that most users are enrolled in early semesters, regardless of degree, implying that students in higher semesters found the DSA as a whole to be of less interest for them compared to students in earlier semesters.

Comparing relative use between Bachelor and Master students, we observed a difference of 10% or more in four of eleven recommenders: *To-Do*, *Funding*, *Evaluation* and *Semester Abroad* recommenders were less frequently activated by Master students compared to Bachelor students. It has to be noted that with N=458 for Bachelor students and N=151 for Master students, this discrepancy in activated recommenders may very well be the result of sampling from populations with different sizes. In the case of the *To-Do* and *Funding* recommenders, we interpret these results to originate from a generally higher proficiency of Master students to organize their studies and their finances during studying. Because Master students were able to build these skills during their Bachelor studies already, the *To-Do* and *Funding* recommender modules are hence of less interest for them. This hypothesis is further strengthened by the fact that the *Learning Organization* recommender module which also focuses on organizing one's studies, is also activated less by Master students compared to Bachelor students (7.5%). Regarding the *Semester Abroad* recommender module, we hypothesize that the divergence between Master and Bachelor student use originates from the circumstance that Master students may have already completed their studies abroad in their Bachelor studies.

Students participating in the design thinking workshop expressed a high interest in the *Academic Contacts* recommender. In parallel, students reported to be especially interested in the *Personality Module* recommender, emphasizing that their user experience was only held back by the lack of transparency of how matches were generated.

Students additionally reported a high degree of helpfulness and comprehensibility of the *Academic Interests* recommender.

4.2 Limitations

A general limitation of the findings from the quantitative approach presented in this work is the inconsistency between sample sets between analysis approaches: Because our analysis methods focus on different properties of users and their interaction with the DSA, insights derived from one method are not necessarily generalizable to all users, but only describe the user experiences of one subset of users. This under sampling of the total underlying user data is a result of the DSA's design regarding data protection and the subsequent possibility of users to carefully select data they want to share with the system. Albeit this design being in line with possible data-protection goals, it also hinders a thorough analysis of usability through quantitative means.

Additional limitations of our findings are related to the *user interface* of the DSA. The order in which the recommender modules are represented for the user may influence their interaction with the recommender modules and their preferences. The latter is especially obvious for the *OER* module. One explanation might be the fact that in the workshops, students were informed during the module presentation that only the concept of *OER* is presented in this module, but that there are no learning materials to be found. One assumption is that students were not aware of this when activating the DSA recommender module, and that the large number of activations can be explained by the fact that students initially assumed that they would find helpful learning material there.

4.3 Future Development

Regarding future development we derive three factors from general recommender usage: firstly, the frequently activated recommender modules *OER*, *Academic Interests*, *Personality Module* and *To-Do* already cover topics of interest for users. These recommenders therefore should be extended in their functionality. Conversely, the often-deactivated recommenders *Academic Contacts*, *Scientific Career*, *Funding*, *Study Abroad* and *Data Ethics* need to be enhanced in their usefulness or evaluated to be removed from the DSA. Because no recommender stands out in terms of non-interaction, we conclude that all recommenders are at least of initial interest for students and therefore, no recommender should be removed on the basis of not being of any initial interest to users.

The semester of enrollment per user shows that most users are in their first semesters. This suggests that the DSA is of primary interest for students in their initial study stages. One future development goal therefore should be to make recommenders more useful for students in low semesters. In parallel, future developments should also focus on identifying, designing, and implementing more useful recommender modules for students of higher semesters, as they are less present in our user data. A recommender module for finalizing a study program and writing a thesis could be a prospective candidate. A similar picture forms regarding the relationship between users and their degrees: Bachelor students are already engaged with the DSA and therefore should be considered as main users. Conversely, Master students are not as engaged with the DSA and therefore new recommenders tending to Master student's wishes should be designed or existing recommenders should be modified to account for them.

As *OER*, *Personality Module* and *Academic Interests* recommender modules already enjoy a high degree of engagement and should be focused on for improvement in future development endeavors. Regarding the recommender module *Academic Contacts*, there is a particular need for optimization in the range of usability. Here, the non-transparency of the matches and the anonymity were criticized during the design thinking workshop. Based on these findings, the creation of personal cards is planned for the further development of this module. In this way, depending on the data students share with other users, they will receive more information about their matches. In addition, the matching function will relate multiple search requests. For example, it will distinguish either by similarity or by complementarity.

ACKNOWLEDGEMENT

We thank all students who voluntarily donated their data.

REFERENCES

Alexander, B., Ashford-Rowe, K., Barajas-Murphy, N., Dobbin, G., Knott, J., McCormack, M., Pomerantz, J., *et al.* (2019), *Educause Horizon Report: 2019 Higher Education Edition.*

Atenas, J., Havemann, L. and Priego, E. (2014), "Opening teaching landscapes: The importance of quality assurance in the delivery of open educational resources", *Open Praxis*, Vol. 6 No. 1, available at: https://doi.org/10.5944/openpraxis.6.1.81.

Broadbent, J. and Poon, W.L. (2015), "Self-regulated learning strategies & academic achievement in online higher education learning environments: A systematic review", *Internet and Higher Education*, Vol. 27 No. April 2015, pp. 1–13.

"Django". (2020), , Django Software Foundation, Lawrence, Kansas, available at: https://www.djangoproject.com/.

Kuckartz, U. (2018), *Qualitative Inhaltsanalyse. Methoden, Praxis, Computerunterstützung*, 4th ed., Beltz Verlagsgruppe, available at: https://content-select.com/de/portal/media/view/5aa7b788-bfd0-4912-a0df-6955b0dd2d03.

Morisano, D. (2013), "Goal setting in the academic arena", in Locke, E.A. and Latham, G.P. (Eds.), *New Developments in Goal Setting and Task Performance.*, Routledge, pp. 519–530.

Morris, R. and Thompson, K. (1979), "Password Security: A Case History", *Commun. ACM*, Association for Computing Machinery, New York, NY, USA, Vol. 22 No. 11, pp. 594–597.

Okita, S.Y. (2012), "Social Interactions and Learning", in Seel, N.M. (Ed.), *Encyclopedia of the Sciences of Learning*, Springer US, Boston, MA, pp. 3104–3107.

Plattner, H., Meinel, C. and Leifer, L. (2010), *Design Thinking: Understand - Improve - Apply*, 1st ed., Springer Publishing Company, Incorporated.

Schippers, M.C., Morisano, D., Locke, E.A., Scheepers, A.W.A., Latham, G.P. and de Jong, E.M. (2020), "Writing about personal goals and plans regardless of goal type boosts academic performance", *Contemporary Educational Psychology*, Elsevier, Vol. 60 No. November 2019, p. 101823.

Schoonenboom, J. and Johnson, R.B. (2017), "Wie man ein Mixed Methods-Forschungs-Design konstruiert", *Kolner Zeitschrift Fur Soziologie Und Sozialpsychologie*, Vol. 69, pp. 107–131.

Stockmann, R. and Berg, A. (2005), "Stud.IP", *Eleed*, Vol. 1 No. 1, available at: http://nbn-resolving.de/urn:nbn:de:0009-5-845.

Stonebraker, M. and Kemnitz, G. (1991), "The POSTGRES next Generation Database Management System", *Commun. ACM*, Association for Computing Machinery, New York, NY, USA, Vol. 34 No. 10, pp. 78–92.

Sweller, J. (1988), "Cognitive load during problem solving: Effects on learning", *Cognitive Science*, Vol. 12 No. 2, pp. 257–285.

Virtanen, P., Nevgi, A. and Niemi, H. (2013), "Self-Regulation in Higher Education: Students' Motivational, Regulational and Learning Strategies, and Their Relationships to Study Success", *Studies for the Learning Society*, Vol. 3 No. 1–2, pp. 20–34.

Zimmerman, B.J. (1990), "Self-regulating academic learning and achievement: The emergence of a social cognitive perspective", *Educational Psychology Review*, Vol. 2 No. 2, pp. 173–201.

EFFECTS OF THE LOCKDOWN ON PERCEIVED STRESS AND WELL-BEING: A STUDY ON ITALIAN UNIVERSITY IN THE FIRST PERIOD OF ISOLATION DUE TO COVID-19

Oronzo Parlangeli, Paola Palmitesta, Stefano Guidi, Ileana Di Pomponio, Margherita Bracci and Enrica Marchigiani
Department of Social, Political and Cognitive Sciences
University of Siena, Italy

ABSTRACT

This study investigated the effect of the isolation during the lockdown period on psychological distress and well-being in a sample of professors (N=150), students (N=150) and technical administrative staff (N=150) from 3 Italian Universities, in the region of Tuscany. We administered a self-reported online questionnaire to collect socio-demographic information, investigate issues in work and study life, and assess the level of perceived stress and psychological well-being. The results of this study indicate that under conditions of isolation perceived stress levels are increased, and this is related to the experience of an unpleasant house environment. This is also significantly predicted by the occurrence of issues with online lectures and administrative activities for university professors or by having issues with managerial support for technical administrative staff. On the other hand, for university students, a good relationship with other students is of great importance to maintain a high level of mental well-being and being male is a protective factor. Evidently, aspects related to the deprivation of opportunities for peer relationships are experienced as particularly problematic.

KEYWORDS

Perceived Stress and Well-Being, Quarantine due to COVID-19, Studying and Working at Distance

1. INTRODUCTION

The pandemic due to coronavirus disease (Covid-19) has forced countries all over the world to take severe social isolation measures to respond to the virus and control its spread. Several countries have been forced to impose many restrictions, social distancing and social isolation measures.

Starting from spring 2020, all Italian Schools and Universities had to transform face-to-face lessons in distance learning. The impact of these measures on behavior and psychological health is not yet clear, though, some researchers have begun to explore the psychological pressure that the pandemic and social isolation have had on general population (Wang et al., 2020), elderly (Mukhtar, 2020) children and adolescents (Shah et al., 2020; Wagner, 2020), university students (Cao et al., 2020; Duan and Zhu, 2020; Odriozola-González et al., 2020; Xiao, 2020).

Past studies have shown the negative impact of social isolation on various individual and organizational outcomes and on emotional and mental health (Courtin and Knapp, 2017; Hossain et al., 2020). All these studies underline that the conditions shared by the different populations under observation, that is isolation, worry for the own health and of their families as well as the concern for the economic impact, can increase the risk of anxiety and mental distress in different groups of people, from children to adults to elderly (Mukhtar, 2020; Rogowska et al., 2020; Shah et al., 2020; Al Issa and Jaleel, 2021).

With regard to university, in addition to the constraints and concerns just mentioned, very recent research highlights the worry for the difficulties that may be encountered in the learning process, teaching and working at a distance (Elmer et al., 2020; Sahu, 2020). On the one hand professors can find it difficult to support motivation and engagement in the learning process, to monitor how students learn or if they encounter difficulties (King et al., 2009; Watson and Sottile, 2010; Parlangeli et al., 2011; Timmis et al., 2016), and the distance teaching strategy exhibited unexpected challenges and concerns among university professors

(Parlangeli et al., 2017; Akour et al., 2020; Sahu, 2020). Moreover, several studies highlighted the need for additional skills for online teaching (Angeli and Valanides, 2005; Kali et al., 2011; Baldwin et al., 2018), including technical and administrative aspects (e.g. using platforms/tools and organizing workflows).

On the other hand, it becomes more challenging for the students to maintain motivation and engagement, to keep up with the pace of study, and to keep in touch and benefit from face-to-face interaction with professors and colleagues (Parlangeli et al., 2018; Elmer et al., 2020; Shah et al., 2020).

Besides all this, technical administrative staff working at university usually have the challenge of attaining high levels of performance and face issues related to limited resources, poor communication and bureaucratic procedures (Kiplangat et al., 2016).

The aim of this study was to investigate the effect of the isolation during the lockdown period on psychological stress and well-being in a sample of university professors, students and technical administrative staff. To this aim several aspects of studying, teaching and working at a distance have been analyzed in order to understand how to implement effective strategies to prevent stress and negative consequences: the environment in which the lockdown period was lived, the adequacy of technological equipment and the distance learning activities.

2. THE STUDY

2.1 Participants and Procedure

The study involved 450 subjects from 3 Italian Universities, in the region of Tuscany, belonging to three groups: professors (N=150), students (N=150) and technical administrative staff (N=150). Participants took part in the study on a voluntary basis. They were invited via their university e-mail address to fill in an anonymous, self-reported online questionnaire that took about 15-20 minutes to be completed. Three versions of the questionnaire have been prepared for the study, dedicated respectively to university students, professors, and technical administrative staff. The delivery of the questionnaire began online in October 2020. The protocol of the study was approved by the Ethics Committee of Human and Social Sciences of the University of Siena.

2.2 Measures

The questionnaire included 55 questions, and it was structured in three sections. The first section was aimed at collecting socio-demographic information about participants. The second section (6 questions) was aimed at gathering information on aspects that were perceived as most problematic such as: attending or holding the lessons at a distance, online exams, the relations with other colleagues, keeping in touch with professors/students/technical administrative staff and obtaining or giving adequate information support from online institutional channels. Problems were rated on a 5-point Likert scale (from 0 = 'not a problem at all' to 4 = 'very much of a problem').

The third section had two scales (18 questions) related to the psychological impact of confinement due to COVID-19 pandemic. The level of perceived stress was measured with the four-item version of the Perceived Stress Scale (Cohen et al., 1983; Warttig et al., 2013), aiming at rating the frequency of perceived stressful situations during lockdown. The answers were collected on a frequency scale from 0 = "Never" to 4 = "Very often". The degree of psychological well-being was measured through the Italian version of the Warwick-Edinburgh Mental Well-Being Scale (WEMWBS) (Tennant et al., 2007; Gremigni and Stewart-Brown, 2011), a 12-item scale, which contains all positively worded items on different aspects of positive mental health, that estimate the individual's ability to manage and get through problematic or difficult situations in life. Answers were collected on a frequency Likert scale, from 1 ("Never") to 5 ("Always"). All the items in the second and third section of the questionnaire were referred to the first lockdown in Italy, March-May 2020.

2.3 Statistical Analyses

Descriptive statistics were computed (mean and standard deviations for numeric variables, frequencies tables for nominal variables) for all the measures of interest. Univariate and Multivariate Analyses of Variance were conducted on quantitative variables while Chi Square Analyses were performed to explore the relation between categorical variables. Correlations were also computed among the different measures of stress, well-being and other issues related to living, studying and working during lockdown. Finally, two multiple regression models were used to assess predictors of stress and well-being.

2.4 Results and Discussion

2.4.1 General Features of the Sample

In the student and T.A. groups, participants were mostly females (76% and 65% respectively), while in the professors' group gender there is no significant difference in gender representativeness. The age range of the total sample was between 18 and 69 years, with different distribution among the three groups. Professors age range was between 27 to 69 years (Mean: 49.92, SD: 10.63), students age range was between 18 and 63 years (Mean: 23.85, SD: 7.5) and technical administrative staff age was between 28 to 66 years (Mean: 51.13, SD: 8.66).

Professors were mostly associate professors (36.7%), researchers (25.3%) and full professors (22%), with a quite homogeneous distribution about seniority and had a full-time commitment (96.6%).

Most of the students (79%) were enrolled in a Bachelor's Degree program, as confirmed also by the fact that most of them were attending in the one of the first 3 years (85.6%).

The distribution of technical administrative staff seniority was very homogeneous.

2.4.2 Information about the Lockdown Period

Table 1 presents distributions of perceptions about problematic conditions concerning the March-May 2020 lockdown period.

Table 1. Variables about quarantine/Isolation

	Professors		**Students**		**T.A Staff**			
Variable	**N**	**%**	**N**	**%**	**N**	**%**	**Chi²**	**p**
Risk of infection								
Low risk	10	6.7%	14	9.4%	6	4.1%		
Intermediate low risk	36	24.2%	**75**†	50.3%	**36**†	24.5%	46,112	0.000
Intermediate high risk	69	46.3%	51	34.2%	69	46.9%		
High risk	34	22.8%	**9**†	6.0%	**36**†	24.5%		
Restrictions								
No restrictions	56	37.3%	46	30.9%	**77**†	52.0%		
No restrictions. DPI	46	30.7%	48	32.2%	47	31.8%	23,517	0.003
Partial isolation	40	26.7%	44	29.5%	**21**†	14.2%		
Total isolation	8	5.3%	11	7.4%	3	2.0%		

Quarantine at University								
No	44	29.3%	**67**†	44.7%	**28**†	19.2%	23,069	
Yes	106	70.7%	**83**†	55.3%	119	81.5%		0.000
Who did you quarantine with								
Family	130	86.7%	132	88.0%	132	88.0%		
Roommates	2	1.3%	3	2.0%	3	2.0%	15,986	0.003
Alone	17	11.3%	15	10.0%	15	10.0%		
How many people did you quarantine with	*Mean*	*SD*	*Mean*	*SD*	*Mean*	*SD*	$F_{(2, 440)}$	
	2.84	1.552	**3.46***	1.349	2.85	1.358	9.157	0.000

Note. † significant standardized residual for Chi Square test. * p value of F (ANOVA) < 0.001. No significant residuals were found for the variable: "*Who did you quarantine with*".

Participants were asked to declare, at the time of the compilation of the questionnaire, the risk of covid-19 transmission within the area they lived, rating the level in: "Low-risk", "Intermediate to low-risk", "Intermediate to high-risk", "High-risk". Students were the least likely to report being in the "high-risk" category, while technical administrative staff were significantly more likely to report to be in a high-risk zone (24.5%). Half the students (50.3%) declared to be in an intermediate low-risk zone, in a significantly higher percentage than other groups.

Half the technical administrative staff (52%) reported that they were not under a form of isolation or restriction (quarantine) when they filled-in the questionnaire.

Almost half the students reported that they didn't spend the March-May 2020 lockdown in the city where their university is located or nearby (44.7%).

The majority of respondents (87%-88%), in all groups, reported having lived with their family during the lockdown period. Students spent the quarantine period averagely in a family of three persons, a number significantly higher than other groups (Mean: 3.46).

2.4.3 Household Environment Features where the Respondents Lived during the Lockdown

We analyzed different aspects of the household environment where the respondents had lived during the first lockdown period, evaluated on a 5-point Likert scale, with the lowest scores indicating a bad quality of environment (e.g.: from less pleasant to more pleasant).

Regarding the quality of the house environment in which they lived during the lockdown, students appeared to be disadvantaged compared to professors and technical administrative staff. Tukey post hoc of the MANOVA revealed that students lived in significantly smaller (Mean: 3.40, SD: 1.14) and more crowded (Mean: 2.72, SD: 1.08) environments, less conveniently positioned with respect to country/city (Mean: 3.83, SD: 1.14) and less pleasant (Mean: 3.83, SD: 1.13).

2.4.4 Technological Equipment that the Respondents Lived during the Lockdown

20% of technical administrative staff, significantly more than the other groups ($p < 0.01$), reported they didn't have a device available for personal use during lockdown. Only 33% of the T.A. has an institutional device (64.8%). However, most participants (80%-95%) had an adequate device and almost all of them (98%) had internet access.

Students had an internet connection moderately adequate for their needs but significantly less adequate than other participants, rated on a Likert scale from 1 = "Adequate" to 5 = "Inadequate" (Mean: 2.68, SD: 1.30, $p < 0.01$).

2.4.5 Issues in Studying and Distance Working

We examined the ratings of the severity of the issues experienced by respondents during lockdown concerning studying and working at distance (rated on a Likert scale, where 0 = "Not at all", 1= "Very little", 2 = "Little", 3 = "Quite", 4 = "Very much"). Multivariate Analysis of Variance (MANOVA) revealed differences between groups (Table 2).

The highest ratings were found about the relationships with students. Students reported more severe issues in their relationship with other students (Mean: 2.75, SD: 1.19) and with professors than other groups (Mean: 2.32, SD: 1.27, $p < 0.01$). Professors reported more severe issues in their relationship with students than administrative technical staff (Mean: 2.68, SD: 1.22, $p < 0.01$). Administrative technical staff, on the other hand, reported less severe relationship issues, either with colleagues or with students.

Table 2. Average scores for the ratings of the difficulties experienced during lockdown concerning studying and working at a distance

	Professors		**Students**		**T.A. Staff**			
Issues	**Mean**	**SD**	**Mean**	**SD**	**Mean**	**SD**	**$F_{(2, 428)}$**	**p**
...in relationships with professors	1.66	1.200	**2.32***	1.270	1.62	1.228	14.855	0.000
...in relationships with students	**2.68***	1.221	**2.75***	1.191	1.38	1.350	54.351	0.000
...in relationships with colleagues	-	-	-	-	1.83	1.326	-	-
... with online exams	2.12	1.256	1.97	1.280	-	-	1.034	0.310
... with online lectures	1.90	1.186	2.14	1.278	-	-	2.636	0.106
... with administrative activities	1.65	1.115	-	-	-	-	-	-
...in receiving administrative and technical support	1.70	1.145	-	-	-	-	-	-
... with research activities	2.55	1.387	-	-	-	-	-	-
... with publications	1.95	1.399	-	-	-	-	-	-
...with administrative procedures	-	-	2.10	1.367	-	-	-	-
...in receiving technical support	-	-	2.34	1.031	-	-	-	-
...with online activities	-	-	-	-	1.90	1.408	-	-
...in receiving managerial support	-	-	-	-	1.61	1.326	-	-

Note. *$p < 0.01$; p-values of Tuckey's post hoc test for MANOVAS.

2.4.6 Stress and Mental Well-being during Lockdown

Table 3 presents descriptive statistics, F and p value of MANOVA about the measures of stress (PSS) and well-being (WEMWBS).

The average level of perceived stress by students (Mean: 9.1, SD: 3.47) was higher than the published normative value (6.7) for a sample of English people in the 19-29 age range (Warttig et al., 2013). Tukey's post hoc test revealed that students had significantly higher scores than other groups ($F_{(2, 447)} = 35.324$, $p < 0.01$).

Students perceived a lower level of mental well-being (Mean: 35.51, SD: 7.99) than professor and administrative technical staff ($F_{(2, 447)} = 24.932$, $p < 0.01$).

The average score for the well-being scale reported by students was lower than the published value (41.5) for Italian students (Gremigni and Stewart-Brown, 2011), while scores reported by the other two groups of participants were in the same range.

Table 3. Average scores for the measures of perceived stress and well-being during lockdown

	Professors		Students		T.A staff			
	Mean	**SD**	**Mean**	**SD**	**Mean**	**SD**	**$F_{(2, 447)}$**	**p**
Perceived stress (PSS)	6.23	3.294	**9.11***	3.473	6.29	3.416	35.324	0.000
Well-being (WEMWBS)	40.32	7.955	**35.51***	7.993	41.62	7.748	24.932	0.000

Note. *p < 0.01; p-values of Tuckey's post hoc test for ANOVAS.

2.4.7 Predictors of Perceived Stress and Well-Being during Lockdown

We investigated the predictive effects of different variables on respondents' perception of perceived stress and well-being using multiple regression models. Table 4 shows Beta coefficient, p value and R^2 of three multiple regression models to analyze predictors of perceived stress by professors, students and T.A. staff.

Table 4. Multiple regression models: predictors of perceived stress by professors, students and T.A. staff

	Professors		Students		T.A. Staff	
Predictors of Perceived Stress (PSS)	**Beta**	**p**	**Beta**	**p**	**Beta**	**p**
gender	-0.155	0.087	-0.101	0.231	-0.096	0.229
age	0.121	0.164	-0.095	0.272	0.055	0.507
risk of infection	0.145	0.088	0.089	0.297	0.022	0.785
restriction/quarantine	-0.099	0.248	0.060	0.465	0.108	0.187
dwelling size	0.039	0.741	-0.029	0.753	-0.042	0.685
housing density	-0.029	0.724	0.116	0.180	0.095	0.259
good position	-0.159	0.067	-0.061	0.483	-0.117	0.181
good equipment	-0.167	0.081	-0.115	0.204	0.097	0.319
pleasantness	**-0.274***	0.023	**-0.314****	0.001	-0.15	0.147
relational issues with professors	-0.051	0.600	-0.100	0.340	0.221	0.079
relational issues with students	-0.173	0.112	0.144	0.114	0.026	0.789
relational issues with colleagues	-	-	-	-	-0.111	0.372
issues with online exams	0.037	0.701	0.009	0.920	-	-
issues with online lectures	**0.297****	0.006	0.181	0.074	-	-
issues with administrative activities	**0.383****	0.000	-	-	-	-
issues with administrative technical support	-0.063	0.540	-	-	-	-
issues with research activities	-0.010	0.935	-	-	-	-
issues with publications	0.192	0.094	-	-	-	-
issues with administrative procedures	-	-	0.141	0.162	-	-
issues with information support	-	-	-0.106	0.280	-	-
issues with online activities	-	-	-	-	0.102	0.233
issues with managerial support	-	-	-	-	**0.253****	0.007
N	129		127		119	
R^2	0.211		0.224		0.305	

Note. *p < 0.05, ** p < 0.01.

Results showed that for professors (Beta: -0.274, $p < 0.05$) and students (Beta: -0.314, $p < 0.01$) experiencing an unpleasant house environment is a predictor of perceived stress.

For professors, having issues with online lectures (Beta: 0.297, $p < 0.01$) and with administrative activities (Beta: 0.383, $p < 0.01$) significantly predicted a high level of perceived stress.

In addition, perceived stress by technical administrative staff is predicted by having issues with managerial support (Beta: 0.253, $p < 0.01$). Table 5 shows Beta coefficient, p value and R^2 of three multiple regression models to analyze predictors of well-being by professors, students and T.A. staff.

Table 5. Multiple regression models: predictors of well-being by professors, students and T.A. staff

	Professors		**Students**		**T.A. Staff**	
Predictors of Mental Well-being (WEMWBS)	**Beta**	**p**	**Beta**	**p**	**Beta**	**p**
gender	0.031	0.753	**0.211***	0.012	0.122	0.124
age	-0.135	0.162	0.117	0.170	0.017	0.835
risk of infection	0.040	0.669	-0.027	0.747	-0.021	0.796
restriction/quarantine	0.073	0.440	0.035	0.659	0.022	0.789
dwelling size	-0.144	0.272	0.003	0.972	0.166	0.107
housing density	0.125	0.171	-0.070	0.407	0.08	0.333
good position	0.035	0.717	0.083	0.332	**0.218***	0.012
good equipment	0.130	0.221	0.055	0.532	-0.007	0.938
pleasantness	**0.269***	0.044	**0.306****	0.001	0.190	0.063
relational issues with professors	-0.032	0.768	0.046	0.652	-0.053	0.669
relational issues with students	-0.055	0.648	-0.214*	0.017	-0.009	0.928
relational issues with colleagues	-	-	-	-	-0.04	0.744
issues with online exams	0.053	0.619	-0.087	0.302	-	-
issues with online lectures	0.012	0.920	-0.068	0.492	-	-
issues with administrative activities	-0.055	0.637	-	-	-	-
issues with administrative technical support	-0.137	0.233	-	-	-	-
issues with research activities	-0.049	0.707	-	-	-	-
issues with publications	-0.117	0.355	-	-	-	-
issues with administrative procedures	-	-	0.040	0.686	-	-
issues with information support	-	-	0.004	0.969	-	-
issues with online activities	-	-	-	-	-0.147	0.084
issues with managerial support	-	-	-	-	**-0.221***	0.016
N	112		127		119	
R2	0.159		0.253		0.322	

Note. *$p < 0.05$, ** $p < 0.01$.

As expected, pleasantness of the house environment is a predictor of high level of well-being for professors (Beta: 0.269, $p < 0.05$) and students (Beta: 0.306, $p < 0.01$).

Having relational issues with other students is a significant negative predictor (Beta: -0.214, $p < 0.05$) of well-being in the student group, while being male is a positive predictor of mental well-being.

On the other hand, for technical administrative employees, being in a good position with respect to country/city (Beta: 0.218, $p < 0.05$) and not having issues with managerial support (Beta: -0.221, $p < 0.05$) are positive predictors of mental well-being.

3. CONCLUSION

University students, teachers, and technical-administrative staff who participated in the study reported different problems with a different level of severity. Aspects related to housing situations are likely to refer to differentiated socio-economic conditions for which social and political interventions are necessary and that can be only marginally influenced by university institutions. In this regard, teachers and students seem to be particularly affected by the level of pleasantness of their housing, while administrative technicians are more likely to suffer from the poor location of their housing. Possible solutions to these problems are not always addressable by higher education institutions which may not have the economic strength to cope with these issues. However, especially for the most fragile, such as students with disabilities, this can be particularly relevant, and interventions aimed at fostering awareness of the need for institutional intervention can produce significant results (Fernández-Gámez et al., 2020).

The main problems for all the three groups of participants, however, are more likely to be related to issues on which it is easier to intervene, because they refer to the possibility of having adequate social relations and receiving efficient informative support. This is particularly relevant for students, who reported alarming levels of stress, and higher than other groups. It is evident that, especially in circumstances of isolation, higher education institutions must know how to organize students' peer support (Gallop and Bastien, 2016) and facilitate participation in online academic social networks. This type of intervention is linked to the possibility of increasing general levels of well-being and limiting the occurrence of marginalization phenomena (Parlangeli et al., 2019; Mishra, 2020). The opportunities that online communication can offer is also relevant for professors and administrative technical staff, even if the needs they express seem less urgent and are, above all, different. For professors, in fact, the need to have adequate ICTs for activities such as online exams and the execution of administrative procedures can be highlighted. The technical-administrative personnel, on the other hand, are suffering from the distance from managers that results in a lack of adequate support. The possibility to have ICTs with an adequate level of usability (Vlachogianni and Tselios, 2021), along with widespread, stable and broadband connectivity opportunities, is a primary need that cannot be further delayed.

REFERENCES

Akour, A. et al, 2020. The Impact of the COVID-19 Pandemic and Emergency Distance Teaching on the Psychological Status of University Teachers: A Cross-Sectional Study in Jordan. *The American Journal of Tropical Medicine and Hygiene*, Vol. 103, No. 6, pp. 2391-2399. DOI: 10.4269/ajtmh.20-0877.

Al Issa, H.-E. and Jaleel, E.M. 2021. Social isolation and psychological wellbeing: lessons from Covid-19. *Management Science Letters*, Vol. 11, No. 2, pp. 609-618. DOI: 10.5267/j.msl.2020.9.006.

Angeli, C. and Valanides, N. 2005. Preservice elementary teachers as information and communication technology designers: an instructional systems design model based on an expanded view of pedagogical content knowledge. *Journal of Computer Assisted Learning*, Vol. 21, No. 4, pp. 292-302. DOI: 10.1111/j.1365-2729.2005.00135.x.

Baldwin, S.J. et al, 2018. Online course design and development among college and university instructors: An analysis using grounded theory. *Online Learning Journal*, Vol. 22, No. 2, pp. 157–172. DOI: 10.24059/olj.v22i2.1212.

Cao, W. et al, 2020. The psychological impact of the COVID-19 epidemic on college students in China. *Psychiatry Research*, Vol. 287. DOI: 10.1016/j.psychres.2020.112934.

Cohen, S. et al. 1983. A Global Measure of Perceived Stress. Journal of Health and Social Behavior Vol. 24, No. 4, pp. 385–396. DOI:10.2307/2136404.

Courtin, E. and Knapp, M. 2017. Social isolation, loneliness and health in old age: a scoping review. *Health & Social Care in the Community*, Vol. 25, No. 3. DOI: 10.1111/hsc.12311.

Duan, L. and Zhu, G. 2020. Psychological interventions for people affected by the COVID-19 epidemic. *The Lancet Psychiatry*, Vol. 7, No. 4, pp. 300–302. DOI: 10.1016/S2215-0366(20)30073-0.

Elmer, T. et al, 2020. Students under lockdown: Comparisons of students' social networks and mental health before and during the COVID-19 crisis in Switzerland. *PLoS ONE*, Vol. 15, No. 7, e0236337. doi: 10.1371/journal.pone.0236337.

Fernández-Gámez M. A. et al, 2020. Innovative interventions and provisions of accommodations to students with disabilities. *European Journal of Special Needs Education*, pp. 1-10. DOI: 10.1080/08856257.2020.1792715.

Gallop, C.J. and Bastien N. 2016. Supporting Success: Aboriginal students in higher education. *Canadian Journal of Higher Education*, Vol.46, No. 2, pp. 206-224. DOI: 10.47678/cjhe.v46i2.184772.

Gremigni, P. and Stewart-Brown, S. 2011. Una misura del benessere mentale: validazione italiana della Warwick-Edinburgh Mental Well-Being Scale (WEMWBS). *Giornale Italiano Di Psicologia.*, Vol. 2, pp. 485–508. DOI: 10.13140/2.1.2425.9203.

Hossain, M.M. et al, 2020. Mental health outcomes of quarantine and isolation for infection prevention: A systematic umbrella review of the global evidence. *Epidemiology and Health*, Vol. 42, pp. 1-11. DOI: 10.4178/epih.e2020038.

Kali, Y. et al, 2011. Researching design practices and design cognition: contexts, experiences and pedagogical knowledge-in-pieces. *Learning, Media and Technology*, Vol. 36, No. 2, pp. 129-149. doi: 10.1080/17439884.2011.553621.

King, C.G. et al, 2009. Online exams and cheating: An empirical analysis of business students' views. *Journal of Educators Online*, Vol. 6, No. 1, pp. 1-11. DOI: 10.9743/jeo.2009.1.1.

Kiplangat, H.K. et al, 2016. Challenges Encountered by University Administrators in Performance Management and Job Satisfaction of Academic Staff in Kenyan Universities The Catholic University of Eastern Africa The Catholic University of Eastern Africa. *Journal of Emerging Trends in Educational Research and Policy Studies*, Vol. 7, No. 6, pp. 383–390.

Mishra S. 2020. Social networks, social capital, social support and academic success in higher education: A systematic review with a special focus on 'underrepresented' students. *Educational Research Review*, Vol. 29, No. 1, 100307, DOI: 10.1016/j.edurev.2019.100307.

Mukhtar, S. 2020. Psychological impact of COVID-19 on older adults. *Current Medicine Research and Practice*, Vol. 10, No. 4, pp. 201–202. DOI: 10.1016/j.cmrp.2020.07.016.

Odriozola-González, P. et al, 2020. Psychological effects of the COVID-19 outbreak and lockdown among students and workers of a Spanish university. *Psychiatry Research*, Vol. 290. DOI: 10.1016/j.psychres.2020.113108.

Parlangeli, O. et al, 2017. Stress and Unethical Behaviour in the Research of the Untenured University Researchers. *ICERI, 10th International Conference of Education Research and Innovation*, Seville, Spain. DOI: 10.21125/iceri.2017.0585.

Parlangeli, O. et al, 2011. The effect of system usability and multitasking activities in distance learning. *Proceedings of the 9th ACM SIGCHI Italian Chapter International Conference on Computer-Human Interaction Facing Complexity - CHItaly*, ACM Press, New York, New York, USA. DOI: 10.1145/2037296.2037314.

Parlangeli, O. et al, 2018. Stress misconduct and reduced ability to express dissent: A study on a sample of students at the University of Siena. in J.B. P.M. Arezes (Ed.), *Occupational Safety and Hygiene*. Vol. VI, CRC Press, Taylor & Francis Group, London, pp. 443–446. DOI: 10.1201/9781351008884-78.

Parlangeli O. et al, 2019. Offensive acts and helping behavior on the internet: An analysis of the relationships between moral disengagement, empathy and use of social media in a sample of Italian students. *Work*, Vol. 63, No. 3, 469-477. DOI: 10.3233/WOR-192935.

Rogowska, A.M. et al, 2020. Examining Anxiety, Life Satisfaction, General Health, Stress and Coping Styles During COVID-19 Pandemic in Polish Sample of University Students. *Psychology Research and Behavior Management*, Vol. 13, pp. 797-811. DOI: 10.2147/PRBM.S266511.

Sahu, P. 2020. Closure of Universities Due to Coronavirus Disease 2019 (COVID-19): Impact on Education and Mental Health of Students and Academic Staff. *Cureus*, Vol. 12, No. 4, e7541. DOI: 10.7759/cureus.7541

Shah, K. et al, 2020. Impact of COVID-19 on the Mental Health of Children and Adolescents. *Cureus*, Vol. 12, No. 8, e10051. DOI: 10.7759/cureus.10051.

Tennant R. et al. 2007. The Warwick-Edinburgh Mental Well-being Scale (WEMWBS): Development and UK validation. *Health and Quality of Life Outcomes*. Vol. 5, No. 63, DOI: 10.1186/1477-7525-5-63.

Timmis, S. et al, 2016. Rethinking assessment in a digital age: opportunities, challenges and risks. *British Educational Research Journal*, Vol. 42, No. 3, pp. 454–476. DOI: 10.1002/berj.3215.

Vlachogianni, P. and Tselios, N. 2021. Perceived usability evaluation of educational technology using the System Usability Scale (SUS): A systematic review. *Journal of Research on Technology in Education*, pp. 1-18. doi: 10.1080/15391523.2020.1867938.

Wagner, K.D. 2020. Addressing the experience of children and adolescents during the CoviD-19 pandemic. *Journal of Clinical Psychiatry*, Vol. 81, No. 3, 20ed13394. DOI: 10.4088/JCP.20ed13394.

Wang, C. et al, 2020. Immediate psychological responses and associated factors during the initial stage of the 2019 coronavirus disease (COVID-19) epidemic among the general population in China. *International Journal of Environmental Research and Public Health*, Vol. 17, No. 5, 1729. DOI: 10.3390/ijerph17051729.

Warttig, S.L. et al, 2013. New, normative, English-sample data for the Short Form Perceived Stress Scale (PSS-4). *Journal of Health Psychology*, Vol. 18, No. 12, pp. 1617-28. DOI: 10.1177/1359105313508346.

Watson, G. and Sottile, J. 2010. Cheating in the Digital Age: Do Students Cheat More in Online Courses?. *Online Journal of Distance Learning Administration*, Vol. 13, No. 1. DOI: 10.1016/j.chbr.2020.100033.

Xiao, C. 2020. A novel approach of consultation on 2019 novel coronavirus (COVID-19)-related psychological and mental problems: Structured letter therapy. *Psychiatry Investigation*, Vol. 17, No. 2, pp. 175–176. doi: 10.30773/pi.2020.0047.

CAN A LEARNING ANALYTICS DASHBOARD PARTICIPATIVE DESIGN APPROACH BE TRANSPOSED TO AN ONLINE-ONLY CONTEXT?

Katia Oliver-Quelennec[1,2,3], François Bouchet[1], Thibault Carron[1] and Claire Pinçon[2]
[1] *Sorbonne Université, CNRS, LIP6, F-75005 Paris, France*
[2] *Univ. Lille, CHU Lille, ULR 2694, METRICS: Évaluation des Technologies de Santé et des Pratiques Médicales, F-59000 Lille, France*
[3] *Univ. Lille, GIVRE, DIP, France*

ABSTRACT

In-person sessions of participative design are commonly used in the field of Learning Analytics, but to reach students not always available on-site (e.g. during a pandemic), they have to be adapted to online-only context. Card-based tools are a common co-design method to collect users' needs, but this tangible format limits data collection and usage. We propose here two steps: first to use an existing co-design card deck-based method for our university context and next to adapt this new method called PADDLE (PArticipative Design of Dashboard for Learning in Education) for an online use.
This article presents key factors and points of attention identified in adapting a card-based co-design method into a digital version for designing learning dashboards. This digital adaptation and the associated tool, ePADDLE, were tested with first year university students divided into 18 groups (N = 58). All groups have successfully designed a dashboard, and using the original evaluation scales, users have evaluated ePADDLE as almost as suitable as the original method. Thanks to the traces provided by the online version, we rely on speech acts to identify favorable conditions for successful collaboration.

KEYWORDS

Learning Analytics Dashboard, Co-Design, Participatory Design, Cards

1. INTRODUCTION

Faced with the massification of higher education, traditional teaching is not always suitable for training an increasingly larger and more heterogeneous student audience. One of the solutions to answer this development is the use of digital technology for (1) training and (2) personalization of training based on the collection of learning data and on their analysis (learning analytics). The dashboard, a classic decision-making aid tool, can support learning and is developing constantly in the field of Technology Enhanced Learning (TEL), mainly for teachers and students (Bodily et al., 2017). The problem remains to be able to provide appropriate Learning Analytics Dashboard (LAD) to this heterogeneous public, meeting their needs.

In the field of human-machine interface, but also more broadly, user-centered design is a design philosophy which aims at really satisfying users' self-expressed needs (Sanders, 2002). Concerning the conception of LAD, several research studies have shown the importance of explaining clearly the pedagogical objectives (Ifenthaler et al., 2005) and of choosing a relevant method (Jivet et al., 2017). To build LADs, participatory design (Ruiz et al., 2018) is a method adapted and often already developed in the design of TEL. However, according to (Prieto Alvarez et al., 2020), students are often absent in the participatory design of TEL, which could explain why some LADs are not always adapted to the learning target. Our first goal was thus to rely on such an existing co-design method for a higher education student context.

Moreover, co-design sessions usually involve an in-person session with participants sitting around a table, which is challenging when social distancing is mandatory, or simply when it is hard to schedule a moment for all stakeholders to be available in a given location. There are reasons to question whether an online version with remote participants would be as efficient, as virtual collaboration can act as a brake on the success of the collaboration by limiting exchanges through text and voice, without facial expressions or body language. (McNair et al., 2010) identified the importance for participants to establish a sense of trust, which can be challenging to establish online. Therefore, our second goal is to verify whether an online co-design approach of dashboard for and by students can lead to successful results by adapting an existing method to an online context assisting in trace recovery. These traces are made of (1) observation data of the use of the method to facilitate its evolution, (2) intermediate data to be able to understand the conditions of effective collaboration, and (3) production results. Finally, we will present the data collected and the results of several experiments showing that this approach might indeed be an efficient replacement for face-to-face sessions. We also explore the new possibilities that the traces provide in order to assess the quality of the interactions and outcomes.

The remainder of this paper is organized as follows. In the next section, we start by presenting previous works on participatory design leading to the conception of LAD, then we present the face-to-face method we chose to adapt, called PADDLE, and our proposal for a digital version, before describing the experiments carried out and the data collected. Next, we present our results before concluding with a discussion about the pros and cons of this digital transposition and by presenting the perspectives opened by this work.

2. PREVIOUS WORK

2.1 Participatory Design

Work by Schneider et al. (2011) has shown that the use of tangible objects (such as cards) can facilitate collaboration and could explain the recurrent use of this format for co-design. However, other works focused on collaboration have also shown that the use of digital technology engages participants in productive processes and in a co-construction framework (Jeong et al., 2016). It is therefore unclear a priori how a digital adaptation of an existing tangible co-design approach will be perceived. On the one hand, the tool can compel users to guide them and help them stay focused on their main task, but on the other hand, it can also limit creativity if it is too direct. Thus, there is a need to find the right balance in its design.

With participatory design, "the user becomes a critical component of the process" (Sanders, 2002), and they can be involved using the appropriate tools, such as card decks (Roy et al., 2019). For learning analytics applications, some card decks-based approaches such as LA-DECK (Prieto Alvarez et al., 2020) have led to successful outcomes in terms of design: "the cards succeeded in playing very similar roles to those documented in the literature on successful card-based design tools". But LA-DECK focuses more on establishing a dialogue between designers, data scientists and users than purely on letting users express their needs.

A literature review of 155 card-based design tools (Roy et al., 2019) shows that this format is widely used: their tangible form combines several ideas, with a limited amount of information, thus providing a good intermediary between structureless tools (post-it) and complete tools (instruction manual). However, this review also points out that only "some of the tools are [...] also available as apps or online." Moreover, the existence of a digital version does not guarantee that traces are recorded, as most methods are more interested in final production than in an analysis of the processes used to obtain them. Finally, when the information was explicitly provided by the authors, it appears that none of these tools was used with remote participants: everyone was always in a face-to-face context around a table. These sessions are often accompanied by a facilitator who introduces the session, presents the cards, answers any questions and concludes the session (Prieto Alvarez et al., 2020). Some studies about co-design (Goldman et al., 2019) uses both online activities and face-to-face time, but as far as we know, none were in online-only context, nor study how to adapt from face-to-face to the full distance.

2.2 Learning Analytics Dashboard

Although the research field around learning analytics dashboards (LAD) is quite young (Schwendimann et al., 2017), there are several reviews of the literature on the LADs already developed (Verbert et al., 2014). LADs allow the learners to be aware of their progress, to create meaning and to take decisions that will impact their learning. But Jivet et al. (2017) explains that LADs are not always developed in line with clear educational objectives, and that making people aware of their journey is not enough to improve learning. In addition, LADs can also cause negative effects (Tan et al., 2017; Teasley et al., 2017), in particular when they provide comparisons with peers for certain student profiles. It is therefore necessary to create LADs adapted to the learning contexts and according to the students' needs. Some works show students' expectations for personalization and the importance of having an adaptable LAD (Roberts et al., 2017; Teasley et al., 2017). There are also early works on the design of adaptive LADs, such as those of Dabbebi et al. (2019) on the design and the dynamic generation of contextual LADs for teachers. All these studies highlight the interest of adaptive LADs but have not been developed for the learners themselves.

To build LADs, participatory design (Ruiz et al., 2018) is a method adapted and often already developed in the design of TEL. As seen before and in the previous works (Lucero et al., 2016; Ruiz et al., 2018; Roy et al., 2019), this approach is generally implemented using cards. The participatory design kit developed by Dabbebi et al. (2019) offers a complete method for designing LADs, the first uses of which were carried out with secondary school teachers. Therefore, it appeared to be the closest to our goals, and we chose to propose an adaptation of this method to students in the context of higher education.

3. THE PADDLE METHOD

To design Learning Analytics Dashboards (LAD), Dabbebi et al. (2019) developed a participatory-based design tool also using card decks which was positively rated by its users. Our adaptation of this method to the context of higher education and focused on co-design by students is called PADDLE (PArticipative Design of Dashboard for Learning in Education). We used an iterative approach to test and propose adaptations of the design kit for our student target. First of all, we practiced with the existing tool by working with its intended audience (teachers) over two sessions, but in a higher education context. This appropriation time have enabled us to confirm the interest of the method in another university context and allowed us to confirm the method was suitable to easily collect users' needs, and that it received positive feedback from participants. We were thus able to define a first variation. The adaptation of this method for higher education includes changes in vocabulary, length of time for the student target and the addition of questions for participants. Vocabulary related to secondary education such as "pupil, class, school, department, academy" has been changed to "student, promotion, institution, regional, national". The second variation was necessary to adapt the tool to students. In order to more easily fit in time slots usually available to them between two classes, we reduced the duration of a session from 150 minutes to 90 minutes, which led to adopting a question-based approach to better guide them and thus save time. For example, the card entitled "Monitoring" initially described by a definition, has been replaced by "How do you keep track of your work? What do you need to track your work?". The participants take turns answering the questions and thus identify their possible needs. Naturally, these adaptations do not prevent from using PADDLE with the initial targets (teachers).

PADDLE allows to co-design LADs in small groups of two to five people. The sessions last from 90 minutes (for students) to 120 minutes (for teachers) and consist of five phases: (1) introduction, (2) choice of the LAD goal, (3) definition of the context, (4) choosing the data to track, the indicators to compute and the associated visualizations to display them, and (5) drawing of the LAD to show how all the visualizations can be associated together in an integrated dashboard.

3.1 Material

The session is supervised by a facilitator who supports debates and helps participants in formalizing their ideas. Nonetheless, the facilitator intervenes only on request or when he/she detects a group is struggling, in order to give participants autonomy. In particular they refrain from giving examples of indicators in a learning context or to express judgment on participants' proposals, in order not to inhibit nor direct the students' discussions. To facilitate transport, pooling and animation, the board has been transformed into convenient cards: PADDLE comes in the form of laminated cards to be able to reuse them and magnetic cards to manipulate them on a whiteboard (cf. Figure 1). Participants must set a goal and then complete a board to describe their context before identifying the relevant data and their graphic representations. Finally, they assemble these elements to design their LAD.

Traces of the sessions are collected using audio recordings of the groups, photos of intermediate stage results, photos of the LAD produced and a paper-based or online evaluation questionnaire.

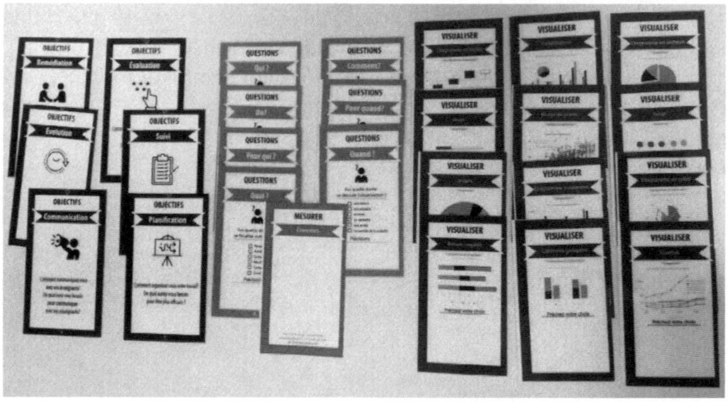

Figure 1. PADDLE Cards

3.2 Method & Data Collected

We carried out with volunteer students three recorded PADDLE sessions followed by a qualitative analysis: (1) two of them with two pairs of 1st year language students enrolled in a training formation dedicated to mastering the university environment, and (2) one with three 5th year pharmacy students in the context of a course using a serious game based on professional simulation. For each session, we recorded the interactions between students, we listed the cards selected, the data they chose to display on their LAD, the final display of the LAD they defined and we asked participants to complete the original evaluation questionnaire (Dabbebi et al., 2019). This evaluation consists in 7 statements to rate using 5-point Likert scale to evaluate their satisfaction both with the process and its outcome (the dashboard they designed). Results are presented in section 5. This data collection was led after declaring it to the university data protection officer (DPO).

As explained in introduction, it could be more convenient to use such a method in remote sessions using online tools, but questions remains open regarding the impact it may have on the quality of the collaboration.

4. REMOTE CO-DESIGN WITH EPADDLE

Scheduling co-design sessions can be difficult, and even impossible in a global pandemic context. Moreover, even when in-person sessions can happen, it is harder to collect traces of activity when tangible objects are manipulated. This led us to propose to transform the PADDLE method and cards deck into the application ePADDLE (cf. Figure 2); a digital format of PADDLE improving the traces collection.

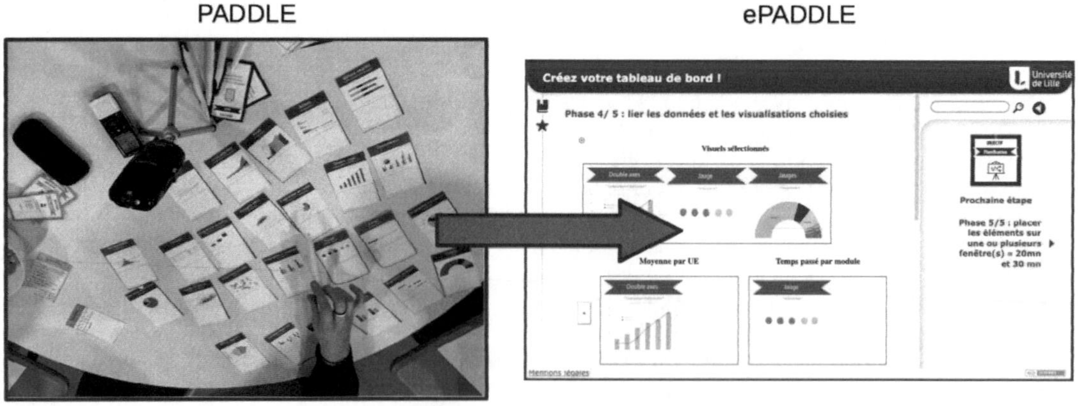

Figure 2. From PADDLE with tangible cards to ePADDLE for remote online co-design sessions

4.1 The ePADDLE Method

4.1.1 Material

The ePADDLE application keeps PADDLE's key elements: (1) its original 5 phases (presentation, decision choice, context, data and visualisation choice and LAD design), (2) the number of participants (2 to 4 in each group), (3) the facilitator whose role is mostly to introduce the goals of the workshop at first, and then to answer to both technical questions and methodological questions. Among the new elements we had to adapt or introduce to organize a remote online session, we can mention: (1) the fact that groups are asked to work together with a web conferencing tool where they can chat, talk by voice and share their screens, (2) two additional specific roles to take into account that it is harder for the session facilitator to keep track of the progression of each group compared with a session where all groups are in the same room: the scribe (whose role is to connect to the ePADDLE app, share their screen and take note of answers from the group), and the time keeper (whose role is to ensure some groups do not spend too much time on some phases), (3) the fact that activities are tracked using the LMS Moodle, commonly used in higher education, as the ePADDLE module is open source and can be embedded into the Moodle[1].

4.1.2 Method & Data Collected

To validate the claim that ePADDLE supports LAD co-design, 4 sessions using ePADDLE were organized, involving overall N=58 first year university students in multimedia design, randomly assigned to 18 groups of 2 to 4 students. During two sessions, there was one facilitator for each group whereas the two other sessions involved only one facilitator who was virtually moving from one group to another.

The audio interactions of each group were recorded. Each participant was asked to fill the same post-session questionnaire used with PADDLE. We also asked participants to fill Belbin team roles questionnaire (Belbin, 2010), to be able to evaluate further on whether the types of roles impacted the quality of the interactions and of the outcome, and asked them to rate how well they knew the other participants in their groups. The Belbin user profiles will be confronted to use of recurrent speech acts patterns in the records (e.g. Question (1) - Answer (1-N) - Acknowledgement of contribution (1-N) or Command – Announcement or again Correct – Accountability) in order to evaluate the collaboration quality. We also proposed a poll to the participants allowing them to vote for the best LAD. In this paper, we focus only on the transposition process of properties identified to enhance trace collection from a face-to-face method to a remote one.

4.2 Transposition of Relevant Properties of PADDLE

We identified 8 properties in the PADDLE method (cf. Table 1) and considered their possible digital transpositions to improve trace collection. These 8 properties were chosen to be generic enough to assume that they would also be relevant for any other adaptation of a card-based co-design method into an online remote version, as none are intrinsically related to mechanics exclusive to PADDLE. We believe however that the way we chose to translate them are not unique, and it is possible that for other methods, other translations would be more relevant than the ones chosen here.

Table 1. Translating the different properties of PADDLE into ePADDLE

Properties	PADDLE	ePADDLE	Additional traces
Initial explanations	Slideshow presented by the facilitator	Slideshow presented by the facilitator	-
Collaboration between participants	Card selection and card annotations by participants	Participating with scribe role and fields to be filled either individually or collectively	Individual and group responses from participants
Scripting collaboration	Ordered cards and regular interventions by the facilitator	Online interface for scripted collaboration	Time spent by phase
Answers to questions	Session facilitator role	Group facilitator or facilitator for the session	Trace questions in the chat

[1] https://padlad.github.io/productions

Time regulation of the session	Session facilitator role	Participating with time master role and follow-up of the session facilitator	-
Visibility of previous decisions	Magnetic cards on the whiteboard and annotation of participants	Summary of the choices made between each phase and via the menu of the digital device	Summary of previous choices and number of times the summary was viewed
Graphical production of the result	Stationery/Office materials (paper, pencil, scotch, ...)	Tool of choice: paper, participant-controlled software or online editing software	Link if online production
Method for results assessment	Questionnaire	Questionnaire with link in the digital device and Belbin profile test for collaboration evaluation	-

More precisely, here are the justifications of our choices; we tried not to lose their primary functionality. The first three properties are only associated to one of the five phases:

- Initial explanations (phase 1): the use of a video makes it easier to collect traces (time spent listening to the video, number of views), but the absence of a human to initiate the activity could be detrimental to the motivation of the group. So, we chose to keep a human briefing.
- Graphic production (phase 5): using digital tools can have potentially more readable results than a handwritten production. In the case of online software use, the link to the productions is saved.
- Evaluation of the method and the results obtained (phase 5): the evaluation method initially developed by questionnaire is adapted to the digital format to facilitate the analysis.

The five following properties are more global and associate to the method overall:

- Collaboration between participants: one option considered consisted in adding RFID chips to identify manipulated cards, to keep the tangible aspect of PADDLE, but it limits the possibility of remote sessions. So, we preferred to force each member of a group to give their opinion by proposing individual fields for some questions. This approach requires all members of the group to participate, reinforcing the commitment in the production process and allowing to collect each participants' traces.
- Scripting collaboration: scripting the digital device reproduces the order of the cards originally proposed and blocks the possibility of inadvertently mixing the cards. The digital format allows collecting information on the time spent on each card, thus allowing to identify for instance the most discussed cards.
- Answers to participants' questions: a chatbot could be considered in order to deal with simple questions, to more easily trace recurring problems as well as guarantee that the provided responses are standardized. However, chatbots can tend to distract participants (who can spend time gaming the system instead of accomplishing the task at hand (Bouchet, 2009)), lead to distrust in the whole approach if the answers are not appropriate, or may over-guide participants in the method. For these reasons, we chose for now to force participants to call the facilitator, even if it may slow down the process.
- Regulation of the session: time regulation is possible to force the transition from one phase to another but may limit rich exchanges, and it is recommended that participants be involved in the regulation of their collaborative activities (McNair et al., 2010). The digital format allows to trace the time spent in each phase.
- Visibility of previous decisions: posting a summary of each phase allows the group to check their choices and change their minds. Access to this screen can be traced to estimate the coordination of decisions with past choices.

5. RESULTS OF THE EXPERIMENTS

Each PADDLE property implementation has either been retained as they originally were, or transposed through an implementation that allows for better tracing. The ePADDLE sessions made it possible to successfully design 18 LADs (one per group - cf. Figure 3), as no group failed to propose a dashboard at the end of the session. Moreover, it allowed to easily collect the data captured during the session, in addition to the traces usually collected with PADDLE. The follow-up of the questions was successfully managed with only one facilitator per session. The regulation can be considered adapted because the duration of the workshops remained mostly in the expected time (from 63 to 115 min, M - 92 min, SD - 18 min). Finally, the visibility of previous decisions and graphic production can be validated by the productions made, which are in line with the choices of the participants.

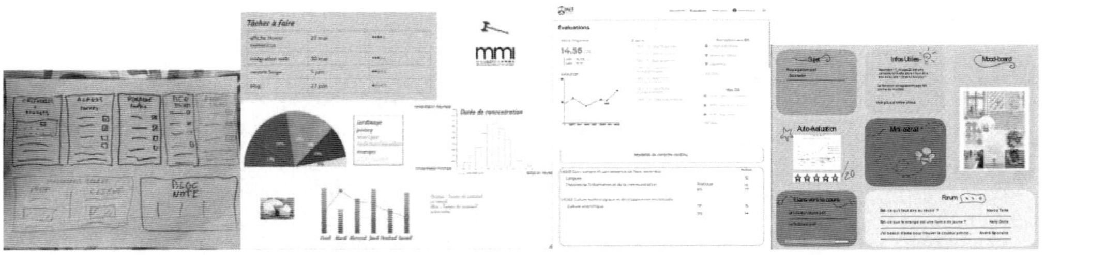

Figure 3. Examples of LAD designed with PADDLE and ePADDLE

However, by reusing the original evaluation questionnaire (Dabbebi et al., 2019), according to user evaluation (see Table 2), ePADDLE was rated a bit lower than PADDLE used in in-person sessions, significantly so regarding help to creativity where the tool could not compete with a real paper whiteboard.

Naturally, these results have to be confirmed with larger samples.

Table 2. PADDLE and ePADDLE user opinions

Properties	Statements to rate using 5-point Likert scale	PADDLE (N=8)	ePADDLE (N=58)	p*
Collaboration	The tool helped you to have a good group dynamic.	M=4.57, SD=0.79	M=4.14, SD=0.98	0.14
	The tool helped you to converge towards a solution.	M=4.29, SD=0.76	M=4.14, SD=0.87	0.27
Scripting	The tool is easy to handle.	M=4.63, SD=0.74	M=4.17, SD=0.75	0.15
	Cards are easily understandable.	M=4.25, SD=0.89	M=3.48, SD=0.90	0.09
	The tool has enabled you to better specify your needs.	M=4.63, SD=0.52	M=3.64, SD=1	0.01
	The tool has enabled you to find original solutions.	M=4.75, SD=0.46	M=3.69, SD=0.98	0.005
	And this solution seems relevant to you.	M=4.71, SD=0.49	M=3.97, SD=0.90	0.01

* The degree of significance of the Mann-Whitney test after Bonferroni correction

6. CONCLUSION AND PERSPECTIVES

Our results with students are encouraging and show the possibility of developing online co-design sessions, and achieve our main goal, co-designing LADs. Indeed, if the main advantage of this digital transposition is to obtain pre-formatted data that allows a rapid processing of these, we can see other benefits, such as remote use. Moreover, this transposition has led to enrichment to the initial method, such as the definition of multiple roles originally all under the responsibility of the session facilitator. However, there are still limits on which this transposition can evolve, such as embedding a graphic production tool which would not only facilitate this activity for participants and standardize the dashboard produced by different group, but also help in collecting traces still poor for this phase (only the final dashboard is collected but not the design process of this dashboard). Another limit relies on the validity of the properties in another context: although chosen to be generic, only transpositions of the same properties in other contexts would confirm it.

The next stages of work will focus on improving the quality of group dynamics, an important point to enable remote collaborative work and fully validate this tool. This initial work should be further developed by testing ePADDLE in other contexts (using different target group, considering the impact of how participants are recruited) and by comparing with adaptations of other co-design methods. These additional studies will help to determine rules to follow for such transpositions to be successful. Future work will also focus on using post-session questionnaires to understand group dynamics and identify potential favourable conditions for successful collaboration through (1) an analysis of speech acts based on (McNair et al., 2010), and (2) finding links with Belbin's collaboration profile. Such analyses could help in enhancing initial group formation or during a session to identify clues indicating a less productive collaboration.

ACKNOWLEDGEMENT

This work is included in the P3 project, developed by Université de Lille and co-financed by the iSite Université Lille Nord-Europe.

REFERENCES

Belbin, R.M., 2010. *Management Teams.* Taylor & Francis.

Bodily, R., Verbert, K., 2017. *Review of Research on Student-Facing Learning Analytics Dashboards and Educational Recommender Systems*. IEEE Transactions on Learning Technologies 10(4), 405–418.

Bouchet, F. 2009. *Characterization of conversational activities in a corpus of assistance requests*. Proc. of the European Summer School for Logic, Language and Information (ESSLLI). pp. 40–50.

Dabbebi, I. et al, 2019. *User Centered Approach for Learning analytics Dashboard Generation.* CSEDU 2019.

Goldman, S. et al, 2019. *Technology-mediated teacher-researcher collaborations.* CSCL 2019.

Ifenthaler, D. and Seel, N., 2005. *The measurement of change: learning-dependent progression of mental models.* Technology, instruction, cognition and learning, vol. 2, no. 4, pp. 317-336.

Jeong, H. and Hmelo-Silver, C.E., 2016. *Seven Affordances of Computer-Supported Collaborative Learning: How to Support Collaborative Learning? How Can Technologies Help?* Educational Psychologist, 51:2, 247-265.

Jivet, I. et al, 2017. *Awareness Is Not Enough: Pitfalls of Learning Analytics Dashboards in the Educational Practice*. In Data Driven Approaches in Digital Education. pp. 82–96. Springer International Publishing, Cham.

Lucero, A. et al, 2016. *Designing with Cards.* In Markopoulos, P., Martens, J.B., Malins, J., Coninx, K., Liapis, A. (eds.) Collaboration in Creative Design: Methods and Tools, pp. 75–95. Springer.

McNair, L. D. et al, 2010. *Towards a Pedagogy of Relational Space and Trust: Analyzing Distributed Collaboration Using Discourse and Speech Act Analysis*. IEEE Transactions on Professional Communication, *53*(3), 233–248.

Prieto Alvarez, C.G. et al, 2020. *LA-DECK: A Card-Based Learning Analytics Co-Design Tool.* In Proc. of the 10th International Conference on Learning Analytics and Knowledge. Frankfurt.

Roberts, L.D. et al, 2017. *Give me a Customizable Dashboard: Personalized Learning Analytics Dashboards in Higher Education*. Technology, Knowledge and Learning 22(3), 317–333.

Roy, R. and Warren, J. P., 2019. *Card-based design tools: A review and analysis of 155 card decks for designers and designing*. Design Studies, *63*, 125–154.

Ruiz, A. et al, 2018. *Participatory design method: Co-Creating user interfaces for an educational interactive system*. In Proceedings of the XIX International Conference on human computer interaction. pp. 1,8. ACM.

Sanders, E., 2002. *From user-centered to participatory design approaches*. In Design and the Social Sciences: Making Connections., pp. 1–7. CRC Press.

Schneider, B. et al, 2011. "Benefits of a Tangible Interface for Collaborative Learning and Interaction," in *IEEE Transactions on Learning Technologies*, vol. 4, no. 3, pp. 222-232.

Schwendimann, B.A. et al, 2017: *Perceiving Learning at a Glance: A Systematic Literature Review of Learning Dashboard Research*. IEEE Transactions on Learning Technologies 10(1), 30–41.

Tan, J.P.L. et al, 2017. *Learner Dashboards a Double- Edged Sword? Students' Sense-Making of a Collaborative Critical Reading and Learning Analytics Environment for Fostering 21st Century Literacies*. Journal of Learning Analytics.

Teasley, S.D., 2017. *Student Facing Dashboards: One Size Fits All?* Technology, Knowledge and Learning. 384.

Verbert, K. et al, 2014. *Learning dashboards: an overview and future research opportunities*. Personal and Ubiquitous Computing 18(6), 1499–1514.

CRITERION VALIDITY AND RELIABILITY OF PERCEIVED STRESS SCALE (PSS) IN A STUDENT POPULATION DURING COVID-19 PANDEMIC

Anna Berardi[1], Ilaria Ruotolo[2], Giovanni Sellitto[2], Francescaroberta Panuccio[2], Antonella Polimeni[3], Donatella Valente[1,4], Marco Tofani[5] and Giovanni Galeoto[1,4]
[1]*Department of Human Neurosciences, Sapienza University of Rome, Italy*
[2]*Sapienza University of Rome, Italy*
[3]*Department of Odontostomatological and Maxillo Facial Sciences, Sapienza University, Rome, Italy*
[4]*IRCSS Neuromed, Via Atinense, 18, 86077 Pozzilli, IS, Italy*
[5]*Department of Intensive Neurorehabilitation and Robotics, Bambino Gesù Children's Hospital, Rome, Italy*

ABSTRACT

BACKGROUND: Because of coronavirus disease 2019 (COVID-19) in Italy, control measures were adopted, such as closure of schools, universities, workplaces, and subsequently lockdown, so everyone's life changed. This is associated with psychological disorders in general public and in particular on students.
OBJECTIVE: To evaluate validity and reliability of the Perceived Stress Scale (PSS) in the assessment of perceived stress of Italian students after the lifestyle changes due to the outbreak of Covid-19.
STUDY DESIGN: Cross-sectional study
METHODS: A mailing list was used for the recruitment of students. Internal consistency was examined through Cronbach's Alpha Coefficient; Criterion validity was evaluated comparing PSS scores to SF-12 values, and Pearson Correlation Coefficient (PCC) was calculated. Correlation analyses were also used to investigate Cross-cultural validity.
RESULTS: The PSS scale was administered to 400 medical and health professionals' students in July 2020. Alpha Coefficient's value was statistically significant, and correlation with the SF-12 health survey was good ($p<0,01$). A correlation was found between Perceived Stress and gender, BMI, and also between PSS scores and time spent sitting and exercising under pandemic.
CONCLUSIONS: The Italian version of PSS scale is a valid and reliable instrument to assess Perceived Stress among medical and health professionals' students.

KEYWORDS

Stress, Covid-19, Pandemic, University Students, PSS

1. INTRODUCTION

Stress is the nonspecific response of the body to any demand made upon it. (Hans Selye, 1973)

Stress considerably impacts the quality of life and is associated with a range of adverse health outcomes. It can also lead to mental illness, which is a burden for the individual but may also cause serious productivity losses with societal implications. Although a stress condition carries substantial difficulties and limitations, it is merely considered a 'risk factor.' In fact, no diagnosis code for stress exists in the 5th version of the Diagnostic and Statistical Manual of Mental Disorders (DSM V) (M. G. Nielsen et al., 2016; American Psychiatric Association, 2013).

Coronavirus disease 2019 (COVID-19) is a new coronavirus that has never been found in humans before. It spread rapidly worldwide, causing severe acute respiratory syndrome. (Hao Tian et al. 2020) The effective control of SARS-CoV-2/COVID-19 required intensive contact tracing, quarantine of people with suspected infection, and the isolation of infected ones (World Health Organization, 2020).

The World Health Organization (2020) declared a pandemic state on 11th March 2020 (A. Babore et al., 2020). In Italy, the Civil Protection Department adopted control measures such as information campaigns, closure of schools, universities, and workplaces, and subsequently a lockdown. (F. Gallè et al., 2020) In this critical situation, everyone's life changed due to restrictions to physical movement and social contacts (A. Babore et al., 2020).

According to a recent rapid review on the quarantine effects, society faces several adverse cognitive and emotional problems, such as confusion, poor concentration, irritability, insomnia, distress, frustration, and anger. People are worried about the quarantine duration, insufficient information availability, economic problems, and stigma. These negative effects may affect individuals' bio-psycho-social functioning and lead to depressive or posttraumatic stress symptoms. (S. M. F. Pizzoli et al., 2020) The outbreak of COVID-19 is associated with considerable psychological disorders (PD) in the general public, specific communities, or medical students, especially when the infection rate and deaths are considerable (Hao Tian et al. 2020).

A recent review of the literature of past epidemics and pandemics highlighted that, when comparing the psychological outcomes of quarantined versus non-quarantined people, the first ones show more psychological distress. A study analyzed psychological distress in Italy's general population during the COVID-19 pandemic and showed that the majority of the increase in distress levels noted in this research was related to the course of the pandemic. (C. Mazza et al., 2020) There is evidence of the current pandemic's psychological and mental health effects on students known to be a vulnerable population. (Changwon Son et al., 2020) The mental health of college students is significantly affected when faced with public health emergencies, and they require attention, help, and support from society, families, and colleges (Xiaoyan Liu, Jiaxiu Liu, Xiaoni Zhong, 2020; Hans Selye, 1973).

Several studies conducted on undergraduate students showed that almost half of them decreased their physical activity, and a reduction in physical activity is known to contribute to stress levels (F. Gallè et al., 2020; F. Gallè et al., 2020; Melling Qi et al., 2020).

The Perceived Stress Scale (PSS) is a widely used instrument for measuring stress. The PSS evaluates the degree to which an individual perceives his life as uncontrollable and overloading during the previous month; it also assesses the ability of students to face external demands (M. G. Nielsen et al., 2016). Thus, PSS could be a suitable tool to evaluate Italian students' perceived stress after the lifestyle changes due to Covid-19 pandemic.

In other countries, PSS was already used among students during the lockdown, such as in Turkey, Colombia, Poland, Arabia, Canada (Fuat Torun, Sebahat Dilek Torun, 2020; J. C. Pedrozo-Pupo, M. J. Pedrozo-Cortés, A. Campo-Arias, 2020; Rogowska AM, Kuśnierz C, Bokszczanin A., 2020; Deemah A. AlAteeq, Sumayah Aljhani, Dalal AlEesa, 2020; C. El Morr et al., 2020).

The primary objective of this study is to evaluate the validity and reliability of the PSS in the assessment of perceived stress of Italian students following lifestyle changes due to the outbreak of Covid-19.

2. METHODS

A research group of Sapienza University of Rome and Rehabilitation & Outcome Measures Assessment (ROMA) association conducted a cross-sectional study to evaluate the psychometric properties of PSS (Amedoro A. et al., 2020; Berardi A et al., 2019; Berardi A. et al., 2020; Galeoto G. et al., 2020; Galeoto G. et al., 2019; Ioncoli M et al., 2020; Panuccio F. et al., 2020; Tofani M et al., 2019; Tofani M. et al., 2018).

The institutional review board of Sapienza University of Rome approved the study and guaranteed ethical standards and procedures. Informed consent was asked to all the participants, and they were fully anonymized.

The datasets analyzed during the study are available from the corresponding author.

The inclusion criteria were to be Medical or Health Professionals university students in Italy.

2.1 Outcome Measures

The PSS was originally developed as a 14-item scale that assesses the perception of stress by asking the individual to indicate the frequency of feelings and thoughts related to events and situations over the previous month. There are also two short forms, the PSS-4 and PSS-10, with 4 and 10 respectively selected items from the original PSS-14 form. (E. Andreou et al., 2011) PSS-10 scores are obtained by reversing the scores on the four positive items 4, 5, 7, and 8. Total scores range from 0 to 40, and higher scores indicate greater overall distress. (Müge Çelik Örücü, Ayhan Demir, 2009) The PSS was compared to the SF-12 survey.

The SF-12 is a generic short form health survey developed in the USA from SF-36. It includes two summary measures evaluating physical and mental self-perceived health: Physical Component Summary and Mental Component Summary.

2.2 Procedures and Data Analysis

The research group recruited participants according to the inclusion criteria. A mailing list was used to recruit university students attending the faculty of Medicine and Surgery or Health Professions in several Universities in Italy. All participants gave informed consent and then completed the PSS questionnaire.

2.3 Reliability

Internal consistency indicates the correlation between different items in the same tool. It was examined through Cronbach's Alpha Coefficient: 0,7 is the significant value recommended to show homogeneity between items.

2.4 Validity

Criterion validity was evaluated by comparing PSS scores to SF-12 values. The two assessment tools were administered together, and the Pearson Correlation Coefficient (PCC) was calculated. PCC can be interpreted as follows: 0 indicates no linear relationship; +1/-1 indicates perfect positive/negative linear relationship; between 0 and ±0.3 weak relationship; between ±0.3 and ±0.7 moderate relationship; between ±0.7 and ±1.0 strong relationship. All statistical analyses were conducted using Statistical Package for Social Sciences (SPSS).

Correlation analysis was used to investigate Cross-cultural validity, in particular between PSS scores and gender of participants, University of origin (North, Central, and South Italy), BMI results, and the total scale scores were also compared to the number of hours spent sitting and exercising during the lockdown.

3. RESULTS

The PSS scale was administered to 400 medical and health professionals' students recruited by the Department of Human Neurosciences of Sapienza University of Rome in July 2020, together with the SF-12. The demographic characteristics of the sample are summarized in Table 1.

Table 1. Demographic Characteristics of the sample

	Mean (SD)
Age	22.9 (5.08)
Body Mass Index	22.44 (4.44)
How many hours a day did you spend sitting during the Lockdown (March 2020-May 2020)?	8.18 (3.89)
How many hours a day did you exercise during the Lockdown period (March 2020-May 2020)?	1.65 (1.96)
Gender	**Frequency (Percentage)**
Men	98 (24.5%)
Women	302 (75.5%)

3.1 Reliability

Table 2 contains results from an analysis of internal consistency. Alpha Coefficient's value was 0,856. That is a statistically significant value.

Table 2. Internal consistency: Cronbach's alpha coefficient

	Mean	St. Deviation	Cronbach's Alpha if Item Deleted
Item 1	1.34	1.190	0.842
Item 2	1.58	1.213	0.828
Item 3	2.53	1.090	0.835
Item 4	1.75	1.020	0.856
Item 5	2.05	1.010	0.843
Item 6	2.22	1.155	0.840
Item 7	2.05	0.953	0.857
Item 8	1.91	0.968	0.844
Item 9	2.05	1.081	0.843
Item 10	1.78	1.210	0.832
Total Scale			0.856

3.2 Criterion Validity

Correlation with the SF-12 health survey was measured using the Pearson Correlation Coefficient analysis, which showed a good linear correlation ($p<0.01$) except for the correlation between Stress and Physical Component Summary of SF-12. Pearson values are respectively 0,013 for correlation between PCS12 and PSS, and -0,390 for those between MCS12 and PSS, with this one significant at the 0.01 level (2-tailed).

3.3 Cross Cultural Validity

A correlation was found between perceived stress and the gender of participants, BMI, and also between PSS scores and time spent sitting and exercising during the pandemic. [Figure 1-4] In particular, time spent sitting is significantly correlated with the BMI of participants and PSS scores, as shown in Table 3.

Table 3. Cross Cultural Validity: Pearson's correlation coefficient

	Gender	Age	University of Italy	BMI	PSS
How many hours a day did you spend sitting during the lockdown (March 2020-May 2020)?	-0.114*	-0.110*	-0.003	0.129**	0.161**
How many hours a day did you exercise during the lockdown (March 2020-May 2020)?	0.025	-0.104*	-0.022	-0.037	-0.112*
**. Correlation is significant at the 0.01 level (2-tailed).					
*. Correlation is significant at the 0.05 level (2-tailed).					

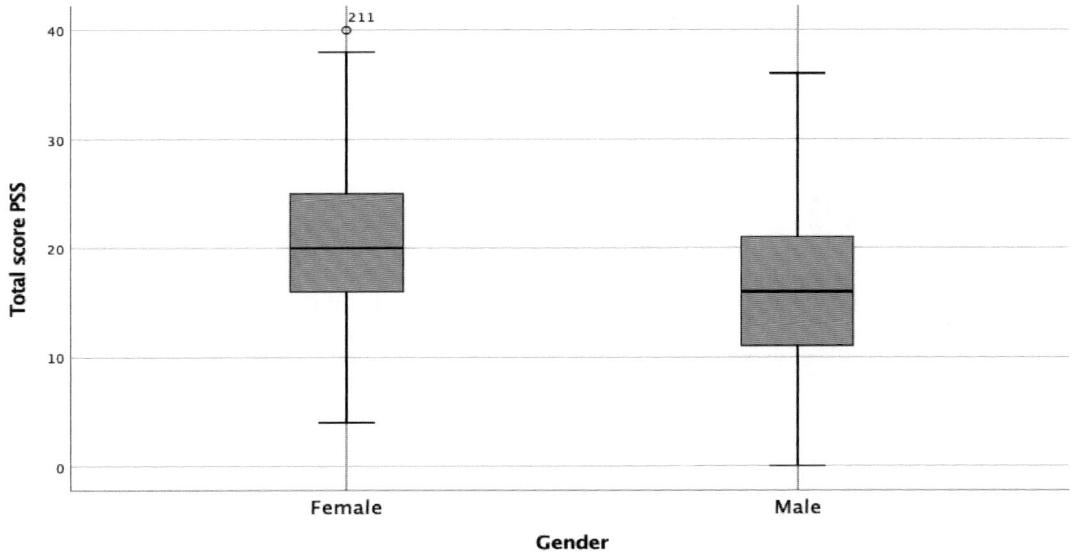

Figure 1. Correlation between gender and PSS total score

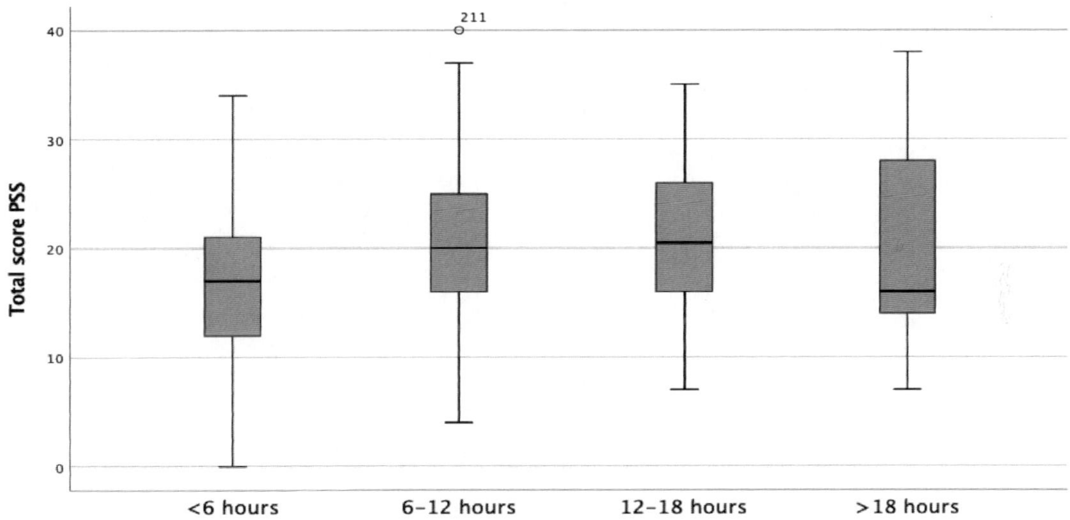

Figure 2. Correlation between time spent sitting and PSS total score

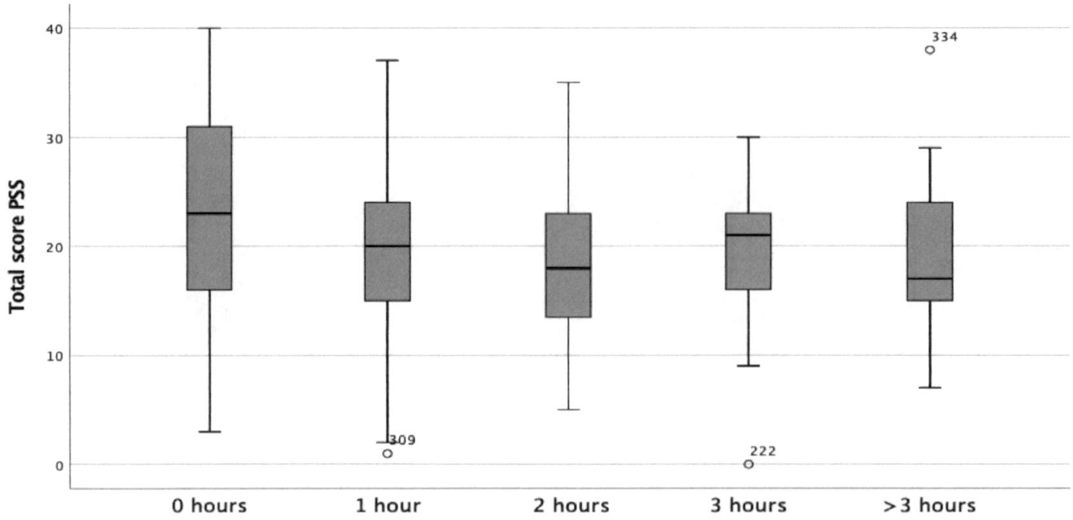

Figure 3. Correlation between time spent exercising and PSS total score

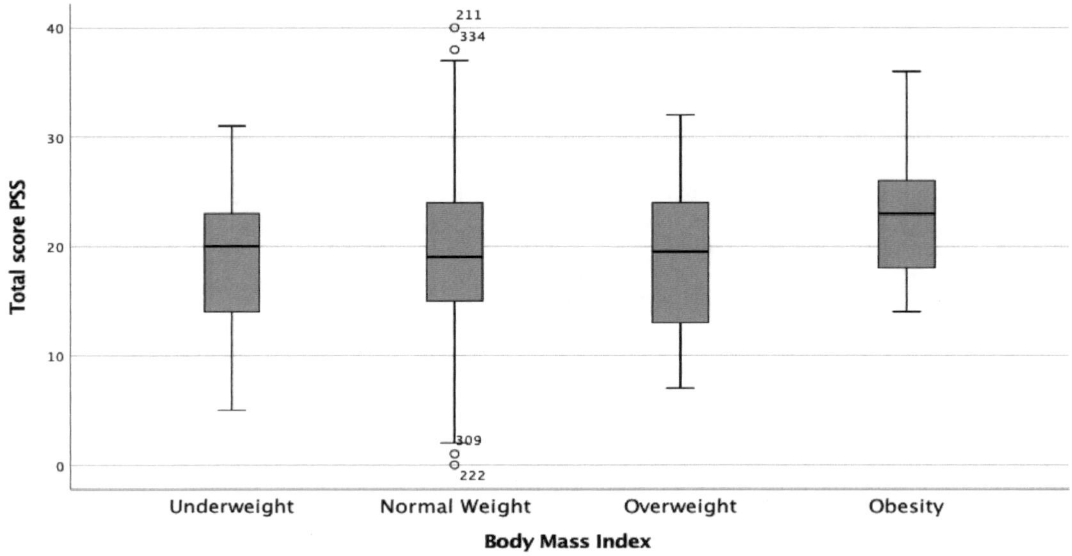

Figure 4. Correlation between BMI and PSS total score

4. DISCUSSION

Results show that there is a correlation between PSS scores and the gender of participants. Female students totalized higher scores than males, which means that their distress level was greater than the males. [Figure 1]. Recent studies that investigated the impact of COVID-19 in China have also suggested that gender was a consistent predictor of psychological outcomes. Females were more significantly affected by psychological distress than males who showed moderate anxiety levels (C. Mazza et al., 2020).

5. CONCLUSION

This study showed that the Italian version of the PSS scale is a valid and reliable instrument to assess perceived stress among medical and health professional students.

The authors report no conflict of interest.

REFERENCES

A. Babore et al., 2020. Psychological effects of the COVID-2019 pandemic: Perceived stress and coping strategies among healthcare professionals. *Psychiatry Research,* https://doi.org/10.1016/j.psychres.2020.113366

Amedoro A. et al., 2020. The effect of aquatic physical therapy on patients with multiple sclerosis: A systematic review and meta-analysis. *Mult Scler Relat Disord.*

American Psychiatric Association, 2013. *Diagnostic and Statistical Manual of Mental Disorders (DSM-5®),* Fifth Edition.

Berardi A et al., 2019. Internal consistency and validity of the Jebsen-Taylor hand function test in an Italian population with hemiparesis. *NeuroRehabilitation.*

Berardi A. et al., 2020. Tools to assess the quality of life in patients with Parkinson's disease: a systematic review. *Expert Review of Pharmacoeconomics and Outcomes Research.*

C. El Morr et al., 2020. Effectiveness of an 8-Week Web-Based Mindfulness Virtual Community Intervention for University Students on Symptoms of Stress, Anxiety, and Depression: Randomized Controlled Trial. *JMIR Publications.*

C. Mazza et al., 2020. A Nationwide Survey of Psychological Distress among Italian People during the COVID-19 Pandemic: Immediate Psychological Responses and Associated Factors. *Environmental Research and Public Health,* PMID: 32370116 PMCID: PMC7246819 DOI: 10.3390/ijerph17093165

C. Moreno et al. 2020. How mental health care should change as a consequence of the COVID-19 pandemic. *The Lancet Psychiatry,* DOI: https://doi.org/10.1016/S2215-0366(20)30307-2

Changwon Son et al., 2020. Effects of COVID-19 on College Students' Mental Health in the United States: Interview Survey Study. *JMIR publications*, doi: 10.2196/21279 PMCID: PMC7473764 PMID: 32805704

Deemah A. AlAteeq, Sumayah Aljhani, Dalal AlEesa, 2020. Perceived stress among students in virtual classrooms during the COVID-19 outbreak in KSA. *Journal of Tibah University Medical Sciences*, https://doi.org/10.1016/j.jtumed.2020.07.004

E. Andreou et al., 2011. Perceived Stress Scale: Reliability and Validity Study in Greece. *Environmental Research and Public Health*, https://doi.org/10.3390/ijerph8083287

F. Gallè et al., 2020. Understanding Knowledge and Behaviors Related to CoViD–19 Epidemic in Italian Undergraduate Students: The EPICO Study. *Environmental Research and Public Health,* doi: 10.3390/ijerph17103481

F. Gallè et al., 2020. Sedentary Behaviors and Physical Activity of Italian Undergraduate Students during Lockdown at the Time of CoViD−19 Pandemic. *Environmental Research and Public Health*, https://doi.org/10.3390/ijerph17176171

Fuat Torun, Sebahat Dilek Torun, 2020. The psychological impact of the COVID-19 pandemic on medical students in Turkey. *Pakistan Journal of Medical Sciences,* PMCID: PMC7501012 PMID: 32968408 doi: 10.12669/pjms.36.6.2985

Galeoto G. et al., 2019. Evaluation of the psychometric properties of the Barthel index in an Italian ischemic stroke population in the acute phase: A cross-sectional study. *Funct Neurol.*

Galeoto G. et al., 2020 Levels of Cognitive Functioning Assessment Scale: Italian cross-cultural adaptation and validation. *Ann di Ig.*

Hans Selye, 1973. The Evolution of the Stress Concept: The originator of the concept traces its development from the discovery in 1936 of the alarm reactions to modern therapeutic applications of syntoxic and catatoxic hormones. *American Scientist* Vol. 61, No. 6

Hao Tian et al. 2020. Humanistic care and psychological counseling on psychological disorders in medical students after COVID-19 outbreak. A protocol of systematic review. *Medicine (Baltimore),* doi: 10.1097/MD.0000000000021484 PMCID: PMC7437756 PMID: 32871994

Ioncoli M et al., 2020. Crosscultural Validation of the Community Integration Questionnaire-Revised in an Italian Population. *Occup Ther Int.*

J. C. Pedrozo-Pupo, M. J. Pedrozo-Cortés, A. Campo-Arias, 2020. Perceived stress associated with COVID-19 epidemic in Colombia: an online survey. *Saude Publica*, https://doi.org/10.1590/0102-311X00090520

M. G. Nielsen et al., 2016. The construct validity of the Perceived Stress Scale. *Journal of Psychosomatic Research,* DOI: 10.1016/j.jpsychores.2016.03.009 PMID: 27095155

Melling Qi et al., (2020). Physical Activity, Health-Related Quality of Life, and Stress among the Chinese Adult Population during the COVID-19 Pandemic. *Environmental Research and Public Health*, https://doi.org/10.3390/ijerph17186494

Müge Çelik Örücü, Ayhan Demir, 2009. Psychometric evaluation of perceived stress scale for Turkish university students. *Stress and Health*, https://doi.org/10.1002/smi.1218

Panuccio F. et al., 2020. Development of the Pregnancy and Motherhood Evaluation Questionnaire (PMEQ) for evaluating and measuring the impact of physical disability on pregnancy and the management of motherhood: a pilot study. *Disabil Rehabil* [Internet]. 4;1–7.

Rogowska AM, Kuśnierz C, Bokszczanin A., 2020. Examining Anxiety, Life Satisfaction, General Health, Stress and Coping Styles During COVID-19 Pandemic in Polish Sample of University Students. *Psychology Research and Behavior Management,* DOI: https://doi.org/10.2147/PRBM.S266511

S. M. F. Pizzoli et al., 2020. An Internet-Based Intervention to Alleviate Stress During Social Isolation with Guided Relaxation and Meditation: Protocol for a Randomized Controlled Trial. *JMIR Research Protocols*, DOI: 10.2196/19236 PMCID: PMC7301689 PMID: 32530814

S. M. Skevington, M. Lotfy, K. A. O'Connell, WHOQOL Group, 2004. The World Health Organization's WHOQOL-BREF quality of life assessment: psychometric properties and results of the international field trial. A report from the WHOQOL group. *Quality of Life Research*, DOI: 10.1023/B:QURE.0000018486.91360.00 PMID: 15085902

Tofani M et al., 2019. Validation of the Pediatric Evaluation of Disability Inventory in an Italian Population with Autism Spectrum Disorder: a Cross-Sectional Study. *Clin Ter.*

Tofani M. et al., 2018. The psychosocial impact of assistive device scale: Italian validation in a cohort of nonambulant people with neuromotor disorders. *Assist Technol*.; 25:1–6.

Tofani M. et al., 2019. A study validating the Italian version of the Level of Sitting Scale in children with cerebral palsy. *Clin Rehabil.*

Tofani M. et al., 2019. The Italian version of rheumatoid arthritis pain scale (IT-RAPS): psychometric properties on community and clinical samples. *Reumatismo.*

World Health Organization, 2020. Coronavirus disease (COVID-19) pandemic. https://www.who.int/emergencies/diseases/novel-coronavirus-2019

Xiaoyan Liu, Jiaxiu Liu, Xiaoni Zhong, 2020. Psychological State of College Students During COVID-19 Epidemic. *The Lancet Global Health.*

Yinjian Ge, Shimeng, Xin, Dechun Luan, Zhili Zou, Mengting. Liu, Xue Bai, Qian Gao (2019). Association of physical activity, sedentary time, and sleep duration on the health-related quality of life of college students in Northeast China. *Health and Quality of Life Outcomes*, DOIhttps://doi.org/10.1186/s12955-019-1194-x

A COMPARATIVE ANALYSIS OF APPROACHES TO DESIGN AND CAPITALIZE DATA INDICATORS

Albane Gril[1,2], Madeth May[1], Valérie Renault[2] and Sébastien George[1]
Le Mans University, [1]LIUM-EA4023, [2]CREN-EA2661, France

ABSTRACT

In Technology Enhanced Learning field, learning analytics cover multiple research challenges, among which tracking data analysis and data indicator design and visualization. Part of our research effort is dedicated to changing their design process, in order to capitalize them. This would allow us to meet a need in cost savings of design workflow and to encourage the adoption by users throughout their implications in a simplified design process. A study of the state of the art has been made to explore various solutions which could be exploited in the capitalization of indicators on both levels, design and implementation. It sets a direction toward a user-centered approach, aiming at a better control of users over their observation needs and the use of their data.

KEYWORDS

Learning Analytics, Capitalization, Indicators, Traces, User-Centered Design, Comparative Analysis

1. INTRODUCTION

In a context where the use of digital environments has become unavoidable, educational practitioners use TEL systems (Technology Enhanced Learning) on a daily basis, generating at the same time a massive quantity of traces. Numerous works exploit these traces with data analysis and visualization mechanisms, transforming raw traces into visual data indicators that are much more comprehensible to users. Our research effort falls into this research area and has been carried out along with a multi-party university project since 2018. The main objective of the latter is to promote students' success via a learning platform to support them in developing their skills in French writing. Our research aims to study how to provide the participants in the project with a technological solution built upon trace analysis and data indicator visualization.

An indicator, according to Dimitrakopoulou (2004), is "a variable in the mathematical sense to which a series of characteristics is assigned". In a pedagogical context, it is an effective way for both teachers and students to take full possession of this digital dimension of learning, as shown by Alowayr and Badii (2014). The design process can be broken down into three steps: defining the observation needs, computing data indicators and data exploitation. However, each of these steps is highly dependent on the context. For example, the environment and the user target the data indicators are designed for, have an important influence on the definition of the indicator (Papamitsiou *et al.* 2012). The intervention of an analyst in the process is therefore necessary. It makes their design resource-intensive. Given this complexity, it is interesting to limit the repetition of the whole process to each new need or context in order to make the design more cost-effective. There is also a limit to their adoption. A feeling of inadequacy of the proposed indicators in relation to the requirements of the end users is sometimes noticed. The difficulty of identifying the observation needs of the various users and the difficulty of extracting the information can be a deterrent (Littlejohn *et al.* 2009).

An approach based on the capitalization of indicators aims to respond to the need in cutting down the design costs, thus enabling a better use of both technical and human resources. We seek to develop a process for the design of indicators that allows their capitalization by the users of the TEL system. Indeed, by allowing a simplification of the design process, the direct collaboration of users is facilitated.

To meet this goal, the issue has been approached using two complementary methods. To initiate a co-design process with users, a protocol for collecting needs is being validated. This is meant to better grasp the involvement users can, and want to, have in the workflow. This will be detailed in another article. In parallel, a state of the art of indicator design approaches has been conducted. The study helps us consolidate the definition of capitalization, before isolating specific challenges to focus on. By using low level criteria to identify indicator capitalization, we can get closer to the user's pragmatic needs. A higher level of interpretation of those requirements will, then, allow us to confront our primary conception of capitalization in a process of consolidating the definition of the notion.

This paper is structured as follows. First, we point out the need for data indicator capitalization and make an attempt to provide a definition of the latter. Then we specify how we established a list of criteria aiming at comparing different approaches of indicator design. Section 2 is dedicated to the description of the approaches chosen for this state of the art. The comparative study is made later in the same section.

2. CAPITALIZATION STUDY

2.1 Defining Data Indicator Capitalization

The concept of capitalization is usually tied to monetary valuation. Here, the capitalization is considered as a valuation of the data itself and the value its information provides. When it comes to capitalized data indicators, their value can be defined by several factors including how relevant an indicator is, or how easy to use and reuse the existing indicators are, according to users and contexts.

Capitalizing indicators would be about keeping and multiplying their value in time, contexts and users, while maintaining the reusability. Our approach considers the latter as objects with challenges to overcome, like production cost or user validation. Indeed, they have a complex design process, highly dependent on context. Even with the many intents to simplify design workflow for analysts, or observation needs' expression for users (Laforcade et al. 2009), the adoption of indicator in learning practice for both teacher and student remains challenging. On top of that, while the usefulness of dashboards has been demonstrated in Verbert et al. (2013) to back up educational practitioners in any type of pedagogical scenario, many barriers remain to fully assimilate indicators as a common pedagogical resource (Surry et al. 2005). The inadequacy of user's implication and expertise with the current solutions have only recently been considered as a design workflow issue. The commitment to create an adequate solution has led to the rise of co-design processes with users (Dollinger *et al.* 2019). Another reflection often left aside resolves around data privacy and ethic of e-learning. Although its impact on users' perception and even performance is not negligible (May et al. 2017). These challenges are those addressed through indicator capitalization.

This approach of capitalization is therefore the combination of several concepts, as illustrated in Figure 1. The first concept is "appropriability", often used in human sciences (Ollagnier-Beldame *et al.* 2010) and in the field of HCI (Human-Computer Interaction). For instance, when adopting the indicators, users can apprehend and customize them without the intervention of experts. Then, comes the idea of "reusability", that is, indicators must be designed to work with similar context. Next, "adaptability" is needed, meaning modifications can be made to other contexts or meet different needs. Finally, "shareability" must be ensured between users, thus, allowing users to access and share capitalized indicators within the system.

The association of all those concepts under the idea of indicator capitalization aims to tackle the identified challenges and encourage a broader use of capitalized data indicators in e-learning practices. In order to verify the achievement of those four concepts, each was broken down into concrete technical properties as validation criteria, as presented hereafter.

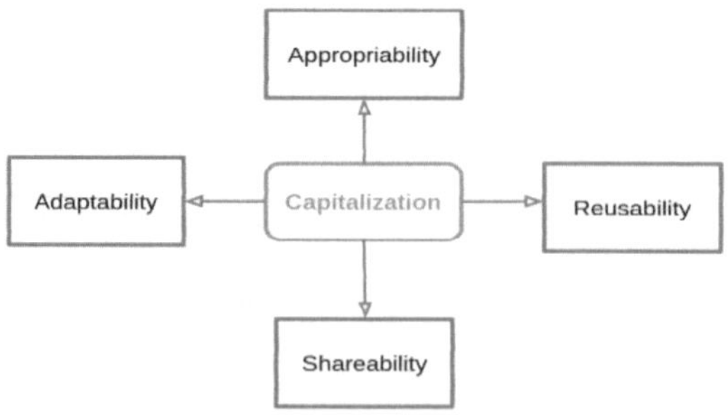

Figure 1. Concepts forming indicator capitalization

2.2 Criteria to Compare Indicator Design Approaches

The criteria of this comparative analysis are intended to specify how an existing approach can achieve indicator capitalization. Several iterations have been made to better define each criterion.

In order to come up with a solution suitable to the platform's users, communication with the project's stakeholders has been maintained right from the start of the design process. Working groups, held primarily with teachers, allowed us to identify some of their needs and expectations. This observation work did not include any presentation of the indicator capitalization process. The subject was tackled through the prism of pedagogical information, their use and challenges, creating a real involvement of the teachers, even without specific knowledge in learning analytics. This will allow us to create a relevant protocol for further experimentations. The preliminary list of needs that emerged was used as a basis to compose a series of technical properties, necessary for the verification of capitalization's concepts (Table 1). The existing criteria are meant to be fed from the experience of different users' context and profiles. The multiple iteration of user need gathering does not affect the existing criteria, but rather help create a hierarchy among the identified needs.

The properties formulated are low level to get closer to functionalities and make the validation process easier. Indeed, an abstract concept is too open to interpretation to be used in a comparative approach. But to formulate technical properties generic enough to apply to different kinds of approaches is no less tedious. Here after a detailed list of all currently selected technical properties classified between the four concepts:

2.2.1 Appropriability

Users need to regain control over the information available to them, which means that anyone can use the system, regardless of specific technical skills.

- **Granularity of entities**: The idea that each complex entity can be broken down into smaller and less complex entities. The more levels of decomposition, the better. This gives the opportunity to consider a nesting architecture to simplify the notions being handled.
- **Visualization choices**: Is an important part of data exploitation, a formalism should be able to specify how an indicator will be visualized, and an implementation should give the possibility to change it. A tool should have customizable visualization options.
- **Categorization of entities**: By classifying all entities, users will be able to access them more easily. It is even more efficient on multiple levels or with a tag system.
- **Search in existing indicators**: Users can access and select existing indicators for their own use.
- **Filtering of indicators**: A variety of indicators can be specified and narrowed down, allowing a better choice for the most relevant indicators for each user's need.

2.2.2 Reusability

Any entity created has to be valued within the system, without losing its value through time.

- **Description of entities**: Any information is useful. It can be considered as meta-data of any sort. It is important for meta-data not to be mandatory, but it's availability, updatable by any user, is a plus. This co-construction raises the question of community regulations to maintain a high level of reliability.
- **Knowledge evolution**: Evolution of the existing entities has to be eased. An existing indicator can be modified to create multiple new ones, without losing any previously created entities.
- **Versioning system**: The idea of keeping track of the indicator's construction through the different steps, as well as its evolution as it passes from user to user. The functionality will allow "Knowledge evolution" without loss of value through time.
- **Interlinking of indicators**: The possibility to create more complex indicators not only from traces but also from other indicators, all entities should be linkable and those links modifiable. It is an easier way to promote "Knowledge evolution" by using some kind of "Granularity of entities".
- **Storage of entities**: It is necessary to store the existing and created entities to ensure their future reuse. This is not necessarily handled by the tool itself, but needs to be considered when designing a system.

2.2.3 Shareability

To promote community and co-construction, communication between the user of the system can be achieved through different means.

- **User access management**: To create a system open to many types of user, being able to handle role and permission, on access or edition is necessary. Also, from an ethical perspective, an open system has to consider anonymization of data on distinct levels.
- **Circulation of indicators to users**: In an effort to co-build knowledge, spreading of the created and existing entities will allow different levels of user commitment and real cost saving. Ideally, any entities or set of entities can be shared to any related group of users.
- **Rating of indicators**: To promote reuse of existing entities and help newcomers to navigate the potentially great quantity of entities. It can be done in many ways, including assessing different aspects of the indicators, such as their usefulness and their relevance.
- **Comments**: Can be made on any indicator. Users participate through the commenting system in describing indicators and their properties.

2.2.4 Adaptability

The system has to provide a strong support to the expansion of indicator use.

- **List of existing entities**: It is required for many previous properties to have an available list of all existing entities. An entity includes indicators but also traces, operators, analysis processes or even users.
- **Import of external traces**: In a new context, traces and data in general, won't necessarily be the same, adding new information has to be facilitated by design.
- **Context of the indicator**: If the context changes, the one in which an indicator has been created has to be specifically detailed in its description. That context is among other things about the pedagogical situation and the environment' setting of the TEL system.
- **Abstraction of indicators**: Regardless of the context of use, each indicator can be created independently.
- **Modular data computing**: The calculation process needs to be easily adaptable to a new context, if possible automatically by the system, requiring a rigorous formalism set in "Abstraction of indicators".

These technical properties are classified between the four concepts defining capitalization. However, most of this classification can be questioned. For instance, the possibility to search and filter indicators can both enable appropriation, but are related to properties classified in other concepts. In order to search among existing entities, it is necessary to have an available list of the existing ones. This related property "List of existing entities" is placed in the "Adaptability" category. In the meantime, an implementation of a formalism allowing access to existing entities does not necessarily have a search functionality either. Likewise, if the filtering property is strayed forward in a tool, for a formalism it means that indicators have specifications they can be filtered on. Therefore, "Categorized entities" or "Description of entities" are considered related properties without being interdependent.

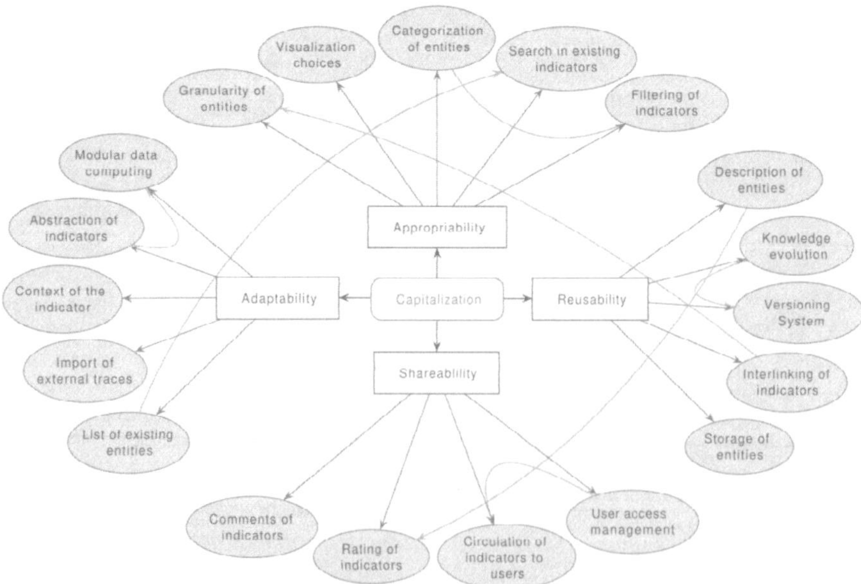

Figure 2. Related criteria for capitalization

Considering the relation of some criteria (Figure 2), their classification was adjusted within multiple iterations of the literature review. The lack of information and inadequate wording was also taken into account to make criteria relevant to the contexts encountered.

With this list of capitalization properties, we seek to experiment how design workflow responds to the identified requirements. Comparing existing solutions through this new perspective and the present grid of criteria will allow us to consolidate the definition of data indicator capitalization within the current context.

3. LITERATURE REVIEW

3.1 Selection of Indicator Design Approaches

Approaches and tools for designing indicators described in various research works have been selected. The starting point was the state of the art carried out in the Thematic Groups of the Digital Education Directorate by Cherigny *et al.* (2020), completed by additional research. Once this initial list of tools had been compiled, those closest to the criteria described above were chosen, distinguishing between formalisms of various kinds and tangible implementations.

Our project's platform is meant for students' online training before a certification, depending on the level reached. It is also meant for teachers to follow the class's progress and help them through available resources. All the approaches selected are relevant in the specific context of our project, removing many tools designed exclusively for interaction analyses, same for laboratory classes and applied work. Likewise, some work specialized on innovative hardware interfaces (tablets, surface tables, VR glasses, …) were discarded as irrelevant to our work.

Each of these approaches were selected for their relevance in a capitalization of indicator design, but also for the diversity of their nature and solution provided.

Rule-based systems (Schauer 2002) reproduce the cognitive mechanisms of an expert in a particular domain. They are based on facts and modifiable rules, which offers flexibility in data computing and the opportunity for knowledge evolution. It has been implemented in GINDIC (Generator of INDICators). Designers can use this tool to define indicators, the calculations performed on the traces and their visualization (Gendron et al. 2012).

The UTL 2 language (Choquet and Iksal 2007) is an XML-based meta-language describing the traces of a scenario. It uses the description of observation analysis methods to facilitate their capitalization. It can be used for indicator modeling with a strong attachment to pedagogical situations.

The trace-based systems, TBS, (Settouti *et al.* 2009) consider traces as a temporal sequence of observed events along with a capitalizable model. Traces in heterogeneous formats can thus be manipulated to create different indicators abstracted from environment' setting of tools. TBS-IM (Djouad and Mille 2010) is an TBS implemented for the indicator calculation in the Moodle learning platform. Another TBS is DDART (Michel *et al.* 2017), a dynamic dashboard based on activity traces and reports in the form of a Moodle plug-in. Learners can create customizable indicators related to their activities.

The Reusable Indicator Template of David *et al.* (2005) is composed of a computational function of traces and metadata explaining the reuse conditions, including the function's domain of definition, the learning situation and a description. The EM-AGIIR tool (David *et al.* 2005) proposes an implementation of the RIT and an open multi-agent architecture to apply the indicators with new traces.

The ontological framework of Lebis (2018) is used to capitalize the analysis processes of learning traces in a so-called narrative way. It is not meant for indicator capitalization, but its originality motivated us to compare it with the rest. It is part of a larger set of tools built for analysis process capitalization.

The Academic Analytics Tool (Ross *et al.* 2017), was developed for the Moodle Analytics project. AAT is a software allowing users to access and analyse student behaviour data in learning systems. Course Insights is a Learning Analytics Dashboard that provides filterable and comparative visualizations of aggregated students' daily activity and learning events to teachers. (Shabaninejad *et al.* 2020). The flexibility of those tools, which are not based on a studied formalism, are interesting from a user perspective.

We looked into indicators design approaches from the Learning Analytics domain, but it seems relevant to expand this search into other domains where context is equally important. Overall, few tools offer a solution for capitalization by the system as well as the users themselves.

3.2 Literature Review Grid

This state of the art is synthesized in Table 1. Our proposal is based on four levels of validation of a criterion: [V] validated with respect to our work, [PV] partially validated, [NV] not validated and [NR] not relevant, in case of inadequacy with a criterion. The number of "not relevant" criteria is due to the effort to compare objects of different nature with a common grid. The formulation of the criteria as technical properties is interpreted in a distinct way depending on whether the analysed object is a theoretical formalism or a tangible implementation. For instance, "Visualization options" would be the information stored for a language, the display handled for an architecture and real visualizations for implemented tools. In some cases, the property does not apply for some level of abstraction, hence the use of "not relevant".

Validation of each criterion was done through a careful analysis of the literature. Nonetheless, the collected information for our analysis can be limited, as each tool we studied is not always meant for data indicator capitalization. The grid's filling considers interconnection of criteria in the implementation level to fill the information gaps. It may occur that specific information contradicts those supposed interconnections, for instance no filtering implemented even where categorization is permitted.

Table 1. Comparison of formalisms and implementations of indicator capitalization

	Formalisms	Rule -based System (Schauer 2002)		Trace-base system (Settouti *et al.* 2009)			Reusable Indicator Template David *et al.* 2005)		UTL 2 language (Iksal and Choquet 2007)	Narrative ontological framework (Lebis 2018)		
	Implementations		**GINDIC (Gendron et *al.* 2012)**		**TBS-IM system (Djouad and Mille 2010)**	**DDART (Michel et al. 2017)**		**EM-AGIIR (David et *al.* 2005)**			**Academic Analytics Tool (Ross et *al.* 2017)**	**Course Insights (Shabaninejad et al. 2020)**
Appropriability	**Granularity of entities**	NV	NV	V	PV	PV	PV	PV	V	V	V	V
	Visualization choices	NV	V	NV	NV	V	NV	PV	NV	NR	NV	PV
	Categorization of entities	NV	V	PV	NV	V	V	V	V	V	V	NV
	Search in existing indicators	V	V	PV	NV	NV	NR	V	NR	NR	V	V
	Filtering of indicators	NV	PV	PV	NV	NV	NR	NV	NR	NR	V	V
Reusability	**Description of entities**	V	V	PV	PV	PV	V	V	V	V	V	PV
	Knowledge evolution	V	V	V	V	PV	NV	V	V	V	NV	PV
	Versioning System	PV	PV	PV	NV	NV	PV	PV	V	NV	NV	NV
	Interlinking of indicators	V	V	PV	NV	NV	NV	NV	V	V	V	V
	Storage of entities	V	V	V	V	V	NR	V	NR	NR	V	V
Shareability	**User access management**	PV	V	PV	NV	NV	NR	V	NR	NR	V	PV
	Circulation of indicators to users	NR	PV	NR	NV	PV	NR	NV	NR	NR	NV	NV
	Rating of indicators	NV	V	NV	NV	NV	NV	NV	NV	NR	NV	NV
	Comments of indicators	PV	NV	PV	NV	NV	PV	PV	PV	PV	PV	NV
Adaptability	**List of existing entities**	V	V	V	V	V	NR	V	NR	NR	V	V
	Import of external traces	V	V	V	V	V	NR	PV	NR	NR	V	V
	Context of indicator	V	V	NV	NV	NV	V	V	V	V	PV	PV
	Abstraction of indicators	V	V	V	V	V	V	V	V	V	V	PV
	Modular data computing	PV	V	V	V	V	V	PV	V	V	V	PV

In this table 1, it can be seen that a rule-based system does not offer any specific means to categorize entities, whereas GINDIC does include the dimension and the nature of the created indicators. On this part, the Reusable Indicator Patron provides three types, Cognitive, Social and Affective, which are here considered as categorization. To take another example, "User access management" may seem a stray forward functionality for an implemented tool, therefore, it can be seen that three out of five of them have it implemented. Then for the formalisms, both rule-based system and trace-based system are considered as partially validating the criterion by suggesting a system architecture in which the property could be easily added, but this concern has not been found in the studied documentation and therefore not fully validated. For the rest of the formalisms, their nature is too disconnected from such a functionality to be considered relevant. A similar reflection has been followed for each criterion in the grid, while studying the available documentation.

Regarding the criteria suggested for the capitalization of indicators, some limits in the design solutions can be noticed. It would be interesting to look for an approach which facilitates the sharing of existing indicators without losing the flexibility of their design. Indeed, the criteria for appropriation and sharing of indicators are the least developed. The usability of an approach is not directly included in this grid, but this important factor of user adoption can be partially assessed through the present criteria.

It can also be noted that an implementation does not necessarily preserve all the technical properties of the corresponding formalism. Some other properties do not seem to be related to the implemented indicator design formalism. However, the chosen formalism clearly has an impact on the implemented functionality. Thus, the conception model for an indicator design approach should not be taken lightly.

4. CONCLUSION

The democratization of data indicators in the learning practice face challenges with high design cost and limited user adoption. Capitalization as a solution to those challenges requires a closer look at the user's needs regarding data collection, transformation, computation, exploration and visualization. The multiplicity of users' level of interaction with the TEL system, the pedagogical information and the data indicator make the design of a common approach more complex. Numerous issues as data privacy and ethics must be assimilated in the design process to reach a thorough user-adapted proposition. The recycling process of an object must be considered at the design stage. However, capitalization also requires the active involvement of users. They need to be proactive for successful indicators' assimilation in the learning practices. This proactivity has to be supported and promoted by the process itself.

With this perspective, a co-design process has been initiated with working groups to identify technical criteria for the capitalization of indicators. These criteria will be a means of validating our approach while relying on a state of the art in the field. This last one shows the necessity to accentuate the accessibility of the entities used by the users to ensure the durability of our approach.

The work presented here allows us to draw some initial analyses, but some limits are to be underlined. First, the domain and project context in which the choice of design approaches remains narrowed. This choice was also due to size constraints, but it would be interesting to extend this analysis to new design solutions. The lack of experimentation to validate the grid's fulling has also been pointed out, and an analysis carried out exclusively through the literature would need to be further investigated. Finally, the criteria developed here are based on a user-centered approach that has only been initiated.

Further work with users will be carried out to validate the initial conclusions. The consolidation of our definition of data indicator capitalization will involve users in the construction of this approach through the organization of focus groups. The grid provided here will allow us to rely on a predefined but enhanceable list of criteria to provide an evolutive approach to indicator design.

ACKNOWLEDGEMENT

Our work is carried out within the French project PIA écri+ (n° ANR-17-NCUN- 0015) <http://ecriplus.fr/>.

REFERENCES

Alowayr, A., Badii, A., 2014. Review of Monitoring Tools for E-Learning Platforms. *International Journal of Computer Science and Information Technology*, 6, 79–86.

Cherigny, F., El Kechai, H., Iksal, S., Lefevre, M., Labarthe, H., Luengo, V., 2020. L'analytique des apprentissages avec le numérique. *Groupes thématiques de la Direction du numérique pour l'Éducation* (DNE -TN2) (Research Report).

Choquet, C., Iksal, S., 2007. Modeling Tracks for the Model Driven Reengineering of a TEL System. *Journal of Interactive Learning Research*, 18.

David, J.-P., Adam, J.-M., Diagne, F., Lejeune, A., Luengo, V., Pernin, J.-P., 2005. Design patterns for recording and analysing usage of learning systems: State of art of tracking and analysing usage.

Dimitrakopoulou, A., 2004. State of the art on Interaction and Collaboration Analysis.

Djouad, T., Mille, A., Reffay, C., Mohamed, B., 2009. Engineering of activity indicators using modelled traces for Computer Supported Collaborative Learning. *STICEF*, 16.

Dollinger, M., Liu, D., Arthars, N., Lodge, J., 2019. Working Together in Learning Analytics Towards the Co-Creation of Value. *Journal of Learning Analytics*, 6, 10–26.

Gendron, E., Pourroy, F., Carron, T., Marty, J.-C., 2012. Towards a structured approach to the definition of indicators for collaborative activities in engineering design. *Journal of Engineering Design*, 23, 195–216.

Ji, M., Michel, C., Lavoué, E., George, S., 2014. DDART, a Dynamic Dashboard for Collection, Analysis and Visualization of Activity and Reporting Traces, in: Rensing C., de Freitas S., Ley T., Muñoz-Merino P.J. (Eds) *Open Learning and Teaching in Educational Communities*. Presented at the EC-TEL 2014, Springer, Cham.

Laforcade, P., Zendagui, B., Barré, V., 2009. Specification of Observation Needs in an Instructional Design Context - A Model-Driven Engineering Approach. *CSEDU*, pp. 111–118.

Lebis, A., Lefevre, M., Luengo, V., Guin, N., 2018. Capitalisation of analysis processes: enabling reproducibility, openness and adaptability thanks to narration. *LAK '18: Proceedings of the 8th International Conference on Learning Analytics and Knowledge*, pp. 245–254.

Littlejohn, A., Margaryan, A., Milligan, C., 2009. Charting Collective Knowledge: Supporting Self-regulated Learning in the Workplace. *Proceedings of 9th IEEE International Conference on Advanced Learning Technologies,* 208–212.

May, M., Iksal, S., Usener, C.A., 2017. The Side Effect of Learning Analytics: An Empirical Study on e-Learning Technologies and User Privacy. in: Costagliola, G., Uhomoibhi, J., Zvacek, S., McLaren, B.M. (Eds.), *Computers Supported Education, Communications in Computer and Information Science*. Springer International Publishing, Cham, pp. 279–295.

Michel, C., Lavoué, E., George, S., Ji, M., 2017. Supporting awareness and self-regulation in project-based learning through personalised dashboards. *IJTEL* 9, 204.

Ollagnier-Beldame, M., 2010. Footprinting e-learners' activity: A first step to help their appropriation of the training system? *International Journal of Knowledge Management*, 6, 65–77.

Papamitsiou, Z., Economides, A., 2014. Learning Analytics and Educational Data Mining in Practice: A Systematic Literature Review of Empirical Evidence. *Educational Technology & Society*, 17, 49–64.

Ross, T., Chang, T.-W., Ives, C., Parker, N., Han, A., Graf, S., 2017. The Academic Analytics Tool: Workflow and Use Cases. *Lecture Notes in Educational Technology*, pp. 231–236.

Schauer, F., 2002. *Playing by the Rules: A Philosophical Examination of Rule-Based Decision-Making in Law and in Life*. Oxford University Press.

Settouti, L.S., Prié, Y., Marty, J.-C., Mille, A., 2009. A Trace-Based System for Technology-Enhanced Learning Systems Personalisation, Proceeding of *9th IEEE International Conference on Advanced Learning Technologies. IEEE,* Riga, Latvia, pp. 93–97.

Surry, D., Ensminger, D., Haab, M., 2005. A model for integrating instructional technology into higher education. *British Journal of Educational Technology*, 36, 327–329.

Verbert, K., Duval, E., Klerkx, J., Govaerts, S., Santos, J., 2013. Learning Analytics Dashboard Applications. *American Behavioral Scientist*, 57.

UNDERSTANDING STUDENT SLIDE READING PATTERNS DURING THE PANDEMIC

Boxuan Ma, Min Lu and Shin'ichi Konomi
Kyushu University
Japan

ABSTRACT

The COVID-19 pandemic has resulted in school closures all across the world, and lots of students have shifted from conventional classrooms to online learning. With the help of ICT technologies nowadays, learning online can be more effective in a number of ways. However, most of the online learning environments without instructors' attention may result in different learning patterns compared to the traditional face-to-face classroom. In this paper, we aimed at detecting the slide reading behaviors of the students by analyzing operational event logs from a digital textbook reader for a lecture offered in our university. We compared reading patterns between traditional face-to-face lectures and hybrid online lectures, our results show that online lectures lead to more off-task behaviors. Our analysis provides a rich understanding of e-book reading and informs design implications for online learning during the pandemic. The findings can also be used to improve the instruction designs and learning strategies.

KEYWORDS

Reading Patterns, E-book Event Stream, Educational Big Data, Online Lecture

1. INTRODUCTION

The COVID-19 pandemic has changed education in many aspects. It has resulted in school closures all across the world and students are forced to learn out of the classroom. As a result, education has changed dramatically, with the distinctive rise of e-learning, whereby teaching is undertaken remotely and on digital platforms. Even before COVID-19, there existed substantial infrastructure for online education in many countries. However, no university was ready for a complete shift to online education. Many universities are now delivering course content through various platforms and professors are using online educational platforms, videoconferencing software, and social media to teach their courses (Patricia, 2020; Chakraborty et al, 2020; Bao, 2020). Online educational platforms, like Google Classroom (Iftakhar, 2016) and Moodle (Costa et al, 2012), allow professors to share notes and multimedia resources related to their courses with students. The online educational platforms also allow students to turn in their assignments and professors to keep track of the progress of the students. Videoconferencing tools, like Google Meet, Zoom, and Microsoft Teams, help in organizing online lectures and discussion sessions. Some universities are also disseminating course material through their websites and their own learning management system. While some believe that the unplanned and rapid move to online learning will result in a poor user experience that is unconducive to sustained growth, others believe that a new hybrid model of education will emerge, with significant benefits. The success of MOOCs shows evidence that learning online can be more effective in a number of ways. This is mostly due to the students being able to learn at their own pace, going back and re-reading, skipping, or accelerating through concepts as they choose.

Nevertheless, others argue that homeschooling and online learning are difficult for the students because a structured environment is missing and they are more easily distracted. With regard to traditional face-to-face classrooms, online learning environments that without instructors' attention may lead to more off-task behaviors. Off-task behaviors can be defined as any actions that a student exhibit in the learning environment that is not according to the tasks given by the lecturer. Off-task behavior is a common problem that online classrooms often face. For example, without instructors' attention, devices like computers, mobiles, tablets, etc. can be a reason for distraction because students may play games, use other applications, and browse the internet. Engaging with off-task behaviors has also been shown to be associated with poor learning (Baker, et al, 2004; Cocea et al, 2009).

Not only different from the traditional face-to-face classroom but also the fully time-free MOOC course, understanding how students learn in such a new hybrid model is still a challenge for researchers. Besides, students are using different study approaches to achieve a specific learning task. Understanding these approaches is important for designing further interventions.

In this paper, we aimed at investigating student reading patterns by using students' reading logs that were collected from a digital textbook reader and compared their reading patterns in traditional face-to-face lectures and hybrid online lectures. Our analysis provides a rich understanding of e-book reading and informs design implications for future e-learning and e-book systems in the age of online learning. The findings can also be used to improve the instruction designs and learning strategies. In addition, by analyzing the different reading patterns of students, interventions can be designed to help off-task students.

2. RELATED WORK

Analyzing learning patterns is important for a better understanding of learners' behaviors and experience, which can help researchers facilitate the design of learning systems, materials, or activities (Sutcliffe et al, 2016). With the increasing use of digital learning materials in higher education, the accumulated operational log data provide opportunities to analyzing how students learn with e-books.

Many researchers focus on studying user reading patterns and their implications from the log data recorded when learners interact with e-book systems to better understand how students read and what they need when reading learning materials. Oi et al. (2015) reported their analysis results of preview and review patterns in undergraduates' e-book logs. Ma et al. (2020) conducted a study to understand the page-flip behavior of students, their results show that students have different page-flip preferences. Shimada et al. (2016) conducted a study based on non-negative matrix factorization and identified five kinds of browsing patterns. Taniguchi et al. (2019) found that highlighters marked by the users on e-textbooks are useful and they provide highlighter recommendations on e-textbooks to help students with better learning. Cheng and Tsai (2014) collected video-recorded data, and used clustering to analyze "Book reading action patterns." Akçapinar et al. (2020) explored students' study approaches and identified three groups of students who have different study approaches, including deep, strategic, and surface. In their study, the relationship between students' reading behaviors and their academic performance is also investigated by using association rule mining analysis. Yin et al. (2019) grouped students were into four clusters using k-means clustering, and their learning behavioral patterns were analyzed.

Based on user behavior analysis, some researchers also find strong correlations between user behaviors and student performance. Brinton et al. (2015) use clickstream data and learner behaviors to predict student performance in a MOOC platform. Okubo et al. (2017) propose a method for predicting final grades of students by a Recurrent Neural Network (RNN) from the log data stored in the educational systems. In addition, Crossley et al. (2016) use click-stream data with NLP tools to predict MOOC completion. Goda et al. (2015) collected data from an e-learning system and used statistical methods to analyze the "Learning pace patterns" of the learners and their relationship to learning outcomes. Seven distinct types of learning behavior were identified, including procrastination, learning habit, random, diminished drive, early bird, chevron, and catch-up. Their results imply that regulated learning could increase learning effectiveness and lead to better learning outcomes.

While existing works provide access to learning log data, they are either aimed at MOOCs or traditional classroom settings, which may differ from the online lecture settings during the pandemic situation. Our analysis focuses on a hybrid online lecture setting, where the instructor gives the course by a videoconferencing tool, and students using an e-book system to read learning materials. Also, we want to compare reading patterns between traditional face-to-face lectures and online lectures.

3. METHOD

3.1 Dataset

The data used in this study were reading logs collected during a 90-minute-long data science course. The instructors and each student used BookRoll (Ogata et al, 2017) (the e-book system in our university) to access teaching slides from a web browser on their personal devices (computer, smartphone, etc.). Other learning activities, such as assignments, quizzes, forum discussions, and so on, were mainly conducted on a Moodle course page. The course lasts for 2 weeks and every lecture has 2 learning materials (teaching slides). Each teaching slide will be used for 45 minutes. In addition, at the end of each lecture, students took part in the quiz related to content. The course was offered to mostly first-year undergraduate university students. In 2019, this course was conducted in a traditional face-to-face classroom. A total of 225 students (mostly freshmen) attended the course in 2019. However, due to the Covid-19 situation, this course was conducted fully online via online meeting software (Zoom) in 2020, the students use BookRoll to access teaching slides at home, keep their microphones muted and cameras off, and listen to the instructor online. A total of 225 students (mostly freshmen) attended the course in 2020. Note that even one is face-to-face and the other is online lecture, the instructors and course contents are all the same in 2019 and 2020.

Figure 1 is the screenshot of BookRoll interface, the basic operation is to flip the page. Students can click the previous button to move to the previous page, and click the next button to move to the subsequent page, they also could use a slider to change pages. Besides that, there are features like bookmark, marker, memo annotating, search, etc. that students can use for learning. All click-stream were recorded in a database that is related to students' interaction with BookRoll. The collected click-stream data contained the following fields. user_id: anonymized student user id. operation_name: the action that was done, e.g. open, close, next, previous, jump, add markers, add bookmarks, etc.). page_no: (the current page where the action was performed), marker: (the reason for the marker added to a page, e.g. important, difficult), role: (the role of the user, including student and teacher), device_code (the type of device used to view BookRoll, e.g. mobile, pc), and operation_date: (the timestamp of when the operation occurred). Table 1 is the description of our dataset.

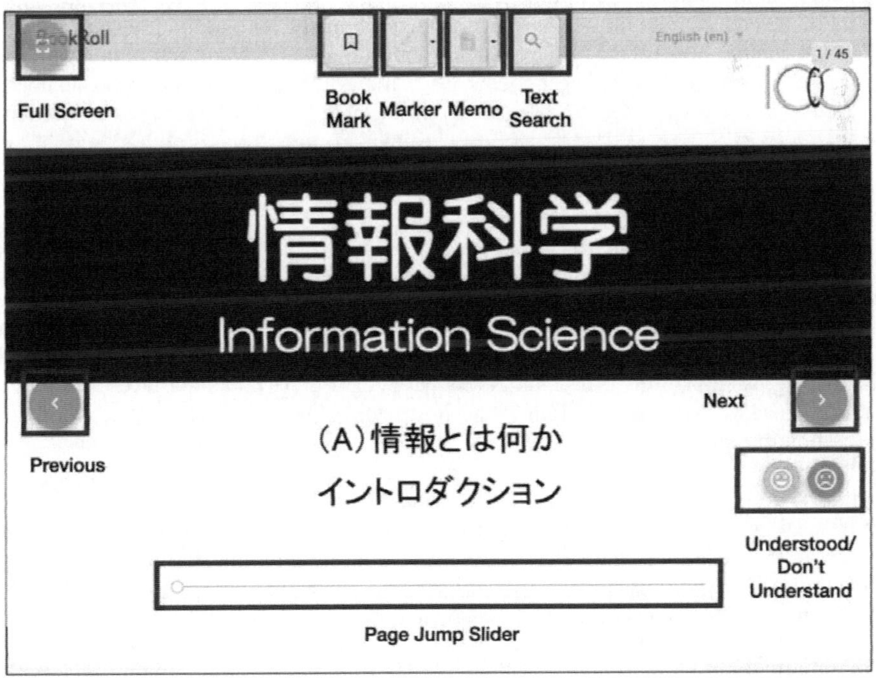

Figure 1. The screenshot of BookRoll interface

Table 1. Description of the Event Stream Dataset

Year	Week	Category	Type	Number
2019	Week 1	Student	Total Student #	175
		Lecture	Lecture Time	90 min
		Operation event	Total Event # (Slide A)	45,141
			Total Event # (Slide B)	31,710
	Week 2	Student	Total Student #	164
		Lecture	Lecture Time	90 min
		Operation event	Total Event # (Slide A)	39,815
			Total Event # (Slide B)	26,846
2020	Week 1	Student	Total Student #	147
		Lecture	Lecture Time	90 min
		Operation event	Total Event # (Slide A)	14,030
			Total Event # (Slide B)	9,656
	Week 2	Student	Total Student #	103
		Lecture	Lecture Time	90 min
		Operation event	Total Event # (Slide A)	12,629
			Total Event # (Slide B)	12,833

3.2 Data Preprocess

For the analysis, we used operation_date (the timestamp of when the operation occurred), page_no (the current page where the action was performed), and role (the role of the user, including student and teacher) columns. First, we grouped the data into 1-minute intervals, then we extracted the pages for all the users, including the instructor and each student. If a user does not have a log for the specific time interval, we assumed that she/he is on the same page where she/he was in the last time. As a result, we got a time-page table for both the instructor and students.

After transforming students' click-stream data into the time-page data, we first calculated all students' reading patterns and relative reading patterns by taking the instructor's reading pattern as a baseline. Next, k-means cluster analysis was used to group students with similar reading patterns. For cluster analysis, we try to group students with similar reading patterns in each teaching slide. The optimal number of clusters is decided based on the elbow method. The details and results will be described in the next section.

4. RESULTS

We visualized all students' reading patterns. Visualizations can be seen in Figure 2. The left is one of the online lectures in 2020 and the right is one of the face-to-face lectures in 2019. The X-axis shows the time, Y-axis shows the page of the books. The intersection of the Time and Page shows the current page of the student at a specific time. Each red line shows the reading patterns of the different students, and the blue line shows the reading patterns of the instructor. As shown in the figure, no matter face-to-face or online lecture, most students' reading pattern is to follow the instructor as we expected, that is, the number of pages increases as time progresses. However, we also observed that there are some students who have different reading patterns.

Enlighted by Akçapınar et al. (2019), we calculated the relative reading patterns of all students to have a better understanding of student reading patterns. To do this we took the instructor's reading pattern as a baseline since the expected reading behavior of students is to follow the instructor during the lecture. The relative reading pattern will be calculated based on the distance of the student's reading pattern and the instructor's reading pattern. For instance, if a student is on page 20 while the instructor is on page 23, then the student's relative distance will be -3. If a student is on page 26, then the relative distance will be +3. And if the student is on page 23 (same page as the instructor), it will be 0.

The results of this calculation are shown in Fig.3. The left is one of the online lectures in 2020 and the right is one of the face-to-face lectures in 2019. The X-axis shows the time of the lecture, while Y-axis shows the student's relative distance from the page where the instructor is currently in. As shown in the figure, both in face-to-face lecture and online lecture, there are some students' reading patterns were ahead of the teacher, some of them tried to follow the teacher, and some were behind of the teacher.

After calculating students' relative distances from the instructor's pattern, we conducted cluster analysis using k-means method to find and compare the common reading patterns in two different learning environments.

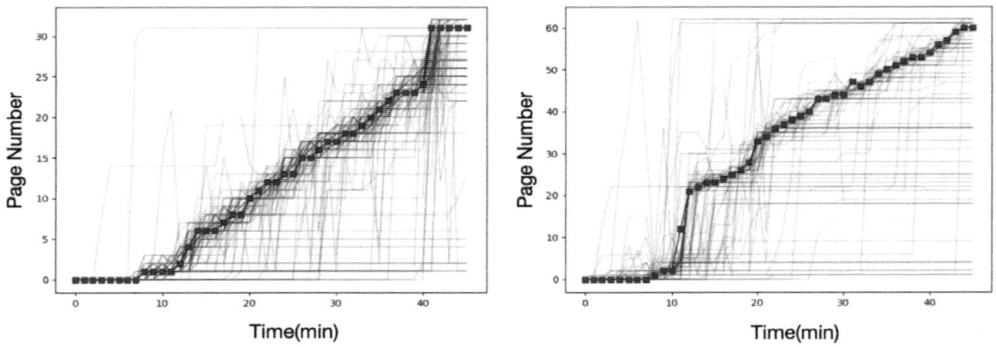

Figure 2. Students' reading patterns across the lecture. Left: 2020 (online lecture). Right: 2019 (face-to-face lecture)

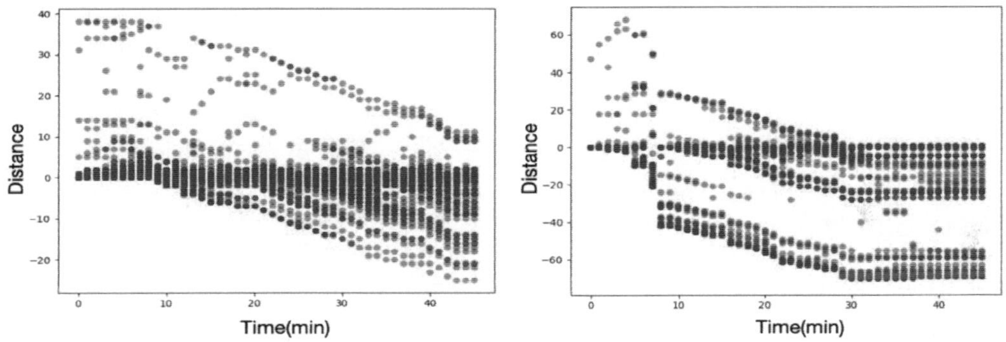

Figure 3. Students' relative reading patterns across the lecture. Left: 2020 (online lecture). Right: 2019 (face-to-face lecture)

4.1 Clustering Result

In order to identify the optimal number of clusters, we have performed the elbow method (Bholowalia et al, 2014) and the number of clusters is set to 4 based on the results. To see the common reading patterns of the students in these clusters, we visualized cluster means as well. Results can be seen in Figure 4. The left is one of the online lectures in 2020 and the right is one of the face-to-face lectures in 2019. The X-axis shows the time of the lecture, while Y-axis shows the cluster means of student's relative distance from the page where the instructor is currently in. From Figure 4, we found four similar patterns both for face-to-face lecture and online lecture. It can be seen that students in cluster 1 (C1) reading the slide even faster than the instructor, while students in cluster 2 (C2) are following the instructor from the beginning until the end of the lecture. In contrast to cluster 2, students in cluster 4 (C4) could be labeled as Off-Task students since they no longer follow the instructor after 15 minutes from the beginning of class. In addition, the relative distance is increased until the end of the course. More interesting thing is that students of cluster 3 (C3), seem to try to catch up with the instructor, and their relative distance is increased first and then decreased.

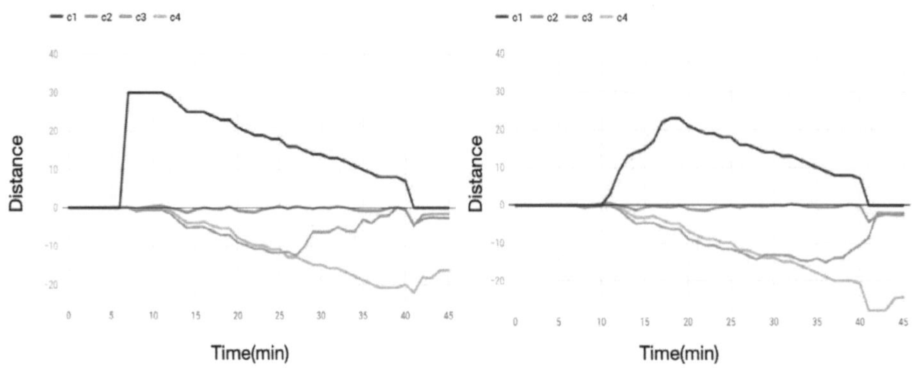

Figure 4. Students' relative reading patterns based on cluster results. Left: 2020 (online lecture). Right: 2019 (face-to-face lecture)

Table 2. Clustering results for 2020 (online lecture)

Category	C1	C2	C3	C4
Week 1 (Slide A)	2%	3%	7%	**88%**
Week 1 (Slide B)	17%	2%	5%	**76%**
Week 2 (Slide A)	14%	7%	3%	**76%**
Week 2 (Slide B)	7%	10%	4%	**79%**

Table 3. Clustering results for 2019 (face-to-face lecture)

Category	C1	C2	C3	C4
Week 1 (Slide A)	20%	31%	5%	**44%**
Week 1 (Slide B)	23%	**43%**	5%	29%
Week 2 (Slide A)	21%	23%	4%	**54%**
Week 2 (Slide B)	26%	24%	14%	**36%**

The percentage of students in each cluster is shown in Table 2 and Table 3. The results in Table 2 highlighted that most of the students had difficulty follow the instructor during the online lectures, more than 76% of students (C4) could not follow the instructor after the first fifteen-minute of the lecture. Only a few students (C2) could follow the instructor all the way during the class. One possible reason could be that a structured environment is missing and they are more easily distracted without the attention of the instructor. The results in Table 3 also show that many students (C4) could not follow the instructor after the first fifteen-minute of face-to-face lectures, however, the percentage of students is lower compared to online lectures. Besides, the percentage of students in C2 is much higher than in online lectures, which hints that students could follow the instructor more easily in face-to-face lectures. Our results show that online format has a significant negative impact on students' persistence in sticking with courses, such an environment that without instructors' attention leads to more off-task behaviors compared to the traditional face-to-face classroom.

4.2 Student Academic Performance

As mentioned before, students took the quiz (full marks=10) at the end of each lecture. We compared the quiz performance of the students in different clusters. Results are shown in Table 4 and Table 5. Since the data were not normally distributed, we used the Mann-Whitney test to compare every two groups. We can see that both for face-to-face lectures and online lectures, students of cluster 2 (C2) get a significantly higher score compared to other clusters, while students of cluster 4 (C4) get a significantly lower score. It is not surprising that students who follow the instructor's reading pattern are more engaging and focusing on the class, and students who give up following the instructor are much easier get distracted during the class and thus receive a low score. However, although leads to more off-task behaviors, our analysis results showed no significant difference in student performance between online and face-to-face students.

Table 4. Clustering results of students' read pattern records for 2020 (online lecture)

Week	Category	C1	C2	C3	C4
Week1	Average Score (SD)	6.09(2.65)	**6.61**(2.55)	5.23(1.81)	5.02(1.97)
Week2	Average Score (SD)	5.16(2.89)	**5.33**(1.39)	4.42(2.58)	3.89(2.68)

Table 5. Clustering results of students' read pattern records for 2019 (face-to-face lecture)

Week	Category	C1	C2	C3	C4
Week1	Average Score (SD)	5.73(1.11)	**5.91**(0.31)	5.51(0.71)	5.18(1.78)
Week2	Average Score (SD)	4.91(1.72)	**5.54**(1.61)	4.45(1.51)	3.91(1.41)

5. CONCLUSION

This research aims to tackle the reading patterns of students while using the e-book system to seek a better understanding of how students read and learn in online lectures and traditional face-to-face lectures. Through the analytics of e-book event stream data, we first calculated all students' reading patterns and relative reading patterns by taking the instructor's reading pattern as a baseline. Next, we conducted a cluster analysis to find the common reading patterns of students. Finally, we compared the quiz performance of the students in different clusters.

The experiment found that both in online and face-to-face lectures there are four reading patterns of students. The results highlighted that online format has a significant negative impact on students' persistence in sticking with courses, such an environment that without instructors' attention leads to more off-task behaviors compared to the traditional face-to-face classroom. Only a few students could follow the instructor all the way during the online lecture. In terms of quiz performance, students follow the instructor received higher score and students show off-task behaviors are associated with poor performance.

Our analysis provides an understanding of e-book reading and informs design implications for learning in the age of online learning. The findings can also be used to improve the instruction designs and learning strategies. In addition, by analyzing the different reading patterns of students, interventions can be designed to help off-task students in online lectures, such as provide early warning settings.

This study has some limitations. First, the sample size is relatively small, which limits the generalizability of the obtained results. Second, while our analysis methods identified e-book reading patterns, we cannot make a strong claim that these clusters are accurately representing students' real intent as reading patterns might depend on other pedagogical methods such as problem sets, discussion, presentation quality, and storyline. Further validation with additional data is required. For future work, we plan to analyze more courses and data streams to analyze the differences in the reading patterns between traditional face-to-face classes and such hybrid online lectures and explore different learning environment's effects on student behavior and learning outcome.

ACKNOWLEDGEMENT

This work was supported by JSPS KAKENHI Grant Numbers JP16H06304, JP20H00622, JP20K19939.

REFERENCES

Akçapinar, G., Chen, M. R. A., Majumdar, R., Flanagan, B., & Ogata, H. (2020, March). Exploring student approaches to learning through sequence analysis of reading logs. In Proceedings of the Tenth International Conference on Learning Analytics & Knowledge (pp. 106-111).

Akçapınar, G., Hasnine, M. N., Majumdar, R., Flanagan, B., & Ogata, H. (2019). Using learning analytics to detect off-task reading behaviors in class. In Companion Proceedings of the 9th International Conference on Learning Analytics and Knowledge (LAK'19) (pp. 471-476). Society for Learning Analytics Research (SoLAR).

Baker, R. S., Corbett, A. T., Koedinger, K. R., & Wagner, A. Z. (2004). Off-task behavior in the cognitive tutor classroom: when students "game the system". Paper presented at the Proceedings of the SIGCHI Conference on Human Factors in Computing Systems, Vienna, Austria.

Bao, W. (2020). COVID-19 and online teaching in higher education: A case study of Peking University. Human Behavior and Emerging Technologies, 2(2), 113–115.

Bholowalia, P., & Kumar, A. (2014). EBK-means: A clustering technique based on elbow method and k-means in WSN. International Journal of Computer Applications, 105(9).

Boxuan Ma, Jiadong Chen, Chenhao Li, Likun Liu, Min Lu, Yuta Taniguchi and Shin'ichi Konomi (2020). Understanding Jump Back Behaviors in E-book System. Comanion Proceedings of the 10th International Conference on Learning Analytics & Knowledge (LAK20), pp. 623-631.

Brinton, C. G., & Chiang, M. (2015). MOOC performance prediction via clickstream data and social learning networks. In 2015 IEEE conference on computer communications (INFOCOM) (pp. 2299-2307). IEEE.

Chakraborty, P., Mittal, P., Gupta, M. S., Yadav, S., & Arora, A. Opinion of students on online education during the COVID-19 pandemic. Human Behavior and Emerging Technologies.

Cheng, K. H., & Tsai, C. C. (2014). Children and parents' reading of an augmented reality picture book: Analyses of behavioral patterns and cognitive attainment. Computers & Education, 72, 302 312.doi:10.1016/j.compedu.2013.12.003

Cocea, M., Hershkovitz, A., & Baker, R. S. J. d. (2009). The Impact of Off-task and Gaming Behaviors on Learning: Immediate or Aggregate? Paper presented at the Proceedings of the 2009 conference on Artificial Intelligence in Education: Building Learning Systems that Care: From Knowledge Representation to Affective Modelling.

Costa, C., Alvelos, H., & Teixeira, L. (2012). The use of Moodle e-learning platform: a study in a Portuguese University. Procedia Technology, 5, 334-343.

Crossley, S., Paquette, L., Dascalu, M., McNamara, D. S., & Baker, R. S. (2016). Combining click-stream data with NLP tools to better understand MOOC completion. In Proceedings of the sixth international conference on learning analytics & knowledge (pp. 6-14). ACM.

Goda, Y., Yamada, M., Kato, H., Matsuda, T., Saito, Y., & Miyagawa, H. (2015). Procrastination and other learning behavioral types in e-learning and their relationship with learning outcomes. Learning and Individual Differences, 37, 72-80.

Iftakhar, S. (2016). Google classroom: what works and how. Journal of Education and Social Sciences, 3(1), 12-18.

Ogata, H., Oi, M., Mohri, K., Okubo, F., Shimada, A., Yamada, M., ... & Hirokawa, S. (2017). Learning analytics for e-book-based educational big data in higher education. In Smart Sensors at the IoT Frontier (pp. 327-350). Springer, Cham.

Oi, M., Okubo, F., Shimada, A., Yin, C., & Ogata, H. (2015). Analysis of preview and review patterns in undergraduates' e-book logs. In 23rd International Conference on Computers in Education, ICCE 2015 (pp. 166-171). Asia-Pacific Society for Computers in Education.

Okubo, F., Yamashita, T., Shimada, A., & Ogata, H. (2017). A neural network approach for students' performance prediction. In LAK (pp. 598-599).

Patricia, A. (2020). College students' use and acceptance of emergency online learning due to COVID-19. International Journal of Educational Research Open in press.

Shimada, A., Okubo, F., & Ogata, H. (2016). Browsing-Pattern Mining from e-Book Logs with Non-negative Matrix Factorization. In EDM (pp. 636-637).

Sutcliffe, A., & Hart, J. (2016). Analyzing the role of interactivity in user experience. International Journal of Human–Computer Interaction, 33(3), 229–240. doi:10.1080/10447318.2016.1239797

Taniguchi, Y., Shimada, A., Yamada, M., & Konomi, S. I. (2019). Recommending Highlights on Students' E-Textbooks. In Society for Information Technology & Teacher Education International Conference (pp. 874-880). Association for the Advancement of Computing in Education (AACE).

Yin, C., Yamada, M., Oi, M., Shimada, A., Okubo, F., Kojima, K., & Ogata, H. (2019). Exploring the relationships between reading behavior patterns and learning outcomes based on log data from e-books: A human Factor Approach. International Journal of Human–Computer Interaction, 35(4-5), 313-322.

MATHEMATICS EDUCATION IN LOWER SECONDARY SCHOOL: FOUR OPEN ONLINE COURSES TO SUPPORT TEACHING AND LEARNING

Alice Barana[1], Francesca Casasso[1], Cecilia Fissore[2], Marina Marchisio[1] and Fabio Roman[1]
[1]*Department of Molecular Biotechnology and Health Sciences, University of Turin, Via Nizza 52, 10126 Torino, Italy*
[2]*Department of Foreign Languages, Literatures and Modern Culture, University of Turin, Via Verdi 41, 10124 Torino, Italy*

ABSTRACT

In the light of an educational emergency aggravated by the health emergency following the COVID-19 pandemic, the DELTA (Digital Education for Learning and Teaching Advances) Research Group developed four open online courses available to lower secondary school students and teachers. The four courses, devoted respectively to Numbers, Space and Shapes, Data and Predictions, Relations and Functions, contain interactive materials to support the teaching and learning of Mathematics. We have made the four open online courses available to teachers, tutors, and students within two projects. Both projects are aimed at lower secondary school students, especially those with difficulties in Mathematics. In this paper we discuss the methodologies and technologies used to develop the online courses and we show an example of the interactive materials that can be found within the courses. The results show the appreciation of the resources by teachers, tutors and students, a sign that open online educational resources can foster a change in Mathematics teaching and learning.

KEYWORDS

Digital Education, Digital Learning Environment, Lower Secondary School, Mathematics Teaching, Open Educational Resources, Open Online Courses

1. INTRODUCTION

Education at every school level was strongly affected by the COVID-19 pandemic. The educational institutions' closures to reduce the spread of contagion during the first half of 2020 have had an effect on around 1.5 billion learners. In fact, in almost 100 countries schools were closed for several weeks, leaving more than a billion students at home (UNESCO, 2021). Several closures also took place during the school year 2020-21, further aggravating the situation. In light of this educational emergency, our University has proposed, during the school year 2020-2021, some projects intended to lower secondary school, aimed at reducing inequalities and further penalization of those students who were already at risk of exclusion.

One of the main projects, in collaboration with De Agostini Foundation, named "compiti@casa, curare la fragilità educativa" (i.e., "homework, curing educational fragility"), intends to support, through the modality of a distance tutoring, girls and boys in lower secondary school who need support in learning. The tutoring activities take place in an integrated digital learning environment and are carried out by tutors, university students selected by the University of Turin. The project addressed 100 students of the first and second year of lower secondary schools and involved 55 tutors. The participating students came from three different Italian cities: Novara, Turin and Milan. Students were divided into little groups of maximum three people and they were supported in their afternoon personal study of scientific subjects at home for two hours a week from February to May.

Another important project (Project 2016 ADR 00310 Con i Bambini - impresa sociale srl), named "Ragazzi Connessi: in rete per sviluppare talenti e offrire opportunità di apprendimento" (i.e., "Connected children: networking to develop talents and offer guidance opportunities"), is designed to tackle educational poverty, providing integrated interventions for the application of innovative learning methodologies in schools. This project has involved 113 students of lower secondary schools of Genoa with learning difficulties in Mathematics. Students were divided into groups of five to ten members. They were helped by eight tutors, for one hour a week, with Mathematics homework and review. Within both projects we also offered an online training course to the teachers of the students involved. The training meetings were aimed at introducing teachers to the innovative methodologies proposed within the projects and to basic training in the use of new technologies. The courses were attended by a total of 14 teachers of scientific subjects. Within these projects, our research group has designed and implemented four open online courses in Mathematics, containing materials and interactive activities for students and teachers of lower secondary schools and for tutors, who could use them in their afternoon remedial actions. These are Open Educational Resources, OERs, always available and accessible to facilitate the right to education for all citizens.

The four courses, aligned to the four areas of Mathematics established by the Italian National Indications (Numbers, Space and Shapes, Relations and Functions, Data and Predictions), have the main purpose of providing innovative didactic materials and interactive activities for learning and teaching Mathematics. At the end of the two projects we asked teachers, students and tutors to evaluate the materials of the four courses in terms of their effectiveness in supporting Mathematics teaching. In this paper we present and discuss the courses we implemented to support the teaching of Mathematics, and the tools we used for creating the interactive materials. The paper is structured as follows: Section 2 depicts the theoretical framework we referred to; Section 3 illustrates the research question and describes the methodology; Section 4 is devoted to the presentation and the discussion of the results; and Section 5 contains some concluding remarks.

2. THEORETICAL FRAMEWORK

In the last years, the use of technology for education in schools has increased quantitatively and qualitatively together with the improvement of technology itself. E-learning provides many advantages (Moreno and Mayer, 2007; Ross et al., 2010; Helder et al., 2017): it offers a variety of freely available materials; it allows students a more accessible education because all they need is an internet-connected device; it can accommodate everyone's needs; it provides adaptive learning. In fact, using the information technologies to support learning can be an effective way for the realization of the declaration of Rights to Education primer (Tomaševski, 2001), which explains the essential features of all types of education: availability, accessibility, acceptability and adaptability. Nowadays several research projects are rising in the field of open digital education (Cronin and MacLaren, 2018), (OPAL, 2011). The main reason of this choice is the easy access to the World Wide Web via many kinds of devices everywhere and at all times. In this context, many institutions, and in particular universities, are devoting much of their research to the preparation of Open Educational Resources. Furthermore, the OERs play a central role in the new Digital Education Action Plan (2021-2027) (European Commission, 2020), that is a European Union (EU) policy initiative to support the sustainable and effective adaptation of the education and training systems of EU Member States to the digital age. The Digital Education Action Plan has two strategic priorities:

1. Fostering the development of a high-performing digital education ecosystem: this includes, among other things, creating high quality learning content, user-friendly tools and secure platforms that respect privacy and ethical standards.
2. Enhancing digital skills and competences for the digital transformation, that means basic digital skills and competences from an early age and advanced digital skills, to produce more digital specialists.

In this context, the use of the OERs is of fundamental importance for several reasons. First, they are characterized by accessibility, inclusiveness and a learner-centered design. Furthermore, OERs promote higher pedagogical and educational quality and respect students' diversity and cultural richness. Indeed, their use can certainly facilitate the development of a digital education ecosystem. The Digital Education Action Plan builds on the experiences of online and distance learning during the COVID-19 crisis to fully understand the needs that emerged in schools and rethink education and training for the digital age at all school levels. Before the COVID-19 pandemic, OERs were already widespread for higher education. There were already many providers of Massive Online Open Courses (MOOC), like EdX (https://www.edx.org/) and Coursera (https://www.coursera.org/). Many universities in North Europe and North America use these open platforms to make their courses available online. Also in Italy, there are platforms that provide online courses, like

EduOpen (Rui, 2016) and Federica (Calise and Reda, 2017). EduOpen is a project founded by the Italian Ministry of Education, University and Research that hosts several online courses about basic and professional disciplines and professional scientific research. Federica is the e-learning project of the University of Naples Federico II, with more than 300 free courses, available at any time, with contents organized in training modules.

Since the beginning of new century, also the University of Turin has taken an interest in digital education and in the creation of open resources, especially for university contexts and for upper secondary schools. One of the main projects providing numerous online, open, and free lessons is "start@unito" (Marchisio et al., 2019). It allows to follow courses while attending high school, before enrolling at university, and also during university career. The courses cover disciplines in almost all the University's study programs: from Physics to Sociology, from Computer Science to Zoology, from Law to Languages, designed specifically for those who are approaching university studies and for those who wish to study independently. In addition, many courses are taught entirely in English to promote internationalization. Other projects promoted by the University of Turin that make open and online materials available are "Orient@mente" (Barana et al., 2017b), "PP&S Problem Posing and Solving" (Brancaccio et al., 2015b) and the project "SMART Science and Mathematics Advanced Research for good Teaching" (Brancaccio et al., 2015a).

3. RESEARCH QUESTION AND METHODOLOGY

By considering the contexts exposed before, we have formulated one main research question, which has acted as motivation for our work:

How is it possible to integrate the teaching and learning of Mathematics in lower secondary school with the support of Open Educational Resources, with a particular focus on recovery actions?

3.1 OERs within a Digital Learning Environment

The four courses have been developed by our research group following principles consolidated by the experience in the field of e-learning for scientific disciplines gained in recent years by the University of Turin in online and blended courses (Barana et al, 2020). In other recovery actions, like "Scuola dei Compiti" project (Barana et al., 2017a), we already adopted a Digital Learning Environment (DLE). This indicates a learning ecosystem in which teaching, learning and the development of competence are fostered in classroom-based, online, or blended settings. Using a DLE can be very effective as it consists of two components: the human component and the technological component, and the interrelations among the two. Its human component, consisting of one or more learning communities, is focused on the interactions between teachers and students and among students themselves (Barana and Marchisio, 2021); its technological component includes a Learning Management System (LMS) along with other integrated tools, such as an Advanced Computing Environment (ACE) and an Automatic Assessment System (AAS). These allow the adoption of specific methodologies such as problem solving (Samo et al, 2017), supported by the use of an ACE and the formative assessment (Black and Wiliam, 2009; Hattie and Timperley, 2007) implemented by the use of an AAS. We used the Moodle LMS Moodle (https://www.moodle.org), the Maple ACE Maplesoft (https://www.maplesoft.com), and the Möbius Assessment AAS DigitalEd (https://www.digitaled.com), as it was already experimented for instance in (Marchisio et al, 2020) and in (Galluzzi et al, 2021). In particular, we made use of the ACE in order to create interactive materials, and of the AAS to create adaptive questions and adaptive assignments. Adaptive questions are composed of sections that are shown to the student depending on the previous given answer. In particular, it consists in a first section where the main problem is posed and the correct solution is directly asked. Students who answer correctly in the first sections receive a positive feedback and complete the question. Students who give a wrong answer are led to the solution step-by-step, one small question at a time with which a possible process for solving the task is shown (Barana et al, 2021). Adaptive assignments are composed of questions divided into groups according to their difficulty level, usually in number of three. Students start at one level, usually the middle one, and then they are promoted to the upper level if they answer correctly to a minimum number of questions. If they make a minimum number of mistakes, they drop to the lower level.

3.2 Structure of the Courses

We now describe the structure of our courses in relation to the design principles presented before. The four courses have been designed for students in lower secondary school and they are dedicated respectively to: Numbers; Space and Shapes; Data and Predictions; Relations and Functions. Indeed, we referred the Italian National Guidelines in which the objects of Mathematics studies are divided in these four categories. Each course is divided into sections, one for each topic, chosen from the main topics listed in the National Guidelines. In particular, we decided to focus on the following topics:

- In the course "Numbers": Fractions, Powers, Expressions and Mathematization, Percentages, Proportions, Scientific Notation;
- In the course "Space and Shapes" (shown in Figure 1): Angles, Triangles, Quadrilaterals, Pythagoras and Euclid, Similitudes, Solid Geometry;
- In the course "Data and Predictions": Statistics, Statistical Graphs, Average Values, Probability;
- In the course "Relations and Functions": Set theory, Proportionality, Equations, Functions, Symbolic Calculation.

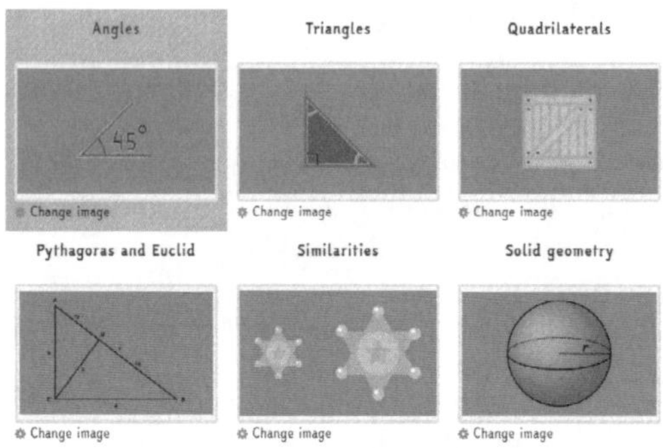

Figure 1. (left) : The "Space and Shapes" course and the relative sections

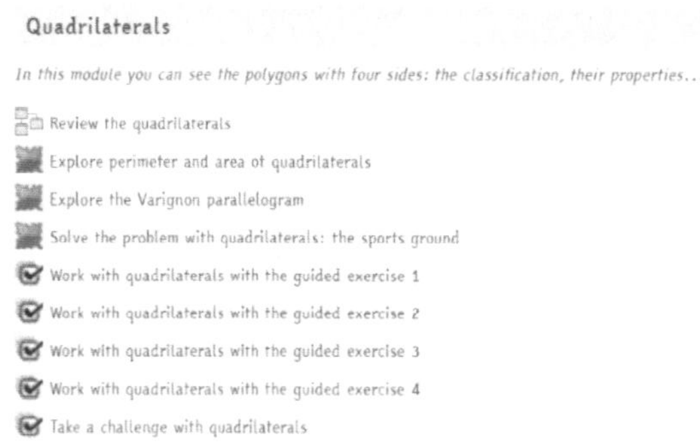

Figure 2. (right) : An example of the structure of a section in the course

Each section has a fixed structure (shown in Figure 2) and it contains:

- A lesson: it contains a theoretical review of the topic of the section, interspersed with short quizzes to verify learning. This material was created using a Moodle "book".
- Interactive exploratory materials: they allow to interactively explore one or more concepts of the topic studied in the lesson. These materials were created with the Maple ACE.
- Interactive problems: they allow to face the guided and interactive resolution of a problem. They are problems contextualized in real life that allow students to explore different situations that can occur in a particular mathematical context. They were also created with the Maple ACE.
- Tests and problems with automatic assessment: they allow to verify the learning of the subject. They provide immediate feedback and, if repeated several times, they present different data. They are mainly adaptive questions and adaptive assignments created with the Möbius Assessment AAS.

Students can browse freely through the four courses, and they can choose the order in which to address the contents. Moreover, students can try tests and problems with automatic assessment more than once, because they have algorithms so that the values change at every attempts. On the platform, the students can monitor their work: a progress bar shows clearly which materials have already been opened, and which ones are still to be done. Furthermore, students can also see the gradebook of all the results of the completed tests and, for each one, all the answers they gave, together with the correct answer and feedback comments so that they can better understand their mistakes. We now present some examples of activity that can be found within the four courses. Figure 3 shows an interactive exploratory activity of the section "Quadrilaterals" through which students can explore the area and the perimeter of different geometric shapes. In the worksheet students can chose a specific quadrilateral and visualize it, along with its perimeter and area formulas. Then, students can choose, through some sliders, the values of some lengths relative to the quadrilateral, and calculate perimeter and area, verifying the correct value. In this way, students become protagonists of their own learning, exploring the object of study independently. Figure 4 shows an adaptive question of the section "Quadrilaterals" through which students can test their previously acquired knowledge. The question presents a main problem focused on the area of a square. If students answer incorrectly, the questions release two more sub-questions that can help them understand how to answer the initial question correctly and recognize their own mistakes. Furthermore, the question is an algorithm-based question, so that students can try the question again finding different numbers, verifying learning.

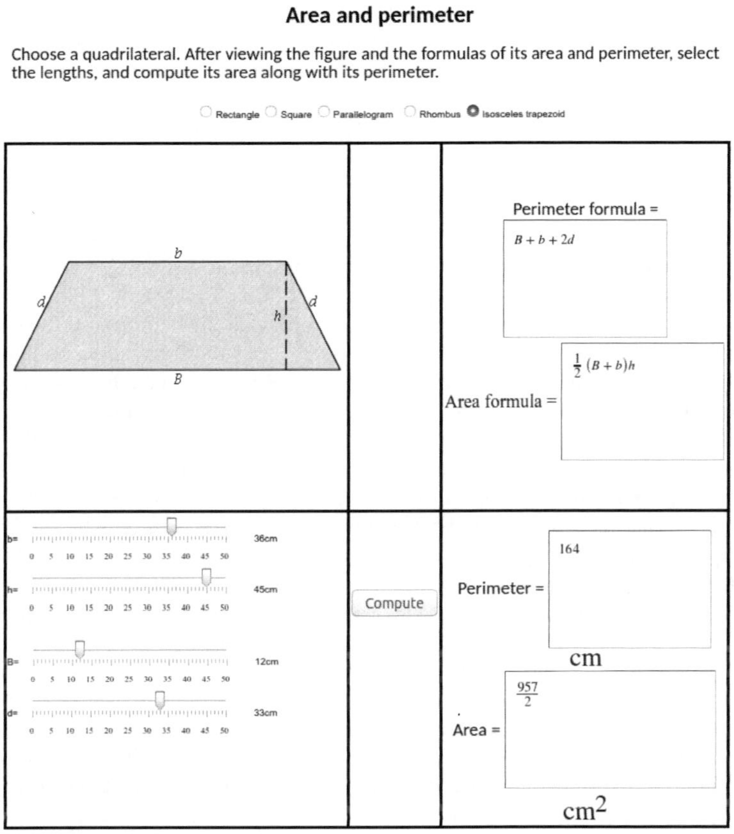

Figure 3. An example of an interactive exploratory material in the section "Quadrilaterals" of the course "Space and Shapes"

We made the four courses available as part of two projects aimed at reducing educational poverty through remedial actions in the afternoon. The tutors who helped students learn Mathematics had the interactive materials at their disposal, and so had the students, and they could use them to tackle new topics and review old ones. The students' teachers also had access to the four courses so that they could use them in the classroom. Indeed, in order to test the effectiveness of our four courses, we presented them in the two teacher training courses. We asked teachers to evaluate the courses materials to bring out strengths and weaknesses. In particular, we asked them to choose one interactive material made with *Maple* and one question with the automatic assessment and then we asked them to fill in a satisfaction questionnaire for each of them. At the end of the project, we also asked all the tutors and students involved their opinion on the materials they had available through a questionnaire.

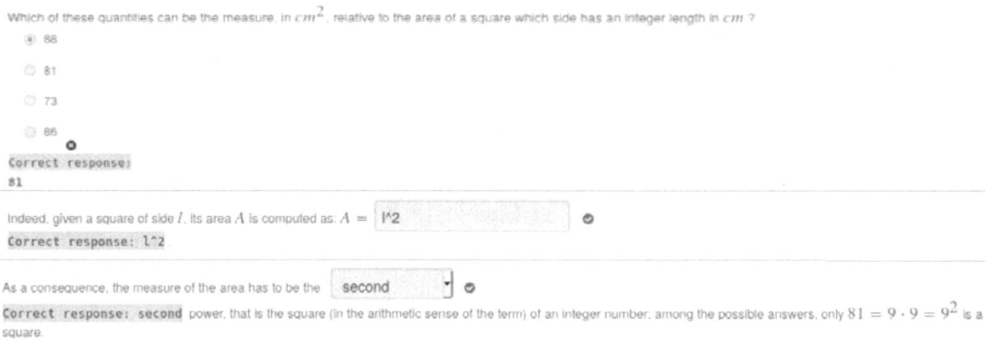

Figure 4. An example of an adaptive question in the section "Quadrilaterals" of the course "Space and Shapes"

The four courses are available at the link: https://ragazziconnessi.i-learn.unito.it/.

4. RESULTS AND DISCUSSION

All the 14 teachers responded to the questionnaires we submitted to them. The first questionnaire was about interactive materials created with the ACE. It emerged that 100% of the teachers liked the materials and would use them in class with their students. The questionnaire asked what the benefit of these interactive materials is, compared to a traditional lesson. Some of the answers were: "It is very engaging and allows students to both practice and self-correct their mistakes", "It captures the attention, allows the learner to explore, to work hands on" and "The possibility of using it at home and reviewing it several times and the presence of small quizzes to check comprehension of the subject". They were then asked how they would use the interactive resources with the students: 50% of teachers said they would use them to review topics before a test and for consolidation of concepts; 40% said they would use them to introduce a new topic; the rest would use them to keep their students' attention during the lessons. Finally, the questionnaire asked teachers for advice on how to improve the interactive resources and it emerged that it would be better to add color and a more readable font, especially for those students with visual difficulties. The second questionnaire concerned tests with automatic formative assessment. It emerged that 100% of the teachers would use the material in class with their pupils and that 100% felt that the tests were well designed. The questionnaire asked what the added value of these tests is, compared to a traditional lesson and some of the answers were: "Variety, adaptability, captures attention visually, offers immediate feedback, and because of this, shortens the distance between the subject and the student", "It allows students to get immediate feedback on their answer and indicates where they went wrong" and "By having immediate feedback, the learner is encouraged to look for the right answer, to reason and to get involved without waiting for external feedback. This should help the student to self-discipline". All teachers said they would use this material as a pre-test review and as homework. Finally, the teachers suggested improving the design of the tests, in order to catch the students' attention, adding color, images and video, and increasing the number of tests within the four courses.

At the end of the projects, tutors and students were also asked for their opinion on the interactive materials they could use in the afternoon meetings. A total of 61 tutors and 171 students filled in the questionnaires. By considering the questions relative to the interactive materials, 95% of the tutors stated that the afternoon tutoring sessions, in which they used the digital resources, helped the students to improve in Mathematics, not only in terms of their final grade, but also in terms of confidence, motivation and awareness. Subsequently, tutors were asked to respond about the usefulness of the didactic material available. In a Likert scale from 1 to 5, where 1 means "not at all" and 5 means "very much", 51% of the tutors responded 3 or more, thus finding the interactive materials provided by us useful. The questionnaire then asked tutors for advice on how to improve the interactive materials. Some tutors highlighted the difficulty of using the materials due to the limited time they had with the students, thus preferring to give it as homework. Other tutors suggested creating other materials, to cover all the topics studied during lower secondary school. In addition, certain tutors complained that the vocabulary in some teaching materials was too difficult for lower secondary school students.

Nevertheless, there was a relevant number of tutors who was generally satisfied of them, and did not ask for specific improvements. In the students' questionnaire, we asked them how useful they perceived tests with automatic assessment. In the same Likert scale as before, 53% students responded at least 4 and 78% at least 3. Then we asked them about the usefulness of interactive exploratory materials and problems. Students were satisfied, even more than before: 62% of students responded at least 4 and 85% at least 3. Table 1 shows some statistics about these questions, along with two other ones regarding their use of the materials.

Table 1. Statistics about use and appreciation of the materials by students

Question	Average	Median	St. Dev.
Did you use the materials on the platform during the meetings?	3.27	3	1.17
Did you use the materials on the platform independently, outside meetings?	2.68	3	1.31
How useful were the tests with automatic assessment?	3.46	4	1.17
How useful were the interactive review materials?	3.65	4	1.08

In light of the results obtained, it can be stated that the materials we created were able to satisfy all the stakeholders involved, with particular regard to teachers and students; about the latter, it has to be noted how they preferred their use *during* the afternoon meetings, showing some difficulty in using them individually, for example while doing homework. This can be explained by the fact that all the students involved had underlying difficulties, which required some time to be leveled; during the project, they were inevitably still affected by them, thus resulting in having moderately less interest and less capabilities in the autonomous fruition of the resources and the activities, although their use was anyway present. On the other hand, tutors were a little bit more critical about the materials, nevertheless giving some valid advice, and being in general eager to have them as available, even if sometimes they did not make use of them, for the above-discussed reasons. The motivation for which tutors expressed critics that teachers did not mention can be related to their different relation with the students, due to various factors such as a less marked age-difference, and a more informal setting of the afternoon meetings compared to the lectures students have with their teachers.

5. CONCLUSIONS

The emergency situation highlighted a pre-existing educational poverty and underlined the need for recovery action in a completely different way from what the school was used to before. So, this work sought to understand how it is possible to integrate the teaching and learning of Mathematics in lower secondary school with the support of Open Educational Resources, with a particular focus on recovery actions. Bearing in mind the University of Turin's past experiences in the field of remedial action, even before the pandemic, we proposed four open online courses within a Digital Learning Environment. In this way, the materials were easy for students to access, always available, and interesting thanks to their interactivity. The materials within the courses were implemented using an ACE for the creation of exploratory files and interactive problems and an AAS for the creation of questions with automatic formative assessment. All the resources we have made available to teachers, tutors and students have been appreciated and have helped the students to catch up in Mathematics, not only in terms of grades, but also in terms of their approach to the subject. The courses we presented, along with all the results and the observations collected, provided a possible valid answer to the research question enunciated at the beginning of Section 3. The next steps we want to take are to take advice from teachers, tutors and students to improve the four open courses. In particular, we appreciated the suggestion to make the resources attractive by adding color, images and videos where possible, and to simplify the language to make it more suitable for lower secondary school students, aspects which can constitute a future work on the materials. Furthermore, we want to create similar courses for nonmathematical sciences as well, in order to provide OERs for all STEM subjects covered in lower secondary school. The Science courses are already in the works, in order to help students also in the recovery of Physics, Chemistry, Biology and Geology. Finally, we would like to make our four open courses as widely known as possible so that they can be useful to as many students and teachers as possible, and in light of this a complete translation to English of all the resources and activities would be a good direction to follow.

REFERENCES

Barana, A. and Marchisio, M., 2021. Analyzing interactions in Automatic Formative Assessment activities for Mathematics in Digital Learning Environments. *CSEDU 2021. Proceedings of the 13th International Conference on Computer Supported Education*, *1*, 497–504. https://doi.org/10.5220/0010474004970504

Barana, A. et al, 2017a. Adaptive teaching supported by ICTs to reduce the school failure in the Project "Scuola dei Compiti", *Proceedings of IEEE 41st Annual Computer Software and Applications Conference (COMPSAC)*, IEEE, Tokyo, Japan, pp. 432-437.

Barana, A. et al, 2017b. Open platform of self-paced MOOCs for the continual improvement of academic guidance and knowledge strengthening in tertiary education, *Journal of e-Learning and Knowledge Society*, Vol. 13, No. 3, 109-119. doi:10.20368/1971-8829/1383

Barana, A. et al, 2020. An online math path to foster the transition of students between lower and upper secondary school, *The 16th International Scientific Conference eLearning and Software for Education,* Bucharest, Romania, pp. 568-575.

Barana, A. et al, 2021. Interactive Feedback for Learning Mathematics in a Digital Learning Environment. *Education Sciences*, Vol. 11, No. 6, 279. https://doi.org/10.3390/educsci11060279

Black, P. and Wiliam, D., 2009. Developing the theory of formative assessment. *Educational Assessment, Evaluation and Accountability*, 21(1), pp. 5-31.

Brancaccio, A. et al, 2015a. Matematica e Scienze più SMART per l'Insegnamento e l'Apprendimento, *MONDO DIGITALE*, Vol. 14, No. 58, pp. 1-8.

Brancaccio, A. et al, 2015b. Problem Posing and Solving: Strategic Italian Key Action to Enhance Teaching and Learning Mathematics and Informatics in the High School. *Proceedings of IEEE 39th Annual Computer Software and Applications Conference (COMPSAC)*, IEEE, Taichung, Taiwan, pp. 845–850. https://doi.org/10.1109/COMPSAC.2015.126

Calise, M. and Reda, V., 2017. In and Out. Federica experience in the rugged terrain of MOOCs inclusion in institutional strategies of university education. Proceedings of EMOOCs 2017-WIP

Cronin, C. and MacLaren, I., 2018. Conceptualising OEP: A review of theoretical and empirical literature in Open Educational Practices. *Open Praxis*, Vol. 10, No. 2, pp. 127-143.

European Commission, 2020. Communication from the Commission to the European Parliament, the council, the European economic and social committee and the committee of the regions. *Digital Education Action Plan 2021-2027: Resetting education and training for the digital age* (COM/2020/624 final). https://ec.europa.eu/education/sites/default/files/document-library-docs/deap-communication-sept2020_en.pdf

Galluzzi, F. et al, 2021. Mathematics in higher education: a transition from blended to online learning in pandemic times, *Proceedings of IEEE 45th Annual Computer Software and Applications Conference (COMPSAC)*, IEEE, virtual, in press.

Hattie, J. and Timperley, H., 2007. The Power of Feedback, *Review of Educational Research*, 77(1), pp. 81-112.

Helder, E. et al, 2017. Adaptive Intelligent Learning Environments. In: Erik Duval, M. Sharples, R. Sutherland, *Technology enhanced learning: Research themes*, pp. 109–114.

Marchisio, M. et al, 2019. Start@unito: Open Online Courses for Improving Access and for Enhancing Success in Higher Education. *Proceedings of the 11th International Conference on Computer Supported Education* (CSEDU 2019), Vol. 1, pp. 639-646.

Marchisio, M. et al, 2020. Teaching Mathematics in Scientific Bachelor Degrees Using a Blended Approach, *Proceedings of IEEE 44th Annual Computer Software and Applications Conference (COMPSAC)*, IEEE, virtual, pp. 190-195.

Moreno, R. and Mayer, R., 2007. Interactive Multimodal Learning Environments. *Educational Psychology Review*, Vol. 19, No. 3, pp. 309–326.

OPAL, 2011. Beyond OER: Shifting focus to open educational practices. OPAL Report 2011. *Open Education Quality Initiative,* Essen, Germany.

Rui, M., 2016. EduOpen: Italian Network for MOOCs, First Three Months Evaluation after Initiation. *Universal Journal of Educational Research*, Vol. 4, pp. 2729-2734.

Samo, D.D. et al, 2017. Culture-Based Contextual Learning to Increase Problem-Solving Ability of First Year University Student. *Journal on Mathematics Education 2017*, 9, doi:10.22342/jme.9.1.4125.81-94.

Tomaševski, K., 2001. Human Rights Obligations: making education available, accessible, acceptable and adaptable, *Right to education primers n. 3*.

UNESCO, 2021. Education: From disruption to recovery. https://en.unesco.org/covid19/educationresponse

STUDENTS' PREFERENCES AND VIEWS ABOUT LEARNING IN A SMART MOOC INTEGRATED WITH INTELLIGENT TUTORING

Gizem Karaoğlan Yılmaz[1], Mustafa Tepgeç[2], Cennet Terzi Müftüoğlu[3], Sema Sulak[1], Muhittin Şahin[4], Furkan Aydın[5], Ramazan Yılmaz[1] and Halil Yurdugül[6]
[1]*Bartın University, Turkey*
[2]*Hacettepe University; Mustafa Kemal University, Turkey*
[3]*Tokat Gaziosmanpasa University, Turkey*
[4]*Ege University, Turkey; University of Mannheim, Germany*
[5]*Kahramanmaras Sutcu Imam University, Turkey*
[6]*Hacettepe University, Turkey*

ABSTRACT

Massive Open Online Courses (MOOCs) have become widespread all around the world since their conceptualization, both in terms of the number of students enrolled and the number of courses available. Some issues or learner needs in these environments, such as accreditation, quality of assessment and scaffolding for left-behind learners, have also surfaced as a result of rise in popularity. Profiling learners, using scaffolding strategies, structuring the assessment in a dynamic and effective manner, monitoring performance, and providing feedback/feedforward based on learning analytics are all expected to be valuable solutions to these issues. In this study, it is aimed to describe student views on the MOOC platform, which has the above-mentioned features and was designed and developed according to the AGILE software development model. Participants of this case study consist of 53 undergraduate students from three different universities. The data was collected using a questionnaire and semi-structured form both of which were developed by the researchers. The findings obtained were considered under these themes: benefits, disliked aspects, preferences in different learning contexts, ease of use, features open to improvement. Findings based on both quantitative and qualitative interpretations are presented on each theme. The findings of this study are limited to student views. In the later stages, authentic usage circumstances can be presented by taking into log data as a data source.

KEYWORDS

MOOCs, Intelligent Tutoring, Learning Analytics, AGILE Model

1. INTRODUCTION

MOOCs (Massive Open Online Courses) allow learners from all over the world, regardless of their location or educational institution, to specialize in specific subjects and receive certifications. In such environments, learners can progress at their own pace without being constrained by a curriculum, study at anytime and anywhere, and regularly test themselves. Since the term was first used in 2008, the use of MOOCs has grown exponentially around the world, in terms of both the number of courses available and the number of students enrolled (Wong et al., 2019). MOOCs' initial target audience was learners who were excluded from higher education; however, in recent years, the target audience has shifted to primarily higher education students (Lambert, 2020). Agreements between well-known MOOC providers, such as edX, and educational institutions have facilitated in the increase of enrolled students in such environments in higher education. Existing MOOCs, on the other hand, have limited capacity to adapt learners' individual characteristics (Aleven et al., 2017). In addition, one of the most remarkable issues in these environments, which are described as disruptive technologies, is the discrepancy between course enrollment and completion rates. MOOCs are likely to be more effective if they can personalize instruction based on learner characteristics, such as prior knowledge or personal interests. They could also be more effective if they included more learning-by-doing activities (Aleven et al., 2017). Integrating existing adaptive learning technologies such as Intelligent Tutoring Systems into

MOOCs is one way to make them more adaptive, with a wider range of learning-by-doing activities. In addition to personalization of instruction, accreditation issues, assessment quality, scaffolding for left-behind learners, and performance monitoring deficiencies are just a few of the challenges.

Accreditation has been one of the major issues that has limited the widespread use of MOOCs since their beginnings (Danka, 2020). In other words, the fact that the learners' competencies they mastered in these environments were not valuable outside of these environments hampered learners' adoption. In line with the needs and expectations of the learners, providers such as Coursera, Udacity and edX have run their certification processes, but the advantages of these certificates have been found to be limited (Lambert, 2020). Another issue that contributes to this limitation is the assessment processes. A significant part of the competence in the current courses is tested with a few static questions or peer reviews at the end of the episode (Xiong & Suen, 2018). Therefore, some of the higher education institutions have not adopted MOOCs due to the inability to perform this assessment effectively (Zhang et al., 2019). The most important goal of MOOCs in the early years was to reach a large mass, and it is possible to say that it has been accomplished by reaching millions of people today. The next goal should be to adapt the system and assessment processes to the needs of the millions of people it reaches, which can help with the previously mentioned assessment and accreditation issues (Wong et al., 2019). Not only in MOOCs, but also in all online learning environments, adaptively performing both the tutoring and assessment processes can be a solution to the scaffolding problem for students whose self-regulation is insufficient. However, it is critical to provide scaffolding for learners who feel more autonomous in MOOCs than in any other online environment. Because control of learning in MOOCs has moved from educational institutions or cultures to the individual - often an isolated individual - (Swinnerton et al., 2017). Another problem that comes up frequently in MOOCs is performance monitoring, which is linked to the scaffolding and assessment issues mentioned previously. In recent years, learning analytics dashboard (LAD) has made performance monitoring more widely available. However, in commonly used MOOCs, these dashboards are generally limited to the display of progress. As a result, providing the feedback and feedforward needed by learners, particularly those who are left behind or at risk of dropping out, through LAD will make a significant contribution to solving this problem. In summary, it is expected that profiling learners in MOOCs, providing scaffolding support to left-behind learners, structuring the assessment in a dynamic and effective manner, monitoring performance and providing feedback and feedforward accordingly, can all be significant solutions to the issues mentioned above.

As previously stated, MOOCs are platforms with deficiencies when it comes to effective teaching. In order to provide effective teaching in these environments, it is necessary to integrate adaptive learning technologies. Therefore, the aim of the research is to examine student views on the design of an intelligent MOOC platform based on an adaptive, dynamic, supported by learning analytics and intelligent tutoring. This research is expected to guide designers, teachers, and educational institutions in both designing and developing solutions for common problems in MOOCs, as well as evaluating these solutions from the perspective of students. Secondary aim of the study is introducing the authors' MOOC platform, which was developed using HTML, PHP, JavaScript, and MySQL. In the system architecture, learners can choose content types based on their preferences. The system also includes PowerPoint presentations, e-books, infographics, and alternative videos as alternative learning materials in addition to video lectures. Learners can utilize descriptive analytics to see their current situation, as well as predictive analytics to assess their next learning experience. Learners' entire interaction data are stored, and the system presents the required information via learning analytics dashboard. To do this, the system employs both classification and clustering algorithms in this process. The system also functions as an intelligent tutoring system while the learners are taking the competency test. The system will direct the learner to this module if he fails the competency test without help. The goal of this module is to improve learners' problem-solving skills by using scaffolding strategies like hints and worked examples.

2. METHOD

2.1 Research Model

The model of the research was based on case study, one of the qualitative research designs. The most basic feature of the qualitative case study is the in-depth investigation of one or a few situations (Yin, 2013). The Smart MOOC Integrated with Intelligent Tutoring environment has been developed by considering the AGILE software development model. In the first stage of the model, the literature was examined and the student needs for MOOC environments were tried to be revealed. Then, based on the findings in the literature, the design and development stages of the Smart MOOC Integrated with Intelligent Tutoring environment, which was supported by learning analytics and based on an adaptive, dynamic, intelligent tutoring system, were carried out. In the next step, usability tests of the developed Smart MOOC Integrated with Intelligent Tutoring environment have been completed. After usability tests, the assessment process, which is the last stage of the first cycle of the AGILE model, was started. The pilot implementation process (evaluation phase of the AGILE model) took eight weeks. At the end of the eight-week implementation process, students' opinions about the advantages, disadvantages and aspects of the Smart MOOC Integrated with Intelligent Tutoring environment were obtained from the students.

2.2 Study Group

The participants consist of undergraduate and graduate students from three different state universities. The total number of participants was 53 and the gender composition was 62.2% (n = 33) male and 37.8% (n = 20) female. Of the participants 51% (n = 27) were undergraduate students and 49% (n = 26) were graduate students. At the beginning of the study, the participants were given information as in regard to the Smart MOOC Integrated with Intelligent Tutoring environments and data collection process.

2.3 Data Collection Tools and Data Analysis

The data was collected using a questionnaire and semi-structured form both of which were developed by the researchers. In the questionnaire, there are questions to determine the demographic characteristics of the students (gender, department of education, university, etc.). The semi-structured interview form consisted of questions asking to determine students' views regarding the Smart MOOC Integrated with Intelligent Tutoring environment. The draft of the semi-structured form questions was developed based on literature review. Five faculty members specialized in educational technologies examined the form and provided feedback. The form aimed to determine liked and disliked features, ease of use of the system and whether the system would be recommended to friends.

In order to analyse the qualitative data content analysis was utilized. The qualitative data was coded by the researcher and recoded by another rater. The reliability of the coding was done by calculating proportion of common codes and total number of codes. The coding reliability was 91%. For the remaining 9% difference, the coders came together and reached a consensus.

3. FINDINGS

3.1 Student Views on the Benefits of the Smart MOOC Integrated with Intelligent Tutoring Environment

The students were asked in what ways they found the developed Smart MOOC Integrated with Intelligent Tutoring environment beneficial. The opinions of the students are given in Table 1.

Examining the students' views in Table 1, it is seen that the students liked the dynamic assessment feature of the Smart MOOC Integrated with Intelligent Tutoring environment the most. In addition, the students expressed that they liked the Smart MOOC Integrated with Intelligent Tutoring environment that it offers multiple alternative content such as e-books, presentations, videos, infographics, and learning tasks. Students stated that they liked the short and concise narration of the videos in the MOOC environment. Students state that another feature of the system that they like is that the system gives advice, hints, and guidance messages through feedback. In addition, the simple and useful interface feature of the developed MOOC environment is stated as another preferred aspect of the system. These are the most admired features of the system developed by the students.

Table 1. Students' views on the benefits of the Smart MOOC Integrated with Intelligent Tutoring environment

Sub-Theme	Frequency
Teaching the subject by reinforcing the questions and tips in the dynamic assessment system	22
Contain alternative learning contents	12
Teaching subjects with short and concise narration in videos	10
The use of the system is simple and straightforward	9
Making it easy to learn	8
Guiding the student in the learning process	7
Detecting learning deficiencies	6
Providing the opportunity to progress according to the student's individual pace and preference	6
Enabling the student to self-monitoring with learning analytics	6
The proficiency test is adaptable	5
Leave the feedback preference to the user (being adaptable)	4
Having a fun structure	3
Being able to predict whether the student is competent in a subject or not	2

Some students, on the other hand, stated that the other features of the system are guiding the student, detecting learning deficiencies, providing the opportunity to progress according to the student's individual pace and preference, providing the student with the opportunity to make self-monitoring with learning analytics, and the system has an adaptable structure. Some of the student views are as follows:

S1: *"It is easier for us to understand the subjects because they are told briefly and concisely. And since it supports the subjects with tests, the system helps us to fully understand the subject."*

S3: *"One of the features I like is that it graphically shows my interaction and my tendency towards the subjects I work on. The fact that he presents my individual performance in a summary manner enables me to monitoring myself more clearly."*

3.2 Student Views on the Disliked Aspects of the Smart MOOC Integrated with Intelligent Tutoring Environment

Students were asked in what ways they disliked the Smart MOOC Integrated with Intelligent Tutoring environment developed. The opinions of the students are given in Table 2.

Table 2. Students' views on the disliked aspects of the Smart MOOC Integrated with Intelligent Tutoring environment

Sub-Theme	Frequency
There is no defect in the system	22
The low number of questions in the system	4
Failure to solve more questions after seeing the decision in the competency test	4
The lecture part is a little insufficient / not detailed	3
Not knowing how many questions to be competent in determining competence	3
Feedback given in some questions is not appropriate	3
The system is inadequate in terms of visual design	2
Low interaction in learning contents	2
Low number, quality and variety of learning tasks for implementation	2
Graphics showing learning analytics are not sufficient in terms of interpretation	2

When the views of the students in Table 2 are examined, the majority of the students stated that there is no feature about the system that they do not like. Some students stated that the number of questions in the dynamic assessment section of the system could be increased, and they would find it useful to allow the system to allow the system to solve questions after the competence of the student in the adaptive test was determined. Some of the student views are as follows:

S2: *"There were very few questions on some issues, the number of questions may be more."*

3.3 Student Views on the use of Smart MOOC Integrated with Intelligent Tutoring Environment Developed in Different Learning Contexts

The students were asked whether you can use the developed Smart MOOC Integrated with Intelligent Tutoring environment in the context of different courses and learning, apart from the statistics course. Students' answers are given in Figure 1.

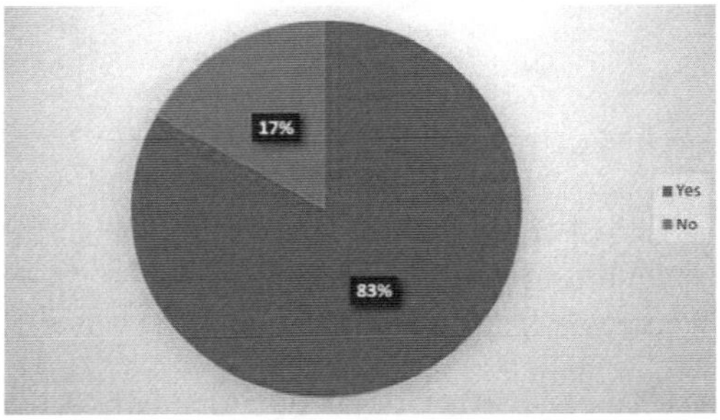

Figure 1. Students' Preferences in Different Learning Context Using the Smart MOOC Integrated with Intelligent Tutoring Environment

When Figure 1 is examined, it is seen that 83% of the students stated that they will use the Smart MOOC Integrated with Intelligent Tutoring environment developed within the scope of different courses and learning contexts. Students were asked why they would like to use this system in the context of different courses and learning contexts. The answers of the students are given in Table 3.

Table 3. Reasons for students to choose the Smart MOOC Integrated with Intelligent Tutoring environment within the scope of different courses and learning contexts

Sub-Theme	Frequency
Because it facilitates learning	13
Since it provides repetition and reinforcement in courses	13
Because it is a self-monitoring system	7
Because the smart system makes decisions about the student	3
Because it increases my competence in a subject	2
As it helps a lot	2
Because the system is easy to use	2
As it provides videos and documents	2
Because I can instantly access information about myself with learning analytics	2
Since it has an adaptable structure	2

When Table 3 is examined, it seems that the most dominant reason for students to prefer the Smart MOOC Integrated with Intelligent Tutoring environment developed in different courses and learning contexts is that the system facilitates learning, provides repetition and reinforcement in courses, and offers self-monitoring. Some of the student views are as follows:

S2: *"Yes because everything is learned more easily this way."*

S3: *"I would use it. Because even the hardest things to learn can be learned easily from this system."*

3.4 Student Views on the Ease of use of the Smart MOOC Integrated with Intelligent Tutoring Environment

The students were asked whether they found the developed Smart MOOC Integrated with Intelligent Tutoring environment easy to use or not. Students' answers are given in Figure 2.

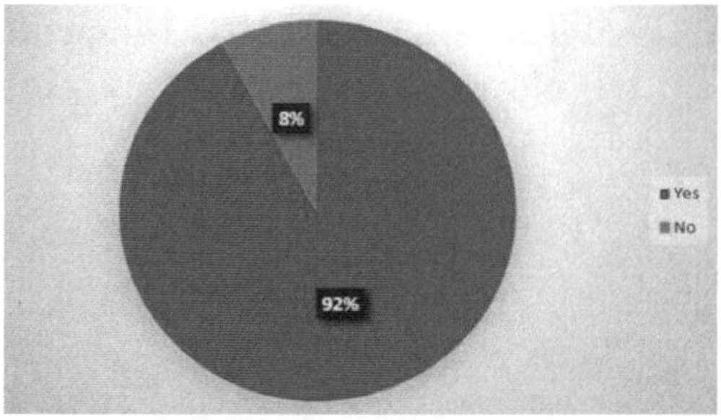

Figure 2. Students' Views Regarding the Ease of Use of the Smart MOOC Integrated with Intelligent Tutoring Environment

When Figure 2 is examined, it is seen that 92% of the students find the developed Smart MOOC Integrated with Intelligent Tutoring environment easy to use. It was observed that 8% of the students found the use of the developed Smart MOOC Integrated with Intelligent Tutoring environment to be moderate.

3.5 Suggesting Situations of Students to use the Smart MOOC Integrated with Intelligent Tutoring Environment to their Friends

The students were asked if you would recommend them to their friends to use the Smart MOOC Integrated with Intelligent Tutoring environment. Students' answers are given in Figure 3.

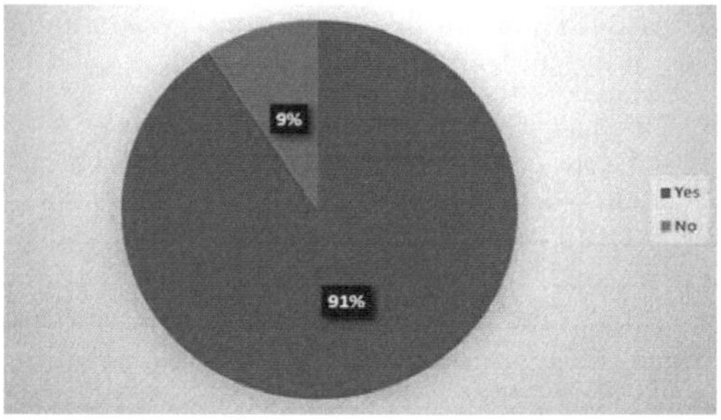

Figure 3. Suggesting Situations of Students to Use the Smart MOOC Integrated with Intelligent Tutoring Environment to Their Friends

When Figure 3 was examined, it was seen that 91% of the students stated that they would recommend them to their friends to use the developed Smart MOOC Integrated with Intelligent Tutoring environment. It is seen that 9% of the students would not recommend them to their friends to use the developed Smart MOOC Integrated with Intelligent Tutoring environment. The students were asked about the reason for this situation. Students' answers are given in Table 4.

Table 4. Reasons for recommending students to their friends to use the Smart MOOC Integrated with Intelligent Tutoring environment

Sub-Theme	Frequency
Because it helps and facilitates learning a lot	18
Because it reinforces and supports learning	15
Because the system is easy to use	10
As it provides an individualized learning environment	9
As it has a rich and alternative content in terms of learning materials	5
To benefit from the problem solving feature of the system	4
Because it adds curiosity and interest to the course	3
Because the lectures are clear and understandable	2
For level determination on the subject	2
As it provides learning analytics and advisory system support	2
Because the videos have a short and concise narrative	2
Because it increases the permanence of what has been learned	2

When Table 4 is examined, it is seen that the main reasons why students recommend the developed Smart MOOC Integrated with Intelligent Tutoring environment to their friends are that the system helps and facilitates learning, reinforces and supports learning, is easy to use, and provides an individualized learning environment. Some of the student views are as follows:

S1: *"Yes, because the lectures are clearly understandable, the tests increase the memorability, so I would recommend them."*

S2: *"I recommend, yes, because thanks to this system, I both reinforced my issues and determined my shortcomings."*

3.6 Students' Views on the Aspects of the Smart MOOC Integrated with Intelligent Tutoring Environment that are Open to Improvement

The students were asked what aspects of the developed Smart MOOC Integrated with Intelligent Tutoring environment could be open to improvement. The opinions of the students are given in Table 5.

Table 5. Students' views on the aspects of the Smart MOOC Integrated with Intelligent Tutoring environment that are open to improvement

Sub-Theme	Frequency
I have no suggestions as it is great.	10
Uploading video of the topics in a little more detail	9
Interface design should be improved	8
It can be motivating for users to see other users' data.	3
There may be more questions	2

When Table 5 is examined, it is seen that the students stated that the lecture videos could be more detailed, the interface design could be improved, it would be useful to see the class average of the users in the dashboard regarding learning analytics, and the number of questions in dynamic assessment could be increased. Some of the student views are as follows:

S1: *"I can wait for the videos to be uploaded in a little more detail."*

S3: *"It can show our ranking among those who use the system."*

4. CONCLUSION AND DISCUSSION

In this research, students' views on the SMIT environment that is based on the adaptive and dynamic intelligent tutoring system supported with learning analytics were analyzed. Each component of this environment was grounded and developed by taking the solution offers for the problems commonly introduced in the literature regarding the MOOCs as references. Following the general assessment of the findings obtained, it is possible to state that the views of the students concerning the system are positive. Upon the analysis of the findings in detail, the dynamic assessment present in the system and multiple alternative contents provided such as e-book, presentation, video, infographics, and learning tasks stand out as the positive features. The students are given scaffolding questions or tips as feedback when they cannot solve a problem and it is aimed for them to reach competence by doing so. This process is called dynamic/interactive assessment (Tzuriel, 2000). There is also a dynamic assessment module in the SMIT environment intended for providing the students with the support they need during problem-solving. The support to be provided to the students at the time when they cannot solve a problem is important to achieve the learning. Students' opinions refer to the importance of this support.

The positive views of the students about providing alternative content can be assessed within the context of flexibility. The universal learning design built on the idea of creating flexibility in the curriculum (Meo, 2008) recommends enabling the variety of expression for students during their performances through various learning tasks and using different presentation forms such as voice, text, and visual in transferring information in order to achieve flexibility (Meyer and Rose, 2006). In the system developed, the flexibility achieved through alternative content became a significant design component regarded positively by the students following the dynamic assessment. Considering the students'views, it can be expressed that the students have expectations towards videos provided as the alternative content to have a brief expression and the system meets this expectation. It was observed that the students have positive intentions to use the developed SMIT environment since it facilitates the learning in different courses and learning contexts and provides repetition and reinforcement in the courses.

The research was limited with liked and disliked features of the SMIT environment, its preferability for various learning contexts, and opinions on the ease of use of the system. In the next stage, it is considered to analyze the student's acceptance structures regarding the developed SMIT based on the real usage data on the basis of technology acceptance models. In addition, the research was conducted in accordance with the case study, which is one of the qualitative research designs. As the continuation of this research, it is projected to carry out a study on a systematic analysis of the students' perspectives on SMIT environment through Q-methodology, which has a predominant qualitative aspect, however, regarded as a mixed-method since it involves a principal components analysis stage.

ACKNOWLEDGEMENT

This study is financially supported by the Scientific and Technological Research Council of Turkey (TUBITAK grant ID: 119K430).

REFERENCES

Aleven, V., Baker, R., Blomberg, N., Andres, J. M., Sewall, J., Wang, Y., & Popescu, O. (2017, May). Integrating MOOCs and Intelligent Tutoring Systems: EDX, GIFT, and CTAT. In *Proceedings of the 5th Annual Generalized Intelligent Framework for Tutoring Users Symposium, Orlando, FL, USA*.

Danka, I. (2020). Motivation by gamification: Adapting motivational tools of massively multiplayer online role-playing games (MMORPGs) for peer-to-peer assessment in connectivist massive open online courses (cMOOCs). *International Review of Education, 66(1), 75-92.*

Lambert, S. R. (2020). Do MOOCs contribute to student equity and social inclusion? A systematic review 2014–18. *Computers & Education, 145*, 103693.

Meo, G. (2008). Curriculum planning for all learners: Applying universal design for learning (UDL) to a high school reading comprehension program. *Preventing School Failure, 52* (2), 21–30.

Meyer, A. & Rose, D.H. (2006). The future in the margins: The role of technology and disability in educational reform. In D.H. Rose, A. Meyer & C. Hitchcock (Eds.), *The universally designed classroom: Accessible curriculum and digital technologies* (13–35). Cambridge, MA: Harvard Education Press.

Swinnerton, B., Hotchkiss, S., & Morris, N. P. (2017). Comments in MOOCs: who is doing the talking and does it help?. *Journal of Computer Assisted Learning, 33*(1), 51-64.

Tzuriel, D. (2000). Dynamic assessment of young children: Educational and intervention perspectives. *Educational Psychology Review, 12*(4), 385–435.

Wong, J., Baars, M., Davis, D., Van Der Zee, T., Houben, G. J., & Paas, F. (2019). Supporting self-regulated learning in online learning environments and MOOCs: A systematic review. I*nternational Journal of Human–Computer Interaction, 35*(4-5), 356-373.

Xiong, Y., & Suen, H. K. (2018). Assessment approaches in massive open online courses: Possibilities, challenges and future directions. *International Review of Education, 64*(2), 241-263.

Yin, R. K. (2013). *Case study research: Design and methods*. Sage publications.

Zhang, J., Hao, B., Chen, B., Li, C., Chen, H., & Sun, J. (2019, July). Hierarchical reinforcement learning for course recommendation in MOOCs. In Proceedings of the AAAI Conference on Artificial Intelligence (Vol. 33, No. 01, pp. 435-442).

THE USAGE OF BLACKBOARD LEARN COMMUNITY OF PRACTICE IN HIGHER EDUCATION INSTITUTIONS IN UAE

Lina Daouk and Nafeth Hamdi Al Hashlamoun
Higher Colleges of Technology
P.O.Box: 41012, Abu Dhabi, UAE

ABSTRACT

UAE Higher education institutions were among the first institutions in the Middle East to adopt Blackboard Learn (BBLearn) as the learning management system for their e-learning activities. Regardless of the large investments spent of BBLearn, the adoption of this system among the faculty is still slow. This qualitative case study research aimed to investigate the need for the creation of a BBLearn community of practice (CoP) in a public higher education institution in the United Arab Emirates, its anticipated benefits and its positive impact on increasing the adoption of BBLearn among the computer department faculty. A qualitative case study research methodology was used, and data was collected from faculty of the public higher education institution. The findings revealed that the faculty support the creation of a BBLearn CoP and they identified its anticipated benefits and listed them. The findings also confirmed that the creation of a BBLearn CoP will have positive impact on the adoption of BBLearn among the computer department faculty. This study confirmed the importance of communities of practice and their roles in sharing and advancing knowledge. It also revealed the need to create a BBLearn CoP to address the slow adoption of BBLearn among faculty.

KEYWORDS

Community of Practice, CoP in a Public Higher Education Institution in UAE

1. INTRODUCTION

Over the last decades, the investment of higher education institutions (HEI) in e-learning instructional technologies have witnessed a continuous steady increase (Gunn, 2010). Similar to other business organizations, HEI have realized that the key to success in the new digital age is to leverage the benefits from e-learning instructional technologies (Wang, Wang, & Shee, 2007). It is commonly understood that e-learning instructional technologies refer to the usage of information technology in learning and teaching (Czerniewicz & Brown, 2009; Salmon, 2005). Following the international e-learning trends, the investment of United Arab Emirates (UAE) HEI in e-learning instructional technologies witnessed a similar increase over the last decades (Vrazalic, Macgregor, Behl, & Fitzgerald, 2009) with millions of dollars being spent on managing e-learning platforms (Daghfous & Barkhi, 2009; Kats, 2010).

BBLearn is one of the most commonly used LMS in HEI in UAE ("Blackboard | Education Technology & Services," n.d.-a). While most of UAE HEI have reported an increase in the implementation of BBLearn, the lack of effective professional development for faculty has been identified by many researchers as one of the main reasons for the slow adoption process of BBLearn among faculty (Abdullah & Ward, 2016; Kassim, Jailani, Hairuddin, & Zamzuri, 2012; Mirza & Al-Abdulkareem, 2011; Tarhini, Hone, Liu, & Tarhini, 2017; Wang et al., 2007).

The concept of CoP was first developed by Jean Lave and Etienne Wenger (Lave & Wenger, 1998). Wenger (2000) in his book "Communities of practice: The key to knowledge strategy" stated that one of the main reasons for CoPs to emerge is the existence of common interest or problem among a collection of people. The rate of adoption of BBLearn among the faculty in in the computer department of public higher education institution is slow when compared to the investment committed by our college. In this paper, I attempt to study the need for the creation of a BBLearn CoP at the public higher education institution using a case study research methodology.

2. BODY OF PAPER

2.1 Research Problem

Considering the large investment in BBLearn and its slow adoption among the computer department faculty, the issue of creating a BBLearn community of practice for the faculty in the higher education institution to address this problem merits special attention (Dlamini, 2015; Vrazalic et al., 2009).

2.2 Purpose of the Study

The purpose of this qualitative research is to investigate the need for the creation of a BBLearn CoP in the institution, its anticipated benefits and its positive impact on increasing the adoption of BBLearn among the faculty. To achieve this objective, a case study research methodology approach will be conducted in the institution. Four of the faculties will be interviewed and the collected data along with the literature review will be used to answer the research questions. The institution is considered to be part of the HEI in UAE with around 23,000 full time students in more than one campus serving all emirates of UAE and was among the first institutions to implement e-learning systems.

2.3 Research Questions

The overarching research question of this study is to investigate the need for the creation of a community of practice for Blackboard Learn from the perspective of the computer department faculty and the anticipated benefits. The particular research questions that will be addressed in this study are:

RQ1. What do the faculty of the institution believe are the anticipated benefits from the creation of a BBLearn CoP?

RQ2. How should the BBLearn CoP creation be managed?

RQ3. How will the creation of the BBLearn CoP affect the adoption of BBLearn among faculty?

2.4 Literature Review

This literature review aims to provide an overview on CoPs and their corresponding social learning theory. The literature review is organized as follows: the characteristics and benefits of CoPs are examined first. The factors that affect the success and failure of CoPs are examined after that. This is followed by a discussion about the need for e-learning CoPs among the faculty of HEI and their anticipated benefits. The literature review concludes by identifying the literature gaps on e-learning CoPs.

2.4.1 Communities of Practice: Characteristics and Benefits

A community of practice (CoP) evolves when a group of people who have a common interest in a particular domain come together or it can be created based on a specific goal of sharing information and experiences between group members (Cho, 2016). During this process, CoP members learn from each other which create opportunities for them to advance and grow professionally and personally (Wenger, McDermott, & Snyder, 2002). Probst and Borzillo (2008) stated that a CoP is a specific form of intra-organizational networks. Members use these specific intra-organizational networks for the development and sharing of knowledge and practices across organizational departments. McDermott (1999) called these specific intra-organizational networks in organizations as cross functional teams. In addition, Wenger et al. (2002) stated that CoP should be created voluntary. This voluntary structure of CoP should be able to generate excitement, relevance and more important value to engage members and attract new ones. Furthermore, Hearn and White (2009) stated that a CoP creates a specific environment that allow members to reflect, interpret and give their feedback enriching the relationships between the members which lead to generating and liking knowledge, policy and practice.

The concept of CoP was developed by Jean Lave and Etienne Wenger (Lave & Wenger, 1998; Etienne Wenger, 2000) as a basis of a social theory of learning (Eckert, 2006). The CoP term was invented by Jean Lave and Etienne Wenger while they were investigating apprenticeship as a learning model (Wenger, 2006).

Wenger (2006) stated that there are three main characteristics that are essential to create a CoP: the domain, community and practice. The domain is what distinguish a CoP from a group of friends of colleagues coming together. Membership implies a commitment to the domain and hence members have a shared competence that distinguishes them from other people (Wenger, 2006). The community indicates that members pursue their interest in their domain. Members engage in joint activities and discussion, work with each other, and share information and experiences. The practice implies that members are practitioners and not simply group of people who share a common interest. They share stories, experiences, tools, ways of addressing common recurring problems related to their domain. Cambridge, Kaplan and Suter (2005) listed four main benefits that member of a CoP expect: *Connection, shared context, dialogue* and *collaborative processes*. Jakovljevic (2012) stated that one of the main characteristics of a CoP is that it must be psychologically safe and secure environment. The author maintains that CoP creates a safe environment for members to drop their fear of criticism, ridicule and retrenchment and unleash their creativity to address common domain problems.

In summary, the main characteristics of a CoP are *the domain*, *the community*, *the practice*, and the *safe innovative environment*. The main benefits are: connections, *shared context, dialogue* and *collaborative processes*.

2.4.2 Communities of Practice: Success and Failures Factors

Probst and Borzillo (2008) investigated 57 CoPs in major European and US companies such as Siemens, Oracle, IBM, Holcim, Mazda, eCoopers, SwissRe, and the world bank to identify the antecedents of their success and failures. The authors listed three major differences between CoPs and regular project team, operational teams, or purely informal network. The first difference is that in CoPs members' roles are not assigned formally and the delineations of these roles are not even clear. Secondly, CoPs members have no formal contractual obligations of any sort. Thirdly, CoPs members share a common interest to develop their practices in their specific domain whereas in other business team structures the members' interest will only last as long as its members find it beneficial to the business. Probst and Borzillo (2008) identified ten commandments of CoP governance that lead to the successful and sustainable development of CoPs and five major reasons for CoPs.

Van Rensburg, Botma, Heyns, and Coetzee (2016) explored the experiences of a group of nurses who started a support group and transformed it to a successful community of practice. Using a case study design guided by the theory of action (Allen, 1984; Coleman, 1986), the authors identified four themes that illuminated and explicated the experiences of the group of nurses, namely shared domain of interest, informal network, formal work group and community of practice. The four themes identified by Van Rensburg et al. (2016) support the ten commandments identified by Probst and Borzillo (2008) particularly having clear strategic objectives and a governance committee with sponsors and CoP leaders to guide the CoP.

Liberatore, Bowkett, Macleod, Spurr, and Longnecker, (2018) investigated the factors that affect the creation of a successful social media CoP for the New Zealand Garden Bird. The authors used a case study design to investigate seven principles for cultivating a successful social media CoP which are: (1) design for evolution, (2) foster open dialogue between inside and outside perspectives, (3) provide public and private community space, (4) enable multiple levels of participations, (5) focus on value, (6) combine familiarities and excitement, and (7) create a rhythm for the community. The seven principles identified by Liberatore et al. (2018) supports the findings of Probst and Borzillo (2008) particularly promoting access to outsiders to general new interests.

Kirkman, Mathieu, Cordery, Rosen, and Kukenberger (2011) developed and empirically tested a CoP effective model using data from 32 CoPs in a United Stated based firms. The authors concluded that the following factors have positive impact of the effectiveness of CoPs: (1) the existence of external community leaders, (2) empowerment, (3) recognition of CoPs as "core" by the organization, and (4) task independence. Kirkman et al. (2011) empirical study confirms again the finding of Probst and Borzillo (2008).

In summary, the antecedents identified by Probst and Borzillo (2008) and supported by Van Rensburg et al. (2016), Liberatore et al. (2018), and Kirkman et al. (2011) provide a summary of the factors that affect the success and failures of CoPs.

2.4.3 Communities of Practice and e-Learning

Using a case study research design, Chang, Chen, and Li (2008) investigated the benefits of an e-learning CoP for a programming course at their university. Chang et al. (2008) argued for the construction of a web-based coursework environment with the aim to promote knowledge sharing, improve the quality of students' coursework and advance learning performance. Again using a case study research design, Cho, (2016) studied the benefits of a bilingual online CoP for pre-service teachers. The findings of this empirical study revealed that mutual engagement, joint enterprise, and shared repertoire were among the features that have positive impact on the creating a beneficial learning experience for these pre-service teachers. Similar to the previous two studies, Clarke (2009) used a case study design to investigate the outcomes of a professional online district CoP of student teachers' professional learning online. Clarke (2009) work empirically shows the power of e-learning CoPs of teachers to create new learning curriculums that recognize the potential of virtual learning environments for their students.

In summary, Chang et al. (2008), Cho, (2016) and Clarke (2009) presented the features and benefits of e-learning CoPs of teachers. Particularly, Clarke (2009) revealed a new powerful advantage of e-learning teachers' CoPs which is the creation of specific curriculum for virtual learning environment.

2.4.4 A Brief Description of the Gaps

Jean Lave and Etienne Wenger stated that CoPs are everywhere, and that people are involved in a number of them formally or informally. The commandments stated by Probst and Borzillo (2008) formed a governance for successful CoP and researchers like Chang et al. (2008), Cho, (2016) and Clarke (2009) presented the features and benefits of e-learning CoPs. However, there is limited research on the learning management systems e-learning CoPs and in particular about BlackBoard CoPs. In addition, the anticipated benefits from a BBLearn CoP in HEI has not yet been fully explored by researchers. I am confident that this case study will support bridging some of the gaps identified.

2.5 Theoretical Framework

The community of practice theory as developed by Jean Lave and Etienne Wenger (Lave & Wenger, 1998) provides a theoretical guidance that was used to direct this case study. The attributes of the three main conceptual themes of Wenger (2006): the domain, community and practice were used as a conceptual lens to guide the development of my case study research as presented in Figure 1.

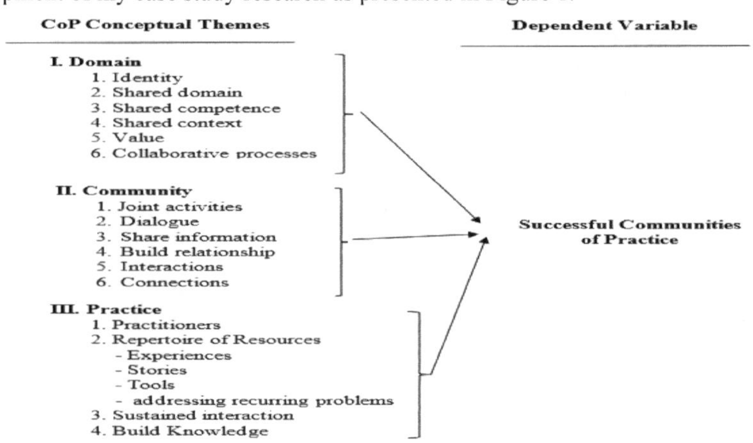

Figure 1. Wenger (2006) communities of practice conceptual themes

2.6 Epistemology and Ontology

Epistemology and ontology are sometimes used interchangeability (Goodson & Phillimore, 2004) but as a researcher I understand fully the difference between them where epistemology is about the way I know things while the ontology is about is what things are. This research is a mini qualitative case study research and hence my ontology is to find out what are the things by analyzing participants answers from the interviews and conducting a literature review about e-learning CoPs. I will continue to have an epistemological stance that by conducting qualitative research I will be able to understand and increase my knowledge about things. This research follows the positivism paradigm where my role is to analyze the data collected and report the findings objectively.

2.7 Research Methodology

The research methodology used in this paper is a case study design. A case study design permits the examining of complex issues and contemporary real-life situations. Researchers have used case study research designs across many disciplines and in particula social scientists used case study designs for their qualitative research to provide a base for the application and extension of ideas (Creswell, 2014; Yin, 2013) and this is the case of this research.

2.7.1 NVivo Coding

One level of coding was used to code the participants' answers in NVivo. A node was created for each question with the answers of the four participants together. Where possible, two queries were run on each node: word frequency queries and text search queries. On all nodes, one minimum text search query using the attributes of Wenger (2006) was executed and where possible a word frequency query was used.

2.8 Data Collection and Analysis

Data was collected from one source which is the open-ended face to face interviews. 10 questions were used in the interviews. Yin (2013) stated that interviews are listed among the most important source of data in case study designs. There are many types of interviews that can be used in case study (Leedy & Ormrod, 2010). The most common types are those that are open ended and semi structured. The design of the interviewing questions was of semi-structured types as described by Yin (2013) with few central questions. The Semi structured design allowed me to questions participants about facts and their opinions and to follow up on certain answers. All of the interviews conducted took maximum one hour to complete. All data collected were text generated from the immediate transcription of the participants' answers.

Four of my colleagues agreed to participate in this research. Participants were all from the computer department who are currently involved in developing courses using BBLearn. The participants were two male and two female faculty. Two of them were lecturers and two were assistant professors. This reflects the overall gender distribution in the department that is equally split between male and female reflecting the nature of the Abu Dhabi Women's College. A linear hierarchical approach was used to analyze the collected data by building from bottom to the top with multiple interactions between the steps (Patton, 2001; Shank, 2005). In the first step, I organized and prepared the collected data for analysis. I read through all the collected data and reflected on its overall meaning in the second step. In the third step, I started a coding process using the themes presented by Wenger (2006). I used the NVivo ("NVivo," n.d.) software to analyze he collected data.

2.9 Quality and Trustworthiness of the Study/Findings

In order to improve the quality and trustworthiness of the collected data, the four colleagues were selected from three different subdivisions in the computer department. While triangulation of evidences by collecting data from other sources like documents, policies and artifacts was not possible due to the time frame of this research, the selection of colleagues from different sub-division in the computer department combined with the literature review on the CoPs should be enough to cover the quality and trustworthiness of this research.

2.10 Ethical Issues and Limitations

All Data collected will be used only for the purpose of this research and will not be shared with anyone. No personal information will be identified. I will keep the digital data for three years and then it will be deleted. This research is under the exempt research type as described by Cozby (2008) since the risk to harm the participants is not greater than the risk they encountered during my normal working activities.

2.11 Findings

This section reports the findings of the interviews that were conducted with four faculty of the computer department. The interviews were conducted using interviews of 10 questions. The first six questions covered the three conceptual themes as presented by Wenger (2006). The last four questions covered the proposed way to manage the BBLearn CoP and any foreseen barriers.

2.11.1 Sample Demographics

The following was collected from the participants to form the demographic profile of the participants: age, gender, total years of experience, BBLearn usage experience, job titles, department / subdivision, and education. The participants are referred with their alias as P1, P2, P3, and P4. The sample demographics are summarized in table 1 below.

Table 1. Summary of the sample demographics

	Age	Gender	Total experience	BBL experience	Job Title	Department	Education
P1	45	Male	16	3	Assistant Professor	CIS / Security and Forensics	PhD
P2	48	Male	15	3	Assistant Professor	CIS / Application development	PhD
P3	44	Female	14	2	Lecturer	CIS/ Business Solution	MS
P4	51	Female	20	4	Lecturer	CIS / Business Solution	MS

Note: This table summarizes the sample demographics of the 4 participants.

Table 2 summarizes the descriptive statistics of the sample demographics.

Table 2. Descriptive statistics of the sample demographics

Descriptive statistics					
	N	Minimum	Maximum	Mean	Standard deviation
Age	4	44	51	47	3
Total experience	4	14	20	16	2.6
BBL experience	4	2	4	2.9	0.8
Valid N (list wise)	4				

The mean of the age of the participants is 47 and the mean of the total years of teaching experiences is 16 which reflect a high level of maturity of the participants as professional instructors with years of experience who can provide reliable and up to date information about their experiences in e-learning and BBLearn. With 2.9 years of mean experience of BBLearn usage, this again gives a high level of confidence that the participants have enough relevant years of experiences in using BBLearn.

2.11.2 Analysis of the Interview Answers

Question 1: What do you think a community of practice for Blackboard learn is all about?

All four participants answered the first question with details. Each member gave his opinion about what a BBLearn CoP is about. Starting from the responses of the third participant, the understanding of BBLearn CoP notion started to repeat itself. This is a good indication that saturation was achieved, and the participants have reached a common notion about what is BBLearn is all about.

The answers of the first question received from the 4 participants were coded in NVivo software. Table 3 lists the results of the top 10 frequently used words in the complete answers of question 1.

Table 3. Top 10 used words in the answers of question 1

Word	Length	Count	Weighted Percentage (%)	Similar Words
participant	11	43	2.55	participant, participate, participation
community	9	40	2.37	communication, communities, community
cop	3	40	2.37	cop, cops
learn	5	37	2.19	learn, learned, learning, learning'
members	7	34	2.02	member, members, members'
share	5	26	1.54	share, shared, sharing
people	6	25	1.48	people
different	9	23	1.36	difference, different
practice	8	23	1.36	practice, practices, practicing
experience	10	21	1.25	experience, experiences
discussion	10	20	1.19	discuss, discussion, discussions

The words participation, learn, share, practice, experience and discussion were among the most repeated used words by the four participants in describing the BBlearn community of practice. The result of this query are in line with the attributes listed by Wenger (2006) about the characteristics of CoPs.

A text search query on the word CoP in the participants answers for question 1 provide a summary of what the participants think are the main characteristics of a BBLearn CoP. The results of this query are shown in figure 2 below.

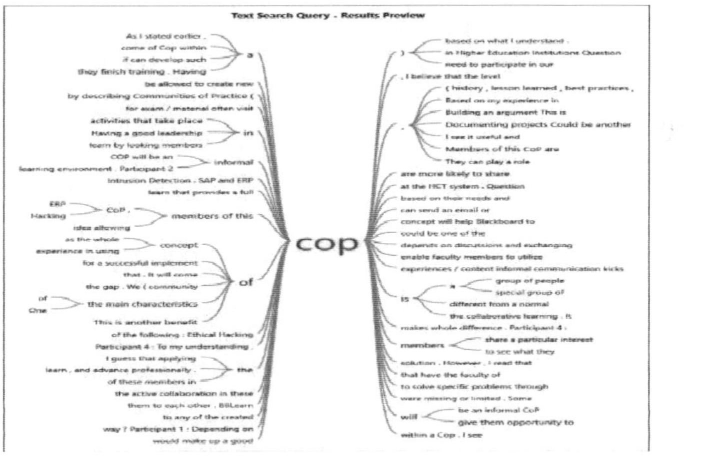

Figure 2. The text search results on word *CoP* and its relationship with the other most repeated words used in the complete answers of question 1

Question 2: How do you know that a community of practice for Blackboard Learn at our college will provide you with the professional development you need and in an accurate way?

All the four participants answered this question with full details. 280 words were used to answer this question by the 4 participants. Collaborative learning and sharing resources and learning from each other were among the most repeated words on how the BBLearn CoP will provide the professional development needed. A text search query using NVivo on the word learn in the participants answers for question 2 provide a summary on how collaborative learning in the BBLearn CoP will provide the professional development needed for faculty to increase their usage of BBLearn. The text search relationship between the word learn and other words in the answers is presented in figure 3 below.

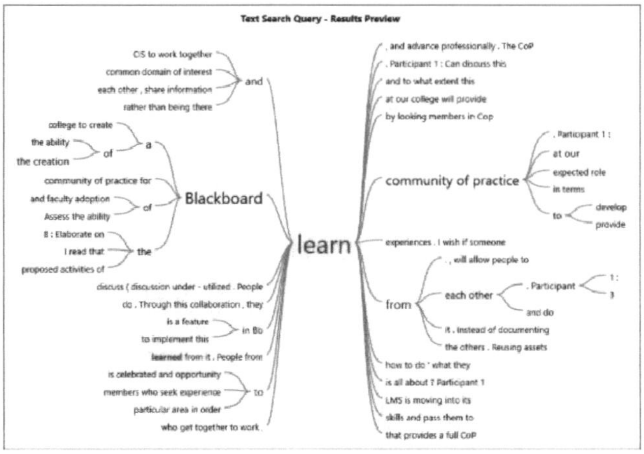

Figure 3. The text search results on word *learn* and its relationship with the other most repeated words used in the complete answers of question 2

The analysis of questions 3 to 10 followed the same procedure used in the analysis of questions 1 and 2.

Question 3: Evaluate the following proposed activities of the Blackboard Learn community of practice in terms of addressing the particular needs for your job.

All four participants answered this question. Three of the four participants considered all the listed activities as beneficial to their work. Only one participant thought that two of the activities are not applicable to his domain. Apart from that, all participants agreed that the proposed activities of BBLearn will address their needs for their jobs. A summary of the words used by all the participants to evaluate the proposed activities is presented in table 4.

Table 4. Summary of the words used to evaluate BBLearn proposed activities

Proposed activities	Words used by participants
Problem solving	Great idea, efficient, success
Request for information	Needed, helpful, accessible
Seeking experience	Learning, repertoire, sharing
Re-using assets	Best practice, knowledge
Coordination and synergy	Needed, very important, sharing knowledge
Building an argument	Natural, focused, a place to voice opinions
Growing confidence	Not applicable, highly important, good.
Discussion and developments	Needed, required
Documenting projects	Good place, important activity, supportive culture
Visits mapping knowledge and identifying gaps	Not applicable, relevant and helpful, useful in bridging gaps.

Question 4: Elaborate on the existence of a shared domain of interest between the faculty of our* department *to create a Blackboard Learn community of practice.

All participants answered this question and provided full details. From the answers of the four participants we noticed that they all agree on the existence of a shared domain of interest between the faculty of the computer department at the public higher education institution to create a BBLearn CoP. A query of the frequently used word in the complete four answers received from the participants using NVivo reveals that the word *practice* with its stemmed words and its synonyms was repeated 86 times. In addition, the words experience, share, collaborative, and value were repeated 62, 47, 14, and 7 respectively. This is a clear indication that the most repeated words in answering this question are the attributes listed by Wenger (2006) in describing the shared domain of CoPs. The results of the query as produced by NVivo are presented in table 5.

Table 5. The frequency of the most repeated words in the answers of question 4

Word	Length	Count	Weighted Percentage (%)	Similar Words
Practice	8	86	2.50	applying, do', good, much, practice, practices, practicing, skill, skilled, skillful, skills, use, used, useful, using
Share	5	47	1.97	contribution, part, share, shared, sharing
Experience	10	62	1.89	experience, experiences, feel, get, know, knowing, receive, see
collaboration	13	14	0.65	collaborate, collaboration, collaborative
Value	5	7	0.30	assess, assessing, evaluate, measure, value, values

Question 5: Describe the ability of a Blackboard Learn community of practice to provide its member with a space to interact, help each other, share information and learn from each other.

The answers received for this question showed different opinions between the participants about the BBLean capability to provide a space for the members to interact. Two participants did not know if such capabilities exist in BBLearn, and the other two though that discussion boards and other similar features in BBLearn can provide the needed CoP features. Overall, there is agreement between the participants that if BBLearn cannot provide the needed CoP capabilities in term of a space to interact to share information, at least it can provide them with a private space to share information among faculty and learn from each other.

Question 6: Assess the ability of Blackboard Learn community of practice to develop a shared practice that help members to share their repertoire of resources, experiences, stories, tools, and their ways of addressing recurring problems.

All participants answered this question with full details. There is common agreement between participants on the positive ability of BBLearn CoP to develop a shared practice among its members. The participants listed Loyalty, feel of belonging, achievement, recognizing of efforts, management support among the shard practice attributes that will support the members. A text search query using NVivo on the word practice in the participants answers for question 6 provide a summary on the ability of BBLearn CoP to develop a shared practice among the faculty of the computer department in the public higher education institution. The text search relationship between the word practice and other words in the answers is presented in figure 4 below.

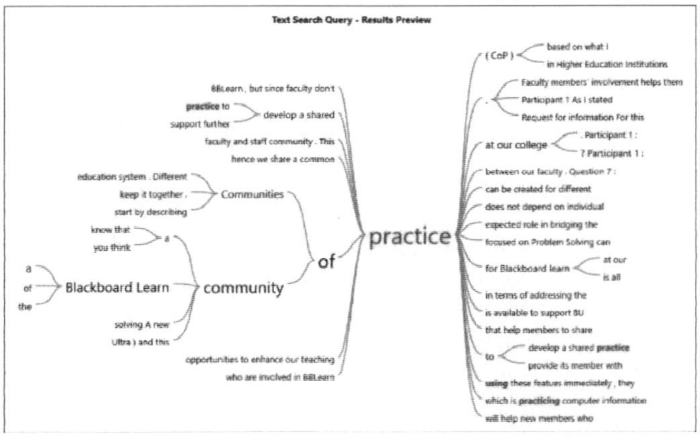

Figure 4. The text search results on word practice and its relationship with the other most repeated words used in the complete answers of question 6

Question 7: Delineate on how to manage the creation of a Blackboard Learn community of practice at our college.

Different responses were received on the possible ways to manage the BBLearn CoP. Two participants considered this as part of the management role and stated that the management of the CoP can be done by the educational department at the college. The other two participants stated that this should be managed by the members of the CoP and one participants acknowledged the role of external members and sponsors in the management of the CoP. Overall, we can conclude that the answers received about the management of the BBLearn are in line with the commandments identified by Probst and Borzillo (2008).

Question 8: Elaborate on the Blackboard Learn community of practice expected role in bridging the gap between the professional training and faculty adoption of Blackboard Learn.

There is agreement between the four participants on the positive role that the BBLearn CoP will play in bridging the gap between the professional training and the adoption of Blackboard learn at the college. Participants shared the opinion that while the professional development they receive provide them with the skills they need, the lack of practice and the lack of a place to share information and request further help are among the main reasons for the slow adoption among faculty. The participants agreed and confirmed that a BBLearn CoP will be able to bridge that gap by complementing the professional development they receive and provide its member with a place to share and advance knowledge.

Question 9: Can you please explain what do you believe are the barriers to the creation of a Blackboard Learn community of practice at our college?

The participants answered this question with full details. They listed culture and environment among the most difficult barrier to the creation of the BBLearn CoP. We did not have time to elaborate on these barriers, but one participants stated openness and another stated management support and a third participant stated that this might be the job of the management. We can conclude form the responses received, that the participants are fully aware of the barriers and this show an alignment of their answers between understanding first the need of this CoP, listing its benefits after that and finally identifying the barriers.

Question 10: As a faculty at our college, how are you planning to overcome the barriers to the creation of a Blackboard Learn community of practice at our college?

All participants answered this question by listing at least one solution to overcome the barriers. Solutions received were to address the barriers listed above. Two participants stated that changing the culture as a solution. Another participant stated involvement of management and recognizing efforts of faculty as a possible solution. The fourth participants stated faculty should create the BBLearn CoP regardless and work on solving the barriers as they arise.

3. CONCLUSION

This case study research revealed the existence of a collective need among the faculty of the computer department of the public HEI to establish a BBLearn community of practice. It confirmed that the faculty of the computer department of the public HEI use the attributes of the three themes presented by Wenger (2006) to measure the anticipated benefits from the creation of the BBLearn. Particularly this case study established the existence of a common domain, a sense of community and a shared practice among the faculty of the computer department of the public HEI. In addition, this case study revealed that while the faculty of the public HEI don't have a clear idea on how this BBLearn CoP will be managed, they understand the barriers to the creation of this CoP and they have a plan to address them.

This case study research revealed the existence of a shared domain among the faculty of the the computer department of the public HEI. The faculty of computer department believe that they have a common identify for their shared domain. The faculty implied a commitment to their domain and even suggested sub-committees for the proposed BBLearn CoP such as a security related one and an SAP one. The computer department of the public HEI were able to identify a shared competence that distinguishes them from the rest of the faculty at the college. Finally, the case study confirmed that the faculty of the computer department of the public HEI value their collective competence and are ready to learn from each other.

This case study research also confirmed the existence of a community feeling among the faculty of the computer department. Faculty are engaged in joint activities, they value dialogue and they understand the importance of sharing BBLearn information. This research confirmed the existence of healthy interactions and connections among the faculty of the computer department that is necessary to create a community for the faculty who are pursuing their interest in their common domain.

In addition, this case study confirmed the practice theme among the faculty of the computer department. They don't only have a common domain and feeling of community, but also they are practitioners. In working with BBLearn, the computer department faculty develop a shared repertoire of resources such as experiences, stories, tools, way of addressing recurring problem, and problem-solving techniques. This research confirmed that the computer department faculty have a shared practice. In summary, this case study research confirmed the existence of the three themes that support the need for creating successful CoP as presented by Wenger (2006). This addresses the purpose of this research that was to investigate the need for the creation of a BBLearn community of practice in the computer department of the public HEI and confirms it.

As per the findings above, this research case study answered the first research question by identifying a list of the anticipated benefits from the creation of the BBLearn CoP. The list included the activities listed in the characteristics of successful CoPs as presented by Wenger (2006). Knowledge sharing, learning from each other, bridging the professional development gaps, open dialogue and increasing BBLearn adoption are among the listed benefits of the BBLearn CoP.

On the other hand, this case study research answered the third research question by confirming that the BBLearn CoP will encourage the computer department faculty to increase their usage of BBLearn. This research revealed that while the faculty of computer department are receiving adequate professional training on BBLearn. The lack of practice has been identified as one of the main reasons for the slow adoption of BBLearn. BBLearn CoP will address this lack of practice by providing a shared space for the faculty to practice the BBLearn features they learned. This confirmed that the creation of a BBLearn Cop will have positive impact the adoption of BBLearn among the computer department faculty. Finally, this case study revealed that the faculty of computer department believe that the BBLearn CoP should be managed by the faculty and sponsor and extremal members are essential to the success of this CoP.

In conclusion, this case study research study explored and investigated the need for the creation of a BBLearn community of practice in the computer department of the public HEI, its anticipated benefits and its positive impact on increasing the adoption of BBLearn among the computer department faculty. Further research is needed to extend the findings of this study to other departments in the public higher education institution where the study took place.

REFERENCES

Abdullah, F., & Ward, R. (2016). Developing a General Extended Technology Acceptance Model for E-Learning (GETAMEL) by analysing commonly used external factors. *Computers in Human Behavior*, *56*, 238–256.

Allen, J. F. (1984). Towards a general theory of action and time. *Artificial Intelligence*, *23*(2), 123–154.

Andrea Liberatore, Erin Bowkett, Catriona J. Macleod, Eric Spurr, & Nancy Longnecker. (2018). Social Media as a Platform for a Citizen Science Community of Practice. *Citizen Science: Theory and Practice*, *3*(1). https://doi.org/10.5334/cstp.108

Blackboard | Education Technology & Services. (n.d.). Retrieved February 9, 2018, from http://www.blackboard.com/index.html

Cambridge, D., Kaplan, S., & Suter, V. (2005). Community of practice design guide: A step-by-step guide for designing & cultivating communities of practice in higher education. *EDUCASE Learning Initiative*.

Chang, C. K., Chen, G. D., & Li, L. Y. (2008). Constructing a community of practice to improve coursework activity.(Report). *Computers & Education*, *50*(1), 235–247. https://doi.org/10.1016/j.compedu.2006.05.003

Cho, H. (2016). Under co-construction: An online community of practice for bilingual pre-service teachers. *Computers & Education*, *92*, 76–89.

Clarke, L. (2009). The POD model: Using communities of practice theory to conceptualise student teachers' professional learning online. *Computers & Education*, *52*(3), 521–529. https://doi.org/10.1016/j.compedu.2008.10.006

Coleman, J. S. (1986). Social theory, social research, and a theory of action. *American Journal of Sociology*, *91*(6), 1309–1335.

Cozby, P. (2008). *Methods in Behavioral Research* (10 edition). Boston: McGraw-Hill Humanities/Social Sciences/Languages.

Creswell, J. W. (2014). *Research Design: Qualitative, Quantitative, and Mixed Methods Approaches*. SAGE Publications.

Czerniewicz, L., & Brown, C. (2009). A study of the relationship between institutional policy, organisational culture and e-learning use in four South African universities. *Computers & Education*, *53*(1), 121–131.

Daghfous, A., & Barkhi, R. (2009). The strategic management of information technology in UAE hotels: An exploratory study of TQM, SCM, and CRM implementations. *Technovation*, *29*(9), 588–595.

Dlamini, R. S. (2015). The role of the strategic and adaptive Chief Information Officer in higher education. *Education and Information Technologies; New York*, *20*(1), 113–140. http://dx.doi.org.ezproxy.hct.ac.ae/10.1007/s10639-013-9269-5

Eckert, P. (2006). Communities of practice. *Encyclopedia of Language and Linguistics*, *2*(2006), 683–685.

Enrollments. (n.d.). Retrieved April 27, 2018, from http://www.hct.ac.ae/en/about/factbook/enrollments/

Goodson, L., & Phillimore, J. (2004). *Qualitative research in tourism: Ontologies, epistemologies and methodologies*. Routledge.

Gunn, C. (2010). Sustainability factors for e-learning initiatives. *ALT-J*, *18*(2), 89–103.

Hearn, S., & White, N. (2009). *Communities of practice: Linking knowledge, policy and practice*. Overseas Development Institute London (UK).

Jakovljevic, M. (2012). A model of creativity, innovation and invention (MCII) from knolwedge management perspective for interdisciplinary education. *Knowledge Management Innovations for Interdisciplinary Education: Organizational Applications by S Buckley: USA: IGI Global Publishers.*, 66–87. https://doi.org/10.4018/978-1-4666-1969-2.ch004

Kassim, E. S., Jailani, S. F. A. K., Hairuddin, H., & Zamzuri, N. H. (2012). Information system acceptance and user satisfaction: The mediating role of trust. *Procedia-Social and Behavioral Sciences*, *57*, 412–418.

Kats, Y. (2010). *Learning Management System Technologies and Software Solutions for Online Teaching: Tools and Applications: Tools and Applications*. IGI Global.

Kirkman, B. L., Mathieu, J. E., Cordery, J. L., Rosen, B., & Kukenberger, M. (2011). Managing a New Collaborative Entity in Business Organizations: Understanding Organizational Communities of Practice Effectiveness. *Journal of Applied Psychology*, *96*(6), 1234–1245. https://doi.org/10.1037/a0024198

Lave, J., & Wenger, E. (1998). Communities of practice. *Retrieved June*, *9*, 2008.

Leedy, P. D., & Ormrod, J. E. (2010). *Practical Research: Planning and Design* (9 edition). Boston: Pearson.

McDermott, R. (1999). Learning across teams. *Knowledge Management Review*, *8*(3), 32–36.

Mirza, A. A., & Al-Abdulkareem, M. (2011). Models of e-learning adopted in the Middle East. *Applied Computing and Informatics*, *9*(2), 83–93. https://doi.org/10.1016/j.aci.2011.05.001

NVivo: The Qualitative Data Analysis & Research Software. (n.d.). Retrieved February 22, 2015, from http://www.qsrinternational.com/products_nvivo.aspxhttp://atlasti.com/

Patton, M. Q. (2001). *Qualitative Research & Evaluation Methods* (3rd edition). Thousand Oaks, Calif: SAGE Publications, Inc.

Probst, G., & Borzillo, S. (2008). Why communities of practice succeed and why they fail. *European Management Journal*, *26*(5), 335–347.

Salmon, G. (2005). Flying not flapping: a strategic framework for e-learning and pedagogical innovation in higher education institutions. *ALT-J*, *13*(3), 201–218.

Shank, G. D. (2005). *Qualitative Research: A Personal Skills Approach* (2 edition). Upper Saddle River, N.J: Pearson.

Tarhini, A., Hone, K., Liu, X., & Tarhini, T. (2017). Examining the moderating effect of individual-level cultural values on users' acceptance of E-learning in developing countries: a structural equation modeling of an extended technology acceptance model. *Interactive Learning Environments*, *25*(3), 306–328.

Van Rensburg, G., Botma, Y., Heyns, T., & Coetzee, I. (2016). Establishing a Community of Practice: from Outsiders to Insiders. *Gender & Behaviour*, *14*(1), 7028–7039.

Vrazalic, L., Macgregor, R. C., Behl, D., & Fitzgerald, J. (2009). E-learning barriers in the United Arab Emirates: Preliminary results from an empirical investigation.

Wang, Y.-S., Wang, H.-Y., & Shee, D. Y. (2007). Measuring e-learning systems success in an organizational context: Scale development and validation. *Computers in Human Behavior*, *23*(4), 1792–1808.

Wenger, E. (2000). Communities of practice: The key to knowledge strategy. In *Knowledge and communities* (pp. 3–20). Elsevier.

Wenger, E. (2006). *Communities of practice: A brief introduction. Retrieved March 26, 2010*.

Wenger, E., McDermott, R. A., & Snyder, W. (2002). *Cultivating communities of practice: A guide to managing knowledge*. Harvard Business Press.

Yin, R. K. (2013). *Case study research: Design and methods*. Sage publications.

LEARNING ANALYTICS AND ITS DATA SOURCES: WHY WE NEED TO FOSTER ALL OF THEM

Dirk Tempelaar
Maastricht University School of Business and Economics
Tongersestraat 53, 6211 LM, Maastricht, Netherlands

ABSTRACT

The search for rigor in learning analytics applications has placed survey data in the suspect's corner, favoring more objective trace data. A potential lack of objectivity in survey data is the existence of response styles, the tendency of respondents to answer survey items in a particular biased manner, such as yeah saying or always disagreeing. Making use of multiple survey instruments that exhibit similar types of response styles, our empirical study identifies response style bias by estimating the aggregate level of a set of response styles, amongst them the Acquiescence Response Style and the Dis-Acquiescence Response Style. We next demonstrate that trace variables are indeed bias-free in that their estimated response style components are small in size, accounting for minimal explained variation. Remarkably, course performance data is not bias-free, implying that predictive modelling for learning analytics purposes will, in general, profit from the inclusion of these bias components or apply survey data containing such response style bias to increase predictive power.

KEYWORDS

Learning Analytics, Trace Data, Survey Data, Course Performance Data, Response Styles

1. INTRODUCTION

What makes data rigorous for Learning Analytics (LA)? That data-related question is one of several in the quest for rigour in LA, opened by the editors in chief of the Journal of Learning Analytics: Knight, Wise, and Ochoa (2019). First directions in that quest are enclosed in the eight SOLAR webinar titled 'What Do We Mean by Rigour in Learning Analytics?' (SOLAR, 2020). Those directions pertain to several facets of LA research: beyond data, data types, data sources and data collection, also research methods and analysis procedures are concerned. The data orientation for LA as provided in the SOLAR webinar is voiced by Philip Winne, as part of the perspective of rigour in statistical approaches in LA research. In his contribution, Winne focuses on types of data being good enough for LA, with a clear suggestion for its direction: "*What is a goal for LA? LA might strive to accurately and responsibly predict achievement and motivation from event data so that we can dispense with, get rid of, tests and surveys. Can I tell whether you have learned by just observing what you do as a learner and how you feel about yourself as a learner by just looking at what you do?*" (SOLAR, 2020).

Banning all data from LA other than computer-logged event data indeed satisfies a crucial aspect of rigour: its restrictiveness. But does it do justice to the goal of accurately and responsibly predicting achievement and motivation? A wealth of empirical LA research applies other data types than event data in successfully predicting learning-related phenomena (for an overview of data types that contribute to LA-based predictions (see e.g., Ifenthaler and Yau, 2020; Dawson et al., 2019). There is even a branch within LA, called Dispositional LA, that entirely builds on the potential of combining event data with survey-based disposition data (Buckingham Shum and Deakin Crick, 2012). It is unclear what criteria would suggest that each and any research within this research tradition lacks rigour.

If anything, a candidate for such a criterion is subjectivity: computer-logged event data are objective, self-report survey data are subjective. For a moment renouncing that all data is subjective in the sense of being fabricated and thus containing bias (SOLAR, 2020; Winne, 2020), the popular view is that subjective data is biased, in contrast to objective data, and therefore objective data is to be preferred. A view easy to unravel: also objective data is subject to error. A simple example is connect-time in a digital learning system: a very objective measure, but as soon as it is applied as a measure of time-on-task, it contains the bias of including idle time not used to work on the task at hand. However, in this contribution, we aim to follow a different rationale: that of profiting from the fact of a bias component within subjective data. The rationale has two distinct features. First, it is often possible to operationalize the bias component and by doing so, correct the subjective measure for the bias. Second: the bias component itself may have predictive power towards crucial response variables in our prediction model, in which case predictive power increases by including the bias estimate together with the corrected measure in our prediction model, or include the uncorrected, biased predictor variable only, when model parsimony of prediction models matters.

Our contribution is directed at the estimation and subsequent correction for one specific bias in self-reported survey data: the presence of response styles in survey data. Response styles represent characteristic patterns in the answers to surveys that act as personality traits, such as the tendency to yeah saying or to give extreme responses. Response styles in survey data are extensively analysed in different academic disciplines, like marketing (Baumgartner and Steenkamp, 2001; Weijters, Cabooter, and Schillewaert, 2010), cultural studies (Cheung and Rensvold, 2000) and psychometrics (Bolt, Lu, and Kim, 2014; Henninger and Meiser, 2020a, 2020b). Different solutions to assess the presence of response styles type of bias have been proposed, like the introduction of neutral, bias-free items that serve as standards for the biased items, the anchoring vignettes (Bolt et al., 2014) or the use of item-response theory models (Henninger and Meiser, 2020a). This contribution builds on previous research of the authors (Tempelaar, Rienties, and Nguyen, 2020), where we use an aggregated measure of response styles as to identify the 'bias component' in different types of data. Estimating such an aggregate response style score is possible by the availability of data from multiple survey instruments and the relative invariance of these instrument-specific response styles (Tempelaar et al., 2020). In this contribution, we focus on the role of the three oldest response styles described in the literature: the Acquiescence Response Style, the systematic tendency to confirm item statements, the Dis-Acquiescence Response Style, the tendency to disagree with item statements, and the MidPoint Response Style, the tendency to respond neutrally. The role of these response styles in building predictive models is the main focus of the current study.

2. METHODS

2.1 Response Styles

Response styles refer to typical patterns in responses to Likert response scales questionnaire items (Baumgarten and Steenkamp, 2001; Weijters et al., 2010). Response styles are induced by the tendency of respondents to respond in a similar way to items, independent of the content of the item, such as yeah saying, or seeking for extreme responses. In the literature, eleven common types of response styles are distinguished:

- Acquiescence Response Style, ARS: the tendency to respond positively
- Dis-Acquiescence Response Style, DARS: the tendency to respond negatively
- Net-Acquiescence, NARS: ARS-DARS
- MidPoint Response Style, MRS: the tendency to respond neutrally
- Non-Contingent Response, NCR: the tendency to respond at random
- Extreme Response Scale, ERS: the tendency to respond extremely
- Extreme Response Scale, ERSpos and ERSneg: the tendency to respond extremely positively or extremely negatively
- Response range, RR: the difference between the maximum and minimum response
- Mild Response Style, MLRS: the tendency to provide a mild response.

Longitudinal research into the stability of response styles concludes that response styles function as relatively stable, individual characteristics that can be included as control variables in the analysis of questionnaire data (Weijters et al., 2010). Empirical studies tend to focus on the role of ERS only; for that reason, our previous study (Tempelaar et al., 2020) stayed in that tradition. Response styles constitute a collinear set of observations, by definition: for example, mild responses are the complement of extreme responses.

2.2 Dispositional Learning Analytics

Dispositional learning analytics proposes a learning analytics infrastructure that combines learning data, generated in learning activities through the traces of technology-enhanced learning systems, with learner data, such as student dispositions, values, and attitudes measured through self-report questionnaires (Buckingham Shum and Deakin Crick, 2012). In our dispositional learning analytic research (Tempelaar et al., 2020), we operationalised dispositions with the help of instruments developed in the context of contemporary social-cognitive educational research, as to make the connection with educational theory as strong as possible. Another motivation to select these instruments is that they are closely related to educational interventions. These instruments include:

- The expectancy-value framework of learning behaviour, encompassing affective, behavioural, and cognitive facets;
- The motivation and engagement framework of learning cognitions and behaviours that distinguishes learning cognitions and learning behaviours of adaptive and maladaptive types;
- Aspects of a student approach to learning (SAL) framework: cognitive processing strategies and metacognitive regulation strategies;
- The control-value theory of achievement emotions, both about learning emotions of activity and epistemic types, at the affective pole of the spectrum;
- Goal setting behaviour in the approach and avoidance dimensions;
- Academic motivations that distinguish intrinsically versus extrinsically motivated learning.

2.3 Context of the Study

This study took place in a large-scale introductory course in mathematics and statistics for first-year students in a business and economics course in the Netherlands. The education system can best be described as 'blended' or 'hybrid'. The face-to-face component is Problem-Based Learning (PBL), in small groups, coached by a tutor. The online component of the mix was two e-tutorials to learn and practice mathematics and statistics. Since most of the learning occurs in outside class self-study through the e-tutorials or other teaching materials, the teaching time is used to discuss advanced problem-solving, as in flipped-classroom design.

The subject of this study is the entire cohort of students in 2018/2019, i.e. all students who registered for the course and responded to the learning dispositions instruments: a total of about 1100 students. There was a great diversity in nationality in the student population: only 22% were educated in the Dutch secondary school system, in total of 57 nationalities were present. International education systems differ widely, especially in mathematics and statistics. Therefore, it is crucial that this current introductory module is flexible and allows for individual learning pathways, which is why we opt for a blended design with a lot of learning feedback from the students through the application of dispositional learning analytics.

In this research, we combine data from different types: course performance, Learning Management System (LMS) and e-tutorial trace variables, and learning dispositions variables measured with self-report questionnaires, in line with Winne's taxonomy of data sources (Winne, 2020).

The self-report questionnaires applied in this research are fully described in our (open-access) previous study (Tempelaar et al., 2020); for reasons of space, we will provide only a short overview here.

- Learning activity emotions from the AEQ instrument: Enjoyment, Anxiety, Boredom, Hopelessness, and their direct antecedent, Academic Control.
- Epistemic emotions, EES instrument: Surprise, Curiosity, Confusion, Anxiety, Frustration, Enjoyment, and Boredom.
- Achievement goals, AGQ instrument: Task-Approach, Task-Avoidance, Self-Approach, Self-Avoidance, Other-Approach, Other Avoidance, Potential-Approach, and Potential-Avoidance Goals.
- Motivation and engagement, MES instrument: Self-belief, Value of school, Learning focus, Planning, Study management, Persistence, Academic buoyancy, Anxiety, Failure avoidance, Uncertain control, Self-sabotage, and Disengagement.
- Attitudes to learning, SATS instrument: Affect, Cognitive competence, Value, No difficulty, Interest, and Effort.

- Approaches to learning, ILS instrument: Memorising and rehearsing, Analysing, Relating and structuring, Critical processing, Concrete processing, Self-regulation of learning processes and results, Self-regulation of learning content, External regulation of learning processes, External regulation of learning results, and Lack of regulation.
- Academic motivations, AMS instrument: Intrinsic motivation to know, to accomplish, to experience stimulation, Identified, Introjectd and External regulation, and Amotivation.

The final course performance measure, Grade, is a weighted average of the final exam score (87%) and the quiz score (13%). The performance in the exam has two components of equal weight: the math exam score (MathExam) and the exam score statistics (StatsExam). The same decomposition refers to the aggregated performance in the quizzes for both subjects: MathQuiz and StatsQuiz.

Trace data from technology-enhanced learning systems related the LMS BlackBoard and two e-tutorials systems for mathematics and statistics. BBClicks as the total number of clicks in BlackBoard is most predictive for performance. From the trace variables available from the two e-tutorial systems, we selected process variables representing the number of attempts to solve exercises: MathAttempts and StatsAttempts, and total time on task: MathTime and StatsTime. The math e-tutorial system then archives the feedback strategies that students use when solving an exercise, resulting in additional process variables MathHints, the total number of hints requested, and MathSolutions, the number of worked examples requested.

2.4 Data Analysis

All disposition questionnaires were administered with items of the Likert 1…7 type. A set of 11 response styles was calculated for all seven questionnaire administrations: ARS, ARSW, DARS, DARSW, MRS, NARS, NARSW, RR, NCR, ERSneg, and ERSpos. By definition, this set of response styles was strongly collinear, making a selection necessary. In this study, we opted for ARS, DARS and MRS.

After estimating aggregated ARS, DARS, and MRS levels for all students in the sample, we applied an instrumental variables approach. All variables were regressed on the ARS and DARS response styles (MRS is left out for collinearity), allowing to decompose all variables into two, orthogonal components: the part of the variable explained by the response styles and the part that is left unexplained (the residual of the regression). The beta weights describe that decomposition. To provide an example: the AEQ variable learning anxiety (LAX), when regressed on the response styles ARD and DARS, generated the following regression equation: $LAX = 0.100(ARS) - 0.537(DARS)$, $R^2 = 0.367$.

This procedure was applied to all variables under study, including the 'objectively' measured variables. That is, self-report constructs, trace variables of the process and product types, and course performance variables were all assigned variable-specific scores for ARS and DARS.

3. RESULTS

3.1 Response Styles Descriptives

Descriptive statistics of response styles of different instruments are provided in Table 1. There are considerable differences in these statistics between the instruments, which can be explained by the balance between adaptive or positive items in the instrument on the one side and negative or maladaptive items on the other side. For instance, the highest ARS score is for the achievement goal instrument AGQ, since all its items correspond to achievement motives that are part of most students' goal-setting behaviour. In contrast, DARS scores are high for the AEQ instrument, which counts several items relating to negative emotions.

There exists collinearity amongst the set of response styles, resulting from the overlap in their definitions. For instance, MRS is the complement of ARS and DARS, and therefore we will restrict the subsequent analysis to ARS and DARS, leaving aside MRS.

Table 1. Descriptive statistics of response styles measures and the overall mean and median of all response styles

	Mean	Median	MES	EES	AGQ	ILS	AEQ	AMS	SATS
ARS	0.56	0.56	0.57	0.45	0.80	0.61	0.33	0.61	0.54
DARS	0.28	0.28	0.33	0.30	0.08	0.22	0.51	0.25	0.31
MRS	0.16	0.15	0.10	0.24	0.12	0.18	0.16	0.14	0.15
NARS	0.28	0.28	0.24	0.15	0.73	0.39	-0.18	0.36	0.23
RR	5.17	5.14	5.86	4.34	3.49	4.84	5.03	5.68	6.95
NCR	1.16	1.15	0.76	1.69	1.13	0.98	1.28	1.07	1.22
ERSneg	0.15	0.13	0.26	0.16	0.04	0.09	0.34	0.06	0.20
ERSpos	0.34	0.34	0.40	0.19	0.63	0.28	0.13	0.42	0.35
MRLS	0.49	0.49	0.34	0.66	0.32	0.63	0.54	0.52	0.45

3.2 Individual Response Style Scores

The next step after determining response style scores for each individual student in each disposition instrument was to average these scores over all seven instruments, generating aggregate ARS and DARS scores for all students. The pattern that arises is pictured in Figure 1: all 1113 students are included in the scatter. Overall, there is a clear negative relationship between ARS and DARS scores: the correlation equals $r = -.646$. Such a negative relationship is natural: the more items a student answers in the acquiescence range, the fewer items are left over to provide answers in the dis-acquiescence range or neutral. In this paper, we will not discuss individual response style scores in more detail but only use these scores as instruments to derive the response style composition of variables.

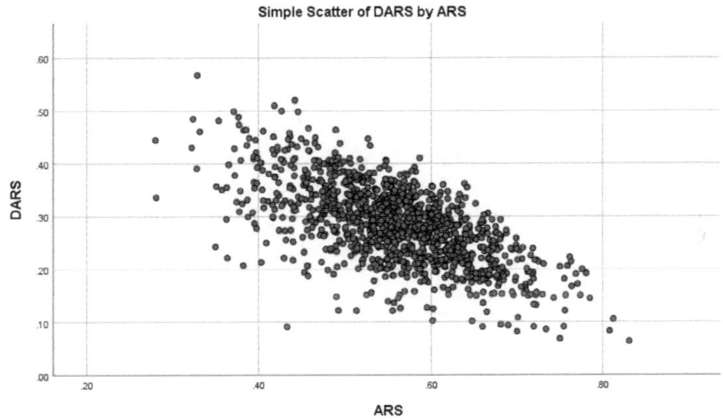

Figure 1. Scatterplot of aggregated ARS, acquiescence scores versus aggregated DARS, dis-acquiescence scores, for all 113 students

3.3 Classification of Variables based on Response Styles

The availability of response style measures allows new ways to categorise our data in educational studies. Rather than using the dichotomy of self-reported data versus objectively scored, we can position each variable of each data type in a two-dimensional plane of response styles: ARS and DARS. The data required for this presentation is in Table 2. It provides for all variables in the analysis the two response style components: the betas of the regression of the variable on ARS and DARs, representing the share of ARS and the share of DARS in explained variation. That explained variation is provided in the last column of Table 2, as the R^2 percentage.

Table 2. Response style components of course performance variables, trace variables and disposition variables, together with explained variation by the ARS and DARS response styles

	ARS	DARS	R^2		ARS	DARS	R^2
Course performance				Trace variables			
Grade	0.129	0.405	11.3%	BBclicks	0.093	0.017	0.7%
MathExam	0.090	0.345	8.6%	StatsTime	0.056	-0.080	1.5%
StatsExam	0.138	0.387	9.9%	StatsAttempts	0.098	-0.033	1.5%
MathQz	0.137	0.304	5.8%	MathTime	0.096	-0.048	1.8%
StatsQz	0.088	0.250	4.2%	MathAttempts	0.093	-0.115	3.5%
Motivation & Engagement Scale				MathSolutions	0.013	-0.217	5.1%
Self-Belief	0.423	0.404	12.1%	MathHints	0.024	-0.037	0.3%
Persistence	0.422	0.235	10.5%	Learning strategies			
Learning Focus	0.517	0.213	17.0%	Relating & structure	0.546	0.230	19.1%
Value School	0.481	0.214	14.4%	Critical process.	0.337	0.078	8.6%
Study Managm	0.328	0.099	7.5%	Memorise & rehear	0.338	-0.040	13.3%
Planning	0.351	0.095	8.9%	Analysing	0.486	0.115	17.8%
Ac Buoyancy	-0.044	0.264	8.7%	Concrete proc.	0.456	0.111	15.6%
Disengament	-0.308	-0.362	8.1%	SelfRegulatingProc	0.466	0.056	18.7%
Self Sabotage	-0.197	-0.331	6.4%	SelfRegulatingCont	0.291	-0.060	11.1%
Uncert Contr	-0.100	-0.466	16.7%	ExternalRegulProc	0.367	0.018	12.7%
Failure avoid	0.023	-0.341	12.5%	ExternalRegulCont	0.543	0.236	18.7%
Anxiety	0.142	-0.408	26.2%	Lack of Regulation	-0.005	-0.496	24.3%
Epistemic Emotions				Achievement Goals			
Curious	0.405	0.151	10.8%	Task Approach	0.382	0.267	8.6%
Surprised	0.185	-0.187	11.3%	Task Avoid	0.339	0.127	7.6%
Confused	0.036	-0.445	22.0%	Self Approach	0.484	0.143	16.6%
Anxious	0.111	-0.503	33.8%	Self Avoid	0.447	0.096	15.4%
Frustrated	-0.083	-0.498	20.2%	Other Approach	0.288	0.029	7.3%
Excited	0.299	0.164	5.3%	Other Avoid	0.343	0.011	11.1%
Bored	-0.290	-0.381	8.7%	Potential Approach	0.438	0.166	12.6%
Activity Emotions				Potential Avoid	0.435	0.092	14.6%
Learn Anxiety	0.100	-0.537	36.7%	Academic Motivation Scale			
Learn Boredom	-0.317	-0.435	11.3%	IntrinMotivKnow	0.516	0.125	19.9%
Learn Hopeless	-0.106	-0.618	31.0%	IntrinMotivAccom	0.528	0.027	26.1%
Learn Enjoym	0.381	0.161	9.2%	IntrinMotivStim	0.358	-0.113	19.4%
Acad Control	0.236	0.585	22.1%	ExtrinMotivIden	0.422	0.137	12.2%
Attitudes towards learning math & stats				ExtrinMotivIntro	0.414	-0.117	24.7%
Affect	0.078	0.515	21.9%	ExtrinMotivExt	0.311	0.035	8.4%
CognCompeten	0.107	0.490	18.4%	Amotivation	-0.234	-0.344	7.0%
Value	0.368	0.404	10.7%				
No Difficulty	-0.192	0.111	7.7%				
Interest	0.395	0.175	9.8%				
Effort	0.382	0.094	10.8%				

There exist large differences in the role of the ARS and DARS response styles in all variables. As could be expected, their role is neglectable in the trace variables: as the obvious example of 'objective' data, these measures are not influenced by response styles. For example, ARS and DARS explain less than 1% of the variation of BlackBoard clicks. In contrast: there are variables for which response styles account for more than

25% of the variation at the other side of the spectrum. The different facets of anxiety are a great example. The Anxiety variable part of the MES instrument finds 26.2% of its variation explained by response styles, Anxious as a scale of epistemic emotions even more than one-third of explained variation and Learning Anxiety, scale of activity emotions, champions with 36.7% explained variation. However, the most remarkable observations in the left upper part of Table 2 refer to the course performance variables. Where one would have intuitively expected these variables to act as an objective measure, similar to the trace variables, they do no. For the three most crucial performance scores, the two examination scores and the final grade, explained variation by ARS and DARS is around 10%, indicating that response styles have an undeniable role in predicting course performance.

Figure 2 provides a graphical representation of these data in the ARS versus DARS plane. Each dot represents a disposition variable, each square represents a course performance variable, and each diamond represents a trace variable. Where space allows, variable names are added. Such space is not available for the trace variables: they cluster around the origin, all carry relatively small ARS and DARS components. Course performance variables also cluster together, distant from the origin, having a relatively small, positive ARS component but a larger, positive DARS component. The only type of variable that occupies all quadrants of the ARS-DARS plane is the survey-based disposition type. We find two learning attitudes, Cognitive Competence and Affect, together with Academic Control, in the neighbourhood of the course performance variables, in the first quadrant: positive ARS and positive DARS components. All of these, together with Self-Belief, are self-efficacy type of variables. Only two variables occupy the second quadrant: negative ARS, positive DARS: NoDifficulty and Academic Buoyancy. We find many more variables, all of the maladaptive type, in the third quadrant: negative components of ARS and DARS. The epistemic and activity versions of Boredom, Hopelessness, and Disengagement are all examples. In the fourth quadrant, we find the above-mentioned group of anxiety-related variables and Confusion. These variables carry a positive ARS component and a negative DARS component. A large group of disposition variables is located at the right: large, positive ARS components, small, mostly positive DARS components.

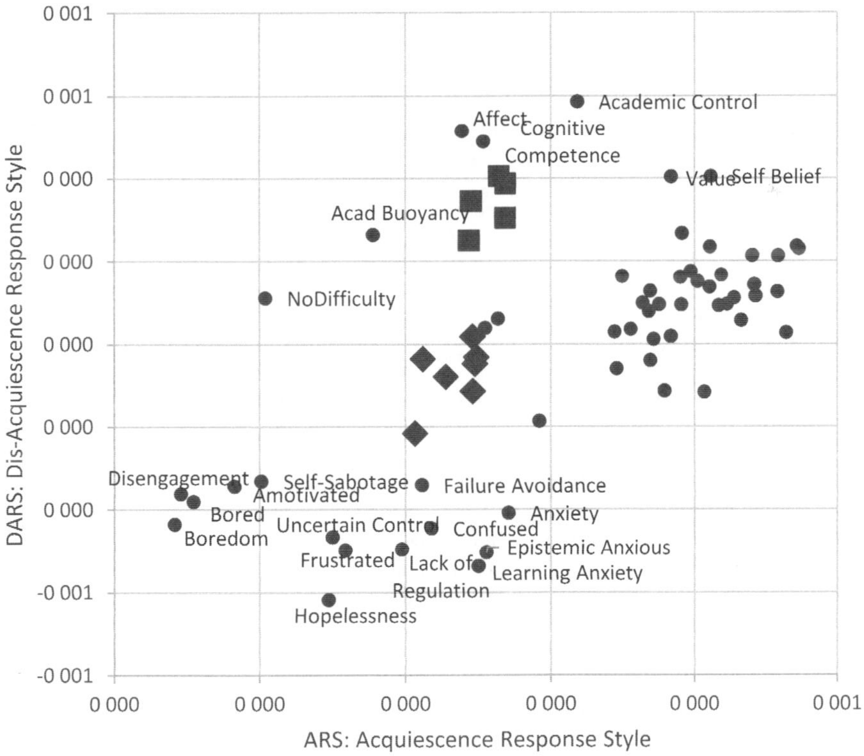

Figure 2. Regression betas of ARS and DARS from regressions of performance variables, denoted ■, trace variables, denoted ♦, and disposition variables, denoted ●, on ARS and DARS

4. DISCUSSION AND CONCLUSION

The most appealing and successful learning analytics functionality is that of developing prediction models, signal students at risk of dropout or discover the optimal individual learning feedback. One can represent the task of predictive modeling with the help of the graphical representation provided above, realizing that the figure is limited to variation within the ARS-DARS dimensions: find a combination of trace and disposition variables that best approximates the course performance variable one wishes to predict. If we apply two predictors, this comes down to searching for two trace or disposition points in the graph that, once connected through a line, hit the point representing the performance variable to be predicted. Inspection of Figure 2 clarifies that the trace variables will never be part of such set of predictors: all situated around the origin of the ARS-DARS plane, they are not instrumental in predicting the response style component in the performance variables. Given the position of these performance variables, the preferred combination of predictors will be taken from the first quadrant, the adaptive, self-efficacy-based dispositions, and the third quadrant, the maladaptive dispositions.

A second conclusion refers to the consistency of the typology of related scales. Although the timing of the epistemic emotions instrument at the start of the course differs strongly from the activity emotions instrument halfway's timing, all three anxiety-related scales consistently position themselves in the same quadrant of the ARS-DARS plane. Making the bias coming with response styles predictable, thus accountable.

Given the response style component in performance variables, optimal prediction models take these ARS and DARS components into account. One can do this by isolating these components from the disposition data and adding them to the set of trace variables, but seeking parsimonious models, one better applies these dispositional variables themselves. In other words: optimal LA prediction models are composed predictor variables of trace and disposition types, where dispostions are best taken as a mixture of adaptive variables, such as self-belief, and maladaptive variables, such as boredom or disengagement.

REFERENCES

Bolt, DM, Lu, Y, & Kim, JS 2014, 'Measurement and control of response styles using anchoring vignettes: A model-based approach', *Psychological Methods*, vol. 19, no. 4, pp. 528–541. DOI 10.1037/ met0000016.

Buckingham Shum, S & Deakin Crick, R 2012, 'Learning Dispositions and Transferable Competencies: Pedagogy, Modelling and Learning Analytics', in S Buckingham Shum, D Gasevic, & R Ferguson (eds.), *Proceedings of the 2nd International Conference on Learning Analytics and Knowledge*. ACM, New York, NY, USA.

Cheung, GW, & Rensvold, RB 2000, 'Assessing extreme and acquiescence response sets in cross-cultural research using structural equations modeling'. *Journal of Cross-Cultural Psychology*, vol. 31, no. 2, pp. 187–212. DOI 10.1177/0022022100031002003.

Dawson, S, Joksimovic, S, Poquet, O & Siemens, G 2019, 'Increasing the Impact of Learning Analytics', in Proceedings of the 9th International Conference on Learning Analytics & Knowledge (LAK19), Association for Computing Machinery, New York, NY, USA, pp. 446–455. DOI 10.1145/3303772.3303784.

Henninger M, & Meiser T 2020, 'Different approaches to modeling response styles in divide-by-total item response theory models (part 1): A model integration', *Psychological Methods*, vol. 25, no. 5, pp. 560-576. DOI 10.1037/met0000249. PMID: 33017166.

Henninger M, & Meiser T 2020, 'Different approaches to modeling response styles in divide-by-total item response theory models (part 2): Applications and novel extensions', *Psychological Methods*, vol. 25, no. 5, pp. 577-595, DOI 10.1037/met0000268. PMID: 33017167.

Ifenthaler, D, & Yau, JYK 2020, 'Utilising learning analytics for study success: a systematic review', *Educational Technology Research and Development*, vol. 68, no. 4, pp. 1961–1990, DOI10.1007/s11423-020-09788-z.

Knight, S, Wise, A, & Ochoa, X 2019, 'Fostering an impactful field of learning analytics', *Journal of Learning Analytics*, vol. 6, no. 3, pp. 1–4. DOI 10.18608/jla.2019.63.1.

SOLAR 2020, Webinar eight: What Do We Mean by Rigour in Learning Analytics? (https://www.solaresearch.org/community/webinars/). Recordings available at https://www.youtube.com/watch?v=RxGa6MvCX6Y&feature=youtu.be.

Tempelaar, D, Rienties, B, & Nguyen, Q 2020, 'Subjective data, objective data and the role of bias in predictive modelling: Lessons from a dispositional learning analytics application', *PLOS ONE*, vol. 15, no. 6: e0233977, DOI 10.1371/journal.pone.0233977.

Winne, PH 2020, 'Construct and consequential validity for learning analytics based on trace data', *Computers in Human Behavior,* vol. 112, no. 106457, DOI 10.1016/j.chb.2020.106457.

A REVIEW OF EDUCATIONAL RECOMMENDER SYSTEMS FOR TEACHERS

Mbarek Dhahri[1] and Mohamed Koutheair Khribi[2]
[1]*Higher School of Sciences and Technologies of Tunis, University of Tunis, Tunisia*
[2]*Technologies of Information and Communication Lab*
Higher School of Sciences and Techniques of Tunis, University of Tunis, Tunisia
5, Av. Taha Hussein, B.P. 56, Bab Mnara 1008, Tunis, Tunisia

ABSTRACT

Recommender Systems (RS) in e-learning has attracted several researchers aiming basically at scaffolding learners in locating relevant learning resources that meet their learning needs and profiles. Whereas a number of review studies have been carried out in the area of educational recommender systems, there is a limited information in the literature review in the specific domain of recommendation systems for teachers. The objective of this work is to summarize the current research efforts in the field of teacher-oriented recommender systems. By performing this systematic review, 32 papers were selected for further analysis. The obtained results show that educational portals and repositories are widely used as learning environments where recommendations occur. The finding of this review further show that personalized recommendations for teachers and teaching practices improvements are the main issues addressed by RS for teachers. Furthermore, the hybrid approach for recommendation and the evaluation by experiment are the most used, occurring in 43,75% of the selected reviewed papers. We are availing the key findings of this work to propose a teacher recommender system that provides teachers with the most relevant open educational resources (OER) retrieved from collections of resources aligned to the UNESCO ICT Competency Framework for Teachers (CFT).

KEYWORDS

e-Learning, Recommender System, Personalization, Teacher Recommendation, ICT Competencies for Teachers, Online Learning Environments

1. INTRODUCTION

Recommender systems (RSs) can be defined as software tools which provide suggestions for the most relevant items to particular users (Lu *et al.*, 2015). They have been implemented in a wide range of application areas including e-commerce, e-library and e-learning. Commonly used recommendation techniques include Content-based filtering (CBF), Collaborative filtering (CF), knowledge-based (KB) and hybrid approaches (Verbert *et al.*, 2012).

In the context of Technology Enhanced Learning (TEL), recommender system has become more and more popular during the last decade, especially with the widespread of online learning environments and repositories (Lu *et al.*, 2015). Educational recommender systems aim basically (1) to help learners/teachers to find different types of learning materials through the learning/teaching process based on their individual interests; (2) to recommend learning pathways or educational scenarios; (3) to suggest users with same profiles (i.e., peers); (4) to predict appropriate rates and ranks, etc. (Khribi *et al.*, 2015). The majority of existing TEL RS targets learners and attempts to integrate their personal attributes in the recommendation process (Sergis *et al.*, 2014a). On the other hand, as there is an increased interest by teachers to improve their information and communication technology (ICT) in education competencies and their learning and teaching practices availing learning technologies, some existing researches have been conducted attempting to recommend adequate training content and educational resources for teachers based on their profiles and needs.

In this paper, we present a systematic review of existing recommender systems for teachers during the period 2009 to 2021. The objective of this review is threefold: (1) identify learning environments where recommendation to teachers occur, (2) investigate addressed issues, and (3) determine which recommendation approaches and related evaluation methods were used.

The rest of the paper is organized as follows: Section 2 details the research method, Section 3 provides proposed answers to key research questions as well as discusses the main raised issues. Finally, Section 4 presents the conclusion and future work.

2. METHODOLOGY

The proposed review has been carried out based on the methodological provided by (Kitchenham and Charters, 2007), (Rivera *et al.*, 2018) and (Pinho *et al.*, 2019). This method highlights several steps that guide the systematic reviews: identification of research questions, formulation of the research strategy, selection of primary studies according to inclusion/exclusion criteria, and the mapping study findings. These steps are further featured in the remainder of this section.

2.1 Research Questions

The research questions addressed by this study are:

1. What are the major types of online learning environments in which recommendation systems are included? This research question aims to spot the most prominent types of online learning environments in which recommendations occur, to name but a few: Learning Management System (LMS), Courseware, Repositories, Learning Activity Management System (LAMS), etc. Findings related to this question would help a lot to identify the most common online learning environments in which the teacher-oriented recommender systems are integrated, and those which are so far overlooked.
2. What are the main issues addressed by teacher recommendation systems? In this research question, issues refer to the challenges addressed by the teacher RS, e.g., personalized recommendations for teachers, improving teaching by recommending suitable practices, etc. Results of this question would help understanding RS added values and strengths when integrating a teacher-oriented RS in such learning environment.
3. What recommendation approaches are mostly used in teacher recommendation systems? This research question aims to investigate major approaches used to generate recommendations such as Content-Based Filtering (CBF), Collaborative Filtering (CF), etc. which would be understanding commonly used approaches and techniques applied in teacher-oriented recommendation systems.
4. What evaluation methods are applied to prove the efficiency of teacher recommendation systems? This research question aims to indicate which validation strategies are applied to recommendation systems e.g. survey, experiment, etc. This would help shedding light on how existing teacher-oriented recommendations are evaluated.

2.2 Search Process

Searching and locating suitable resources for the study were established through online search from the following digital sources: IEEE Xplore, ScienceDirect, SpringerLink, Taylor & Francis and Google Scholar. We set our database search query using the following terms with the combination operator "AND" and "OR" as: Education AND (Teacher OR Educator) AND "Recommender System". The number of studies found was 602 eventually relevant papers. We read the papers' titles, abstracts, and keywords. This filtering procedure produced a total of 32 papers (note that the same paper may occurs in more than one source). The selected primary studies were then read and analyzed. The research was undertaken in April 2020 and updated in January 2021.

2.3 Selection of Criteria

In this step, in order for the selection of existing studies to be ensured seamlessly, we defined exclusion criteria to decide whether a paper is directly linked to search query:

- Papers not written in English.

- Papers not targeting teacher-oriented RS.
- Duplicates studies: only the most current included.
- Summary articles, tutorials, workshop reports.

If the study met at least one of the criteria listed below, it would be excluded from the process. The table 1 shows the number of studies retrieved and relevant after the application of the exclusion criteria.

Table 1. Summary table of search results

Source	Number of studies	Selected
Springer	254	11
IEEE Xplore	70	9
ScienceDirect	180	5
Google Scholar	First 30 results	5
Taylor & Francis	68	2
Total	**602**	**32**

3. REVIEW OF EXISTING RS FOR TEACHERS

In this section, we present an overview of selected articles and results of our survey on teacher-oriented recommender systems.

3.1 Overview

Authors in (García *et al.*, 2009) affirmed that educational RSs can help teachers to improve learning performance. Authors in (Manouselis *et al.*, 2010) concluded in their study that as opposed to movie or music recommender, the field of learning resources is very diverse and complex due to the variety in the potential educational uses of learning resource. In (Garcia-Valdez *et al.*, 2010), the authors explored the use of fuzzy approach in educational recommender systems. (Brusilovsky *et al.*, 2010) demonstrated how social navigation can be implemented in the context of a large distributed educational digital library. (Zapata *et al.*, 2011) proposed a hybrid recommendation method to assist teachers in the search and selection process in learning objects repositories. (Bahritidinov *et al.*, 2011) proposed a recommendation algorithm that recommends relevant collaborative teams of teachers to the coordinators of courses or units of learning. In (Ferreira-Satler *et al.*, 2012), the authors demonstrated how a fuzzy ontology can be used to represent teacher profile into a recommender engine and enhances the teacher's activities into e-learning environment. (Fazeli *et al.*, 2012) proposed a social recommender to assist young teachers to find most suitable peers to address their problems. In other work (Fazeli *et al.*, 2014), the authors enhanced a trust-based recommender algorithm with social data obtained from monitoring the activities of teachers in order to help them to find the most learning resources. Another peer-based recommender system has been proposed by (Miranda *et al.*, 2012) that combines collaborative and content filtering and enriched with contextual information to recommend online comments written by teachers to their peers about their experience related to educational activities in an online educational community. (Limongelli *et al.*, 2013) addressed the problem of helping teachers to retrieve didactic material from a repository through a didactic social network where teachers with similar teaching styles can assist each other to find educational material. In other work (Limongelli *et al.*, 2016), the authors presented a recommender system to assist teachers to build their courses through the Moodle learning management system. (Mottus *et al.*, 2013) identified the goal of generating a visual dashboard for teachers to allow them easy access to complex educational information. (Gallego *et al.*, 2013) proposed a new model to produce proactive context-aware recommendations on resources while creating a new learning object (LO) that a teacher performs by using an authoring tool. (Cobos *et al.*, 2013) proposed a recommendation system of pedagogical patterns allowing teachers to access to patterns that provide solutions to the different problems they meet and assist them to accomplish their goals related to their courses. (Soldatova *et al.*, 2014) addressed the issue of recommending e-learning tools for teaching stuff of engineering disciplines by defining criteria that will be used to create an e-learning recommender system. In

(Sergis *et al.*, 2014b), (Sergis and Sampson, 2015) and (Sergis and Sampson, 2016), the authors tackled the problem of ignoring the potential benefits of profiling teachers' particular professional characteristics. They proposed a recommender system to help teachers to find LO from existing repositories in a unified manner namely by automatically constructing their ICT complex profiles and exploiting these profiles for more efficient LO selection. (El-Bishouty *et al.*, 2014) developed a smart e-course recommender tool to support teachers to extend their existing e-courses in learning management system by adding a list of recommended LOs to courses. (Zervas *et al.*, 2015) proposed a recommender system to support teachers to find and select the suitable remote and visited labs based on core pedagogical elements of their learning designs and their information and communication technology competences profiles. (Tewari *et al.*, 2015) proposed a recommender system that analyses learner's opinions about contents and recommends the teachers who have uploaded the content of the web site to modify the particular portion of the subject topic which is difficult to understand by learners using opinion mining. In (Revilla Muñoz *et al.*, 2016), the authors defined and implemented a recommender system to support teachers to find the most suitable solutions to their ICT problems from others teachers. (Karga and Satratzemi, 2018) and (Karga and Satratzemi, 2019) found in their research that Mentor, a recommender system integrated into learning activities management system, facilitates the sharing of good practices and help teachers to find a good learning design to rely upon for creating their own.

It is noteworthy that the current review represents the second milestone of an ongoing research aiming at developing a teacher recommender system that is intended to suggest relevant OER aligned to the UNESCO ICT competency framework. The first milestone of the project (Dhahri and Khribi, 2021) explored teachers' ICT competency assessment realm by identifying and analyzing existing tools and approaches for assessing teachers' ICT competency level.

3.2 Answers to Research Questions

In this section, we present the results grouped by research questions.

3.2.1 Learning Environments

In table 2 we show the results of the first research question found in the selected papers.

Table 2. Distribution by learning environment

Learning Environment	Number of studies	%
Learning Management System (LMS)	7	21,88
Educational Portal	10	31,25
Repository	8	25,00
Collaborative Authoring Tool	1	3,13
Social Platform	2	6,25
Learning Content Management System (LCMS)	1	3,13
Digital ecosystems	1	3,13
Learning Activity Management System (LAMS)	2	6,25

LMSs are software tools that provide mainly course management functionality and basic facilities of course authoring tools (Soldatova *et al.*, 2014). Educational portal is a web-based interface with learning resources (Manouselis *et al.*, 2010). Repositories are digital libraries for publishing, searching and retrieval of instructional resources (Zapata *et al.*, 2013). Collaborative authoring tools provide environments that facilitate teacher participation in knowledge sharing activities, retrieving, and reusing of materials and activities created by colleagues (Bahritidinov *et al.*, 2011). Social platforms are online social networks designed to support professional development (Fazeli *et al.*, 2012). LCMS provide spaces where teachers publish, catalog and download learning resources (Ferreira-Satler *et al.*, 2012). Digital ecosystems can be considered as platforms for cooperation, sharing and access to knowledge in order to facilitate learning (Mohamed Ali *et al.*, 2017). LAMS are tools for designing, managing and delivering sequences of learning activities (Karga and Satratzemi, 2018).

Results show that around 31% of the papers reviewed choose educational portals to make recommendation to teachers due to the user feedbacks (ratings, comments, tagging) that offer a portal. These forms of feedback demonstrated their ability to guide portal users to relevant resources (Brusilovsky et al., 2010). Other primary studies (around 25%) focused on Learning Objects (LOs) recommendation and personalization into LO repositories. In the educational field, there is a lot of repositories and courseware where teachers can share their resources and locate educational material of interest to reuse (Limongelli et al., 2013). Furthermore, there are around 22% of the reviewed papers which referred to learning management systems to provide recommendations. As can be seen in Figure 1, few reviewed studies have been focusing on collaborative authoring tools and social platforms. On the other hand, there is a significant interest in using educational portals, then repositories, and learning management systems to provide recommendations for teachers.

3.2.2 Recommendation Issues

In table 3 we show the results of the second research question found in the selected papers. Personalized recommendations for teachers and improving teaching practices are the main issues addressed by teacher-oriented RSs (around 34% for each one). Instead of simple recommendation which provides Top-N items, in a personalized recommendation, the teacher attributes (i.e., prior knowledge, learning style, etc.) are used in the process of recommendation (Sergis and Sampson, 2016). Studies like (Sergis *et al.*, 2014b), (Zervas et al., 2015) and (Sergis and Sampson, 2016) proposed teachers' ICT competence-based LO recommendations. Other studies addressed different issues: social navigation (12.5%), prediction accuracy, teaching capacity building, support program on ICT for teachers, proactive contextaware recommendations in e-learning.

Table 3. Distribution by issue

Issue	Number of studies	%
Improve teaching practices	11	34,38
Personalized recommendations for teachers	11	34,38
Social navigation	4	12,50
LO personalized search	2	6,25
Proactive contextaware recommendations in e-Learning	1	3,13
Prediction accuracy	1	3,13
Support program on ICT for teachers	1	3,13
Teachers' capacity building	1	3,13

Figure 2 show the comparative panorama between the results. Therefore, user profiling in teacher-oriented recommender systems should be an important consideration for educational recommendation systems for teachers.

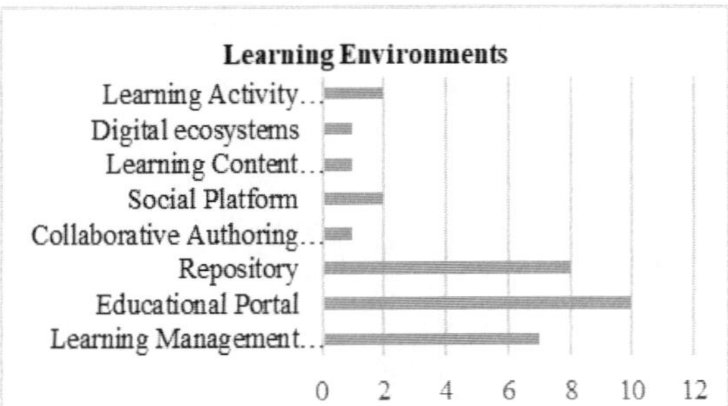

Figure 1. Learning environments

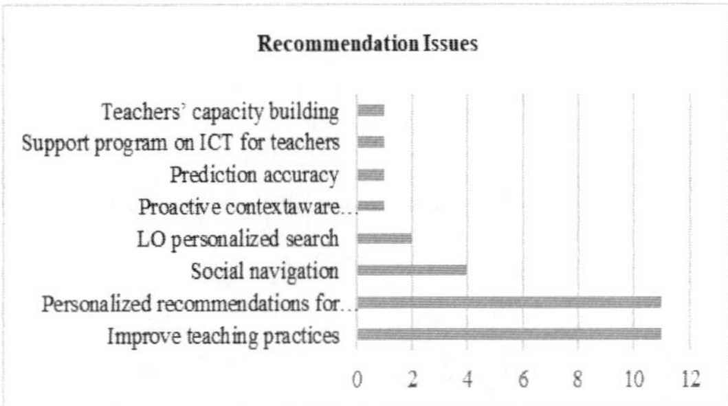

Figure 2. Recommendation issues

3.2.3 Recommendation Approaches

The results discovered in the selected articles related to the third research question are shown in table 4.

Table 4. Distribution by recommendation approach

Approach	Number of studies	%
Hybrid Filtering	14	43,75
Content-Based Filtering	9	28,13
Collaborative Filtering	8	25,00
Fuzzy-Based	1	3,13

The analysis of the results demonstrates that the hybrid approach is frequently used in teacher-oriented RS. As can be seen in Figure 3, around 44% of the papers reviewed combine several recommendation techniques. Others recommendation approaches used include collaborative filtering (25%) and content-based filtering (around 28%). Collaborative filtering recommendation approaches assist users to make their choices based on the opinions of others users who share same interests (Lu *et al.*, 2015). However, content-based filtering recommendation approaches suggest items that are similar to items already preferred by a specific user (Lu *et al.*, 2015). Other less commonly used approach is fuzzy-based RS. For example, (Ferreira-Satler et al., 2012) utilize fuzzy ontology to represent user profiles into a recommender engine. The most preference of a hybrid approach is to enhance the efficiency of the recommender model and get over the issues of other types of recommender such as collaborative and content-based filtering.

3.2.4 Evaluation Methods

The analysis of the results of the fourth research question indicates that around 22% of the selected studies did not carry out any evaluation method as shown in table 5. Around 44% of the studies had been evaluated through an experiment. For instance, (Sergis and Sampson, 2016) performed experiments with data from three repositories to demonstrate the benefits of the proposed system. Around 19% of selected papers reported case study. (Manouselis *et al.*, 2010) conducted a case study to understand the teacher's perceived usefulness and quality of the resources they accessed. Around 16% of the studies proposed RSs which had been evaluated via a survey. (Hariharan et al., 2019) presented a questionnaire to understand the level of acceptance and support for the recommendation method.

Table 5. Distribution by evaluation method

Evaluation method	Number of studies	%
Case study	6	18,75
Survey	5	15,63
Experiment	14	43,75
None	7	21,88

As can be seen in Figure 4, the analysis of the results demonstrates a tendency amongst researchers in the experiment evaluation method as a method of approval of their proposals.

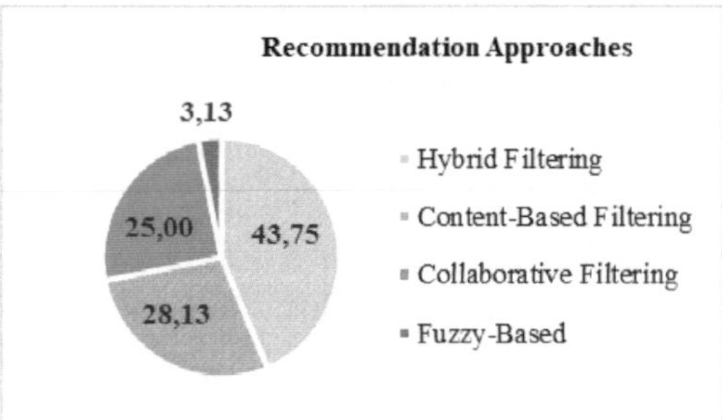

Figure 3. Recommendation approaches

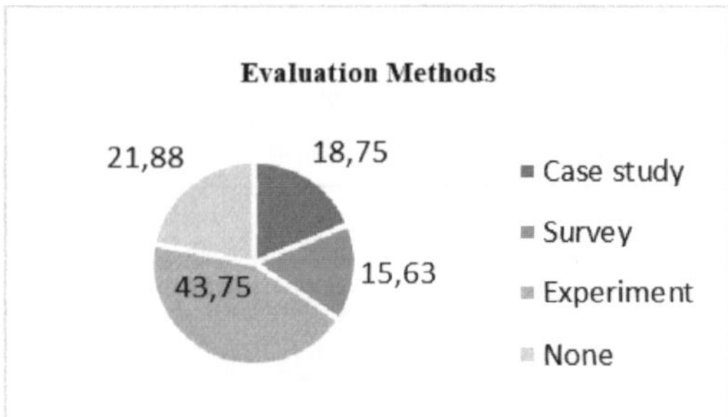

Figure 4. Evaluation methods

4. CONCLUSION

The objective of this review is to conduct a literature review to examine existing recommendation systems for teachers. It represents an important milestone towards proposing an ICT-CFT recommender system for teachers that recommends training material based on teachers' ICT competencies. In this review, 32 primary studies were selected and examined. Then, selected papers were classified according to a set of selected features namely: learning environments, recommendation issues, recommendation approaches and evaluation methods.

This study has revealed that educational portals, repositories, and learning management systems are the widely learning environments used for recommending educational resources to teachers. Results further showed that personalized recommendations for teachers and improving teachers' practices are the main issues addressed by these RS. Moreover, the hybrid approach is the most frequent type of recommender system used in teacher-oriented recommendation systems. In order for the recommendation approaches efficiency to be validated, the method of evaluation by experiment is the mostly used one.

In our future work, we propose to develop a teacher recommender system based on ICT-CFT harnessing OER, that can be embedded in portals and repositories gathering collections of various ICT-CFT aligned resources.

REFERENCES

Bahritidinov, B. *et al.* (2011) 'Recommending teachers for collaborative authoring tools', in *11th IEEE International Conference on Advanced Learning Technologies, ICALT 2011*, pp. 438–442. doi: 10.1109/ICALT.2011.137.

Brusilovsky, P. *et al.* (2010) 'Social navigation for educational digital libraries', *Procedia Computer Science*, 1(2), pp. 2889–2897. doi: 10.1016/S1877-0509(10)00330-3.

Cobos, C. *et al.* (2013) 'A hybrid system of pedagogical pattern recommendations based on singular value decomposition and variable data attributes', *Information Processing and Management*, 49(3), pp. 607–625. doi: 10.1016/j.ipm.2012.12.002.

Dhahri, M. and Khribi, M. K. (2021) 'Teachers' Information and Communication Technology (ICT) Assessment Tools : A Review', in *IEEE 21th International Conference on Advanced Learning Technologies, ICALT 2021 (accepted)*.

El-Bishouty, M. M. *et al.* (2014) 'Smart e-course recommender based on learning styles', *Journal of Computers in Education*, 1(1), pp. 99–111. doi: 10.1007/s40692-014-0003-0.

Fazeli, S. *et al.* (2012) 'Exploring social recommenders for teacher networks to address challenges of starting teachers', in *8th International Conference on Networked Learning 2012*, pp. 74–80.

Fazeli, S. *et al.* (2014) 'Towards a Social Trust-Aware Recommender for Teachers', in Manouselis, N. et al. (eds) *Recommender Systems for Technology Enhanced Learning: Research Trends and Applications*. Springer, New York, NY, pp. 177–194. doi: 10.1007/978-1-4939-0530-0.

Ferreira-Satler, M. *et al.* (2012) 'Fuzzy ontologies-based user profiles applied to enhance e-learning activities', *Soft Computing*, 16(7), pp. 1129–1141. doi: 10.1007/s00500-011-0788-y.

Gallego, D. *et al.* (2013) 'Enhanced recommendations for e-Learning authoring tools based on a proactive context-aware recommender', in *Frontiers in Education Conference, FIE*, pp. 1393–1395. doi: 10.1109/FIE.2013.6685060.

Garcia-Valdez, M. *et al.* (2010) 'Fuzzy inference for Learning Object Recommendation', in *International Conference on Fuzzy Systems, Barcelona*, pp. 1–6. doi: 10.1109/FUZZY.2010.5584322.

García, E. *et al.* (2009) 'An architecture for making recommendations to courseware authors using association rule mining and collaborative filtering', *User Model User-Adap Inter*, pp. 99–132. doi: 10.1007/s11257-008-9047-z.

Hariharan, M. *et al.* (2019) 'Teaching Style Recommender using Machine Learning', *1st IEEE International Conference on Advances in Information Technology, ICAIT 2019*, pp. 238–244. doi: 10.1109/ICAIT47043.2019.8987364.

Karga, S. and Satratzemi, M. (2018) 'A hybrid recommender system integrated into LAMS for learning designers', *Education and Information Technologies*, 23(3), pp. 1297–1329. doi: 10.1007/s10639-017-9668-0.

Karga, S. and Satratzemi, M. (2019) 'Using explanations for recommender systems in learning design settings to enhance teachers' acceptance and perceived experience', *Education and Information Technologies*, 24(5), pp. 2953–2974. doi: 10.1007/s10639-019-09909-z.

Khribi, M. K. *et al.* (2015) 'Recommendation systems for personalized technology-enhanced learning', in Kinshuk and Huang, R. (eds) *Ubiquitous Learning Environments and Technologies*. Springer-Verlag Berlin Heidelberg, pp. 159–180. doi: https://doi.org/10.1007/978-3-662-44659-1_9.

Kitchenham, B. and Charters, S. (2007) *Guidelines for performing Systematic Literature Reviews in Software Engineering, EBSE Technical Report*. doi: 10.1541/ieejias.126.589.

Limongelli, C. *et al.* (2013) 'A teaching-style based social network for didactic building and sharing', *Lecture Notes in Computer Science (including subseries Lecture Notes in Artificial Intelligence and Lecture Notes in Bioinformatics)*, 7926 LNAI, pp. 774–777. doi: 10.1007/978-3-642-39112-5-110.

Limongelli, C. *et al.* (2016) 'A recommendation module to help teachers build courses through the Moodle Learning Management System', *New Review of Hypermedia and Multimedia*, 22(1–2), pp. 58–82. doi: 10.1080/13614568.2015.1077277.

Lu, J. *et al.* (2015) 'Recommender system application developments: A survey', *Decision Support Systems*, 74, pp. 12–32. doi: 10.1016/j.dss.2015.03.008.

Manouselis, N. *et al.* (2010) 'Collaborative recommendation of e-learning resources: An experimental investigation', *Journal of Computer Assisted Learning*, 26(4), pp. 227–242. doi: 10.1111/j.1365-2729.2010.00362.x.

Miranda, C. *et al.* (2012) 'A hybrid peer recommender system for an online community of teachers', in *CEUR Workshop Proceedings*.

Mohamed Ali, B. A. *et al.* (2017) 'Recommendation of pedagogical resources within a learning ecosystem', in *9th International Conference on Management of Digital EcoSystems, MEDES 2017*, pp. 14–21. doi: 10.1145/3167020.3167023.

Mottus, A. *et al.* (2013) 'Visualization and interactivity in the teacher decision support system', in *IEEE 13th International Conference on Advanced Learning Technologies, ICALT 2013*, pp. 502–503. doi: 10.1109/ICALT.2013.163.

Pinho, P. C. R. *et al.* (2019) 'Developments in Educational Recommendation Systems: A systematic review', in *2019 IEEE Frontiers in Education Conference, FIE* 2019. pp. 1-7. doi: 10.1109/FIE43999.2019.9028466.

Revilla Muñoz, O. *et al.* (2016) 'The Skills, Competences, and Attitude toward Information and Communications Technology Recommender System: An online support program for teachers with personalized recommendations', *New* Review *of Hypermedia and Multimedia*, 22(1–2), pp. 83–110. doi: 10.1080/13614568.2015.1036132.

Rivera, A. C. *et al.* (2018) 'Recommendation Systems in Education: A Systematic Mapping Study', in *International Conference on Information Technology & Systems (ICITS 2018)*, pp. 138–147. doi: 10.1007/978-3-319-73450-7.

Sergis, S. *et al.* (2014a) 'ICT competence-based learning object recommendations for teachers', *11th International Conference on Cognition and Exploratory Learning in Digital Age, CELDA 2014*, (October 2015), pp. 150–157.

Sergis, S. *et al.* (2014b) 'Towards learning object recommendations based on teachers' ICT competence profiles', in *IEEE 14th International Conference on Advanced Learning Technologies, ICALT 2014*, pp. 534–538. doi: 10.1109/ICALT.2014.156.

Sergis, S. and Sampson, D. G. (2015) 'Enhancing learning object recommendations for teachers using adaptive neighbor selection', in *IEEE 15th International Conference on Advanced Learning Technologies, ICALT 2015*, pp. 391–393. doi: 10.1109/ICALT.2015.50.

Sergis, S. and Sampson, D. G. (2016) 'Learning Object Recommendations for Teachers Based on Elicited ICT Competence Profiles', *IEEE Transactions on Learning Technologies*, 9(1), pp. 67–80. doi: 10.1109/TLT.2015.2434824.

Soldatova, E. *et al.* (2014) 'E-Learning Recommender System for Teaching Staff of Engineering Disciplines', *International Journal of Engineering Pedagogy (iJEP)*, 4(3), p. 42. doi: 10.3991/ijep.v4i3.3478.

Tewari, A. S. *et al.* (2015) 'e-Learning Recommender System for Teachers using Opinion Mining', *Lecture Notes in Electrical Engineering*, 339, pp. 777–784. doi: 10.1007/978-3-662-46578-3.

Verbert, K. *et al.* (2012) 'Context-aware recommender systems for learning: A survey and future challenges', *IEEE Transactions on Learning Technologies*, 5(4), pp. 318–335. doi: 10.1109/TLT.2012.11.

Zapata, A. *et al.* (2011) 'A Hybrid Recommender Method for Learning Objects', *International Journal of Computer Applications*.

Zapata, A. *et al.* (2013) 'A framework for recommendation in learning object repositories: An example of application in civil engineering', *Advances in Engineering Software*, 56, pp. 1–14. doi: 10.1016/j.advengsoft.2012.10.005.

Zervas, P. *et al.* (2015) 'Towards Competence-Based Learning Design Driven Remote and Virtual Labs Recommendations for Science Teachers', *Technology, Knowledge and Learning*, 20(2), pp. 185–199. doi: 10.1007/s10758-015-9256-6.

IMPLEMENT ADAPTATION IN A CASE BASED ITS

Nikolaj Troels Graf von Malotky and Alke Martens
University of Rostock
Albert-Einstein-Str. 22, 18059 Rostock, Germany

ABSTRACT

ITSs have the requirement to be adaptive to the student with AI. The classical ITS architecture defines three components to split the data and to keep it flexible and thus adaptive. However, there is a lack of abstract descriptions how to put adaptive behavior into practice. This paper defines how you can structure your data for case based systems in a way that adaptivity is easier to achieve while maintaining the classical splitting of the system and reducing the data footprint. Building a case based system from a collection of exchangeable steps is also possible with this approach. Two variants of adaptivity based on the data structure are explored and both can be used in conjunction.

KEYWORDS

ITS, Adaptation, Case Based System

1. INTRODUCTION

ITSs (Intelligent Tutoring System) can look back at a comparably long tradition. The first ITSs have been developed in the 1970s, which is a long time ago. At this time, the main idea of ITS was to provide a maximum of expert knowledge. Nowadays, given the modernization of technical devices and the digitalization processes, the main task of the ITS and the part which makes it different then all the other teaching and training software types, is the adaptivity. Regarding this aspect, the ITS is a teaching program that has the highest scores (Mendicino 2009) (Beal 2010) (Singh 2011) (Van Lehn 2011). Adaptation as different facets, like adaptation of the content, adaptation of the navigation, adaptation to a given student (Pirolli 2013) or adaptation of help and correction. Not all these facets of adaptation are necessarily realized in an ITS - adaption can exist in multiple ways in such a system. Some ITS manage only initial adaption to a student, some provide for runtime adaptability. However, independent of the way adaptation is realized, the software system itself has to manage different groups of data to achieve this task. Regarding the basic idea of adaption, the groups of data can be categorized according to the questions: What shall be adapted to whom or to which process and in which way. On the software engineering level these ideas are reflected in different designs (Graf von Malotky 2020), but mainly the idea is constructed around the availability of data for steering the adaptation and for adaptation itself. The classical groups of data for an ITS is the domain knowledge, the pedagogical knowledge and the student knowledge (Nkambou 2010). These three groups represent the knowledge we want to teach, the knowledge about the teacher's behavior and the student knowledge. The teaching material consists of the domain knowledge, which is the content we want to teach and the pedagogical knowledge which is needed to make good decisions as a teacher. The student knowledge is needed to track the student, so that the system adapts to his preferences and skills. Authoring teaching material that is marked as domain and pedagogical knowledge, makes it possible that domain experts can edit the domain knowledge only, with less thinking about the pedagogical consequences of the material, achieving the goal of making authoring easier (Murray 1999). It is a more modular approach that sees the domain knowledge as a collection of material that can be used as teaching material, without having a certain place in a defined learning sequence of the student.

Since the definition of the data groups (domain, pedagogical, student) are so generalized, one data group cannot expect specific data elsewhere when only designing them separately. Therefore, it is important that the basic structure of the teaching material and the student knowledge are harmonized with one another. Harmonizing the data groups reduces the amount of data we need to gather about the student, since we already know what data is needed for the adaptation. Instead of using big data to get clues out of a massive amount of data from the student, we think about what we need from the student while creating the teaching material. There is a large variety of possible ITS types (Graf von Malotky 2019), by focusing on one ITS type, it is possible to specifically define what should be saved in each data group.

It is rare that there is an abstract definition of how a splitting of the teaching material in pedagogical and domain knowledge can be implemented. In this paper it is shown how to structure your data and additional algorithms to accomplish adaptive teaching material consisting of the classical knowledge components in a case based system, since a case based system is inherently already split up into elements which can be filtered and reasoned about (Funk 2002).

2. DATA OF THE STUDENT

Before we can adapt the teaching material to the student, we need to know what is best suited for the student. This can be a combination of several aspects, like for example his personal learning preferences (e.g. more pictures), his level of expertise (e.g. beginner), and also his performance in former cases. Additionally, we have aspects like the performance at runtime. To abstract this, we split the student knowledge data in two: Student style preferences and student skills. We define the style preferences of a student as the attributes of teaching material which will make him more likely to stay motivated and are subjective to the student. A loss in motivation can partly be measured by checking if the student is active and or performing well in a given time period, but it is not very accurate, since there are many other factors that could influence that. Some students tend to be engaged but are less measurable active. Without knowing what the student is thinking and staying away from forcing the student to interact with the system just to check their motivation. This is not a good solution. Additionally, there is still the problem of slowly decreasing performance when the motivation decreases, even though the student could do better. We decided that the student can decide which explanation style is used for the presentation of the domain knowledge. All these explanation styles are generated from the same domain knowledge. This mostly boils down to the presentation style preferred by the student, for example having a style preference for graphical content. If available, the system chooses the domain knowledge with the matching style. If the student has not decided, the system automatically chooses one where the student performed best and makes a switch if the performance does decrease more than a threshold. Since the student cannot game the system by choosing a different style preference (scoring is not affected), we are letting him select and change it at any time.

We define the student skill as the part of the domain knowledge the student has already learned. Skills are determined only by the student's performance and are therefore easier to track. The goal is that the student fully learns all the skills available. Which skills they may learn at one point in time, is inferred by the skills already estimated to be obtained and saved in the student knowledge. How good a student is in a certain skill is saved by the skill levels, which are set through the evaluation of their performance in different sessions of the available cases for that skill. Since you cannot game the system to give you higher scores, students have the option to choose which teaching material they want to learn that has their current difficulty level. Asking the student which skills he has obtained opens up the possibility to game the system (d Baker 2006). Even ignoring this fact, it is expected that some student misjudges themselves. The student should not be required to know the correct dependencies of the skills. Even though a skill might seem to be easy for a student, the system expects also the dependencies. Students outperforming by a large margin will be recognized and their skill updates much faster. It may be beneficial to have short estimation tests for expert students, to speed up the process for them to get a higher difficulty level.

Reducing the amount of data gathered improves the systems disk space, performance and protects the student's privacy. Only the parts of data of the student which are required to make good assumptions about his skills and style preferences are necessary. Since we expect the system to handle teaching by cases, we can save a history of all the cases the student interacted with, including all necessary information that are relevant to judge the performance of the student. At the minimum, it is enough data, when you can generate an estimation of how good the student is at the different skills, which has to include the student's history (Zhou 1999). The system cannot easily track the skills of the student directly, but instead the system can easily track what the student does. As an example, how this can be achieved is shown in the following: it is possible to use just three data sets, which are

- Duration of each step of a case (which implies if the case was started and finished)
- Inputs for each step of the case (to check the correctness and the number of inputs)
- Score achieved in each step of case (which is automatically also the progress)

3. BUILDING THE TEACHING MATERIAL

The teaching material consists of instructionally elaborated training cases. This material is split into domain knowledge and pedagogical knowledge, i.e. the underlying expert knowledge and the instructional aspects related to and embedded in the constructed training case respectively. The training cases often are related to real live cases, which can be extended, anonymized and then integrated in the knowledge modules.

In contrast to other teaching and training system (e.g. mathematics or chemistry), we are developing a system based on these cases, which means the idea of the training cases influenced the software system design. In contrast to non case based training, in case based training we always find the above mentioned combination. Always these cases contain aspects of knowledge of the domain, e.g. in clinical medicine, we find overall medical information, medical information about anatomy and symptoms. This allows us to integrate a large amount of pre-existing databases. As for example the medical knowledge domain consists of facts and rules, we can integrate parts of this as universal information parts. Additionally, we have case-related information, e.g. in the medical domain, an x-ray of an elderly male thorax with lung disease after 30 years of smoking is a special picture with a related special diagnosis related, and which cannot be re-used in an arbitrary way. However, this is still not the pedagogical knowledge. The pedagogical knowledge can in such a case consist of certain related facts and special rules, like level required, skills, sequence of steps, but also of question/answer sets of different presentation styles (Graf von Malotky 2017). Moreover, here we have set goals: Which knowledge we want to teach which each case. This means we need different tasks grouped together to teach some predefined skills.

A case can be represented as a graph with each node of it being a step in the case (see figure 1). There is always one starting node (no incoming edges), at least one end node (no outgoing nodes) and all nodes are reachable by edges. To keep it simple, in this model a step is associated with a display of content on the level of the human-computer-interface (e.g. the monitor). The navigation from one step to another (the edges in the graph) are the navigation buttons or menus in human-computer-interface. To graph shows all the potential ways navigating through the pages of a training case. The steps exist at least once and, in our example, cases as graphs are often simple enough to not need to think about complex graph theories. Generally, the complexity is realized in the training case to switch the nodes. Sometimes, content of steps can be designed in a way that a step can re-occur in different branches of the tree (e.g. in the medical domain, some examinations are not dependent on the time in the training case, some can even be repeated).

To successfully complete the case the student has to view or solve steps and come to a step where there are no outgoing edges. Each step can be a passive explanation or an interactive task to be solved by the student. The passive steps are for the preparation of the student for the next task and can additionally feature storytelling aspects to merge the different tasks into one motivating case. The tasks in the case can be embedded in a story which progresses step by step. The story makes the tasks more interesting and motivating.

The domain knowledge contains teaching content visible to the student while the pedagogical knowledge is the added data. For the case it is the graph, the available style preferences and skills and how they are connected to each case. For the step it is its difficulty, the style of the step and whether it can be used as a passive or interactive step. The style for the passive steps can for example be clean text, comic images or 3D-Model instructions. The only "interaction" here is that the student has to read the information. No additional action like selecting, clicking, marking or whatever are included. These types of interactions are realized in the so-called interactive tasks. For the interactive tasks there are the typically used single or multiple choice questions, drag and drop, draw lines, text with drop down fill holes and so on.

In figure 1 you can see an example graph, where passive steps are squares and interactive steps are circles. In this example passive and interactive steps alternate. The passive steps show knowledge embedded in a story which should be learned, while the interactive steps tests the skills of the student, so the student is forced to think about what they are showing, instead of only remembering. The starting (A) and the ending step (K) start and finish the included story. Dependent on the difficulty more or less information in the passive steps is shown, important parts highlighted and kept for later look up. The same goes for interactive steps, where help is reduced with higher difficulty.

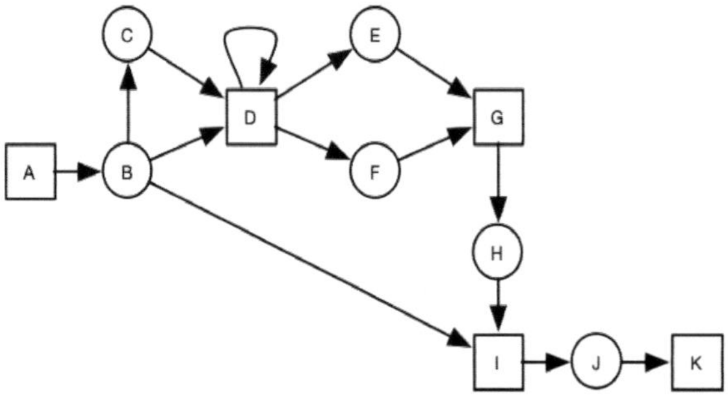

Figure 1. Example case graph with passive elements as squares and interactive elements as circles

With this approach, the idea is to build up a collection of steps that can be reused and exchanged. Each step has enough additional information to make an educated decision which step to use for a given student in his current situation. An idea was to create the graph automatically from the dependencies of the nodes to each other so there would be a dynamic graph, but that creates the problem that each node has to know other nodes or that there exists some sort of general, detailed, wide applicable node classification to use for all steps. To maintain the simplicity and the modularity of the steps the graph of the case is static. This means that the structure is a fixed attribute of the case which is represented by the graph and will not adapt to a student or changing steps. The graph can of course be still changed by authors of teaching content. The case itself is not adaptive, but is built in a way that each step can easily be exchanged at runtime. The adaptation algorithm has to decide which steps to choose. In another variation, the adaptation algorithm can also decide which steps are possible for a given case, but this is not the focus of the paper. This automation needs a lot more understanding of the system, e.g. which content is inside a step and which shall be used for the student according to which rules.

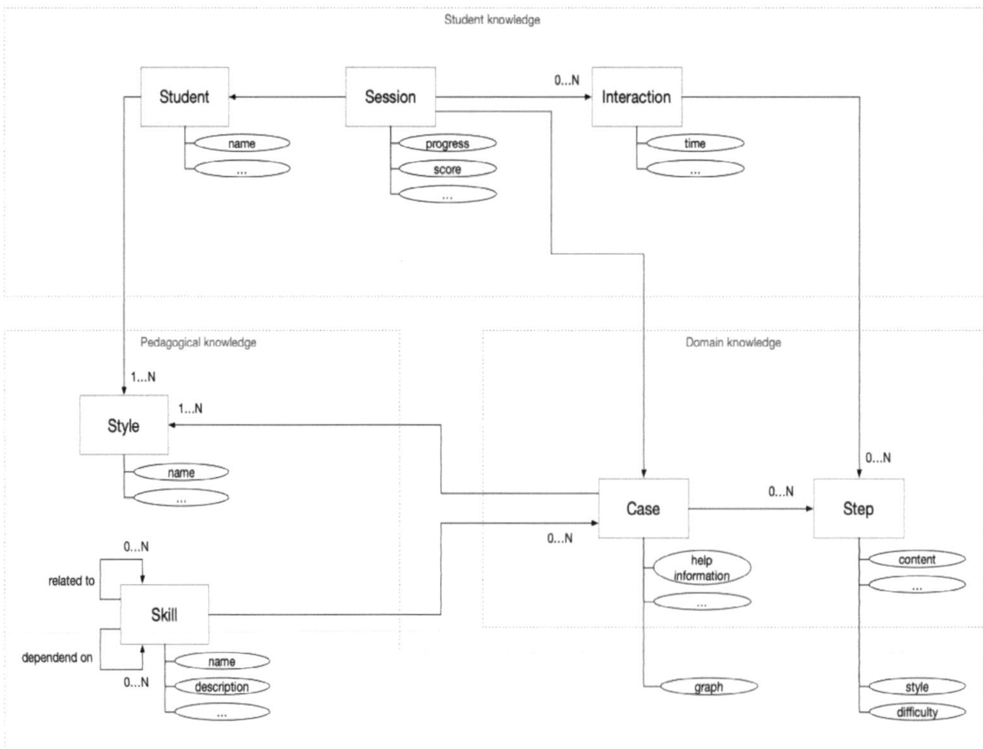

Figure 2. Database structure of a case based ITS

The reduced structure of the general data needed for the system is shown in figure 2. To be reusable we explain the system in an abstract way. There is a separation of domain knowledge and pedagogical knowledge, which allows authors to modify only one of them. The cases are exchangeable, as are their steps. Instead of defining which concrete case is dependent on other cases, this information is extracted into its own part, the skills that the student should learn.

As we already defined the student knowledge, we have to associate the student knowledge with the teaching material. To track the progress in the observed skill of the student, we save the interactions of the student with the steps to evaluate a score. With the score, the progress and the time of each interaction in one case session it is possible to estimate the student's skill.

4. ADAPTATION

Now that the teaching material is structured in a way that it is ready to collect the necessary data about the student, while also being built in a way that the student's data is enough to be used as input to adapt the teaching material, we can use adaptation methods. In its raw form the student knowledge is not informative enough. We additionally need to calculate the student's overall skill levels from the sessions the student completed. The skill level of a student is just a number based on the progress, score, number of interactions and duration of his session history. For the score the difficulty of the steps is included. The difficulty could be a number from 0.0 to 1.0 and be used as a multiplier in the score calculation. To be able to compare the student's skill level to a difficulty/scores and showing the progress, it is important that the algorithm for the skill level does not change and is built together with the adaptation methods. It has to be clear for the system, what a high and low score is. The teaching material also needs additional data if it did change. This includes the dependencies/relations between skills and implies the dependencies/relations between cases, the possible difficulties of each case, the possible styles of each case and the selection of available styles and skills. Two possibilities are explored how to adapt to the student. The first option is that adaption is realized by the selection of domain knowledge that matches the preferences and skills of the student; in the second option the adaptation is realized through adjustments on the shown domain knowledge.

For the first option we need a case to teach the student. Each case has skills and styles associated with it. Dependency of cases to each other is calculated beforehand by the skills each case requires. Therefore, the selection of matching teaching material comes first. We want students which use our system to show matching learning material, but avoid to show the exact same material again. Additionally the teaching material should also take into account what style preferences and skills the student has. So the task is to select teaching material which is less often seen, has matching style and is about skills that are related to and dependent on skills that the student already has.

Currently there is a problem for students, that do not learn in the set speed of existing static teaching material: If they learn slower, they will be presented with the same teaching material repeatedly. That means that some students may pass only because they learned about how the material is structured. They learned the answers but did not understand all necessary parts for it. The difference here is between "putting it into the brain" without grasping them deeper meaning, in contrast to the student's knowledge construction and deeper learning, which is the target of all good structured learning material. If a student who does not pass a test after reading a book the first time is shown the exact same test over and over again, he will pass it eventually, but maybe does not really understand the underlying content. That problem also applies to digital content, if not prevented with varying content. Instead of showing complete new content we can exchange only some part of the content to adapt on a finer grained level to the learning speed of the student. Adjustments of the teaching material allows not only to have a better matched difficulty but has also the benefit of varying the case if used multiple times by the same student. Creating variations for a case has a higher change of requiring the requested skills, not knowledge about how the case is structured. We can reuse the teaching material by modifying it enough so that the student is more likely to think about the problem instead of remembering the already given solution from previous sessions.

The second option is the adaptation of teaching material itself. It allows the ITS to be more suited to the liking of the student to increase motivation or to address problems with improper difficulty settings. Adjustments on the case by exchanging steps to select a matching style, get the correct difficulty and the less seen steps. By allowing to have exchangeable tasks in the case we can adapt the content and difficulty of the case without changing what the goal of teaching of the case is. Another way that such a system can adapt the difficulty is to show less additional information from the case itself. To give a more concrete example of how the rules could look like the following list of rules could help. The system searches through the cases and selects the steps to build a case that matches as many as possible of the existing rules preferred in the given order (most preferred are on the top). A threshold for skills can be set to define how good a student has to be in one skill to progress to the next.

- Cases that can be built from steps matching difficulty to the student's skill level
- Cases that can be built with steps that match the student's style preference
- Cases that are related to cases already in the student's history (ordered by highest score)
- Cases that are directly dependent to cases already in the student's history above score threshold (ordered by highest score)
- Cases with no progress (unseen case)
- Cases that can be built with steps without scores (unseen steps)
- Cases that can be built with steps with score below threshold
- Cases with incomplete progress
- Cases with a higher than threshold score but are completed long time ago (ordered by days since last session)

5. CONCLUSION AND OUTLOOK

There are multiple ways of achieving adaptivity in an ITS. Both shown methods of adaptation that were explored in this paper have their benefits and they can both be implemented side by side. With the presented structure this is possible in a reusable way for a case based system which can then be fitted with more details of the given domain. The presented steps to create an adaptive case based system allow for a general way to achieve the set goals for an ITS without demanding domain specific details. The data structure respects the subjective preferences of a student as well as his objective performance goals for skills while maintaining a minimal data footprint. Both of which can be fitted to many available domains. The presented adaptive methods work on the defined data structure and can easily be implemented with very simple algorithms and grow more complex as the system gets more sophisticated. We have explored this in the context of our DigiCare Project and the training cases in our project are developed based on the above mentioned algorithm.

DigiCare is a project about supporting the Healthcare and Healthcare management students at the University of Applied Sciences Neubrandenburg and at the University of Rostock. Together with the DZNE (German Center for Neurodegenerative Illnesses), a threefold approach is realized in the funding period of 2019 to 2022. The first steps have been the collection and digitalization of teaching and training material, which has gained double speed in the pandemic situation starting in 2020. Currently, large parts of the curriculum are digitalized and recorded with the purpose of distance education. On the long run, the University of Applied Sciences Neubrandenburg will keep open the opportunity for the students to combine distance and presence studs. The second step has been to integrate the system SCARLET (Nicolay 2020) as part of the lectures. SCARLET is a software which allows for the interactive annotation of lectures by students, via using hashtags. An automatic analysis of the lecture slides based on the LDA (Latent Dirichlet Algorithm) allows to grasp the underlying content structure of the slides. The resulting model shows the required domain knowledge, which should be mediated to the students. A mapping of the student's hashtag annotations with the resulted graph structure allows the students or even a supervisor to see how close the students' understanding is to the intended understanding. The third step is the Intelligent Tutoring System, as sketched above. The ITS in DigiCare has been developed for the purpose that in healthcare, student have to work with real life cases from very early stages of their professional development. However, given the traditional lectures at the University, this can only take place on a very abstract level. Moreover, in the pandemic situation, students are not allowed for practical parts of their study. Thus, to allow them at least a small glance into the patient situations, the ITS was developed. Our ITS consists of three main aspects:

- It is a case-based ITS, thus is contains only patient related training cases. The training cases are based on real existing cases, e.g. patients with dementia. These training cases, same as the underlying knowledge structures of the expert knowledge in the ITS are provided by the DZNE partner in the project, in close co-operation with the University partners.
- The case-based ITS contains also a natural language and dialog component, which is described in several other publications (Sosnowski 2020)(Abuazizeh 2020). The main underlying idea is here, that patients with dementia show a very good observable behavior in communicative situations. Examples reach from 'answering aggressively' to 'not answering at all'. The communication training is perceived to be one important part of the education, which admittedly cannot be reached in the traditional educational formats like lectures. Thus, an ITS can be at least a bit helpful in this context.
- There exists a bunch of material, which can be re-used in different training cases, and which represents main parts of the necessary education in health care, e.g. how to fill in medical records, which rules apply during patient contact etc. This content can be re-used in diverse settings and allow the student to close the gap between theoretical and practical knowledge. In the above-mentioned graph, these step types are examples of re-occurring or re-usable steps.

The ITS is developed based on software engineering aspects and is based on the framework for Intelligent Tutoring Systems. This component based generative framework is the first all-purpose framework for ITS, as it has been shown that especially ITS lack general and re-usable structures.

Our future work will be to refine the existing ITS, to close the gap between the dialogue and the other content of the ITS. Currently, the dialog is perceived to be one step in the abovementioned graph. Thus, knowledge gain in the course of the dialogue is not yet part of the adaptation process. Additionally, the next steps will also be to allow for even more adaptability and flexibility in the training cases.

ACKNOWLEDGEMENT

This paper is part of the research project "DigiCare". This joint research project "DigiCare" is supported by the European Social Fund (ESF), reference: ESF/14-BM-A55-0018/19, and the Ministry of Education, Science and Culture of Mecklenburg-Vorpommern, Germany. We thank all our cooperation partners!

REFERENCES

Abuazizeh, M.D., Kirste, T. and Yordanova, K., 2020, June. Computational state space model for intelligent tutoring of students in nursing subjects. In *Proceedings of the 13th ACM International Conference on PErvasive Technologies Related to Assistive Environments* (pp. 1-7).

Beal, Carole R. et al., 2010, Evaluation of AnimalWatch: An intelligent tutoring system for arithmetic and fractions, *Journal of Interactive Online Learning*, volume 9, issue 1, pages 64-77, ISSN 1541-4914.

d Baker, R.S. et al., 2006, June. Adapting to when students game an intelligent tutoring system. In *International conference on intelligent tutoring systems* (pp. 392-401). Springer, Berlin, Heidelberg.

Graf von Malotky, Nikolaj Troels et al., 2017, Synthesis of pedagogical annotations, *9th annual International Conference on Education and New Learning Technologies (EDULEARN)*, EDULEARN17 Proceedings, ISBN 978-84-697-3777-4, ISSN 2340-1117, DOI 10.21125/edulearn.2017, pages 3655-3661.

Graf von Malotky, Nikolaj Troels, Martens, Alke, 2019, Analyzing the usage of the classical ITS software architecture and refining it, *15th international conference on intelligent tutoring systems (ITS2019)*, pages 40-46, DOI 10.1007/978-3-030-22244-4_6, Springer, Cham, Online ISBN 978-3-030-22244-4, Print ISBN 978-3-030-22243-7.

Graf von Malotky, Nikolaj Troels, Martens, Alke, 2020, General ITS software architecture and framework, *16th International Conference on Intelligent Tutoring Systems (ITS2020)*, Springer.

Funk, P. and Conlan, O., 2002, September. Case-Based Reasoning to Improve Adaptability of Intelligent Tutoring Systems. In *ECCBR Workshops* (pp. 15-24).

Mendicino, Michael et al., 2009, Comparison of Traditional Homework with Computer Supported Homework, *Journal of Research on Technology in Education* 41(3), pages 331–359.

Murray, T., 1999, Authoring intelligent tutoring systems: An analysis of the state of the art. *International Journal of Artificial Intelligence in Education* (IJAIED), 10, pp.98-129.

Nicolay, Robin, Martens, Alke, 2020, Synthesis of Knowledge Tracing Models Using Natural Language Processing on Lecture Content, *EDULEARN20 Proceedings*, pp. 1659-1666.

Nkambou, Roger et al., 2010, Advances in intelligent tutoring systems, *Springer Science & Business Media*, volume 308, ISBN 3642143628.

Singh, Ravi et al., 2011, Feedback during web-based homework: the role of hints, *International Conference on Artificial Intelligence in Education*, Springer, Berlin, Heidelberg.

Sosnowski, T., Yordanova, K., 2020, June. A probabilistic conversational agent for intelligent tutoring systems. In *Proceedings of the 13th ACM International Conference on PErvasive Technologies Related to Assistive Environments* (pp. 1-7).

Van Lehn, Kurt, 2011, The relative effectiveness of human tutoring, intelligent tutoring systems, and other tutoring systems, *Educational Psychologist* 46.4, pages 197-221.

Zhou, Yujian Zhou, Evens M. W., 1999, A practical student model in an intelligent tutoring system, Proceedings 11th *International Conference on Tools with Artificial Intelligence*, pp. 13-18, doi: 10.1109/TAI.1999.809759.

MAXIMIZING THE POTENTIAL OF TRANSPARENT SIMULATIONS BY COMBINING PERFORMANCE GOALS WITH LEARNING GOALS AND EXPLORATORY GUIDANCE IN A DYNAMICALLY COMPLEX TASK

Carlos Capelo[1] and Renato Pereira[2]
[1]*Universidade Europeia, Estrada da Correia, 53, 1500-210 Lisboa – Portugal*
[2]*Iscte Business School, Instituto Universitario de Lisboa, Avenida das Forças Armadas, 1649-026 Lisboa – Portugal*

ABSTRACT

Simulation-based learning environments have been proposed by researchers, as educational tools to support learning in complex business systems. However, studies have evidenced that subjects may nevertheless have great difficulty understanding and managing dynamic systems. Previous research has revealed positive learning and performance effects of using transparent simulations (that is, revealing users the structure and behaviour of the simulator model). This study explores the effects of combining exploratory guidance, learning goals, and performance goals in a transparent simulation of a dynamically complex system. We present a set of hypotheses about the influence of different goal-setting conditions on participants' performance and comprehension of the system dynamics. In a simulation experiment, participants interacted with a system dynamics model representing the growth of a business venture. Participants who previously worked higher learning goals under exploratory guidance and were then submitted to higher performance goals (compared to vague goals) achieved higher performance and demonstrated better comprehension of the model dynamics. However, participants who were only subjected to more specific, high performance goals (compared to vague performance goals) did not improve their outcomes and revealed larger differences within the treatment group. Two out of the four hypotheses were confirmed. In a transparent simulation of a dynamically complex system, setting specific, high learning goals, previously worked through exploratory guidance, positively moderates the impact of the level of performance goals on the comprehension of the model dynamics and performance.

KEYWORDS

Simulation-Based Learning, System Dynamics, Model Transparency, Exploratory Guidance, Discovery Learning, Goal-Setting Theory

1. INTRODUCTION

1.1 Model Transparency

Simulator transparency refers to the extent the structure and behaviour of the underlying computational model is shown to students using the simulation. In "black-box" or opaque simulations, students can explore a system's behaviour, but the underlying computational models remain hidden and can only be inferred by what appears on the screen. Studies have suggested that this type of ''black-box'' situation could lead students to form wrong mental models, interfering with proper learning. "Glass-box" or ''transparent'' simulations have alternatively been proposed to obviate the above-described problems, as the relations among their variables are accessible to students. Transparent simulators have been used in system dynamics (SD) learning environments, detailing through their stocks-and-flows diagram (SFD) the causal structure of the underlying system. By using this approach, students may trace the cause and effect structure and understand the relationships between structure and behaviour, and they are in a position of understanding even counterintuitive system behaviours.

Research shows that structural knowledge provided by transparent simulations has the potential to improve leaning and task performance (Capelo and Silva, 2020).

1.2 Learning and Performance Goals in Complex Tasks

The goal setting, a theory of motivation in organizational psychology, states that setting specific and high goals leads to higher performance than easy goals, no goals, or even general goals, namely "to do one's best" (Locke & Latham, 2013). The assumption in the education is that a simulation task with no clear learning and performance goals may disorient and fail to stimulate students' attention and interest. The positive effects of goals operate through cognitive and affective mechanisms, including attention, effort, persistence, self-efficacy, motivation, and learning (Locke & Latham, 2013). In this context, goal setting is viewed as a promising technique to provide attention and motivation towards learning and to avoid situations in which the students merely play the game (Nebel et al., 2017). Goals stimulate cognitive activities to support simulation-based learning such as attending to instruction, developing task strategies to attain the goals, and processing and integrating relevant knowledge (Yang et al., 2017).

On the other hand, previous studies have shown that providing no specific goals at all could benefit learning in problem-solving tasks (Sweller, et al., 1998). According to the cognitive load theory (CLT) (Sweller, 2020), learning is compromised when the total cognitive load exceeds available working memory capacity. That goal-free effect, which is derived from CLT, states that learning and performance will improve by setting vague goals, and thus avoiding unnecessary load resulted by distant, specific goals (Sweller et al., 1998). These cognitive costs may generate distraction and deteriorate students' learning and performance outcomes (Crouzevialle & Butera, 2017). Gary et al. (2017) did not find main effect of stretch goals on performance and concluded that stretch goals (compared with moderate goals) generate large attainment discrepancies that increase willingness to take risks, undermine goal commitment, and generate lower risk-adjusted performance.

Goal-setting theory distinguish two types of goals (Locke & Latham, 2013): learning goals, which focus on acquiring the required task knowledge, and performance goals, which specify desired task outcomes. Performance goals may lead to the situation in which students only attempt to reach their goals rather than acquiring the knowledge and skills needed. Whereas learning goals may lead to more learning-oriented behaviour such as focussing attention on mastering a task, discovering task-relevant strategies, and achieving learning objectives. The results of Nebel et al. (2017) showed that specific learning goals decrease cognitive load and improve motivation.

In a complex task, learners lack the necessary knowledge to perform effectively because task elements are highly interrelated, and the consequence of possible actions is often ambiguous (Gary & Wood, 2011). Empirical studies revealed that when there is a high complex task that requires previous learning so that it can be performed effectively, a general goal (e.g., ''to do one's best'') leads to better outcomes than a specific performance goal. In that stage, wherein the requisite knowledge needs being acquired, the approach proposed consists of assigning learning goals first, and then assigning performance goals later once subjects sufficiently learn about the task (Chen & Latham, 2014; Latham et al., 2008; Yang et al., 2017).

1.3 Exploratory Guidance and Discovery Learning

Simulation-based learning is frequently considered a method to promote inquiry-based learning and discovery learning (Alfieri et al. 2011). However, the literature on simulation-based learning suggests that students perform better when some form of guidance is provided (Landriscina, 2013). Instructional guidance refers to the support provided to students during simulation in the form of questions, procedures, steps, or materials. According to Mayer (2004), instructional methods involving guided discovery have been more effective in helping students learn, as they involve cognitive activity. In such instructional strategy, students discover the underlying rules through exploratory guidance, this is, at each stage, learning goals are presented, and students are free to explore the learning environment. Studies have found that students achieve deeper understanding of subject matter when using scientific reasoning (Clement, 2008). They have the opportunity to iteratively act, appreciate the consequences of their decisions, reflect, and test their comprehension of the cause-effect relations.

However, some studies on inquiry learning with computer simulations (e.g. de Jong, 2006) have shown that students operating in complex environments generally have difficulty in all phases of the inquiry process. In a simulation task, the complexity of the model may exceed the working memory limits of students. To obviate these cognitive load problems, de Jong et al. (2018) suggest that instructional method be integrated with 'cognitive tools' aimed at guiding and supporting students' activities. More recently, the results of the experiment conducted by Capelo and Silva (2020) indicated positive learning effects of using transparent simulations and exploratory guidance involving model progression, worked examples, and task segmentation. Debriefing sessions may also be incorporated in the instructional method, by discussing with the students about their difficulties related to the comprehension of the model structure and behaviour (between simulation runs). This approach can stimulate students to reflect on the simulation experience and help them to overcome misconceptions about dynamic and complex tasks (Capelo et al., 2020).

2. RESEARCH HYPOTHESES

The present study investigates whether an instructional approach of simulation-based learning that includes exploratory guidance, learning goals, and performance goals can improve the learning potential of transparent simulations in a dynamically complex task, which consists of starting and growing a business venture.

According to a model-based learning perspective, the learnings outcomes refer to the students' comprehension of the simulated system and to their performance in the simulation task. The students' comprehension is assessed on the basis of their ability to deal with specific dynamic aspects of the simulation model. As students interact with the simulator dynamics, they interpret the situation, mentally simulate the consequences of selected actions, and then they define and implement courses of action which reflect their comprehension about the structure and behaviour of the simulator model.

The expected relations and hypotheses are based on the following variables: (i) LPG - Level of Performance Goals. This variable indicates in what extent the instructional method includes the setting of specific, high performance goals. (ii) LLGEG - Level of Learning Goals and Exploratory Guidance. This variable indicates in what extent the instructional method includes the setting of specific, high learning goals, worked under exploratory guidance. (iii) Comprehension of model dynamics (CMD). This variable reflects how students comprehend the structure of the simulation model and are able to infer its dynamical behaviour. (iv) Performance. The performance of this simulation task is measured in terms of the financial value created by the venture.

The following hypotheses are defined: H1a - LPG positively influences CMD; H1b - LPG positively influences Performance; H2a - LLGEG positively moderates the effect of LPG on CMD; H2b - LLGEG positively moderates the effect of LPG on Performance.

3. METHOD

3.1 Simulator, Participants, and Procedure

The SBLE used in this experiment incorporates a system dynamics (SD) model that was developed and utilized in previous research (Capelo et al., 2018; 2020), which represents the growth of a business venture. By interacting with this simulator, students would be able to appreciate the dynamical complexity involved in a business venture and the performance effects caused by system misconceptions. The SBLE provides a transparent interface, which includes six screens. The first screen (the panel control) allows participants to adjust simulation parameters and includes tables presenting critical measures. The panel control provides the information included in a stock and flow diagram. The second and third screen present the historical behaviour over time for key variables. The other screens show the causal loop diagram (CLD) and selected stock and flow diagrams (SFDs) of the simulator model.

In order to test the hypotheses, we conducted a laboratory experiment using three treatment groups: a control group (CG) of students who interacted with a transparent simulator, without learning and performance goals - low LPG and low LLGEG; an experimental group (E1) of students who used a transparent simulator, had performance goals, and did not have learning goals - high LPG, and low LLGEG; and an experimental group (E2) of students who used a transparent simulator, had performance goals, and had learning goals previously worked under exploratory guidance - high LPG, and high LLGEG.

This research was conducted at Iscte Business School in Lisbon, Portugal. The experiment involved three classes of entrepreneurship courses with 68 students in total. Groups CG (with 22 students), E1 (with 24 students), and E2 (with 22 students). One of the authors acted as instructor in these classes.

To succeed in this simulation task, students need to identify and understand the cause-and-effect relationships among critical variables, particularly those included in the CLD and selected SFDs provided in the simulator interface. That model complexity has been demonstrated to negatively influence both formation of accurate mental models and task performance. Moreover, subjects who are not familiarized with systems dynamics have additional difficulties in recognizing and comprehending dynamical structures as they are not able to properly read and interpret causal-loop-diagrams and stocks-and-flows diagrams (Davidsen & Spector, 2015). In order to obviate these problems, model transparency is complemented with structural and behavioural debriefings (Capelo et al., 2020). The students from all the groups participated in a debriefing session (after the first simulation run) focused on the model variables and relations. Then (after the second simulation run) they were involved in discussions about the relation between model structure, courses of action, and behaviour.

The experiment procedure involved two sessions and had the following steps (Figure 1).

Treatment		Experimental Procedure								
		a) Lecture on CLD and SFD	b) Simulator and task description	c) First simulation run	d) Structural debriefing	e) Second simulation run	f) Behavioural debriefing	g) Learning goals and simulation with exploratory guidance	h) Performance goals	i) Third simulation run
CG	Low LPG, low LLGEG	●	●	●	●	●	●			●
E1	High LPG, low LLGEG	●	●	●	●	●	●		●	●
E2	High LPG, high LLGEG	●	●	●	●	●	●	●	●	●

Figure 1. Experimental procedure

Session 1. a) The students received a lecture on CLDs and SFDs, so that they were able to read and interpret the CLD and SFDs available in the simulator interface. During the simulation task, all the participants were encouraged to read and interpret the CLD and SFDs available in the game interface.

Session 2. In this session, students performed the simulation task using three simulation runs (for approximately 20 to 25 minutes each). b) They read the introduction with the overall description and the objectives of the simulation task. Participants then read the instructions for accessing, starting, and running the simulator. Some simulation rounds were conducted to become familiar with the simulation. c) They performed the first simulation run. d) The students, after performing the first simulation run, participated in a structural debriefing (lasting approximately 35 minutes). The instructor described the CLDs and SFDs in the game interface in a form of a step-by-step guided tour and cleared all the doubts raised by students concerning the model variables and their relations. e) Participants then performed the second simulation run. f) The second simulation run is followed by a behavioural debriefing. This debriefing (lasting approximately 50 minutes) focused on the relation between the model structure, courses of action, and corresponding dynamical behaviour. g) The students from experimental group E2 (submitted to learning goals, exploratory guidance, and performance goals) were assigned some specific learning goals related to three different simulation phases. For each simulation phase, they were asked to identify and write a description of a possible strategy to overcome certain challenges and maximize value creation. The participants were free to explore the simulator, performing all the simulation runs they need. They analysed the challenges to be addressed, hypothesised strategies and scenarios, adjusted the decision parameters, ran the simulator, interpreted the results, defined new strategies and scenarios, and repeated the process. Once students identified and wrote down the strategy requested, they moved to the next simulation phase. They spent approximately 60 minutes working through the three simulation phases. h) The participants from experimental groups E1 (submitted to performance goals) and E2 (submitted to learning goals, exploratory guidance, and performance goals) were given high performance goals to be addressed in the final simulation round. i) Finally, they performed the third and final simulation run. The students from group E2 were asked to implement the strategies they had identified in order to achieve the performance goals.

3.2 Research Variables

This section summarises the use of the variables that were defined in the research model.

Level of Performance Goals (LPG). This variable features two degrees. In the low degree, students perform the simulation task with a global, vague performance goal. They are to maximize value creation. In the high degree, students have specific, high performance goals. They are to achieve certain outcomes in terms of clients and value creation for each simulation phase.

Level of Learning Goals and Exploratory Guidance (LLGEG). This variable features two degrees. In the low degree, students perform the simulation task without specific learning goals and they are not submitted to exploratory guidance. In the high degree, the students are submitted to specific, high learning goals, combined with exploratory guidance. They are free to explore the simulator, performing all the simulation runs they need. This experiment condition is designed to promote discovery learning with appropriate aids. They are asked to identify and test strategies to address specific business challenges. The students reflect on each issue, formulate some hypotheses about model behaviour, and define scenarios to test those hypotheses. They run the simulator, interpret the results, test the hypotheses, and determine the cycle repeats.

Comprehension of the model dynamics (CMD). This variable indicates how students understand the structure and behaviour of the simulation model. The measurement of this variable is based on students' patterns of action throughout the final simulation round, by analysing how they consistently deal with certain dynamical structures of the simulation model. This variable is calculated as the average of four components that are rated in a continuous scale (from 0 to 1) against reference values.

Performance. The performance of this simulation task is measured in terms of the financial value created by the venture, indicated by the value of the parameter MVA (market value added) achieved in the final simulation round. This variable is rated in a continuous scale (from 0 to 1) against reference values of MVA.

4. RESULTS AND DISCUSSION

Table 1 presents the mean values, standard deviations, and sample sizes for the variables CMD and Performance corresponding to the three experimental treatments. Table 2 displays the results of an independent sample *t* tests of significance for differences in means between pairs of treatment groups.

The lowest mean values for the variables CMD and Performance were found in participants from experimental group E1 (submitted only to high performance goals). On average, the participants from group E2 (submitted to high learning goals, exploratory guidance, and high performance goals) exhibited the highest values for both the dependent variables. These results suggest that participants learn and perform more effectively if the transparent simulation combines specific, high learning goals, previously worked under exploratory guidance, with specific, high performance goals.

The students from control group (CG) and those from the group E1 (submitted only to high performance goals) were submitted to equivalent guidance conditions. The difference between those treatment groups is that while students from control group had a vague performance goal (to maximize value creation), students from group E1 had specific, high performance goals to be achieved throughout the simulation task. The statistical testing presented in Table 2 (pair E1-CG) shows that the average outcomes from those groups are not significantly different (CMD mean difference = -0.070, $p = 0.117$; Performance mean difference = -0.097, $p = 0.157$). The comparison between treatment groups CG and E1 presented in Tables 1 and 2 demonstrates that setting high performance goals did not cause the participants to reveal better outcomes. Instead, high performance goals compared with vague performance goals increased the variance in CMD and performance. That means that participants from group E1, who received specific, high performance goals for each phase throughout the simulation task, on average, did not improve their comprehension of the model dynamics and performance, and revealed larger differences within the treatment group. One possible explanation is that some students may lack of proper knowledge about the complex structure and behaviour of the simulator model in order to effectively deal with those high performance goals. Thus, those students from group E1, in such poor understanding condition, may experience additional pressure and cognitive load as they monitor their progress and perceive a persistent and increasing distance from the desired performance level, which reduce the availability of their limited cognitive resources. These cognitive costs may generate distraction and deteriorate learning and performance outcomes, which erodes motivation and goal commitment. These findings are somehow consistent with the results reported by Gary et al. (2017) that, in a complex task, stretch goals (compared with moderate goals) did not produce a significant main effect on performance and increased its variance.

Table 1. Means and standard deviations for variables CMD (comprehension of model dynamics) and Performance for each treatment group

			CMD - Comprehension of the Model Dynamics		Performance	
Treatment	Description	N	Mean	SD	Mean	SD
CG	Low LPG, low LLGEG	22	0.458	0.144	0.455	0.196
E1	High LPG, low LLGEG	24	0.388	0.153	0.358	0.254
E2	High LPG, high LLGEG	22	0.564	0.122	0.622	0.259

LPG - Level of Performance Goals; LLGEG - Level of Learning Goals and Exploratory Guidance

Table 2. Independent sample t-tests of significance for differences in means for the variables CMD and Performance between pairs of treatment groups

	CMD - Comprehension of the Model Dynamics			Performance		
Pair	Mean Difference	SD	p-value	Mean Difference	SD	p-value
E1-CG	-0.070	0.044	0.117	-0.097	0.067	0.157
E2-CG	0.105*	0.040	0.012	0.167*	0.069	0.021
E2-E1	0.176**	0.041	0.000	0.264**	0.076	0.001

*p<0.05, **p<0.01

On the other hand, the difference between treatment groups E1 and E2 is that students from the latter group received previously some specific challenges and learning goals to be addressed through exploratory guidance. As shown in Table 2, the comparison between group CG and group E2 (pair E2-CG) reveals positive differences in means for CMD and Performance (CMD mean difference = 0.105, p = 0.012; Performance mean difference = 0.167, p = 0.021). Consequently, the variable LLGEG seems to positively moderate the impact of LPG on CMD and Performance. Students submitted to high performance goals demonstrate, on average, an increasing comprehension of the model dynamics and a better performance if they addressed previously high learning goals through exploratory guidance. As students explored the simulator to resolve the challenges associated to the learning goals, they were engaged in an inquiry process and had opportunity to accelerate and consolidate their learning about the structure and behaviour of the simulated system.

Table 3 shows the results of multivariate regression analyses of CMD and Performance on the independent variables. The regressions were run on standardised values for all the variables to directly compare the relative effects of each independent variable on the dependent variable. As presented in Table 4, regression analysis for CMD on the independent variables shows a low significant negative effect for LPG (β=-0.212, p=0.095) and no significant effects for LLGEG (β=-0.176, p=0.174). Regression analysis of

Performance shows strong significant positive effects for LPG (β=0.529, p<0.001) and LLGEG (β=0.4792, p<0.001).

In the present teaching approach and corresponding experiment design, the learning goals and exploratory guidance are applied as complementary methods to increase the effectiveness of performance goals setting. Thus, high LLGEG only occurs with high LPG. Consequently, we are only able to identify moderation effects of LLGEG on the relation between LPG and CMD/Performance. As such, the significant positive correlation found between LLGEG and CMD/Performance means that LLGEG positively moderates the relation between LPG and CMD/Performance.

Table 3. Regression results for all independent variables

	Dependent Variables			
	CMD - Comprehension of Model Dynamics		Performance	
Independent Variables	Stand. Beta	p-value	Stand. Beta	p-value
LPG - Level of Performance Goals	-0.212*	0.095	-0.176	0.174
LLGEG - Level of Learning Goals and Exploratory Guidance	0.529**	0.000	0.479**	0.000
Adjusted R^2	0.194		0.154	

*p<0.1, **p<0.01

These results confirm two of the four hypotheses. As indicated by Table 2, the mean values of CMD and Performance for experimental group E1 (high LPG and low LLGEG) are not significantly different from those for the control group (low LPG and low LLGEG). Also, the regression (Table 3) does not show significant positive effects (at 0.05 significance level) of LPG on CMD and Performance. On contrary, regression for CMD reveals a low significant negative effect for LPG (at 0.1 significance level). Consequently, our research does not provide support for hypotheses H1a/b - the level of performance goals positively influences the comprehension of the model dynamics and the performance in transparent simulations of a complex system. As discussed previously, the results presented in Table 2 suggest that LLGEG positively moderates the impact of LPG on CMD and Performance. Additionally, as the learning goals and exploratory guidance condition (high LLGEG) complements the performance goals condition (high LPG), a significant effect of LLGEG on CMD and Performance (Table 3) also confirms the existence of that moderation effect. Consequently, these findings support hypotheses H2a/b - the level of learning goals and exploratory guidance positively moderates the impact of the level of performance goals on the comprehension of the model dynamics and on the performance in transparent simulations of a complex system.

5. CONCLUSION

This study is based on an educational experiment aimed at testing hypotheses about the effects of setting learning and performance goals on students' learning and task performance in a transparent simulation of a dynamically complex system. It was predicted that (1) setting specific, high performance goals (compared to vague, moderate performance goals) and (2) setting additionally specific, high learning goals, previously worked through exploratory guidance, would benefit learning and task performance, in a transparent simulation of a dynamically complex system.

The results from regression analysis confirm two of the four hypotheses. The hypotheses H1a (the level of performance goals positively influences the comprehension of the model dynamics) and H1b (the level of performance goals positively influences the performance) are not supported. This finding is consistent with some of the literature on learning from complex simulations. For example, Gary et al. (2017) also reported that, in a complex task, stretch goals (compared with moderate goals) did not produce a significant main effect on performance. A possible explanation, in the view of CLT, is that the extra pressure and cognitive load, caused by the persistent and increasing distance from the high goals, reduce the availability of students' cognitive resources, deteriorate learning and performance outcomes, and erode motivation and goal commitment.

By previously working specific, high learning goals, under exploratory guidance, students significantly improved comprehension and task performance, supporting hypothesis H2a (the level of learning goals and exploratory guidance positively moderates the impact of the level of performance goals on the comprehension of the model dynamics) and H2b (the level of learning goals and exploratory guidance positively moderates the impact of the level of performance goals on the performance). As we hypothesised, the results strongly evidence that setting specific, high learning goals (to be previously worked under exploratory guidance) gave participants a powerful means to reflect and learn on model structure and behaviour, which accelerated and consolidated their learning about the dynamics of the simulated system and enhanced performance. This conclusion is in line with previous research about the goal setting effects on performance in high complex tasks (e.g. Chen & Latham, 2014; Latham et al., 2008; Yang et al., 2017), which articulates that in situations where primarily the acquisition of knowledge and skills is required, a specific challenging learning rather than an outcome goal should be set.

REFERENCES

Alfieri, L., Brooks, P. J., Aldrich, N. J., & Tenenbaum, H. R. (2011). Does discovery-based instruction enhance learning? *Journal of Educational Psychology, 103*(1), 1–18.

Capelo, C., Dias, J., & Pereira, R. (2018). A system dynamics approach to analyse the impact of energy efficiency policy on ESCO ventures in European Union countries: a case study of Portugal. *Energy Efficiency, 11*, 1-33.

Capelo, C., Pereira, R. & Dias, J. (2020). Performance effects of structural and behavioural debriefings in transparent simulations. In Sampson, D. G., Ifenthaler, D., & Isaías, P. (Eds.), Proceedings of the IADIS international conference on cognition and exploratory learning in the digital age. IADIS: Lisboa, Portugal, pp 149-156.

Capelo, C. & Silva, A. (2020). Optimizing the learning potential of simulations through structural transparency and exploratory guidance. *Simulation & Gaming.*

Clement, J. J. (2008). *Creative model construction in scientists and students. The role of imagery, analogy, and mental simulation.* Springer.

Chen, X. & Latham, G. (2014). The effect of priming learning vs. performance goals on a complex task. *Organizational Behavior and Human Decision Processes, 125*, 88-97.

Crouzevialle, M. & Butera, F. (2017). Performance Goals and Task Performance - Integrative Considerations on the Distraction Hypothesis. *European Psychologist, 22*(2), 73-82.

Davidsen, P. & Spector, J. (2015). Critical Reflections on System Dynamics and Simulation/Gaming. *Simulation & Gaming*, *46,* 430-444.

de Jong, T. (2006). Technological advances in inquiry learning. *Science, 312*, 532–533.

de Jong, T., Lazonder, A., Pedaste, M., & Zacharia, Z. (2018). Simulations, games, and modelling tools for learning. In F. Fischer, C. E. Hmelo-Silver, S. R. Goldman, & P. Reimann (Eds.), *International handbook of the learning sciences* (pp. 256–266). Routledge, Taylor and Francis.

Gary, M., & Wood, R. (2011). Mental models, decision rules, and performance heterogeneity. *Strategic Management Journal, 32*(6), 569–594.

Gary, M., Yang, M., Yetton, P., Sterman, J. (2017) Stretch Goals and the Distribution of Organizational Performance. *Organization Science, 28* (3), 379-595.

Landriscina, F. (2013). Simulation and learning: *A model-centered approach*. Springer.

Latham, G. P., Seijts, G., & Crim, D. (2008). The effects of learning goal difficulty level and cognitive ability on performance. *Canadian Journal of Behavioural Science, 40*(4), 220–229.

Locke, E. A., & Latham, G. P. (2013). New developments in goal setting and task performance. London: Routledge.

Mayer, R. E. (2004). Should there be a three-strikes rule against pure discovery learning? *American Psychologist, 59*(1), 14–19.

Nebel, S., Schneider, S., Schledjewski, J., & Rey, G. (2017). Goal-Setting in Educational Video Games: Comparing Goal-Setting Theory and the Goal-Free Effect. *Simulation & Gaming, 48*(1), 98-130.

Sweller, J. (2020). Cognitive load theory and educational technology. *Educational Technology Research and Development, 68*, 1-16.

Sweller, J., van Merrienboer, J. G., & Paas, F. W. C. (1998). Cognitive architecture and instructional design. *Educational Psychology Review, 10*, 251-296.

Yang, M., Jiang, H., & Gary, M. (2017). Challenging learning goals improve performance in dynamically complex microworld simulations. *System Dynamics Review, 32*, 204–232.

ONLINE UNIVERSITY ORIENTATION MODELS FOR STUDENT TRANSITION BETWEEN SECONDARY AND TERTIARY EDUCATION

Francesco Floris[1], Marina Marchisio[1], Matteo Sacchet[1], Tiziana Margaria[2] and Sergio Rabellino[3]
[1]Department of Molecular Biotechnology and Health Sciences, University of Turin, Via Nizza 52, 10126 Turin, Italy
[2]Department of Computer Science and Information Systems, University of Limerick, Lero, the Irish Software Research Centre, Tierney Building, V94 T9PX Limerick, Ireland
[3]Department of Computer Science, University of Turin, C.so Svizzera 185, 10149 Turin, Italy

ABSTRACT

The transformation of higher education practices needs to be accompanied by the deployment of university guidance. This is especially important when activities have to be carried online and remotely. Online students expect to receive precise information to be successful learners, just as they would if they were in a face-to-face setting, but even more, due to the large capabilities of digital services. Worldwide universities provide free and open access to educational content online, but this is effective for guidance only if it is the main objective of courses and resources. One way to address student transition has been experimented by the University of Turin with the action Orient@mente that helps students in their transition from secondary school to university. In Orient@mente, students can find useful information, guidance activities, automatically graded tests to prepare for university admittance, online courses for revising basic knowledge, resources for foreign students, and information about the Erasmus program. This action has already proven its usefulness and it is expanding as a transversal and international model. Soon a new action will be fully developed, Eirenteering, a name mixing Eire (the Irish name for Ireland) and Orienteering. This paper discusses the methodologies adopted in Orient@mente and the forthcoming Eirenteering, together with results obtained with Orient@mente concerning the usage and the usefulness of the service.

KEYWORDS

Digital Learning Environment, Online Orientation, Secondary to Tertiary Transition, University Admittance, University Guidance, University Orientation

1. INTRODUCTION

The transformation of higher education practices generates new challenges for university guidance. Many changes arose after the Bologna process, a series of ministerial meetings aimed at bringing more coherence to higher education systems across Europe and at making higher education more inclusive, accessible, attractive, and competitive worldwide. The Bologna Follow Up Group has identified three key commitments: the implementation of the three-cycle degree structure, the recognition of qualifications, and quality assurance (European Commission/EACEA/Eurydice, 2018). Beyond these three commitments, we can find other areas of intervention, such as Opening higher education, which deals with education barriers, disadvantaged students, difficulties in completing higher education, and dropout rates. In this framework, student transition to university is an area leading to ongoing challenges that different stakeholders in institutions need to face. The transition between secondary school and the university very often occurs over a difficult time frame. The challenges in this phase are still unclear (Gueudet, 2008), both in STEM and in other disciplines. Possible barriers to study success are individual, social, due to the education system, or to personal conditions. Students need to feel accompanied in their educational path. After the enrolment, universities usually register many changes of course and abandonment of studies. Dedicated staff should help students in their orientation. Results demonstrated that having a designated office for orientation programs is important for narrowing the academic learning gap between new first-year and transfer students (Mayewh et al., 2010). Institutions try to make orientation a more personalized experience for new students by offering small orientation sessions, making them feel comfortable and connected to both their orientation leader and their peers in the group (Mayewh et al., 2010). In today's educational environments, the use of web-based technologies emerged, with a focus on online course delivery. In this way, orientation activities can take place even remotely and using online courses, tests, and other interactive resources (Barana et al., 2017a; Barana et al., 2017b). This is especially important in times of forced online activity (Alperin et al., 2020), not just for students, but also for working professionals. Online students expect to receive information that will prepare them to be successful learners, just as they would if they were in a face-to-face setting. When supported by institutions, new technologies can be effective for university guidance. Worldwide universities provide free and open access to educational content online. Resources, learning plans, and activities specifically designed for this objective can enhance the effectiveness of online students' guidance. Multimedia, interactive resources, automatic online assessment, Massive Open Online Courses, and the variety of tools integrated into Learning Management Systems allow institutions to contact students, to guide and to connect experts and learners. Online orientation is even more important in times of pandemic, as experienced in 2020 due to Covid-19 when different nations faced lockdown of many educational activities. New funds will be injected in the university system in Italy from the PNRR, the National Plan for Resistance and Resilience, to promote access to university, make the transition easier and faster and strengthen guidance tools in the choice of the university path.

One way to address student transition is by introducing an appropriate form of automatic formative assessment: if well-structured and provided within a proper support environment, it can improve consciousness, self-awareness, confidence, and student experience. Since 2014, the University of Turin has been supporting Orient@mente, an action to help students in the transition from secondary school to university, able to adapt to the specific needs of each student and to encourage them to choose consciously their academic studies using Open Online Courses hosted on a custom Moodle platform. Along with specific discipline contents, students can find various information, guidance activities for courses, preparation tests for university admittance, online courses for revising basic knowledge, resources for foreign students, and advices about the Erasmus program.

Online orientation can easily become international, and a model similar to Orient@mente is going to be developed soon with Eirenteering, a name mixing Eire (the Irish name for Ireland) and Orienteering. In this case, the starting point is Computer Science, since many first-year students are not sufficiently aware of the challenges intrinsic to the specific discipline (such as programming and model-driven design), related topics (such as discrete mathematics), and innovative approaches (such as formative assessment) to guide students through a resolution process whenever they have a gap in their knowledge. Eirenteering, whenever possible, will also support blended courses, because many online contents overlap with first-year modules in the common entry in Computer Science LM121 BSc.

This paper discusses the methodologies adopted and the results obtained in Orient@mente. It will also describe how this model is going to be implemented in the Irish context. After presenting the state of the art of online models for orientation in Section 2, the paper describes the research question and the methodology in Section 3. Section 4 delineates the framework in which these activities have been carried out. The model is fully analyzed in Section 5, while Section 6 reports some results concerning student online activity.

2. STATE OF THE ART

In education, the term guidance is used in the context of lifelong learning, career guidance, counseling, related services that support students, and specific provision of teaching and learning (Hounsell et al., 2008). University teaching can provide students with tools and skills that will help them face their future studies and career (Marchisio et al., 2020). In (Chiteng Kot, 2014), the students who made use of the centralized academic advising reported an increase in their first-term, second-term, and first-year cumulative Grade Point Average. Moreover, students who used centralized advising during the second term experienced a decrease in their probability of first-year attrition. Different studies agree with this research. In (Skaniakos et al., 2019), with self-assessed students' surveys, the authors found that general study guidance is a strong predictor of students' development of academic and generic skills, promoting also working life orientation. This is valid across all different disciplines, with some variation on the impact according to the Department.

In (Sun and Yuen, 2012) the authors discuss the adoption in China of orientation models that have been developed and mainly used in Europe or the US. The authors discuss the content, the implementation, the problems that arose, and ways of improving the university actions in China. They underline the importance of local factors such as the job market, the employment system, the educational philosophy, and the social value system. They propose different steps to achieve the objective of a good orientation: the construction of a student talent database, more participatory and with interactive forms of career guidance, and the establishment of a team of teachers with relevant expertise relevant for college students.

From the point of view of online orientation activities, one of the main issues is the ability to build digital capacity at a large scale. For example, according to the European frameworks, the DigComp 2.1 (Carretero et al., 2019) identifies five areas of digital competence as key components: Information and data literacy, Communication and collaboration, Digital content creation, Safety, and Problem solving. All these features are essential to the success of online activities. The Digital Education Action Plan (DEAP, 2020) deals with digital competencies, too. The communications report state the needs of a vast and growing array of digital technologies together with digital competencies for all learners. In (Herridge et al., 2020), findings suggest that students who attend online out-of-class orientation activities were more likely to become engaged in group study and preparation, having more knowledge of the institutional and academic advising support. The authors identified four recommendations for practitioners: Orientation programming should continue to enhance efforts related to student knowledge of institutional support; Practitioners should be innovative in how they construct orientation programming whether online or in traditional settings; Advising support should be central to online and traditional orientation; Institutions should engage in more critical evaluation of orientation programming; Online orientation can make use of new technologies in ICT, like artificial intelligence techniques. In (Kai et al., 2017), the authors made use of machine learning methods in order to develop prediction models to assess the effectiveness of an online orientation course in improving student retention in an online college program.

To summarize what emerged from a literature review on orientation models, various forms of orientation activities can take place. The ones coming from a centralized institutional division can be more efficient. Moreover, online orientation proved its usefulness. These are the main ingredients for the recipe of the orientation support model developed by the University of Turin and adopted by other international universities.

3. RESEARCH QUESTION AND METHODOLOGY

The question that motivated this research is the following: how can institutions set up an orientation process to guide students to achieve better outcomes in their university path? To understand this, we analyzed the model developed by the University of Turin with the action Orient@mente, which was recently adopted by the University of Limerick with the action Eirenteering. First, we are going to describe the framework in which those actions took place, also taking into account different indicators: Accessibility, Adaptability, Availability, Consistency, Control, Digital Environment, Open Access, Staff training, Support and communication, Sustainability. These indicators are compliant with a model of student orientation and with previous work by the research group on this topic (Barana et al., 2017a; Barana et al., 2017b). Second, we are going to present statistics from the student population of the University of Turin, especially in comparison with the usage of Orient@mente. We will underline the kind of users that interact with the online environment.

4. THE FRAMEWORK

A net is stronger when the strings are tightly woven together. The same applies to networks of collaboration, and this is why many universities create connections. In our specific context, we describe a growing partnership network that spans heterogeneous and interdisciplinary partners:

- the Department of Computer Science and the Department of Molecular Biotechnologies and Health Sciences (DMBHS) of the University of Turin, Italy;
- the Department of Computer Science and Information Systems (CSIS) of the University of Limerick, Ireland, as well as two national research centers: Lero - the Irish Software Research Centre and Confirm - the Smart Manufacturing Research Centre.

The main topic of the partnership is the transition between secondary and tertiary education. This is addressed with online resources and paths, openly available to students. The University of Turin (UNITO) has a long-lasting experience in the use of Digital Learning Environments (DLE), with the adoption of the Moodle platform since 2003 and its large-scale adoption for blended teaching and online projects. One of these projects, called “Orient@mente” (Barana et al., 2017a; Barana et al. 2017b), is aimed at encouraging students to make a more conscious and informed decision about the choice of their university studies. UNITO reinforces classic orientation activities for incoming students through a model involving interactive guidance to courses, testing with automatic evaluation, and online tutoring. The action of Orient@mente have reinforced actual orientation activities, shared tools, and data with the pre-existing ICT services of the University. Orient@mente offers a growing number of Open Online Courses (OOCs) containing information and guidance activities for university courses, free admission tests, courses for revising basic high school knowledge, and specific resources for foreign students and Erasmus students. The adopted model is an example of mutual entailment between the academic world and social networking: students are guided to face their academic decisions, while the University monitors their progress, provides feedback about their current abilities, and tries to meet their information and self-assessment needs. This model was shown to be useful for Italian students (Floris et al., 2020). Other actions that have been carried out inside Orient@mente concern a disciplinary formative orientation, with programs that let student discover specific topics and their relation with other subjects. There is also a series of actions devoted to teachers, a course to train University Ambassadors, close guide for students.

The University of Limerick (UL) requires similar – potentially adapted – initiatives, since many first-year Computer Science (CS) students are not sufficiently aware of the specific challenges related to the discipline. For example, surveys of first-year CS students in the LM121 BSc Hons program show that only 50% of them have previous programming experience. Studies about programs in CS education (McInerney et al., 2017) show that there is a gender difference in CS and STEM education. An internal analysis in UL has shown that success is not gender-related in first-year CS, while the transition from secondary to tertiary education is one of the possible causes for the high attrition in year one. Success in the first year is essential to a positive student experience, which is a pivotal aim both in the specific UL setting and at the Irish national level. For example, the National Forum Strategic Priorities (Strategy 2019-2021) and the Third Level Computing Forum work in this direction. On the ground, the special orientation and mentorship for incoming students are addressed in UL in general by assigning faculty as personal mentors to each student. Specifically, in CS, the first-year LM121 students are additionally peer-mentored by second-year volunteers students in the CSIS-CTL co-led pilot intervention project “Making the Leap: a Pathway to Success”, now in its third year. The collaboration is between the CSIS Department and the Centre for Teaching and Learning in Computer Science, which “support and promote active learning among the students of ICT related programs in UL, via the use of proven learner support approaches, tutoring innovation, research, and evaluation, to develop learners who are confident and effective ICT practitioners.” So far, there is no self-assessment offer for students and prospective students.

The model of Orient@mente and, consequently, Eirenteering, provides different features.

- Accessibility. Developed contents are possibly accessible. Moreover, the platforms adopt system-wide the high-legibility font “EasyReading” designed for people with dyslexia.
- Adaptability. The model, structure, and tools can be applied to different university requirements, various disciplinary areas (as of 2020, Orient@mente lets students explore almost the entire offer of the University of Turin) and different students’ learning approaches.
- Availability. From the point of view of time, both actions operate as continual services to let students access anytime. From the point of view of space, learners from all over the world can benefit from materials.
- Consistency. The platform that students navigate is the same technology that supports university modules and is adopted by many universities around the world. Students become familiar with a system that they will meet continuously throughout their careers. Moreover, the integration of multiple kinds of resources facilitates ongoing research on new technology.
- Control. Institutions and related stakeholders perform periodical analysis to understand the learning behavior of students and provide possible improvements to the action, adapting it to students’ needs.
- DLE with integrated tools. The online provision of contents allows the integration with different tools with a Learning Management System (LMS), such as an Advanced Computing Environment (ACE) useful for students of STEM disciplines that require a scientific approach, and an Automatic Assessment Systems (AAS) to monitor students’ results and give proper feedback whenever possible. Students are facilitated in autonomously overcoming their insecurities by immediate feedback.
- Open Access. There is no cost in accessing the online resources. This is in line with the Open Educational Resources (OER) paradigm. Moreover, when accessing the platform for the first time,

users must accept the privacy policy that specifies their own rights about personal data, according to the European General Data Protection Regulation.

- Staff training and teamwork. Different actors were involved in the design and implementation of online contents: university professors, graduate students, PhDs, and students with master's degrees. All these people attended a training course in the use of digital tools and online learning methodologies, coordinated by expert instructional designers and by university module leaders. Thus, highly qualified staff designed the point of contact between students and the university.
- Support and communication. The platforms link to the main source of information, which lies in the official university web pages, creating synergy with other orientation activities. Moreover, the collaboration with Regional School offices plays an essential role in promoting the actions.
- Sustainability. Students pay nothing to access the service. The university sustains all the costs for the production of materials and services, as well as the costs for recruiting staff.

Different kinds of students can fruitfully use these actions.

- Secondary school students, who are the main target of these actions and need to make informed choices at the time of enrolment.
- University students, who need to fulfil a supplementary educational obligation (for example, those who score poorly in admission tests).
- Secondary school teachers, who can count on an up-to-date environment with online contents and provide accurate suggestions to their students.

Table 1. Needs of students in transition between secondary and tertiary education and strategies adopted by Orient@mente and Eirenteering

Need	Orient@mente	Eirenteering
Recover gaps in the knowledge	Realignment courses in scientific disciplines	Most secondary students do not study Computer Science, first-year modules are introductory courses
Attend university modules	This is done by start@unito, another action of UNITO	First-year open online courses in Computer Science
Prepare for admission tests	Test area, plus an area dedicated to medical sciences and healthcare professions	There is no admission test in Computer Science
Explore degree programs	Area to explore almost all degree programs at UNITO	Students can explore Computer Science Common Entry

To summarize, these actions answer to some of the needs of students that triggered a response from the university. In Table 1, we summarize some of these needs and highlight the answer given by each action. As stated in the table, some of the students' needs in the transition to university are provided by other actions, too. As an example, at UNITO there is also start@unito, a platform that delivers 50 open online courses prepared specifically for students who are attending a university module for the first time (Bruschi et al., 2018; Marchisio et al., 2019).

5. RESULTS

In this section, we are going to report subscriptions, logins, and other data collected from platform usage to give an idea of the action Orient@mente. The data were collected in July 2021. The platform hosts 69,398 users, 11% of which are students at UNITO (7888 users) because they use the institutional student email address. In all the other cases, the detection of the correspondence between UNITO students and Orient@mente users is not straightforward, because the only identifier in joining the two datasets is represented by the email address, and the same person may use multiple accounts. Open access sometimes means difficulties in joining with other data sources.

To understand the impact of Orient@mente, we performed a comparison between users' subscriptions and the number of first-year students at UNITO. The numbers are shown in Table 2. The size of the numbers is comparable. The number of first-year students has increased across the years, while the number of Orient@mente users has initially grown, and then slightly decreased.

Table 2. Yearly new subscriptions to Orient@mente compared with UNITO first-year students

Year	Orient@mente subscriptions	UNITO first-year students	Ratio
2015	4,307	17,800 (Academic Year 2014/2015)	24%
2016	6,613	18,500 (Academic Year 2015/2016)	36%
2017	11,358	20,800 (Academic Year 2016/2017)	55%
2018	17,270	22,400 (Academic Year 2017/2018)	77%
2019	15,693	23,100 (Academic Year 2018/2019)	68%
2020	11,119	23,600 (Academic Year 2019/2020)	47%
2021	7,552	26,000 (Academic Year 2020/2021)	29%

Orient@mente alone does not equal the numbers of all first-year students, but on average around 48% of first-year students made use of the support, which is quite an interesting result.

As explained in the previous sections, students can navigate into different areas: Area 1, online courses to recover gaps in the knowledge and fulfil additional education duties (17,479 subscriptions), Area 2, courses devoted to exploring the degree programs at the University of Turin (22,886 subscriptions), Area 3, courses to prepare for admission tests (83,554 subscriptions), and a new specific area (Area 4) for admission tests in medical sciences and healthcare professions (1,408 subscriptions). Moreover, the platform devoted another area for the TARM test, Assessment Test of Minimum Requirements, which was delivered by Orient@mente. This area is now no longer supported (18,247 subscriptions) because the university decided to ask an external agency to organize the TARM and the admission test.

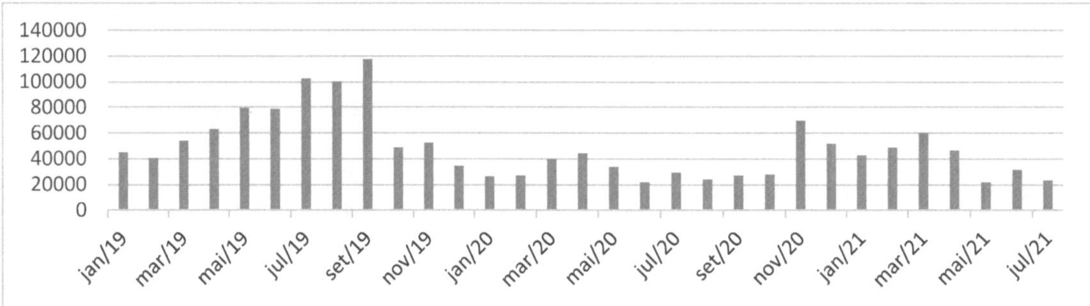

Figure 1. Number of user logins in Orient@mente divided by month from January 2019 to July 2021

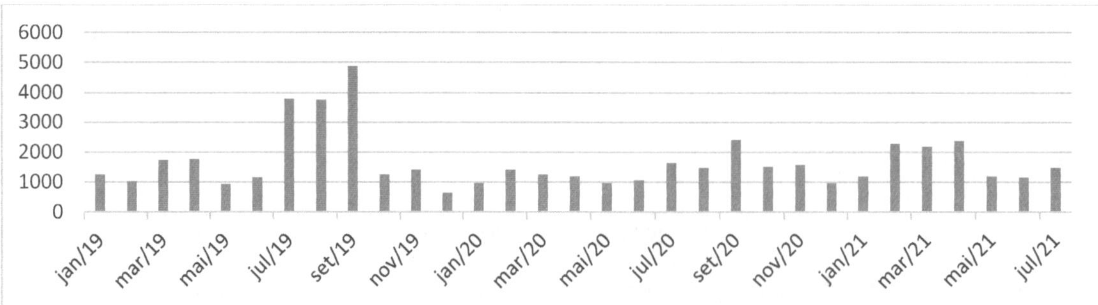

Figure 2. Number of unique user logins in Orient@mente divided by month from January 2019 to October 2020

Figure 1 considers the number of user logins. In the period January 2019-July 2021, the average number of monthly student logins was 48,857. On the other side, Figure 2 considers the number of distinct user logins. In the period January 2019-July 2021, the average number of monthly student distinct logins was 1,670. The numbers suggest that many students use the online platform, even though the numbers are not increasing over time. This depends also on actions that are carried out by the university and the project managers: when there is something new in the platform, there is an advertisement and more users subscribe.

The time that students spend surfing the platform can vary significantly. It is worth noting that half of users subscribed and viewed contents just for one day (54.5%). This is quite reasonable for students who simply wish to explore the various degree programs or attempt the admission tests just once successfully. Excluding users that subscribed and viewed the platform just for one day, the time difference between the first and the last access is on average 133 days. This number is more related to students who attend the online courses to remediate gaps in their knowledge, in fact 116 days is a suitable time for studying.

6. CONCLUSION

There are different objectives behind the improvements in the organization of university's orientation actions: facilitate students' transition between different education systems, prevent the dropout in the study program, and improve students' responsibility towards their academic studies. The present paper fully describes and explains the setup of the orientation processes. The model provides different features that all together lead to a positive and fruitful experience. Furthermore, it is applicable and sharable among different universities.

The adaptive learning path containing the remedial procedure created to assess and fill learning gaps in Computer Science does indeed retain the features of the University of Turin model and the related literature. The features acted as a guideline in designing new learning paths.

The actions are alive and continuously developing. On one side, Orient@mente in 2020 has extended the number of interactive paths to all courses at the University of Turin. Even the test area was expanded, with numerous activities to prepare admission tests to medical degrees, which are, in Italy, very restrictive. On the other side, Eirenteering is still in its infancy, with two interactive first-year modules in Computer Science. More online resources are currently under development, in particular in collaboration with the team of ISE, the new integrated BSc/MSc Immersive Software Engineering that will start in Limerick in September 2022. Future work in Eirenteering concerns the development and delivery of adaptive assessments in an open online learning environment. Considering the most up-to-date trends in education (openness, mobile learning, adaptive learning, etc.), the platform contents provide individual orientation to prospective first-year students and help them consciously make their choice about an academic career in Computer Science. This way, prospective students will test their skills and competencies for the first time in advance of their application, while evaluating different possible career paths. This new opportunity will also directly affect students that have difficulties in attending classes, such as working students or students with limited mobility. Learning Analytics create new opportunities for student orientation, delivering early warnings that alert teachers, instructors, and students when there is a risk of not meeting academic goals, especially for people who often work directly with students, but usually not in classroom settings, like academic advisors in higher education and other professionals in the K-12 system (Ocumpaugh et al., 2017). Data collection analysis and learning analytics techniques (Marchisio et al., 2019) applied to the fine granular data obtained from the online platform is likely to provide new insights into how students learn on their own time, thus helping us to improve teaching and learning in Computer Science.

ACKNOWLEDGEMENT

This research was funded, from the Orient@mente side, by the bank foundation "Compagnia di San Paolo". From the Eirenteering side, the research was funded by the Science Foundation Ireland grant 13/RC/2094 by Lero - the Irish Software Research Centre (www.lero.ie), HEA/NF SATLE 2019 Funding from the Irish National Forum for the Enhancement of Teaching and Learning in Higher Education.

REFERENCES

Alperin, L. et al., 2020. The Role of Orientation Programs to Prepare Students for Online Learning: A Case Study from an Executive MPH Program. *Pedagogy in Health Promotion*, 6(4), pp. 239-245. doi:10.1177/2373379920953375

Barana, A. et al., 2017a. Open platform of self-paced MOOCs for the continual improvement of academic guidance and knowledge strengthening in tertiary education. *Journal of e-Learning and Knowledge Society*, 13(3), pp. 109-119. doi:10.20368/1971-8829/1383

Barana, A. et al., 2017b. Self-paced approach in synergistic model for supporting and testing students: the transition from Secondary School to University. *Proceedings of 2017 IEEE 41st Annual Computer Software and Applications Conference (COMPSAC)*. Torino, Italy, pp.404-409. doi:10.1109/COMPSAC.2017.211

Bruschi, B. et al., 2018. Start@unito: a Supporting Model for High School Students Enrolling to University. *Proceedings of the international conference on Cognition and Exploratory Learning in Digital Age (CELDA 2018)*, Budapest, Hungary, pp. 307-312.

Carretero, S. et al., 2017. DigComp 2.1: The Digital Competence Framework for Citizens with eight proficiency levels and examples of use. *EUR 28558 EN*. doi:10.2760/38842

Chiteng Kot, F., 2014. The Impact of Centralized Advising on First-Year Academic Performance and Second-Year Enrollment Behavior, *Res High Educ* 55, pp. 527-563. doi:10.1007/s11162-013-9325-4

DEAP, 2020. Digital Education Action Plan 2021-2027 – Communication September 2020, retrieved from https://ec.europa.eu/education/sites/default/files/document-library-docs/deap-communication-sept2020_en.pdf, last accessed July29th, 2021.

European Commission/EACEA/Eurydice, 2018. The European Higher Education Area in 2018: Bologna Process Implementation Report. *Luxembourg: Publications Office of the European Union*. doi:10.2797/265898

Floris, F. et al., 2020. Learning analytics to evaluate the effectiveness of higher education student failure prevention. *Proceedings of 17th international conference on Cognition and Exploratory Learning in the Digital Age (CELDA 2020)*, pp. 265-272.

Gueudet, G., 2008. Investigating the secondary-tertiary transition. Educational Studies in Mathematics, *Springer Verlag*, 67 (3), pp. 237-254. doi:10.1007/s10649-007-9100-6

Herridge, A. S. et al., 2020. Online Orientation among Community College Students: Academic Engagement and Sense of Belonging. *Journal of Applied Research in the Community College*, 27(1), pp. 17-31.

Hounsell, D. et al., 2008. The Quality of Guidance and Feedback to Students. *Higher Education Research & Development* 27 (1), pp. 55-67. doi:10.1080/07294360701658765

Kai, S. et al., 2017. Predicting Student Retention from Behavior in an Online Orientation Course. *International Educational Data Mining Society (EDM)*.

Marchisio, M. et al., 2019. Boosting up data collection and analysis to learning analytics in open online contexts: an assessment methodology. *Journal of E-Learning and Knowledge Society*, 15(3), pp. 79-89. doi: 10.20368/1971-8829/1135048

Marchisio, M. et al., 2019. Start@unito: Open Online Courses for Improving Access and for Enhancing Success in Higher Education. *Proceedings of the 11th International Conference on Computer Supported Education (CSEDU 2019)*, Vol. 1, Heraklion, Greece, pp. 639-646. doi:10.5220/0007732006390646

Marchisio, M. et al., 2020. Teaching Mathematics in Scientific Bachelor Degrees Using a Blended Approach. *Proceedings of 2020 IEEE 44th Computer Software and Applications Conference (COMPSAC),* Madrid, Spain, pp. 190-195. doi: 10.1109/COMPSAC48688.2020.00034

Mayhew, M. J., 2010. A Multi-Level Assessment of the Impact of Orientation Programs on Student Learning, *Res High Educ* 51, pp. 320-345. doi:10.1007/s11162-009-9159-2

McInerney, C. et al., 2017. Computing Camps for Girls - A First-Time Experience at the University of Limerick. In A. Tatnall & M. Webb (A c. Di), Tomorrow's Learning: Involving Everyone. Learning with and about Technologies and Computing, *Springer International Publishing*, pp. 494-505. doi:10.1007/978-3-319-74310-3_50

Ocumpaugh, J. et al., 2017. Guidance counselor reports of the ASSISTments college prediction model (ACPM). *Proceedings of the 7th International Learning Analytics & Knowledge Conference (LAK '17).* New York, USA, pp. 479-488. doi:10.1145/3027385.3027435

Skaniakos, T. et al., 2019. Study guidance experiences, study progress, and perceived learning outcomes of Finnish university students. *European Journal of Higher Education*, 9(2), pp. 203-218. doi:10.1080/21568235.2018.1475247

Sun, V. J. and Yuen, M., 2012. Career Guidance and Counseling for University Students in China, *Int J Adv Counselling* 34, pp. 202-210. doi:10.1007/s10447-012-9151-y

A CASE STUDY OF STUDENTS' VIEWS ON THE DIGITAL SKILLS NEEDED FOR THE LABOUR MARKET

Anda Zeidmane and Anna Vintere
Latvia University of Life Sciences and Technologies
Liela Street 2, Jelgava, Latvia

ABSTRACT

New digital technologies are changing entrepreneurship. Digital entrepreneurship includes new ways how to find customers for business, how to design new products, how to generate revenue, how to collaborate with platforms and partners and so on. Today's labour market requires staff with foundation digital skills, ICT general skills, ICT specialist skills and ICT complementary skills. Improving digital competences is also a major challenge for the European higher education system. The aim of the study is to determine students' views on what digital skills students need to improve in order to enter the future labour market as well as learn and identify opportunities for students to develop their digital skills. Based on the research on digital competences, a questionnaire was developed for students of the Latvia University of Life Sciences and Technologies (LLU). This reassessment was also compared among the faculties of LLU. According to students, the most important digital skills needed for the labour market are as follows: use and manage information (69.84%), evaluation of information (67.19%) and access to information (65.15%). The comparison among the specialties show that students of agricultural engineering and forest science and forestry engineering programmes have the lowest evaluation of their digital skills, but, of course, the specialty "Information technologies for sustainable development" has the highest. Based on the obtained results, the authors suggest that the study course "Informatics" should be regularly reviewed and updated, the development of digital skills should be promoted in all study courses, as well as the study course "Introduction to the specialty" should be used to reduce the gap between ICT skills for the first-year students.

KEYWORDS

Digital Skills and Competences, Digital Entrepreneurship, Self-Assessment

1. INTRODUCTION

With the development of the technological age, the possibilities to solve various everyday needs and situations electronically are constantly increasing - everyday life is unthinkable without communication with peers online. In addition, the number of public services that can be received digitally is also increasing. To take full advantage of these opportunities, well-developed skills in the use of digital technologies are needed. According to the European Commission, more than a third (37%) of Europeans of working age do not have sufficient digital skills, but 13% do not have them at all. If we talk about the situation in Latvia, then the results of the Eurobarometer survey conducted in Latvia show that only a quarter of the public (25%) believe that their e-skills meet every day needs. Meanwhile, 8% of respondents consider their e-skills to be rather insufficient, while 13% admit that their skills are too weak.

Digital competence is not just the ability to surf the Internet, it can be broken down into many smaller components. The European Commission has developed the Digital Competences Framework for Europeans (DigComp), which is divided into five areas: information and data literacy; communication and cooperation; digital content creation; safety; and problem solving. Today, digital competences are no longer just about access to and use of information communication technologies (ICT), they are also about ICT knowledge, skills and attitudes. It should be noted that digital competence, can be seen also as a transversal competence, also helps to develop other essential skills, such as communication, language skills or basic knowledge in mathematics or science.

In the context of developing the skills needed for today's labour market, it should be noted that the digital era is introducing the need for a new business model with new skill requirements, new ways of working, and a more flexible work culture. According to the IBM finding, "The digital era has provided the opportunity and the need for speed – and that, in turn, has led to new ways of working. Remote working, always-on access, transparency, less hierarchy, pop-up teams operating across functional and organizational boundaries, and organizations operating within an ecosystem of partners all require a cultural agility and, in turn, new skills for the workforce" (IBM, 2019).

2. MATERIALS AND METHODS

To develop the methodology of this study, a study of the scientific literature and documents on digital competence was performed in the light of the above circumstances. Based on the findings, a questionnaire was created to identify students' views on the digital competence necessary for the labour market.

2.1 Theoretical Background of the Study

Students studying at a university should be aware of the need to develop their digital skills for successful integration into the labour market. The first step is to understand what digital entrepreneurship means and what the key factors are. In its Entrepreneurship 2020 Action Plan, the European Commission intends to drive the transformation of the business environment through new digital technologies (Entrepreneurship, 2013). The term Digital Entrepreneurship is used, which is different from traditional entrepreneurship. The European Commission (EC,2015) has defined: "Digital entrepreneurship embraces all new ventures and the transformation of existing businesses that drive economic and/or social value by creating and using novel digital technologies". Digital enterprises make very intensive use of new digital technologies, especially social, big data, mobile and cloud solutions.

The developed conceptual model of digital entrepreneurship (EC,2013) identifies five "pillars":

1) Digital knowledge base and ICT market - which will contribute to the improvement of the digital innovation, commercialization and ICT sector
2) Digital business environment - which will strengthen the digital infrastructure, the regulatory framework and simplify business
3) Access to finance - which will facilitate access to finance and digital investment
4) Digital skills and e-leadership - which will promote the development of e-leadership skills through education and training
5) Entrepreneurial Culture – which creating a supportive entrepreneurial culture

Digital entrepreneurship is recognized as a new and growing field of research (Zhao & Collier, 2016), and students need to be ready to integrate into digital entrepreneurship today.

The European Commission's study report (Shaping Europe's digital future, 2021) highlighted issues of digital skills in the workplace, even the impact of ICT on the workplace, as well as the transformation of ICT skills. The study found that most jobs require basic digital skills, including software developers, engineers, doctors, teachers, construction workers, accountants, lawyers, journalists, civil servants, sales staff, agricultural workers and more. Studies have shown that most workplaces require special digital skills such as technicians, professionals - 50% of cases, managers -30%. The lack of digital skills affects more than 38% of jobs and the main negative effects are lost productivity (46%) and declining customer numbers (43%). It was also found that 88% of workplaces have not taken any action to address the digital skills shortage *of* employees.

To reduce the risk of unemployment and growing inequality, a change in ICT skills development policies is necessary. ICT skills development policy should aim to:

- strengthen initial learning,
- increase the use of staff skills,
- stimulate further education.

The Organization for Economic Co-operation and Development (OECD) has highlighted four types of ITC-related skills needed in the workplace (Background report, OECD, 2016). These are: 1) ICT generic skills, 2) ICT specialist skills 3) ICT complementary skills 4) foundation skills (see Figure 1).

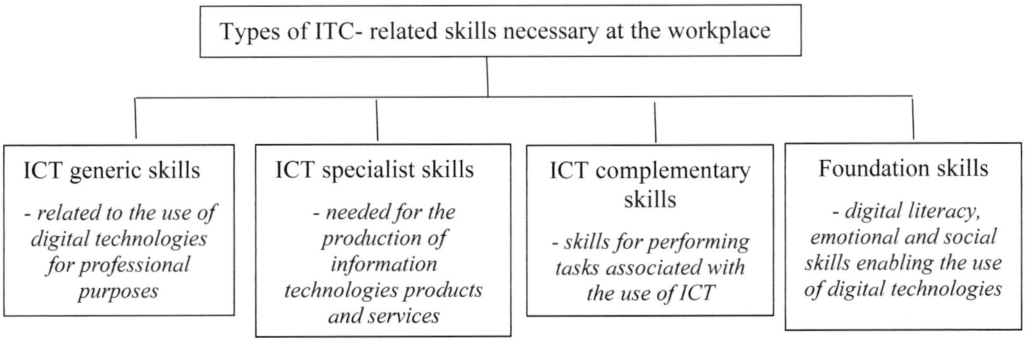

Figure 1. Types of ITC-related skills needed in the workplace (OECD,2016)

Based on the advice of experts and stakeholders, the European Commission (Background report, OECD, 2016) also makes recommendations on how to improve digital skills in the workplace to support labour market transformation. The most important of them are:

- Bridging the digital divide between citizens (especially those lacking ICT skills);
- Raise awareness of the need for digital skills;
- Use loans, grants and other mechanisms to improve and support access to digital technologies, especially for small businesses;
- Expand access to digital skills through the education and training system by renewing programs at all levels and in all sectors of education.
- Promote employers' access to training through sectoral organizations and associations;
- Integrate digital skills into a broader skills strategy that includes other transversal skills relevant to employers.

Based on the above and including social and emotional skills, the higher use of ICT in the labour market is also associated with tasks that require greater interaction with workers and clients.

Correlations between daily use of ICT at work and other tasks include aspects such as (Jobs and skills in the digital economy, 2016):

- Horizontal interaction *(information sharing, training others, giving presentations)*;
- Client interaction *(selling a product or service, advising others)*;
- Self-direction *(planning own activities; organising own time)*;
- Managerial skills *(planning activities of others)*;
- Influence *(persuading people; negotiating with people)*;
- Problem solving *(problem solving in less than 5 minutes, thinking about a solution for at least 30 min)*;
- Physical skills *(working physically)*;
- Manual skills *(using skills or accuracy with hands or fingers)*;
- Information-processing skills *(reading, writing, numeracy)*.

Improving digital competences is also a major challenge for the European higher education system. Universities need to focus on three areas (Torres-Coronas & Vidal-Blasco, 2014): the computer hardware, the operating system, and the specific software. Students must be able to adapt their communication style to the new technological environment and be able to work collaboratively in virtual teams.

In order to develop the digital skills needed in the labour market, the curriculum needs to be reviewed, the ITC infrastructure needs to be adapted to the digital change, and the acquisition of ICT skills in disadvantaged groups needs to be promoted (Kiss M, 2017). The Fast Track for Information Technology programme for long-term unemployed (FIT) in Ireland is a good example. The tasks of FIT are (FIT):

- Upskilling job seekers:
- Increasing access to in-demand technology training:

- Promoting smart people with smart skills:
- Training for employment (commencing careers);
- Putting policy in action.

The website "CV Market" has compiled six digital skills that are necessary for a modern professional in the labour market in Latvia: e-mail communication, the ability to adapt to the use of new tools, media literacy and information research skills, information presentation skills, social media skills and information technology (IT) and data security fundamentals. The research methodology was developed in accordance with these skills, as the goal of higher education institutions is to increase the qualification of young specialists for successful entry into the labour market.

2.2 Methodology of the Study

Considering the above-mentioned research results on the digital competence, a research methodology which includes a questionnaire for students was developed to identify key areas of Digital Competence (information, communication, content creation, safety and problem solving) and students' self-assessment of their achievements in these relevant areas of competences as well as to identify what digital skills students need to improve in order to enter the future labour market. In this article answers to the questions in the last section are analyzed, namely, the assessment of skills needed for the labour market, to determine the importance of the given skills and do self-assessment of those skills.

The questionnaire included six different digital skills needed for the labour market *(access to information, evaluation of information, use and management of information, information coding and programming, use of ICT for a specific purpose and use of ICT legally and ethically),* and students had to assess them from three perspectives: the importance of given skills, to what extent they have them and the need to improve these skills. The evaluation was performed in a three-stage Likert scale. The questionnaire contained closed questions.

The survey was conducted at the university of the authors of this article, asking students of different specialties to fill in an electronic questionnaire "Self-assessment of digital abilities", which is available at: https://ej.uz/DigCom. The sample of the study was 216 students from different specialties: civil engineering (14.93%), economics (19.40%), agricultural engineering (14.93%), forest science and forestry engineering (32.84%), information technologies for sustainable development (10.45%) and computer control and computer science (7.46%). Most of them (82.86%) were the first-year students and only 17.14% represented the second-year students.

According to the scientific literature, in order to improve the performance of higher education and promote learning, the study used the self-assessment method, which is recognized as the most powerful tool for identifying strengths and weaknesses (Andrade & Valtcheva, 2009).

3. FINDINGS

The results of the study show that according to the evaluation of students, the most important skill in the labour market is the use and management of information. 69.84% of all respondents consider it to be very important. This is followed by evaluation of information (67.19%) and the ability to access the information (65.15%). Slightly more than a quarter of respondents (26.15%) stated that the least important skill is information coding and programming (Table 1).

Table 1. The importance of digital skills for the labour market, answers in % (n =216)

Digital skills for the labour market	Unimportant	Moderately important	Very important
Access to information	7.58	27.27	65.15
Evaluation of information	7.81	25.00	67.19
Use and management of information	9.52	20.63	69.84
Information coding and programming	26.15	40.00	33.85
Use of ICT for a specific purpose	20.31	48.44	31.25
Use of ICT legally and ethically	21.88	42.19	35.94

Students were asked to rate the extent to which they have digital skills by three statements: *I lack such skills; this skill is average*; *this skill is at a high level.* The results of the survey show that only 37.88% of the surveyed students have the highest level of skills to access information, but 6.06% lack these skills (Table 2). About a third of students have a high level of ability to use and manage the information (32.31%) and to evaluate information (29.69%). Information coding and programming is a skill that is lacking in almost half of the students (46.15%). Although this skill is considered insignificant, it is at a high level of 10.77% (Table 2).

Although educational research has already shown that students have a high level of skills in using mobile phones, smartphones, laptops and other devices, and in using social networking software, they have problems using this technology in their studies (Khoza & Manik 2015). In this study, similar results were obtained: 34.38% of respondents lack the skills to use ICT for a specific purpose, which greatly influenced the distance learning process during the Covid-19 pandemic constraints. Issues of legitimacy of the use of ICT as well as ethical issues are also problematic for 24.19% of interviewed students.

Table 2. Self-assessment of digital skills needed for the labour market, answers in % (n =216)

Digital skills for the labour market	I lack such skills	This skill is average	This skill is at a high level
Access to information	6.06	56.06	37.88
Evaluation of information	7.81	62.50	29.69
Use and management of information	7.69	60.00	32.31
Information coding and programming	46.15	43.08	10.77
Use of ICT for a specific purpose	34.38	50.00	15.63
Use of ICT legally and ethically	24.19	59.68	16.13

Assessing the three most important digital skills needed both in the labour market and in everyday life by specialty, it can be concluded that more than a third of civil engineering students consider that they lack all of these skills; agricultural engineers lack information assessment skills (44.44%) and use and manage information (25%), but as regards forest science and forestry engineering students, 11.11% of respondents consider they lack the skill of use and management of information.

As shown in Table 3, these skills are at a high level for students majoring in IT or computers. It should be noted that more than a third of economics students (36.36%) have highly developed skill to access the information as well as to use and manage information.

Table 3. Assessment of digital skills "This skill is at a high level" by specialties, answers in % (n =216)

Specialty	Access to information	Evaluation of information	Use and management of information
Economics	36.36	18.18	36.36
Civil engineering	10.00	20.00	30.00
Forest science and forestry engineering	22.22	16.67	22.22
Agricultural engineering	0.00	22.22	12.50
Computer control and computer science	57.14	33.33	33.33
Information technologies for sustainable development	88.89	66.67	55.56

Today, higher education like all other sectors in the world has been influenced by different types of technologies, especially digital technologies (Khoza & Manik, 2015). Therefore, the ability to use digital technologies in higher education is crucial to ensure the development of the competences needed for the labour market. Thus, the questionnaire also included a question on what digital skills students need to improve in order to enter the future labour market.

Results show that 30.77% of respondents really need to improve information coding and programming skill, as this skill was missing most often. Although the evaluation and use and management of information were ranked at a very high level by almost a third of respondents, almost a fifth (18.77%) of them felt a great need to improve this skill (Table 4). 15.78% of those students who answered that this skill is at a high level, still wanted to improve this skill being aware of its importance in the labour market.

The least number of students think that it is necessary to improve the skills of using ICT for a specific purpose (12.50%) and the use of ICT legally and ethically (9.38%), although the data shown in Table 2 show that these skills were missing most often.

Table 4. Self-assessment of the need to improve the digital skills needed for the labour market, answers in % (n =216)

Digital skills for the labour market	I don't need to improve this skill	I should improve this skill	I really need to improve this skill
Access to information	26.15	60.00	13.85
Evaluation of information	23.44	57.81	18.75
Use and management of information	25.00	56.25	18.75
Information coding and programming	24.62	44.62	30.77
Use of ICT for a specific purpose	18.75	68.75	12.50
Use of ICT legally and ethically	23.44	67.19	9.38

The analysis of the results by specialty show that all skills could be improved almost equally for students majoring in economics.

The results show that there is a real need to improve their ability to access information as well as use and manage of information for 50.00% of agricultural engineering students and access to information for 40.00% of forest science and forestry engineering.

Table 5. High need to improve digital skills by specialty, answers in % (n =216)

Specialty	Access to information	Evaluation of information	Use and manage of information
Economics	18.18	27.27	36.36
Civil engineering	20.00	30.00	20.00
Forest science and forestry engineering	40.00	11.11	11.11
Agricultural engineering	50.00	33.33	50.00
Computer control and computer science	14.29	16.67	16.67
Information technologies for sustainable development	11.11	11.11	11.11

Students were asked to name what opportunities they use to develop their digital skills. In the questionnaire a choice of following options was offered: paid courses (formal education in the field), use of free online training, self-study (trial and error of applications, software, technology, etc.), peer help who can demonstrate in person how to use a specific app or asking for advice from older people using the field.

The results show that self-study was the opportunity most often used by students to promote digital skills - 88.6% of cases. It should be noted that self-study skills are also one of the determining factors in the labour market. As students have fairly good communication and collaboration skills (Zeidmane & Vintere, 2021), more than a half of the students (57.1%) used the opportunity "Help from peers who can demonstrate in person how to use a particular application / technology" and one quarter (25.7%) used "Seek advice from older people who use the area".

4. CONCLUSION

According to students' opinion, the most important digital skills needed for the labour market are as follows: use and manage information (69.84%), evaluation of information (67.19%) and access to information (65.15%).

For the surveyed students, the ability to access information is the most often developed at a high level (37.88%), but the ability of information coding and programming skills (46.15%). There is also a greatest need (30.77%) for skills development in this area.

About a third of civil engineering students lack all of these digital skills.

As regards students majoring in economics, all the mentioned skills are developed at either an intermediate or high level, however, about one third of respondents really need to improve these skills.

The greatest need to improve the ability to access information is for agricultural engineering and forest science and forestry engineering students, respectively: 50.00% and 40.00%.

This was a case study and used a self-assessment method, therefore the results are based on the respondents' opinion and can't be generalized. The study can be used to identify problems / directions for in-depth research.

The authors' recommendations are based on findings:

- the study course "Informatics" should be regularly reviewed and updated,
- the development of digital skills should be promoted in all study courses;
- the study course "Introduction to the specialty" should be used to reduce the gap between ICT skills for first-year students.

REFERENCES

Andrade H. and Valtcheva A., 2009. Promoting learning and achievement through self-assessment. *Theory into Practice*, no. 48, pp. 12-19, 2009.

DigComp 2.0: The Digital Competence Framework for Citizens. https://ec.europa.eu/jrc/en/digcomp/digital-competence-framework

Entrepreneurship 2020 Action Plan. European Economic and Social Committee, plenary session, 2013. https://www.eesc.europa.eu/en/our-work/opinions-information-reports/opinions/entrepreneurship-2020-action-plan

European Commission 2013. European Commission (EC), Digital Entrepreneurship study; Project Description, 2013. https://ec.europa.eu/growth/tools-databases/dem/monitor/project-description

European Commission 2015. European Commission (EC), Digital Transformation of European Industry and Enterprises; A report of the Strategic Policy Forum on Digital Entrepreneurship. http://ec.europa.eu/DocsRoom/documents/9462/attachments/1/translations/en/renditions/native

FIT https://fit.ie/what-we-do/

Jobs and skills in the digital economy. OECD Ministerial meeting, panel 4.2., June 2016, Mexico https://www.oecd.org/digital/ministerial/meeting/Skills-for-a-Digital-World-discussion-paper.pdf

Khoza, S. B., Manik, S., 2015. The recognition of 'digital technology refugees' amongst post graduate students in a higher education institution. *Alternation*, 17(2015), 190–208.

Kiss M. Digital skills in the EU labour market. European Parliamentary Research Service, 2017. https://op.europa.eu/en/publication-detail/-/publication/cb9ff359-e2c9-11e6-ad7c-01aa75ed71a1/language-en -8

Shaping Europe's digital future. New report shows digital skills are required in all types of jobs,2021. https://digital-strategy.ec.europa.eu/en/news/new-report-shows-digital-skills-are-required-all-types-jobs

Skills for a Digital World, OECD, 2016. https://www.oecd.org/els/emp/Skills-for-a-Digital-World.pdf

Skills for a Digital World, 2016. Ministerial meeting on the digital economy. Background report, OECD, 2016 https://read.oecd-ilibrary.org/science-and-technology/skills-for-a-digital-world_5jlwz83z3wnw-en#page6

Torres-Coronas T., Vidal-Blasco M.A., 2014. Students and employers perception about the development of digital skills in higher education, pp 63-89. https://silo.tips/download/students-and-employers-perception-about-the-development-of-digital-skills-in-hig

Zeidmane A. and Vintere A., 2021. Digital competences of students for the implementation of remote studies. *EDULEARN21 Proceedings*, Italy, pp. 5128-5136.

Zhao F and Collier A., 2016. Digital entrepreneurship: research and practice. *Proceedings of the 9th Annual Conference of the EuroMed Academy of Business,* pp. 2173-2182. https://www.researchgate.net/publication/309242001_Digital_Entrepreneurship_Research_and_Practice

PROMOTING SELF-REGULATED LEARNING STRATEGIES FOR FIRST-YEAR STUDENTS THROUGH THE COMPER SERVICE

Laëtitia Pierrot[1], Christine Michel[1], Julien Broisin[2], Nathalie Guin[3], Marie Lefevre[3] and Rémi Venant[4]
[1]Université de Poitiers, TECHNE EA 6316, F-86073 Poitiers, France
[2]Université Toulouse 3 Paul Sabatier, IRIT, UMR 5505, F-31062 Toulouse, France
[3]Université de Lyon, CNRS, LIRIS UMR 5205, F-69622 Villeurbanne, France
[4]Le Mans Université, LIUM EA 4023, F-72085 Le Mans, France

ABSTRACT

Implementing remote and blended higher education courses motivated the design for new support services for autonomous learning. Thus, combining a competence-based approach and self-regulation, the COMPER project offers a service to be used in addition to the courses. It consists of a graphical presentation of the learners' competency profile (following the open learner model's approach) and a personalized resources recommendation system. To assess its usefulness and usability, we conducted a study to test the COMPER service on 181 first-year students (from a two-year university diploma in computing), in addition to practical work carried out remotely. Based on a survey (usage data and scales) analysis, our study shows that globally the learners perceive the service as useful, especially those who favor working individually. Finally, our findings showed how much attention must be paid before implementing an independent OLM into an existing learning environment, especially for learners lacking SRL competencies.

KEYWORDS

Self-Regulated Learning, Usability, Utility, Autonomous Learning, Competency-Based Approach

1. INTRODUCTION

One of the many students' challenges relates to the competencies they need for organizing or achieving work. However, most students entering the university have no training in the implementation of these methods. Indeed, a study on prospective students' habits (Panadero *et al.*, 2020) shows that the most common learning strategy (70.7% of the sample) is the organization and transformation of instructional content through creating summaries or concept maps. Marginal strategies are information seeking (6.7%), goal setting and planning (4%), or asking teachers for help (4%). Only one participant reported seeking help from peers. Other strategies (self-assessment, monitoring, environmental structuring) are non-existent. Thus, there is a need to provide learners with support for autonomy in their learning activities. This problem is even more critical considering that most of these activities shifted to emergency remote mode with the health crisis.

To address this problem, helping students self-regulate (Zimmerman, 2000) and competency-based approaches (CBA) are two of the many existing strategies. Schunk (1994) defines self-regulation of learning as "a set of processes by which subjects activate and maintain goal-directed cognitions systematically, affects, and behaviors."

Our study measured the usability and relevance of combining two tools, available during face-to-face and distance courses, and designed to support students' self-regulation strategies based on CBA: access to a self-training platform and the visualization of a competency profile. We observed the use and opinions of 181 first-year students from a two-year university diploma in computing engaged in an introductory Shell programming course that gave access to these tools. We cross-referenced these with their self-regulated learning (SRL) profiles. This paper presents our findings and recommendations for designing and implementing services articulating self-regulation and CBA.

2. SUPPORTING STUDENTS' AUTONOMOUS WORK AT THE UNIVERSITY

Self-regulation skills have been found as a factor for learners' performance. Using these skills allows them to efficiently control and modify their actions to reach set goals (Pintrich, 2000). Instead of simply responding to environmental stimuli, learners organize their environment according to their targets. This approach includes different strategies that the learners can implement: self-assessment, studying training resources, asking for help or defining objectives, and planning their work, among many (Zimmerman and Pons, 1986).

2.1 Promoting SRL Strategies

The tools proposed to measure and promote self-regulation have evolved in three waves (Panadero, 2017). The first employed learners' self-reported data from questionnaires, the second trace data from learners' interactions with learning platforms. In both cases, the data's exploitation provided learners (or teachers) with global pictures useful for making diagnoses and adapting their behaviors. The third wave of tools also exploits interaction trace data and adds functionalities that stimulate learners' self-regulation skills. The most common functionalities in current devices (2008-2018) correspond to tools from waves 2 and 3 and include dashboards fed from Learning Analytics (LA) techniques, intelligent agents, and personalized feedback/prompts offered to learners. However, studies (Araka *et al.*, 2020; Panadero, 2017) have pointed out the need to exploit further LA and the lack of models to implement third wave tools.

Schumacher and Ifenthaler (2018) analyzed how different functionalities of interest for SRL can proceed from interaction data. In parallel, they evaluated their usefulness and acceptability to learners. Their study showed that the most useful feature is the invitation to self-evaluate with immediate feedback to support the reflection and performance phases. Indeed, this feature is necessary to assess the state of knowledge and plan the next steps. Furthermore, the following two most useful features are the recommendation of topics and courses to work on based on, for example, the content the learner has already worked on. Finally, the features more oriented towards planning or monitoring the activity are not considered useful or acceptable.

Self-assessment with immediate feedback requires activities or features that allow students to assess themselves against the course objectives. Exercisers (or exercise generators) are a way to diagnose the skills acquired quickly, to perform performance memorization and skill development through trial and error learning based on repetition (Mostow *et al.*, 2004). Since the exerciser environment keeps track of the learning activity and provides immediate feedback, it facilitates the learner's regulation by allowing explicit reflection on the skills worked on (Steffens, 2006). The following section presents specific visualizations of the skills profile useful to help the learners situate themselves under the competency framework.

2.2 Competency Profile Visualization

Dashboards include various information to visualize the skills evolution according to the success in learning activities, especially for an online or hybrid learning context (Kizilcec *et al.*, 2017). Visualizing objectives provides learners with standards against which to position themselves (Sedrakyan *et al.*, 2019). However, these strategies have limitations in terms of effectiveness. Only older learners have the metacognitive skills to implement SRL processes (Kizilcec *et al.*, 2017). Moreover, these strategies must be combined with assessments so that learners can verify the achievement of objectives. Finally, statistical approaches, which are currently widely applied, should be complemented with techniques that incorporate the level of readiness and the dependencies between learning objectives and sub-objectives (Sedrakyan *et al.*, 2019). This type of formalization particularly occurs in CBA.

The OLM is a structured representation of the state of one's correct/incorrect knowledge and difficulties. It allows the learner (and/or others) to visualize information about themselves (Bull and Kay, 2010), according to an awareness process that supports learning (Bodily *et al.*, 2018). Bull and Kay (2010) identified several benefits for the learner, with the OLM supporting metacognitive activities, facilitating consultation and access to related resources, and making the learner more autonomous as they are more responsible for their learning. However, OLMs are generally dependent on a learning device, making them unusable for others (Hooshyar *et al.*, 2020). The simplest forms using color coding are preferred as learners more easily use them. Complex representations, which hierarchically show knowledge structures, are more useful for supporting SRL processes but are also the most difficult to use (Hooshyar *et al.*, 2020). It is, therefore, a challenge to find a good visual representation for an independent OLM. This literature review also shows the difficulties of knowing which visual representation a learner would prefer depending on SRL skills.

In this paper and in the COMPER project, we aim to study different visualization forms of independent OLMs and measure their usefulness and usability according to the SRL skills of the learners.

3. SUPPORTING SELF-REGULATION IN AN INTRODUCTORY SHELL PROGRAMMING COURSE

3.1 Learning Situation Experimented

The COMPER project produced several independent tools to support self-regulation: a competency framework, a personalized resource recommendation system, and a tool for visualizing learner competency profiles (OLM module). Combining these tools allows us to cover the three stages of the SRL cycle.

The OLM module proposed a description of the learner's knowledge, skills, and competency mastery rate, according to the learning objectives defined within the framework. The mastery rate was calculated according to the learner's success in the learning activities, based on the data-trace analysis (if a remote system is used) and/or teachers' opinions. The OLM module also provided a confidence rate to indicate the mastery rates' reliability based on the number of assessments and the assessments' recency. According to previous studies within the COMPER project (Bull *et al.*, 2013; Hooshyar *et al.*, 2020), four different profile visualizations were designed (see Figure 1).

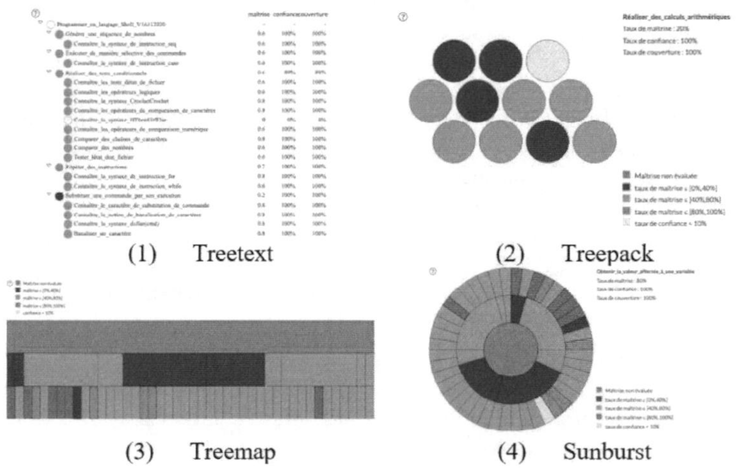

Figure 1. OLM module visualizations in the COMPER project

We experimented with a combination of tools for an introductory Shell programming course offered to first-year university students starting November 2020. A virtual and remote laboratory (Broisin et al., 2017) is usually operated in this course. It provides learners with an infrastructure of virtual machines and networks adapted to the course's needs. We add three tools: a competency framework, the OLM module, and an exercise generator (exerciser platform) (Lefevre et al., 2015) used for several years in university but never in this course. The competency framework represented the 55 competencies "Programming in Shell language" worked in the class. We propose access to the OLM module through the virtual and remote laboratory's interface because this tool is usually used. Finally, the teacher provided a set of exercises for individual training with the exerciser platform.

We implemented this combination to correspond to the learners' preferences (Schumacher and Ifenthaler, 2018) and respect the design recommendations identified previously (Sedrakyan *et al.*, 2019). The exerciser platform (Lefevre et al., 2015) allows teachers to create self-evaluation exercises and provides automatic and instant evaluation, so learners receive immediate feedback. OLM module helps learners to visualize their competency profiles and to supervise knowledge and skills.

3.2 Research Questions

In addition to verifying the feasibility of combining these different tools in an existing training course, this implementation in the programming course aimed to answer several research questions. RQ1: Globally, how useful is the whole combination in terms of self-regulation? More specifically (RQ1.1), is the support useful for all students or just for those who lack SRL strategies? RQ2: Are the tools usable by first-year university students who work autonomously overall and have punctual guidance? More specifically (RQ2.1), are the visualizations proposed in the competency profile easy to understand and use by students?

4. STUDY

4.1 Participants

181 participants took part in this experiment. All of them were students enrolled in the first year of a two-year diploma in computing (French *Diplôme Universitaire de Technologie*), aged between 17 and 19 years old, mostly male (87% male to 13% female). The students followed the training as described above, working alone and remotely.

4.2 Shell Programming Course Organization

Traditionally, this course is on a face-to-face modality, and it was conducted remotely due to the sanitary crisis. Learners had access to the tools during the five remote practical work sessions (once a week), followed by three weeks of revision and a face-to-face exam. Before the course, the teacher defined the course's objectives within the competence framework, the practice exercises within the virtual and remote laboratory, and those carried out with the exerciser platform.

During the practical sessions, the teacher attended learners remotely to complete the practical work and corrected their production at the end of each week. He assessed the learners' skills, calculating the competency profile and updating the framework system elements' mastery rates. Between sessions, learners had access to a list of resources adapted to their competency profile. Resources included course materials and exercises from the exerciser platform. Learners could freely follow the system's recommendations or autonomously choose exercises. All the tools were available during the training phase (during the five weeks of practical work courses) and the revision phase.

To evaluate each profile visualization, all participants were divided, at the beginning of our study, into four experimental groups (45 to 46 students per group) in a balanced way according to their academic level. During the first two weeks of the training phase, each group had only access to a single profile visualization among the four available. After these two weeks, each learner could freely access all four visualizations and switch to the preferred one at any moment.

4.3 Collected Data

In this study, we carried out several measurements through online surveys. First, the EAREL scale (Cosnefroy *et al.*, 2020), which focuses on SRL strategies for distance learning activities, measured learners' SRL skills. Students were asked to indicate their disagreement (1: strongly disagree) or agreement (7: strongly agree) on 4 dimensions of 6 items each, namely procrastination (PROC), control of the learning context (CTXT), cognitive/metacognitive strategies used for learning (COGN), and peer support (PEERS). We used this scale at the beginning (EAREL, n=94) of the experiment to cover RQ1.

According to the System Usability Scale, the second scale evaluates the OLM module's usability (Brooke, 1996). The SUS measures usability through 10 items, consistent with an agreement scale (1: strongly disagree, 5: strongly agree). The score obtained is displayed out of 100. A system's usability is considered correct, but with usability problems when the SUS is between 50 and 70, good when it is between 71 and 85, and excellent if it is above 85. We used this scale to cover RQ2 (SUS, n=73). To balance self-reported data on usability, we used logs from the exerciser platform (n=98) and OLM module (n=82). Each log contains data on the learners' activity (temporally marked interactions with the system).

Besides, we remotely conducted semi-structured interviews with 5 students at the end of the experiment. These interviews aimed to deepen their understanding of the tools, their work strategies, and their wishes for the tools' evolution. In this paper, we use the quotes of 5 students to illustrate and complete the analyses.

5. RESULTS

5.1 Learners' SRL Competencies

According to EAREL scale results, learners show good abilities to organize their learning context. However, they have a high propensity to procrastinate and demonstrate poor communication and work strategies. In addition, the standard deviations and coefficients of variation are high, which indicates a strong population disparity (see Table 1).

Table 1. Mean (m), standard deviation (σ), and coefficient of variation (CV) on EAREL dimensions

SRL strategies	CTXT	PEERS	PROC	STRAT
m before (n=94)	4,84	4,13	4,07	3,24
σ before	1,00	1,56	1,40	1,33
CV before	21 %	38 %	34 %	41 %

We performed a principal component analysis (PCA) and a K-means partition to view various SRL profiles globally. We applied PCA to explore linear relationships among the 24 variables. We found 3 characterizing variables: procrastinating and implementing work strategies (with the highest values on the left side of Axis 1 in Figure 2) and communicating with peers (with the highest values on the top of Axis 2). Contextual control behaviors were not discriminating. The K-means method allowed us to identify four groups of learners structured according to their implementation level of SRL strategies. Figure 2 shows learners' distribution according to the K-means groups in the vector plane composed of PCA axes 1 and 2. Dropouts (class1-blue) do not use any strategy, procrastinate and communicate little with their peers. Followers (class2-yellow) use some strategies but procrastinate and start working by communicating with their peers. Lone enforcers (class3-green) use strategies, do not procrastinate and do not communicate with their peers. Finally, efficient students (class4-orange) use strategies, do not procrastinate and communicate with their peers.

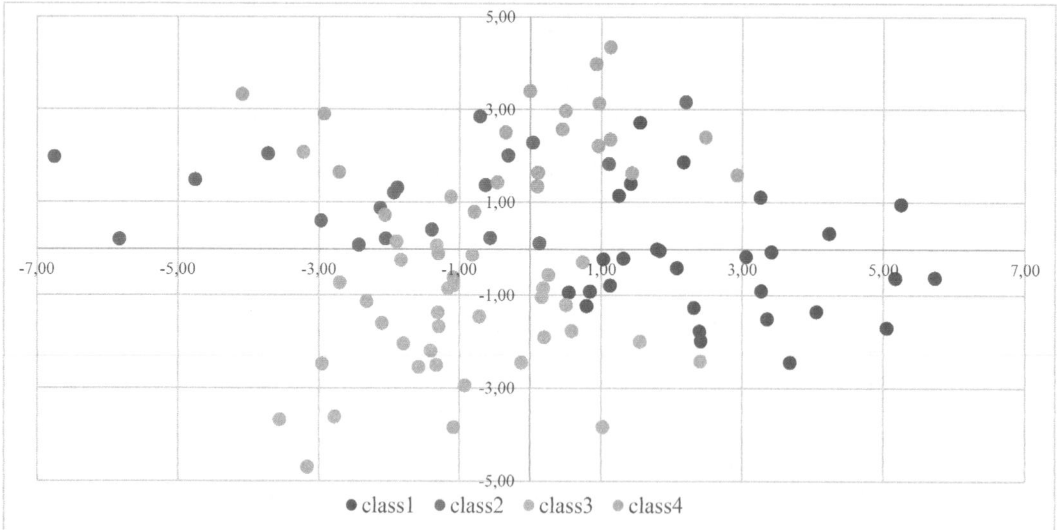

Figure 2. Learners distribution by SRL characteristics (level of procrastination, strategy use, and request for peer support)

5.2 Analysis of COMPER Project's Combination Use and Usefulness

5.2.1 Analysis of the Exerciser Platform Use and Usefulness

According to the exerciser platform's log analysis (cf. figure 3a), half of the students did not use it (83/181), mostly because they lacked time. However, 83.56% of the learners who declared using it found it useful (see figure 3b). Most of the learners who used the exerciser platform are the least communicative: class1 (dropouts) and class3 (lone-enforcers). "I practice until I get it. I do sequential work" self analyzes a class1-student while a class3-student mostly acts out of a performance quest: "if I really can't do it, I'll get help, but otherwise I try to succeed on my own". This use was motivated by the students' desire to position themselves in their learning process (to check if they have understood and know where they stand) and target and work on specific skills. "I try to follow and learn in class so that I can limit the amount of work I have to do at home, and for the exams, it's the same" explains a class4-student.

5.2.2 Analysis of the OLM Module Use and Usefulness

The OLM module log analysis showed that an even larger proportion of students did not use the OLM module (102/181, see figure 4a). The OLM module was considered not useful (at 45.83%) and difficult to use (at 55.55%) (see figure 4b). Also, some students reported being unaware of the service and relying on other resources, such as direct feedback from the instructor, to assess their progress. A class1-student reported: "Actually, I think I didn't understand how to use the competency profile because I didn't see it changing much, so I stopped looking at it". The other class1-student found the OLM module adequate to practical works, but he explained not using it since he didn't like "having to prove" what he learned. When used, it was mostly at a low level (see Figure 4a). A class2-student explained how he used the OLM module after the course: "I would look to see if it turned green. It reassured me to know that the system said I understood". Learners used the tool to monitor their overall progress on the course, knowing that the teachers' previous week's assessment was added into the competency profile.

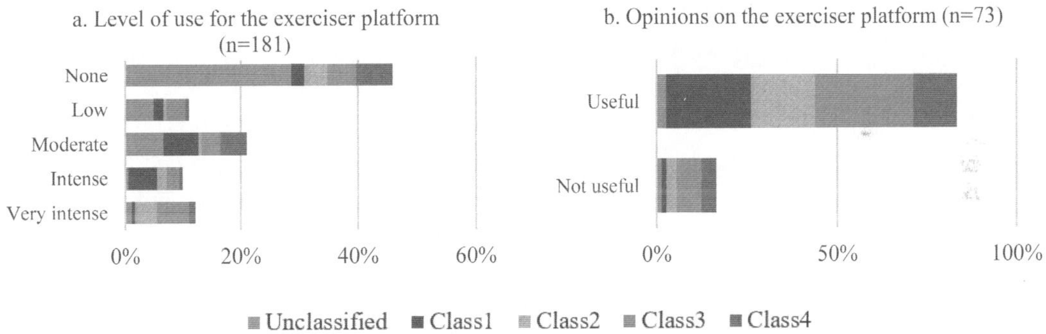

Figure 3. Level (a), and students' opinion (b) for the exerciser platform. Unclassified group shows logs activity from students who did not complete the EAREL scale

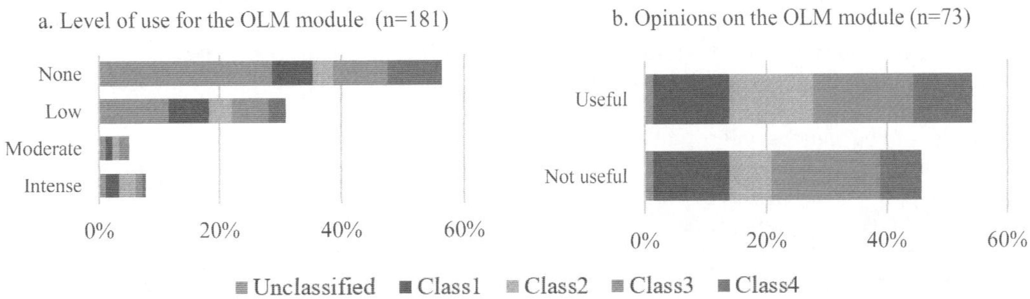

Figure 4. Level (a), and students' opinion (b) for the OLM module

5.3 Opinions about the OLM Module Design

5.3.1 OLM Module Usability

If the exerciser platform was found easy to use (49 out of 73 learners who declared using it), only half of students found the OLM module easy to use (32 out of 64 learners who declared using it). Indeed, the OLM module obtained a SUS score of 59.49/100. The OLM module has, therefore, correct but limited usability. These limitations are the need for technical support (average score of 3.167/4) and difficulties in using OLM (items "I thought there was too much inconsistency in this system" average score of 3.056/4, and "I find this service very cumbersome to use" average score of 3.022/4). However, the analysis of the trace data activity on the OLM module showed that only a minority of the logs concern technical errors encountered by the students, either when displaying a skill or changing the visualization. The type of difficulties encountered is thus more related to the type of visualization. On the other hand, students expressed feeling unconfident with the information displayed (average score of 1.8/4) and did not find the service well integrated (average score of 2/4). Another explanation may be related to a misunderstanding of some SUS items.

5.3.2 Comparison of the Four Visualizations

According to the activity logs, the students consulted the Treetext visualization (46%). When learners chose the four visualizations, they systematically replaced the sunburst visualization with another, mainly the Treetext (52%). The opinions expressed in the questionnaire confirm this and show that the preferred view is the Treetext (for 37 learners out of 47). For them, this visualization is easy to read and understand, and it allows them to grasp quickly each targeted skill, which was confirmed by four of the five students interviewed. On the other hand, 5 out of 47 learners preferred the Treemap presentation. Like with the Treetext visualization, the Treemap offered "clear" and "comprehensive" information. However, one student expressed his concerns about the other two visualizations, mentioning how they were not enough "intuitive and too esthetic." In contrast, another explained how Treetext and Treemap visualizations were less complex for them. A few students (5 out of 47) preferred the two other visualizations (conversely, 3 for the Sunburst visualization, 2 for the Treepack one). In that case, these visualizations were the first ones they have had access to.

4. DISCUSSION

The students' SRL profile played an important role in the use of the tools. "Dropout" students, characterized by a lack of SRL strategies, mainly used reinforcement exercises, but the OLM module was not yet usable for them. The "followers" and "efficient" students were less likely to use the COMPER service. The "effective" ones, already using SRL strategies, consider these tools not very useful for additional help. The "followers" mostly used profile visualization during practical work courses, which suggests that it was at the teacher's request. Thus, the COMPER service appears to address the needs of some students who are isolated and have little or no SRL strategies in place. It would be interesting to compare the learners' goals (mastery or performance) to see if, as for Lust *et al.* (2013) or Matcha *et al.* (2019), they guide the preference of use towards monitoring tools (such as the OLM module) or testable materials (such as the exerciser platform).

The exerciser platform was found to be more usable than the OLM module, considered difficult to understand. However, its use, which did not stop, and the statement about the Treetext visualization, judged easy to read and understand, invites further development. Indeed, the results confirm the link between perceived usability and the tools' actual usefulness: the students who most favorably evaluated the tools were also those who used them the most and for the longest time. Further research is needed to understand what design features lead learners to believe that this visualization is easier to use.

In this study, although the OLM module was implemented directly in the learning environment that students were used to, it was conceived as an independent OLM. This choice was made since the overall COMPER project aims to design and implement generic tools to existing learning situations. Yet, our usability findings showed that the module was not perceived as part of their usual environment for some learners. Still, Hooshyar *et al.* (2020) recommend maintaining the OLM module independent or open to various resources or materials. Lust *et al.* (2013) showed that much attention needs to be provided before students start using a new SRL tactic. Thus, the scaffolding (offered by the teacher at the beginning of the experiment and by the system through the profile captions) may not have been sufficient for learners to adopt the tools fully. The analysis of the scaffolding means seems to be a good research perspective to improve the design and implementation of such services. The editable aspect of the exerciser platform, which was much more used than the OLM module, invites us to consider adding more personalized/inspectable features to further development of the OLM module.

5. CONCLUSION

This article describes the COMPER service's experimentation by first-year students in computing, articulating a competency-based approach and self-regulation to support autonomous work. The experimentation showed that both tools (exerciser platform and OLM module) were globally useful and usable, but in different ways according to the learners' SRL profiles. The tools mainly address the learners' needs who have not developed SRL strategies. The research also shows that the other SRL profiles used the set of tools less. Exploiting the data from the questionnaires and the activity logs confirmed the global approach's relevance with students in autonomous learning situations. Our future work will focus on better understanding learners' motivations for using these services and how best to adapt the design and implementation according to their needs and the characteristics of learning sessions.

ACKNOWLEDGEMENT

This experimentation and the design of the tools were carried out in the context of the French National Research Agency COMPER project (ANR-18-CE38-0012).

REFERENCES

Araka, E., Maina, E., Gitonga, R., Oboko, R., 2020. Research trends in measurement and intervention tools for self-regulated learning for e-learning environments—systematic review (2008–2018). RPTEL 15, 6.

Bodily, R., Kay, J., Aleven, V., Jivet, I., Davis, D., Xhakaj, F., Verbert, K., 2018. Open learner models and learning analytics dashboards: a systematic review. pp. 41–50. https://doi.org/10.1145/3170358.3170409

Broisin, J., Venant, R., Vidal, P., 2017. Awareness and Reflection in Virtual and Remote Laboratories: the case of Computer Education. International Journal of Technology Enhanced Learning 9, 1.

Bull, S., Kay, J., 2010. Open Learner Models, in: Nkambou, R., Bourdeau, J., Mizoguchi, R. (Eds.), Advances in Intelligent Tutoring Systems, Studies in Computational Intelligence. Springer Berlin Heidelberg, Berlin, Heidelberg, pp. 301–322. https://doi.org/10.1007/978-3-642-14363-2_15

Bull, S., Kickmeier, M., Vatrapu, R., Johnson, M., Hammermueller, K., Byrne, W., Hernandez-Munoz, L., Giorgini, F., Meissl-Egghart, G., 2013. Learning, Learning Analytics, Activity Visualisation and Open Learner Model: Confusing? https://doi.org/10.1007/978-3-642-40814-4_51

Cosnefroy, L., Fenouillet, F., Heutte, J., 2020. Construction et validation de l'Échelle d'autorégulation des apprentissages en ligne (EAREL). Canadian Journal of Behavioural Science / Revue canadienne des sciences du comportement 52, 255–260.

Hooshyar, D., Pedaste, M., Saks, K., Leijen, Ä., Bardone, E., Wang, M., 2020. Open learner models in supporting self-regulated learning in higher education: A systematic literature review. Computers & Education 154, 103878. https://doi.org/10.1016/j.compedu.2020.103878

Kizilcec, R.F., Pérez-Sanagustín, M., Maldonado, J.J., 2017. Self-regulated learning strategies predict learner behavior and goal attainment in Massive Open Online Courses. Computers & Education 104, 18–33.

Lefevre, M., Guin, N., Cablé, B., Buffa, B., 2015. ASKER : un outil auteur pour la création d'exercices d'auto-évaluation, in: Atelier EAEI (Évaluation Des Apprentissages et Environnements Informatiques) - Conférence EIAH 2015. Agadir, Morocco.

Lust, G., Elen, J., Clarebout, G., 2013. Students' tool-use within a web enhanced course: Explanatory mechanisms of students' tool-use pattern. Computers in Human Behavior 29, 2013–2021. https://doi.org/10.1016/j.chb.2013.03.014

Matcha, W., Ahmad Uzir, N., Gasevic, D., Pardo, A., 2019. A Systematic Review of Empirical Studies on Learning Analytics Dashboards: A Self-Regulated Learning Perspective. IEEE Transactions on Learning Technologies PP, 1–1. https://doi.org/10.1109/TLT.2019.2916802

Mostow, J., Beck, J., Beyi, J., Cuneo, A., Sison, J., Tobin, B., Valeri, J., 2004. Using automated questions to assess reading comprehension, vocabulary, and effects of tutorial interventions. Tech. Inst. Cognition and Learning 2, 103–140.

Panadero, E., 2017. A Review of Self-regulated Learning: Six Models and Four Directions for Research. Front. Psychol. 8, 422.

Panadero, E., García-Pérez, D., Fernández-Ruiz, J., Sánchez-Centeno, H., 2020. A Transitional Year Level to Higher Education: Challenges, Experiences and Self-regulatory Strategies during the Final Year of the University Preparatory Level. Estudios sobre Educación 39, 109–133.

Pintrich, P.R., 2000. The role of goal orientation in self-regulated learning, in: Handbook of Self Regulation. Academie Press, San Diego, pp. 451–502.

Schumacher, C., Ifenthaler, D., 2018. Features students really expect from learning analytics. Computers in Human Behavior 78, 397–407.

Schunk, D., 1994. Self-regulation of self-efficacy and attributions in academic settings, in: Self-Regulation of Learning and Performance: Issues and Educational Applications. Hillsdale, NJ: Lawrence Erlbaum, pp. 75–99.

Sedrakyan, G., Mannens, E., Verbert, K., 2019. Guiding the choice of learning dashboard visualizations: Linking dashboard design and data visualization concepts. Journal of Computer Languages 50, 19–38.

Steffens, K., 2006. Self-Regulated Learning in Technology-Enhanced Learning Environments: lessons of a European peer review. European Journal of Education 41, 353–379.

Zimmerman, B.J., 2000. Attaining self regulation. A social cognitive perspective, in: Handbook of Self Regulation. Academie Press, San Diego, pp. 13–39.

Zimmerman, B.J., Pons, M.M., 1986. Development of a Structured Interview for Assessing Student Use of Self-Regulated Learning Strategies. American Educational Research Journal 23, 614–628.

A MULTI-LAYER ARCHITECTURE FOR AN E-LEARNING HYBRID RECOMMENDER SYSTEM

Lisa Roux, Pantxika Dagorret, Patrick Etcheverry,
Thierry Nodenot, Christophe Marquesuzaa and Philippe Lopisteguy
Université de Pau et des Pays de l'Adour/E2S UPPA,
Laboratoire d'Informatique de l'Université de Pau et des Pays de l'Adour, EA3000, 64000 Pau, France

ABSTRACT

Distance computer-assisted learning is increasingly common, owing largely to the expansion and development of e-technology. Nevertheless, the available tools of the learning platforms have demonstrated their limits during the pandemic context, since many students, who were used to "face-to-face" education, got discouraged and dropped out of school. In this context, a main issue is to conceive tools that would allow the teachers to supervise their students at a distance, by monitoring their progress and ensuring follow-up action as required. Another issue is to equip the learning platforms with intelligent systems able to guide the students involved in pedagogic activities.

In this work, we propose a novel architecture of recommender system for vocational higher education that provides the students with personalized advice and the teacher with suitable information, in order to make the task of monitoring easier and involving them in the machine learning. Our system is supposed to act in a hybrid environment, and, for this purpose, has to explain its predictions in an interpretable and faithful manner, both to the students and the teachers, so that the former can determine the relevance of what is suggested and the latest can act on the future analyses and recommendations. This is a multi-layer architecture, so that each step of the recommendation process is meaningful, thus explicable to the users. The design of this architecture is a preliminary stage of a recommender system. It is designed on top of a learning digital infrastructure exploited since 2018 by the 1000 students of Bayonne Institute of Technology.

KEYWORDS

Recommender Systems in Vocational Higher Education, Supervised Classification, Explainable AI, Hybrid Learning Context

1. INTRODUCTION

This paper relies on the assumption that the future of vocational higher education will be hybrid. If there was still a need for evidence, one year and a half of COVID pandemy in our university has demonstrated that the learning interactions offered by available Learning Management Systems (LMS) to students (e.g. Moodle and its available plugins) are useful, especially when lecturers and teachers are accompanied by pedagogical engineers ; but used as a whole, these LMS are considered quite inappropriate by teachers to foster and support active learning in and out of the classroom. In the works presented in this paper, we use the Moodle Platform as an organised container providing the students with learning opportunities (description of available exercises) and with resources in relation with the competences addressed by these exercises: course contents, wikis, forums, tutorials, quizzes... Nevertheless, in our institute, most of the available exercises are realized outside of the Moodle environment, face to face for half of a group (8 from 16 or 15 from 30 in the COVID context) and also at a distance for the second half of a group and thus, thanks to dedicated virtual environments offering the required professional tools. For example in the context of a computer-science curriculum in our institute, students are called to practice C++ exercises with a code editor including a debugger, some test scenarios. Those at a distance can reach these programming tools thanks to a single internet connection, then also can cooperate in a synchronous way through screen-sharing and showcase facilities; and all the students (those in the campus and the others at a distance) can also take advantage from the Moodle resources also put at their disposal. This stuff can be later used by students to go deeper by themselves into the learning material. From a pedagogical viewpoint, this hybrid approach for practising on authentic exercises and on teaching through practice has demonstrated all its strengths all this year-long but also the following important weakness: teachers have encountered difficulty to succeed in eliciting which students to tutor in priority, which students should be considered as a single group to advice at a given stage of a session, ... They asked for a system that could assist them in managing the learning process followed by their students and the most motivated teachers agreed to spend time and provide us with their pedagogical expertise in a an applied research focusing on a recommender system for learning from authentic learning situations.

Different directions have been proposed to design such recommender systems. Some studies have shown an initial relationship between personality profiles and meaningful learning profiles (e.g. [arruda2019]), so that it is important to provide the students with student-centered environments and propose them stimulating activities in which they take an active part. Moreover, many AI works in e-learning aim at conceiving auto-adaptive platforms, where different environments are available, so that one of them can be assigned to a student depending on them profile, obtained from tests or questionnaires (e.g. [klavsnja2011, schiaffino2008, wolf2003]: on the basis of standard learning profiles, such as those defined by Honey and Mumford [honey1989] or Kozma [kozma1991] for example, several potential interfaces or sequences of pedagogical activities are designed, each of them being associated to a defined profile.

Nevertheless, these applications address total automation, while numerous researches aim at teaming AI with people in order to improve joint performance and efficiency. In particular, in the context of e-learning, hybridization ensures that the teachers can follow each student's progress despite the distance, which deprives the teachers of direct view on their work: without AI, this would be a very onerous and time-consuming task. This is why an intelligent system is required to detect the students who need particular attention and increased monitoring (e.g. students at risk of dropping out of school, or experiencing significant difficulties). But we assume that the principal responsibility for helping and guiding students should remain with teachers and not placed on the AI authority: the teaching practices, the pedagogical support, the human capacity to tailor their actions to the individual situation cannot be replaced with machine learning and algorithms, since many factors, such as motivation, are hardly automatically measurable. The very issue of learning profiles appears questionable [claxton2013, rohrer2012, stahl2002], since assigning a student to one single profile and, therefore, one type of interface or sequence, means reducing them to one way of learning, when students can have various learning behaviors, strategies, and needs depending on situations. Yet, one of the main challenging issues in the conception of dynamic recommender systems is to take into account the possible conceptual shifts (e.g. user preferences, item popularity) in order to adapt the system to the user's evolving behavior and expectation [rana2015]: this is a key factor of the recommendation improvement [vinagre2015].

Thus the purpose of our system is not to propose a predefined and static model of pedagogical activities to a student according to their assessed type, but recommend them suitable activities at a given time, depending on the difficulties they meet and what they have done so far. Indeed, while the distance learning enables the students to work when they want (i.e. gives them the ability to manage their own time) and gives them access to a multitude of activities and resources to practice and learn, this makes the real-time and exhaustive monitoring hardly possible and requires the assistance of a AI.

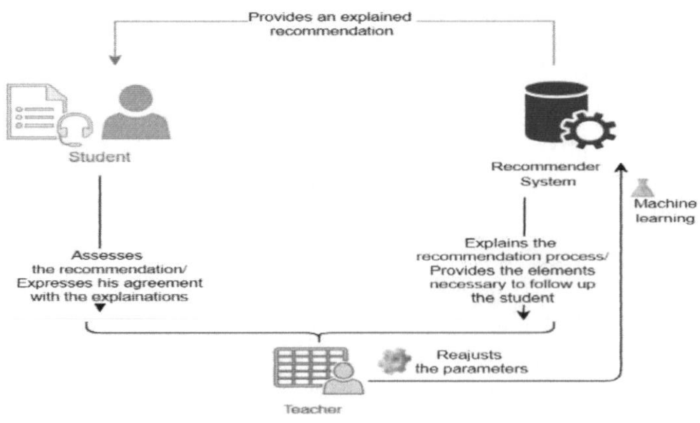

Figure 1. System operation

For these purposes, it operates at two levels, which are interwoven. A first level, which is based on an improvement detection system, aims at guiding the students who are engaged in a task and proposing them suitable activities according to the encountered problems and the situation of the student. A second level update a teacher's configurable scoreboard that indicates the recommendations that the system has done, the students' behaviors and feedbacks, and highlights those who need particular attention. According to the feedbacks and their own expert analysis of what is reported, the teacher can decide to change the recommendations or rectify the class allocation (i.e. choose which category the student should have been placed in).

Regarding the AI designed to operate in a hybrid context, accuracy is far from being the only preoccupation [grosz1996]. In spite of the accuracy decreasing that such a multi-layered architecture can imply, it allows a better understanding of how AI works, thus better control. If accuracy has been regarded as the major development for years and is still a major research issue, much recent concern has been focused on trust in AI, especially for the conception of successfully creating human-AI teams. Indeed, recent research has demonstrated that an increasing AI accuracy does not always translate to a better general team performance [yin2019, lai2019] because it is closely linked to the quality of the relationship between the human and the AI (i.e. trust, knowledge of the limits and the potentials of the AI, understanding of system operation, etc.). That is why it is important to find a compromise between accuracy and comprehensibility - and that is what why try to reach in this study.

2. OVERVIEW OF THE RECOMMENDER SYSTEM

2.1 The Recommendation Process

Our recommender system is designed to help students in choosing relevant activities depending on their situation. Its main purpose is to recommend useful and interesting resources or tasks to e-learners based on their different learning and gesture behavior, and other meaningful attributes. It is integrated in the Moodle environment, because this is free Open Source software package, widely used at our University and others. Moreover, we can use the Moodle logs to track student activity, thus have relevant information about their attendance, attempts, preferences, etc. When the systems used in e-commerce, vod platforms, social networks, etc. mainly implement content-based, knowledge-based or collaborative filtering techniques to recommend items, these methods cannot be directly applied to the e-learning area. Indeed, in e-learning, recommendations must take into account that the learning courses, activities, and materials need to be proposed in order to ensure that the prerequisites of some courses are met and that they match their particular in-time needs. Hybrid recommender systems (i.e. recommender systems combining different techniques) are more popular for e-learning than single recommendation method-based systems for avoiding the drawbacks of individual recommendation methods. Since our system has to adaptively model and respond to the change of the learner profile and propose them adequate activities, it has to find similarities between users to determine which kind of activities are interesting and relevant for the target user at a given time, taking into account the strong influence of the context, but also consider the complex pedagogical relationship between items in e-learning. We consider that students can experience difficulties in some subjects but feel very comfortable with others, and this may change over time, depending on the addressed notions, their personal lives, the course organization, etc. It is therefore necessary to take into account all aspects, either external and internal, that can dynamically contribute to the emergence of the student's specific need, and that have to be identified to detect this need. That is why our approach needs to both recommend activities that have been proven to be relevant for learners with close profiles in similar contexts and integrate knowledge-based techniques. Moreover, since the learner cannot be described by one single class but may adopt various cognitive and metacognitive strategies and approaches, have different levels of cognitive engagement and motivation over time, for example depending on courses and tasks, we will use classification methods based on fuzzy-logic [isaza2006, roux2015]. Moreover, we will use supervised classifications firstly because the class design can rely on a precise knowledge that teachers have about their students and that they therefore can put at our disposal. Moreover, the formalization of this knowledge will be based on classifications recognized in the field of educational sciences.

Despite this system is designed as a general recommender system for different types of courses, the first completely implemented and tested version will be for an introductory C++ programming course, since the reflection needed to be contained within the framework of one particular pedagogical situation, so that, as the teachers involved in this class, we can study how we recommend activities to students during the in-person classes, thus how the AI could do it in our place. Therefore, some tools used for the improvements detection in a C++ program are not suitable for any other type of task, but the architecture is thought to be generic. As we can see on the figure 2, a first step is to detect the possible improvements to the student's work. This can be done in an automatic way or through a questionnaire. The questionnaire is designed by the teachers, who select the relevant questions that enable the system to measure or assess the achievement of task objectives. The questions can be tailored for every single exercise or automatically assigned through a labelling system: a set of questions can be initially written by the teacher for one label, so that he only has to tag a task with this label to associate the questions to it. For example, in the case of a C++ programming task, the questions could be: "Do your variable names describe what your variables are for?", "What kind of structure do you use to implement your sorting function?" "Try to assign 0 to this variable. Does it work?". There are checkboxes for each question on the questionnaire, and the answers allow direct detection of improvements. Questions can be added later, if the teacher notices that some important aspects to assess are missing. This tool has two main objectives. Firstly, as we have just mentioned, it is a detection mechanism. Secondly, it allows the active implication of the student in the understanding of the possible improvements of what they have done. By answering the questions, they operate a structured review of their own work, assess their practices by confronting it to the explicit objectives of the task, check for missing exception cases processes, etc.

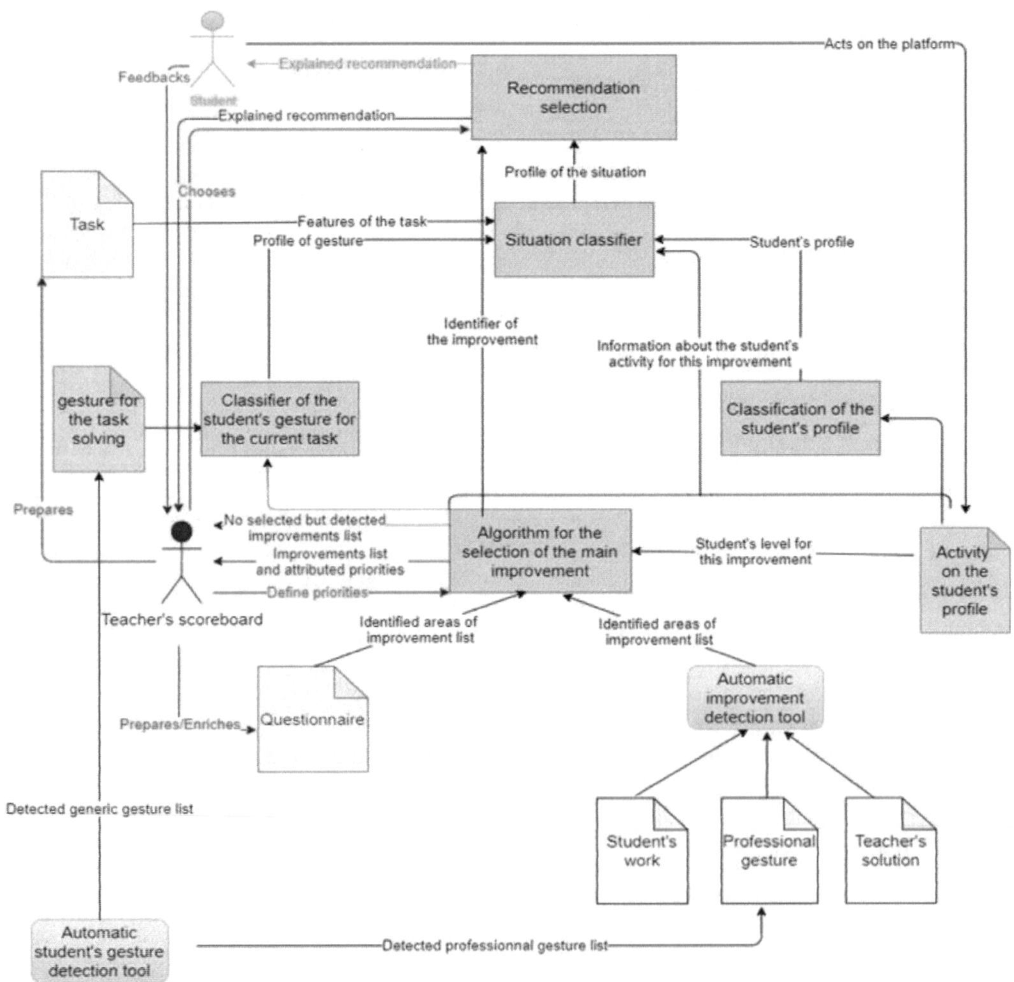

Figure 2. Architecture of the system

There is another detection tool, which is completely automatic, based on three elements. The first element is the student's work, that can be, to some extent, assessed by an automatic tool designed for what we want to check (e.g. spell and syntactic checker, anti-plagiarism system, parser generator tool that builds a concrete syntax tree of a program), sometimes by comparing it to a second element, which is the teacher's solution. The third element is the professional gesture, which permits to detect whether the student has adopted the good practice (i.e. the professional practice, as taught in their courses) during the task. For example, in a programming task, the examined issues can be: Has the code been progressively written, by validating each step with a compilation operation? Has the student used the debugger to analyse the execution errors? Is the code structured and developed in an incremental way? The information about the professional gesture is got from a tool that we will describe more precisely in section IV.

Both improvement detection tools are complementary. Indeed, some questions are hardly detectable in an automatic way, thus the questionnaire appears to propose a more complete check. Nevertheless, the student may have not checked the right box (i.e. the box associated to their situation) for several reasons, such as they have not understood the question or improvement that could be done, or also because they do not want the improvement to be detected. With the automatic detection tool, some improvements will be detected despite this, and a conflict situation will be raised so that the teacher is informed.

The student's situation, whose description is necessary to recommend them a suitable activity, depends on three main elements: how they feel during the task (i.e. does he seem confident, hesitating, etc.?), the quality of their learning process, and their historical relationship to the selected improvement. Thus, the system integrates four distinct processes, which are, on a first level, the selection of the main improvement, the student's quality of learning, and the student's gesture analysis. This student's gesture (i.e. hesitating, confident, etc.) is different from the professional gesture that we have mentioned above, since the former is dedicated to describe how confident or hesitating a student feels during a task, and the latter describes how much the student has assimilated the taught professional practice. Once the detection is completed, the list of improvements is processed by a selection algorithm, which chooses one improvement regarded as a priority issue. The teacher will be able to know every improvement detected if they are interested in; moreover, the information about which improvement is selected and which are not is stored in the database to feed further processing. The algorithm will be described more precisely in section III. In the same time, a classification allows to allocate the student's gesture to a class, and another permits to identify to what class belongs the student's quality of learning. Both classifications will be described in section IV. Those three processes will allow to get the student's situation class through a third classification process. Then, the system is able to recommend to the student an appropriate activity thanks to the predefined teacher's recommendations: this last step requires that the teacher has precised, for every possible situation (i.e. every class provided by the situation classification), which activities would be relevant. Those are generic activities that refer to available Moodle activities (e.g. reading a lesson, asking to a classmate, doing an exercise, posing a question on a forum); among them, the recommander system is able to choose which are available for this specific improvement (i.e. which resources and tasks have a label related to the improvement one) and relevant for the particular situation of the student (i.e. what the student has already done or not).

2.2 Explainable Recommendations

Once the recommendation is done, the student can choose to follow it or not, and is invited to assess its quality: does it meet their needs? Are they happy with their gesture assignation? Do they agree with the improvement? These feedbacks allow the teacher to improve the system, in particular by improving the questionnaire, modifying the weights they have associated to the possible improvements, and assigning the student's gesture or the student's learning quality to the suitable classes if the previous classifications appear to be inaccurate. In this way, the teacher is actively involved in the student monitoring: they can choose what recommendations are made depending on situations, know which difficulties are met by every student, and reajust the classification processes from their own analysis and observations. Thus AI explains its decisions to the teacher by providing them with every information it has used to take them, and, this doing, ensures that they can keep control on the recommendation process, and tailor them to their pedagogical practices. Similarly, the student can understand why this recommendation, for which improvement, etc, to help them become more aware of them and learn how to step back and assess their own work more effectively - in order to make them be gradually more autonomous. This allows to increase the user's trust in the system and keep them being actors of the student monitoring for the former, and their learning for the latter.

2.3 Labels and Tags

The system requires that the teacher has conceived a skill graph for their course. This is a directed graph, in which they indicate what are the skills learnt and practiced during the course, in what sequence (i.e. which ones are prerequisites necessary for others). Each skill corresponds to one label, so that every improvement, every resource, every task should be tagged by the corresponding label (i.e. the skill to which it refers). The more detailed it is, the more precise the recommendation can be; nevertheless, the skill graph can be improved and developed over the years.

3. SELECTION OF THE MOST IMPORTANT IMPROVEMENT

Among all the detected improvements, the recommendation concerns one of them, which is regarded as primary, so that the student can concentrate on every point one by one, with the computed priority order. The algorithm take five parameters into account: the situation of the improvement in the skill graph, the student's skill level, the priority level assigned by the teacher to the different improvements, how many times the improvement has appeared over the past ten recommendations, how many times the improvement has been selected over the past five recommendations.

Situation of the improvement in the skill graph: This indicates how they articulate relative to one another, depending on the number of skills that they require among the skills associated to the selected improvements.

Student's average skill level: Students have to acquire the skills taught in a course to validate it. For every skill of the course, they can further it by completing tasks tagged by the associate label. There are five skill levels, related to a value between 0 and 4: not started (0), beginner (1), workable (2), mastering (3), expert (4).

Priority level assigned by the teacher to the different improvements: If they want, the teacher can assign priority levels to the possible improvements, either generically or specifically to a task. This is an optional indicator, since the teacher could prefer letting the algorithm decide on the basis of the other information, or have no time for this. They can also assign a priority level to a handful of improvements.

Number of times the improvement has appeared over the past ten recommendations: In order to foster the selection of the repeating improvements, the system takes into account the number of times an improvement has appeared in the student's works over the past ten analyses done on them. Only the past ten recommendations are taken into account to avoid outliers.

Number of times the improvement has been selected over the past five recommendations: We assume that the subject of recommendation has to change regularly to facilitate learning and avoid fatigue: a break can be necessary, because learning is a process that can take time. When an improvement has been selected many times over the recent recommendation, the likelihood of being selected for the current one decreases. We only consider the five last recommendations in order to ensure a good turnover and avoid outliers.

4. IDENTIFICATION OF THE SITUATION AND PERSONALIZED RECOMMENDATION

4.1 Identification of the Student's Gesture

In interviewing teachers, we found out that a first factor that generally determines which kind of help a teacher would provide to a student is their ease to achieve a task: are they actively involved in the task solving? how much is the student hesitant or confident? Are they trying to solve the difficulties they meet by themselves? Do they know how to face the problems and where to look for the needed information? The study of the student's gesture aims to assess how confident and proactive the student is during the task. In order to assess the student relationship to the group, we can use an automatic detection tool that collects in XML format all their actions: clicks, written characters, open windows, etc. These tracks can then be processed and used to provide our system with useful and meaningful information. This tool allowed us to compose five indicators, related to the above questions: the rate of activity, the rate of research, the rate of research related to the selected improvement, the rate of erasure, the frequency of the work verification.

Rate of activity: This indicator assesses how much the student is active on the computer, using the keyboard or the mouse. It is calculated as time using them, divided by the total task time.

Rate of research: It shows whether the student tries actively to solve the problems he meets, by searching on the Internet or the online course material. It is calculated by dividing the research time online by the total activity time.

R*ate of research related to the selected improvement*: It indicates whether the main improvement detected by the system has been identified by the student as a problem in their work. It is calculated by dividing the research time about the improvement online, divided by the total research time.

Rate of erasure: This assesses the student's certainty about what they write. It is calculated by dividing the number of erased characters by the number of written characters.

Frequency of the work verification: This indicators shows whether the student regularly checks the validity of their work. In the case of a programming task, it is calculated by dividing the number of times the student has launched the compilation operation by the number of complete structures in their program. This is an optional indicator, since not all software programs can offer such a functionality.

Therefore, data are described by a 4 or 5-dimensional vector and can be classified to indicate how much the student encounter difficulty during the task and how much they try to solve them.

4.2 Identification of the Student's Profile

A second factor that influences the teacher's behavior is the general quality of the student's learning process, assessed by the means of seven indicators, which are: the rate of achieved tasks, the rate of successful tasks, the rate of consulted course material, the average skill level, the average duration of task completion, the number of improvements by complete task, and the rate of started but unfinished task.

Rate of achieved tasks: The first indicator used to classify the student's profile is the number of achieved tasks by the total number of available tasks (i.e. all the open tasks among the past and current courses taken by the student). It shows whether the student is determined to get involved in the available tasks through the end.

Rate of successful tasks: It indicates how many tasks are successfully completed by the student among the total number of available tasks. We chose to consider the total number of available tasks instead of the completed tasks, in order to get a better idea of their overall comprehension and mastering of the course.

Rate of consulted course material: This indicator is meant to show whether a student seeks to understand the theoretical aspects of a course, how much they try to consult the available course material to master the content.

Average skill level: As mentioned above, there are five possible levels for each skill. This indicator refers to the mean value of the achieved levels for every skill that should have been started at this point of course.

Average duration of task completion: For every completed task, the normalized duration is calculated by dividing the amount of time spent by the student on the task by the average amount of time spent on the same task by all the students. Thus, the average duration of task completion is the mean of all these normalized lengths of time. This indicator shows whether a student generally complete quickly their tasks.

Number of improvements by completed task: This indicates how many improvements are detected for every task a student achieves, in order to assess the average quality of the final works. This corresponds to the average value.

Rate of started but unfinished tasks: This indicator expresses whether a student often gives up an ongoing work. It is measured among the total number of available tasks the total number of started tasks.

4.3 Identification of the Situation

A recommendation is made to a student according to who they are in general, but also how they are faring with the specific current task, and their historical relationship with the detected main improvement, in particular the theoretical and practical course contents related to this improvement. Thus, in order to classify the situation of the student, we take into account five indicators: the student's gesture such as obtained under the step described in IV.A, the student's profile obtained under the step described in IV.B, how long they have already spent doing the task, the number of times they have consulted the course material related to the improvement, the number of tasks related to the improvement they have already completed, the number of times the improvement has appeared over the past ten recommendations (see III).

Time spent on the current task: This indicator is normalized in relation with the average duration of the task. It indicates whether the current task takes a lot of time to the student. Indeed, in order to avoid fatigue and discouragement, the teacher often adapt their recommendation depending the time that the student has already spent doing the task. Generally, the longer is the task completion, the more steering is the provided help. For example, in some cases, the teacher could advise the student to consult the course material whether they think they can and have time to solve the problem themselves; on the contrary, a teacher could prefer providing a student with an extract from their own solution when they think that they encounter too difficult matters for the current task and spend too much time on it.

Number of accesses to the course material related to the improvement: This indicates whether the student has already consulted the related course, and how many times they have, in order to determine whether they are familiar with the theoretical aspects of the current matter they face.

Number of completed tasks related to the improvement: This indicates whether the student has already complete tasks related to the detected improvement, and how many times they have, in order to determine whether they have already faced and addressed this issue, and how much they are familiar with its practical aspects.

4.4 Assignment of a Recommendation Depending on the Student's Situation

Once the different situation classes are defined, the teacher will be able to assign them generic recommendations, i.e. specifying what kinds of activity they would suggest to a student in that situation or what kinds of resources they would provide to them. The teacher is free to set priorities to the recommendations associated to each class. In a given situation, for a specific task, some recommendations will be applicable and some other will not, for example whether there is no material course for the concerned skill. If possible, two possible activities will be recommended to the student each time, in order to let them judge which activity is most convenient for them and record their preferences. Therefore, during the recognition process, the system will chose among the different available possibilities, among those defined by the teacher, depending on different indicators, such as the assigned priorities if applicable. The system will also take into account what the student, and the students in the same situation as them, did during the previous recommendations, whether they have followed the recommendation or not, what was their assessment, depending on the type of activities or resources that was proposed to them. The recommendation will be first chosen randomly, then willing to leave the opportunity for chance in order to avoid convergence and foster the diversity of the suggested activities, this information will be used to weight this random selection.

5. DISCUSSION AND CONCLUSION

The study introduces the conception of a recommender system that operates in a hybrid context, in which the teacher has total control on the involved parameters and the system is an assistant to facilitate the monitoring and provide the students with a work companion. This is meant to ensure a constant support for student within the framework of elearning. The system is thought to be enriched over time through the overhauls and refinements by the teacher, who will be able to rely on the student's feedbacks. The multi-layered architecture allows the segmentation of the computation in several meaningful thus easily describable and explainable steps.

The next step will be to carry out several experiments on an educational dataset in order to test our system first within the framework of a C++ programming course, and define meaningful classes of student's gesture, quality of work, and situation. Then it will be extended to other courses as a robustness test. A mid-term objective is therefore to compare the evolution of the classes throughout the different kind of courses.

REFERENCES

Claxton, G., 2013. *What's the point of school?: Rediscovering the heart of education*. Simon and Schuster Publishers, London, England.

Ennouamani S, Mahani Z, 2017. An overview of adaptive e-learning systems. 2017 Eighth International Conference on Intelligent Computing and Information Systems (ICICIS) IEEE, pp. 342-47.

Grosz, B. J., 1996. Collaborative systems, (aaai-94 presidential address). *AI magazine*, Vol. 17, No.2, p. 67.

Haruna K. et al., 2017. Context-aware recommender system: A review of recent developmental process and future research direction. *Applied Sciences,* Vol. 7, No. 12, p. 1211

Honey P. et al, 1989. *Learning styles questionnaire*. Organization Design and Development, Incorporated, Peter Honey Publications Limited, England.

Isaza, C., et al., 2006, An optimization method for the data space partition obtained by classification techniques for the monitoring of dynamic processes. *Proceedings of the 2006 conference on Artificial Intelligence Research and Development*, pp.80-87.

Klašnja-Milićević A. et al, 2011. E-Learning personalization based on hybrid recommendation strategy and learning style identification. *Computers & education*, Vol. 56, No. 3, pp. 885-899.

Kozma, R. B., 1991. Learning with media. *Review of educational research,* Vol. 61, No.2, pp. 179–211.

Lai, V. and Tan, C., 2019. On human predictions with explanations and predictions of machine learning models: A case study on deception detection. *Proceedings of the Conference on Fairness, Accountability, and Transparency*. pp. 29–38.

Rabiu I. et al, 2020. Recommender system based on temporal models: a systematic review. *Applied Sciences*, Vol. 10, No.7, p. 2204.

Rana C. et al, 2015. A study of the dynamic features of recommender systems. *Artificial Intelligence Review,* Vol. 43, No. 1, pp. 141–153.

Rohrer D. et al, 2012. Learning styles: Where's the evidence? *Online Submission*. Vol. 46, No. 7, pp. 634–635.

Roux, E., 2015. Développement d'un outil d'aide au diagnostic pour la production de maïs permettant la réduction de la consommation en eaux d'irrigation et en traitements phytosanitaires. Doctoral Dissertation, INSA de Toulouse.

Schiaffino, S. et al, 2008, Eteacher: Providing personalized assistance to e-learning students. *Computers & Education*, Vol. 51, No. 4, pp. 1744–1754.

Stahl S. A., 2002. Different strokes for different folks. *Taking sides: Clashing on controversial issues in educational psychology*, pp. 98–107.

Vinagre J. et al, 2015. An overview on the exploitation of time in collaborative filtering. *Wiley interdisciplinary reviews: Data mining and knowledge discovery*, Vol. 5, No. 5, pp. 195–215.

Wolf, C., 2003. iWeaver: towards 'learning style'-based e-learning in computer science education. *Proceedings of the fifth Australasian conference on Computing education*, Vol. 20, pp. 273-279.

Yin M. et al, 2019, Under-standing the effect of accuracy on trust in machine learning models. *Proceedings of the 2019 chi conference on human factors in computing systems*, pp. 1–12.

THE AGENT'S SMILE: IMPACTS OF ARTIFICIALLY GENERATED PEDAGOGICAL AGENTS ON RISK-TAKING

Patrick Jost
Department of Computer Science,
Norwegian University of Science and Technology, Trondheim, Norway

ABSTRACT

Educators are increasingly confronted with technology-driven learning scenarios. Even before the push from the current pandemic, digital learning apps became an integrated didactic tool. Advanced computing can thereby support the digital content creation for educational courses offered on mobile platforms. Computed media content such as natural voices or generated images of real looking but non-existent persons has become easy to access and feasible to use. Particularly in exploratory learning approaches, natural environments and lifelike characters could be utilised to create compelling instructional scenarios or reality-oriented training assignments. However, there is still a limited understanding of the effects such generated lifelike persons used as Pedagogical Agents (PAs) may have on cognition and behaviour.
This study presents the findings of an international field test on the Google Play Store that investigated the effects of an artificially generated instructor's facial expression on risk-taking in a decision-making task. In the field study, an established measure of risk propensity, the Balloon Analogue Risk Task (BART), was extended to include instructions by an artificially generated lifelike persona with different facial expressions. The resulting research game for mobile phones was internationally distributed on the app store for a two-month between-subjects field experiment. The participants were instructed either by a smiling female pedagogical agent, the same agent with a neutral expression or no agent while deciding to risk further pumping up a balloon for more profit or safely collect balloons for realising a current, more modest profit.
The results (n = 379) indicate that instructions presented by a smiling female agent reduce risk propensity in decision-making compared to instructions presented with a neutral facial expression. Instruction design considerations and experiences from the distribution of a research game on Google Play are summarised in the concluding implications.

KEYWORDS

Instructional Design, Artificial Tutors, Pedagogical Agents, Risk-Taking, Google Play Store, Field Experiment, Serious Game

1. BACKGROUND AND RESEARCH OBJECTIVES

Remote and mobile learning are increasingly important scenarios in educational practice. The required digital content creation for educational apps stretches from illustrations to instructional videos and virtual tutor characters (i.e. pedagogical agents) (Clark & Mayer, 2016). While publishing apps on mobile stores has become feasible even in small-scale education scenarios, designing instructional content adequate for mobile and distributed learning remains challenging. It is well known that content presentation and interaction influence cognition and can, for example, create extraneous cognitive load (Jost et al., 2020).

These influences can impact learning gain and are critical to regard when designing for learner evaluation. Reduced personal interaction between educators and students in remote/mobile learning further complicates the design of instructions and assignments.

Advanced computing may help create educational content for mobile apps by generating visually realistic learning scenarios or lifelike instructors who act as mentors, facilitators, or examiners. Generative Adversarial Networks (GAN), a machine learning technique, has been developed intensively during recent years and can now create photorealistic pictures of non-existing persons with different facial expressions and lifelike video portraits (Liu et al., 2021). Moreover, services offer generative APIs and royalty-free, pre-generated portraits (e.g. www.generated.photos) that can be used as pedagogical agent (PA) in educational or research-oriented mobile apps at no charge. Using such artificially generated media allows for learning or training apps with a lifelike instructional PA without copyright concerns or photo shootings. In addition, the parametric flexibility in creating specific facial expressions provides numerous opportunities to emphasise instructions, highlight critical pitfalls in trainings or create a more sympathetic and engaging learning environment.

However, there is currently limited insight into how such lifelike-generated personas impact cognition or behaviour. A better understanding of these influences is needed to realise the full potential of generated PAs for designing instructional apps. This study, therefore, investigates how the facial expressions of a generated lifelike PA affect risk-taking in a decision-making task to inform instructional design for educational and research mobile apps.

1.1 Pedagogical Agents in Digital Learning and Examination Scenarios

Commonly understood by a PA is a visually represented character used in digital learning to instruct and guide learners (Veletsianos & Russell, 2014). The impact of pictured (Khan & Sutcliffe, 2014), animated (van der Meij et al., 2015) and voiced PA (Domagk, 2010) has been researched in a broad area of instructional applications. Thereby PAs have been found to improve learning outcome and performance (e.g. Atorf et al., 2019; Schroeder et al., 2013). Researchers also investigated how realism in depicting the PA impacts learning gain and found that a more realistic PA representation leads to higher learning gains (Salehi & Teymouri Nia, 2019). Moreover, studies found low or no impact on extraneous cognitive load when instructing by PA through gestures (Davis, 2018) or in multiple-choice scenarios (Schroeder, 2017). The influences of PAs in multiple-choice decision-making are of particular importance in the mobile learning context. Typing longer texts on the phone is tedious, and learner assessment is therefore often designed with choice dialogues or quizzes presented by a PA (e.g. Oyelere et al., 2018). In this regard, studies have found that risk propensity is influencing decision-making in multiple-choice exams (Biria & Bahadoran, 2015; Yang & Tackie, 2016). The reported findings suggest that multiple-choice exams are disadvantageous for students with lower risk propensity and suspect a gender bias preferring male students.

Studies applying PA instructions have also reported various impacts on emotions and behaviour. Dinçer and Doğanay (2017) found positive effects on motivation when applying instructive PAs in teaching software skills. Additionally, some researchers found gender-specific motivational benefits on math learning from animated (Arroyo et al., 2011) and cartoon-illustrated (Bringula et al., 2018) PA instructors with female students profiting more than male. Kahn and Sutcliffe (2014), on the other hand, investigated the influences of PA attractiveness on persuasion and found a positive correlation. The influences of different PA facial expressions have been explored on the notion of human mimicry (Chartrand & Van Baaren, 2009) and emotional contagion (Hatfield et al., 1993). Tsai and colleagues (2012) have looked at smiling virtual agents in association with decision-making and concluded that the detected emotional contagion effect is repealed by strategic reasoning.

Investigations on PA smile frequencies/timings by Krämer et al. (2013) further confirmed emotional mimicking and found it also occurs when people were not consciously aware of the PA facial expression. DeMelo et al. (2012) analysed decision-making in a negotiating process with a PA with different facial expressions. Their results indicated that people were more likely to accept a deal when the PA expressed joy. Liew et al. (2016) researched the influences on learner motivation between neutral and smiling PA portraits in virtual learning environments. They concluded that the smile of the PA was perceived as non-genuine by the participants and thus affected motivation negatively.

However, PA visualisations generated by GAN, which are virtually indistinguishable from natural persons/photographs, have only recently become available for research in instructional scenarios. A recent study examining the influences of such lifelike PA portraits showed that persons instructed by a smiling male PA took higher risks in their decisions than those instructed by a smiling female PA (Jost, 2020c). This present study extends on these results and further investigates the suggested impact of lifelike female PA instructors on decision-making.

1.2 Research Objectives

The focus of this research is to investigate how the smiling and non-smiling of a lifelike female PA might influence risk-taking in a decision-making task. Using an established behavioural measure of risk-taking, the Balloon Analogue Risk Task (BART) (Lejuez et al., 2002), and extending it with instructions from the generated PA, a mobile research game is created and deployed in an international field test in the Google Play Store. The research objectives of this field study were thereby twofold:

1. Investigating the influences of artificially generated smiling and non-smiling female instructor personas on risk propensity in a decision-making exercise to inform instructional design practice.
2. Providing practical insights into improving the design of games for research purposes distributed via mobile app stores.

2. EMPIRICAL RESEARCH APPROACH

2.1 Creating and Configuring the Research Game for Mobile Phones

The creation of the mobile research balloon task closely followed the conduct and constructs of the original BART experiment (Lejuez et al., 2002). The BART presents a setting where participants can pump up a balloon. For each pump, a fixed amount of virtual currency (e.g. five dollars) is added to a temporary account, but only when the participant decides to collect the balloon, the amount gets transferred to a permanent account. If the user decides to take a higher risk, further pump up the balloon, and it explodes in the process, the accumulated temporary amount is lost, and the next balloon starts.

Since the initial BART experiment, the validity of the constructs for assessing individual risk propensity has been demonstrated in numerous studies concerning decision-making in mobile and other scenarios (Lauriola et al., 2014; Li et al., 2020; MacLean et al., 2018). Similarly, the author's prior field study on generated female/male PA influences employed the BART constructs by creating a mobile app with a research game framework (Jost, 2020a, 2020c). The same framework – the Quest Game-Frame – with scripted components for the Unity game engine (unity.com) was thus used to create and configure the mobile research game for this study to allow for comparison of results and research process.

The provided logging modules were utilised to protocol the BART risk parameters (see section 2.2). Data was stored in a database under the researchers' authority in a GDPR-compliant manner without personal references using a participation token and secure https connection. Informed consent form and privacy policy were shown as an introductory screen before the game. Participants were asked to give active consent and indicate age group and gender via drop-down before proceeding to the game task. The BART research scenario was designed as described by Lejuez et al. (2002), using the same text/terminology, interaction buttons and general screen layout. Instructions were presented as in the original experiment with only a text without a PA in experimental *condition A*; *condition B* was extended by a generated non-smiling, female PA instructor. In *condition C,* the same artificial instructor persona was shown with a smiling facial expression (Figure 1).

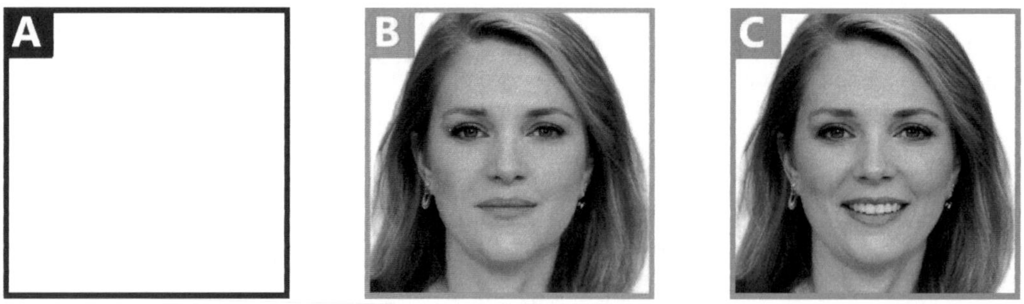

Figure 1. Experimental conditions: A – no PA; B – generated non-smiling, female PA; C – generated smiling female PA

The female PA was randomly selected on *www.generated.photos/faces* where GAN generated, non-existent person portraits are offered free of charge with attribution. Since the offered collection of over 2.5 million generated portraits included "beautified" portraits, a selection filter was set to include only natural, front-facing portraits of adults. As the previous study on male/female PA influences was conducted with a PA of white ethnicity, this pre-selection was also made to maintain comparability. With these inclusion criteria set, the first portrait of a female persona featuring both a neutral and joyful expression was selected as PA for the study (Figure 1). The PA portraits were included in the mobile game to instruct the BART rules and report the score in the decision-making exercise (Figure 2).

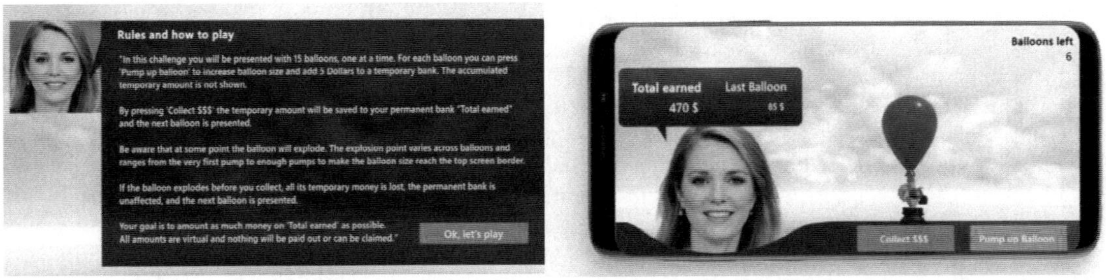

Figure 2. Mobile instruction app with generated smiling female pedagogical agent (condition C)

Following the preceding study (Jost, 2020c), the task featured 15 balloons to pump up with a pump range between 1 and 64. As in the original BART trials, the average breaking point (i.e. on which pump the balloon explodes) for each balloon was pre-calculated to improve the validity of the experiment. Integer series with values 1 to 64 were shuffled until a collection of 15 series was found with the exact breakpoint average of 32. The balloon would pop at the random position of number 1 in each of the series. However, opposed to the BART laboratory experiment, the mobile game could be played as much as players liked. After each trial with 15 balloons, the players could immediately retry the task or finish for now and come back at a later point to play again. Players were informed that the balloon may burst at each pump and that the maximum size to which the balloon can be inflated is the top border of the screen. For assessing PA influences between the three conditions, only each participant's first trial was evaluated in the between-subjects research design. Logging was used to ensure an even distribution of the experimental conditions by assigning the next participant the variant with the lowest number of participations. The assigned condition was kept the same for the participant also in case of retries. The created mobile research game was published internationally on the Google Play Store for a two-month field test.

2.2 Research Design, Hypothesis and Data Collection

The game was configured to measure the BART risk constructs, mean pumps before collection/explosion and total collected/exploded balloons (Figure 3). Lejuez et al. (2002) found that each of the constructs represents valid measures of risk propensity. However, the total collected/exploded balloons are mutually exclusive, meaning a collected balloon cannot be exploded, and an exploded balloon cannot be collected. The two measures can, therefore, essentially be seen as representing a quota of 15 balloons.

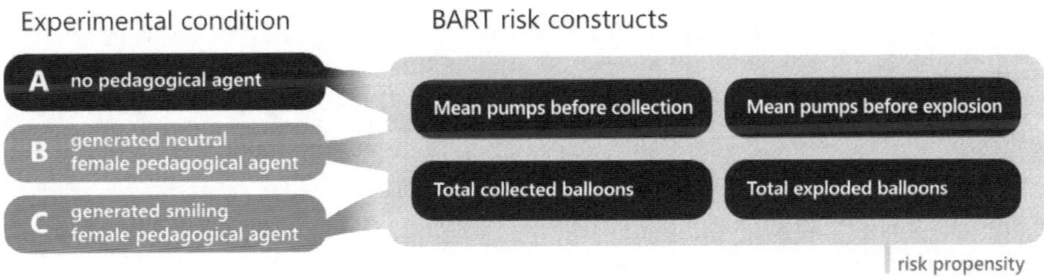

Figure 3. Experimental design for investigating PA expression influences with the mobile balloon risk task

The three independent experimental conditions to investigate influences on risk propensity were designed to show either no PA as in the original BART (*condition A*), the generated non-smiling female PA (*condition B*) or the smiling female PA (*condition C*) as instructor and announcer of progress (score) in the task. It was hypothesised that there would be a difference in the conditions since the preceding study had found effects when displaying a female instructor PA (Jost, 2020c). Accordingly, the null hypothesis for the field study was established as:

H_0: 'There are no significant differences in the measured BART risk propensity constructs when instructing participants with either a smiling, non-smiling or no generated female persona visualisation.'

The mobile game was internationally published in English on the Google Play Store. For the field study, the app ran two months from February to the same day in April 2021. An international Google Ad was run with an increase of budget compared to the prior study from 0.5 €/day to 4.7 €/day as suggested by the Google algorithm. The app was presented in the store as a research game that gives some insight into individual risk propensity compared to other players. In contrast to the prior study, the average score and the total high score of all players were shown after each trial run of 15 balloons before participants could choose to either quit or play again. The Google Play Store analytics showed that the research game was compatible with 17807 different devices and offered in the store of 177 countries. Users could only proceed to the balloon game exercise after giving active, informed consent and stating age-group and gender in the introductory screen. Contrary to the previous study, reporting the country where the game was played was no longer asked from the player, as this data was available through Google Play Store analytics. The BART risk constructs were only stored in the database after a completed game run with 15 balloons either collected or exploded. The collected data were statistically analysed after the field test period with IBM SPSS Statistics 27.

3. RESULTS

3.1 Field Experiment Participation

Throughout the two months, 7595 persons from 83 different countries installed the research game. About 48% identified themselves as female participants, 40% as male and 12% indicated their gender as other. However, only 5% converted to valid participation in the balloon decision exercise (Table 1). The majority dropped out before giving informed consent. About 48% of the recorded balloon test results were repeated trials from the same person identified by the participation token.

Table 1. Participant distribution of the two-month field experiment

	n	*Quota*	*A (no PA)*	*B (neutral PA)*	*C (smiling PA)*
Installations from Google Play Store	7595	100%	-	-	-
Unique participations	464	6%	149	157	158
Valid participations	379	5%	115	136	128

Eventually, 464 records were unique/first trial balloon test results. From these unique trials, 85 were excluded as they either had less than 20 pumps (61 entries) during the whole task or the average time between each pump decision was 0 (14 entries) or over 20 seconds (10 entries). These cases were identified as invalid as the participants either rushed through the steps without making a serious effort or were considerably distracted.

3.2 BART Risk Constructs

The requirements analysis indicated that the recorded valid data were not normally distributed and showed heteroscedasticity of variances. However, analysis of variance (ANOVA) is considered robust against the normality assumption for large sample sizes ($n > 30$) (Field, 2017). Particularly when distributions show only moderate skewness and kurtosis between -1 and 1 (Blanca et al., 2017). Furthermore, as Field (2017) pointed out, Welch's F test does not assume equal variances while having greater statistical power than non-parametric alternatives. Following these indications, Welch's ANOVA was conducted for analysis ($a = 0.05$).

Table 2. BART results

	A (*no PA*)	*B* (*neutral PA*)	*C* (*smiling PA*)
Mean collected balloons	10.9	*10.4	*11.5
95% CI lower / upper	10.3/11.4	9.8/11.1	11.0/12.0
Mean exploded balloons	4.1	*4.6	*3.5
95% CI lower / upper	3.6/4.7	3.9/5.2	3.0/4.0
SE collected & exploded balloons	0.3	0.3	0.3
Mean pumps before collection	4.5	4.8	4.9
SE pumps before collection	0.5	0.5	0.5
Mean pumps before explosion	25.4	24.5	24.4
SE pumps before explosion	0.7	0.8	0.9

**Significant differences between conditions B and C, p = .034*

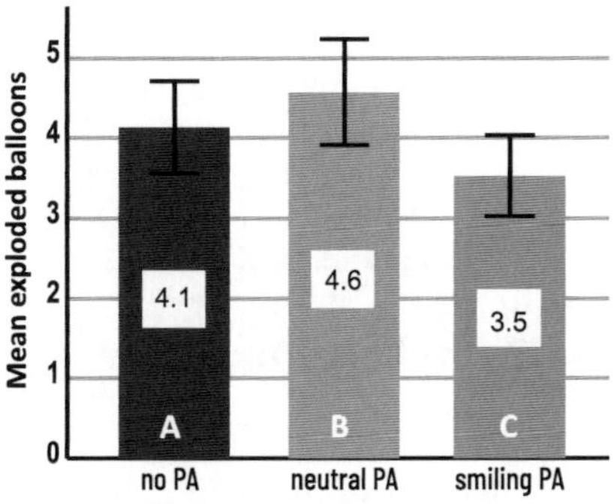

Figure 4. Significantly less exploded balloons with smiling female PA [+/- 2 SE]

Analysis showed no significant differences between the instruction scenarios for mean pumps before collection, F (2, 249.9) = 0.189, p = .828 and mean pumps before explosions, F (2, 249.0) = 0.439, p = .645. However, the balloon test outcome differed significantly between the three instruction conditions regarding collections/explosions of balloons, F (2, 247.9) = 3.35, p = .037. Pairwise comparisons with Games-Howell post-hoc procedure was then conducted to determine which of the A, B and C scenarios resulted in significantly different means of collected/exploded balloons. The results revealed that participants decided differently in the B and C conditions where they were instructed by the neutral or smiling generated female PA. As displayed in Table 2 and Figure 4, participants were on average more inclined to collect balloons than pump them further and risk explosion when instructed by the smiling PA compared to the non-smiling PA (mean difference exploded balloons = -1.04; 95% CI = -2.02, -0.06; p = .034) with a small to medium effect size of Cohen's d = 0.3. Consequently, statistical analysis indicates to reject H_0.

4. DISCUSSION

4.1 Interpretation of PA Influences on Instructional Design

When interpreting the results regarding the *first research objective* about the impact of an artificial PA's facial expressions, the study disclosed mainly three insights to inform instructional design.

First, the outcome confirms prior findings that instructions presented by a lifelike generated PA can impact taking chances in decision-making tasks. As previously found with male/female PA instructors (Jost, 2020c), differences in participants' decision making were also found when a PA with a neutral or a smiling facial expression instructed them. While participants inflated the balloons on average to a similar extent, the group instructed by the smiling PA collected the balloons more frequently and thus risked less of the balloons exploding.

Second, the impact of PA facial expressions could be utilised as subtle nudging mechanism in digital learning scenarios. This finding on facial expression influence supports the results of Kahn and Sutcliffe (2014), who found that more attractive PA pictures are more persuasive. In the BART scenario, the collecting action that grants the money could be seen as offer from the PA, which was more often accepted by the participants shown the smiling PA. On the other hand, it is also possible that the participants were subconsciously in a more positive mindset due to emotional contagion originating from the smiling PA (Krämer et al., 2013), resulting in more active avoidance of explosions. Further research is required to investigate this distinction and the nature of the more cautious decision-making when instructed by a smiling PA. In any case, the subtle influences from PA expressions on risk-taking present various instructional design opportunities. Educational content creators could, for example, use generated PA instructors with sympathetic expressions that support more cautious practices in training applications.

Third, the emotional impact of PA facial expressions needs to be considered when creating instructional apps that assess learner progress or include research objectives. Generated lifelike PA also present an opportunity for designing exploratory or game-based learning where they could be applied in instructional, assessment or motivational functions. However, the reported PA influences require careful consideration when assessing learner progress. Results from dialogue prompts presented by a generated PA may be confounded by different PA facial expressions or gender, which is of particular concern when also including research-oriented assessment (Jost, 2020b).

4.2 Implications for the Creation of Mobile Research Games

In general, utilising the Quest Game-Frame facilitated the iterative adaption of the research scenario and republishing the research game to the Google Play Store, which could be done within a couple of hours. In relation to the *second research objective*, the study confirmed and highlighted some design considerations from practice for the creation of mobile research games.

First of all, consent to data collection discourages most users from engaging in a research game. Only 5% of installations converted to valid participations. Most users that installed the app did not engage in playing but dropped out at the consent page even though it was simplified for this study. Thus, researchers must consider a high conversion drop-out quote when planning GDPR conform field trials with a mobile game.

Next, advertising the mobile app with an online ad campaign is required but also feasible and can be controlled by budget increase. The preceding field trial employed a Google Ad campaign with a budget of 0.5 €/day that generated 20.6 installations per day. Increasing the budget to 4.7 €/day generated 128.7 daily installations. An approx. 10-fold higher budget led to a 6-fold higher installation volume. Thus, raising the ad budget effectively controls the participation rate when also considering the drop-out quote.

Finally, showing participants a comparative score of other players can considerably increase the replay rate. If the research includes repetitive trials, it can be supported by showing participants the average score and current high score combined with a retry button after each round of play. Providing this information to players led to an increase in replays in this field study compared to a preceding one, from 22% to 48%.

4.3 Limitations and Further Research Trails

This study and its findings are limited in several aspects that must be addressed. The Google Play Store was used to distribute and advertise the mobile game internationally in 177 countries. However, the interface language was English only. As the research game was played in 83 countries, several people with limited understanding of the instructions will likely have participated in the trials. Moreover, influences originating from different cultural backgrounds were not considered since only a PA of white ethnicity was pictured. Another aspect to consider for all field studies is the limited control of the context of play. Although extreme values could be identified by time logging, other more subtle contextual influences and distractions could have contributed to the group differences. Further research on influences from artificially generated PAs should include more controllable research designs such as laboratory studies. Psychophysiological measurements, including skin conductance or eye-tracking, could thereby provide further insight into how features of a generated PA affect decision-making.

5. CONCLUSION

The reported result from the two-month field study confirmed previous studies that found influences from pedagogical agents on decision-making. Participants took a less risky approach in the mobile game based on the balloon risk task if a generated smiling PA instructed them compared to a non-smiling variant. The generation of lifelike personas as portraits and video content offers vast opportunities for instructional design in education and research. Knowing the impact of facial expressions allows adapting tutor design to support pedagogical and research-oriented strategies. The findings suggest that sympathetic generated female PAs could be utilised in digital training applications to unobtrusively support more cautious decision-making where it is helpful. Moreover, the study demonstrated the utility of a mobile game as research instrument. The international field experiment on an app store was feasible and controllable while creating valuable insight for instructional design of artificial PA instructors. However, the high drop-out rate due to informed consent and other field study constraints requires careful planning of research conduct. Ultimately, artificially generated PAs and their features need to be further investigated for their potentials. Therefore, field studies should be complemented with controlled laboratory experiments to learn more about how generated lifelike PAs can be used beneficially for education and research.

ACKNOWLEDGEMENT

This research was supported by the Research Council of Norway (Norges Forskningsråd) by funding the IKTPLUSS project ALerT, #270969.

REFERENCES

Arroyo, I., Woolf, B. P., Cooper, D. G., Burleson, W., & Muldner, K. (2011). The Impact of Animated Pedagogical Agents on Girls' and Boys' Emotions, Attitudes, Behaviors and Learning. *2011 IEEE 11th International Conference on Advanced Learning Technologies*, 506–510. https://doi.org/10.1109/ICALT.2011.157

Atorf, D., Kannegieser, E., & Roller, W. (2019). Study on Enhancing Learnability of a Serious Game by Implementing a Pedagogical Agent. *International Conference on Games and Learning Alliance*, 158–168.

Biria, R., & Bahadoran, A. (2015). Exploring the role of risk-taking propensity and gender differences in EFL students' multiple-choice test performance. *Canadian Journal of Basic and Applied Sciences*, *3*(05), 144–154.

Blanca, M. J., Alarcón, R., Arnau, J., Bono, R., & Bendayan, R. (2017). Non-normal data: Is ANOVA still a valid option? *Psicothema*, *29*(4), 552–557.

Bringula, R. P., Fosgate Jr, I. C. O., Garcia, N. P. R., & Yorobe, J. L. M. (2018). Effects of Pedagogical Agents on Students' Mathematics Performance: A Comparison Between Two Versions. *Journal of Educational Computing Research*, *56*(5), 701–722.

Chartrand, T. L., & Van Baaren, R. (2009). Human mimicry. *Advances in Experimental Social Psychology*, *41*, 219–274.

Clark, R. C., & Mayer, R. E. (2016). *E-learning and the science of instruction: Proven guidelines for consumers and designers of multimedia learning* (Fourth edition). Wiley.

Davis, R. O. (2018). The impact of pedagogical agent gesturing in multimedia learning environments: A meta-analysis. *Educational Research Review*, *24*, 193–209. https://doi.org/10.1016/j.edurev.2018.05.002

de Melo, C. M., Carnevale, P., & Gratch, J. (2012). The Effect of Virtual Agents' Emotion Displays and Appraisals on People's Decision Making in Negotiation. In Y. Nakano, M. Neff, A. Paiva, & M. Walker (Eds.), *Intelligent Virtual Agents* (pp. 53–66). Springer. https://doi.org/10.1007/978-3-642-33197-8_6

Dinçer, S., & Doğanay, A. (2017). The effects of multiple-pedagogical agents on learners' academic success, motivation, and cognitive load. *Computers & Education*, *111*, 74–100.

Domagk, S. (2010). Do pedagogical agents facilitate learner motivation and learning outcomes?: The role of the appeal of agent's appearance and voice. *Journal of Media Psychology: Theories, Methods, and Applications*, *22*(2), 84.

Field, A. (2017). *Discovering statistics using IBM SPSS statistics* (5th edition). SAGE Publications.

Hatfield, E., Cacioppo, J. T., & Rapson, R. L. (1993). Emotional contagion. *Current Directions in Psychological Science*, *2*(3), 96–100.

Jost, P. (2020a). The Quest Game-Frame: Balancing Serious Games for Investigating Privacy Decisions. In *Proceedings of the 11th Scandinavian Conference on Information Systems (SCIS2020)* (pp. 1–17). Association for Information Systems (AIS). https://aisel.aisnet.org/scis2020/5/

Jost, P. (2020b). Because it is Fun: Investigating Motives of Fake News Sharing with Exploratory Game Quests. In D. G. Sampson, D. Ifenthaler, & P. Isaías (Eds.), *17th International Conference on Cognition and Exploratory Learning in the Digital Age (CELDA 2020)* (pp. 35–42). IADIS Press.

Jost, P. (2020c). Pedagogical agents: Influences of artificially generated instructor personas on taking chances. *Proceedings of the Norwegian Conference for ICT-Research and Education (NIKT 2020)*, *4*, 1–14.

Jost, P., Cobb, S., & Hämmerle, I. (2020). Reality-based interaction affecting mental workload in virtual reality mental arithmetic training. *Behaviour & Information Technology*, *39*(10), 1062–1078.

https://doi.org/10.1080/0144929X.2019.1641228

Khan, R. F., & Sutcliffe, A. (2014). Attractive agents are more persuasive. *International Journal of Human-Computer Interaction*, *30*(2), 142–150.

Krämer, N., Kopp, S., Becker-Asano, C., & Sommer, N. (2013). Smile and the world will smile with you—The effects of a virtual agent's smile on users' evaluation and behavior. *International Journal of Human-Computer Studies*, *71*(3), 335–349. https://doi.org/10.1016/j.ijhcs.2012.09.006

Lauriola, M., Panno, A., Levin, I. P., & Lejuez, C. W. (2014). Individual differences in risky decision making: A meta-analysis of sensation seeking and impulsivity with the balloon analogue risk task. *Journal of Behavioral Decision Making*, *27*(1), 20–36.

Lejuez, C. W., Read, J. P., Kahler, C. W., Richards, J. B., Ramsey, S. E., Stuart, G. L., Strong, D. R., & Brown, R. A. (2002). Evaluation of a behavioral measure of risk taking: The Balloon Analogue Risk Task (BART). *Journal of Experimental Psychology: Applied*, *8*(2), 75.

Li, X., Pan, Y., Fang, Z., Lei, H., Zhang, X., Shi, H., Ma, N., Raine, P., Wetherill, R., & Kim, J. J. (2020). Test-retest reliability of brain responses to risk-taking during the balloon analogue risk task. *NeuroImage*, *209*, 116495.

Liew, T. W., Zin, N. A. M., Sahari, N., & Tan, S.-M. (2016). The effects of a pedagogical agent's smiling expression on the learner's emotions and motivation in a virtual learning environment. *The International Review of Research in Open and Distributed Learning*, *17*(5).

Liu, M.-Y., Huang, X., Yu, J., Wang, T.-C., & Mallya, A. (2021). Generative Adversarial Networks for Image and Video Synthesis: Algorithms and Applications. *Proceedings of the IEEE*, *109*(5), 839–862.

https://doi.org/10.1109/JPROC.2021.3049196

MacLean, R. R., Pincus, A. L., Smyth, J. M., Geier, C. F., & Wilson, S. J. (2018). Extending the Balloon Analogue Risk Task to Assess Naturalistic Risk Taking via a Mobile Platform. *Journal of Psychopathology and Behavioral Assessment*, *40*(1), 107–116. https://doi.org/10.1007/s10862-017-9628-4

Oyelere, S. S., Suhonen, J., Wajiga, G. M., & Sutinen, E. (2018). Design, development, and evaluation of a mobile learning application for computing education. *Education and Information Technologies*, *23*(1), 467–495.

https://doi.org/10.1007/s10639-017-9613-2

Salehi, V., & Teymouri Nia, F. (2019). Effect of levels of realism of mobile-based pedagogical agents on health e-learning. *Future of Medical Education Journal*, *9*(2), 40–45.

Schroeder, N. L. (2017). The influence of a pedagogical agent on learners' cognitive load. *Journal of Educational Technology & Society*, *20*(4), 138–147.

Schroeder, N. L., Adesope, O. O., & Gilbert, R. B. (2013). How effective are pedagogical agents for learning? A meta-analytic review. *Journal of Educational Computing Research*, *49*(1), 1–39.

Tsai, J., Bowring, E., Marsella, S., Wood, W., & Tambe, M. (2012). A Study of Emotional Contagion with Virtual Characters. In Y. Nakano, M. Neff, A. Paiva, & M. Walker (Eds.), *Intelligent Virtual Agents* (pp. 81–88). Springer. https://doi.org/10.1007/978-3-642-33197-8_8

van der Meij, H., van der Meij, J., & Harmsen, R. (2015). Animated pedagogical agents effects on enhancing student motivation and learning in a science inquiry learning environment. *Educational Technology Research and Development*, *63*(3), 381–403. https://doi.org/10.1007/s11423-015-9378-5

Veletsianos, G., & Russell, G. S. (2014). Pedagogical Agents. In J. M. Spector, M. D. Merrill, J. Elen, & M. J. Bishop (Eds.), *Handbook of Research on Educational Communications and Technology* (pp. 759–769). Springer. https://doi.org/10.1007/978-1-4614-3185-5_61

Yang, Z., & Tackie, M. (2016). Risk Preference and Student Behavior on Multiple-Choice Exams. *Economics Bulletin*, *36*(1), 58–67.

ESTIMATING LEARNING ASSISTANCE SKILLS USING LEARNING ANALYTICS

Hiroyuki Watanabe[1], Yoshiko Goda[2], Atsushi Shimada[3] and Masanori Yamada[4]
1Faculty of Arts and Science, Kyushu University, 744, Motooka, Nishi-ku, Fukuoka 819-0395, Japan
2Research Center for Instructional Systems, Kumamoto University, 2-39-1, Kurokami, Chuo-ku, Kumamoto, 860-0862, Japan
3Faculty of Information Science and Electrical Engineering, Kyushu University, 744, Motooka, Nishi-ku, Fukuoka 819-0395, Japan
4Faculty of Arts and Science, Kyushu University ,744, Motooka, Nishi-ku, Fukuoka 819-0395, Japan

ABSTRACT

Learning assistance is an essential part of higher education. Tutors, the core of the assistance staff, need to have learning assistance skills. If the potential for these skills can be identified when selecting tutors, the training method will be more efficient. Also, learning assistance skills are thought to be related to learning skills. Therefore, in this paper, we used previous research to identify the relationship between learning skills and learning assistance skills to clarify this. Then, using learning analytics, we explored whether learning support skills can be determined from learning skills.

KEYWORDS

Learning Skills, Learning Assistance Skills, Learning Analytics, CRLA, ITTPC

1. INTRODUCTION

Lack of student preparation for college is not a new phenomenon in higher education in the United States (US) (Sheets 1994). Therefore, "widely used academic support programs aimed at improving student retention and persistence rates (Brooks 2006)" have become indispensable. Among them, tutoring has become a standard service in the ongoing support for students to graduate (Colver and Fray 2015).

The programs cover topics such as textbook reading, time management, effective note-taking, use of resources such as libraries, and preparation for exams (Wernersbach et al. 2014). Learning assistants are also often referred to as peer tutors in the US (Maxwell 1997). Peer tutors provide course-specific content and study skills to support undergraduate students across the curriculum (Keller 2020). It can also refer to the various ways in which learning takes place through interaction with peers (Rae and Baillie 2005).

One of the reasons for the recent increase in peer tutoring in universities is the decreasing resources and increasing student numbers. In other words, there is a growing interest in peer tutoring as a means of doing more with less, while improving the quality of education (Topping 1996). Maxwell surveyed the literature on tutoring in 1990 and noted that training of peer tutors was essential to the success of tutoring programs in universities (Maxwell 1990).

Thus, learning assistants have to be trained. The training method will be more efficient with the information on their potency for learning assistance skills when selecting them. Of course, the higher the potential, the more advanced will be the learning and the more competent they will be as learning assistants. As a way to measure the potential, it is desirable to understand whether the learning skills of students, the possible learning assistants, are sufficient in their usual study.

Therefore, in this study, based on the review of learning assistance skills, the relationship with learning skills will be discussed. Moreover, based on the analysis of recent learning behavior, we will explore the possibility of estimating the degree of learning assistance skills using learning analytics (Schumacher and Ifenthaler, 2018), which aims to improve the learning environment.

2. PREVIOUS RESEARCH REVIEW

2.1 Learning Assistance Skills from the Perspective of Learning Assistance Programs

Many universities are now adopting various programs to help students adapt and succeed in higher education.

These programs focus on topics such as time management, reading textbooks, taking effective notes, using resources such as the library, and exam preparation. The study also found that students enrolled in study skills courses initially had lower levels of self-efficacy. However, after testing, they reached levels equal to or higher than those of comparison students (Wernersbach et al. 2014).

Moreover, success courses for university students are designed to help develop effective self-regulated learning (SRL) skills. Therefore, students believed that time management and motivation are important for becoming effective college students (Hoops, 2016). Similarly, in the case of distance education, study skills, motivation, time management, exam preparation, and coping with exam stress affect students' success (Poyraz 2013).

Next, regarding programs and their effectiveness, Dakhiel et al. (2019) found the effectiveness of training programs in developing study skills and improving the English language proficiency of 10th grade students. To examine learning skills, the students were classified into five independent sub-skills according to the list developed by Dennis (2010). According to this list, these were procedurally defined as grades in each skill (i.e., textbook, memory, test preparation, concentration, and time management skills).

O'Reilly and Sabatini (2016) introduced a cognitive science intervention for students who struggled with reading, and Salame and Thompson (2020) found that methodical note-taking can benefit students by providing a specific way of learning and help them perform better in their courses. They also said that there is a correlation between note-taking and grade point average (GPA) of students as those who are good note-takers also have a higher GPA. Akkaraju (2018) stated that writing by hand is a multisensory process that enhances learners' memory, concentration, focus, and cognition, making it a valuable learning skill.

Along with the effectiveness of mutual learning, Stigmar (2016) analyzed how tutors and tutees benefited from peer teaching. The most common research design was the use of quasi-experimental pre- and post-tests. The main educational beliefs and theories are social constructivism. The main conclusion was that generic skills development and metacognitive training benefited from peer teaching. It has also been shown to have positive effects on student tutors and tutees (Keller 2020).

Wolfe (2018) investigated the impact of a peer tutoring model in information technology foundations (ITF), an introductory computer science course at a high school in South Carolina. The results showed improved post-test scores, increased completion of assignments, lesser time spent waiting for support when there was confusion, and improved cooperative learning skills as students had to learn to communicate in a meaningful way while respecting each other. Reporting that student participants benefited in various ways, Yaman (2019) examined the characteristics of peer tutoring in a first-year engineering calculus I course and found that tutors and tutees had three types of relationships that depended on the skills of the tutor and peer personality (interdependent, mutual support, and tutoring).

Thus, learning assistance programs include topics such as SRL, time management, note-taking, reading, and exam preparation which are effective for tutors and tutees in terms of mutual and cooperative learning. However, the boundary between them and learning skills is not clear. Therefore, in the next section, we will approach the issue from the perspective of the skills needed by peer tutors and learning supporters.

2.2 Standards for Learning Assistance Programs by CRLA

In the 1980s, several national associations for professionals in the learning assistance field emerged. This was because of the rapid increase in the number of faculty and learning assistance centers. Training tutors created a need for a new category of staff to work in universities and to provide a forum for them to discuss their professional development with colleagues and experienced leaders in learning assistance (Colver and Fry 2016). College Reading and Learning Association (CRLA; https://www.crla.net/index.php/membership/about-us) is one of the organizations that emerged from this process. It was here that the International Tutor Training Program Certification (ITTPC), announced in 1986 to certify the quality of tutor training programs, was considered. The concept was developed over three years and became the CRLA's ITTPC (originally ITCP) in 1989 (Sheets 2012). Today, certification for tutor training programs is more widely recognized as a means of providing consistent and quality learning support. The ITTPC sets the standard for tutor training.

This program is divided into levels one to three according to the skills and experience of the tutors. The ITTPC is unique as it does not certify individual tutors, but the institutions that train them. Since 1989, more than 1,000 university tutor training programs around the world have taken the ITTPC at one or more levels, and thousands of people from these programs have been certified as tutors, advanced tutors, or master tutors. Table 1 shows the items required at Level 1 of the ITTPC.

Table 1. ITTPC Topics (Level 1)

No.	Topics	Learning skills
1	Definition of tutoring and tutor responsibilities	No relations
2	Basic tutoring Guidelines/ Tutoring Do's & Don'ts	No relations
3	Techniques for beginning and ending a tutoring session	No relations
4	Adult learners and/or learning theory and/or learning styles.	No relations
5	Assertiveness and/or Handling Difficult Situations.	No relations
6	Role Modeling	Relations
7	Setting Goals and/or Planning	Relations
8	Communication Skills	No relations
9	Active Listening and Paraphrasing	No relations
10	Referral Skills	No relations
11	Study Skills	Relations
12	Critical Thinking Skills	No relations
13	Compliance with Ethics and Philosophy of the Tutoring Profession &/or Compliance with Sexual Harassment concerns &/or Compliance with Plagiarism concerns.	No relations
14	Problem Solving	No relations

2.3 Relationship between Learning and Learning Assistance Skills

Learning assistance skills were discussed in sections 2.1 and 2.2, and their relationship with learning skills will be summarized here. Learning analytics captures and analyzes the learning behavior of individuals, and although it is possible to estimate learning skills, it is difficult to trace the behavior that supports others' learning from the learning behavior. Therefore, to estimate whether an individual has learning support skills, we analyzed if learning skills were strongly related to the support skills.

We will now discuss ITTPC's Topic 6, 7, and 11, which we believe are related to learning skills.

First, "Topic 6: Role Modeling" is based on the criteria such as being a role model for learners, using a calendar to make appointments and take notes, practicing specific learning methods, creating a personal schedule that supports sufficient study time, and communicating with faculty (through email and face-to-face). In other words, it is related to an important aspect of learning skills, time management. This shows that students can create a schedule that takes into account their fixed schedule, classes, and study time, and create a study plan before the final exam period.

Next, "Topic 7: Setting Goals and/or Planning " means that tutors can effectively help learners plan and set their personal academic goals according to the criteria set in the tutor training. This corresponds to time management study skills. If students do this type of time management, it is possible to help them.

The last topic, "Topic 11: Study Skills," states that tutors develop a repertoire of effective study skills and strategies to facilitate the learning of new information (e.g., effective time management, organization, note-taking, test-taking, motivation, mastery, retention, performance, and reducing anxiety), which is a learning skill.

The above three topics are the ones that overlap with learning skills, and if these can be estimated from the logs, it may be possible to estimate learning support skills indirectly.

3. CAN LEARNING ANALYTICS BE USED TO ESTIMATE LEARNING ASSISTANCE SKILLS?

Recent advances in Information and Communication Technology (ICT) have made it possible to trace the behavior of learners using the learning analytics approach. Watanabe et al. (2020a) organized the learning skills that can be traced by the LA approach, focusing on the types of learning behaviors, especially lecture-style classes in educational institutions. The systems used here include e-book viewers (Teasley 2017) and learning management systems (LMS). Moreover, a personalized learning analytics dashboard (LAD) for students was developed by integrating data from a student information system into a basic algorithm (Ogata et al. 2017, Chen et al. 2019, Lu et al. 2020). The LAD can visualize information about the acquisition and use of learning skills. Chen et al. (2020a) listed two effects of LAD: "First, students' perceptions of visual attraction for LAD assessment and learning behaviors were related to reflection." "Second, the students' perceptions of behavioral changes for LAD had positive effects on the regulation of cognition dimension." Moreover, Chen et al. (2021) identified (1) appropriate graphic representations; (2) comparison functions; (3) monitoring functions that relate to goal attainment; and (4) consistent feedback" as four important elements of LAD.

At Kyushu University, as specific tools, the LADs used are Real-time Monitoring (Figure1)(Shimada et al. 2018, Owatari et al.2020), Reading Path (Figure 2)(Chen et al.2019, Lu et al. 2020), and MAI Helper (Figure 3) (Watanabe et al. 2021). What kind of learning skills can be estimated by the LA approach?

First, the real-time monitoring shows the markers and words that students are paying attention to in BookRoll, an e-book viewer, and whether they are pressing the "Get it" or "Not Get it" button on each page. This allows the log to show trends about reading for learning skills.

Second, for the reading path, the log shows which pages were viewed during and after the reading class, and how often they were viewed. This also falls under the learning skill reading.

Finally, there is the MAI Helper. This is a system that allows you to list your learning activities, which mainly applies to learning skills related to time management (Watanabe et al. 2020b). It also has memo, reflection, and calendar functions. Thus, using the system's logs, we can check time management, note-taking, reflection, access time, and frequency, all of which are related to learning skills. The system helps students develop study attitudes and habits by allowing them to manage their schedules. Table 2 shows an example of a student schedule log. From these logs, it is difficult to extrapolate learning assistance skills such as "tutor definition and tutor responsibilities," "techniques for starting and ending tutoring sessions," and "active listening and paraphrasing." Therefore, we believe that the basic learning skills of reading, writing, and time management can be estimated.We focused on the strategies of these from a pedagogical perspective. McNamana (2004) indicated that it helped students use logical thinking, or domain-general knowledge, rather than domain-specific knowledge, to understand the text. Palincsar and Brown (1984) showed that through reciprocal teaching, the quality of summarizing and questioning was greatly improved when tutors and learners took turns summarizing (self-reviewing), questioning, clarifying, and predicting the text. Furthermore, regarding time management by making plans and schedules for learning, Pintrich et al. (1993) mentioned that one of the self-regulated learning strategies is the resource management strategy, which includes "time management and environmental composition". Thus, students' basic learning skills are based on learning strategies such as "reading strategies", "writing strategies", and "self-regulated learning strategies". Estimating these basic learning skills can help instructors to understand how students' use their learning (assistance) skills, and to select students to lead group learning in the class, tutors for out-of-class activities.

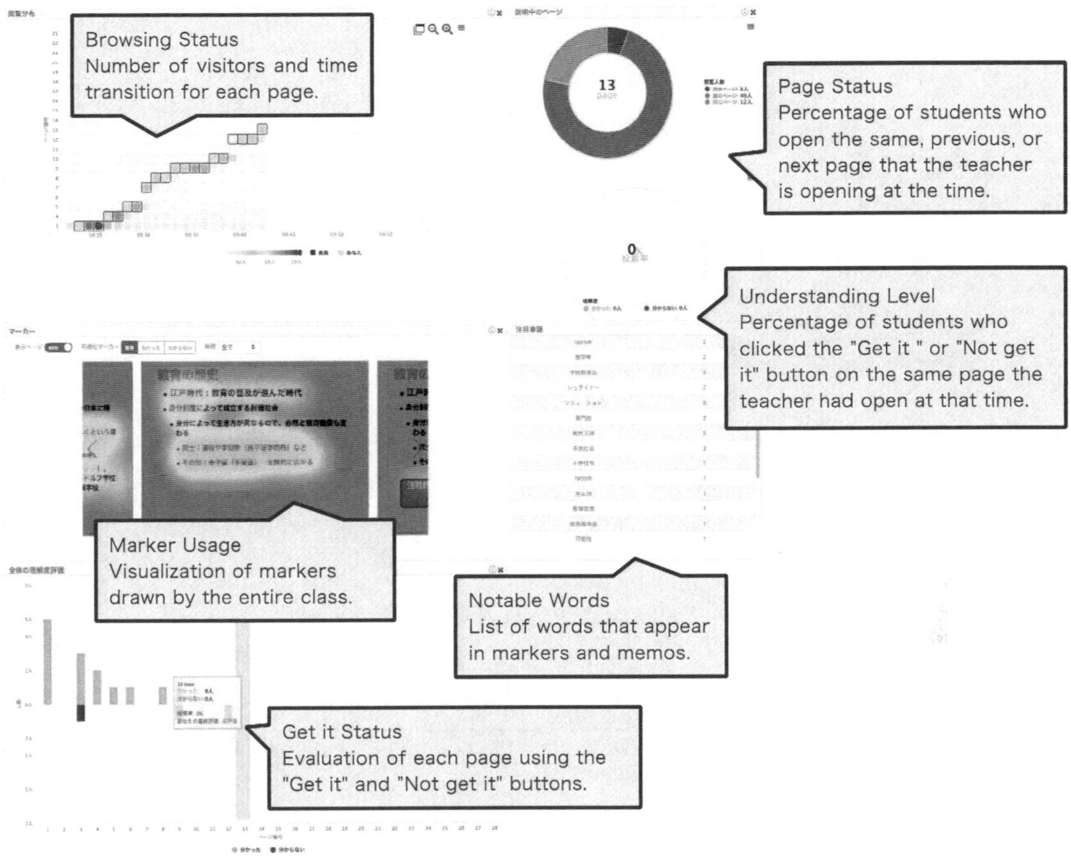

Figure 1. Real-time Monitoring overview

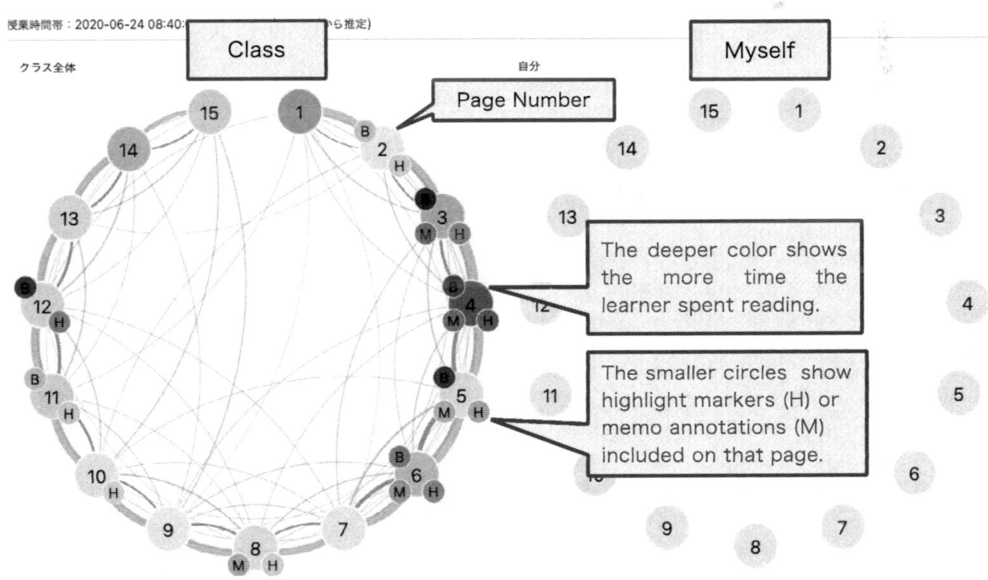

Figure 2. Reading Path overview of Metaboard

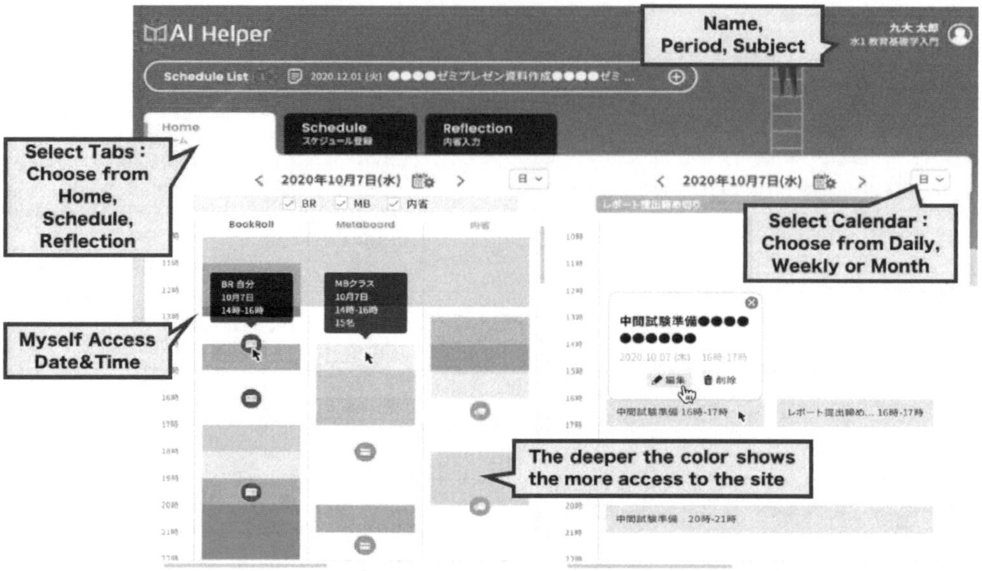

Figure 3. MAI Helper overview of Metaboard

Table 2. Example of Schedule Logs

Student No.	Name	Update type	Schedule title	Start time	End time	Repeat setting contents	E-mail notification time	Log making time
1375	Kyu Taro	Addition	Test 1	2021/1/ 10 10:00	2021/1/10 10:10	every day	2021/1/25 10:00	2021/1/ 10 10:10
1375	Kyu Taro	Addition	Class	2021/1/ 12 13:00	2021/1/12 14:30	every day		2021/1/ 12 14:30
1375	Kyu Taro	Addition	Report	2021/1/ 25 20:00	2021/1/25 21:30	every day	2021/1/30 10:00	2021/1/ 25 21:30
1375	Kyu Taro	Addition	Library	2012/2/ 4 12:00	2012/2/4 16:30	every day		2012/2/ 4 16:30

4. CONCLUSION AND FUTURE WORKS

In this paper, we have discussed whether Learning Analytics can be used to estimate learning assistance skills, based on a review of previous research. We aimed to verify whether this is possible by using log data. We found that it is possible to estimate learning assistance skills from data on learning behavior by using LAD. How should we visualize these?

For example, analyzing students' learning behaviors from log data accumulated from e-Book viewers could be beneficial for instructors and learners. (Yin et al. 2018). It can also be used to develop self-regulated learning skills. Awareness of active time management for learning planning can promote the submission of one-minute papers on time and regular reports earlier than the due date (Yamada et al. 2015).

Moreover, Chen et al. (2020b) designed a science course that aligned with the collaborative problem solving (CPS) process, collected multiple data sources, and examined them in a learning analytics approach. Specifically, they compared the results of high- and low-performing groups, taking into account CPS awareness and factors of learning motivation and learning behavior, as well as individual differences in students' learning abilities.

However, Oi et al. (2017) reported that the findings of the educational big data were only partially replicated in a replication experiment. This result suggests that "to make effective use of learning and teaching analytics, the educational environment needs to be carefully constructed to ensure reproducibility."

In inferring learning assistance skills from these findings, the question for the future is how to build learning assistance models from the data.

ACKNOWLEDGEMENT

This research was supported by JST AIP Grant No. JPMJCR19U1, JSPS Kakenhi JP19H01716, JP20H01727, and JP21K18134, Japan

REFERENCES

Akkaraju, S., 2018. Handwriting to Learn: Embedding a Crucial Study Skill in a Gateway Science Course, *Journal of Effective Teaching in Higher Education,* Vol. 1, No. 1, pp. 55-72.

Beck, K. and Ralph, J., 1994. Patterns Generates Architectures. *Proceedings of European Conference of Object-Oriented Programming. Bologna,* Italy, pp. 139-149.

Bodorik P. et al, 1991. Deciding to Correct Distributed Query Processing. *In IEEE Transactions on Data and Knowledge Engineering,* Vol. 4, No. 3, pp. 253-265.

Campus, P. B., 2012. Enhancing Supplemental Instruction at Brevard Community College: A Review of Peer Tutoring, Its Effectiveness on Learning Outcomes, and the Costs and Methods of Implementation.

Chen L., Lu M., Goda Y., Shimada A. and Yamada M., 2021. *Learning Analytics Dashboard Supporting Metacognition.* In: Ifenthaler D., Sampson D.G., Isaías P. (eds) Balancing the Tension between Digital Technologies and Learning Sciences. Cognition and Exploratory Learning in the Digital Age. Springer, Cham.

Chen, L., Inoue, K., Goda, Y. et al, 2020b. Exploring Factors that Influence Collaborative Problem Solving Awareness in Science Education. *Technology Knowledge Learning,* Vol. 25, pp. 337–366.

Chen, L., Lu, M., Goda, Y., and Yamada, M., 2019. Design of Learning Analytics Dashboard Supporting Metacognition. *In Proceedings of 16th International Conference Cognition and Exploratory Learning in Digital Age (CELDA 2019),* pp. 175-182.

Chen, L., Lu, M., Goda, Y., Shimada, A., and Yamada, M., 2020a. Factors of the Use of Learning Analytics Dashboard that Affect Metacognition. *In Proceedings of 17th International Conference Cognition and Exploratory Learning in Digital Age (CELDA 2020)*, pp. 295-302.

Colver M. and Fry, T., 2016. Evidence to Support Peer Tutoring Programs at the Undergraduate Level, *Journal of College Reading and Learning,* Vol. 46, No. 1, pp.16-41.

Congos, D. H., 2011. *Starting Out in Community College*. McGraw-Hill, Chicago.

Dakhiel, Maysoon A.; Ahmed, Somaya A., 2019 Effectiveness of a Training Program in Improving Study Skills and English Language Achievement among High School Students. *Journal of Educational Issues,* Vol. 5, No. 1, pp. 132-149.

Does tutoring help? a look at the literature. *Review of Research in Developmental Education,* Vol. 7, No. 4.

Keller, P., 2020. A Terminological Study of Peer Education in Higher Education: A White Paper prepared for the College Reading and Learning Association.

Lu, M., Chen, L., Goda, Y., Shimada, A., and Yamada, M., 2020. Development of a Learning Dashboard Prototype Supporting Meta-cognition for Students. *In Companion Proceedings of the 10th International Conference on Learning Analytics & Knowledge (LAK20)*, pp. 104-106.

Maxwell, M., 1990. Does tutoring help? a look at the literature. *Review of Research in Developmental Education,* Vol. 7, No. 4.

McNamara, D. S., 2004. SERT: Self-Explanation Reading Training. *Discourse Processes,* Vol. 38, No. 1, pp.1-30.

O'Reilly, T., and Sabatini, J., 2016. *Using Advances in Cognitive Science to Improve Students Study Skills and Reading Comprehension.* In R. Schiff and R. M. Joshi (Eds). Interventions in Learning Disabilities: Literacy Studies, 13, (pp. 139-158). Switzerland: Springer International.

Ogata, H., Oi, M., Mohri, K., Okubo, F., Shimada, A., Yamada, M., Wang, J., and Hirokawa, S., 2017. Learning Analytics for E-book-based Educational Big Data in Higher Education. *In Smart sensors at the IoT frontier ,* pp. 327-350. Springer, Cham.

Oi, M., Yamada, M., Okubo, F., Shimada, A., and Ogata, H., 2017. Reproducibility of Findings from Educational Big Data: A Preliminary Study. *LAK '17: Proceedings of the Seventh International Learning Analytics & Knowledge Conference*, pp. 536–537.

Owatari, T., Shimada, A., Minematsu, T., Hori, M., and Taniguchi, R. I., 2020. Real-Time Learning Analytics Dashboard for Students in Online Classes. *In 2020 IEEE International Conference on Teaching, Assessment, and Learning for Engineering (TALE)* , pp. 523-529.

Palincsar, S. A., and Brown, L. A., 1984. Reciprocal Teaching of Comprehension-Fostering and Comprehension-Monitoring Activities, *Cognition and Instruction*, Vol.1, No.2, pp. 117-175.

Pintrich, P. R., Smith, D. A. F., Garcia, T., and Mckeachie, W. J., 1993. Reliability and Predictive Validity of the Motivated Strategies for Learning Questionnaire (Mslq). *Educational and Psychological Measurement*, Vol.53, No.3, pp. 801–813.

Poyraz, C., 2013. Investigating Distance Education Students' Study Skills, *Turkish Online Journal of Distance Education,* Vol. 14, No. 4, pp 69-82.

Psychology Teaching Review, Vol. 11, No. 1, pp. 53-63.

Rae, J. and Aubrey Baillie, A., 2005. Peer tutoring and the study of psychology: Tutoring experience as a learning method

Salame, I. I. and Thompson, A., 2020. Students' Views on Strategic Note-Taking and Its Impact on Performance, Achievement, and Learning, *International Journal of Instruction,* Vol. 13, No. 2, pp. 1-16.

Schumacher, C., and Ifenthaler, D., 2018. Features students really expect from learning analytics. *Computers in Human Behavior,* Vol. 78, pp. 397-407.

Sheets, R. A. ,2012. *Peer Tutoring and Tutor Training: A Historical Perspective.* In K. Agee and R. Hodges Handbook for Training Peer Tutors and Mentors, (pp.3-6), College Reading and Learning Association, Mason, USA.

Sheets, R. A., 1994. The Effects of Training and Experience on Adult Peer Tutors in Community Colleges (Doctoral dissertation, Arizona State University).

Shimada, A., Konomi, S. I., and Ogata, H., 2018. Real-time earning analytics system for improvement of on-site lectures. *Interactive Technology and Smart Education,* Vol. 15, No. 4, pp. 314-331.

Stigmar, M., 2016. Peer-to-peer teaching in higher education: A critical literature review. *Mentoring & Tutoring: Partnership in Learning,* Vol. 24, No. 2, pp. 124-136.

Teasley, S. D., 2017. Student facing dashboards: One size fits all? Technology, *Knowledge and Learning,* Vol. 22, No. 3, 377-384.

Topping, K. J., 1996. The Effectiveness of Peer Tutoring in Further and Higher Education: A Typology and Review of the Literature. *Higher Education,* Vol. 32, No. 3, pp. 321-345.

Watanabe, H., Chen, L., Geng, X., Goda, Y., and Shimada, A., 2020b. Design of the Time Management Skills Acquisition System Using Learning Analytics. *In Proceedings of 17th International Conference Cognition and Exploratory Learning in Digital Age (CELDA 2020)*, pp. 67-73.

Watanabe, H., Chen, L., Goda, Y., Shimada, A., and Yamada, M., 2021. Development of a Time Management Skill Support System Based on Learning Analytics. *In Companion Proceedings 11th International Conference on Learning Analytics & Knowledge (LAK21)*, pp. 241-249.

Watanabe, H., Chen, L., Shimada, A., and Yamada, M., 2020a. Toward Identification of Learning Skills from Learning Analytics Approach: A Research Review. *In IEEE International Conference on Teaching, Assessment, and Learning for Engineering (TALE) 2020*, pp. 807-812.

Wernersbach, B.M., Crowley, S., Bates, S., and Rosenthal, C., 2014. Study Skills Course Impact on Academic Self-Efficacy. *Journal of Developmental Education,* Vol. 37, pp. 14-33.

Wolfe, B., 2018. The impact of a peer-tutoring model on the academic performance of secondary students. (Doctoral dissertation).

Yamada, M., Goda, Y., Matsuda, T., Kato, H., and Miyagawa, H., 2015. The Relationship among Self-Regulated Learning, Procrastination, and Learning Behaviors in Blended Learning Environment. International Association for Development of the Information Society. *12th International Conference on Cognition and Exploratory Learning in Digital Age 2015 (CELDA 2015),* pp.67-74.

Yaman, B., 2019. A multiple case study: What happens in peer tutoring of calculus studies? *International Journal of Education in Mathematics,* Science and Technology (IJEMST), Vol. 7, No. 1, pp. 53-72.

Yin, C., Yamada, M., Oi, M., Shimada, A., Okubo, F., Kojima, K., and Ogata, H., 2019. Exploring the Relationships between Reading Behavior Patterns and Learning Outcomes based on Log Data from E-books: A Human Factor Approach. *International Journal of Human–Computer Interaction*, Vol. 35, No. 4-5, pp. 313-322.

USING ADAPTIVE MASTERY TESTING IN ASSESSMENT MANAGEMENT SYSTEMS

Muhittin Şahin[1], Furkan Aydın[2], Sema Sulak[3], Cennet Terzi Müftüoğlu[4], Mustafa Tepgeç[5], Gizem Karaoğlan Yılmaz[3], Ramazan Yılmaz[3] and Halil Yurdugül[6]
[1]*Ege University, Turkey; University of Mannheim, Germany* *
[2]*Kahramanmaras Sutcu Imam University, Turkey*
[3]*Bartın University, Turkey*
[4]*Tokat Gaziosmanpasa University*
[5]*Hacettepe University; Mustafa Kemal University, Turkey*
[6]*Hacettepe University, Turkey*

ABSTRACT

The use of technology for teaching and learning has created a paradigm shifting in learning environments and learning process, and also the paradigm shifting has also affected the assessment processes. In addition to these, online environments provide more opportunities to assess of the learners. In this study, the Adaptive Mastery Testing (AMT) system in Assessment Management System was designed and developed in which students can test themselves, recognize their strengths and weaknesses, and determine their learning objective based competencies. AMT environment is structured in accordance with the rapid prototyping software developing model. In this environment, there are questions for the students about four learning objectives, which are among the basic subjects of the Statistics course. AMT environment consists of presentation, assessment, domain and learner model. Pilot implementation was carried out with 98 undergraduate students. In order to evaluate of the environment; number of tests taken, number of correct answer, number of wrong answer and number of total answer data were used. According to the findings, it is seen that most of the students are masters in the learning objectives presented to them. In addition, it was found that half of the students took an average test to become a master. In other words, half of the learners participating in the study were determined as masters by the system in the first test they took for each learning objective.

KEYWORDS

E-Assessment, Adaptive Mastery Testing, Assessment Management System, Rapid Prototyping, Statistic, Log Data

1. INTRODUCTION

The use of technology for teaching and learning has created a paradigm shifting in learning environments and learning process, and also the paradigm shifting has also affected the assessment processes. With this paradigm shifting, it's expected that learners be aware of their learning processes and guide their learning processes. In the literature, it is stated that students who cannot guide their own learning processes cannot make use of e-learning processes adequately (Gibbons, 2003). In other words, it can be said that e-learning environments work in favor of autonomous learners (Grow, 1991). In this context, individual online learning environments and assessment environments and designs that recognize and guide the learner, enable them to learn at an individual pace, come to the fore. Assessments within the scope of increasing learners' awareness of learning and monitoring learning processes are considered as formative assessment (Yurdugül & Bayrak, 2014). Formative assessment aims to contribute to the learner's learning process by providing information to the learner about their performance (Sadler, 1998). However, it seems that this assessment cannot be made effectively in physical environments (Mok, 2010). Online environments provide more opportunities to assess of the learners (Oosterhof, Conrad, & Ely, 2008). In this context, e-learning environments where students can test themselves and make a judgment about themselves contribute to the e-assessment process (Bayrak, 2014). In this study, the Adaptive Mastery Testing (AMT) in Assessment Management System (AMS) was designed and developed in which students can test themselves, recognize their strengths and weaknesses, and determine their learning objective based competencies. This system design is based on the Learning Management System

(LMS) architecture. It is thought that such AMS systems can be integrated with LMS in the further researches. Besides this, the AMS expression was used in the research due to the use of metrics in the assessment tasks of the students. In addition, in the research, 98 undergraduate students used this system as a pilot study and the findings according to the use of the system by students were included.

1.1 Adaptive Mastery Testing (AMT)

The key feature of adaptive tests is that each respondent is tested based on their ability (Eggen, 2004; Wainer,1990; Weiss, 1983). The most important adaptive testing application is Computerized Adaptive Testing (CAT) which is based on Item Response Theory (IRT). The critical component of adaptive tests is the selection of the items that convey the significant information regarding the ability of the examinee as well as the fact that each respondent receives items that adapted. Thus, adaptive test applications require a large item pool of computed parameters. (Kingsbury & Zara, 1991; Van Der Linden & Glas, 2000). Despite adaptive item administration is a significant feature of a learning system, models utilizing a unidimensional representation of ability, such as the standard IRT model, are not capable of exploring what aspects of the material the individual has mastered or not mastered (Deonovic et al, 2018).

On the other hand, variable-length mastery tests maximize the possibility of making correct classification decisions as well as shorten the test length (Lewis, Sheehan; 1990). Adaptive Mastery Testing (AMT) is a method in which item selection methods from variable-length mastery tests and test termination rules are applied adaptively (Kingsbury & Weiss, 1983). Mastery testing is performed to decide whether an individual is master or non-master according to the test result observed in a learning objective/subject (Vos & Glas, 2000). There are two basic approaches called sequential and adaptive mastery tests in mastery testing where the number of items is uncertain (Vos & Glas, 2000). Within the scope of the research, an AMT environment was designed and developed to decide the master or non-master levels of the students on a learning objective. The Sequential Probability Ratio Test (SPRT) algorithm has been administered to determine the master/ non-master levels of the students. Item-examine incompability is employed as the item-selection algorithm. These processes take place until it is decided the examinee is a master/nonmaster. This rule, introduced by Wald (1947), is widely used for IRT-based adaptive computer testing. When this test is utilized, it is possible to reach more consistent and optimal results with fewer questions (Spray & Reckase, 1996). Since one of the limitations of the study is the number of questions, the SPRT algorithm, which is thought to provide an optimal solution, was utilized to determine the master /non-master levels of the students.

2. METHOD

Adaptive Mastery Testing e-assessment environment which determine whether the students are master or non-master was developed. This environment was developed based on the rapid prototyping software development process (Figure 1).

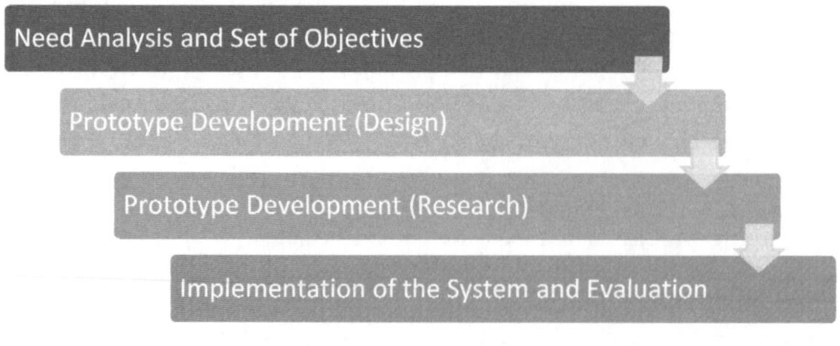

Figure 1. The steps of rapid prototyping software development process (Tripp & Bichelmeyer, 1990)

As seen in Figure 1, this process starts with the needs analysis and ends with the implementation and evaluation phase of the system. In this section, information about the participants, AMT e-assessment environment, data collection tools and data analysis were presented.

2.1 Participants

Participants of the study consist of 98 undergraduate and graduate students at different state universities. 65% (64) of these students are female and 35% (34) are male students.6

2.2 Adaptive Mastery Testing Environment

In this research, AMT in an AMS which determine whether students master or non-master about a learning objective was developed and presented to the students. In this environment, students take the tests on basic concepts, data summarization, central tendency measures and distribution measures in the basic statistics course. This AMS system is structured on the basis of LMS architecture and system architecture and processes is presented in Figure 2.

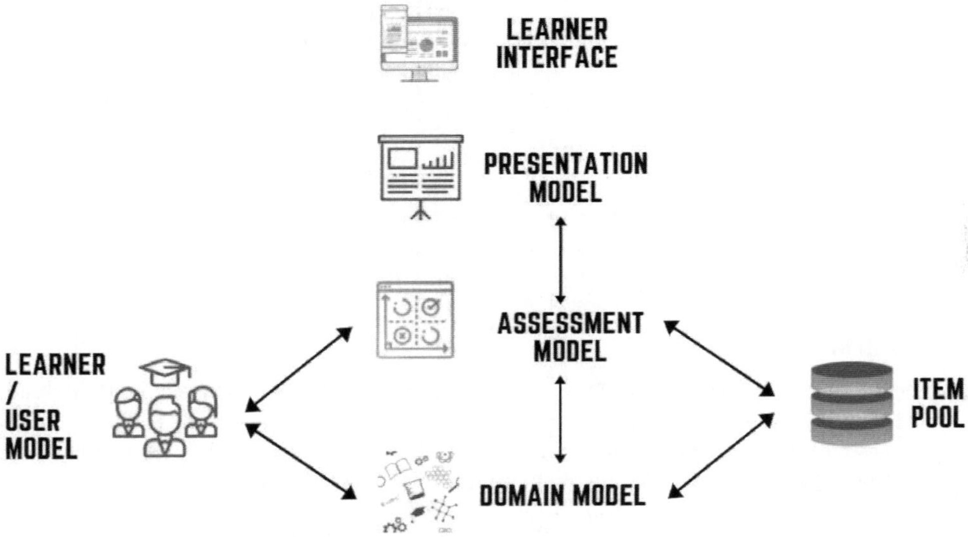

Figure 2. System architecture

In seen Figure 2, AMT consists of learner model, assessment model, domain model, item pool, presentation model, and learner interface. seen in Figure 2, AMT consists of learner model, assessment model, domain model, item pool, presentation model, and learner interface.

2.2.1 Presentation Model and Learner Interface

Students can access the system through learner interface. Students can login to the system by entering their username and password. These usernames and passwords created by the researchers and were delivered to the students. After login to the system, students can see the learning objectives whether they are master or non-master. Then they can take to test and test themselves. The screenshot of the AMT environment is presented in Figure 3.

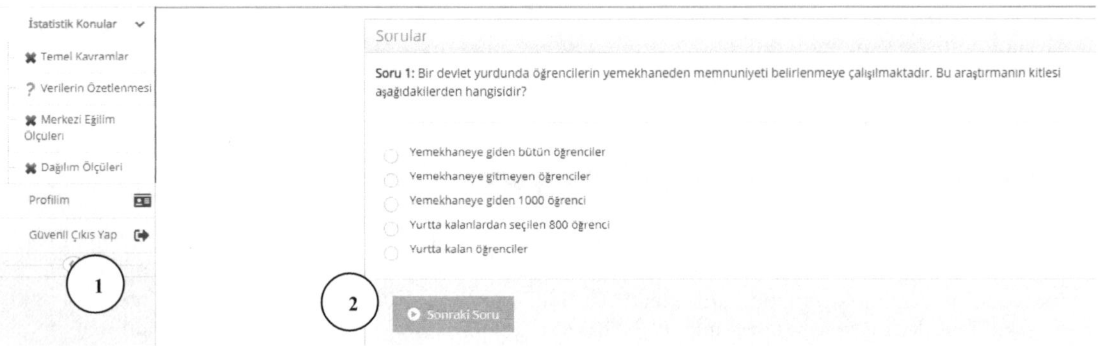

Figure 3. Screenshot of the adaptive mastery testing environment

Area 1 shows the learning objectives of the students. Here (x) sign indicates that the student has taken the test for that learning objective but is not a master, (?) Has not yet taken any test for the learning objective, and (√) indicates the learning objective that the students is master. The number 2 area shows where questions are presented to the students.

2.2.2 Learner/User Model

A learner / user model was created in order to access students to interact with the system and to store and update learner information. In this model, data is stored about the users such as a) usernames, b) user passwords, c) user codes, and d) information about the individual characteristics of the users. This model is associated with the presentation model, evaluation model and domain model.

2.2.3 Assessment Model

This model consists of the rules when configuring AMT. Within the scope of this system, SPRT algorithm has been utilized. There are more advanced versions of SPRT algorithms such as EXSPRT, EXSPRT-I, but these algorithms require item parameters. Therefore, the SPRT algorithm has been utilized within the scope of the research in order to get faster and more effective results. SPRT can produce more efficient results than CAT with fewer items (Rudner, 2001). SPRT uses the information which points located above or below the threshold score determine the classification status (Parshall et al., 2002) then, decide students is master or non-master on this subject. The test terminates when the individual is classified in one of the predetermined categories (Thompson, 2007). SPRT was used as a termination rule. There are two hypotheses for the SPRT such as H_0 (null hypothesis) and H_1 (alternative hypothesis) and presented below:

$$H_0: \theta_i \leq \theta_0 - \delta = \theta_1$$

$$H_1: \theta_i \geq \theta_0 + \delta = \theta_2$$

θ_i: ability level; θ_0: cut point; δ: indifference region

According to these hypotheses, the decision is made by the system, and the test is terminated. Learners were classified as master or non-master about the subject in the context of this research.

2.2.4 Domain Model

This model focused on the learning objective which are the smallest part of the learning process, and the competence of the learners (master or non-master) is revealed for these learning objectives. Domain model consists of a) course, b) unit, c) topic, d) learning objective (subject).

2.2.5 Item Pool

The item pool has been structured in suitability with the system. While structuring the item pool, each question was structured in accordance with the relevant learning objective and appropriate meta-data structures were used in this context.

2.3 Data Collection Tools and Data Analysis

Within the scope of this research, the system was presented to use 98 students and the log data of these students' system usage was collected as the log data. The data consists of a) the number of take test by students, b) the number of correct answer, c) the number of incorrect answer, and d) the total number of attempt to response. In addition, new metrics were calculated from these metrics. Detailed information about this metrics is presented in the findings section. Descriptive information about the log data obtained from the system was included in the analysis of the data.

3. FINDINGS

Information about the log data of the students that used the system Table 1. This information consists of number of different learning objective, number of master learning objective, number of test by taking students, number of correct answer, number of incorrect answer, and number of total response.

Table 1. Information about the log data obtained from the system usage

	N	Min	Max	X_{ave}	SD
Number of different learning objective	98	1	4	3.33	1.05
Number of master learning objective	98	0	4	2.63	1.40
Number of taking test	98	1	12	4.86	2.72
Number of correct answer	98	0	86	32.56	18.20
Number of incorrect answer	98	0	70	20.89	17.84
Number of total response	98	4	153	53.45	33.73

While in total four learning objectives were presented to the students, it can be stated that students had taken the learning objective on average approximately 3 (3.33). It's drawn the attention that the number of master learning objective is 2.63. It's seen that the number of test which taken by students is 4.86. The reason why the number of tests taken is higher than the number of learning objective is that non-master learners can take the tests over and over again. It is seen that the students responded 53.45 items on average and approximately 32.56 of these responses were answered correctly. In addition, students' total correct answer rate was 63%, and the rate of incorrect answers was 37%. On the other hand, new metrics are also calculated in order to obtain more detailed information according to these system metrics. For this purpose, learning objective ratio (Figure 4) and attempt ratio (Figure 5) were calculated.

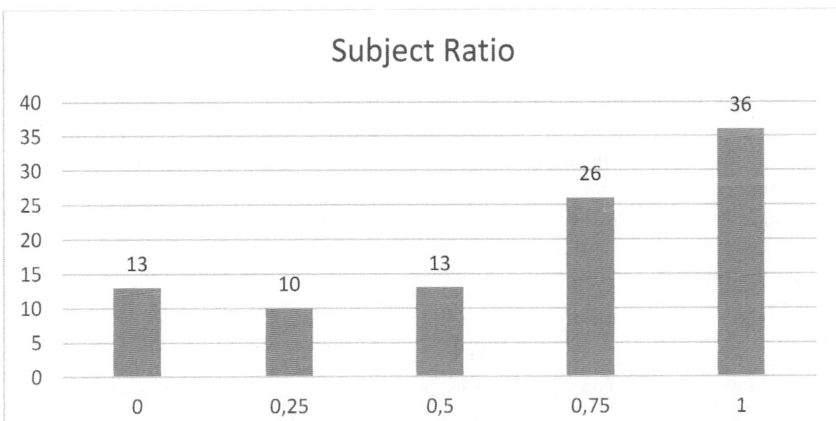

Figure 4. Learning objective/subject ratio

The learning objective/subject ratio was obtained by dividing the number of master learning objective by the total number of learning objective. If this ratio is high, it means that the student is so successful on the basis of learning objective. According to the results, it is understood that a) 37% (36) of the students in the system are masters in all learning objectives, b) 27% (26) in three learning objectives, c) 13% (13) in two learning objectives, d) 10% (10) in one learning objective. It can be stated that 13% (13) of the students are non-masters in any of the learning objectives.

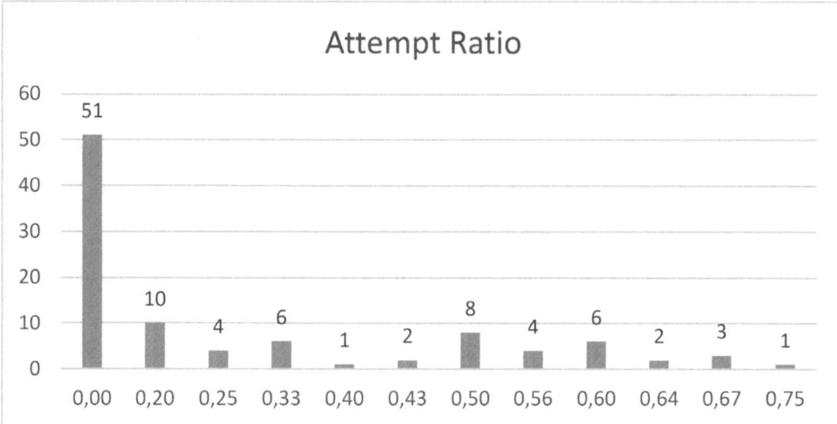

Figure 5. Attempt ratio

In order to calculate the attempt ratio in the first step, the number of learning objectives is divided by the number of tests. Then this value obtained was subtracted from 1. If the value is increasing it means that students take tests many times in the same learning objective. It shows that 52% (51) of the students were determined as a master by the system for the first time.

4. CONCLUSION

In the system developed within the scope of the research, the learning management system architecture was grounded due to the integration of these kinds of systems with learning management systems in the future. The competencies of students can be monitored and students' learning awareness can be increased through AMT during the learning processes provided that LMSs and AMSs using the same learner model are integrated. The literature reveals that the mainly used metrics in the learning analytics are learning performances, that is to say, test results (Aguilar et al., 2021; Kia et al., 2020; Tan et al., 2016). It is projected that this kind of integration will enrich learning analytics.

The AMT environment was developed in order to determine the students' master/non-master status according to a learning objective within the scope of this research. Components in this environment and results obtained from the pilot application were included. Sequential Probability Ratio Test (SPRT) algorithm was used in order to classify the students as master or non-master and item-examine incompatibility was set to work as the item-selection algorithm. The students were submitted with tests concerning four achievements towards the statistics course. According to the obtained results, it can be expressed that most of the students interacted with most of the achievements submitted to themselves. In addition, the fact that more than half of the students were determined as the master in the first test they received for each achievement is another finding we obtained.

The AMT developed as part of the research is limited to the SPRT algorithm. Alternatively, it is possible to use more advanced algorithms such as EXSPRT or EXSPRT-I using the item parameters. Another limitation of the study is the usage of log data only in order to evaluate the system. In the next stage, it is projected to perform an analysis in terms of system usability and student satisfaction.

ACKNOWLEDGEMENT

This study is financially supported by the Scientific and Technological Research Council of Turkey (TUBITAK grant ID: 119K430).

REFERENCES

Aguilar, S. J., Karabenick, S. A., Teasley, S. D., & Baek, C. (2021). Associations between learning analytics dashboard exposure and motivation and self-regulated learning. *Computers & Education*, 162, 104085.

Bayrak, F. (2014). The effectiveness of perceived self-intervention in web based self-assessment system. Hacettepe University (Unpublished doctoral dissertation), Ankara, Turkey.

Deonovic, B., Yuseldon, M., Bolsinova, M., Attali, M., and Maris, G. (2018). Learning meets assessment. Behaviormetrika, 45, 457-474. doi: 10.1007/s41237-018-0070-z

Eggen, T. J. H. M. (2004). Contributions to the theory and practice of computerized adaptive testing (Doctoral dissertation). University of Twente, Enschede.

Gibbons, M. (2003*). The self-directed learning handbook: Challenging adolescent students to excel.* John Wiley & Sons.

Grow, G. O. (1991). Teaching learners to be self-directed. *Adult Education Quarterly, 41*(3), 125-149.

Kia, F. S., Teasley, S. D., Hatala, M., Karabenick, S. A., & Kay, M. (2020, March). How patterns of students dashboard use are related to their achievement and self-regulatory engagement. *In Proceedings of the Tenth International Conference on Learning Analytics & Knowledge* (pp. 340-349).

Kingsbury, G. G., Zara, A. R. (1991). A comparison of procedures for content-sensitive item selection in computerized adaptive tests. Applied Measurement in Education, 4, 241-261

Kingsbury, G.G. & Weiss, D.J. (1983). A comparison of IRT-based adaptive mastery testing and sequential mastery testing procedure. In D.J. Weiss (Ed.), New horizons in testing: Latent trait test theory and computerized adaptive testing (pp. 257–283), New York: Academic Press

Lewis, C., & Sheehan, K. (1990). Using Bayesian decision theory to design a computerized mastery test. *Applied Psychological Measurement*, 14, 367-386.

Mok, M. M. C. (2010). *Self-directed learning oriented assessment: Assessment that informs learning & empowers the learner*. Hong Kong: Pace Publications.

Oosterhof, A., Conrad, R. M., & Ely, D. P. (2008). Assessing learners online. New Jersey: Pearson.

Parshall, C. G., Spray, J. A., Kalohn, J., & Davey, T. (2002). Practical considerations in computer-based testing. Springer Science & Business Media.

Rudner, L. M. (2001). Measurement Decision Theory.

Sadler, D. R. (1998). Formative assessment: Revisiting the territory. *Assessment in Education: Principles, Policy & Practice*, *5*(1), 77-84.

Spray, Judith A. & Reckase, Mark D. (1996). Comparison of SPRT and Sequential Bayes Procedures for Classifying Examinees into Two Categories Using a Computerized Test. *Journal of Educational and Behavioral Statistics*, 21(4), 405-14.

Tan, J. P. L., Yang, S., Koh, E., & Jonathan, C. (2016, April). Fostering 21st century literacies through a collaborative critical reading and learning analytics environment: user-perceived benefits and problematics. *In Proceedings of the sixth international conference on learning analytics & knowledge* (pp. 430-434).

Thompson, N. A. (2007). A practitioner's guide for variable-length computerized classification testing. *Practical Assessment, Research, and Evaluation, 12*(1), 1.

Tripp, S. D. & Bichelmeyer, B. (1990). Rapid prototyping: An alternative instructional design strategy. *Educational Technology Research and Development, 38*(1), 31-44.

Van der Linden, W. & Glas, C. (2000). Computerized adaptive testing: Theory and Practice. Dordrecht, The Netherlands: Kluwer Academic Publishers

Wainer, H. (Ed.). (1990) Computerized adaptive testing: A primer. Hillsdale. NJ: Lawrence Erlbaum Associates.

Wald, A. (1947). Sequential analysis. New York: Wiley

Weiss, D. J. (Ed.). (1983) *New horizons in testing.* New York: Academic Press

Yurdugül, H., & Bayrak, F. (2014). The acceptance of web based formative assessment system for primary school students. *Journal of Educational Sciences & Practices*, *13*(26).

ACTION RESEARCH TO STUDY PROBLEM SOLVING SKILLS OF PRIMARY SCHOOL PHYSICS STUDENTS

Jörgen Ivar Sikk and Kairit Tammets[1]
Tallinn University, Narva mnt 25, 10120 Tallinn, Estonia
[1]Senior Researcher

ABSTRACT

PISA studies have concluded that while the level of knowledge, amongst students in Estonia, is good the level of higher order thinking skills is lower, especially in natural sciences, which is accompanied by lower study motivation. In order to study the level of higher order thinking skills and what influences those skills, an action research was conducted. The research was done in Tallinn 21. school with 90 students from 8th grade. The students studied, using ICT enhanced study material specifically made to increase their higher order thinking skills. In order to study the effects of the study material, student's problem solving skills were measured before and after using the new study material. Also, the students had to answer a questionnaire, which was measuring their study motivation and self-confidence. The research concluded that the study material has an effect on the level of higher order thinking skills, but the statistical evidence was lacking to clearly understand the role of the new study material.

KEYWORDS

Action Research, Problem Solving Skills, ICT Learning Materials

1. INTRODUCTION

Estonia's success in the PISA tests is the fruit of the cooperation, to which parents, school leaders and teachers have contributed. Despite the good results, student struggle with higher order thinking skills (Schleicher, 2018), a result which was already hinted at in the 2006 PISA tests. Developing of higher order thinking skills are supported by activating and research-based learning methodologies (Rohatgi, et al., 2016). Although teachers are aware of these methodologies in Estonia (Kikas, E., 2015; Henno, et al. 2017), they are rarely applied in class (Schleicher, 2018; Le Donne, et al., 2018), especially in natural sciences (Henno, et al., 2017).

However, higher cognitive thinking skills need to be addressed in order for students to cope in the information age. In addition to reading, arithmetic, and writing, students must be able to think critically, solve problems, communicate, and collaborate, and they must acquire skills that will ensure their ability to learn and retrain in the future (Johnson, P., 2011). To this end, it is important to use information and communication tools (ICT), as the ability to use these tools will continue to be important, and they have certain advantages over traditional learning materials (Genlott & Grönlund 2016; Jolliffe, et al., 2001). Learning materials created with ICT tools and the methods applied through them have shown advantages over other tools in the development of higher order thinking skills and more precisely in problem-solving skills (Heikkilä & Lonka, 2006). Although ICT-based tools have an advantage, there are also problems (Genlott and Grönlund, 2016; Lndblom-Ylänne & Lonka, 1999) and because the development of higher order thinking skills also depends on the subject context (Shabrina & Kuswanto, 2018), one should take a lot of care when creating teaching materials addressing those skills.

Due to the relative lack of focus on higher order thinking skills in natural sciences, this action research focused on improving them, through teacher curated study materials. The following research questions were posed: 1) Which kind of higher order thinking skills are necessary in the context of natural sciences? 2) How to evaluate student's higher order thinking skills? 3) What is the effect of created study-material on student's higher order thinking skills?

2. LITERATURE REVIEW

2.1 Higher Order Thinking Skills

Higher Order Thinking Skills (HOTS) go beyond basic observation of facts and memorization and can be considered to be the more demanding cognitive skills of Bloom's Taxonomy, such as Analysis, Synthesis and Evaluation (Krathwohl & Anderson, 2001). Concepts of critical thinking, problem solving skills and creative thinking are also included as HOTS and, in general, the concept has a wide variety of sub-contexts and overlaps (Brookhart, 2010). Despite the plurality, all the HOTS depend on the context they are applied to, which means that developing HOTS requires also the understanding of contextual space (Zohar, 1996). In the current study the focus was set on metacognitive, problem solving and critical thinking improvement., because they are rarely applied in natural sciences (Henno, et al., 2017), but found important in strategic planning of education (Republic of Estonia, 2020). Metacognitive thinking requires the student to be involved in analyzing and regulating their learning process (Bransford et al., 1999) and thus is also an important part of HOTS. Metacognition develops the students capability of choosing the right means and strategies to overcome problems. As such, it is an important skill to have in modern times, due to everchanging skillset requirements and adaptation issues (Brinkley, 2019). Moreover students with higher metacognitive skills tend to be better at guiding their studies (Rohatgi, et al., 2006), finding better strategies in order to solve problems (Herawaty, et al., 2018) and over all be more involved in the studying process (Rohatgi, et al., 2016; Desoete, et al., 2019). Although further research is needed to understand the carry-over effect of metacognitive skills in various disciplines (Tanner, 2017).

Tied together with metacognitive skills are problem solving and critical thinking skills, which have gotten a lot of attention from researchers. Problem solving skills have strong ties with Bloom's "Analysis" and "Evaluation" categories (Krathwohl & Anderson, 2001), while critical thinking is more-so a process of evaluating strategies in order to find the best solution to a problem (Bransford, et al., 1999).

2.2 Fostering the Development of HOTS and Problem Solving Skills

In order to hone and develop those skills cognitively activating strategies and supporting of metacognitive processes should be applied (Snyder & Snyder, 2008). Such strategies do exist already and mainly fall under constructivist or cognitive teaching methods, where the teacher is more supporting the process of learning, and to a lesser extent leading it (Le Donne, et al., 2016). Methodologies like flipped classroom can give students practical problem solving and critical thinking skills, even if the teacher themselves is not so familiar with it (Smith, et al., 2018), or guided group work (Fung, 2017). Such inclusive methodologies also affect problem solving capabilities of students (Lin, et al., 2014), additionally it can bring better results in terms of activating the students (Lonka & Ahola, 1995), while depending on the teachers readiness for that way of teaching (Henno, et al., 2017).

The inclusion of ICT capabilities, especially one's that students are familiar with (like smart phones), tend to have a positive effect on the students critical thinking (Ismail, et al., 2018). That familiarity can also allow students easier means of self-reflection, which, as a metacognitive skill, can aid in building problem solving skills (Kim & Kim, 2019). An important aspect of online environments is their plurality, in which games (Lin, et al., 2014), interactive simulations (Ceberio, et al., 2016) and other visual media are all capable of enhancing the learners absorption of information and skills. While this study focuses on problem solving, it is important to note the „across the board" positive effect of ICT on the development of higher order thinking skills and its sub theories. One interested in developing learning materials for it, should not leave these tools unnoticed.

As mentioned, the improvement of problem solving skills demands a closer look at the learning materials, since the learning materials create the context, and context influences HOTS (Zohar, 1996) and thus problem solving skills. While previously discussed ICT environments can help in improving the students problem solving skills the learning materials should create a helping narrative for it. More precisely the narratives should be engaging by being actual and pose interesting questions (Dori, et al., 2003). For lack of a better word they should introduce a problem, which is easily relatable. Although a more simple worksheet can also be feasible (Verdina & Sulastri, 2018), or the narrative doesn't have to be text based at all (Lin, et al., 2014). What ever the form of narrative, it will drive the meaningful acquirement of information and help the student in their self-guided learning (Sanchez-Marti, et al., 2018). The use of ICT should have some advantages over classical study materials (Jolliffe, et al., 2001; Genlott & Grönlund, 2016), both in audio-visual information and also from the point of student engagement (Hakkarainen, 2000; Genlott and Grönlund, 2016).

In conclusion, the learning material's context and narrative should be intertwined to create an engaging and reflective learning process for the student, while also employing visual and active media, through ICT to help achieve needed learning goals.

3. METHODOLOGY

3.1 Research Design

In order to research the effects of ICT enhanced study materials on student's problem solving skills an action research in an Estonian elementary school was conducted during a period of one month in spring of 2020. The experiment was done in physics class, since in that curricula constructivist practices are seldom used and tend to not include the development of higher order thinking skills, at least in Estonia (Henno, et al., 2015). The study included 90 students from 8th grade (age 14-15). The students were divided randomly to groups of three and each group was assigned, at random, a study material. There were three types of study materials:

1) ICT enhanced problem solving skill focused study material
2) ICT enhanced classical study material
3) Classical study material

The purpose of the new study material (Group 1) was to develop the student's problem solving skills, while also following the criteria of national curriculum. The study material follows the recommendations of Broadbear (2003) and McMahon's (2009) to increase the cohesion between subject context and developing problem solving skills. Amongst exercises are also metacognitive reflective parts, which followed the structure and recommendation of Tanner (2017), Herawaty (2018) and Desoete, et al., (2019). The exercises sometimes lacked a clear definitive answer, and as such demanded more analytical and comparative approach. Such strategy is important when developing critical thinking and problem solving skills, since one should be able to choose between and evaluate different viable strategies (Bransford, et al., 1991). Additionally, students had to find the right information in situations where there was too much extra information, or the important information was given in a non-standard way, in an attempt to foster engagement (Dori, et al., 2003). Included were guiding comments by the teacher, never revealing the answer, but encouraging to look for help or guide the thought process. Moreover, a curated choice of simulations and other visual-media was added to the study material to help with visualizing the physics problem and finding the correct solution, since there is additional benefit of using ICT to engage students (Masiello, et al., 2005; Ismail, et al., 2018; Lin, et al., 2014; Ceberio, et al., 2016).

The ICT enhanced classical study material (Group 2) is an online environment developed by a publisher in Estonia, who is also responsible for writing the work- and study books for general schools. The environment (opiq.ee) has the same structure and exercises as their books, with the added benefit of integrated videos and interactive exercises. The classical study materials (Group 3) are the official work- and study books that are used in physics classes all over Estonia. In physics their structure is the same for every topic. The student is given the theory and definitions, then a few examples and in the end some exercises. Exercises are mostly focused on physics formulas, with few experiments and team-orientated problems.

Comparing results from the first two groups should give an idea on the effect of ICT on problem solving skills. The third group is a control group, in which the students use their already familiar study books and exercises there-in.

Action research in education can also be called teacher research (Manfra, 2019), due to its ulterior motive being to improve the teachers teaching capabilities. In this research the teachers role consisted of a) following the process of student groups, b) evaluating the group work and c) giving live feedback to student's if they were struggling with semantical or group related issues. Due to COVID-19 restrictions, the student's conducted the work online and the live feedback part of the role was somewhat weaker than initially planned, but later, when classes resumed an open forum way of discussing the study material and its impact was done. Due to it the wording of evaluative tests was changed. Additionally, further changes were made to the study material based on student feedback, but since the current research paper focuses on the results of the first round of testing, then the changes aren't included in this paper.

3.2 Procedure and Data Collection

Before using the study materials on a new topic, the student groups had to do a pre-test to determine their level of problem solving skills. The pre-test was made in the context of the curriculum that they had already gone through, so the physics theory and formulas were already familiar. But, unlike their usual physics tests this one focused on problem solving skills and metacognitive aspects. The pre-test was made following examples from 2006 PISA test and research papers that have evaluated problem solving skills before (Whiley, et al., 2017; Snyder & Snyder, 2008). The test consisted of four exercises each one being gradually more complex.

After the pre-test, students in their groups of three were tasked to study for a new topic, using the materials and procedures given by the teacher (the materials mentioned before in this paper). Due to COVID-19 regulations the classes were online and the students had to organize their group work by themselves. The teachers role was to make sure the group work was happening and every person was involved. The groups had one week to use the study materials.

The post-test was to measure the student's problem solving skills and was identical in structure to the pre-test. The difference being that the context was reflecting the new physics topic. The post-test was to give an idea on the change (or lack of) of students' problem solving skills after using the study materials.

The qualitative data gathered from the pre-, and post-tests were analyzed using standardized evaluation of Estonian physics exercises and following the example of Karatas & Baki (2013), in which problem solving skills are evaluated in phases. Only student groups who completed both problem-solving tests and finished the study materials were included in the analysis (27 student groups out of 30). Since there were three different distinct groups then in the analysis we use the following abbreviations:

A) VIII.1 - Student groups who used ICT enhanced HOTS focused study material;
B) VIII.2 - Student groups who used ICT enhanced classical study materials;
C) VIII.3 - Student groups who used classical study materials.

4. RESULTS

4.1 Problem Solving Pre-Test

The problem solving pre-test was evaluating student's current level of higher order thinking skills in the context of physics class that they were already familiar with. On average the different student groups performed quite similarly on the pre-test (VIII.1 – 45%; VIII.2 – 51%; VIII.3 – 43%). After doing an ANOVA test on the pre-test results, we found that the results were statistically insignificant (Sig. 0.81; F – 0.212, df = 2), meaning the difference in scores wasn't due to the assigned group.

Table 1. Problem solving skills pre-test results of different study material groups in the context of exercises

	Problem solving skills test 1		
	VIII.1 (%)	VIII.2 (%)	VIII.3 (%)
Exercise 1	75	75	45
Exercise 2	55	85	45
Exercise 3	46	60	57
Exercise 4	35	28	30

The text questions were numbered based on their relative difficulty level, Exercise 1 being easier than Exercise 2 and so on. The results were more similar between VIII.1 and VIII.2, with VIII.3 showing, relative to others, lower average.

4.2 Problem Solving Post-Test

The problem solving post-test results differed significantly from the pre-test ones. VIII.1 group average score was 77%: VIII.2 group average score 60% and VIII.3 group's average was 18%. ANOVA test showed that the assigned group did have an effect on the test scores (Sig. = 0.0001, $\alpha = 0.016$) and that approximately 46% of the dispersion in results was due to it ($\eta_p^2 = 0.461$).

When looking at the data from the point of view of individual exercises then we see the relative progress of groups VIII.1 and VIII.2 to group VIII.3. The biggest difference between the groups being the most complex exercise 4.

The post-test score was statistically significant (df = 2, F – 23.157, Sig. 0.00001), but when making a two tailed T-test we see that the difference between VIII.1 and VIII.2 isn't.

Table 2. T-test of groups' post-test results. df = 2, F - 23.157

Groups	P(T<=t) two-tail	α	Significant
VIII.1 and VIII.2	0.0616	0.0160	No
VIII.1 and VIII.3	4.57E-05	0.0160	Yes
VIII.2 and VIII.3	0.0011	0.0160	Yes

Table 3. Problem solving skills post-test results of different study material groups in the context of exercises

	Problem solving skills test 2		
	VIII.1 (%)	VIII.2 (%)	VIII.3 (%)
Exercise 1	100	90	20
Exercise 2	70	50	15
Exercise 3	55	62	10
Exercise 4	70	49	20

5. DISCUSSION

While the pre-test showed quite similar results across the board, the post-test showed a significant shift. The group VIII.1, who received the new ICT enhanced study material improved their results significantly, while the results of VIII.2 showed minor improvement and the group VIII.3 results showed a steep decline. The main difference between the groups was the addition of ICT for groups VIII.1 and VIII.2 and another was the difference of study material (VIII.1 vs the rest). Considering that the t-test didn't show any statistical difference between VIII.1 and VIII.2 then one explanation could be that the inclusion of ICT capabilities and their quality plays a role in developing higher order thinking skills. More so, due to there being no statistically important difference between VIII.1 and VIII.2, even though the former deployed a HOTS focused study material. Perhaps a bigger sample size should be used.

An important element of this group work was communication between group members. The novel study material of group VIII.1 was developed keeping that nuance in mind. That meant that the information and exercises required discussion amongst each member. The classical study material of VIII.3 is developed as a thorough theoretical work, meaning that it doesn't require the reader to make the connections themselves. As a study material it fosters passive learning and requires the student to think for themselves only at the end of the chapter in form of questions, and even then mostly checking the students lower order thinking skills. Such an approach is effective when we, as educators, are interested in relaying enough information with the least amount of time (and time is an important constraint in education). However, such material is lacking when we want the student to develop their higher order thinking skills.

There can be couple of reasons for the decline of VIII.3 group: a) usually their study material is used together with teacher instruction and b) they learned new information using study materials that don't incorporate higher order thinking skills as much. This would mean that, even though their problem solving test results declined it didn't happen because their problem solving skills declined, but that their weak contextual knowledge didn't allow their higher order thinking skills to be applied. Further evidence of that is shown with the results of Exercise 3, where the students had to find the right answer from with-in the text (thus using their functional reading skills and making generalisations), which in turn requires a good grasp on the theory, and as such is quite unusual for a physics problem (which classically require an application of a formula). Considering that a person's functional reading ability doesn't change rapidly then we can guess that the decline in the results of Exercise 3 means that the students lacked generalisation ability in the context of that physics topic. An important distinction is that groups VIII.1 and VIII.2 used different ICT environments and capabilities, and as such definite conclusions on the effects of ICT on study motivation is hard to draw is in this study. Additionally group VIII.2 used an ICT environment that was already familiar for them, while group VIII.1 used novel environments. Considering that time spent in an online study environment has a positive effect on the study results (McMahon, 2009) then it is even harder to evaluate the true connection between ICT and study motivation in this research.

6. CONCLUSION

Problem solving skills are important tools, which should be taught to students, while also considering the context of curriculum. However, the attention these skills receive, is lacking (Henno, et al., 2015). The current action research aimed to alleviate this issue by creating study materials, which could be used in a standard natural science class, with all its time and curriculum constraints. The study material aimed to be engaging by offering various ICT-enhanced aids and was built on a narrative. The study material was compared with other study materials to evaluate the effect of it on students' problem solving skills. The results showed that while the study material does have an effect on problem solving skills it is difficult distinguish the difference between ICT enhanced study material and ICT enhanced problem solving skills study material. Further research should be conducted, and, for statistical assurance, number of study groups should be increased. Nevertheless, the role of study materials remains an important part of developing student's (higher order thinking) skills, maybe even more so with the advances in ICT technology and its ease-of-use.

REFERENCES

Anderson, L.W. and Krathwohl, D.R., 2001. *A taxonomy for learning, teaching, and assessing: A revision of Bloom's taxonomy of educational objectives*. Longman,.

Binkley, M. et al., 2012. Defining twenty-first century skills. In *Assessment and teaching of 21st century skills* (pp. 17-66). Springer, Dordrecht.

Bransford, J. et al., 1999. *How people learn: Brain, mind, experience, and school*. National Academies Press.

Broadbear, J., 2003. Essential elements of lessons designed to promote critical thinking. *Journal of the Scholarship of Teaching and Learning*, pp.1-8.

Brookhart, S.M., 2010. *How to assess higher-order thinking skills in your classroom*. ASCD.

Ceberio, M. et al., 2016. Design and application of interactive simulations in problem-solving in university-level physics education. *Journal of Science Education and Technology*, *25*(4), pp.590-609.

Desoete, A. et al., 2019. Metacognition and motivation as predictors for mathematics performance of Belgian elementary school children. *ZDM*, *51*(4), pp.667-677.

Dori, Y.J. et al., 2003. Teaching biotechnology through case studies—can we improve higher order thinking skills of nonscience majors?. *Science Education*, *87*(6), pp.767-793.

Fung, D., 2017. The pedagogical impacts on students' development of critical thinking dispositions: Experience from Hong Kong secondary schools. *Thinking Skills and Creativity*, *26*, pp.128-139.

Genlott, A.A. and Grönlund, Å., 2016. Closing the gaps–Improving literacy and mathematics by ict-enhanced collaboration. *Computers & Education*, *99*, pp.68-80.

Hakkarainen, K. et al., 2000. Students' skills and practices of using ICT: Results of a national assessment in Finland. *Computers & Education*, *34*(2), pp.103-117.

Heikkilä, A. and Lonka, K., 2006. Studying in higher education: students' approaches to learning, self-regulation, and cognitive strategies. *Studies in higher education*, *31*(1), pp.99-117.

Henno, I. et al., 2017. Eesti loodusainete õpetajate uskumused, õpetamispraktika ja enesetõhusus TALIS 2008 ja 2013 uuringu alusel. *Eesti Haridusteaduste Ajakiri*, *5*(1), p.268.

Herawaty, D. et al., 2018, September. Students' metacognition on mathematical problem solving through ethnomathematics in Rejang Lebong, Indonesia. In *Journal of Physics: Conference Series* (Vol. 1088, No. 1, p. 012089). IOP Publishing.

Ismail, N.S. et al., 2018. The effect of Mobile problem-based learning application DicScience PBL on students' critical thinking. *Thinking Skills and Creativity*, *28*, pp.177-195.

Johnson, P., 2009. The 21st century skills movement. *Educational Leadership*, *67*(1), p.11.

Jolliffe, A. et al., 2012. *The online learning handbook: Developing and using web-based learning*. Routledge.

Karatas, I. and Baki, A., 2013. The effect of learning environments based on problem solving on students' achievements of problem solving. *International Electronic Journal of Elementary Education*, *5*(3), pp.249-268.

Kikas, T.E. and Toomela, A., 2015. Õppimine ja õpetamine kolmandas kooliastmes. Üldpädevused ja nende arendamine.

Kim, J.Y. and Lim, K.Y., 2019. Promoting learning in online, ill-structured problem solving: The effects of scaffolding type and metacognition level. *Computers & Education*, *138*, pp.116-129.

Kuswanto, H., 2018. Android-Assisted Mobile Physics Learning Through Indonesian Batik Culture: Improving Students' Creative Thinking and Problem Solving. *International Journal of Instruction*, *11*(4).

Le Donné, N. et al., 2016. Teaching strategies for instructional quality: Insights from the TALIS-PISA link data.

Lin, C.F. et al., 2014. Developing a problem-solving learning system to assess the effects of different materials on learning performance and attitudes. *Computers & Education*, *77*, pp.50-66.

Lindblom-Ylänne, S. and Lonka, K., 1998. Individual ways of interacting with the learning environment—are they related to study success?. *Learning and instruction*, *9*(1), pp.1-18.

Lonka, K. and Ahola, K., 1995. Activating instruction: How to foster study and thinking skills in higher education. *European journal of psychology of education*, *10*(4), pp.351-368.

Manfra, M. M. (2019). Action research and systematic, intentional change in teaching practice. *Review of Research in Education*, *43*(1), 163-196.

Masiello, I. et al., 2005. Attitudes to the application of a Web-based learning system in a microbiology course. *Computers & Education*, *45*(2), pp.171-185.

McMahon, G., 2009. Critical thinking and ICT integration in a Western Australian secondary school. *Journal of Educational Technology & Society*, *12*(4), pp.269-281.

Republic of Estonia 2020, Haridusvaldkonna arengukava 2021-2035, Ministry of Education and Science, viewed 04.05.20, <https://www.hm.ee/et/kaasamine-osalemine/strateegiline-planeerimine-aastateks-2021-2035/eesti-haridusvaldkonna-arengukava>

Rohatgi, A. et al., 2016. The role of ICT self-efficacy for students' ICT use and their achievement in a computer and information literacy test. *Computers & Education*, *102*, pp.103-116.

Sánchez-Martí, A. et al., 2018. Implementation and assessment of an experiment in reflective thinking to enrich higher education students' learning through mediated narratives. *Thinking Skills and Creativity*, *29*, pp.12-22.

Schleicher, A., 2019. PISA 2018: Insights and Interpretations. *OECD Publishing*.

Smith, T.E. et al., 2018. Teaching critical thinking in a GE class: A flipped model. *Thinking Skills and Creativity*, *28*, pp.73-83.

Snyder, L.G. and Snyder, M.J., 2008. Teaching critical thinking and problem solving skills. *The Journal of Research in Business Education*, *50*(2), p.90.

Tanner, K.D., 2012. Promoting student metacognition. *CBE—Life Sciences Education*, *11*(2), pp.113-120.

Verdina, R. and Gani, A., 2018, September. Improving students' higher order thinking skills in thermochemistry concept using worksheets based on 2013 curriculum. In *Journal of Physics: Conference Series* (Vol. 1088, No. 1, p. 012105). IOP Publishing.

Whiley, D. et al., 2017. Enhancing critical thinking skills in first year environmental management students: a tale of curriculum design, application and reflection. *Journal of Geography in Higher Education*, *41*(2), pp.166-181.

Zohar, A., 1996. Transfer and retention of reasoning strategies taught in biological contexts. *Research in Science & Technological Education*, *14*(2), pp.205-219.

COMPUTATIONAL TECHNIQUES FOR DATA SCIENCE APPLIED TO BROADEN THE KNOWLEDGE BETWEEN CITIZEN SCIENCE AND EDUCATION

Miriam Calvera-Isabal, Nuria Varas and Patricia Santos
Research group on interactive and distributed Technologies for education, Pompeu Fabra University
Plaça de la Mercè, 10-12. 08002 Barcelona, Spain

ABSTRACT

This paper describes a preliminary study of how computational methods allow us to know more about citizen science and its connection with education. Citizen science is a practice involving a general public in scientific tasks and generating knowledge and scientific results. Previous studies have shown that the education sector can take benefit of the knowledge and activities organized or resources generated in CS projects. Previous studies have shown that the education sector can take advantage of the knowledge and activities organized in CS projects. In this papers, we analyze three citizen science platforms (Eu.Citizen science platform, Observatorio de la ciencia ciudadana and Oficina de la ciència ciutadana) with computational analytics techniques to provide initial insights of how educators can take benefit of the analysis of large amounts of data from CS. Finally, different visualizations and dashboards have been developed as illustrative examples of tools to support educators and learners. These tools provide information about citizen science projects, an overview of scientific vocabulary, access to validated resources and examples of technology used in scientific inquiry that can be used with educational purposes.

KEYWORDS

Citizen Science, Education, Data Analysis

1. INTRODUCTION

The objective of this paper is to show the potential that analytic computational techniques have to better understand the practice of citizen science (CS) and how the data extracted/analyzed can be used with educational purposes. There is a need to know more about the practice of CS, especially since there are more and more CS projects and interest in this field in Europe (Vohland et. al., 2021). The information of these CS projects is distributed online all over the world in many websites which causes that knowledge is not centralized and it is more difficult to have an overview.

Despite data analysis algorithms have been applied to many scientific fields (McNamara 2011, Koh and Tan 2011), there is a lack of knowledge of how to apply computational analytic techniques to better understand the gap of knowledge about CS projects practices and the connection with Education (Ginger et al. 2020, Lambers et al. 2019). For this research, data of 377 CS projects and resources available in three key CS platforms has been extracted. This preliminary study will also contribute to bringing citizen science closer to the education sector and equipping it with new tools and data to support the educational process. The study shows how this connection can be established and states the bases of many new analyses on citizen science, from another perspective than participating in scientific projects.

2. BACKGROUND

2.1 Citizen Science

The term Citizen Science is not clearly defined because there is no consensus on the various definitions proposed by the community (Auerbach et al. 2019, Haklay et al. 2021). Even so, we select the following definition: “Citizen science broadly refers to the active engagement of the general public in scientific research tasks” (Vohland, V et. at. 2021).

CS can be applied to many different scientific disciplines such as natural sciences, social sciences, or humanities (Tauginienė et al. 2020) although it depends on the scientific objectives of the CS project. There is a long history of citizens contributing to science (i.e., Christmas Bird Count or The American Association of Variable Star Observers (AAVSO)) which causes an impact on policies, human health or in society (Hecker et al. 2018). CS promotes citizen participation and interest in science in addition to other qualities related to learning about science (Shah and Martinez 2016).

2.2 Citizen Science & Education

There is a lot of evidence showing how CS can contribute to Science, Technology, Engineering and Maths (STEM) career motivation (Hiller and Kitsantas 2014). CS promotes values such as ecology, knowledge about the environment (Kobori et al. 2016, Ballard, Dixon and Harris 2017, Kelemen-Finan, Scheuch and Winter 2018) or critical thinking (Masterson et al. 2019).

In general, the scientific objectives of CS projects are not educational, but a common practice is to create educational materials and adapt practices to support learning (National Academies of Sciences, Engineering, and Medicine 2018, Schuttler et al. 2019). Posters, videos or guides are the most common educational resources created by projects to support participants during their participation in scientific research (Brossard, Lewenstein and Bonney 2005) These materials are helpful to support literacy, understand how investigation will be developed, know the timings, promote open discussions and advance in scientific knowledge and improve scientific skills (Bonney et al. 2009). Citizen science involves a participatory process which implies, for instance, events to train volunteers or workshops, carried out during the development of the project (Cohn, 2008).

2.3 Citizen Science Platforms

Since CS is attracting more and more attention every year (Bautista et al. 2019), several associations are being created to help in the development and management of CS. Divided by geographical areas, we could say that there are three key CS associations: the Citizen Science Association (CSA, North America), the European Citizen Science Association (ECSA, Europe) and the Australian Citizen Science Association (ACSA, Australia) (Storksdieck et al. 2016). Covering regional areas, we can find national or regional associations like Observatorio de la ciencia ciudadana in Spain or Flemish Knowledge Center for Citizen Science in Belgium (SCivil). These associations have a website or online digital platform containing information about CS projects, events, related resources and sometimes have a space for communications (i.e., news, forum, etc) (Sanz, Gold and Mazzonetto 2019). In ‘The science of citizen science’ it has been defined five different types of online CS platforms; in this preliminary study are analysed two National CS platforms (Observatorio de la ciencia ciudadana and Oficina de ciència ciutadana) and one European CS platform (EU.Citizen science) (Vohland et. al., 2021). These online portals, act as a repository having metadata information about regional CS projects in a structured or unstructured way, but only few of them use the metadata standards (i.e., PPSR metadata standard (https://core.citizenscience.org/)). The fact that the data is distributed in many platforms, in different languages and data structures, makes the process of analyzing and exploring the data from CS more complicated.

2.4 Data Extraction, Analysis and Visualization

In order to address the problem defined in the previous section, we propose to apply web scraping techniques. These are typically used for extracting data automatically from websites and storing it structured in a database or file. Web scraping software or personalized ones (also called robots or crawlers) is used in many fields like arts and humanities or biology (Diouf et al. 2019). In the context of CS, these techniques have been used to analyze citizen participation in online project forums (Ponti et al. 2018). However, there is no evidence of having used it to obtain metadata about CS projects although it has been proved a powerful tool to extract and classify data (Karthikeyan et al. 2019).

Data mining techniques such as Natural Language Processing (NLP), Sentiment Analysis or Machine Learning is applied in combination with web scraping to better understand data retrieved. These analytical techniques are typically used in CS projects to analyze the data obtained from volunteers' participation (Caruana et al. 2006, Fink and Hochachka 2012). Nevertheless, although many qualitative studies are done to analyze CS projects metadata (Bonney et al. 2009), there is a lack of knowledge related to the application of other automatic methods (i.e., text mining) to analyze CS online data.

In addition to computation analytic methods, data visualization is useful to validate hypotheses, get insight from the data (i.e., identifying patterns) and as a communication tool for end-users. Depending on the type of data (i.e., one-dimensional or two-dimensional), visualization technique (i.e., Standard 2D/3D displays) and the interaction (i.e., filtering or zooming), many techniques can be applied to the linked data such as the one extracted for the study presented in this paper (Keim 2002). Due to the number of different visualizations that can be created using this data, dashboards are a good solution that facilitate the monitoring of the data by integrating them into a single tool. For example, it has been shown the positive impact of dashboards to help educators to improve as professional facilitators, analysts, and designers. Moreover, these tools also support the learning process of students (Michaeli, Kroparo and Hershkovitz 2020).

3. METHODOLOGY

Three CS platforms have been selected: The Eu.Citizen science platform, The Observatorio de la ciencia ciudadana and Oficina de la ciència ciutadana. The purpose of this analysis is to know the connections between citizen science and education and identify information that can support the education process. Data from these three platforms has been analyzed to better understand what information is shared, vocabulary used and resources available that could be used in an educational context. To automate the manual work of extracting data from websites, web scraping tools are used to extract this data from multiple sites and store it, structured, in a database or file (Zhao 2017).

In order to provide rules to this web scraping process, a Robots Exclusion Protocol (REP) was defined. This protocol defines a regulatory framework that allows site administrators to decide which crawlers are or are not allowed to access a specific part of the website (Sun, Zhuang and Giles 2007). These specifications have to be informed for each website in the robots.txt file with a certain structure for crawlers to read it before scraping the site and check if data can be extracted or not.

For this preliminary study, a crawler has been developed with python (https://www.python.org/). Selenium (https://selenium-python.readthedocs.io/) has been chosen as the main web scraping software. The Observatorio de la ciencia ciudadana and The Oficina de ciència ciutadana websites have been scraped with that crawler to obtain the data. The EU.citizen science website has its own Application Programming Interface (API) (https://eu-citizen.science/swagger/) so, a code has been developed with python to get the data through it. Once the data has been collected, it has been stored in different files (by platform) in a structured way by classifying it by type of data (Saurkar, Pathare and Gode 2018). To analyze the data again an algorithm developed with python and other data science libraries and tools (i.e., pandas, re or nltk) and Jupyter notebook (https://jupyter.org/) were used.

To pre-process the data before performing the analysis, different methods of text mining have been applied (i.e data cleaning, tokenization or lemmatization) (Vijayarani and Janani 2016). When the data has been prepared to be analyzed, a Term Frequency - Inverse Document Frequency technique (TF-IDF) has been applied to count the number of occurrences for a given word in a document (TF) it measures if a term is common or not in a collection of documents (IDF) (Dillon 1983). With this method, the most relevant words for a document can be computed. After that, Name entity recognition (NER) has been applied to identify people's names or institutions from text.

Finally, to continue with the data analysis data has been categorized. The way to classify projects or resources using text fields is generating a list of words that refer to a topic, for example, and looking if that project description contains any of those words. In order to extract correlations among variables such as projects topics and status, those variables need to be converted into numerical values. Therefore, label encoders must be used to determine which number corresponds to a specific type.

The same process has been applied to online resources metadata. In case of texts that contain a description of the resource, as the previous section explains, text mining has been used to obtain the abstract word cloud, length distribution and the most relevant terms for each resource (with TF- IDF). For resources has been developed an analysis of metadata information of the timeline of when the resource was published.

Dashboards with Tableau (https://www.tableau.com/es-es) have been generated to show conclusions about the data analyzed of the project's information and resources. This is a very useful data visualization tool to make data more understandable by creating interactive dashboards and visualizations.

4. STUDY OF THREE CITIZEN SCIENCE PLATFORMS: RESULTS AND ANALYSIS

Figure 1 shows a comparative analysis of the data from the three different platforms (Eu.Citizen science, Observatorio de la ciencia ciudadana and Oficina de Ciència ciutadana).

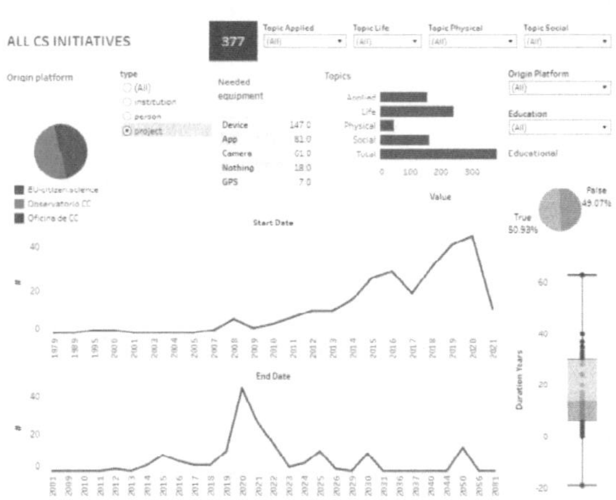

Figure 1. Information of CS projects of all platforms

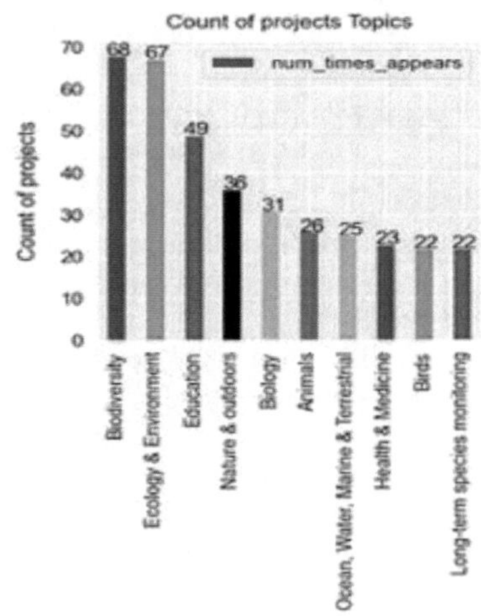

Figure 2. List of Topics obtained from CS projects information of the EU.Citizen science platform

As a result, data from 377 CS projects have been extracted from the 3 different CS platforms analyzed. The Spanish platform is the one with more content (188 CS projects), followed by the European one (176 CS projects) and the one from Barcelona (13 CS projects). Some data (16 CS projects) are duplicated within Spanish and European platforms.

First of all, data has been analyzed and related to education. CS projects that contain educational keywords (i.e., schools, education or classrooms) have been classified in the category "Education". 241 over 468 projects (51,5%) meet the criteria. As a result, a filter has been designed for educators or learning designers to rapidly visualize specific data of CS projects related to educational initiatives.

In order to obtain a deeper understanding of the CS projects, the topics information have been distinguished in four different groups (depending on their science types) that correspond to the primary disciplines of citizen science projects: Applied sciences, social sciences, life sciences or physical sciences. To sum up, Life science is the discipline more common in the data being Biodiversity and Ecology & Environment the topics from this category most frequent in the Eu.Citizen science platform is (Figure 2).

As a result, data from 377 CS projects have been extracted from the 3 different CS platforms analyzed. The Spanish platform is the one with more content (188 CS projects), followed by the European one (176 CS projects) and the one from Barcelona (13 CS projects). Some data (16 CS projects) are duplicated within Spanish and European platforms.

First of all, data has been analyzed and related to education. CS projects that contain educational keywords (i.e., schools, education or classrooms) have been classified in the category "Education". 241 over 468 projects (51,5%) meet the criteria. As a result, a filter has been designed for educators or learning designers to rapidly visualize specific data of CS projects related to educational initiatives.

Considering an educational perspective, we could say that topics of CS initiatives are similar to those addressed in the curriculum. This analysis has special interest to the educational community when exploring specific data of the project. We have analyzed the terminology related to citizen science projects for each platform and project. Figure 3 shows a word cloud graph with the most relevant words in the Eu.Citizen science platform.

Figure 3. A word cloud with the most common stemmed terms of the Eu.Citizen science platform

Aristeidou and Herodotou (2020) states that by participating in citizen science projects communication skills and vocabulary are improved. In Figure 4 the most important terms used by the citizen science projects of the European platform can be explored. They can also be filtered by project category (previously analyzed), which provides added value since it allows the words to be classified by scientific typologies. By exploring specific terminology, learners can improve functional science literacy (Utami, Saputro and Masykuri 2016).

Name	Word 1	Word 2	Word 3	Word 4	Word 5	Word 1 aim	Word 2 aim	Word 3 aim
Dragonfly Conservation Program ..	visit	vitoria	gasteiz	dragonfli	juli	dragonfli	danger	water
100&CIA for Vitoria-Gasteiz	conserv	program	memori	coordin	bird	conserv	gather	municip
Advancing work on Public Particip..	metadata	standard	repositori	interoper	conduct	ppsr	standardis	metadata
ALPTREES iNaturalist	alptre	inaturalist	org	alpin	tree	tree	nativ	non
Ambassadors of Biodiversity Emb.	seed	varieti	bank	grower	orchard	ambassador	cita	protagonist
Asteroid Hunters	asteroid	object	hunter	astronom	detect	asteroid	earth	disastr
Atlas of Estonian mammals	collat	histor	input	mammal	form	mammal	estonian	systemat
BeBirds: Belgian Ringing Scheme	ring	bird	bebird	ringer	wild	li	strong	ringer
Big Garden Birdwatch	garden	bird	number	thrush	rspb	garden	bird	rspb
Big Seaweed Search	seawe	uk	sea	issu	distribut	seawe	search	british
BioBlitz a tutti i costi	bioblitz	tutti	costi	quot	outdoor	bioblitz	tutti	costi

Figure 4. Dashboard with the keywords extracted from CS projects description of the Eu.Citizen science platform

Another aspect analysed is the use of information and communication technology (ICT, also called materials) by participants. Depending on the objective of the project and how the participation in the scientific process was designed, there are multiple tools used to conduct research (i.e., MammalNet: Watch Wildlife for Science (https://www.mammalnet.com/)). In general, the most common tools used in citizen science are ICT devices (i.e., smartphones) and cameras (Figure 5). ICT tools applied in an educational environment have an impact on student's scientific literacy (Luu and Freeman 2011). Knowing which technologies are useful according to certain scientific tasks helps teachers select which ones to use with their students.

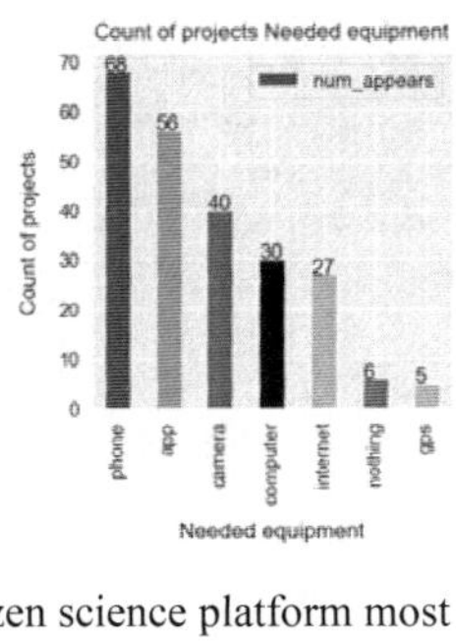

Figure 5. Eu.Citizen science platform most required ICT tools

Finally, the two temporal graphs (Figure 1) show when projects start and end. The first illustrates the growing interest that citizen science has because of the number of projects that started in the last ten years.

These dates can be used to understand how actualized the data and the material used are because the more recent the start date, the more innovative the project will be and the more interest it will have in current problems.

Figure 6 shows how many of the 212 resources extracted belong to each platform (62% are from the European platform and 38% are from the Spanish platform). The information has been classified into categories, depending on the typology of resources (most of them are guidelines, reports, websites or educational resources). Additionally, it has been informed if they are linked to a citizen science project or not (40% of the total are, while the remaining 60% are not).

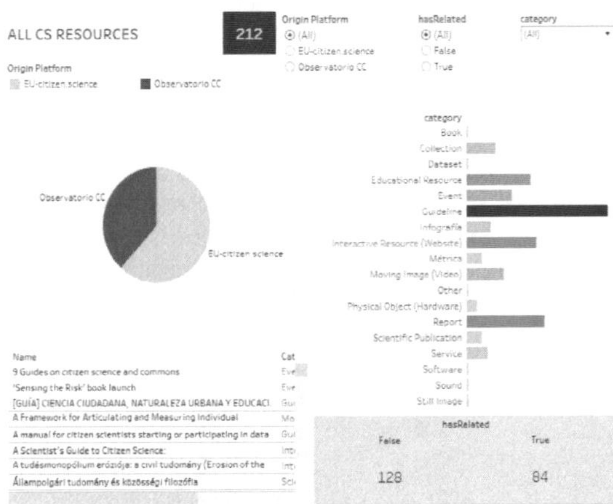

Figure 6. CS projects resources available in platforms

5. CONCLUSION AND FUTURE WORK

The goal of this preliminary study has been to use Data Science techniques to extract and analyze data from CS projects, create visualizations and analyze the connections and possibilities of the data with an educational perspective. The analysis done in this paper shows the potential to analyze large amounts of data to understand better the CS practice, and in particular how this data can be used with educational purposes.

The main limitation observed in this study is that there are inconsistencies on the data structure of CS platforms and the metadata standard use. This implies that specific algorithms have to be designed and implemented based on specific website structures. This limitation, along with the use of different national languages, entails a time consuming process and high cost of resources. In addition to this, another limitation of this preliminary study is that so far educators have not been involved in this research.

The lessons learned from the process followed in this study allowed us to identify four different potential benefits that can be further explored in the future: (1) Access to CS projects information ordered by different categories, (2) Overview of scientific vocabulary, (3) Access to scientific validated resources (4) Technologies that can be used in scientific inquiry.

Having access to CS projects information classified by different disciplines. This can potentially help teachers to design learning activities/content as it can be used as a source of scientific information. Besides that, the students that explore the information could find many examples about different scientific projects motivating or stimulating to learn more about scientific topics.

Having an overview of scientific vocabulary supports teachers during the teaching process and students to easily identify science concepts. Suggate et.al (2012) concluded that there is a positive significant correlation between lexicon and later literacy development. The combination of the use of scientific terms and specific teaching strategies during learning activities implies better vocabulary development by students and will affect literacy (Hong and Diamond 2012).

Enhance the accessibility to scientific validated resources that can be used by a non-academic audience to support the learning process in science. Teachers use resources available online to design their own learning design materials or activities or to use it as main materials.

Identifying technologies that can be used in scientific inquiry will help teachers to define which strategies follow on the use of ICT in the classroom. Many examples of how technology is being used in CS projects for specific tasks can be found in the graphs developed. There is much evidence of how the use of ICT affects positively in students' learning (Fu 2013). Taking into account that one of the barriers of using technology in class is the self-confidence of teachers, it is important to bear in mind that, in many cases, there will be additional resources developed by projects to explain how to use it.

For future work, we plan to organize co-design workshops, as proposed by Scanlon, McAndrew and O'Shea (2015), to understand the needs of educators and students when interacting with Dashboards as the ones proposed in this paper. From the citizen science viewpoint, having CS projects metadata in a single repository will help the CS and Education communities in the analysis and expansion of knowledge of different aspects like CS projects communication or volunteer tasks and how participation is conducted. Additionally, we want to expand the amount of data by extracting information on more platforms to have more information about CS projects.

ACKNOWLEDGEMENT

This work has been partially funded by the CS Track project, European Union's Horizon 2020 research and innovation programme under grant agreement No 872522. Patricia Santos acknowledges the support by the Spanish Ministry of Science and Innovation under the Ramon y Cajal programme.

REFERENCES

Aristeidou, M., & Herodotou, C. (2020). Online citizen science: A systematic review of effects on learning and scientific literacy. Citizen Science: Theory and Practice, 5(1), 1-12.

Auerbach, J., Barthelmess, E. L., Cavalier, D., Cooper, C. B., Fenyk, H., Haklay, M., ... & Shanley, L. (2019). The problem with delineating narrow criteria for citizen science. Proceedings of the National Academy of Sciences, 116(31), 15336-15337.

Ballard, H. L., Dixon, C. G., & Harris, E. M. (2017). Youth-focused citizen science: Examining the role of environmental science learning and agency for conservation. Biological Conservation, 208, 65-75.

Bautista-Puig, N., De Filippo, D., Mauleón, E., & Sanz-Casado, E. (2019). Scientific landscape of citizen science publications: Dynamics, content and presence in social media. Publications, 7(1), 12.

Bonney, R., Cooper, C. B., Dickinson, J., Kelling, S., Phillips, T., Rosenberg, K. V., & Shirk, J. (2009). Citizen science: A developing tool for expanding science knowledge and scientific literacy. BioScience, 59(11), 977-984.

Brossard, D., Lewenstein, B., & Bonney, R. (2005). Scientific knowledge and attitude change: The impact of a citizen science project. International Journal of Science Education, 27(9), 1099-1121.

Caruana, R., Elhawary, M., Munson, A., Riedewald, M., Sorokina, D., Fink, D., ... & Kelling, S. (2006, August). Mining citizen science data to predict orevalence of wild bird species. In Proceedings of the 12th ACM SIGKDD international conference on Knowledge discovery and data mining (pp. 909-915).

Cohn, J. P. (2008). Citizen science: Can volunteers do real research?. BioScience, 58(3), 192-197.

Dillon, M. (1983). Introduction to modern information retrieval. Information Processing & Management, 19(6). Vijayarani, S., & Janani, R. (2016). Text mining: open source tokenization tools-an analysis. Advanced Computational Intelligence: An International Journal (ACII), 3(1), 37-47.

Diouf, R., Sarr, E. N., Sall, O., Birregah, B., Bousso, M., & Mbaye, S. N. (2019, December). Web Scraping: State-of-the-Art and Areas of Application. In 2019 IEEE International Conference on Big Data (Big Data) (pp. 6040-6042). IEEE.

Fink, D., & Hochachka, W. M. (2012). Using data mining to discover biological patterns in citizen science observations. In Citizen science: public participation in environmental research (pp. 125-138). Ithaca, NY: Comstock Publishing Associates.

Fu, J. (2013). Complexity of ICT in education: A critical literature review and its implications. International Journal of education and Development using ICT, 9(1), 112-125.

Ginger Tsueng, Max Nanis, Jennifer T Fouquier, Michael Mayers, Benjamin M Good, Andrew I Su, Applying citizen science to gene, drug and disease relationship extraction from biomedical abstracts, Bioinformatics, Volume 36, Issue 4, 15 February 2020, pp 1226–1233.

Haklay, M. M., Dörler, D., Heigl, F., Manzoni, M., Hecker, S., & Vohland, K. (2021). What Is Citizen Science? The Challenges of Definition. The Science of Citizen Science, 13.

Hecker, S., Haklay, M., Bowser, A., Makuch, Z., Vogel, J., & Bonn, A. (2018). Innovation in open science, society and policy–setting the agenda for citizen science. Citizen science: innovation in open science, society and policy. UCL Press, London, UK, 1-23.

Hiller, S. E., & Kitsantas, A. (2014). The effect of a horseshoe crab citizen science program on middle school student science performance and STEM career motivation. School Science and Mathematics, 114(6), 302-311.

Hong, S. Y., & Diamond, K. E. (2012). Two approaches to teaching young children science concepts, vocabulary, and scientific problem-solving skills. Early Childhood Research Quarterly, 27(2), 295-305.

Karthikeyan, T., Sekaran, K., Ranjith, D., & Balajee, J. M. (2019). Personalized content extraction and text classification using effective web scraping techniques. International Journal of Web Portals (IJWP), 11(2), 41-52.

Keim, D. A. (2002). Information visualization and visual data mining. IEEE transactions on Visualization and Computer Graphics, 8(1), 1-8.

Kelemen-Finan, J., Scheuch, M., & Winter, S. (2018). Contributions from citizen science to science education: An examination of a biodiversity citizen science project with schools in Central Europe. International Journal of Science Education, 40(17), 2078-2098.

Kobori, H., Dickinson, J. L., Washitani, I., Sakurai, R., Amano, T., Komatsu, N., Kitamura W., Takagawa S., Koyama K., Ogawara T. & Miller-Rushing, A. J. (2016). Citizen science: a new approach to advance ecology, education, and conservation. Ecological research, 31(1), 1-19.

Koh, H. C., & Tan, G. (2011). Data mining applications in healthcare. Journal of healthcare information management, 19(2), pp 65.

Lambers, K., Verschoof-van der Vaart, W. B., & Bourgeois, Q. P. (2019). Integrating remote sensing, machine learning, and citizen science in Dutch archaeological prospection. Remote Sensing, 11(7), pp 794.

Luu, K., & Freeman, J. (2011). An analysis of the relationship between information and communication technology (ICT) and scientific literacy in Canada and Australia. Computers & Education, 56(4), 1072-1082.

Masterson, J., Meyer, M., Ghariabeh, N., Hendricks, M., Lee, R. J., Musharrat, S., Newman G., Sansoms G. & Van Zandt, S. (2019). Interdisciplinary citizen science and design projects for hazard and disaster education. International journal of mass emergencies and disasters, 37(1), 6.

McNamara, D. S. (2011). Computational methods to extract meaning from text and advance theories of human cognition. Topics in Cognitive Science, 3(1), pp 3-17.

Michaeli, S., Kroparo, D., & Hershkovitz, A. (2020). Teachers' Use of Education Dashboards and Professional Growth. The International Review of Research in Open and Distributed Learning, 21(4), 61-78.

National Academies of Sciences, Engineering, and Medicine. (2018). Learning through citizen science: enhancing opportunities by design. National Academies Press.

Ponti, M., Hillman, T., Kullenberg, C., & Kasperowski, D. (2018). Getting it right or being top rank: Games in citizen science. Citizen Science: Theory and Practice, 3(1).

Sanz, F., Gold, M., & Mazzonetto, M. (2019). D2.3: Platform Functionality Requirements & Specification Report (Version Version Final Submitted draft). Zenodo.

Saurkar, A. V., Pathare, K. G., & Gode, S. A. (2018). An overview on web scraping techniques and tools. International Journal on Future Revolution in Computer Science & Communication Engineering, 4(4), 363-367.

Scanlon, E., McAndrew, P., & O'Shea, T. (2015). Designing for educational technology to enhance the experience of learners in distance education: how open educational resources, learning design and MOOCs are influencing learning. Journal of interactive Media in education, 2015(1).

Schuttler, S. G., Sears, R. S., Orendain, I., Khot, R., Rubenstein, D., Rubenstein, N., Dunn R. R., Baird E., Kandros K., O'Brien T. & Kays, R. (2019). Citizen science in schools: Students collect valuable mammal data for science, conservation, and community engagement. Bioscience, 69(1), 69-79.

Shah, H. R., & Martinez, L. R. (2016). Current approaches in implementing citizen science in the classroom. Journal of microbiology & biology education, 17(1), 17.

Storksdieck, M., Shirk, J. L., Cappadonna, J. L., Domroese, M., Göbel, C., Haklay, M., ... & Vohland, K. (2016). Associations for citizen science: regional knowledge, global collaboration. Citizen Science: Theory and Practice, 1(2).

Suggate, S., Schaughency, E., McAnally, H., & Reese, E. (2018). From infancy to adolescence: The longitudinal links between vocabulary, early literacy skills, oral narrative, and reading comprehension. Cognitive Development, 47, 82-95.

Sun, Y., Zhuang, Z., & Giles, C. L. (2007, May). A large-scale study of robots. txt. In Proceedings of the 16th international conference on World Wide Web (pp. 1123-1124).

Tauginienė, L., Butkevičienė, E., Vohland, K., Heinisch, B., Daskolia, M., Suškevičs, M., ... & Prūse, B. (2020). Citizen science in the social sciences and humanities: the power of interdisciplinarity. Palgrave Communications, 6(1), 1-11.

Utami, B., Saputro, S., & Masykuri, M. (2016, January). Scientific literacy in science lesson. In Proceeding of International Conference on Teacher Training and Education (Vol. 1, No. 1).

Vohland, K., Land-Zandstra, A., Ceccaroni, L., Lemmens, R., Perelló, J., Ponti, M., ... & Wagenknecht, K. (2021). The Science of Citizen Science Evolves. The Science of Citizen Science, 1.

Zhao, B. (2017). Web scraping. Encyclopedia of big data, 1-3.

EXPLORING PREDICTING PERFORMANCE OF ENGINEERING STUDENTS USING DEEP LEARNING

Imran Zualkernan
Computer Science and Engineering
American University of Sharjah, UAE

ABSTRACT

A significant amount of research has gone into predicting student performance and many studies have been conducted to predict why students drop out. A variety of data including digital footprints, socio-economic data, financial data, and psychological aspects have been used to predict student performance at the test, course, or program level. Fairly good prediction results have been achieved using both traditional machine learning and more recently deep learning methods. While using diverse sets of data has achieved good results, this data is often difficult and expensive to collect, and may have privacy-related issues. This paper explores the extent to which only prior performance data readily available with registrars in most Universities can be used to predict student performance in future terms. Twenty term data from 789 students enrolled an engineering program at an American University were used to train long term short term (LSTM), Bi-directional LSTM and Gated Reference Units (GRU) models to predict student performance in future terms. The results are that all three types of models were able to reasonably predict the next term's performance (F1-score of about 0.70) regardless of the number of terms a student had spent the University. The models generally did not overfit. The prediction was reasonable until about trying to predict performance on seventh term in the future, but the performance dropped beyond this point primarily due to lack of sufficient data (F1-score of about 0.2).

KEYWORDS

Performance Prediction, Higher Education, Engineering, Deep Learning, LSTM, GRU

1. INTRODUCTION

Predicting student performance is a classical problem in educational data mining. A recent survey showed that student success could be predicted based on a number of variables including information from digital platforms, student demographics, socio-economic status, prior academic performance, course load, relationship to the educational institutions, access to counselling, and psychological factors, etc. (Ifenthaler and Yau, 2020). For example, engagement data from a learning analytics platform was a good predictor of student success for first year students (Foster and Siddle, 2020). Family commitments, financial strain, time management, expected study load, and work commitments were also found to be related to early dropout (Nieuwoudt and Pedler, 2021). A student's relationship to the educational institution also played a role as students who were strongly 'fused' with their university were more likely to not dropout (Talaifar et al., 2021). Institutional fit, high school performance, and financial aid were also significant predictors of dropout (Elder, 2021). Prior academic performance is important in predicting success. For example, first year grades were found to be the best predictor of graduation at the University level (Willoughby et al., 2021). A host of psychological factors like academic exhaustion, satisfaction with education and dropout intention have also been explored as well (e.g., (Casanova et al., 2021)).

Data required to predict performance can be divided into three broad categories. First, some data like digital platform data, or prior performance is readily available with the academic information technology (IT) systems. Second, other data like financial aid data can be requested from external information providers. Thirdly, data related to socio-economic factors and psychological factors may require conducting surveys or deploying similar instruments to collect and create data. In most higher education environments, the performance data including students' GPA on every course taken must be collected and retained by the registrar and hence this data is always available in most higher education contexts and does not require any additional effort or cost for collection.

In higher education, students' performance can be predicted within a course, across semesters or across programs. For example, based on performance on a few quizzes, one can predict how a student will perform on final examination or overall, in the course. Similarly, one could also use performance on multiple courses within some number of terms (e.g., first four terms) to predict how well they will perform in the next term or subsequent terms. Finally, one could also compare students' performance to others to determine how well they will perform in the program overall. For example, would they be able to graduate or not. This paper explores if prior performance data alone can be used to predict future performance of students based on course GPA's from a set of terms. The primary contribution of this paper is building time-based models to predict student performance in future terms based on course GPA data alone.

Rest of the paper is organizes as follows. Related work is discussed next. This is followed by a decription of the methodology used. Results are presented next, and the paper ends with a discussion and a conclusion.

2. RELATED WORK

Prior research has shown that most work in machine learning (38%) is about predicting the final grade within a course, this is followed by work (14.7%) to predict an exam grade. The other predictive variables include program retention (13.4%), predicting the GPA (12.2%) and performance on a specific assignment (11.4%) (Hellas et al., 2018). Machine learning has achieved significant performance (e.g., 90-95% accuracy) in some cases but also has also failed to perform in many others (48-76% accuracy) (Namoun and Alshanqiti, 2021). A wide range of machine learning methods have been used for predicting student performance. Traditional regression models have been used to predict student dropout (Hippel and Hofflinger, 2021). Traditional machine learning methods like Support Vector Machines (SVM) and Boosted Trees with ensemble methods were used to achieve accuracies ranging from 71% to 93.5% depending on the term in which prediction was made; earlier terms yielding lower accuracies (Hannaford et al., 2021). Boosted trees were also used achieve an accuracy of 91% to predict student dropout (Oreshin et al., 2020). Similarly, AutoML was used with ensemble models on admission data of students to achieve accuracy rates of about 75% (Zeineddine et al., 2021). Similarly, SVM and Random Forest were used to predict first year student dropout with an accuracy of 85% (Del Bonifro et al., 2020). Other traditional machine learning techniques like Bayesian Belief Network (BBN) have been used to predict student performance with an accuracy of 76% (Delen et al., 2020). Finally, Naïve Bayes was used to achieve an accuracy of 76% across two cohorts.

Neural networks have also been used to predict performance. For example, multi-layered perceptron was also used to predict student failure with an F1-Score of 0.83 (Karimi-Haghighi et al., 2021). Similarly, neural networks were used to predict students at risk with an accuracy of 83.7%. At the course level a neural network outperformed traditional machine learning methods like SVM, K-NN etc. and achieved an F1-Score of 0.96 (Tomasevic et al., 2020). In order to explicitly cater for time-nature of performance (activity on a campus) recurrent networks and SVM have been used to predict student performance (Wang et al., 2020). One problem with performance data is the small size of these educational data sets. The ICGAN-DSVM algorithm combined Generative Adversarial Networks (GANs) with SVM to achieve better performance than supervised learning methods alone (Chui et al., 2020).

3. METHDOLOGY

3.1 Data

The data used for this paper was drawn from the registration system of an engineering program of a college of engineering at an American University. The data ranged from 2014 to 2019. Only the courses taught in the engineering program were considered. For example, humanities, Math, and other courses were excluded. The data included accumulated hours, grade point average (GPA) in each course taken, the instructor for each course, academic status, and the admitting cohort of the student. The data consisted of 789 students who had registered in a total of 10,508 individual courses over this time. Many students had only taken one course so far with a maximum of 43 courses taken and a mean of 13.318 courses attempted per student. The total number of courses available to students in this engineering program was 64. Students could register for multiple courses in a term and four terms (including the summer terms) were counted per year. Regardless of cohort, the data was normalized for each student to start in term 1.

3.2 Neural Network Models

Since the purpose of this paper was to use the timed sequence of student performance to predict future performance, three commonly used time-based neural network prediction models were used. Each is described below.

3.2.1 Long Short-Term Memory Networks (LSTM)

Since their proposal in 1995, recurrent neural networks with long short-term memory (LSTM) have been successful in handling sequential data in a variety of domains (Greff et al., 2017). LSTM architecture is based on a memory cell that maintains its state over time. LSTM uses nonlinear gating units that regulate the flow of information in and out of the cell. An LSTM can take an *n* sized input sequence $x^1, x^2, .. x^n$ where each element of the sequence x^i can be represented by a fixed set of features $f_1^i, f_2^i, .. f_k^i$. In this paper, since the input to LSTM consisted of a sequence of terms with associated GPA in each course, x^i represented the *i*th term while the GPA in each course was represented by a feature f_l^i. For example, the engineering program considered had a total of 64 upper-level courses (i.e., $k = 64$) which were typically attempted by each student. The second term (i.e., x^2) for a particular student was hence represented by the feature vector $f_1^2, f_2^2, .. f_{64}^2$ where each f_j^2 either represented the GPA in a course that was attempted in this term or a very small number ($\varepsilon = 0.0001$) indicating that course was not attempted in this term.

Within this formulation, the LSTM was trained using variable length sequences $x^1, x^2, .. x^l$ as input and performance to be predicted in future terms $p(x^l), p(x^{l+1}), p(x^{l+3})$,.. etc. For example, one could use the data from the first term only (i.e., x^1) to predict performance in the third term (i.e., $p(x^3)$). Performance can either by the actual cumulative GPA of the student in the said term or a classification into a performance category based on the cumulative GPA. For a term x, this paper defined p as shown in Eq. (1). In other words, if the student's cumulative GPA in term x was less than 2 out of 4, then they were classified as weak with a code of 1, and so on; the student's performance was categorized in one of the three categories depending on their cumulative GPA.

$$p(x) = \begin{cases} 1 & 0 <= cgpa(x) <= 2 \\ 2 & 2 < cgpa(x) <= 3 \\ 3 & 3 < cgpa(x) <= 4 \end{cases} \quad (1)$$

The training data for the LSTM consisted of batches of variable length sequences of terms (e.g., first two terms) followed by a predicator based on a subsequent term. For example, one set of training data consisted of $< x^1, p(x^2) >$ in predicting student performance in the second term based on the GPA of courses taken in the first term (i.e., x^1) only. Similarly, $< x^1, x^2, .. x^p, p(x^q) >$ represents a training set that used the data from the first p terms to predict performance in the qth term where $q > p$. All such valid sequences were used to train a single LSTM for each p and q.

After the LSTMs were trained, given the performance of a student $x^1, x^2, .. x^p$ as input the respective LSTM could predict the performance $p(x^q)$ in the qth subsequent term.

Figure 1 shows the number of terms completed verses the number of batches when predicting performance in the next term. Each batch consists of data of the form $< x^1, x^2, .. x^p, p(x^q) >$ for some p and q. For example, for each p terms (e.g., one term) completed, Figure 2 has data in the form of $< x^1, x^2, .. x^p, p(x^{p+1}) >$ as we are trying to predict the GPA in the next (i.e., *p+1*) term. As the figure shows, the number of batches is reduced as we get closer to higher terms because fewer students have taken that many courses.

Figure 2 shows graphical representation of various inputs $< x^1, x^2, .. x^p, p(x^{p+1}) >$ for $p = 15$. Each colored dot represents a grade point average (GPA) in a course. As the Figure shows, lighter colors mean higher GPA. The Figure also demonstrates that there does not seem to be an obvious pattern on how the various students choose to attempt the courses within the same engineering program.

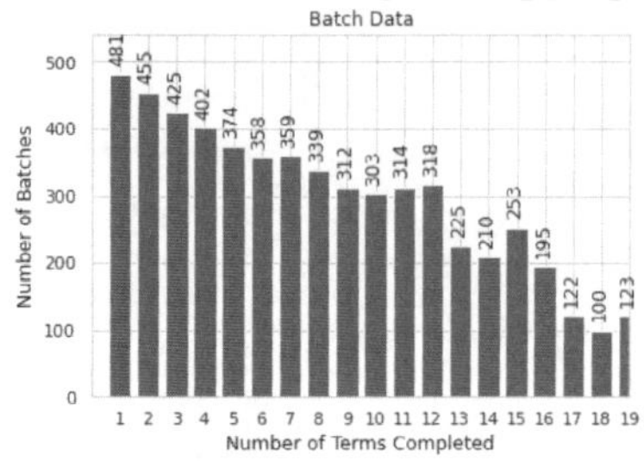

Figure 1. Number of batches completed to predict performance in the next term

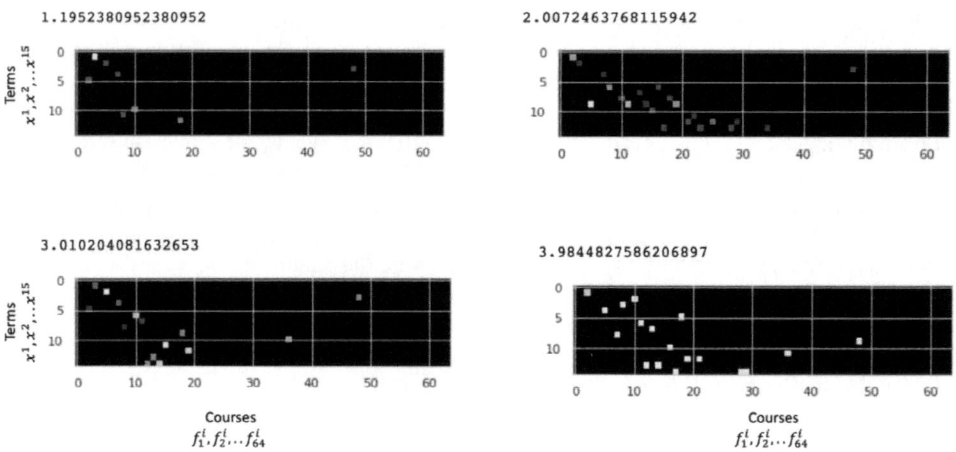

Figure 2. Randomly selected students with different cumulative GPAs for batch size = 15 terms

3.2.2 Gated Reference Units (GRU)

Recurrent networks with gated recurrent units (GRU) emerged in 2014 as a simpler form of LSTM and are more efficient (Chung et al., 2014). Since the basic formulation is the same as the LSTM, the same data was used for training as the LSTM but replacing the LSTM with a GRU.

3.2.3 Bi-Directional LSTM

Bi-directional LSTM is another version of an LSTM that processes the input sequence both forward and in backwards direction to make the predictions (Graves and Schmidhuber, 2005). Since the the basic formulation is the same as a normal LSTM, the same data was used for training as an LSTM but the LSTM was replaced with a bi-directional LSTM.

3.3 Training

One model of each type (e.g., LSTM) for each forward prediction capability was trained on the data set. The data set used an 80:20 split for training/testing and a 70:30 split of training data into training/validation sets.

In each case a two-level stacked model with 16 internal nodes was found to work best. The learning rate was 0.001. 20% dropout was used between the two stacks to prevent overfitting. Each model was trained for 50 epochs and a batch size of 16 was used. Generators were used to dynamically feed batches to the models for training. For example, if the model was to predict *n* terms ahead, then the model was trained on various batches $< x^1, x^2, .. x^p, p(x^{p+n}) >$ where *p* could vary from 1 to the maximum number of terms available that allowed prediction to $p(x^{p+n})$. For example, since only data for 20 terms was available, one could only use data from the first 4 terms to be able to predict 16 terms forward. Hence, the models that were trying to predict farther in the future had lesser data available for training.

4. RESULTS

Figure 3 shows the multiple performance metrics for the various models trained for each predict forward capability. As the Figure shows, the LSTM model to predict performance one term ahead was quite reasonable with a macro F1 Score of 0.70. However, as the prediction horizon becomes longer the performance deteriorates and the macro F1 Score drops to drops to 0.19 for predicting 17 terms ahead. Similarly, GRU performed similarly to the LSTM with a macro F1 Score of 0.72 for one term look ahead. The performance dropped to a macro F1 Score of 0.22 for predicting 17 terms ahead. Finally, Bidirectional LSTM models also performed similarly with an F1-score of 0.72 for one term look ahead. The performance drops to 0.24 for predicting 17 terms ahead.

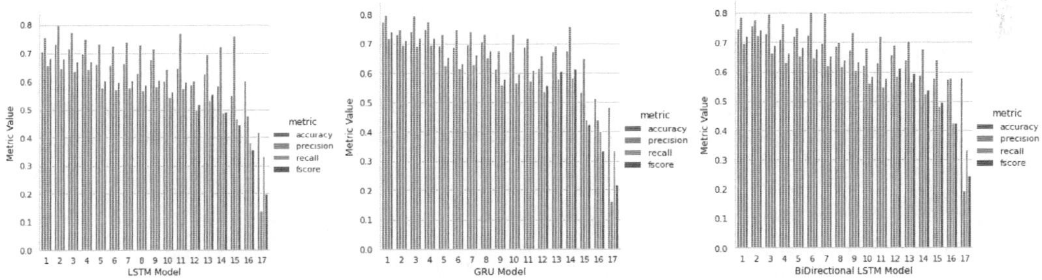

Figure 3. Performance metrics for various models with different forward predictions

As Figure 4 shows, the LSTM models are robust under overfitting as the validation and the training loss follow each other. However, overfitting begins to occur when the number of data points for training become quite small as shown in Figure 6 (f) where validation loss diverged from the training loss.

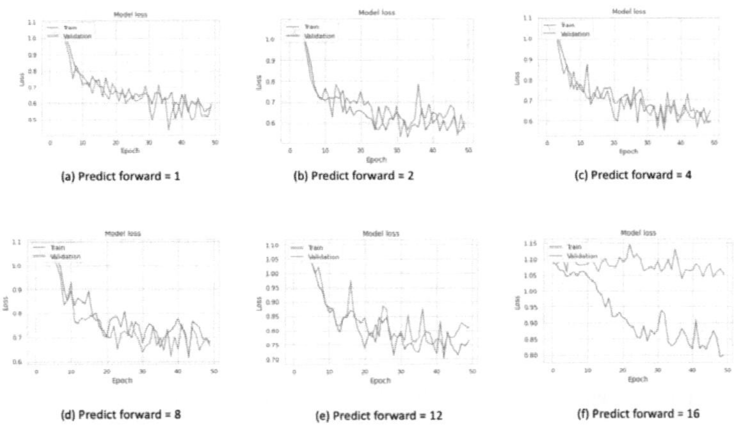

Figure 4. Loss while training for various LSTM models with different forward predictions

Similarly, as Figure 5 shows, like the LSTM, the GRU models also did not overfit. In fact, in this particular training regimen the GRU models did not seem to overfit even for very low amount of data. This can perhaps be attributed to the fact that GRU models generally require much lesser number of parameters as opposed to an LSTM. Finally, as Figure 8 shows, like the normal LSTM, the Bi-Directional LSTM also begins to overfit when the amount of training data becomes very small. However, it tends to not overfit until even when trying to predict 12 terms ahead.

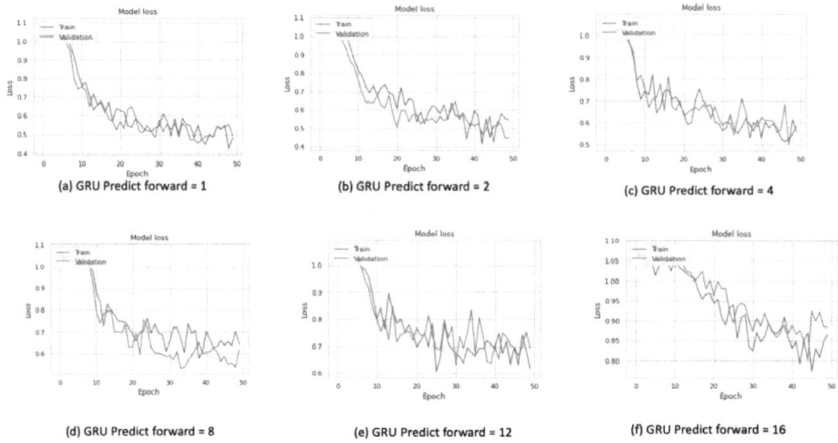

Figure 5. Loss while training for various GRU models with different forward predictions

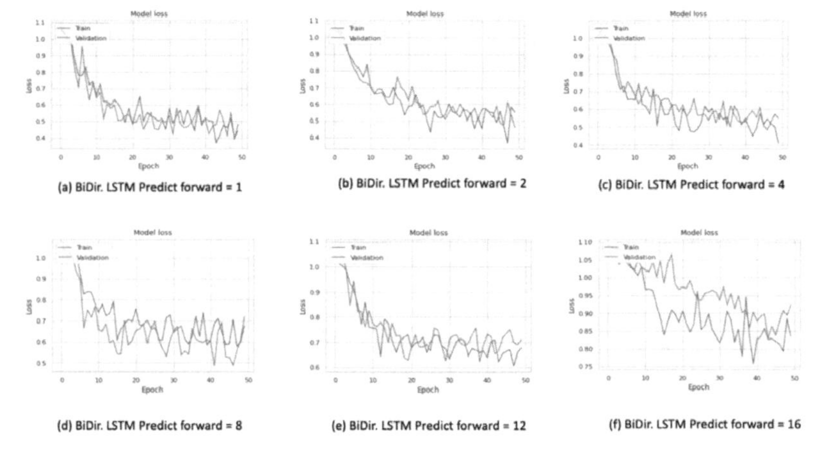

Figure 6. Loss while training for various Bi-directional LSTM models with different forward predictions

5. DISCUSSION

As Figure 7 shows, all three model types performed similarly with respect to the macro F1 Score. For all three model types, the performance dropped significantly when trying to predict beyond seven terms in the future. The results are not spectacular as many have achieved much higher performance by using a variety of data sources. However, given that only performance data was used and that a single model can predict performance in the future regardless of how many terms are counted as input, these initial results are promising.

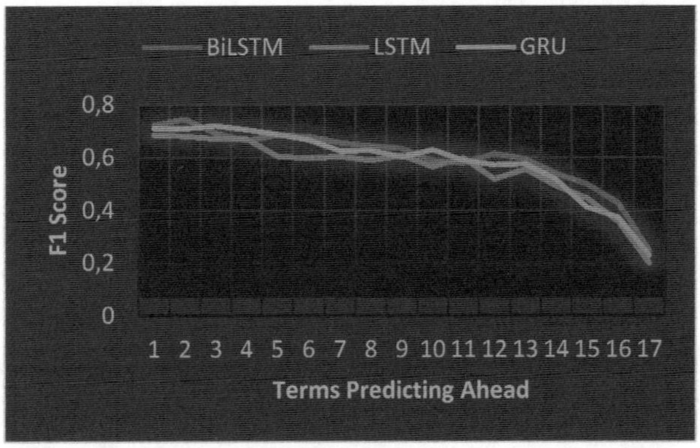

Figure 7. Macro F1 Scores for models trying to predict various terms in the future

6. CONCLUSION

This paper has explored the extent to which course-level GPA alone within an engineering program could be used to predict student performance in future terms. Several models were built based on the how far in the future predictions were to be made. Each model could be used to predict performance even if the student had spent a few terms in the University. The results are reasonable for predictions into up to seven terms in the future. Obviously, the results are limited to one engineering program alone. It will be interesting to compare the results with traditional machine learning techniques like SVM that seemed to have performed well elsewhere using a wider set of data. Similarly, GAN-based architectures to augment data could perhaps also be explored to cater for the low amount of data available in such educational environments

REFERENCES

Casanova, J.R., Gomes, C.M.A., Bernardo, A.B., Núñez, J.C., Almeida, L.S., 2021. Dimensionality and reliability of a screening instrument for students at-risk of dropping out from Higher Education. Studies in Educational Evaluation 68, 100957. https://doi.org/10.1016/j.stueduc.2020.100957

Chui, K.T., Liu, R.W., Zhao, M., De Pablos, P.O., 2020. Predicting Students' Performance With School and Family Tutoring Using Generative Adversarial Network-Based Deep Support Vector Machine. IEEE Access 8, 86745–86752. https://doi.org/10.1109/ACCESS.2020.2992869

Chung, J., Gulcehre, C., Cho, K., Bengio, Y., 2014. Empirical Evaluation of Gated Recurrent Neural Networks on Sequence Modeling. arXiv:1412.3555 [cs].

Del Bonifro, F., Gabbrielli, M., Lisanti, G., Zingaro, S.P., 2020. Student Dropout Prediction, in: Bittencourt, I.I., Cukurova, M., Muldner, K., Luckin, R., Millán, E. (Eds.), Artificial Intelligence in Education, Lecture Notes in Computer Science. Springer International Publishing, Cham, pp. 129–140. https://doi.org/10.1007/978-3-030-52237-7_11

Delen, D., Topuz, K., Eryarsoy, E., 2020. Development of a Bayesian Belief Network-based DSS for predicting and understanding freshmen student attrition. European Journal of Operational Research, Featured Cluster: Business Analytics: Defining the field and identifying a research agenda 281, 575–587. https://doi.org/10.1016/j.ejor.2019.03.037

Elder, A.C., 2021. Holistic factors related to student persistence at a large, public university. Journal of Further and Higher Education 45, 65–78. https://doi.org/10.1080/0309877X.2020.1722802

Foster, E., Siddle, R., 2020. The effectiveness of learning analytics for identifying at-risk students in higher education. Assessment & Evaluation in Higher Education 45, 842–854. https://doi.org/10.1080/02602938.2019.1682118

Graves, A., Schmidhuber, J., 2005. Framewise phoneme classification with bidirectional LSTM networks, in: Proceedings. 2005 IEEE International Joint Conference on Neural Networks, 2005. Presented at the Proceedings. 2005 IEEE International Joint Conference on Neural Networks, 2005., pp. 2047–2052 vol. 4. https://doi.org/10.1109/IJCNN.2005.1556215

Greff, K., Srivastava, R.K., Koutník, J., Steunebrink, B.R., Schmidhuber, J., 2017. LSTM: A Search Space Odyssey. IEEE Transactions on Neural Networks and Learning Systems 28, 2222–2232. https://doi.org/10.1109/TNNLS.2016.2582924

Hannaford, L., Cheng, X., Kunes-Connell, M., 2021. Predicting nursing baccalaureate program graduates using machine learning models: A quantitative research study. Nurse Education Today 99, 104784. https://doi.org/10.1016/j.nedt.2021.104784

Hellas, A., Ihantola, P., Petersen, A., Ajanovski, V.V., Gutica, M., Hynninen, T., Knutas, A., Leinonen, J., Messom, C., Liao, S.N., 2018. Predicting academic performance: a systematic literature review, in: Proceedings Companion of the 23rd Annual ACM Conference on Innovation and Technology in Computer Science Education, ITiCSE 2018 Companion. Association for Computing Machinery, New York, NY, USA, pp. 175–199. https://doi.org/10.1145/3293881.3295783

Hippel, P.T.V., Hofflinger, A., 2021. The data revolution comes to higher education: identifying students at risk of dropout in Chile. Journal of Higher Education Policy and Management 43, 2–23. https://doi.org/10.1080/1360080X.2020.1739800

Ifenthaler, D., Yau, J.Y.-K., 2020. Utilising learning analytics to support study success in higher education: a systematic review. Education Tech Research Dev 68, 1961–1990. https://doi.org/10.1007/s11423-020-09788-z

Karimi-Haghighi, M., Castillo, C., Hernandez-Leo, D., Oliver, V.M., 2021. Predicting Early Dropout: Calibration and Algorithmic Fairness Considerations. arXiv:2103.09068 [cs].

Namoun, A., Alshanqiti, A., 2021. Predicting Student Performance Using Data Mining and Learning Analytics Techniques: A Systematic Literature Review. Applied Sciences 11, 237. https://doi.org/10.3390/app11010237

Nieuwoudt, J.E., Pedler, M.L., 2021. Student Retention in Higher Education: Why Students Choose to Remain at University. Journal of College Student Retention: Research, Theory & Practice 1521025120985228. https://doi.org/10.1177/1521025120985228

Oreshin, S., Filchenkov, A., Petrusha, P., Krasheninnikov, E., Panfilov, A., Glukhov, I., Kaliberda, Y., Masalskiy, D., Serdyukov, A., Kazakovtsev, V., Khlopotov, M., Podolenchuk, T., Smetannikov, I., Kozlova, D., 2020. Implementing a Machine Learning Approach to Predicting Students’ Academic Outcomes, in: 2020 International Conference on Control, Robotics and Intelligent System, CCRIS 2020. Association for Computing Machinery, New York, NY, USA, pp. 78–83. https://doi.org/10.1145/3437802.3437816

Talaifar, S., Ashokkumar, A., Pennebaker, J.W., Medrano, F.N., Yeager, D.S., Swann, W.B., 2021. A New Pathway to University Retention? Identity Fusion With University Predicts Retention Independently of Grades. Social Psychological and Personality Science 12, 108–117. https://doi.org/10.1177/1948550619894995

Tomasevic, N., Gvozdenovic, N., Vranes, S., 2020. An overview and comparison of supervised data mining techniques for student exam performance prediction. Computers & Education 143, 103676. https://doi.org/10.1016/j.compedu.2019.103676

Wang, X., Yu, X., Guo, L., Liu, F., Xu, L., 2020. Student Performance Prediction with Short-Term Sequential Campus Behaviors. Information 11, 201. https://doi.org/10.3390/info11040201

Willoughby, T., Dykstra, V.W., Heffer, T., Braccio, J., Shahid, H., 2021. A Long-Term Study of What Best Predicts Graduating From University Versus Leaving Prior to Graduation. Journal of College Student Retention: Research, Theory & Practice 1521025120987993. https://doi.org/10.1177/1521025120987993

Zeineddine, H., Braendle, U., Farah, A., 2021. Enhancing prediction of student success: Automated machine learning approach. Computers & Electrical Engineering 89, 106903. https://doi.org/10.1016/j.compeleceng.2020.106903

EVALUATING VISUALIZATION FOR SLIDE-BASED INVESTIGATIVE LEARNING WITH CONNECTION BETWEEN PRESENTATION SLIDES

Mitsuhiro Goto and Akihiro Kashihara
The University of Electro-Communications
1-5-1, Chofugaoka, Chofu, 182-8585, Tokyo, Japan

ABSTRACT

Presentation documents have been increasingly used not only as supplementary presentation materials but also as contents for investigative learning. In learning a presentation document, learners generally need to select a number of slides from the document, which describe what they want to learn or should learn. However, it is not so easy to find out the slides to be learnt since what each slide represents is not concisely stated and what connections exist between the adjacent slides are not explicitly expressed. They accordingly take more time for learning and finish learning with incomplete knowledge. In order to address this issue, this paper introduces a map called slidemap for visualizing the logical connections between the slides. This map helps learners identify the sequence of slides to be learnt from the presentation document and grasp the structure embedded in the document in a shorter time. This paper also demonstrates a tool for presentation slides-based investigative learning with slidemap. In addition, this paper reports a case study involving 16 participants with the tool, whose purpose was to ascertain whether using slidemap could be more beneficial for understanding the presentation document than using PowerPoint user interface. The results of the study show the effect of increasing learning time and visiting frequency for slides to be learnt, and promoting learners' understanding of presentation documents in a shorter time.

KEYWORDS

Presentation Slides, Slides-Based Investigative Learning, Visualization, Slide Map

1. INTRODUCTION

In recent years, the opportunities of investigative learning with presentation documents (referred to as "P-documents") have been increased since the Web services such as SlideShare (LinkedIn, 2006) allow the learners to search and investigate P-documents in various fields to learn. Corbeil states “For university students familiar to ICT, P-documents are more effective learning media than textbooks (Crebeil, 2007).” In addition, P-documents usually consist of slides, and the contents of a presentation are often summarized clearly and precisely on the slides utilizing figures or images so that the audience can easily comprehend the contents. By using such P-documents, it is possible to learn about the latest research with texts, figures or images in the slides, although those do not exhaustively describe it. For example, researchers in educational technology can learn the contents of slides describing "evaluation methods" from a P-document on research similar to their theme in order to understand "the latest evaluation methods to claim the usefulness of the system." We call such learning with P-documents "slide-based investigative learning (SBI-learning)". Web-based investigative learning has been proposed in our previous work (Kashihara & Akiyama, 2013). In SBI-learning, on the other hand, learners learn the slides of P-documents instead of web resources, in which they do not always investigate all of the slides included in a P-document, but select a number of slides according to the viewpoint from which they want to learn. They then extract concepts included in slides as keywords to combine them and construct knowledge. Even if the P-document does not contain enough information for learning, they could explore other P-documents related to the viewpoint with the Web services such as SlideShare.

In this work, we have designed a model of SBI-learning that consists of the following three phases: (1) slides investigation phase, (2) knowledge construction phase, and (3) P-documents investigation phase. We have also proposed the method for supporting SBI-learning based on this model. In this paper, we focus on slides investigation phase, and introduce a supporting method in this phase. P-documents targeted in this model have a relatively large number of slides (several dozen or so), and can be divided into several semantic segments that embody the main topic of presentations (Shibata et al., 2013), such as sub-themes and topics. Each segment also contains a series of one or more slides, which are logically connected to each other. Furthermore, the slides can be classified into two according to their roles, such as "slides describing the main topic of a presentation" and "slides supplementing the main topic".

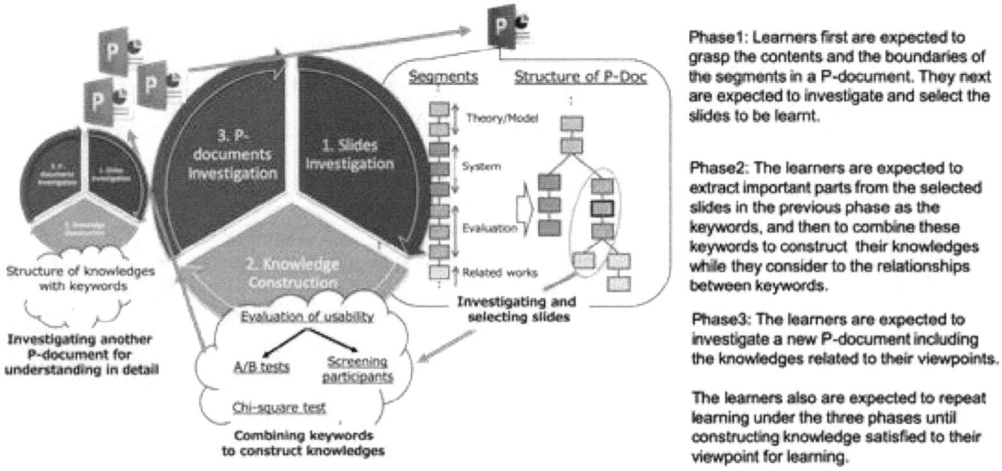

Figure 1. An overview of SBI-learning model

In order to efficiently find out slides to be learnt in a P-document, it is necessary to grasp the contents and boundaries of the segments in the document, and to select the slides based on the segments grasped. However, it is not so easy for learners to identify the segments and to find out slides from P-documents since the roles of slides or the logical connections between the adjacent slides are not explicitly represented. As a result, they take more time for learning, and finish learning with incomplete knowledge.

In this work, we propose a map that visualizes the structure of a P-document involving the roles of each slide and the logical connections between the adjacent slides. This map makes it easy to identify the contents and boundaries of segments in a P-document and to find out slides to be learnt. We also implemented a tool for investigating slides based on the map.

2. SLIDE-BASED INVESTIGATIVE LEARNING

2.1 Overview

By using P-documents for technical reports, conferences, etc., learners can learn the latest content that is not published in textbooks. During SBI-learning, the learners are expected to investigate a number of slides, which are related to their viewpoints from which they want to learn, and to extract important parts from the slides as keywords that are necessary for learning. They are then expected to combine these keywords to construct their knowledge. Unlike textbooks, these P-documents do not often provide a table of the contents with which the learners can readily detect a number of slides to be learnt and decide the order of learning the slides. Therefore, the learners need to grasp the contents and boundaries of the segments in a P-document considering the roles of the slides and the logical connection between the slides, and to select slides based on the segments grasped by themselves.

Kashihara and Akiyama proposed a model and a cognitive tool of knowledge construction from Web resources that do not often provide a table of contents (Kashihara & Akiyama, 2013). Referring to this model, in this paper, we have designed a model of learning processes for SBI-learning. The model consists of three phases as shown in Figure 1. In this model, learners are expected to repeat investigating and understanding slides under these phases until they finish constructing knowledge satisfied to their viewpoint for learning. In the above three phases, it is very important to find out slides necessary for learning in the first phase because they will finish learning with incomplete knowledge in the subsequent phases if they cannot find out the slides. In the following section, we will accordingly focus on the slides investigation phase.

2.2 Problem Addressed

As Kohlhase (Kohlhase, 2007) states, "PowerPoint is a tool that optimizes the creation of graphical slides", P-document tools such as PowerPoint and Keynote seem to focus on supporting the creation of individual slides. On the other hand, there are few tools that consider the relationship between segments and slides, and that provide only limited functionality, such as outline view by slide title and adding sections. Therefore P-documents created using these tools tend not to explicitly represent the roles of each slide and the logical connection between slides. Hence, when learners investigate slides from these P-documents, they need to identify whether the role of each slide represents "the main topic" or "supplementary of the main topic", and whether there are logical connections between slides such as causal or inclusion relationship while they grasp the content of each slide in detail and the structure of the P-documents. However, it is very complicated and difficult for the learners to identify the connections and the roles of slides, and to select slides from the P-document while overviewing the contents of all dozens of slides. As a result, it requires a lot of time for slides investigation.

3. SUPPORTING TO INVESTIGATING SLIDES

As described in 2.2 section, it is necessary to concurrently understand the content of the slides and the structure between the slides in SBI-learning, in which the cognitive load would be quite high. Following Mayer's cognitive theory of multimedia learning (Mayer, 2004), we accordingly propose a visualization that enables learners to understand the structure between slides with an appropriate cognitive load.

The proposed visualization allows learners to overview the roles of slides (explanation of the main topic, supplementary explanation of the main topic) and the logical connections between slides (such as causal and inclusive relations). These roles and connections are provided to the learners as a map called slidemap so that they can seamlessly grasp the contents and the boundaries of the segment, and select slides necessary for learning.

3.1 Visualization of the Roles of Slides

As described above, slides in a P-document have two roles. The role of "supplementary explanation of the main topic" can be also divided into two types: One is to present the contents that support the main topic (support explanation), and the other is to present the contents that rebut the main topic (rebuttal explanation)". In the slidemap, these roles are visualized as shown in Figure 2 (a).

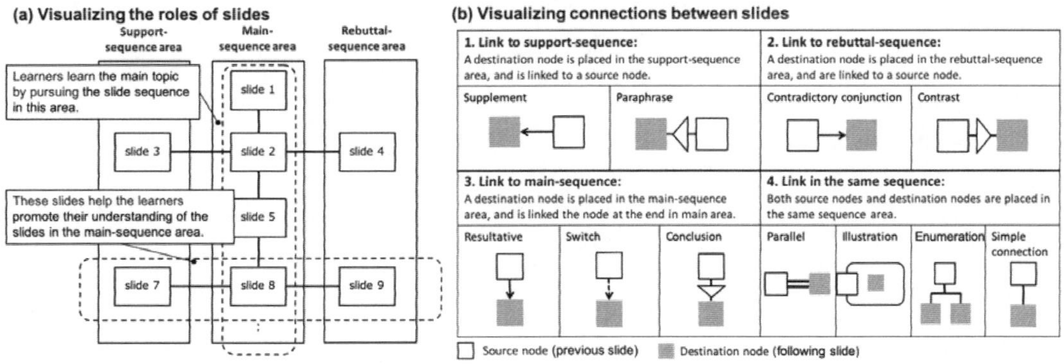

Figure 2. An example of visualization the roles of the slides and the logical connections

This map consists of three areas, which are main-sequence area, support-sequence area and rebuttal-sequence area. Each slide is also represented as node and the connection between slides is represented as link between the corresponding nodes, as shown in Figure 2 (a). The main-sequence area includes the slides, which describe the main topic. The learners are allowed to pursue the slide sequence in this area to learn the main topic of the P-document. The support-sequence area also includes the slides, which describe the contents supporting the main topic for the slides in the main-sequence area. On the other hand, the rebuttal-sequence area includes the slides, which describe the rebuttal of the main topic in the main-sequence area. The slides in the support-sequence and rebuttal-sequence areas are useful for them to promote their understanding of the slides in the main-sequence area.

3.2 Visualization of Connections between Slides

In order to represent the logical connections between the adjacent slides, this paper adopts the functions of conjunctions. The functions of conjunctions allow us to represent the logical connections independent of the slide contents. In this work, we follow the classification of conjunctions in Japanese by Ishiguro (Ishiguro, 2006) to define 10 types of logical connections. Moreover, the connection between the adjacent slides beyond the functions of conjunctions is defined as simple connection. These 11 connection types are visualized as shown in Figure 2 (b), which allow learners to grasp the structure embedded in a P-document in a shorter time. For example, if there is an "Illustration" relationship between two slides, it implies that the including slide represents "a certain content" and the included one represents "a specific example". This allows learners to grasp the relationship of the two slides.

Links representing the logical connections are changed according to the conjunction types as shown in Figure 2 (b). There are four categories of link representations, and the placement area of the destination node is decided according to the category. In addition, segments are not explicitly represented in the slidemap. Learners are expected to become aware of the boundaries of the segments by means of the link representation in the map.

3.3 Visualizer Tool for Investigating Slides

This tool is implemented as an add-in for Microsoft PowerPoint 2013, and runs standalone in the PowerPoint on a Windows PC. This tool provides learners with the map representation displaying together on the normal user interface of PowerPoint in order to support the slide investigation.

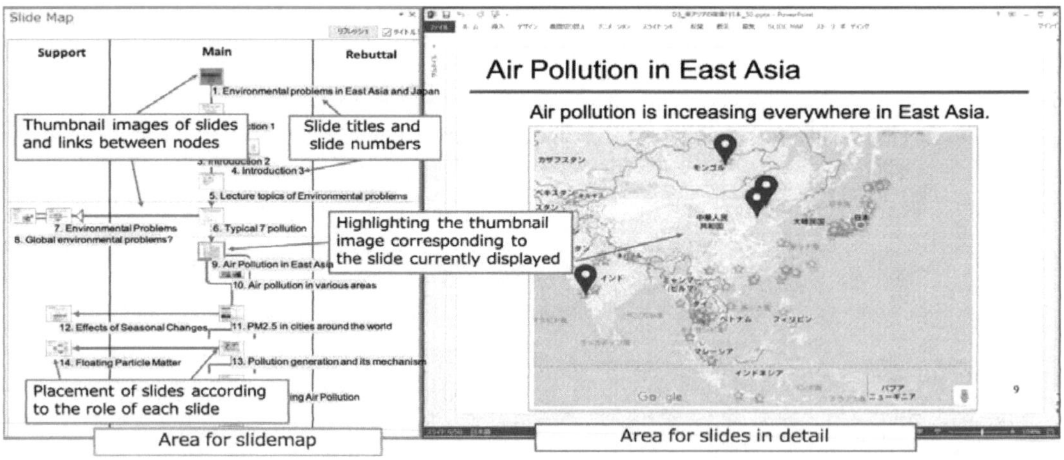

Figure 3. An overview of the proposed tool

As shown in the left of Figure 3, the slidemap displays the structure of the P-Document with the thumbnail images of each slide as nodes and the connections between slides as links. The thumbnail images of slides are placed in the area for slidemap, and the slide numbers and slide titles are displayed near the corresponding thumbnail images. These representations allow learners to overview each slide without confirming the details of each slide. The thumbnail image in the map is highlighted corresponding to the slide currently displayed in the area for slides on the right of Figure 3. This feature allows the learners to visually confirm the conjunctive relationship between a slide which they confirm in detail and the ones surrounding it. Wang and Sumiya proposed a quick browsing tool that generates a word cloud based on the texts in a slide to help learners understand the content of each slide (Wang & Sumiya, 2013). It aims not to grasp the segments but to overview the contents of each slide.

4. CASE STUDY

We conducted a case study with 16 participants to confirm whether the proposed tool was effective in the slide investigation phase of SBI-learning. In this case study, we evaluated the differences in learning time and test results between the two conditions, which were slide investigation with normal PowerPoint user interface (referred to as PowerPoint-UI) and slide investigation with the proposed tool (referred to as Slidemap-UI).

4.1 Preparation

The participants were 16 undergraduate and graduate students of information engineering (3rd year to 2nd year of master's degree; male: 12, female: 4; mean age: 22.7±1.2). The P-documents used in this case study were two documents obtained from SlideShare (Linkdeln, 2016). One was a document on renewable energy (referred to as Doc 1), and the other was a document on zoology (referred to as Doc 2). Two conditions were set: one for learning Doc 1 with PowerPoint-UI (referred to as "C-Cond"), and the other for learning Doc 2 with Slidemap-UI (referred to as "P-Cond"). The size of the slides displayed in both UIs was the same, and the participants in C-Cond were instructed slide investigation using a thumbnail view of PowerPoint-UI, in which thumbnail images lined up in a row.

The number of slides in each document was 55 slides, the number of segments included in each document was 6 segments, and the average number of slides in a segment was 9.2 slides. The number of slides in each sequence area was almost the same. We also confirmed that prior knowledge about the contents each participant had was almost the same by means of 5-point Likert scale questionnaire. As a result, we believed that the difference of P-documents has little impact on the learning results.

We prepared viewpoints for learning in the experiment, and the participants were instructed to investigate slides related to the viewpoints provided, and to understand the details of the slides. Table 1 shows two viewpoints provided with the participants in each condition. Each condition had two sessions. In Session 1, the participants were given the first viewpoint, and then were required to investigate and learn slides. In Session 2, they were given the second viewpoint, and then were required to conduct investigative learning. In other words, we conducted a within-participants design, and required each participant to do two sessions under each condition. The reason for conducting two sessions under one condition was to evaluate the effectiveness of the slide map under the first use of P-document and the second use of the same P-document with some knowledge of the structure.

Table 1. The viewpoints provided with the participants in each session

	First session	Second session
C-Cond	The environmental loads compared to depletable energy	The problems in spreading the use of solar power in Japan
P-Cond	The layout of exhibition of great academic significance in zoos	About animals that can only exhibit their herd in females

4.2 Procedure

First, the participants practiced the operation of each UI with a sample P-document that was different from Doc1 or Doc2 until they had no unclear point in using it. The experimenter next instructed the participants as follows: (1) You were required to investigate and learn slides according to the viewpoint provided using the UI specified by the experimenter. The learning time was within 20 minutes in one session. If you finished learning earlier than 20 minutes, you were also required to tell the experimenter when you finished, (2) After learning in one session, you were required to answer an understanding test about the viewpoint provided, (3) After learning in one condition, you were required to answer a questionnaire about the System Usability Scale (SUS) (Brooke, 1996) of UI that you used, and (4) you were finally required to answer the five Likert scales of questionnaire about the subjective usability of each UI as shown in Table 2.

Table 2. Each question item of subjective questionnaire

Q1	How easy was the UI to find the slides needed to learn a given viewpoint?
Q2	How much was the UI useful to identify the contents and the boundaries of segments in the P-document?
Q3	How much was the UI useful to comprehend the overall structure of the P-document such as the connections between slides?
Q4	How much was the UI useful to identify the role of each slide, such as representing the main or the supplementary?

In this study, we also recorded the learning time and the viewing frequency of each slide by each participant as quantitative metrics to evaluate the effectiveness of the slide investigation, which were captured by the logger implemented in each UI. The hypotheses we set up in this study were as follows:

H1: The Slidemap UI encourages learners to investigate the slides related to the viewpoint in a shorter time than the PowerPoint-UI,

H2: The Slidemap UI encourages learners to more intensively investigate the slides that are suitable for understanding the viewpoint than the PowerPoint-UI and

H3: The Slidemap UI has higher usability for investigating the slides than the PowerPoint-UI.

4.3 Results

The results were analyzed by Wilcoxon signed-rank test for each session or each condition, the symbols in the graphs represent significant differences at †: $p < .10$, *: $p < .05$, **: $p < .01$ and r represents effect size ($0.1 <= r < 0.3$: small, $0.3 < r <= 0.5$: medium, $r > 0.5$: large) respectively.

4.3.1 Learning Time and Viewing Frequency

Figure 4 (a) shows the average of the total learning time in each session. In the first session of each condition, the average time in P-Cond was about one minute shorter than C-Cond, but there was no significant difference ($Z = -1.24$, $p = 0.21$, $r = 0.31$.) In the second session of each condition, however, the average time in P-Cond was about the half of the average time in C-Cond, and there was a significant difference ($Z = -3.46$, $p < .01$, $r = 0.87$.)

Figure 4 (b) shows the ratio of the average learning time of the slides related to the viewpoint to the time of all slides in each session. If this ratio is higher, it suggests that the participants spent more time for learning the slides related to the viewpoint. In the first session of each condition, the ratios in C-Cond and P-Cond were 21.8% and 35.9% respectively. In the second session of each condition, the ratios in C-Cond and P-Cond were also 59.1% and 82.1%. There was no significant difference in the first session and was significant difference in the second session between P-Cond and C-Cond (in the first session: $Z = 1.24$, $p = .21$, $r = 0.31$, in the second session: $Z = -2.89$, $p < .01$ $r = 0.72$.)

Figure 4 (c) shows the ratio of the average viewing frequency of the slides related to the viewpoint to the frequency of all slides in each session. If this ratio is higher, it suggests that the participants more repeatedly view the slides related to the viewpoint. In the first session of each condition, the ratios in C-Cond and P-Cond were 20.6% and 15.5%, and there was no significant difference ($Z = -1.29$, $p = .20$, $r = 0.32$.) In the second session of each condition, the ratios in C-Cond and P-Cond were 30.8% and 56.2%, and there was a significant difference ($Z = -2.84$, $p < .01$, $r = 0.71$.)

We also compared the average of the viewing frequency of all slides in C-Cond with the one in P-Cond. In the first session, the frequency in C-Cond was 82.1 times and the one in P-Cond was 93.6 times. This result suggests that the participants tended to overview more slides in the P-document. In the second session, the frequency in C-Cond was 51.6 times and P-Cond was 26.5 times. This result suggests that the participants more intensively investigate the slides related to the viewpoint based on some knowledge about the structure of the P-document grasped in the first session (Due to the space limitation, the graph is not shown here.)

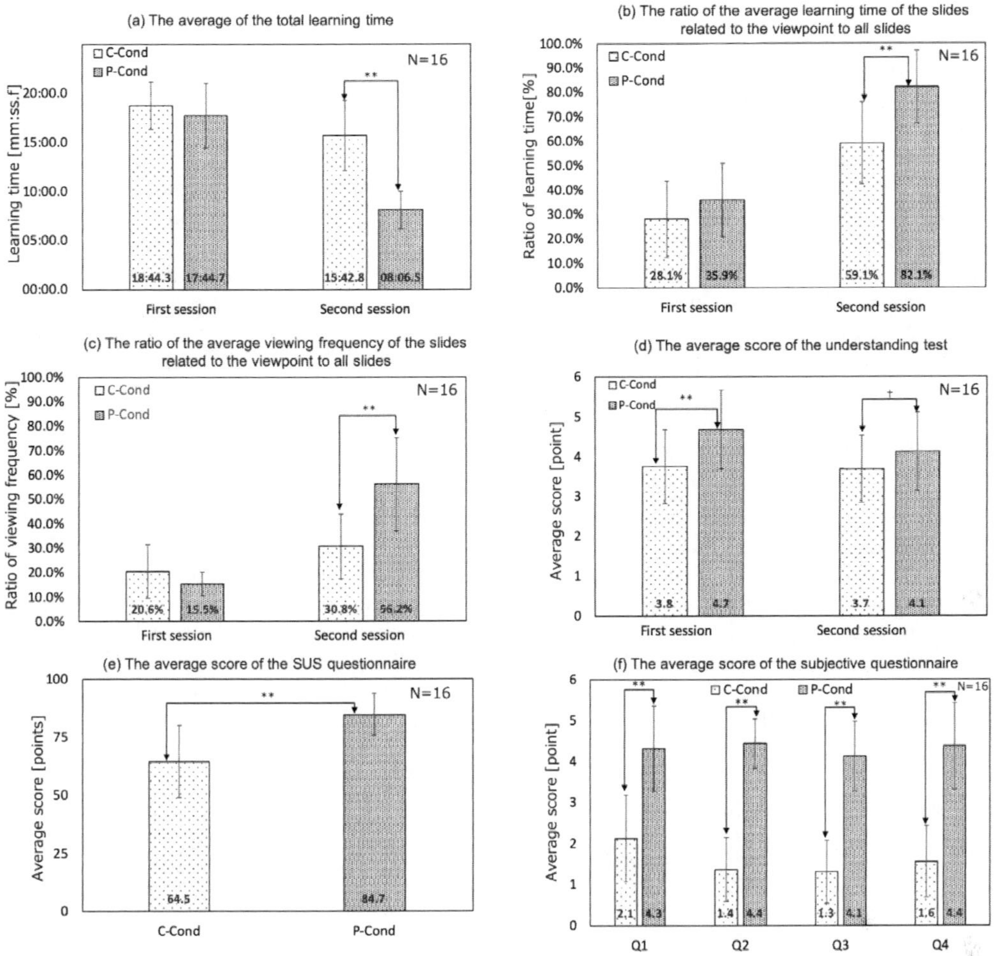

Figure 4. Results of the case study

4.3.2 Understanding Test

The understanding test consisted of five questions about the contents of the slides, each of which was given one point, for a total of five points. When a question is answered with multiple elements, the score is divided by one. For example, if a question is answered with two elements, the score is 0.5. Figure 4 (d) shows the average scores of the test for all the participants in each condition. In the first session, the average scores of understanding test in C-Cond and P-Cond were 3.8 points and 4.7 points respectively. In the second session, the average score in C-Cond and P-Cond were 3.7 points and 4.1 points. There was a significant difference in the first session and was a tendency of significant difference in the second session between P-Cond and C-Cond (in the first session: $Z = -3.01$, $p < .01$ $r = 0.75$, in the second session: $Z = -1.67$, $p < .10$, $r = 0.42$.)

4.3.3 Usability of User Interface

Figure 4 (e) shows the average scores of the SUS questionnaire for all participants in each condition. The average scores in C-Cond and P-Cond were 64.5 points and 84.7 points, and there was a significant difference. SUS is the metrics to evaluate the usability of information systems, and the range of score is from 0 to 100. If the score is closer to 100, it indicates a higher usability. P-Cond accordingly makes an impression of a good UI to the participants. Figure 4 (f) shows the results of the subjective questionnaire for each condition. For all questions from Q1 to Q4, the average score in P-Cond was higher than the one in C-Cond, with significant differences (Q1: Z = -3.05. p < .01 r = 0.76, Q2: Z = -3.24, p < .01 r = 0.81, Q3: Z = -3.53, p < .01 r = 0.88, Q4: Z =-3.49, p < .01, r = 0.87).

Following the results described above, we confirm whether the hypotheses H1, H2, and H3 are valid. From the average of total learning time in one session (Figure 4 (a)) and the scores of the understanding test (Figure 4 (d)), the Slidemap-UI first allowed the participants to finish learning with a shorter time, and to get higher scores in the understanding test than the PowerPoint-UI not only in the first session but also in the second session. These results support H1. From the ratio of the average learning time (Figure 4 (b)), next, the Slidemap-UI can be more effective than the PowerPoint-UI. From the ratio of the average viewing frequency of the slides (Figure 4 (c)), when the participants have some knowledge about the structure of P-document, the Slidemap-UI allowed the participants to learn more intensively the slides in the second session than in the first session. These results suggest H2. Finally, the SUS score (Figure 4 (e)) and the subjective questionnaire (Figure 4 (f)) for each condition suggest that the Slidemap-UI has higher usability and is subjectively more suitable for supporting investigating slides in SBI-learning than the PowerPoint-UI. These results support H3.

5. CONCLUSION

In this paper, we proposed supporting slides investigation with the slidemap that visualizes the logical connections between slides based on the 11 types of relationships corresponding to the meanings of Japanese conjunctions. We also conducted a case study with 16 participants whose purpose was to confirm the effectiveness of the tool for slides investigation. As a result, the proposed Slidemap-UI allowed the participants to finish learning with a shorter time and higher understanding scores than the PowerPoint-UI. In addition, the proposed UI encouraged the participants intensively to learn the slides related to the viewpoint with higher usability. In future, we will study the algorithm for automatic generation of the proposed slide map, design the UI for knowledge construction and the UI for slides investigation in multiple P-documents.

ACKNOWLEDGEMENT

The work is supported in part by JSPS KAKENHI Grant Number JP17H01992.

REFERENCES

Brooke, J., 1996. SUS: A "quick and dirty" usability scale. *Usability. Evaluation in Industry*, pp. 189-194.

Corbeil, G., 2007. Can PowerPoint Presentations Effectively Replace Textbooks and Blackboards for Teaching Grammar? Do Students Find Them an Effective Learning Tool? *CALICO Journal,* 24(3), pp.631–656.

Ishiguro, K., 2006. *Sentences are connected with conjunction* (in Japanese). Koubunsha, Tokyo, JAPAN.

Kashihara, A. and Akiyama, N., 2013. Learner-created scenario for investigative learning with web resources. *Proceedings of the 16th International Conference on Artificial Intelligence in Education (AIED2013), LNAI7926*, pp.700-703.

Kohlhase, A., 2007. Semantic PowerPoint: Content and Semantic Technology for Educational Added-Value Services in MS PowerPoint. *Proceeding. of World Conference on Educational Multimedia, Hypermedia & Telecommunications (ED-MEDIA2007).* Vancouver, Canada, pp. 3576-3583.

LinkedIn Corporation, *SlideShare*, viewed 20 April 2016, <http://www.slideshare.net/>.

Mayer, R. E., 2014. *Cognitive theory of multimedia learning.* The Cambridge handbook of multimedia learning. Cambridge University Press, pp. 43–71.

Shibata, Y. et al, 2013. Skill transfer from learning to creating presentation documents. *Proceedings of the 12th Information Technology Based Higher Education and Training (ITHET2013).* Antalya, Turkey, pp. 1-6.

Wang, Y., and Sumiya, K., 2013. Dynamic Word Clouds: Context-based Word Clouds of Presentation Slides for Quick Browsing. *Proceedings. of 6th IIMSS2013.* Sesimbra, Portugal, pp. 108-117.

MIND-WANDERING DETECTION MODEL WITH ELECTROENCEPHALOGRAM

Chutimon Rungsilp[1], Krerk Piromsopa[1,2], Atthaphon Viriyopase[3] and Kongpop U-Yen[3]
Chulalongkorn University, Bangkok, Thailand
[1]Department of Computer Engineering, Faculty of Engineering
[2]Research Group on Applied Digital Technology in Medicine
[3]Future Innovation Science and Technology

ABSTRACT

The study of mind-wandering is popular since it is linked to the emotional problems and working/learning performance. In terms of education, it impacts comprehension during learning which affects academic success. Therefore, we sought to develop a machine learning model for an embedded portable device that can categorize mind-wandering state to assist people in keeping track of their minds. We utilize a low-channel EEG to record the brain state and to build the predictive model because of its practicality and user-friendly. Most machine learning experiments in mind-wandering using EEG exhibit good individual-level performance. For the group-level technique, only a few research has developed a model. As a result, the goal of this research is to achieve a high-accuracy group-level model. Thus, Leave One Participant Out Cross Validation (LOPOCV) was used to assess the model correctness. This study shows that using a baseline normalization technique assists feature extraction and improves performance. The model was built using a support vector machine (SVM), and the best model achieved an accuracy value of 75.6 percent.

KEYWORDS

Mind-Wandering, Electroencephalogram, Support Vector Machine, Time-Frequency Analysis

1. INTRODUCTION

Mind-wandering is your thought that does not relate to current activity, commonly occurs in everyday life (Killingsworth and Gilbert, 2010). Your mind flew away to the past, future, or impossible occurrence while doing some tasks repeatedly. If you are mind-wandering during classroom instruction, you will miss out on lessons. This event is a negative impact on your retention and recognition. Some studies supported that it can cause faulty scenes and reduce working performance (Giambra, 1995) . Moreover, some research advocated that mind-wandering correlates with an emotional disorder, such as neuroticism, alexithymia, dissociative, and depression (Watts and Sharrock, 1985, Baer et al., 2006, Jensen et al., 2016). Thus, this study aimed to establish a machine learning model for an embedded portable device that can classify mind-wandering in real-time to help people monitor their minds.

To access mind-wandering sessions, two conceptual protocols are used to collect data. Firstly, it is called probe-caught sampling. This technique collects data by randomly sampling question subjects while doing a determined task repeatedly. The question is whether they are mind-wandering during an experiment in the previous ten minutes (Smallwood et al., 2007). This method has a drawback since people are intermittently aware of mind-wandering (Schooler et al., 2011). So, some sessions of mind-wandering were mistakenly reported (Pelagatti et al., 2020). To get rid of this issue, self-caught sampling was introduced. The self-caught sampling is a method that a subject performs a determined task repeatedly. If the subject is aware of mind-wandering during an experiment, report the mental state by pushing a button. This research used the self-caught sampling method to obtain dataset. The protocol is described in the next section.

After getting the protocol, we selected a biological instrument to record mind-wandering data. Hasenkamp (Hasenkamp et al., 2012) studied mind-wandering using functional magnetic resonance imaging (fMRI), which measures brain activity by monitoring variations associated with blood flow. There is a fluctuation of brain function between focus and mind-wandering during focus-attention meditation with breath counting.

Furthermore, pupil diameter and electroencephalogram (EEG) can detect mind-wandering (Pelagatti et al., 2020, Dhindsa et al., 2019). This study has chosen a few-channel EEG device, which measures electrical activity on the scalp. The reasons are portable usability function and affordable price.

There are several studies on mind-wandering using EEG. Smallwood and Beach et al. studied the effect of mind-wandering on time series EEG signals. They found the different amplitude of the P300 ERP component, which represents brain response of sensory, cognitive, or motor event (Kam et al., 2012). Braboszcz and Delorme discovered that the mind-wandering effect on EEG power frequency bands. Theta (4-7 Hz) and delta band (2-3.5 Hz) are increasing, but alpha (9-11 Hz) and beta band (15-30 Hz) are decreasing (Braboszcz and Delorme, 2011). This study applied machine learning to the EEG dataset. Due to the limitation of the device's resources, we selected the support vector machine (SVM) model. Moreover, SVM is suitable for real-time systems (Anh et al., 2012) and is the best classification performance (Lotte et al., 2007).

2. MATERIAL AND METHOD

This section describes research procedures in five parts, such as data acquisition, data cleansing, feature selection, model classification, and performance evaluation. The explanation is below.

2.1 Subject and Procedure

2.1.1 Subjects

We acquired the data from Future Innovation Research Science and Technology (FIRST) (Viriyopase, 2021, in preparation), which contains datasets from 22 right-handed subjects (male =12, female =10). They got Chulalongkorn University poster information. The subjects are 42.64(SD=7.39) years old on average, without any history of psychological disorder. This is confirmed by a PHQ-9 score below or equal to 4 (Kroenke et al., 2001). The subjects must give informed consent.

2.1.2 Procedure

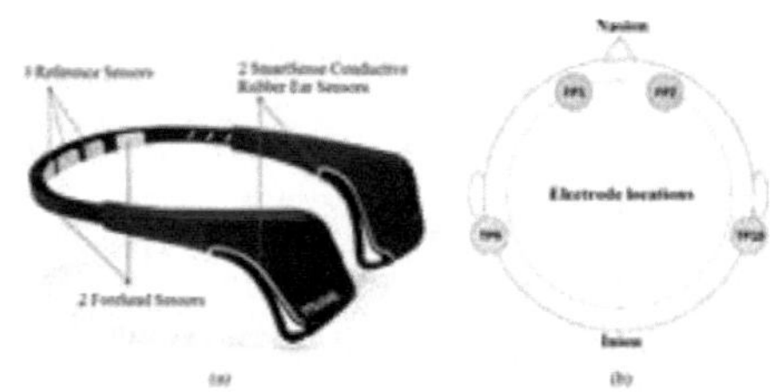

Figure 1. Muse EEG recording device and its electrode positions (Liu et al., 2020)

Recording EEG Data, we used InteraXon MUSE 2016. The signals originate from AF7 and AF8 silver active electrode, and TP9 and TP10 conductive-silicon-rubber active electrode (referenced position with UI 10-10 system)(Jurcak et al., 2007). The instrument and the electrode position are shown in Figure 1. The EEG signal has a 256-Hz sampling rate and 12-bits scale resolution. The protocol for getting data is shown in Figure 2 and can be described as follows.

The data collecting protocol is modified from Braboszcz's study (Braboszcz and Delorme, 2011). A participant sits down, relaxes, and closes his/her eyes for 2 minutes before starting an experiment. The participant pushes a button to start the trial, then the start of trial session sound beeps randomly between 5-10 seconds. After the participants hear the sound, focus on the breath by counting 1 to 10 repeatedly. If he/she is aware that he/she does not concentrate on counting-breath during the trial, presses the button to report a mind-wandering and finished the trial session. All subjects repeatedly experiment for no more than 3 hours to prevent fatigue.

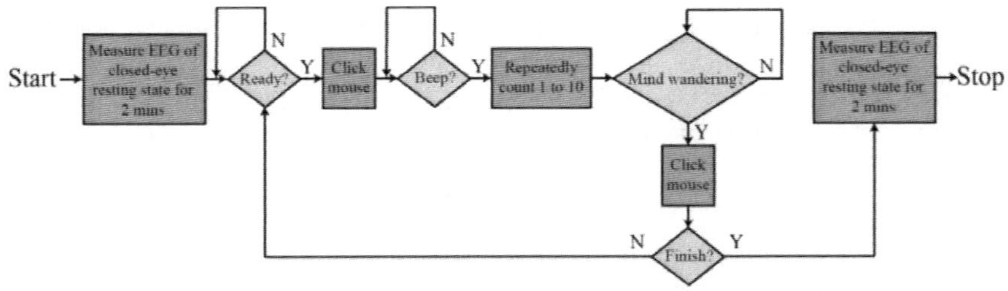

Figure 2. The EEG data acquisition protocol (Viriyopase, 2021, in preparation)

2.1.3 Data Structure

The data of each experiment contains 4-channel EEG time-series data (TP9, AF7, AF8, TP10) with a 512 Hz sampling rate. The data is recorded from EEG between starting session and reporting end session, which is shown in figure 3.

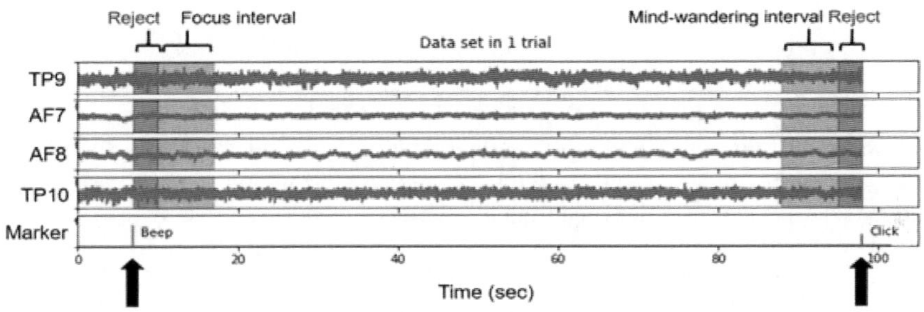

Figure 3. The dataset of each experiment

2.2 Data Cleansing

We considered that the subject was focus (FS) on the breath for 2 to 10 minutes after the short beep occurring. Mind-wandering (MW) is a duration between -10 to -2 minutes before pushing the report. We applied a bandwidth filtering of 0.5-30 Hz and rejected data with the artifact by the following criteria. The average value of electrode TP9 and TP10 with 50ms time window was gradients with greater than 10 μV/ms or difference of more than 100 μV (Krigolson et al., 2017). Finally, we got 990 cleaned interval data from 22 subjects (495 FS and 495 MW samples) which are usable for creating the model.

2.3 Feature Selection

We implemented time-frequency analysis and baseline normalization to create a feature vector of each data sample. Firstly, we select Morlet wavelet convolution in time frequency because of low computational complexity (Cohen, 2019). A complex Morlet wavelte equation is

$$w = e^{2i\pi ft}e^{\frac{-t^2}{2\sigma^2}},$$

when w is a product between a complex sine wave and a Gaussian window. i is an imaginary number. f is the frequency in Hz. t is time in seconds (define t from -2 to +2 seconds). σ is the width of the Gaussian, which are defined as:

$$\sigma = \frac{n}{2\pi f},$$

when n is a number of cycles, which affect the precision of temporal resolution and frequency resolution (define n is 1.5 to 8.0 round at frequency 3 to 30 Hz with linearly increasing (Braboszcz and Delorme, 2011)).

After we acquired time-frequency sample data, it has a problem that the power in all frequency does not have the same scale because of 1/f phenomenal and the difference of person, electrode, and trial. Baseline normalization is used to get rid of this issue. Secondly, we applied three baseline normalization methods (Cohen, 2014).

- Decibel conversion (dB_{tf}) is the ratio between the power activity of each frequency and the baseline power activity of each frequency. The equation is

$$dB_{tf} = 10log10\left(\frac{activity_{tf}}{\overline{baseline_f}}\right),$$

when $\overline{baseline_f}$ is an average of the power activity of each frequency in baseline time. $activity_{tf}$ is power activity of frequency f and time t.

- Percentage change and baseline division ($prctchange_{tf}$) is a percent of the power activity relate to baseline. The equation is

$$prctchange_{tf} = 100\frac{activity_{tf}-\overline{baseline_f}}{\overline{baseline_f}}.$$

- Z-transform (Z_{tf}) is power activity scaling in the standard deviation unit of the baseline period. The equation is

$$Z_{tf} = \frac{activity_{tf}-\overline{baseline_f}}{\sqrt{n^{-1}\sum_{i=1}^{n}\left(baseline_{if}-\overline{baseline_f}\right)^2}},$$

when $baseline_{if}$ is the power activity of baseline at frequency f and time i. This study employs two minutes of closed eyelids before beginning an experiment as a baseline period.

The normalized sample was calculated from the mean power values in five frequency bands with time epoch of 2, 4, 6, and8 seconds.

Eventually, we got five-frequency-band features (size of matrix is 5 features x 990 samples) with varying four-electrode positions, four-time-window size, and three baseline normalization techniques conditions. We would find the best condition for modeling in the performance evaluation topic.

2.4 Model Classification

We select the support vector machine (SVM). This model is a supervised learning model which construct an optimal separating hyperplane for classification. The dataset (D) for the training model contains five features and 990 samples with the defining condition of electrode positions, time window size, and baseline normalization techniques.

$$D = \{(\vec{x}_i, y_i); i = 1,2,\dots,990\},$$

when $\vec{x}_i = [x_{i1}, x_{i2}, \dots, x_{i5}] \in R^5$ is a feature vector of sample i^{th}. $y_i \epsilon \{1, -1\}$ is a class label.

The SVM decision function (f) can be defined as follow.

$$f(x) = sign(\vec{w}.K(\vec{x},\vec{z}) + b),$$

when b is a bias. $\vec{w}$ is the weight vector of the feature vector after converting with a kernel function ($K(\vec{x},\vec{z})$), low-dimensional transforms into the high-dimensional features. We select the linear kernel and radial basis function kernel (RBF), which give high performance in previous BCI application studies (Lotte et al., 2007).

Linear kernel can be defined as

$$K(\vec{x},\vec{z}) = \vec{x}.I,$$

when I is an identity matrix.

RBF kernel can be defined as

$$K(\vec{x},\vec{z}) = [e^{-\gamma\|\vec{x}_1-\vec{z}_1\|^2}, e^{-\gamma\|\vec{x}_2-\vec{z}_2\|^2}, \dots, e^{-\gamma\|\vec{x}_u-\vec{z}_u\|^2}],$$

when $\vec{z} = [\vec{z}_1, \vec{z}_2, \vec{z}_3, \dots, \vec{z}_u]$ is the vector of landmark, assist in feature dimension transformation (5-D to u-D). γ is a parameter that regulates model simplicity.

The optimal separating hyperplane is to maximize the margin of the parallel line. Each line is closed to the support vectors of different class. The margin maximizes when we minimize the following:

$$Minimize\frac{1}{2}\|w\|^2 + C\sum_{i=1}^{N}\xi_i ,$$

when $(w^T K(\vec{x},\vec{z}) + b) + \xi_i - 1 \geq 0$,$\xi_i \geq 0, i = 1,2,\dots,N$. $\xi_i$is an error of the sample ith.C is a parameter that is a trade-off between error smallness and model simplicity.

We used a grid search to find best C and γparameters. This searching technique examines all parameter competitors to get the best performance of the model.

2.5 Performance Evaluation

The studies of machine learning in mind-wandering using EEG mostly achieved high performance in the individual-level analysis (Kawashima and Kumano, 2017, Jin et al., 2019, Dhindsa et al., 2019). Few studies establish a model in the group-level method (Jin et al., 2020). Thus, this study aims to achieve a group-level model with high accuracy score. To accomplish this goal, we suppose that the baseline normalization technique will directly influence the predictive models.

We practiced leave-one-participant-out-cross-validation (LOPOCV) to evaluate the performance of all models with various conditions and parameters. LOPOCV provides a test/train dataset, leave one subject out from the total dataset as testing data and the other 21 subjects as training data. The cross-validation iteratively operates until each participant is test data once. The averaged accuracy values of all cross-validation indicate the model performance. The model had conditions that varied in time window lengths, baseline normalization methods, electrode positions, parameters, and kernel types. The result will discuss in the next section.

3. RESULT

We implement LOPOCV to the model by varying condition on the 990 samples (495 FS and 495 MW samples). We design the study in 3 parts as follows:

3.1 Performance Comparison of Varied Electrode's Position

We used data with a time window length of 8 seconds. The data is not normalized. We create the search gride model of each electrode's position and compare them.

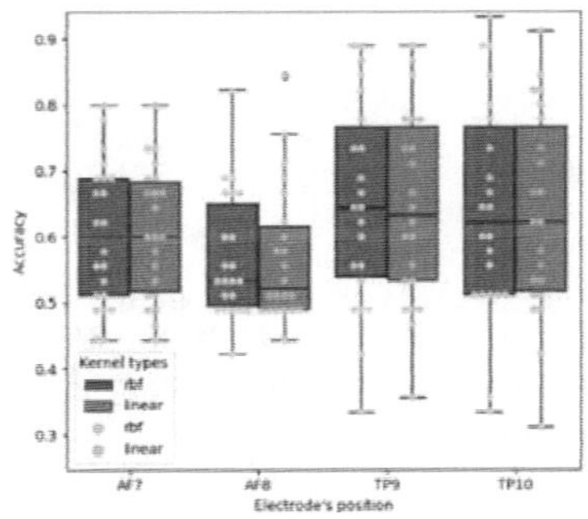

Figure 4. The model cross-validation accuracy values of each electrode and kernel type (without baseline normalization, time window length = 8 seconds)

This collection of boxplots in figure 4 depicts the accuracy distribution of both SVM kernels and the electrode placements of four electrodes. AF7, AF8, TP9, and TP10 have the average linear of SVM accuracy values of 0.61, 0.57, 0.63, and 0.64, respectively, and have average non-linear SVM accuracy values of 0.60, 0.56, 0.64, and 0.65, respectively. For all kernel types, the results show that the electrode positions of TP9 and TP10 perform better than AF7 and AF8.

3.2 Performance Comparison of Varied Baseline Normalization

To study the effect of baseline normalization with the predictive search gride models, we used data with a time window length of 8 seconds, electrode's position (TP9, TP10), and varied baseline normalization types.

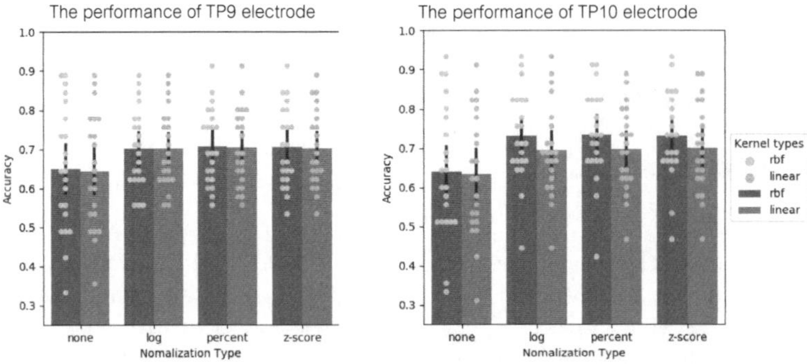

Figure 5. The model cross-validation accuracy values of each baseline normalization method and kernel type (time window length = 8 seconds). The left side is the performance of the TP9 electrode, and the right side is the performance of the TP10 electrode

The performance of each baseline normalization method of TP9 and TP10 location in Figure 5 is shown in bar graphs. The results demonstrate that models constructed from data with normalized baseline perform better than those built from data without normalization in both electrode position TP9 and TP10.

3.3 Performance Comparison of Varied Time-Window Length, Electrode's Position, and Baseline Normalization

The goal of this study was to find the optimum SVM model condition and parameter. To build each model, we change the electrode's location, baseline normalization, and time-window length. The top ten models with the best performance are shown in table 1.

Table 1. The Accuracy, precision, recall, area under curve, baseline normalization, and model parameter of each combination electrodes (top ten best performance)

electrode	Accuracy	precision	recall	area under curve	Baseline	C	γ	$K(\vec{x},\vec{z}$	win
TP10	**Avg = 0.756,** Sd = 0.104	Avg =0.803, Sd = 0.132	Avg = 0.685, Sd = 0.216	Avg = 0.756, Sd = 0.102	z-score	1000	1	rbf	4
TP9,TP10	**Avg = 0.755**, Sd = 0.107	Avg = 0.792, Sd = 0.139	Avg = 0.686, Sd = 0.235	Avg = 0.756, Sd = 0.106	log	100	0.125	rbf	4
AF7,TP10	**Avg = 0.752**, Sd = 0.103	Avg = 0.804, Sd = 0.129	Avg = 0.684, Sd = 0.223	Avg = 0.752, Sd = 0.102	log	100	1	rbf	4
TP10	**Avg = 0.747**, Sd = 0.100	Avg = 0.804, Sd = 0.141	Avg = 0.667, Sd = 0.202	Avg = 0.748, Sd = 0.098	percent	1000	1	rbf	4
TP10	**Avg = 0.745**, Sd = 0.095	Avg = 0.808, Sd = 0.136	Avg = 0.661, Sd =0.198	Avg = 0.746, Sd = 0.094	log	1000	1	rbf	4
TP10	**Avg = 0.743**, Sd = 0.111	Avg =0.806, Sd = 0.148	Avg = 0.651, Sd = 0.241	Avg = 0.744, Sd = 0.111	log	1000	1	rbf	6
TP9,TP10	**Avg = 0.742**, Sd = 0.100	Avg =0.797, Sd = 0.131	Avg = 0.670, Sd = 0.225	Avg = 0.744, Sd = 0.100	percent	100	0.1	rbf	4
TP10	**Avg = 0.742,** Sd = 0.117	Avg =0.790, Sd = 0.173	Avg = 0.659, Sd = 0.240	Avg = 0.743, Sd = 0.116	percent	1000	1	rbf	6
TP10	**Avg = 0.742,** Sd = 0.108	Avg =0.803, Sd = 0.134	Avg = 0.656, Sd = 0.249	Avg = 0.742, Sd = 0.107	z-score	1000	1	rbf	6
All	**Avg = 0.740,** Sd = 0.096	Avg = 0.785, Sd = 0.126	Avg = 0.684, Sd = 0.217	Avg = 0.741, Sd = 0.095	log	100	0.125	rbf	4

The values which indicate the model performance are represented with bold style.
Avg, Average; Sd, Standard division; log, Decibel conversion; percent, Percentage change and baseline division; z-score, Z-transform.

We vary electrodes condition with one, two, and every positions. The result shows that the best model constructs from the dataset of TP10 electrode, 4 seconds time window length, log baseline normalization, and non-linear kernel. The performance measure of the best model is in the Figure 6.

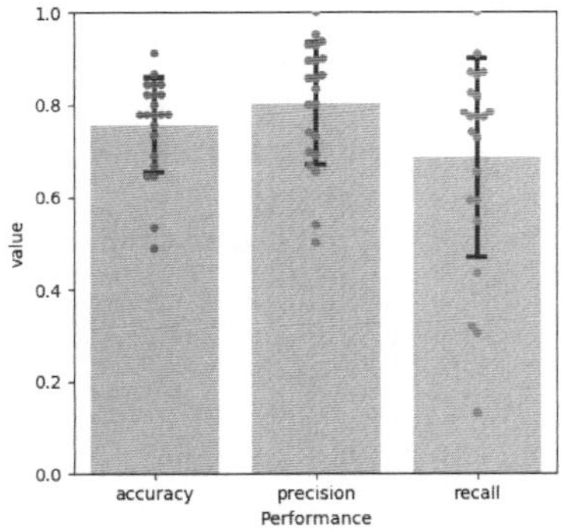

Figure 6. The cross-validation performance values of the best model conditions

In Figure 6, we presented the accuracy, precision, and recall of the best model. The model evaluates via LOPOCV. The dot plot overlay the bar is the performance of each validation round.

4. CONCLUSION

In this study, baseline normalization is employed for the first time in the feature extraction process for detecting Mw using low-channel EEG data. One advantage of this normalization technique is to enhance the feature for the group-level predictive model. Moreover, the predictive model constructs from low-channel EEG helps the device to convenient and easy to use. We applied LOPOCV to the 22-participant data and find the best conditions and parameters of the model. The study showed that the model with normalized baseline has higher performance than those without normalization. The best accuracy score is 75.6 % with 4-seconds time-window length, z-score baseline normalization, TP10 electrode's position, and non-linear SVM kernel.

Although our group-level analysis model can reveal the pattern of the brain associate with mind-wandering, the number of subjects is 22. In the future study, we would increase the number of participants to make the model more generalize. We hope that the application of this study helps people to observe their though. The students can take advantage of it to improve their cognition and retention. These are good for their learning or education.

REFERENCES

Anh, V. H., et al., 2012. A real-time model based support vector machine for emotion recognition through EEG. In: *2012 International Conference on Control, Automation and Information Sciences (ICCAIS).* IEEE, pp. 191-196.

Bare, R. A., et al. (2006) Using self-report assessment methods to explore facets of mindfulness. *Assessment,* Vol. 13, No. 1, pp 27-45.

Braboszcz, C. and Delorme, A., 2011. Lost in thoughts: neural markers of low alertness during mind wandering. *Neuroimage,* Vol. 54, No. 4, pp 3040-3047.

Cohen, M. X., 2014. *Analyzing neural time series data: theory and practice.* MIT press.

Cohen, M. X., 2019. A better way to define and describe Morlet wavelets for time-frequency analysis. *NeuroImage,* Vol. 199, pp 81-86.

Dhindsa, K., et al., 2019. Individualized pattern recognition for detecting mind wandering from EEG during live lectures. *PloS one,* Vol. 14, No. 9, pp e0222276.

Giambra, L. M., 1995. A laboratory method for investigating influences on switching attention to task-unrelated imagery and thought. *Consciousness and cognition,* Vol. 4, No. 1, pp 1-21.

Hasenkamp, W., et al., 2012. Mind wandering and attention during focused meditation: a fine-grained temporal analysis of fluctuating cognitive states. *Neuroimage,* Vol. 59, No. 1, pp 750-760.

Jensen, C. G., et al., 2016. General inattentiveness is a long-term reliable trait independently predictive of psychological health: Danish validation studies of the Mindful Attention Awareness Scale. *Psychological Assessment,* Vol. 28, No.5, pp e70.

Jin, C. Y., et al., 2019. Predicting task-general mind-wandering with EEG. *Cognitive, Affective, & Behavioral Neuroscience,* Vol. 19, No.4, pp 1059-1073.

Jin, C. Y., et al., 2020. Distinguishing vigilance decrement and low task demands from mind-wandering: A machine learning analysis of EEG. *European journal of neuroscience*.

Jurcak, V., et al., 2007. 10/20, 10/10, and 10/5 systems revisited: their validity as relative head-surface-based positioning systems. *Neuroimage,* Vol. 34, No. 4, pp 1600-1611.

Kam, J. W., et al., 2012. Mind wandering and motor control: off-task thinking disrupts the online adjustment of behavior. *Frontiers in human neuroscience,* Vol. 6, pp 329.

Kawashima, I. and Kumano, H., 2017. Prediction of mind-wandering with electroencephalogram and non-linear regression modeling. *Frontiers in human neuroscience,* Vol. 11, pp 365.

Killingsworth, M. A. and Gilbert, D. T., 2010. A wandering mind is an unhappy mind. *Science,* Vol. 330, No. 6006, pp 932-932.

Krigolson, O. E., et al., 2017. Choosing MUSE: Validation of a low-cost, portable EEG system for ERP research. *Frontiers in neuroscience,* Vol. 11, pp 109.

Kroenke, K., et al., 2001. The PHQ-9: validity of a brief depression severity measure. *Journal of general internal medicine,* Vol. 16, No. 9, pp 606-613.

Liu, R., et al., 2020. A Pilot Study on Electroencephalogram-based Evaluation of Visually Induced Motion Sickness. *Journal of Imaging Science and Technology,* Vol. 64, No.2, pp 20501-1-20501-10.

Lotte, F., et al., 2007. A review of classification algorithms for EEG-based brain–computer interfaces. *Journal of neural engineering,* Vol. 4, No. 2, pp R1.

Pelagatti, C., et al., 2020. A closer look at the timecourse of mind wandering: pupillary responses and behaviour. *PLoS one,* Vol. 15, No. 4, pp e0226792.

Schooler, J. W., et al., 2011. Meta-awareness, perceptual decoupling and the wandering mind. *Trends in cognitive sciences,* Vol. 15, No. 7, pp 319-326.

Smallwood, J., et al., 2007. The lights are on but no one's home: Meta-awareness and the decoupling of attention when the mind wanders. *Psychonomic bulletin & review,* Vol. 14, No. 3, pp 527-533.

Viriyopase, A., 2021(in preparation). Catch mind wandering by deep learning.

Watts, F. N. and Sharrock, R., 1985. Description and measurement of concentration problems in depressed patients. *Psychological Medicine,* Vol. 15, No. 2, pp 317-326.

EXPLORING STUDENTS' COMPUTATIONAL THINKING FOR MATHEMATICAL PROBLEM-SOLVING: A CASE STUDY

Nils Kristian Hansen and Said Hadjerrouit
University of Agder, Institute of Mathematical Sciences, Kristiansand, Norway

ABSTRACT

The purpose of this paper is to investigate students' engagement in computational thinking (CT) and programming with MATLAB when solving a mathematical task in a programming course at the undergraduate level. The data collection method is participant observation of three groups of three students presented with a mathematical task to solve. The study uses a deductive-inductive analysis strategy based on the interplay between the theoretical framework and the empirical data. The results reveal that engaging students in CT for mathematical problem-solving is challenging for many reasons: Lack of mathematical thinking (MT), insufficient experience with CT, and more importantly lack of deeper connection between CT and MT. Conclusions are drawn from the results to promote mathematical problem-solving by means of CT and MT at the undergraduate level.

KEYWORDS

Algorithm, Computational Thinking (CT), Mathematical Thinking (MT), Mathematical Problem-Solving, Programming

1. INTRODUCTION

Computational thinking (CT), mathematical thinking (MT) and programming are increasingly relevant aspects of undergraduate students in science studies. A primary motivation for introducing CT practices into mathematics classrooms is the rapidly changing nature of competencies of the discipline required for future work in society and the professional world. To benefit from CT, students need to investigate the way in which CT interacts with their reasoning about mathematical concepts. This study explores students' engagement in CT, MT and programming activities when solving mathematical problems.

The article is structured as follows. Firstly, the theoretical framework is outlined. Secondly, the context of the study, research question, methods, and task are described. Thirdly, the empirical results are analyzed and discussed. Finally, the limitations of the study and future work conclude the article.

2. THEORETICAL FRAMEWORK

Computational thinking (CT) represents a "universally applicable attitude and skill set everyone, not just computer scientists, would be eager to learn and use'' (Wing 2006, p. 33). Accordingly, CT is a fundamental skill for virtually any discipline, including mathematics, physics, engineering, etc. It may have far reaching practical implications from which mathematics in particular can benefit.

2.1 Computational Thinking (CT)

Wing (2014) characterizes CT as "the thought processes involved in formulating a problem and expressing its solution(s) in such a way that a computer—human or machine—can effectively carry out". Mistfelt & Ejsing-Duun (2015) describes CT as the ability to work with algorithms understood as systematic and structured descriptions of problem-solving and construction strategies. Likewise, Filho and Mercat (2018) defines algorithmic thinking as the process of solving a problem step-by-step in an effective, non-ambiguous and organized way that can be translated into instructions to solve problems of the same type by an individual or a computer. Csizmadia et al. (2015) emphasizes the role of logical reasoning in CT to make sense of problems through thinking clearly and precisely. It allows students to draw on their own knowledge to analyze problems, design algorithms, build, test, debug, and correct programs derived from the algorithm and associated solution to the problem. More precisely, CT means to engage in several cognitive processes with the goal of solving problems efficiently and creatively (Csizmadia et al., 2015; see also Wing (2006)). Firstly, it is the ability to think algorithmically, that is a way of getting to a solution to the problem step-by-step. Secondly, it is a way of thinking about problems in terms of decomposition of their components into manageable units that can be understood, solved, developed, and evaluated separately. Thirdly, CT is associated with generalization in terms of identifying patterns, similarities, and connections, and exploiting those features to generalize the problem-solving process to similar problems. In other words, generalization is a way of solving new problems based on previous solutions, building on prior experience, and generalizing these experiences. Fourthly, CT uses abstraction to make problems easier to think about. Abstraction is the process of making problems more understandable through reducing unnecessary details. Finally, CT makes use of evaluation, which is the process of ensuring that the problem-solving process, whether an algorithm or program, is fit for the purpose.

2.2 Computational Thinking, Mathematical Thinking, and Programming

Connecting CT and programming to MT in a meaningful way is at the heart of tackling mathematical problem-solving in a technological environment. The connection between CT and MT is not new and has a legacy of over 45 years in the theory of constructionism (Papert & Harel, 1991). Likewise, the connection of computer programming and CT with MT has been recognized since the development of the Logo programming language (Shodiev, 2015). In other words, CT and programming complement MT as a way of reasoning to solve mathematical problems (Wing, 2006). According to Shute, Sun, and Asbell-Clarke (2017, p. 145), MT consists of three parts: "beliefs about math, problem solving processes, and justification for solutions". MT involves the "application of math skills to solve math problems, such as equations and functions" (Ibid, p. 145). The authors conclude that MT and CT have a lot of communalities: problem solving, modelling, data analysis and interpretation, and statistics and probability (p. 145). As a result, with the use of CT and computers, the relationship between modelling, analysis, and solution of mathematical problems has changed, and it is becoming increasingly important (Buteau, et al., 2018).

The close connection between MT and CT provides opportunities for building efficient algorithms for mathematical problem-solving as a structured step-by-step construction processes that can be implemented using programming languages (Topallia & Cagiltay, 2018; Wing, 2008, 2014). More specifically, mathematical problem-solving through CT involves expressing a solution by means of decomposition in its parts, abstraction by removing unnecessary details, generalization from previous experiences, algorithmic thinking and transformation into a program that can be evaluated (Csizmadia et al, 2015). The challenge is to engage students in a mathematical problem-solving process through CT by designing effective algorithms that can be translated into efficient computer programs that can be tested, modified, and improved iteratively. There is also a clear connection between CT and coding, but CT is not the same as programming, but being able to program is a result of being able to think computationally (Shute, Sun, & Asbell-Clarke, 2017; Wing 2006). Rooted in these theoretical considerations, a model of mathematical problem-solving is elaborated inspired by Hadjerrouit and Hansen (2020). Figure 1 illustrates the model and demonstrates four points.

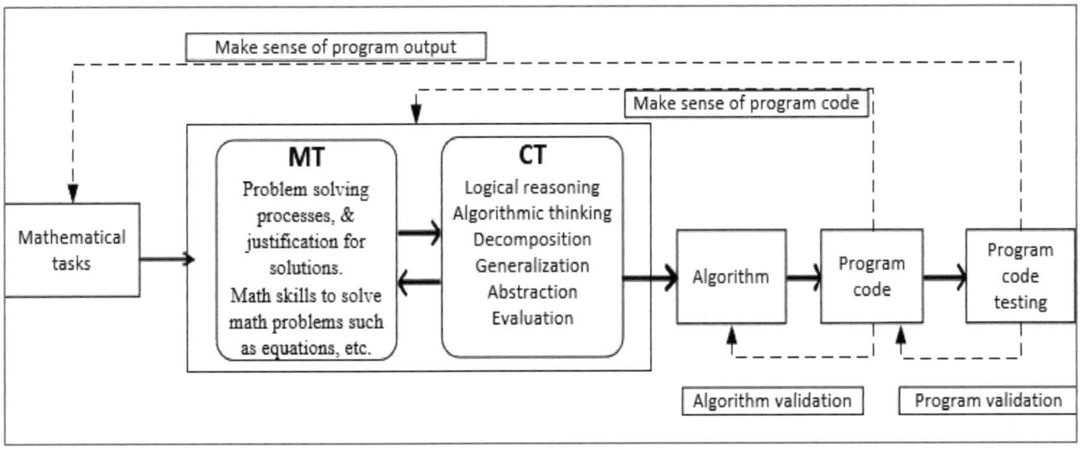

Figure 1. A model for mathematical problem-solving combining MT, CT, and programming and their interactions

Firstly, it is a pre-requisite that students have a good understanding of mathematical concepts and a capability for abstract reasoning and logical deduction to benefit from CT. Secondly, CT should in turn enable students to logically analyze, abstract, and decompose mathematical problems and design an algorithm step-by-step before programming it. Thirdly, students should be able to translate the mathematical solution and associated algorithm into programming code that can be tested and evaluated. Finally, the solution process should be generalized to a variety of similar problems.

This is not a linear model that starts from a mathematical problem and ends up with program code testing. It is rather an iterative model with feedbacks to previous processes to make sense of program output or validating the algorithm, etc. It is also particularly important to consider interactions between MT and CT. Using this model, the goal is to gather and analyze data on students' CT and MT, and programming activities. It is particularly important to look at the way students approach mathematical problem-solving with a range of MT skills in mind such as abstract reasoning and logical thinking, but without thinking computationally automatically, and how CT may help to decompose the problem and making it more understandable through abstraction, and generalization of the problem-solving process.

3. THE STUDY

3.1 Context of the Study, Research Question, and Methods

This work is a single case study conducted in the context of a first-year undergraduate course on programming with applications in mathematics. The participants were a convenience sample consisting of 9 students volunteering from a class of 50, enrolled in the course in 2020. The students had varied knowledge background in mathematics, but no experience with CT. The course introduced the basic constructs of the MATLAB programming language, e.g., single variables, arrays, control flow statements and functions. The course also discussed major steps in systems development, i.e., analysis, design, implementation, and testing. Ultimately programming was used for numerical analysis, and the concept of CT was briefly introduced through a worked example.

The research question addressed in this paper is: How do students engage in CT, MT and programming activities when participating in group work for solving a mathematical problem in a first-year undergraduate course?

The main data collection method is participant observation of three groups, each consisting of three students with varying knowledge in mathematics. The students were presented with a mathematical task to solve, while responding to questions in dialogue with the teacher on the solving process, by means of CT, MT, and programming activities. Open-ended questions were also used to gain a deeper understanding of the process.

The analysis of the results seeks indications of students' engagement in CT and MT when solving mathematical tasks. It uses a deductive-inductive strategy based on the interplay between the theoretical framework and the empirical data (Patton, 2002).

3.2 The Task

The task for the group work was: "Write a MATLAB-function calculating the circumference of a triangle, based on the coordinates of its three corners." This is feasible by calculating the length of each side of the triangle and adding the results, a task which may be considered to be composed of a mathematical and a computational part. The mathematical part consists of calculating the length of a triangle side based on the coordinates of the corners. This may be done by using the Pythagorean theorem, i.e., given two corners, $C_1: (x_1, y_1)$ and $C_2: (x_2, y_2)$, employing the distance formula $D = \sqrt{(x_2 - x_1)^2 + (y_2 - y_1)^2}$, as illustrated in figure 2.

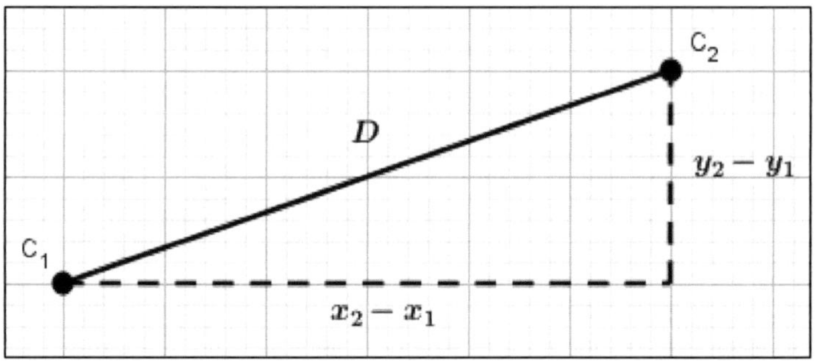

Figure 2. Employing the Pythagorean distance formula

The computational part consists of formulating an algorithm for systematically applying the distance formula to the triangle sides and adding the results. This involves creating a control flow structure for repeated use of the distance formula, i.e., a loop, as well as a selecting a convenient data structure for representing the coordinates of the corners.

3.3 Group Work Activities

The group work consisted of three sessions with three students in each, scheduled for 45 minutes. It took place in the video conferencing system Zoom (https://zoom.us/), due to corona restrictions. The sessions were recorded and transcribed. The task was introduced in the Zoom chat at the beginning of each session, and the students were asked to reflect on it and engage in a discussion on the solving process. When required, the teacher outlined steps, asked questions, and gave hints. In all groups one of the students undertook the task of coding in MATLAB, sharing screen with the others.

4. RESULTS

The results describe how the participating students engaged in solving the task, with focus on the mechanisms outlined in figure 1. During the work, the teacher suggested test coordinates based on the triangle shown in the GeoGebra screenshot in figure 3. In the following the teacher is referred to as T, and the students as S1 – S9.

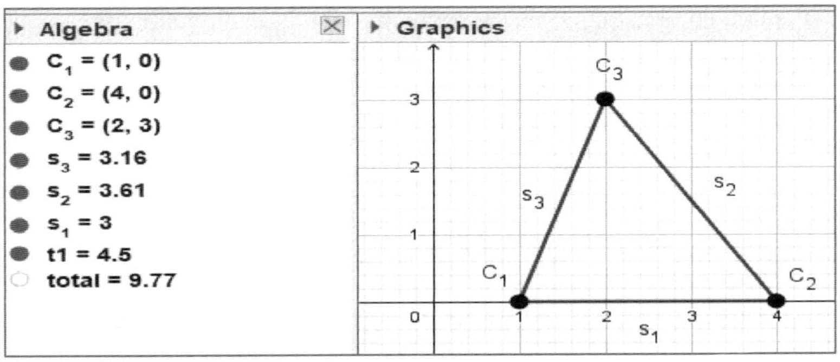

Figure 3. Triangle test coordinates

During work the students faced the problem of the end points of the sides of a triangle being numbered modularly, i.e., 1-2-3-1, whereas the loop variable progresses linearly, i.e., 1-2-3-4. A calculation modulo 3 is a good MT solution to the problem, but because MATLAB array indexing starts at 1 instead of 0, implementing the calculation in program code is a bit awkward. An alternative solution is adding a dummy point 4 with coordinates equal to point 1 to the test data.

4.1 Group 1

T presents the task, and when there is no response, prompts the students for a suggestion on how to attack it.

After a minute S1 suggests calculating the distance between the corners and then adding them. But without a clear distinction between the tasks involved. When T wants to know what to start with, S1 suggests finding a length, though with imprecise wording. At this stage, the students struggle with the initial process of understanding what the mathematical problem consists of, and they are unable to use MT and CT to model and decompose the task.

None of the students are able to suggest a method for calculating the length. When T mentions Pythagoras, S1 argues that the triangle then has to be right-angled, confusing the interior angles of the triangle with the angle to be constructed on each side, as in figure 2. Considerable elaborations from T are required to correct the misunderstanding. This shows that though the Pythagorean theorem supposedly is well known to the students, they are unable to use MT to employ it in practice without lengthy instructions.

Once the idea of calculating the length of a triangle side by Pythagoras is established, an algorithm for doing the calculation may be formulated. However, there is no student initiative to take the process further. T then starts a discussion on what type of variable that would be best suited for the coordinates, thus taking a step into the process of producing program code. S2 and S3 engage in the discussion, and after some hints from T agree to that using an array will facilitate the use of a loop. At this point S2 and S3 show that they now are able to outline the major steps in an overall algorithm:

T: (...) if we have a table, we can have a loop variable, and then we can traverse that table coordinate by coordinate.

S3: Yes.

S2: Yes, and then we do Pythagoras.

T: Yes.

S2: Step by step.

Responding to a question from T on whether it would be easier to generalize the algorithm to a polygon with an arbitrary number of corners, S2 again demonstrates to have grasped the general idea:

S2; When we are using a loop, all that is needed is adding some numbers to the array. Almost.

The students now describe the structure of an algorithm, but it is vague in detail, unsuitable for programming and testing. To continue there is a need to reduce the complexity of the algorithm, typically deciding on starting by calculating the length of one side only. T attempts to discuss this with the students, but eventually needs to suggest the solution:

T: (...) in the first version of the program, would you try to include everything, or would you construct it bit by bit?

S2: Eh, I would have tried to include all at one time. And then checked if it worked or not. And then, after that, if it works, I would have tried to find points where it could be improved.

T: Yes. Do you think a good strategy would be to calculate the length of a single side and make that work first, and then extend it to the triangle?

S2: Yes, that would have been a good idea.

S2 now suggests starting writing program code, and shares screen with MATLAB programming environment. On instructions from T S2 creates arrays with test coordinates based on the triangle in figure 3. With some assistance from T S2 creates a syntactically correct MATLAB function skeleton, but then work stops. T reminds of the suggestion made earlier:

T: Well, what do you feel the next step should be? We did agree not to do everything at the same time?

Still after this allusion to how to simplify the algorithm, there is no response. The students seem unable to perform the transition between algorithm and program code. T suggests calculating the change in x-coordinate between corner one and two. S2 then types "xdiff = x2 - x1". By this S2 appears to have switched to a pure MT-context because, though mathematically sound, the variable names x2 and x1 do not exist in the MATLAB function. S3 appears to see the difficulty, and is able to, assisted by T, instruct S2 on replacing x1 and x2 with the proper array variables. The students are however not able to translate the mathematical distance formula into MATLAB-code without strong hints from T.

The code is now tested, and MATLAB correctly outputs s_1 as in figure 3. When T suggests testing with corners 2 and 3 instead, S2 is able to replace the array indexes and test again. The test is successful.

Now an entire cycle in figure 1 is completed. MT has been used to determine that Pythagoras may be used to calculate the distance between two corners, CT has been used in producing an algorithm, the algorithm has been implemented in MATLAB-code, the code has been tested, and the output has been verified to make sense mathematically, in form of the length of triangle sides.

T now wants the students to engage in extending the program to calculate the circumference of the entire triangle, but work does not progress, not even when T reminds of the consensus on using a loop. T has to provide detailed instructions on how to merge the distance formula with the loop. But then S3 realizes that the loop variable, n, must be used to identify the triangle corners, and S1 employs MT to establish that if n is a natural number, the subsequent natural number is $n + 1$, and uses CT to apply this to two succeeding corners.

S3 now states that there will be a range error when $n = 3$. T postpones the problem by suggesting setting the upper loop boundary to $n = 2$.

To make the students attack the problem of making the algorithm accumulate the side lengths, strong engagement from T is again required. But finally, S3 is able to instruct S2 on how to implement the mechanism required. The program is tested, and correctly outputs $s_1 + s_2$ as in figure 3.

When T brings up the problem of the index becoming 4, S1 again employs MT and suggests modulo calculations. T acknowledges the idea but suggests using CT and adding a test corner 4 with equal to test corner 1. The program is tested and correctly outputs the circumference of the triangle, $s_1 + s_2 + s_3$, as in figure 3.

When T ends the session by asking the students to sum up the steps taken in creating the final MATLAB program, there is no response. They thus seem unable to articulate the process of using MT and CT in problem solving.

4.2 Group 2

At the start of the group work S6 suggests Pythagoras as a method to calculate the length of the triangle sides. T suggests tables as variable types for the coordinates. There is some confusion on how to provide test data, so T asks if somebody can start MATLAB. By doing this T goes straight to the programming phase, without prior elaboration on MT and CT.

S4 starts MATLAB, sharing screen. When T invites the students to suggest test data, S6 gives an odd comment:

S6: (...) We probably want some coordinates that are equal, some that are negative, some that are positive.

One may suspect that S6 here mechanically refers to a test strategy appropriate in the context of previous exercises, without abstracting, generalizing, and adapting the strategy to the context in question.

T provides the test coordinates from figure 3. S6 and S4 now engage in a discussion, and are able to create a function skeleton with only a few hints from T.

T then reverts to MT and demonstrates on figure 2 how the length of a triangle side may be calculated from the corner coordinates.

The students are unable to give a reasonable suggestion on how to split the task into subtasks, and T suggests starting by calculating a single side length. Now the students will need to use CT to implement this calculation. S6 is able to instruct S4 on what to type with very little intervention from T. The result is correct apart from that the length calculated is not assigned to the function's return variable. S4 is however able to correct the problem when T draws attention to MATLAB warnings.

The program is tested and correctly outputs the length of s_1 as in figure 3. Now T asks the students what the next step should be. S6 responds:

S6: We should probably do that for the rest of … find an expression then… probably a loop doing this for the remaining sides.

T: Yes, why do you suggest a loop?

S6: Because then you can take from point one to point three, or side one to side three.

T: Yes.

S6: A for-loop then, since you know the fixed values and the fixed steps between. That performs that operation three times, so that you do not have to write that operation for the three different points.

Though the students initially were unable to suggest loop as a control flow structure, S6 is now able to describe it in detail. Thus, after producing some program code, S6 reverts to CT and is able to extend the algorithm.

With only a few hints from T S6 instructs S4 on how to program the loop. A transition to MT/CT is then required to employ the loop variable, n, in indexing the corners. When T suggests replacing index 2 with $n + 1$, S4 is able to replace all four indexes correctly without further instructions.

The code is tested, and MATLAB outputs an array-out-of-bounds message. S6 immediately identifies the problem as $n + 1 = 4$ when $n = 3$, but suggests correcting it by setting $n = 2$ as upper loop bound, apparently unaware that this will cause the third triangle side to be skipped. T however allows the correction.

MATLAB now outputs the length of s_2 as in figure 3. When T demonstrates on figure 3 that s_1 and s_2 are not added, S6 is able to use CT and describe the algorithm extension required.

MATLAB now outputs the length of $s_1 + s_2$ as in figure 3. To include s_3, S6 first reverts to CT and suggests adding an extra instance of the distance formula. But when T relates the indexes to the triangle sides, S6 employs MT and suggests using a modulus calculation. T accepts this as a good strategy but suggests adding a corner 4 equal to corner 1, as a quick fix. MATLAB now outputs the correct circumference of the triangle as in figure 3.

When summing up S6 is able to describe how to extend the function to work on an arbitrary polygon, and also to articulate the steps undertaken in the task just completed. S6 is however not quite able to articulate a test strategy.

4.3 Group 3

When the group initially is asked to reflect on how to attack the task, S7 correctly suggests calculating the distances between the corner points and adding them, though incorrectly referring to the distances as "absolute values". T comments that S7 has mentioned two subtasks, but none of the students seem able to use CT in a systematic way to identify the tasks, even after hints. And only after a 3-minute demonstration from T on figure 2 does S9 suggest using Pythagoras to calculate a side length.

Also, even after strong hints from T, the students are unable to suggest neither test strategy nor a suitable data structure for test coordinates. Temporary single variable test coordinates are then created for corner 1 and 2.

S9 starts programming in MATLAB, sharing screen, and is able to establish a syntactically correct function skeleton, but work progresses no further. When T suggests calculating change in x-value, S9 makes the same mistake as S2 in group 1, using non-existent variable names. T is required to point out the problem, but S9 then is able to make corrections. After T uses MATLAB warnings to point out that the calculated distance is not assigned to the return variable, S9 corrects this also, and a test run outputs the length of s_1 as in figure 3.

T now invites the students to consider a more suitable data type for the coordinates. S7 and S9 realizes there will be a problem "to get in all the coordinates" but have no further suggestions. When T suggests arrays, S9 is however able to, with hints from T, implement the necessary changes in the MATLAB-code. S9 now raises the question of the sequence of the two corners used to calculate dx and dy:

S9: Is it number two minus number one, or what?

T: Does it really matter? Does anybody have an opinion on that? What would have happened if we swapped 1 and 2?

S7: We would have gotten another number.

S9: It would be negative.

T: Yes. We would have gotten opposite sign.

S9: Minus two. Yes.

The discussion continues, but the students are unable to employ MT to articulate that swapping two corners simply causes a change in sign, which is unimportant since the value later is squared.

Work stops. On request from T on a natural next step, S7 suggests adding the lengths, but there is no further progress. Even when T asks the students to reflect on mechanisms used in previous exercises, nobody realizes the need for a loop. T is required to give detailed instructions.

S9 seems to understand that the loop variable n will have to be used in identifying the corners, and after a hint from T is able to use MT and CT to make the adaptations required.

Now the problem with the loop variable being out of bounds arises. S9 is able to identify the problem, but there is no switch to MT to come up with modulo calculation. T then suggests adding a corner 4 equal to corner 1 to the test coordinate array.

Now a test run outputs s_3 as in figure 3. Referring to the figure, T explains what has been calculated, and what should have been calculated, hinting that the same kind of problem has been solved in previous exercises. S9 realizes that a mechanism for accumulating the side lengths is required but is unable to implement it. S8 suggests employing a variable named "sum-of-series". In the context of many previous exercises this has been a sensible name, but it absolutely does not fit the current context. S8 thus demonstrates a lack of ability to abstract, generalize and adapt a mechanism used in other settings.

Eventually T has to instruct S9 on how to implement the mechanism for adding the side lengths. The program is tested and outputs the correct circumference of the triangle in figure 3.

Ultimately T asks the students how they would attack the problem on their own. S9 would have thought about it a bit, then started to program. When asked about taking all at once, says to go by it part by part, but is unable to identify the parts. When T asks how the solution is generalizable to arbitrary polygons, S9 is able to provide an adequate answer. This demonstrates a certain ability to used CT in solving a task, but the ability has major flaws.

5. DISCUSSION AND IMPLICATIONS

The main findings of this study are twofold. Firstly, the introduction of CT to students at the undergraduate level presents many challenges for teachers committed to improving students' MT. Secondly, the mathematical task presented to the students to develop their MT and CT skills was challenging for novice learners for many reasons, considering their minimum prior knowledge of CT and programming, their varied mathematical knowledge levels, and mathematical problem-solving skills. This study produced interesting findings and implications for further research, which can be summarized as follows according to the categories and key principles of the theoretical framework.

Mathematical problem, MT-CT interactions: Most students struggled with the initial process of understanding what the mathematical problem task consisted of, and as a result were unable to use MT and CT to model and decompose the task without the teacher's guidance. It appears from the students' responses that the lack of MT hindered them in making sense of the task and develop a problem-solving strategy translatable into an algorithm. The transition between MT and CT was also challenging, even though these thinking processes are based on logical reasoning, as stated in the theoretical framework. As a result, the interaction between MT and CT was not straightforward and at times very challenging and incoherent. Most students were unable to identify the problem until the teacher pointed it out. Guided by the teacher, some students were able to translate the identified mathematical expression into correct MATLAB-code, but without the mediation of CT.

Transition algorithm – code: As a consequence of the lack of MT, most students failed to use CT to develop an algorithm step-by-step, or presented a solution only as program code without an explicit algorithm description and associated steps to be taken in obtaining a solution. Some students were able to use CT and describe an algorithm and program code. However, they often switched rapidly to the programming phase, without further elaboration on creating a coherent algorithm. The transition between algorithm and MATLAB-code was thus challenging as the students struggled with implementing the algorithm in the form of MATLAB code.

CT – algorithm-decomposition: When students managed to develop some sort of algorithm, they were often unable to reduce the complexity of the algorithm or simplify it and re-construct it step-by-step or decompose the task in smaller sub-tasks. Likewise, the direct transition from MT to code without the mediation of CT did not work well, e.g., the translation of the mathematical distance formula into MATLAB-code.

Program code: When it comes to programming, many students were able to understand the program after it had been developed under the guidance of the teacher. However, extending the program based on extensions to the algorithm proved difficult. For example, once the need for a loop was established, the students struggled with integrating the loop with the previously coded distance formula. It is worth noting however, that in one case a student, initially unable to see the need for a loop, after producing some preliminary program code was able to revert to CT and describe the mechanism required in detail.

Abstraction – Generalization: The results also show that generalization was difficult, as the students showed low ability to abstract, generalize and re-use programming concepts known from previous exercises in another context. For instance, the students needed strong guidance to see the need for a loop, and in some cases suggested reusing mechanisms unmodified from previous exercises. Likewise, few students were able to generalize the algorithm or extend the program to work on arbitrary polygons.

Code evaluation: Finally, students struggled with code validation and testing. On request from the teacher, most students were initially not able to suggest a test strategy, and ultimately, they were unable to describe the test strategy actually employed during the group work.

Implications from the results indicate that a requirement for engaging in mathematical problem-solving through CT and programming is a solid foundation in both MT and CT, as well as an understanding of the interaction between the two. More precisely, to make MT interact better with CT, a learning environment around first-year undergraduate mathematics courses should be well designed to ensure a smooth integration of CT and MT. Moreover, the learning environment should promote explicit CT processes that expose students to logical and algorithmic thinking, decomposition, generalization, abstract reasoning, and evaluation. This is the key in deciding how to introduce CT at the undergraduate level and assist students in learning to think computationally. A learning environment where students engage in CT associated with appropriate learning activities and varied and intrinsically motivating tasks that are suited to their mathematical knowledge level may lead to greater involvement and learning progression, and hopefully improved learning outcomes as well. Such a learning environment is powerful in providing more opportunities for students to develop their own understanding of CT and programming concepts. In other words, it lays the ground for learning autonomy. On the other hand, student autonomy cannot be fully expected for novices without good knowledge background in MT and familiarities with CT and programming. Moreover, as this study shows, the role of a knowledgeable teacher in MT and CT is still important to assist students in designing algorithms and implementing computational solutions for mathematical problem-solving. In this regard, there will be a need for professional development for teachers that enhances not only their understanding of CT, but also about the ways in which CT interacts with MT. A final implication of this research is the need to reconsider the interactions between MT, CT, and programming because the findings show more overlaps than what was proposed in the model in figure 1. Indeed, a more in-depth examination of the interactions between CT and MT is necessary to highlight their communalities and potential differences and suggest some modifications to the proposed model.

6. LIMITATIONS AND FURTHER WORK

The number of participants (*N=9*) of out of 50 students from one class is limited to generalize the results. Hence, a larger number of participants from one or several classes could have been more appropriate to achieve higher generalization. Nevertheless, the data analysis method used in this article to generate a large and in-depth set of qualitative data seems to be justified for addressing the research question and associated issues on CT, MT, and programming critically.

Future work will include a study exploring the implications of a learning environment with explicit focus on CT and MT in a larger number of groups to ensure more reliability and validity of the results.

REFERENCES

Buteau, C., et al. (2018). Computational thinking in university mathematics education: A theoretical framework. In A. Weinberg, et al. (Eds.), *Proceedings of the 21st annual conference on research in undergraduate mathematics education* (pp. 1171–1179). San Diego, CA: RUME.

Csizmadia, A. et al. (2015). Computational thinking: A guide for teachers. Retrieved from https://eprints.soton.ac.uk/424545/1/150818_Computational_Thinking_1_.pdf

Filho, P., & Mercat, C. (2018). Teaching computational thinking in classroom environments: A case for unplugged scenario. In V. Gitirana, et al. (Eds.). *Proceedings of Re(s)sources 2018 - Understanding Teachers' Work Through Their Interactions with Resources for Teaching* (pp. 296-299). Lyon: France.

Hadjerrouit, S. & N.-K. Hansen (2020). Students engaging in mathematical problem-solving through computational thinking and programming activities: A synthesis of two opposite experiences. *Proceedings of the 17th international conference on cognition and exploratory learning in the digital age (CELDA 2020),* pp. 91-98.

Misfeldt, M., & Ejsing-Duun, S. (2015). Learning mathematics through programming: An instrumental approach to potentials and pitfalls. In K. Krainer, & N. Vondrová (Eds.). *Proceedings of CERME 9* (pp. 2524-2530). Prague, Czech Republic.

Papert, S., & Harel, I. (1991). *Constructionism*. Norwood, NJ: Ablex Publishing.

Patton, M. Q. (2002). *Qualitative research & evaluation methods*. London: Sage Publications.

Shodiev, H. (2015). Computational thinking and simulation in teaching science and mathematics. In M. G. Cojocaru et al. (eds.). *Interdisciplinary Topics in Applied Mathematics, Modeling and Computational Science.* Springer Proceedings in Mathematics & Statistics 117, pp. 405-410

Topalli, D., & Cagiltay, N. E. (2018). Improving programming skills in engineering education through problem-based game projects with Scratch. *Computers & Education 120*, pp. 64-74.

Shute, V.J., Sun, C., & Asbell-Clarke, J. (2017). Demystifying computational thinking. *Educational Research Review*, pp. 1-10.

Wing, J.M. (2006). Computational thinking. *Commun. ACM 49*(3), pp. 33–35.

Wing, J. M. (2008). Computational thinking and thinking about computing. *Philosophical Transactions of the Royal Society of London A: Mathematical, Physical and Engineering Sciences*, *366*(1881), pp. 3717-3725.

Wing, J. M. (2014, January 9). Computational thinking benefits society. *Social Issues in Computing,* 40th Anniversary Blog, University of Toronto. Retrieved from

http://socialissues.cs.toronto.edu/index.html%3Fp=279.html

EXPLORING NUMBAS FORMATIVE FEEDBACK FOR TEACHING AND LEARNING MATHEMATICS: AN AFFORDANCE THEORY PERSPECTIVE

Said Hadjerrouit and Celestine Ifeanyi Nnagbo
University of Agder, Institute of Mathematical Sciences, Kristiansand, Norway

ABSTRACT

The purpose of this article is to explore students' and teachers' perceptions of affordances, and their actualization while interacting with the e-assessment system Numbas and its effect in terms of formative feedback delivery. The article uses affordance theory and a qualitative research design approach to analyze data using semi-structured interviews. Eight interviews were conducted with six students and two teachers. The results reveal the actualization of several affordances such as ease of use and navigation, variation in mathematical contents, congruence to textbook mathematics, support for pen and paper skills, learner autonomy and motivation to engage in mathematical problem-solving. Conclusions and future work based on comparative studies are drawn from the results to promote Numbas formative feedback for teaching and learning mathematics.

KEYWORDS

Affordance Actualization, Affordance Perception, Affordance Theory, Constraint, Formative Feedback, Numbas

1. INTRODUCTION

In recent years, Numbas is becoming increasingly popular due its wide acceptability and integration into mathematics education, which is evident from about thirty institutions around the world, including the United Kingdom and Norway that are currently using the software tool. Clearly, this increased attention on the use of Numbas to provide timely feedback to students learning mathematics underscores the relevance of studies on its affordances. However, except one article (Hadjerrouit, 2020b), there is a lack of research providing an understanding of affordances and constraints of Numbas as a tool of feedback delivery between teachers and students. The aim of the present study is to investigate the affordance perceptions of Numbas (as a tool of formative assessment) by teachers (who employ Numbas for feedback delivery) and students, and the associated constraints in the actualization of the affordance (Nnagbo, 2020). In specific terms, this study aims to address the following research questions: a) What affordances of Numbas are *perceived* by students and teachers? b) How are the affordances of Numbas *actualized* by students and teachers? and c) What are the *constraints for the actualization* of Numbas' affordances by students and teachers?

The article is structured as follows. First, Numbas is described. Second, the theoretical framework is outlined, followed by methods. Then, the results and discussion are presented. Finally, some remarks on limitations of the study and future work conclude the article.

2. NUMBAS

Among the most popular e-assessment systems is Numbas (a typical interface in shown in Figure 1), developed by the e-learning unit of Newcastle university's school of mathematics and statistics with focus on formative e-assessment (Lawson-Perfect, 2015). A test "consists of several questions, each of which consisting of one or more parts which assess an individual answer entered by the student" (Lawson-Perfect, 2015, p. 1).

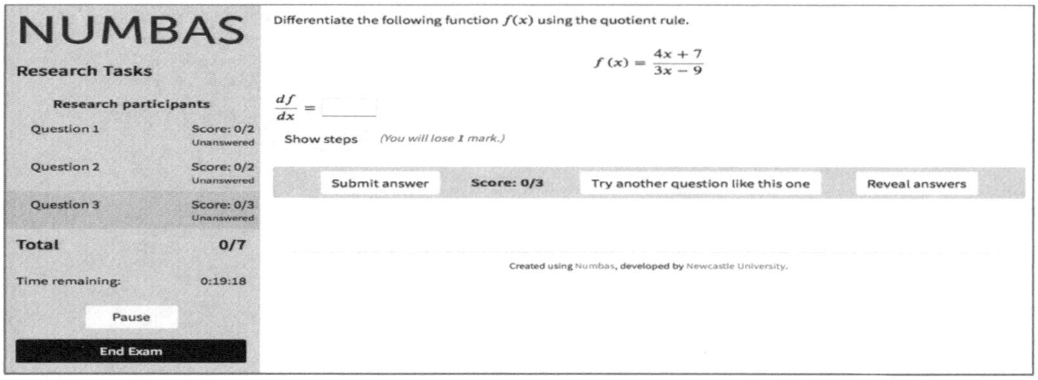

Figure 1. A typical Numbas user interface

The most important features of Numbas are as follows:

Question types - Numbas allows several question-and-answer types such as mathematical expression, Number entry, matrix entry, match text pattern, choose one from a list, choose several from a list, match choices with answers, gap-fill, information only, quantity with units, are supported by Numbas (Lawson-Perfect, 2020). Numbas shows the notation instantly beside the input field, so as students are inputting their answers in the system, simultaneously they see how the system understands their expressions (Figure 2).

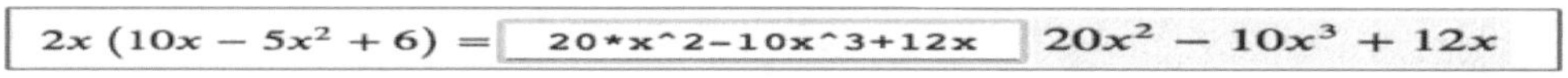

Figure 2. The student's answer and how Numbas reads it

Ease of integrating rich content materials - Numbas supports videos and interactive diagrams to be embedded on the editor before they are distributed along with the final questions. The videos can be uploaded directly, while the interactive diagrams could be included in Numbas questions either by embedding a GeoGebra applet or use JSXGraph (Lawson-Perfect, 2020).

Marking - Numbas uses marking algorithm that is conceptually simple to mark mathematical expressions. For example, in factorizing a quadratic equation, expected answers are often in this form (x+a)(x+b) and not x^2+ax+b, but Numbas marking algorithm is sophisticated enough to understand the later form, mark correctly and give feedback accordingly.

Feedback - Numbas performs marking on the client, which makes its feedback immediate. In order to make its feedback effective, there are multiple ways Numbas gives feedback to both students and instructors. These include submit answer, show steps, reveal answers, try another question like this one.

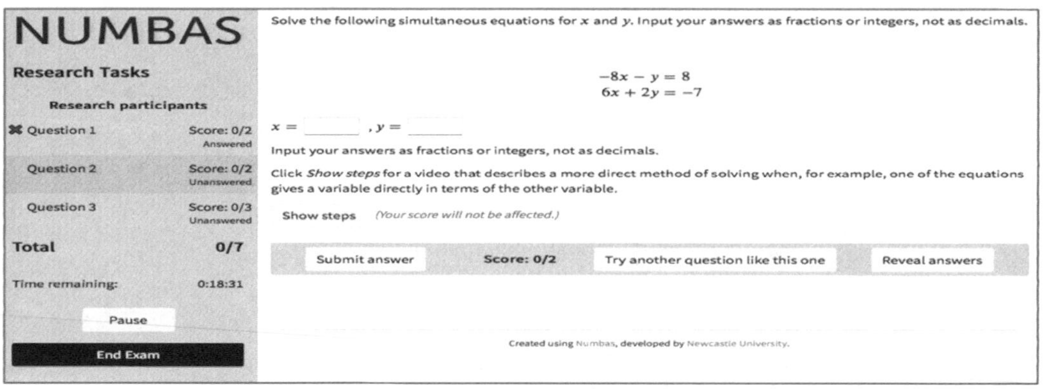

Figure 3. Feedback options

Submit answer - Students get instant feedback as soon as they submit an answer. The feedback simply indicates with a green color 'good' sign if the submitted answer is correct, with red color 'bad' sign indicating that the supplied answer is wrong, or partially correct, with feedback message underneath. The students will also be shown the maximum attainable score for each question, and their own score for the question after they have submitted the answer. The teacher may choose to disable these feedback options.

Show steps - When a student clicks on the show steps, Numbas will give the general solution to that question, it may include video or graphical explanation depending on the kind of feedback the examiner put in there. This is a way of reminding the student to have a look at the formula or the general solution and retry solving the task. Show steps does not give students the exact solution to the particular task.

Try another question like this one - Numbas uses the set of variables defined by arbitrary mathematical expressions to randomly generate questions that are similar. With this, student have the opportunity to attempt similar questions many times until they feel confidence enough to move to the next question.

Reveal answer - This section provides step by step solution that is personalized to the question randomly generated question to the student. When a student decides to explore this option, they lose all the marks and cannot re-attempt the exact question. Again, the instructor may decide to disable this.

Statistics - Numbas stores data of students' performance. This statistical package is particularly helpful to the teachers. They can track how well the students understand the topic through their performances, and they can equally identify the tasks students perform below expectations and reemphasis on them in the next class.

3. THEORETICAL FRAMEWORK

The term 'affordance' was coined by James J. Gibson, a perceptual psychologist, in his book titled '*the Ecological Approach to Visual Perception*', first published in 1977. He proposed the term to describe what the environment offers the animal (Gibson, 1986, p. 127). He argued that affordance can be seen from the properties of the environment that are relative to the animal in question. He further stresses that affordance must be peculiar to the animal it affords; not just any property of the environment or whatever the environment can offer. Affordances can be both objective and subjective, "they are objective because they exist independently of the act of perception, but they are also subjective because the frame of reference is the individual's action capabilities" (Osiurak, Rossetti, & Badets, 2017).

The term "affordance" in the world of Human-Computer Interaction (Norman, 1988) refers to a goal-oriented action potential that emerges as result of interaction between subjects (e.g., students and teachers) and an object (e.g., Numbas). This perspective is in accordance with the conceptualization of affordance by Strong et al. (2014) who defined it as "the potential for behaviors associated with achieving an immediate concrete outcome and arising from the relation between an artifact and a goal-oriented actor or actors" (p. 69). Affordance is neither the property of an object in isolation nor that of the subject. Instead, it emerges as an offshoot of a dynamic interaction between the subjects (students and teachers) and the object (Numbas). It is perceived (i.e., students and teachers are aware of the existence of the action potential of Numbas) in many ways and actualized (i.e., students are able to turn the potential of Numbas into action) to produce effect (i.e., feedback delivery) depending on many factors that include the Numbas platform, its user interface, capability of the students, and their level of preparedness (Markus & Silver, 2008). Moreover, the actualization of Numbas affordance is either facilitated by some enabling conditions or mitigated by some constraints.

Given the emergence of the Numbas affordance, it is legitimate to ask how the affordance is perceived. As such, when students interact with Numbas to facilitate feedback delivery on some mathematics concepts they do so conveniently with the aid of the technical features of the software. During this process, they become aware of the affordance that emerged during the interaction in terms of feedback delivery. The next issue is how they can actualize this affordance. Yet, this issue raises three questions: (a) How do action potentials turn into actions? (b) Are the perception and actualization processes distinct? (c) Does an action potential necessarily need to be perceived before being actualized?

Affordance actualization is a process of turning action potentials (affordances) into real actions to bring an effect in using a particular tool (Anderson & Robey, 2017; Bernhard et al., 2013). In specific terms, affordance actualizations are "the actions taken by actors as they take advantage of one or more affordances through their use of the technology to achieve immediate concrete outcomes in support of organizational goals" (Strong et al., 2014, p. 70). To turn a possibility into an action, it is expected that the user has the ability and capability to harness the potential and there are enabling conditions to facilitate the process. Affordance actualization varies from one individual to another because it is goal-oriented and a process of specificity. As Volkoff and Strong (2017) wrote "actualization relates to a particular individual actor and details regarding the specific actions that actor will take or has taken" (p. 236). Two or more students may interact with Numbas, for instance, and actualize different affordances of the software depending on their respective individual differences and choices.

Some researchers maintain that the two processes are the same and by implication affordance may be actualized without being perceived (Strong et al., 2014; Volkoff & Strong, 2013; Wang et al., 2018). In contrast, some other researchers maintain that actualization is a different process from perception of affordance, as such, affordances are perceived before being actualized (Anderson & Robey, 2017; Bernhard et al., 2013; Pozzi et al., 2014; Thapa & Sein, 2018). This study acknowledges that affordance perception and actualization are two distinct processes, and, in most cases, affordances are perceived before being actualized as shown in Figure 4. Anderson and Robey (2017, p. 102) summarizes this line of thought: "Affordance actualization in practice is not fully explainable through perception and goals alone because there are times when a user is both aware of an affordance and has a current goal that the affordance could support, and yet the affordance is not actualized".

Moreover, it is expected that following the actualization of Numbas affordance are some consequences (effects). These consequences as Bernhard et al. (2013) put it may be "intended by the user and/or those by the original creator of the artefact as well as unintended effects" (p.6). It is important to remark that the perception and actualization of affordances happen very fast, which could be a reason why a clear distinction is not easy to sustain. It is expected that when affordances are perceived and then actualized, then some effects are generated in terms of feedback delivery on mathematical tasks to students. Figure 4 shows the underlying framework that captures the perception, actualization of Numbas affordance, and its effect.

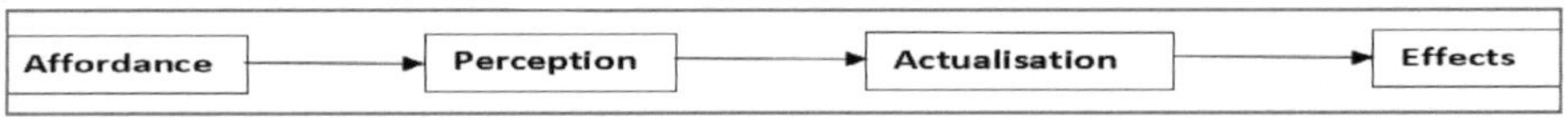

Figure 4. A framework for perception, actualization of Numbas affordance, and its effect

Based on these considerations, this study proposes a framework for assessing Numbas affordances. The framework encompasses the following layers: (a) Technological affordances at the ergonomic level; (b) Pedagogical affordances at three levels: Assessment, mathematics subject, student/mathematics tasks/classroom; and (c) Socio-cultural affordances at the teacher education level. The framework (Figure 5) relies basically on Hadjerrouit (2020a) for the conceptualization of its constituent parts.

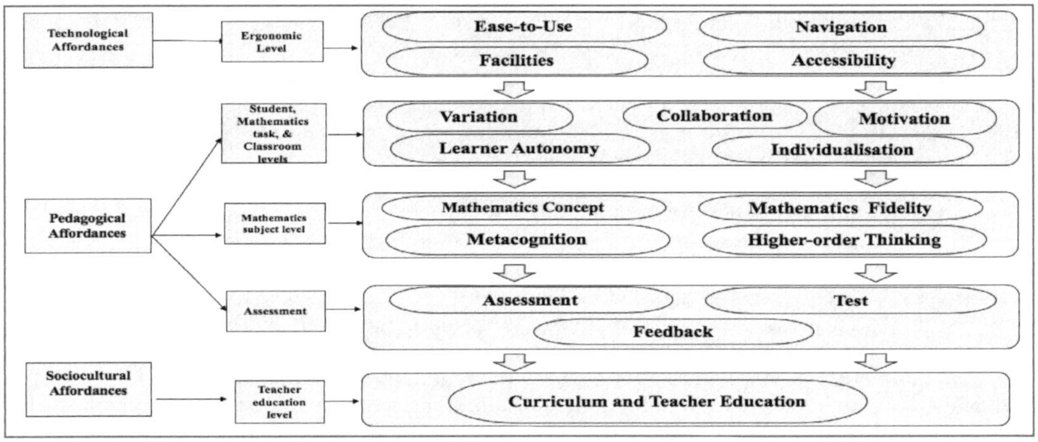

Figure 5. Framework for assessing Numbas affordances and constraints

4. METHODS

A case study design approach is chosen to understand and analyze the affordances perceived by both students and teachers while interacting with Numbas, how they actualized the perceived affordances, and the relevant criteria for the actualization. A case study involves "detailed examination of one setting, or one single subject, (…), or one particular event" (Bogden & Biklen, 1982, p. 58). A case study is the preferred strategy to answer 'how' and 'why' questions, as well as the type of 'what' questions that are expository in nature (Yin, 2009). Thus, these are in line with the research questions of this study.

4.1 Participants

The data collection was done from two set of participants - Two teachers and six students from a mathematics teacher education class of a Norwegian university. The two teachers were considered and selected because they are actively making use of Numbas for formative assessment in their respective classes. The second cohort is six out of about twelve students from one class who willingly volunteered to participate in the study. These participants are master's degree students. They were currently taking a course entitled "Digital tools in mathematics teaching". Both cohorts were familiar with Numbas and affordance theory.

4.2 Data Collection and Analysis Methods

Prior to data collection by means of interviews, a survey questionnaire was used to collect information based on the categories of the theoretical framework for assessing Numbas affordances and constraints (Figure 5). The students' responses to the questionnaire were then used to inform the subsequent interview guide and associated questions in relation to the theoretical framework.

A thematic approach is used to analyze the empirical data by identifying, analyzing, and reporting codes and themes within the data set (Bryman, 2016). Code development takes a deductive-inductive strategy based on the interplay between the empirical data and the pre-defined categories of the framework. The analysis starts with a deductive approach based on the categories of the framework in search for meaningful interpretation of the empirical data following an inductive approach. An example of coding is as follows:

Pre-defined categories from the theoretical framework (Figure 5): *Assessment, Test, and Feedback*

Deductive approach: *Use these pre-defined categories about the feedback Numbas offers to the participants, which includes feedback when teachers are creating tasks and during the period students are solving tasks.*

Inductive approach based on empirical data: *(...) first you can show steps, which show you how you are supposed to do it, not how you supposed to solve that same task, just general solution and general set of rules, and afterwards you can see then the actual solutions, if you want to (...)*

As the process evolves, room was given for the data to express itself by creating new codes that emerged from the data inductively. The development of inductive codes follows reading and rereading of the data carefully and annotating same to identify topics raised by participants themselves. The topics (codes) are refined and validated by checking whether these are repeated by different participants or highlighted by the participants themselves as an important theme (Hennink et al., 2020).

5. RESULTS

5.1 Summary of Results

The findings show that many affordances that emerged were perceived and actualized while some were not actualized at all or partially actualized due to some constraints. Firstly, most students perceived and actualized the technological affordances while interacting with Numbas. They also indicated that they were motivated when they used Numbas. They attributed their motivation to clean interface and good feedback. Furthermore, they think that they can work on Numbas independently but that heavily relies on how comprehensive the feedbacks are. The role of teachers to make these feedbacks was pointed out. Most students believed that collaboration and differentiation are low in Numbas, but that the teacher can make them work by asking the students to work in groups using one computer and creating different levels of tasks that will target different learning abilities of their students. They also expressed that their pen and paper skills develop simultaneously while using Numbas. Finally, they think Numbas can be adapted as part of digital tools in Norwegian schools, specifically for assessing procedural understanding.

Secondly, all the teachers indicated that the technological affordances were perceived and actualized, except the editor's interface which they think is easy to make simple tasks and difficult to make complex tasks. Teachers also agreed that the elements of pedagogical affordances were globally perceived and actualized.

They reported that students are motivated to engage in Numbas due to the instant feedback and other feedbacks. Furthermore, they expressed high satisfaction with the feedback they receive from Numbas in form of statistics of students' activities. Moreover, teachers believed that Numbas cannot guarantee total autonomy. Finally, a constraint also was actualized in the form of wrong marking of some correct answers, though in rare occasions, but this was found to provoke deep mathematical thinking in most of students.

Thirdly, the findings suggest that students and teachers are on the same page in most of the affordances and constraints of Numbas, except for ease of use, learner autonomy and suitability to the new core curriculum. While teachers found Numbas difficult to create 'very good' tasks, students found the user interface simple to use. Teachers further think that their role cannot be replaced by Numbas. Students believed that with comprehensive feedback, they can work independently on Numbas. Teachers are indecisive about adopting Numbas to the Norwegian schools, but the students indicated that Numbas is suitable to part of the digital tools, where it will be used for testing procedural understanding.

5.2 Affordance Emergence, Perception, Actualization, and Effect of Feedback

The goal of this study is to explore how Numbas promotes formative assessment for mathematics teaching and learning by assessing the affordances and constraints that emerge from interactions between teachers/students and Numbas. Having addressed Numbas affordances and constraints (Research question 1 and 2), the next question, which this paper addresses is how these affordances do, from teachers' and students' views, promote formative assessment, and ultimately mathematics teaching and learning. According to the theoretical framework, the actualization of Numbas affordances lead to some effects for teaching and learning of mathematics as a result of formative feedback delivery to the user. The essence of formative assessment is to receive formative feedback that will lead to improvement in teaching and learning. Therefore, formative feedback is vital to improving mathematics teaching and learning (Pereira et al., 2016).

However, the desired goal (formative feedback delivery) does not manifest straight away. In fact, it manifests as a consequence or effect of the actualized affordances. Figure 4 explains this relationship. It shows that achieving the goal (formative feedback delivery) that is needed to improve teaching and learning of mathematics subject depends on perception and actualization of the emerged affordances of Numbas by the students or teachers. If they fail to actualize the affordances, the intended goal may not be achieved.

While the goal of students is to receive feedback from teachers through Numbas. Therefore, formative feedback delivery is the common goal, but the ultimate goal, which is the implication of the formative feedback delivery is to improve teaching and learning of mathematics subjects. From the model, the desired goal (formative feedback delivery) does not manifest straight away. It manifests as a consequence or effect of actualization of Numbas affordances. Recall that the emergence of Numbas affordance is viewed as an offshoot of a dynamic relationship between students/teachers and Numbas, and perception of the emerged affordances concerns its awareness by students/teachers. Whereas actualization is the action taken by the students/teachers to take advantage of the perceived affordances.

When the students/teachers actualize some required affordance(s), then the effect will lead to achieving the goal (formative feedback delivery) and by extension improves teaching and learning. For example, when a student wants to solve formative assessment at home using Numbas, her goal is to achieve formative feedback through Numbas. However, she must first actualize the affordance of accessibility. If the student faces constraint of internet connection, then the effect will be that she will not achieve her goal (formative feedback delivery) because she could not actualize an important affordance required. But if the student actualizes the affordance by accessing the internet, she may achieve the goal, however this is subject to actualizing other feedbacks (e.g., ease of use, navigate) she might also need to successfully achieve the goal.

6. DISCUSSION

The results reveal that first, both teachers and students globally share the same views regarding technological affordances of Numbas. They perceived and actualized ease of use, ease of navigation, accessibility, and facility's affordances of Numbas. The effect of this is that the students' engagement increased; they became motivated to solve more formative assessment tasks in Numbas. The number of times they are allowed to attempt a related task is unlimited. There was no barrier (except lack of Internet) regarding where and when they will solve formative assessment and receive feedback in Numbas. Ultimately, this would lead to improved learning of mathematics. This clearly shows and supports the study finding that technological affordances support pedagogical affordances (Pierce & Stacey, 2010). Pedagogical affordances of any digital tool depend to a large extent on the technological affordances of such tool. If students or teachers find for example the interface of a tool difficult to use, they may likely not use the tool to achieve their pedagogical purpose. One has to find the interface friendly before he/she can use it to learn. If the navigation buttons are hidden, the user might not be able to move to the feedback pages thereby not getting the desired help.

Second, both teachers and students perceived and actualized several pedagogical affordances. They found Numbas to support different mathematical content presentations. With this, teachers can create formative assessment in different representations - diagrams, graphs, matrices, multiple choices etc., also they can create the associated feedbacks in various forms that may cover the students' misconceptions. Formative feedbacks that Numbas give are found useful and motivating by the teachers and students. The main essence of formative assessment according to Weeden et al. (2002) is to identify students' current performance and aid learning, and that one of the ways teachers can achieve this important objective is through feedbacks. This is the reason why formative feedback is done while Numbas is on-going. It is to identify how far the objectives and goals of a tool have been achieved. Teachers and their students mostly undertake this kind of assessment to obtain vital information in form of formative feedback that they will apply to modify and improve the ongoing teaching and learning activity (Black & William, 2010).

The feedback in form of statistics containing students' performance identifies their current performance level, areas of difficulties, strengths and many more, are useful to the teachers for conducting diagnostic teaching. More so, feedbacks from teachers to students regarding their performances, challenges and difficulties are aimed at encouraging and helping them to identify their misunderstandings and misconceptions regarding the topics and concepts and ways to improve. Many studies have link feedback as one the most powerful ways to increase students learning and achievement (Hattie & Clarke, 2018; Hattie & Timperley, 2007). However, delivering it on time is often challenging to the teachers. Findings from this present study reveal that Numbas promotes formative assessment by providing feedback to both students and teachers in a timely fashion. Students receive feedbacks in different forms including instants feedbacks, hints, reveal answers, etc. It provides feedbacks to the teachers in form of the statistical report of the students' activities. With this, enormous time is saved for both the teachers and students.

Formative assessment requires setting learning and monitoring progress towards achieving the goals. This type of regularity in feedback provision helps to achieve learning goal. Findings also reveal that engagement in Numbas enhances students' motivation and increases their mathematical engagements. Students identified among others, the instant feedback to be very motivating. Furthermore, teachers expressed satisfaction that Numbas could save them a whole lot of time. Numbas is equipped with randomization mechanisms. That means, it can generate unlimited similar tasks with corresponding feedbacks. This saves teachers a lot of time and stress. They need not spend hours and days preparing tasks for formative assessment. It also offers students the opportunity to solve many tasks until they master the topic.

7. CONCLUSION

This work is a case study on formative assessment from a mathematics teacher education class using Numbas. It entails in-depth study of one setting. Affordances and constraints of Numbas have been studied in detail using a semi-structured interview, which gave the participants the opportunity to fully express their thoughts. However, the study is not without limitations. Firstly, the participants (*N=8*) are master's students and their teachers from teacher education program of one university. A larger number of participants from one or several classes and universities could have been more desirable to make better generalization and ensure more validity and reliability. However, the chosen number of participants with a large set of qualitative information seems to be justifiable for addressing the research questions and issues critically. The second limitation has to do with the student participants who are not the 'end users' of Numbas. Though they have good knowledge of Numbas and affordance theory, they have studied Numbas in details, used it for assessment (but in a limited form), also they have studied and evaluated other current digital tools in mathematics education. However, it will be difficult to take their opinions and perceptions to pass judgement for students who use Numbas regularly for studies. The findings can be drawn in the light of the use of Numbas in teacher education program. Students using Numbas for day-by-day activities may have a different perspective about the affordance perception and actualization processes. Future research studies involving such set of students would be appropriate to compare with findings of the presents study.

REFERENCES

Anderson, C., & Robey, D. (2017). Affordance potency: Explaining the actualization of technology affordances. *Information and Organization*, *27*(2), pp.100-115.

Bernhard, E., Recker, J., & Burton-Jones, A. (2013) Understanding the actualization of affordances: A study in the process modeling context. In M. Chau, & R. Baskerville (Eds.) *Proceedings of the 34th International Conference on Information Systems (ICIS 2013).* Association for Information Systems (AIS), pp. 1-11.

Bogden, C. R., & Biklen, S. K. (1982). *Qualitative Research for Education: An Introduction to Theory and Methods*, Boston: Ally and Bacon. In: Inc.

Bryman, A. (2016). *Social research methods*. Oxford, United Kingdom: Oxford University Press.

Gibson, J. J. (1986). *The ecological approach to visual perception*. Hillsdale, N.J: Lawrence Erlbaum.

Hadjerrouit, S. (2020a). Exploring the affordances of SimReal for learning mathematics in teacher education: A Socio-cultural perspective. In L. H. Chad; S. Zvacek; & J. Uhomoibhi (2020). *Computer Supported Education. 11th International Conference, CSEDU 2019, Heraklion, Greece. Revised Selected Papers*. Springer Nature, pp. 26-50.

Hadjerrouit, S. (2020b). Exploring the affordances of Numbas for mathematical learning: A case study. *International Network for Didactic Research in University Mathematics (INDRUM 2020)*, pp. 453 - 462.

Hattie, J., & Clarke, S. (2018). *Visible learning: Feedback*. London: Routledge.

Hattie, J., & Timperley, H. (2007). The power of feedback. *Review of Educational Research, 77*(1), pp. 81-112.

Hennink, M., Hutter, I., & Bailey, A. (2020). *Qualitative research methods*. SAGE Publications Limited.

Lawson-Perfect, C. (2015). A demonstration of Numbas, an e-assessment system for mathematical disciplines. *CAA Conference.* Retrieved from https://www.numbas.org.uk/blog/2015/07/a-demonstration-of-numbas-at-caa-2015/

Lawson-Perfect, C. (2020). How Numbas can help during the COVID-19 crisis. Retrieved from

https://www.numbas.org.uk/blog/2020/03/how-numbas-can-help-during-the-covid-19-crisis/

Markus, M. L., & Silver, M. S. (2008). A foundation for the study of IT effects: A new look at DeSanctis and Poole's concepts of structural features and spirit. *Journal of the Association for Information Systems, 9(*10*)*, pp. 609-632.

Nnagbo, C. I. (2020). Assessment in mathematics education using Numbas: Affordances and constraints from an activity theory perspective. [Unpublished master's thesis]. University of Agder, Kristiansand, Norway.

Norman, D. A. (1988). *The psychology of everyday things*. New York: Basic Books.

Osiurak, F., Rossetti, Y., & Badets, A. (2017). What is an affordance? 40 years later. *Neuroscience and Biobehavioral Reviews*, *77,* pp. 403-417.

Pereira, D., Flores, M. A., Simão, A. M. V., & Barros, A. (2016). Effectiveness and relevance of feedback in Higher Education: A study of undergraduate students. *Studies in Educational Evaluation, 49*, pp. 7-14.

Pierce, R., & Stacey, K. (2010). Mapping pedagogical opportunities provided by mathematics analysis software. *International Journal of Computers for Mathematical Learning*, *15*(1), pp. 1-20.

Strong, D. M., Volkoff, O., Johnson, S. A., Pelletier, L. R., Tulu, B., Bar-On, I., ... Garber, L. (2014). A theory of organization-EHR affordance actualization. *Journal of the Association for Information Systems, 15(2),* pp. 53-85.

Volkoff, O., & Strong, D. M. (2013). Critical realism and affordances: Theorizing IT-associated organizational change processes. *MIS Quarterly, 37*(3), pp. 819-834.

Volkoff, O., & Strong, D. M. (2017). Affordance theory and how to use it in IS research. In R. D. Galliers & M.-K. Stein (Eds.). *The Routledge companion to management information systems*. London: Routledge.

Wang, H., Wang, J., & Tang, Q. (2018). A review of application of affordance theory in information systems. *Journal of Service Science and Management, 11*(1), pp. 56-70.

Weeden, P., Winter, J., & Broadfoot, P. (2002). *Assessment*. London: RoutledgeFalmer.

Yin, R. K. (2009). *Case study research: Design and methods*, 4th ed., vol. 5. Applied social research methods series.

INTERNAL CONSISTENCY, RESPONSIVENESS AND MINIMAL DETECTABLE CHANGE OF THE TECO IN THE BACHELOR'S DEGREE COURSE IN PEDIATRIC NURSING AT THE "SAPIENZA" UNIVERSITY OF ROME: A CROSS SECTIONAL STUDY

Giovanni Galeoto[1], Giuliana D'Elpidio[2], Rosaria Alvaro[3], Anna Maria Zicari[4], Donatella Valente[1] and Marianna Riccio[5]

[1]*Department of Human Neurosciences, Sapienza University of Rome, Rome, Italy*
[2]*Bambino Gesù Pediatric Hospital- IRCCS, Piazza Sant'Onofrio 4, Rome, Italy*
[3]*Full-Professor of Tor Vergata University of Rome, Rome, Italy*
[4]*Department of Pediatric, Sapienza University of Rome, Rome, Italy*
[5]*Sapienza University of Rome, Piazzale Aldo Moro 5, Rome, Italy*

ABSTRACT

The Italian Disciplinary section of Test of Competences (TECO-D) project is an important longitudinal study used to analyze learning outcomes of ungraded students and to measure quality of the educational process. The aim of the present study was to evaluate the psychometric properties of the TECO-D in students enrolled in the Bachelor's Degree in Pediatric Nursing at "Sapienza" University of Rome. The other aim was to evaluate if TECO-D is able to assess the changes in skills between students of I and III year of the university course and to calculate the minimal detectable change. The sample was composed by 35 pediatric nursing students and was recruited in October 2019. The test was administered using a digital platform with multiple choice questions (MCQs). The reliability, as internal consistency, was excellent ($\alpha = 0.938$). The responsiveness evaluated by t-test for independent samples, the Standard Error of Measurement (SEM) and Minimal Detectable Change (MDC) was supported by significant differences between two cohorts of pediatric nursing students, and adequate TECO-D is a reliable instrument for assessing the skills of pediatric nursing student evaluating the achievement of university goals and improving the quality of the training provided by the university.

KEYWORDS

TECO, Progress Test, Pediatric Nursing, Students

1. INTRODUCTION

The longitudinal progress testing assessment developed in the early 1970s at the University of Missouri-Kansas City School of Medicine and at the University of Limburg in Maastricht. It has since become increasingly popular internationally due to obvious advantages. Progress test periodically measure entire body of student's knowledge during their learning process. Thus, it is useful for the new medical schools to establish a comparison in terms of achievement with more prestigious medical schools (Schuwirtf, 2012) (Verhoeven, 2002). Progress test can be also used to identify both strengths and weaknesses in student's knowledge and as a self-assessment tool that give cross-sectional measure of individual's performance that each student can compared with their peers. For the administration usually multiple choice questions (MCQs), that are randomly drawn from a database (Verhoeven, 2002) (Wrigley, 2012).

Based on this principle, (Test Of Competence) TECO project coordinated by National Agency for the Evaluation of Universities and Research Institutes (ANVUR) was established in Italy in 2012. The agency avails of academic representatives who compose in working groups (WG) associated by the Executive Council. The TECO project evaluates and monitors the skills of undergraduate students and results of training course.

The aim of testing is to measure and to improve the quality of the educational process by encouraging mechanisms within the academic self-assessment world. Therefore TECO, promotes student centered teaching associated by the analysis of learning outcomes, as recommend by the recent European guidelines (Standards and Guidelines for Quality Assurance, 2015) of the European Area of Higher Education (EHEA). TECO project proposes both Trasversal section (TECO-T) and Disciplinar section (TECO-D) (ANVUR, 2020) (ESG, 2015). TECO-D analyses specific training contents of the course and students are examined with digital platform managed by *Consorzio INteruniversitario pEr il Calcolo Automatico dell'Italia (CINECA)* in classrooms on the university campus. The time testing is established by the ANVUR in collaboration with the CINECA (usually September – December).

The Bachelor's Degree in Pediatric Nursing provides didactic courses and experiences of clinical practice intended for the training of health professionals expertise in the care of healthy and sick children and family/caregivers. The studies objectives allow future pediatric nurses to develop specific care and relation skills in relation to the specific stage of childhood. The medical pediatric specialty is crucial because a pediatric patient has physical, physiological and psychological features quite different from the characteristics of an adult patient. For this reason, health professional expert and specifically trained are necessary to adequately satisfy the needs regarding the nursing of pediatric patient. Therefore, the importance of careful assessment of the skills of future pediatric nurses to ensure quality and safety in care is evident and key. The dawn of pediatric nursing history dates back to 1852-1854 when the doctor Charles West found one of the first pediatric hospitals in the world. He highlighted the need of nurses with a firm grip in the care of sick child. Italian pediatric nursing has one's origins in historical health figure named *"vigilatrice di infanzia"*, officially recognized in 1940. During the mid-twentieth century this first health pediatric figure had an important professional role. The position developed parallel to that of the generalist nurse acquiring greater autonomy and responsibility. It was only in 1997 the profession of pediatric nurse has been was finally regulated by Ministerial Decree n. 70 (FNOPI) (Costamagna, 2010).

For the academic year 2019 – 2020 the test was adopted in "Sapienza" University of Rome for the Bachelor's Degree courses in Pediatric Nursing. This study aimed to evaluate the reliability, as internal consistency and the responsiveness, in term of significant difference in skills between pediatric nursing students of First and Third years in "Sapienza" University, of the TECO-D for Bachelor's Degree courses in Pediatric Nursing (ANVUR, 2020).

2. MATERIALS AND METHODS

2.1 Population and Procedures

The data were gathered from 35 students enrolled in the Bachelor's Degree in Pediatric Nursing at "Sapienza" University of Rome: 15 of First year of course and 20 of Third year of course. The students were approached in October 2019 and were invited and informed about the modalities of test by email. Participation was voluntary. The individual results of tests were communicated to each participating students by certificate available from February 2020 and the outcomes did not affect the evaluation in progress or the final assessment. The accumulated data were transmitted to the responsible coordinators of the study courses involved and to the university board (ANVUR, 2020).

2.2 Instruments

TECO-D for pediatric nursing students was created by specific working group that had reworked 70 questions by database containing 250 questions. Multiple choice questions (MCQs), divided into thirteen care macro areas (Table 1), with only one correct answer composed the TECO-D. The test was administered using a digital platform managed by CINECA (Figure 1 shows the graphic interface) in a university classroom equipped with computers within 90 minutes (ANVUR, 2020).

The process of creation/administration of the test of this institutional platform, in general, requires the participation of three persons with three different roles. There is a different reserved access area for each of the three roles. The University Contact creates and prepares the exam session; the Classroom Tutor opens and closes the administration of the test; the student compiles and sends the test data. The registration on the website Universitaly (a platform of Ministry of education, university and research) by students is an essential requirement in order to do the test. There are present "Summery" pages in each phase that give indications on missing answers and the "Delivery" button that concludes the current phase. Before the conclusion, the student receives a confirmation message that warns him of the impossibility of being able to re-enter the current phase (Galeoto, 2019) (Paterniani, 2019).

Table 1. Macro areas of TECO-D

Number of macro areas	Learning	Number questions
1	Transversal care skills	12
2	Vital critically	8
3	Cardio-respiratory	6
4	Hematology	6
5	Metabolic	2
6	Gastro-intestinal	4
7	Renal	3
8	Neurological Neuropsichiatric	5
9	Surgical	5
10	Health prevention	5
11	Nursing care safety	8
12	Organization	3
13	Ethical responsibility	4

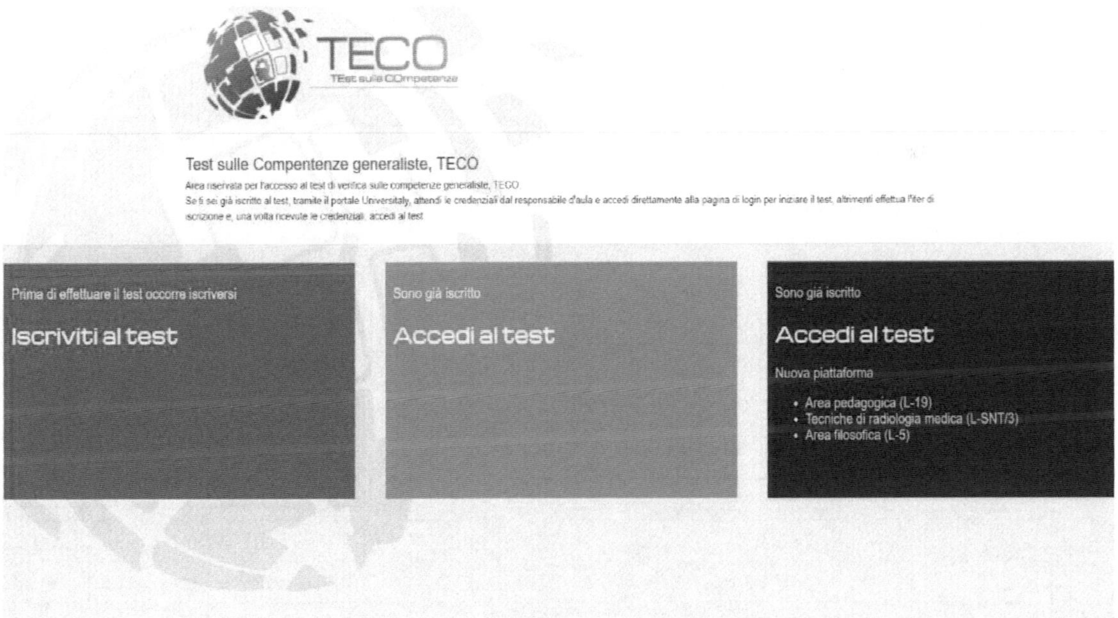

Figure 1. CINECA platform (CINECA, 2020)

2.3 Data Collection and Data Analyses

The data of TECO-D of the two years of course was collected in October 2019. Ethical approval was obtained. Participants were fully informed about the study's aims and gave their consent. Instruments were all anonymous, and participants were assured about data confidentiality.

Analyses were performed using SPSS 23.0 (IBM Corp., Armonk, NY, USA). Descriptive analyses were conducted: continuous and categorical variables were reported as means (± SD) and frequencies (%). The reliability, as internal consistency, of the TECO-D was tested by Cronbach's alpha coefficient, values greater than 0.70 were adequate.

To evaluate the responsiveness, defined as "the ability of an instrument to detect change over time in the construct to be measured" (Mokking, 2010) t-test for independent samples, the Standard Error of Measurement (SEM) and Minimal Detectable Change (MDC) were carried out.

Specifically, in the t-test for independent samples, we compared the TECO-D scores reported in the first and third year by pediatric nursing students. Significant differences indicate that the instrument was able to measure the difference in skills between the two cohorts of student.

The Standard Error of Measurement (SEM), an indication of the absolute reliability, was calculated through the error term from the 2-way model (MSE) of the repeated measures ANOVA. The SEM value lower than Standard Deviation/2 identifies higher reliability of the measure.

The Minimal Detectable Change (MDC), the minimal amount of change that can be interpreted as a real change in acquired competencies for a student during the years, was computed using SEM according to the following formula, $MDC=SEM\times1.96\times\sqrt{2}$.

3. RESULTS

3.1 Population

The sample was composed by 35 students of the Bachelor's Degree in Pediatric Nursing at "Sapienza" University of Rome: 15 of First year of course and 20 of Third year of course. The average age of the participants was 21 years and the predominant gender was female.

3.2 Internal Consistency

The score of internal consistency for the TECO-D was excellent (α=938).

Table 2

Area	Scale Mean if Item Deleted	Scale Variance if Item Deleted	Corrected Item-Total Correlation	Cronbach's Alpha if Item Deleted
1	21.11	192.752	0.712	0.937
2	23.23	200.829	0.637	0.939
3	25.23	213.593	0.701	0.933
4	25.34	210.820	0.879	0.928
5	26.20	227.341	0.772	0.934
6	25.66	216.585	0.813	0.931
7	25.51	213.963	0.832	0.930
8	25.74	225.726	0.710	0.935
9	25.46	213.138	0.812	0.930

10	24.91	219.257	0.631	0.935
11	24.26	190.255	0.870	0.928
12	26.14	227.950	0.683	0.935
13	25.20	212.400	0.752	0.932

3.3 Responsiveness

The evaluation of the responsiveness evaluated by t-test for independent samples showed statistically significant data in the comparison of the results of the two cohorts of pediatric nursing students.

The SEM and MDC and responsiveness are reported in Table 3.

Table 3. Responsiveness and Minimal Detectable Change

Area	Administration 2019 in First year (means ± SD)	Administration 2019 in Third year (means ± SD)	Mean Difference	SEM	p	MDC
1	3.80 ± 2.18	7.45 ± 1.2	-3.65	0.59	0.00	1.63
2	2.07 ± 1.53	5.05 ± 1.99	-2.98	0.61	0.00	1.71
3	0.47 ± 0.64	2.75 ± 1.33	-2.28	0.37	0.00	1.03
4	0.40 ± 0.83	2.60 ± 0.88	-2.20	0.29	0.00	0.81
5	0.00 ± 0.00	1.40 ± 0.68	-1.40	0.18	0.00	0.49
6	0.33 ± 0.72	2.10 ± 1.02	-1.77	0.31	0.00	0.86
7	0.40 ± 0.82	2.30 ± 1.03	-1.90	0.33	0.00	0.90
8	0.47 ± 0.74	1.85 ± 0.75	-1.38	0.25	0.00	0.70
9	0.40 ± 0.83	2.40 ± 1.10	-2.00	0.34	0.00	0.94
10	0.93 ± 1.28	2.95 ± 0.83	-2.02	0.36	0.00	0.99
11	4.10 ± 1.4	0.27 ± 0.46	-3.17	0.53	0.00	1.48
12	1.30 ± 0.98	0.60 ± 0.99	-1.03	0.27	0.00	0.76
13	0.60 ± 0.99	2.70 ± 1.22	-2.10	0.38	0.00	1.06
Total score	11.07±7.57	38.96 ± 7.16	-27.88	2.51	0.00	6.95

*p<0.05 *SD= Standard Deviation *SEM= Standard Error of Measurement *MDC= Minimal Detectable Change

4. DISCUSSION

The study was conducted by a research group from the "Sapienza" University of Rome and from "Rehabilitation & Outcome Measure Assessment" (R.O.M.A.) association (Berardi, 2019) (Galeoto, 2020) (Ioncoli, 2020) (Miniera, 2020) (Panuccio, 2020).

The TECO project is an instrument to evaluate and monitor the skills of undergraduate students and results of training course. It proposes two sections: Trasversal section (TECO-T) and Disciplinar section (TECO-D). This study aimed to evaluate the reliability, as internal consistency and the responsiveness, in term of significant difference in skills between pediatric nursing students of First and Third years in “Sapienza” University, of the TECO-D for Bachelor’s Degree courses in Pediatric Nursing.

The psychometric properties of TECO-D for Bachelor’s Degree in Pediatric Nursing had a very positive evaluation: we defined an excellent internal consistency, which means that the all items of the TECO-D were strongly interrelated with each other and that the TECO-D IS a reliable instrument for assessing the skills of pediatric nursing student.

The analysis of responsiveness and the evaluation of MDC highlighted an improvement statistically significant of TECO- D's results between First and Third years. So we can say that the TECO-D is an instrument sensitive to the change of competences between First and Third years, although the two cohorts of this study were not represented by the same sample.

4.1 Limitation of the Study

This study present several limitations. First we collected data using a convenience sample. Second, it was not possible to assess the change in skills of the same sample of students over time. Third, the responsiveness was analyzed comparing two different cohort (First and Third years) using TECO-D results from the same year of administration (2019). Fourth, a reduced size sample was used to perform analysis. Further studies with larger samples are needed.

5. CONCLUSION

The TECO-D can be considered a reliable tool for assessing the skills of students of the Bachelor's Degree in Pediatric Nursing. The TECO-D test is able to catch statistically significant changes in the skills of pediatric nursing students and the minimal detectable change value necessary for the TECO-D score change to be significant year after year. TECO-D can be useful to achievement of university goals and to improve the quality of the training provided by the university. Therefore, an increasingly widespread and consolidated use of TECO-D can be hoped for in order to intervene in a timely manner if critical issues arise in the learning process. This is a particularly important intervention for the training of those who will carry out a health profession in the future.

CONFLICT OF INTEREST

The authors declare that they have no conflict of interest.

REFERENCES

ANVUR homepage, https://www.anvur.it/attivita/ava/teco-test-sulle-competenze/ last access 2020/07/10 https://enqa.eu/wp-content/uploads/2015/11/ESG_2015.pdf , last access 2020/07/10

ANVUR homepage https://www.anvur.it/attivita/ava/teco-test-sulle-competenze/rilevazioni-teco/ last access 2020/07/10

ANVUR homepage, https://www.anvur.it/attivita/ava/teco-test-sulle-competenze/rilevazioni-teco/la-rilevazione-teco-2019/, last access 2020/07/10

ANVUR https://www.anvur.it/wp-content/uploads/2019/08/TECO-D-Infermieristica-Pediatrica.pdf, last access 2020/07/15

Berardi A. et al, 2019. Internal consistency and validity of the Jebsen-Taylor hand function test in an Italian population with hemiparesis. NeuroRehabilitation, vol. 45, no. 3, pp 331-339.

CINECA https://verificheonline.cineca.it/teco/login_studente.html, last access 2021/01/27

Costamagna G., 2010. Lo sviluppo dell'Infermieristica Pediatrica in Italia. Giornale Italiano di Scienze Infermieristiche Pediatriche, vol. 2, no. 4, pp 116-118.

FNOPI https://www.fnopi.it/aree-tematiche/infermieristica-pediatrica/ , last access 2020/07/28

Galeoto G. et al, 2019. J. The use of a dedicated platform to evaluate health-professions university courses. in Advances in Intelligent Systems and Computing. pp 275-284

Galeoto G. et al, 2020. Levels of Cognitive Functioning Assessment Scale: Italian cross-cultural adaptation and validation. Annali di igiene: medicina preventive e di comunità, vol. 21, no. 1, pp 16-26.

Ioncoli M. et al, 2020. Crosscultural Validation of the Community Integration Questionnaire-Revised in an Italian Population. Occupational Therapy International, vol. 2020, 9816541.

Mokkink L. B. et al, 2010. International consensus on taxonomy, terminology, and definitions of measurement properties: Results of the COSMIN study. Journal of Clinical Epidemiology, vol. 63, no. 7, pp 737–745.alfabet

Miniera f. et al, Measuring Environmental Barriers: Validation and Cultural Adaptation of the Italian Version of the Craig Hospital Inventory of Environmental Factors (CHIEF) Scale. Occupation Therapy Health Care, vol. 34, no. 4, pp 373-385.

Paterniani A. et al, 2019. Electronic Test of Competence Administration: Qualitative Evaluation of Students' Satisfaction on Telematic Platform a Cross Sectional Study. Advances in Intelligent Systems and Computing. Spain, pp 47-54.

Panuccio F. et al, 2020. Development of the Pregnancy and Motherhood Evaluation Questionnaire (PMEQ) for evaluating and measuring the impact of physical disability on pregnancy and the management of motherhood: a pilot study. Disability Rehabilitation, vol. 42, no.4, pp 1–7.

Schuwirtf L., Van der Vleuten C, 2012. The use of progress testing. Prospectives on Medical Education, vol. 1, n. 1, pp. 24-30.

Verhoeven BH. et al, 2002. Growth in medical knowledge. Medical Eduction, vol. 36, n. 7, pp 11–7.

Wrigley W. et al, 2012. A systemic framework for the progress test: Strengths, constraints and issues: AMEE Guide. Medical Teacher, vol. 71, no. 34, pp 683-697.

LESSON LEARNED FROM AN EXPERIENCE OF TEACHING SUPPORT IN HIGHER EDUCATION FOR A DIGITAL TRANSITION IN THE NEW SCENARIO CREATED BY COVID-19

Barbara Bruschi[1], Francesco Floris[2], Marina Marchisio[2] and Matteo Sacchet[2]
[1]*Department of Philosophy and Education Sciences, University of Turin*
Via Sant'Ottavio 20, 10124 Turin, Italy
[2]*Department of Molecular Biotechnology and Health Science, University of Turin*
Via Nizza 52, 10126 Turin, Italy

ABSTRACT

Teaching skills are fundamental for academic positions, which combine research and teaching activities. Thus, universities should look for candidates with excellent research records and teaching experience or skills; another strategy is the training of teaching staff. On the other hand, when dealing with already in-service teachers, the challenges for universities are completely different and it is often difficult to cope with digital technologies for education. Moreover, roles in the education process assume different perspectives. This is the background of this research, which investigates the measures adopted at the University of Turin to deal with the scenario of the Covid-19 pandemic and subsequent periods. 30 young graduates halfway between students and teachers, one per university department, support teachers and the digital transition. Their role ranges from the didactical support (online teaching methodologies and the use of the Learning Management System) to the preparation, delivery, and monitoring of online assessment and exams. These young assistants received a grant for their role and proper training over all these topics and other themes related to online education, such as accessibility, copyright, video editing. At the start of the second semester, a questionnaire was delivered to these grant holders to receive feedback on their activity during the first semester and exam period. We collected 26 answers from the questionnaire. Results show that, among the different roles, they were more involved with online examinations and students' support, while collaborating more with professors and with their peers. Most of these grant holders would like to participate again in such an experience, it being useful for their future career, the teachers of the future.

KEYWORDS

Digital Education, Digital Transition, Higher Education, Teacher Support, Young Assistants

1. INTRODUCTION

As the Covid-19 pandemic was spreading all over the world, local governments took many actions to shut down schools, colleges, and universities, leaving a lot of uncertainties about the future openings. This caused a challenge to the higher education landscape at a magnitude that had probably never been seen before. Online teaching suddenly became the only possible way to keep students engaged in these difficult times. However, this transition to online teaching requires digital technologies to be accessible to every student and teacher, but it is quite clear that it is not the case, even in the most developed countries. Besides this lack of equity in accessing digital devices and education, it soon became necessary to rethink, renovate and redesign the education systems according to the new needs. It is not just a matter of policies and interventions: the discussion must involve all the stakeholders. Teachers, the first line facing disruptive change, require an increasingly larger set of competencies, their digital competencies. This is true at all levels of education. Many works in the literature explain and assess frameworks of digital competencies for educators. Even before the Covid-19 pandemic, there was a lot of work in this sense, because of the rapidly changing scenario in a world where digital technologies are ubiquitous. This is the case of DigCompEdu (Redecker, 2016), which provides a description of the various sets of teachers' competencies for online teaching. This framework is valid for educators both at secondary schools (Fissore et al., 2020) and in higher education. Moreover, the framework aims at guiding policies, implementing regional and national tools and training programs, providing a common soil to help the dialogue and exchange of practices.

This work analyses the experience of teaching support in this new scenario reshaped by Covid-19 at the University of Turin. In line with the recommendations in (UNESCO-IESALC, 2020) to anticipate the possibility of closed institutions, the university introduced 30 new figures to facilitate the transition from traditional to digital education, giving didactical and technical support and helping in the preparation, delivery, and monitoring of online assessment and exams - this last item being one of the main challenges. These grant holders received proper training on all topics and themes related to online and digital education. Training topics are Instructional Design, accessibility, copyright, video editing, usage of the Learning Management System. At the start of the second semester of the academic year 2020/2021, a questionnaire was delivered to these grant holders to receive feedback on their activity during the first semester and the exam period. We collected 26 answers from the questionnaire: almost all grant holders responded. Results show that the experience was positive, with a strong collaboration with professors and with their peers.

The paper is divided into sections as follows. Section 2 describes the state of the art. Section 3 describes the support that was designed and delivered at the University of Turin. Section 4 introduces the research questions and the related methodology. Section 5 presents and discusses the results of this experience.

2. STATE OF THE ART

The perception of education can differ between students and teachers. In (Asikainen et al., 2018) the authors asked Likert-scale and an open-ended question to 68 teachers and 104 students with results that showed significant differences in both students' and teachers' experiences. Teachers experience the support given to students more positively than the students do. In addition, teachers experience the commonality and interaction between teachers and students more positively than the students do. Institutional leaders should pay more attention to the teacher-student relationship at the higher education level, emphasizing abilities to interact with others and social behavior when recruiting staff.

Digital tools support teaching in higher education in a pervasive way. These tools demand new responsibilities on the teacher and influence teacher roles. This has been well known since the first years of the new millennium. In (Wake et al., 2007), the authors investigated a case study about the introduction of a digital tool, which had become fully integrated with the teaching-learning environment, and they highlighted the birth of new teacher roles, one of the most crucial changes being the move from private to public feedback. The study was conducted through interviews and the study of textual artifacts. The use of digital technologies alone does not result in improved educational outcomes and ways of working (Kirkwood, 2009). Students' engagement with e-learning relates to their expectations and conceptions of learning and to assessment demands. Academics need to re-assess their own beliefs and practices concerning teaching and assessment and their impact on the experience of learners. Digitalization in Higher Education institutions does not only concern teachers, but also many educational stakeholders. Digital skills are becoming increasingly relevant in the workplace, especially in education. One of the main objectives for universities is training current and future teachers together with professionals and academic staff. Different countries and institutions proposed policies, initiatives, and strategies. In Germany, researchers at the University of Oldenburg found that both teachers and students use a limited number of digital technology for predominantly assimilative tasks, with the Learning Management System being perceived as the most useful tool (Bond et al., 2018). They based their analysis on two datasets regarding the use and perceptions of students ($n = 200$) and teachers ($n = 381$) on the use of digital tools.

Covid-19 pandemic disruptively changes students' perception regarding online learning. From a study conducted in two of the largest Romanian universities (Coman et al., 2020), the authors revealed that higher education institutions were not prepared for exclusively online learning. When unprepared, the disadvantages of online learning become more prominent. Technical issues were found to be the most important ones, followed by teachers' lack of technical skills and their teaching style improperly adapted to the online environment, up to the lack of interaction with teachers or poor communication with them.

Several programs arose to face such emergency. In (Quezada et al., 2020), the authors discusses how the pandemic created opportunities for their department, students, teachers, school district partner teachers, faculty, and university supervisors to be "changemakers" in the transition from an on-campus face to face teaching and on-school site supervision to remote teaching and supervision of practicum and student teachers. Their program yielded some themes: Technology-Based Instructional Strategies, Technology-Based Support Office Consultation, Alternative Technology-Based Course Assessments, Feedback for Learning and Teaching Improvement, and Social-Emotional Engagement in Courses, and Support of Clinical Placement. The result after a transition week was the Instructional Plan of Action (IPA) to support all full-time and adjunct instructional needs and teacher candidates.

Emotion and mental strength played a role, too. Teachers were strongly affected by the pandemic, and (Pressley, 2021) gained insight into the impact and the factors that lead to teacher anxiety and burnout.

There is research about teacher support in secondary education (Fissore et al., 2020) and in higher education (Floris et al., 2020), but there is also research about teaching and learning practices, see (Carrillo & Flores, 2020) for a review. In particular, there are practice involving Students as Partners in Higher Education. Students can be partners in different aspects, in governance, pedagogy, inclusion. In (Bovill, 2017), the author proposes a participation matrix, a way to be transparent about the different roles of different actors at different stages in the partnership between teachers and students. The teacher should lead the initiative at the start, but at later stages, the teacher is working in partnership with different subsets of the student cohort. A range of challenges arises in this context: establishing and maintaining partnerships, limited contact with students, the large size of many university classes, student or staff skepticism about partnership.

Guidelines for facing challenges in educations appear in (Digital Education Action Plan 2021-2027), which outlines the European Commission's vision for high-quality, inclusive, and accessible digital education in Europe. Its aim is to learn from the COVID-19 crisis and adapt education and training systems to the digital age. Researchers from all over Europe participated to open public consultations on the new action plan from June to September 2020.

At the University of Turn in Italy, the Covid-19 pandemic affected the second semester of the academic year 2019/2020 and the academic year 2020/2021. In the first case, the response was due to the emergency, online teaching was not planned at all and professors had to face the situation with their previous knowledge or work with online learning (Bruschi et al., 2020). In the second case, all stakeholders knew that the new academic year would be a new scenario for higher education generated by the pandemic. The situation has been constantly evolving, and the first period of the academic year was still characterized by a health emergency, but it is now clear that new ways of teaching and learning are opening up. All teachers and students must be prepared.

3. SUPPORT FOR DISTANCE TEACHING

To guarantee permanent support to teachers, which is a trend research theme, the university introduced 30 young figures, young graduates halfway between a student and a professor. They received a grant for their activity as assistants. The choice of young graduates resides in the proximity with students, thanks to a smaller age gap; moreover, it is easier to recruit young graduates than other kinds of teaching assistants, for which competition is required. These grant holders got their workplace inside the staff members of all departments of the university: there are 27 departments at the University of Turin, so one grant holder per department, the residual ones were hired in Interdepartmental centers. Their role is to spread digital education competencies to all areas. Thus, the number of teachers they supported is quite variable, depending on the size of the department. Requirements for a successful application were the knowledge of a specific discipline, the main one of each department, even though disciplines can differ greatly within a department. Because of this, the collaboration between the grant holders was highly encouraged. No particular mastery in teaching was required because these grant holders were trained (online, see Figure 1 for an overview of the online training course) on the various aspects related to their future activity and online teaching. First, they were introduced to the situation at the university and the importance of their role, with an overview of the set of recommendations and university policies for the emergency. They also received proper professional training on online teaching methodologies, how to use the Learning Management System integrated adopted by the University of Turin, how to prepare, deliver and monitor online assessment, how to edit videos, and other topics related to online education, like accessibility and copyright. The training program was carried out following positive previous experiences in training those who will be trainers (Marchisio et al., 2019) especially in the case of open online courses inside the start@unito experience (Bruschi et al., 2021; Marchisio et al., 2020).

4. RESEARCH QUESTION AND METHODOLOGY

The research question that defines the research described in this work is: how can a university support its teaching staff in the transition to digital education, especially in new normal scenarios like the ones arisen during the Covid-19 pandemic?

To answer this question, many focus groups took place to collect needs and specific requests and, at the start of the second semester, a questionnaire was delivered to these grant holders to receive feedback on their activity during the first semester and exam period. The questionnaire is composed of different questions about their perspective, the activities they performed, the usefulness of the training, the importance of this experience for their future job applications. We collected 26 answers from the questionnaire of grant holders hired in 23 different departments. Some qualitative remarks from focus groups with the deputy directors for teaching and the grant holders themselves are reported in the last lines of the results section.

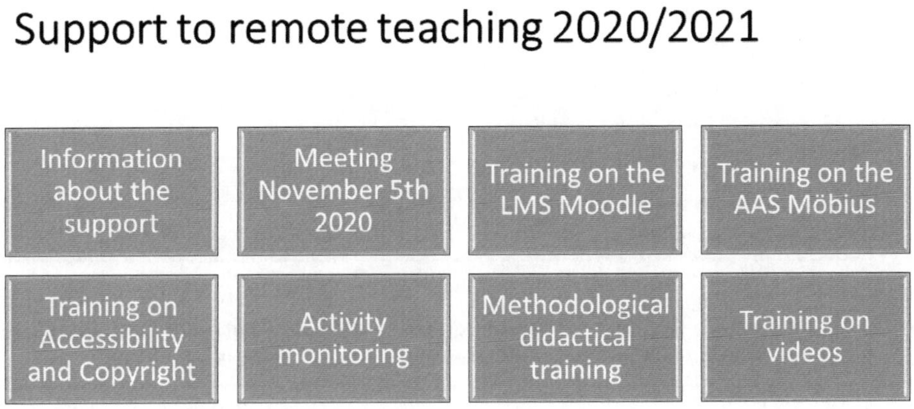

Figure 1. An overview of the training course for grant holders

5. RESULTS

After the training, the grant holders were active resources for their departments, under the supervision of the Department Directors and in collaboration with the local staff. Thus, the first aspect that was thoroughly investigated is the kind of activity they performed. As depicted in Table 1, the main areas of intervention involved supporting online examinations and responding to students' requests (median 4 over a 5-point scale). This is mainly due to the large-scale online examination (the University of Turin has more than 80 thousand students) and to the unavoidable disorientation of first-year students (around 26 thousand students). Since grant holders are familiar with content topics, they were sometimes requested to check online contents and modules and to develop materials and assessments. They were less involved in the design phase or with video making because grant holders arrived after a possible design phase and most of the lessons were carried out through video conferencing systems. They covered also other important activities:

- Review of the web pages of the degree programs, to keep the information up-to-date, also due to the changing rules caused by the Covid-19 period.
- Creation of material for university orientation, especially inside the Orient@mente university action (Barana et al., 2017a; Barana et al., 2017b), an experience of online delivery of open courses for university guidance.

- Training meetings and contents for teachers, to spread what they learned during the training course in the departments.
- Remote exam assistance, especially in large-scale assessment for open online courses delivered by many degree programs. The role of the grant holders was checking identities, camera control, support students with basic immediate help and reassure them.
- Management of a database of all the useful material already prepared and available, to prepare a long-term repository of useful contents.
- Analysis of the results of the exams in the online session, comparing the results with the previous in-person exams.
- Questionnaires for students and teachers, to understand in their local department or degree program the implications of the Covid-19 crisis on students and to collect the needs of teachers.

Table 1. Summary of the answers to "To what extent were you involved in the following activities?" over a 5-point Likert scale, in which 1 = a little, 5 = a lot

Activity	**Median**	**IQR**
Design of online educational paths	2	2
Development of online contents	3	2
Check online contents	3	2
Check modules	3	2.75
Cataloging of online contents	2	2
Preparation of quizzes with automatic evaluation	3	3
Preparation and support in making videos	2	2
Support in the administration of remote examinations	4	2
Respond to support requests	4	2

Table 2. Summary of the answers to "How much did you collaborate with the following categories of people from the university?" over a 5-point Likert scale, in which 1 = a little, 5 = a lot

Category	**Median**	**IQR**
Professors	4.5	1
Students	1.5	1
Researcher	2	2.75
Technicians	3	1
Administrative staff	3	2
Postdoctoral researchers	1	1
Ph.D.	1	1
Other grant holders	4	2

Table 2 shows the main collaborations between other stakeholders inside the university. The grant holders collaborated mostly with professors, but also with other grant holders, as peer support to exchange ideas, documents, and advice. The grant holders collaborated less with researchers, postdoctoral fellows or PhDs. It is possible that they were not aware of the precise academic position of some of their collaborators. This also indicates that older professors are more in need of support for the digital transition in the new scenario, due to less familiarity with new technologies, and due to heavier institutional and research commitments. This table highlights the reciprocal support and the collaborative work with peers, which is one of the aspects that grant holders liked, as written in the open comments. Other particularly appreciated aspects are:

- The perception of usefulness, especially due to the Covid-19 period and to the fact that most grant holders just graduated.
- The gratitude they received from teachers and staff: their work has been perceived as essential.
- Solving problems and provide solutions to teachers' difficulties.
- The chance to manage their work autonomously.

There were of course also some difficulties in their daily duties. Some grant holders highlighted the difficulty to let teachers and staff know that they were there to support and the precise definition of their competencies, which were sometimes overlapping other figures (but that is inside the meaning of support).

Concerning the training, grant holders' participation was mandatory and all of them attended most of the training sessions. Their training was made by experts in digital education and concerned the following topics:

- Accessibility and Copyright
- The Learning Management System
- Automated Assessment System
- Instructional design
- Video editing

Table 3 summarizes grant holders' evaluation of the training. The training they attended was very useful for the support that they had to provide to the departments and professors in order to improve online teaching. They stated that the training provided food for thought and gave them the necessary skills. The young age of these figures allowed them to be easily accepted by the teachers. They are aware of the potential consequences of this experience on their future career, and they think it will be useful (median 3 over a 5-point scale). Moreover, they will gladly apply again for the same position and the same experience (median 4 over a 5-point scale).

Table 3. Summary of the answers to "How do you rate the training received in the following areas?" over a 5-point Likert scale, in which 1 = bad, 5 = good

Category	**Median**	**IQR**
Usefulness	4	2
Relevance with the activities that you will carry out	4	2
Tips for reflection on the activities that you will carry out	4	2
Acquisition of skills	4	2

The topics were all interesting for grant holders, but the most appreciated one is the Learning Management System lesson. This is probably due to the strong basis that a Learning Management System gives to online learning, but also to the practical approach: grant holders had to study hands-on a local platform with more privileges than they had before, particularly interesting for new graduates and for the difficult times of pandemic. Many of the open comments state that grant holders would like to receive more training, even more personalized in their particular area.

A remark that was given by some grant holders concerns their role in the department. In some cases, it was difficult and not clear. Difficult due to established ways of teaching and to the waving amount of work, heavy during classes and exams, relaxed in other periods. Not clear due to the different needs of each department and sometimes to the lack of communications and collaboration between grant holders and teachers, staff, and different offices. Nonetheless, most of the grant holders stated that they would like to repeat the same experience (85%) and that it was very useful or quite useful for their future career (85%).

A final source of feedback about the work of the grant holders comes from focus groups with the deputy directors for teaching, whose role in this field was to manage the grant holders, and with the grant holders themselves. From the first ones, it emerged that grant holders were proactive in their job and delicate with students. They worked on the inclusiveness of online materials and they organized the materials for the remote lessons to make them more usable. Mapping the online materials available to students was another of their duties, so as to intervene when there is a shortage. Grant holders created question archives for remote exams. From the second kind of focus groups with the grant holders, it emerged that they collaborated between fellows from different departments and had many personal appointments with teachers, both for basic and specific requests, in the evening, too, and at times outside the hours of lessons or research or assistance in the departments. Their feedback on teachers was positive; they noted an increase in the autonomy of teachers to prepare materials, such as tests. They would have liked even more training to be able to propose new solutions.

6. CONCLUSION

The analysis of the responses given by grant holders to the questionnaires helps us answer the research question. This is a good starting point to help a higher education institution in facing the challenges of teachers' support and digital transition. The investment made by the university in the recruitment of people dedicated to supporting online teaching and teachers has certainly been a positive experience. One lesson learned from this experience is that such an immediate support is effective because it can be deployed very quickly. Moreover, second lesson learned, a young graduate is easier to train and facilitates the relationship with the teacher. Third lesson learned, this action works on both the two priority areas of the Digital Education Action Plan: grant holders helped in producing content and developing digital skills, together with enhancing and strengthening the digital skills of teachers useful in distance learning, these skills are useful for switching to online teaching. Methodologies combined with new technologies make it possible to adopt new teaching models to respond to open scenarios.

The hurry caused by the Covid-19 pandemic made it difficult to carefully plan all the phases of the intervention. It presented some difficulties in the organization and management of activities since everything took place remotely, with natural implications in communications. Despite this, in addition to facing the academic year more effectively in an uncertain setting, the experience represents a first response to the need for permanent and transversal support for teachers to offer quality and up-to-date teaching in new scenarios. This is not just a response to an emergency, but it is also aimed at spreading innovative methodologies and technologies to university teachers. Another positive effect is the temporary employment of newly graduated people, which could have trouble in finding suitable job opportunities in a time when traveling and interviews are restricted.

Beyond the activities described in this research, other parallel actions are necessary. All this work should be accompanied by an action dedicated to strengthening the infrastructure and it requires the engagement at institution level. Future activities concern a more structured way to face new scenario. The main action that is underway is the introduction of a Teaching and Learning Center to enhance didactics in higher education, hosting permanent figures that can support teachers. Permanent roles are necessary because the transition to the new scenario takes more than one academic year. Other future activities concern the creation of a good internal quality monitoring system, the eventual design and execution of a second round of grant holders for the next academic year, together with a new assessment of this kind of support at the end of the grant.

REFERENCES

Asikainen, H., Blomster, J., Virtanen, V. (2018). From functioning communality to hostile behaviour: students' and teachers' experiences of the teacher–student relationship in the academic community, Journal of Further and Higher Education, 42:5, 633-648, https://doi.org/10.1080/0309877X.2017.1302566

Barana, A., Bogino, A., Fioravera, M., Floris, F., Marchisio, M., Operti, L., Rabellino, S. (2017a). Self-paced approach in synergistic model for supporting and testing students: The transition from Secondary School to University. Proceedings of 2017 IEEE 41st Annual Computer Software and Applications Conference (COMPSAC), 404-409, IEEE 2017. https://doi.org/10.1109/COMPSAC.2017.211

Barana, A., Bogino, A., Fioravera, M., Marchisio, M., Rabellino, S. (2017b). Open Platform of Self-paced MOOCs for the continual improvement of Academic Guidance and Knowledge Strengthening in Tertiary Education. Journal of E-Learning and Knowledge Society, 13(3). https://doi.org/10.20368/1971-8829/1383

Bond, M., Marín, V.I., Dolch, C. et al. (2018). Digital transformation in German higher education: student and teacher perceptions and usage of digital media. Int J Educ Technol High Educ 15, 48. https://doi.org/10.1186/s41239-018-0130-1

Bovill, C. (2017). A Framework to Explore Roles Within Student-Staff Partnerships in Higher Education: Which Students Are Partners, When, and in What Ways?, International Journal for Students as Partners, 1 (1).

Bruschi, B., Marchisio, M., Sacchet, M. (2021) Online Teaching in Higher Education with the Support of Start@Unito During Covid-19 Pandemic. In: Agrati L.S. et al. (eds) Bridges and Mediation in Higher Distance Education. HELMeTO 2020. Communications in Computer and Information Science, vol 1344. Springer, Cham. https://doi.org/10.1007/978-3-030-67435-9_15

Carrillo, C., Flores, M. A. (2020) COVID-19 and teacher education: a literature review of online teaching and learning practices, European Journal ofTeacher Education, 43:4, pp. 466-487. https://doi.org/10.1080/02619768.2020.1821184

Coman, C, Țîru, L. G., Meseșan-Schmitz, L., Stanciu, C., Bularca, M. C. (2020). Online Teaching and Learning in Higher Education during the Coronavirus Pandemic: Students' Perspective, Sustainability 12, no. 24: 10367. https://doi.org/10.3390/su122410367

Communication From The Commission To The European Parliament, The Council, The European Economic And Social Committee And The Committee Of The Regions Digital Education Action Plan 2021-2027 Resetting education and training for the digital age. COM/2020/624 final. Retrieved from https://eur-lex.europa.eu/legal-content/EN/TXT/?uri=CELEX:52020DC0624 , last accessed 2021/05/31.

Fissore, C., Floris, F., Marchisio, M., Rabellino, S., Sacchet, M. (2020). Digital competences for educators in the Italian secondary school: a comparison between DigCompEdu reference framework and the PP&S project experience, MCCSIS2020 - Proceedings of International Conference on e-Learning 2020 (EL2020), pp. 47-54. http://dx.doi.org/10.33965/el2020_202007L006

Fissore, C., Marchisio, M., Rabellino, S. (2020). Secondary School Teacher Support and Training for Online Teaching during the COVID-19 Pandemic, European Distance and E-Learning Network (EDEN) Conference Proceedings, In EDEN Conference Proceedings, No. 1, pp. 311-320.

Floris, F., Genovese, A., Marchisio, M., Roman, F., Sacchet, M. (2020). Teacher support in COVID-19 pandemic to develop blended learning disruptive models in higher education. Paper presented at the 17th International Conference on Cognition and Exploratory Learning in Digital Age, CELDA 2020, pp. 173-180.

Kirkwood, A. (2009). E-learning: you don't always get what you hope for, Technology, Pedagogy and Education, 18:2, pp. 107-121, https://doi.org/10.1080/14759390902992576

Marchisio, M., Rabellino, S., Sacchet, M. (2020). Start@unito as Open Educational Practice in Higher Education. Journal of E-Learning and Knowledge Society, 16(4), 46-55. https://doi.org/10.20368/1971-8829/1135354

Marchisio, M., Sacchet, M., Salusso, D. Instructional Design to "Train the Trainers": The Start@unito Project at the University of Turin, Multi Conference on Computer Science and Information Systems, MCCSIS2019 - Proceedings of the International Conference on e-Learning 2019 (EL2019), pp. 195-202. https://doi.org/10.33965/el2019_201909F025

Pressley, T. (2021). Factors Contributing to Teacher Burnout During COVID-19. Educational Researcher, 50(5), pp. 325–327. https://doi.org/10.3102/0013189X211004138

Quezada, R. L., Talbot, C., Quezada-Parker, K. B. (2020) From Bricks and Mortar to Remote Teaching: A Teacher EducationProgram's Response to COVID-19, Journal of Education for Teaching, 46:4, pp. 472-483. https://doi.org/10.1080/02607476.2020.1801330

Redecker, C. (2017). European Framework for the Digital Competence of Educators: DigCompEdu. Punie, Y. (ed). EUR 28775 EN. Publications Office of the European Union, Luxembourg, https://doi.org/10.2760/159770

UNESCO-IESALC: Coronavirus COVID-19 and Higher Education: Impact and Recom-mendations, https://www.iesalc.unesco.org/en/2020/03/09/coronavirus-covid-19-and-higher-education-impact-and-recommendations/ , last accessed 2021/04/06.

Wake, J. D., Dysthe, O., Mjelstad, S. (2007). New and Changing Teacher Roles in Higher Education in a Digital Age. Educational Technology & Society, 10 (1), 40-51.

Gap in pagination due to formatting issues.

Pages 284-286

ADAPTIVE RELEASE LEARNING PATHS TO MOTIVATE ACTIVE LEARNING AND ENGAGEMENT IN STUDENTS

Pavani Vemuri, Monique Snoeck and Stephan Poelmans
KU Leuven
3000 Leuven, Belgium

ABSTRACT

Learning Analytics (LA), a decade old emerging filed, has the potential to make data-informed decisions to improve the quality of Higher Education (HE). It can be a good tool for HE institutions to tackle problems like student retention and promote student success rates. While LA could involve studying the impact of socioeconomic variables such as age, work, gender, stage, status, etc., on student success; these variables cannot be addressed by a teacher. Study attitude on the other hand, may be affected by instructional design, study counselling and guidance with theory informed teaching interventions. Grounding first year bachelor's students in the culture of active learning in their first year itself, will help develop self-regulation strategies which will thereby improve success and retention for not just the first year but also to complete the bachelor program in the stipulated period. In this study, we analyze data sourced from across all the first-year bachelor's courses of an Economics and Business Faculty. The students are classified into different groups according to their summative scores and their LMS interaction behaviors are studied. in future work, the collection of data across different campuses, courses and student programs allows for a comparative analysis across different dimensions, thus allowing for the investigation of the generalizability of results by means of out-of-sample testing or models built on a single course's data. Additionally, the collection of data across three successive academic years will also allow for the out-of-time validation of findings, including the analysis of the impact of the COVID-19 pandemic on the students' behavior.

KEYWORDS

Technology Enhanced Learning, Learning Analytics, Automatic Feedback, Formative testing, Student retention, Student Success

1. INTRODUCTION

The use of learning management systems (LMS) and other learning technologies in higher education (HE) to improve the quality of education has become common place over past few years. The use of these technologies generates a lot of log data when students access these systems. Learning Analytics (LA) is an emerging field (still nascent, only a decade old) that grew due to the digitalization of education and the maturity of data mining technology (Ferguson, 2012). The HE sector looks to LA for solutions to issues like a student's learning progress, retention, satisfaction; improving teaching quality and innovations which result in an elevated learning experiences there by contributing towards institutional performance and ranking. Nevertheless, it important to know what the immediate goals of LA are, to choose the appropriate methods to be used. In search for factors that are predictive for learner success, our study focuses on factors that can be addressed by a teacher. While studying the impact of socioeconomic variables such as "Age, Work, Gender, Stage, Status" on student success is interesting (Hamoud, Hashim, & Awadh 2018, p. 30), these variables cannot be addressed by a teacher. Study attitude on the other hand, may be affected by instructional design, study counselling and guidance.

Drop-out rates and success rates for first year students are a concern for many HE institutions. The Faculty of Economics and Business (FEB) at KU Leuven is no different as it experiences low success rates with its first-year students (less than half of the student's succeed only after a retake of the failed exams). The problem is not unique to FEB but prevails across all educational programs at KU Leuven (and even in Flanders). There has been a university-wide call for initiatives to find feasible solutions to this problem. The "Adaptive Learning Paths for ACtivation and Assessment of Students" (ALPACAS) project was initiated at FEB in 2019, with the central idea that - if more attention is given to first year students to ground them in the culture of active learning in their debut itself, they will develop self-regulation strategies early on; thereby improve success and retention for not just the first year but also to complete the bachelor program in the stipulated period. Among the key elements to achieve the goals of this project were: to utilize coordinated, uniform communication across all courses in a program; help didactic teams use formative assessments and adaptive learning paths including follow-up and feedback during the semester; and use LA to better inform teachers about their students.

One of the challenges for an institution/faculty-wide LA initiative is that courses even across one faculty may have a variety of teaching approaches as they are usually designed autonomously by their individual instructors or didactic teams; and hence diverse learning strategies maybe required. This diversity also presents an opportunity as different instructional designs can be used to investigate the generalizability of factors found to correlate with student success. In the context of the ALPACAS project, data was collected from all first-year courses across the entire faculty. This allows for the use of LA to investigate student behavior along different dimensions: comparing a same group of students' behaviors across different courses, comparing behavior in a same course across students from different programs or campuses, etc. LA is an appropriate tool in such context, to reflect on student behaviors to predict future behaviors and outcomes of students (Leitner, Khalil & Ebner, 2017). Potential problems can be recognized in an early stage and appropriate teaching interventions can be used to mitigate issues like retention (Palmer, 2013) and promote student success. However, before engaging in predictive analytics and model building, it makes sense to start with an exploratory analysis to verify the assumption that active learning behaviors are associated to better learning outcomes.

The following research questions were tackled by the research presented in this paper:

RQ1: Does the exploratory analysis of the data confirm that different behavior can be associated with different levels of student success?

RQ2: Does exploratory analysis allow to distinguish between different factors correlating with learner success?

The remainder of the paper is organized as follows: Section 2 presents the data collected in the context of the ALPACAS project. Section 3 presents some results of the exploratory analysis. Section 4 discusses avenues for further research and concludes the paper.

2. DATA DESCRIPTION

Each year, approximately 4000+ students enroll into (one of) the 10 programs (taught in English/Dutch languages) offered by FEB at its 4 locations. Each program has 4-5 courses taught each semester summing up to 9-11 courses per year. An instructor or didactic team teaching the course has autonomy over how the course is taught, the pedagogy and use of tools etc. There are 110+ courses taught in the first-year bachelor programs excluding languages. The primary datasets were extracted from the foundation technologies (Gasevic et al., 2019) of an HE institution: the Toledo-Blackboard LMS used at KU Leuven; and the student information systems (SIS). Due to strict GDPR guidelines in Europe, the socio-demographic data was not collected from the SIS but only student enrollment data and their summative scores were sourced. As the datasets are across multiple systems, it was mapped appropriately and pseudonymized in accordance with the university guidelines on data management. Secondary datasets are yet to be sourced from other sources like the Kaltura platform (a video cloud platform that integrates with an LMS) and we are currently also working on collecting longitudinal data across three academic years in the next data extracts. The first extract of the data was transversal in nature collected over the academic year 2019-2020. There are numerous dimensions to consider when analyzing this data. A course can be taught by different teachers on different campuses, in different academic years, or in different semesters. Data was simplified using a hierarchical structure - *students* in *courses* taught by *teachers* in each *semester* belonging to *programs* offered in *campuses*. The Toledo extension of the LMS allows to collect more than just trace data (navigation between webpages). The interaction of students with the LMS is captured in specific clicks termed as Events.

3. PRELIMINARY ANALYSIS

As a part of the preliminary analysis, the student behaviors across the semester were visualized in the courses. First, the content types used in courses were identified. Each course used various content types per the didactic team's choice of the course design. To compare events between courses, and to know the scale of how instructors used the LMS functionalities, (a) the number of learning items per content type and (b) number of events per content type were examined for each course. Next, students were categorized according to their summative scores into four categories (*Student_class*) of students: "*Excellent*" (scores above 16/20), "*Successful*" (between 10 and 15/20), "*Able to Push*" (scores 7, 8 or 9/20), and "*Poor*" students (score below 7/20). Student behavior during the semester was captured as average events per week per *Student_class*.

Figure 1 shows student behavior in two courses *Marketing* and *Global Economy* offered in the business engineering program (HIR). Firstly, we can distinctly notice (also in figure 2) that *Excellent* students worked hard consistently throughout the semester (followed by *Successful*) than any other *Student_class*. We also noticed that this is the general trend across most courses. The *Poor* students work very hard mostly at the semester-end and have the highest number of exam-period events in some courses. These, among other observations of visualizations confirm RQ1 that behavior can be associated with different levels of student success.

Notice that the average events are higher for *Global Economy* with the intensive use of the flipped classroom approach with adaptive paths by offering 11 formative tests with feedback which were actively used (not shown here); compared to *Marketing* which offered no tests at all. While longitudinal studies may give more insights into courses and student behaviors, it is clear that not all courses are built alike and evidently further analysis is needed to understand what makes the success rates of one course higher than others.

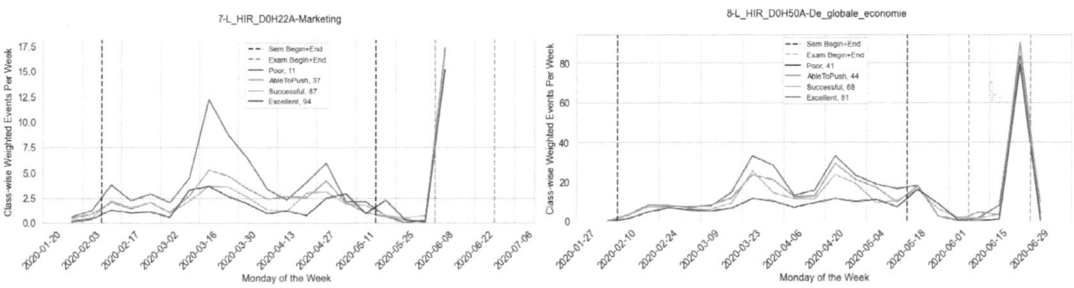

Figure 1. Average events per student group per week in the 'Marketing' (left) & 'Global Economy' (right), HIR Program

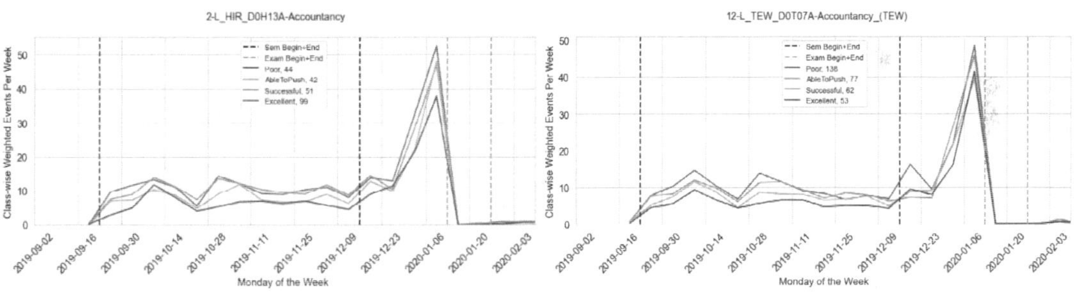

Figure 2. Average events per student group per week: in the 'Accountancy' course, (left) HIR and (right) TEW program

Secondly, consider the Figure 2 which shows student behavior in the *Accountancy* course followed by two distinct cohorts. The management students (TEW) have a lesser stronger quantitative profile than those of the business engineering (HIR). The numbers in the legend of each graph indicate the number of students in that specific *Student_class*. Notice that in both cohorts, class-wise student behaviors are very much alike despite their demographic differences. Perhaps HIR students are more successful in this course due to their quantitative profiles and additional interventions might be required for TEW students. Quantitative profile of a student can be a factor that can predict student success in some courses. Additionally, in both figures 1 & 2, the peaks in activity before the exam periods can be ode to summative assignments, specific formative tests or mock exams. *Excellent* student_class (followed by *Successful*) have higher activity than others as indicated by these pre-exam period peaks. But it is not straight forward to infer from the preliminary analysis (RQ2) or distinguish which other factors affect and are correlated with success without further in-depth analysis.

4. CONCLUSION AND FUTURE WORK

Collecting such a large amount of data, checking its relevance, and analyzing it in HE at a formal university across so many courses and programs is very uncommon. Gasevic et al. (2019) mention that predictive modeling and simulation or analytics informed intervention was not carried out on a large scale at institutions. Herodotou et al. (2019) report a large-scale implementation of predictive LA in HE but at the open university in UK with mostly completely online courses. In future work, our research team plans to conduct predictive analysis to identify at risk students in each course separately; compare how students distribute activity across courses in a semester compare the success of different cohorts of students attending the same courses, analyzing impact of COVID-19 pandemic on student behavior, etc. Especially in the second semester, with the data from first semester behavioral analysis and summative scores; and early prediction analysis with early second semester data; teaching interventions or student counselor interventions can be planned to support at risk students.

The initial exploration of the data demonstrates the data to be rich enough to analyze various aspects of student behavior. It can be inferred from exploratory analysis that different behavior can be associated with different levels of student success. While some factors like quantitative profiles are distinguishable from exploratory analysis as predictors of success, an in-depth analysis is needed for exploring many other factors of prediction. The collection of data across different campuses, courses and student programs allows for a comparative analysis across different dimensions, thus allowing for the investigation of the generalizability of results by means of out of sample testing or models build on a single course's data. Hence on one hand, analysis needs to be conducted multi-dimensionally at the course, semester, program and campus levels. On the other hand, equally important is to equip teachers with the know-hows of making informed teaching interventions. The ALPACAS project also aims to bring the instructors together to learn not just from LA but also each other's practices. As we aim towards capturing longitudinal datasets, the collection and analysis of data across three successive academic years will also allow for the out-of-time validation of findings, including the analysis of the impact of the COVID-19 pandemic.

REFERENCES

Ferguson, R. (2012). Learning analytics: drivers, developments and challenges. *International Journal of Technology Enhanced Learning,* 4(5/6), pp. 304–317.

Gasevic, D., Tsai, Y., Dawson, S., Pardo, A. (2019). How do we start? An approach to learning analytics adoption in higher education. *The International Journal of Information and Learning Technology*, 36(4), pp. 342-353.

Hamoud, A. K., Hashim, A. S., Awadh, W. A. (2018). Predicting Student Performance in Higher Education Institutions Using Decision Tree Analysis. *Intl. Journal of Interactive Multimedia and Artificial Intelligence*, 5(2), pp. 26–31.

Herodotou, C., Rienties, B., Boroowa, A. et al. (2019). A large-scale implementation of predictive learning analytics in higher education: the teachers' role and perspective. *Education Tech Research Dev,* 67, pp. 1273–1306.

Jeroen J. G. M. and Paul A. K. (2017) Ten steps to complex learning: A systematic approach to four-component instructional design.3rd edn. New York: Routledge.

Leitner, Khalil and Ebner (2017). 'Learning analytics in higher education–a literature review' in A. Peña-Ayala (ed.). *Learning analytics: fundaments, applications, and trends*. Springer., pp. 1–24.

Palmer S. (2013). Modelling engineering student academic performance using academic analytics. *Int J Eng Educ* 29(1), pp. 132–138.

DOES THE LEVEL OF POLITENESS USED BY A SOCIAL ROBOT AFFECT CHILDREN'S LEARNING?

Hsiu-Feng Wang
National Chiayi University, Taiwan

ABSTRACT

This study examined the impact of social robot's politeness strategy on the learning outcome and interest of children. The experimental study employed a within-subject design to investigate the effect of social robot's politeness strategy. The dependent variables are children's learning outcomes and learning interests. A total of 40 participants were involved. Participants' learning interests are measured by the Study Interest Questionnaire (SIQ), which included three aspects: feeling, value, and intrinsic. The results showed that there was no significant difference between children's learning outcomes and the level of politeness with social robots. However, in terms of learning interest, a higher level of polite feedback may be more beneficial to children. The findings of this experiment should be of value to people involved in the design of children's learning material with the social robots and those who work on interaction design with children.

KEYWORDS

Politeness Theory, Children, Social Robot, Learning Outcome, Learning Interest

1. INTRODUCTION

Many educators and parents believe that social robots create engaging learning experiences for children. Indeed, social robots are often bought by schools and families to teach younger ones' mathematics, new words and so on. However, despite their growing popularity, there is still limited understanding as to how social robots should interact in order to foster effective learning in children. This study investigates the impact of different level of politeness with social robot's feedback on children's learning outcome and interest.

2. BACKGROUND OF THE STUDY

Brown and Levinson (1987) devised a prominent approach called politeness theory to examine people's communication. According to politeness theory, everybody has a positive and negative "face" cross-culturally. The concept originates from Goffman (1967) described as a constructed self-image. The idea of negative face means that people do not want others to disrupt with their affairs because they do not want to lose their autonomy. The idea of positive face means that people desire others to be appreciated and approved of them. There are some communication acts such as requests or too direct can threaten the people's negative face, they referred to as face threatening acts (FTAs). For example, in this experiment, the direct wording of feedback (such as "It's so easy, everyone should know it.") from social robot can threaten student's negative face and restricting their willingness to work cooperatively with the social robot.

A number of researches based on theories of politeness investigations have since been conducted, seeking to understand the politeness effect in more detail. Ginns *et al.* (2013) reviewed a meta-analysis showed that politeness could enhance learning outcome. They revealed that the possible explanations are that politeness can act as social cues, may increase the perception of a system's (such as: intelligent tutors or social robot) friendliness therefore, enhance learners' effective processing. Another empirical research has similar results. Wang *et al.* (2008) conducted an experiment, they asked college students to learn to play an industrial engineering game named Virtual Factory. In the game, students learn how to assemble line processes efficiently by online tutor. They found that students who received polite feedback from an online tutor learned more than those who received direct (impolite) feedback; however, there were no statistically reliable differences between conditions on ratings of self-efficacy and interest. Wang and Johnson (2008) also found a politeness effect in a web-based tutoring system for teaching foreign language, with adults who were unfamiliar with the cultural context of the language. However, Other studies of politeness effects have found mixed results. A recent study conducted by Mikheeva *et al.* (2019), they recruited 277 students learned mathematics in a web-based intelligent tutor. The tutor provided either polite or direct instructions and feedback to students. The results showed that politeness in feedback influenced learning positively, but politeness in instructions did not have any influence.

The above paragraphs illustrate that there is a lack of consistency in the literature with respect to results that relate to politeness: some experiments support politeness theory while others do not. This suggests that more research is needed in this area. It is hypothesized that: Does social robot's feedback with different levels of politeness affect learning outcomes and interest in children?

3. METHOD

3.1 Participants and Design

Forty Taiwanese primary school children participated in the experiment. The children came from the same rural primary school in Chiayi, Taiwan. The mean age was 11.4 years (*SD =.47*); it comprised 21 boys and 19 girls. All the children attended computer lessons at least twice a week, played computer game and used the Internet. All had passed the school's internal Chinese language examination. The experiment used a within-subject design to discover how different level of politeness of feedback on the social robots affected children's learning outcome and learning interest. The independent variable was the difference level of politeness. The three levels were: high, medium and low politeness. The experiment had two dependent variables: children's learning outcome and learning interest.

3.2 Materials

The experiment uses NUWA Robotic manufactured Kebbi social robots which specifically designed for children. The Kebbi social robots were used for children to watch video (use animation as teaching material) and to conduct the interactive test during this experiment. The narration and feedback was done by a 20-year-old male professional voice. The robot gives facial expression from its build-in databank when giving feedback to match the voice tone.

Table 1. Feedback given in different levels of politeness

Feedback/Level of politeness	High level of politeness	Medium level of politeness	Low level of politeness
Correct feedback (Positive feedback)	Wow! You are awesome.	It's correct.	It's so easy, everyone should know it!
Incorrect feedback (Negative feedback)	Think again.	It's incorrect.	Everyone knows it, and you didn't know!

The video and test questions uses in experiment were designed by three specialists (including two school teachers who had over 7 years of teaching experience and one interaction designer with over 10 years of working experience). They created a set of teaching materials in the form of animation that suifigure for age 11-12 children. The three specialists eventually decided to use the theme "Life of a classical musician" for the content for this experiment. The video is in three parts, after playing each part of video, participants need to touch the social robot monitor to answer 4 questions related the content in the video, and once the answers were given, robot will randomly give feedback from 3 different levels of politeness. For example, when first part of video gives feedback from high level of politeness, the social robot will reply "Wow! You are awesome" (see Table 1), and show a smiling face (see Figure 1a). On the other hand, when answering incorrectly, the social robot will reply "Think again" (see Table 1), and show a sad face (see Figure 1b). The facial expression of social robot from different level of politeness were the same for correct answer, and incorrect answer. The verbal feedbacks were different according to the level of politeness which participants viewed. The feedback given after answering the question was designed according to Mayer *et al.* (2006) 's different levels of politeness.

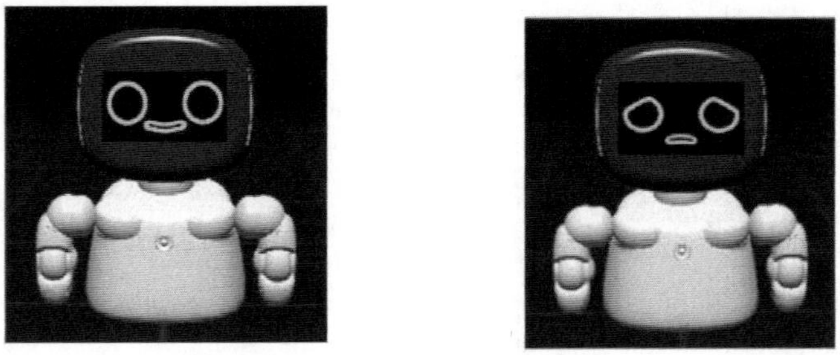

(a) Facial expression for correct answer (b) Facial expression for Incorrect answer

Figure 1. Social robot facial expression used in the experiment

3.2.1 Learning Test

The learning test took the same set of prior-knowledge questionnaire with different questions order. And then answer the test questions on social robot right after reviewing the video. The robot will give feedback with facial and verbal expression according to the answers given by participants.

3.3 Procedure

On arrival at the lab, an experimenter collected participants' consent forms which had their parent/guardian signed in advance of the experiment. Each participant was given his/her own social robots and worked alone. During the experiment, one participant in the classroom at a time with an experimenter. The experimenter gave oral instructions and demonstration of how to operate the social robot. Participants have been told that they can interact with the social robot freely for three minutes to familiar with social robot. Then, each participant started with the practice trial. The practice trial involved the children viewing the video on social robot (mentioned in Section 3.2.1) and answering two multiple-choice questions about each one. The section lasted no more than 10 minutes.

The experiment involved each child viewing video on social robot. The video divided into three parts with approximately equal length, after participants viewing each part of video, four questions will appear randomly. Participants need to answer the questions by touching the robot monitor, the social robot will give feedback with different level of politeness (either high, medium or low); each part have the same level of politeness, so that each participant received equal exposed to the three levels of politeness. The children were told that they could take as long as they wanted to answer the questions and should click the 'Done' button on social robot when finished.

Once everybody had completed the activity a questionnaire was distributed. Each question was explained and the children completed the questionnaire independently. During the sessions no child showed signs of fatigue. Before leaving the room, each child filled out a demographic form and received a stationary gift.

4. RESULTS

A one-way ANOVA was carried out to evaluate the different levels of politeness with respect to mean scores. The means and standard deviations for the scores obtained in the tests are shown in Table 2.

No significant effect of different levels of politeness on the learning outcome scores was found, F (2, 78) =0.27, p=.954. The results revealed that there was a significant difference between children's learning interest and the different levels of politeness, F (2, 78) =11.167, p=.000.

In terms of learning interest ratings, the highest score was given to the high level of politeness, followed by the medium level of politeness, then the low level of politeness. Further multiple comparisons using the Scheffé statistical test showed that the difference between the high level of politeness was significantly higher than the low level of politeness (p=.000); and that the medium level of politeness was significantly higher than the low level of politeness (p=.005). A significant difference was also found between the learning interest ratings for the high level of politeness and medium level of politeness (p=.019).

Table 2. Descriptive statistics for learning outcome and learning interest

	M	*SD*
Learning outcome		
High	1.50	1.02
Medium	1.47	.904
Low	1.45	1.05
Learning interest		
High	3.89	.675
Medium	3.72	.734
Low	2.49	.812

5. CONCLUSION

The experiment examined the politeness strategy on social robot with respect to children's learning interest and learning interest. It tested politeness theory of people's communication which claims that people prefer positive face than negative face. We divided the politeness according its directness into three levels (high, medium, low) on the feedback given by social robot.

The results showed that there was no significant difference between children's learning outcome and the level of politeness with social robot. However, it also showed that politeness had an impact on learning interest: children preferred high levels of politeness. This was in line with politeness theory. These results are comparable to those obtained by Mikheeva *et al.* (2019) and Wang and Johnson (2008), found that politeness in feedback influenced learning positively. This experiment clearly identified that different levels of politeness significantly impact on children's learning interests, but not learning outcome. This research should be useful to educators, instructional designers and social robot developers who create teaching materials for children. Further research is needed to determine how politeness strategy affects children' learning, when different age's children interactive with social robot.

ACKNOWLEDGEMENT

This experiment was kindly supported by a grant from the National Science Council of Taiwan. (Contract number: NSC109-2410-H-415-004).

REFERENCES

Brown, P., & Levinson, S. C. (1987). *Politeness: Some universals in language usage.* Cambridge university press.

Ginns, P., & Martin, A. J. & Marsh, H. W. (2013). Designing Instructional Text in a Conversational Style: A Meta-analysis, *Educational Psychology Review, 25*(4), 445-472.

Goffman, E. (1967). On facework. In E. Goffman (Ed.). *Interaction ritual* (pp. 5–45). New York: Doubleday Anchor.

Mikheeva, M., Schneider, S., Beege, M., & Rey, G. D. (2019). Boundary conditions of the politeness effect in online mathematical learning, *Computers in Human Behavior*, *92*, 419-427.

Mayer, R. E., Johnson, W. L., Shaw, E., & Sandhu, S. (2006). Constructing computer-based tutors that are socially sensitive: Politeness in educational software, *International Journal of Human-Computer Studies, 64*, 36-42.

Wang N., & Johnson W.L. (2008). The Politeness Effect in an Intelligent Foreign Language Tutoring System. In: Woolf B.P., Aïmeur E., Nkambou R., Lajoie S. (eds) Intelligent Tutoring Systems. ITS 2008. *Lecture Notes in Computer Science*, vol. 5091. Springer, Berlin, Heidelberg.

Wang, N., Johnson, W. L., Mayer, R. E., Rizzo, P., Shaw, E., & Collins, H. (2008). The politeness effect: Pedagogical agents and learning outcomes. *International Journal of Human-computer Studies, 66*, 98-112.

DEVELOPING DIGITAL HIGHER EDUCATION IN THE PANDEMIC

Barbara Getto and Franziska Zellweger
Zürich University of Teacher Education
Lagerstrasse 2
8090 Zürich, Switzerland

ABSTRACT

This work-in-progress paper presents a project with focus on the role of digital strategies on higher education development in the context of the pandemic situation. During the pandemic, higher education institutions had to switch to distance learning at very short notice. Motivated by the urgency of the external circumstances, digital media were used to a great extent. Numerous empirical studies have examined the experiences of lecturers and students and pointed to potentials and challenges. The steering efforts of higher education management and strategic implications though, have so far been less in focus. This project will contribute to the discourse on how the systematic further development of digitization efforts can take place in a forward-looking manner and what role digitization strategies play in the further development of studies and teaching in the context of the pandemic.

KEYWORDS

Higher Education Development, Digitization, Digital Strategies, Post Pandemic Development

1. INTRODUCTION

The drastic conversion of face-to-face teaching to distance learning in the wake of the corona pandemic has been accomplished surprisingly quickly and extensively in the higher education landscape. What e-learning specialists had worked towards (more or less) successfully in years of effort was now suddenly possible: Many faculty members have committed themselves to the new tools and have adapted their teaching to the new circumstances. Digital infrastructures were further expanded. In the meantime, it is becoming apparent that the sanitary situation will at least partially allow a return to the campuses soon and the question arises: What will remain of this exceptional experience? Numerous empirical studies have examined the experience of faculty and students and pointed to potentials and challenges. The steering efforts of leaders and strategic implications have received less attention to date. The outlined project is intended to contribute to the discourse on how the systematic further development of digitization efforts can be pursued and what role strategies for digitization play in the further development of higher education in the context of the pandemic.

2. HIGHER EDUCATION DEVELOPMENT IN THE CONTEXT OF THE PANDEMIC

2.1 The Significance of Digitization Strategies

Research on digitization in education has made it clear that digitalization in higher education institutions means an organizational change process that requires a range of measures at different levels (e.g., Seufert et al, 2015). Digitization in higher education is more than the introduction of certain technologies and new teaching methods (Castañeda & Selwyn, 2018). Projects as individual measures and associated investments do not contribute sufficiently to higher education development if they are not integrated into an overarching strategy that is anchored in the organizational development goals (Kerres & Getto, 2015). Therefore, higher education institutions are advised to pursue digitization along the lines of higher education development (Kerres & Getto, 2017).

During the pandemic, however, higher education institutions had to transition to distance learning on very short notice. Motivated by the urgency of external circumstances, the use of digital media occurred almost across the board. A distinction is made between digitally supported teaching and so-called "emergency remote teaching" (Hodges et al, 2020). Nevertheless, the question arises, what influence the experiences from the pandemic will have on the design of higher education in the context of digitization. In this context, we are particularly interested in the extent to which strategic principles guided the way in which this emergency was managed and in what way the experiences are incorporated into the strategic discourse.

2.2 Disruption by the Pandemic?

Findings from many empirical studies on the effects of the pandemic indicate that teaching operations could be maintained in spring 2020 with moderate difficulties in organization (Karapanos, Pelz, Hawlitschek, & Wollersheim, 2021). Students appreciated the flexibility of online learning but missed the contact with instructors and fellow students. Mulders and Krah (2021, p. 40) note that preferences for synchrony, self-structuring, collaboration, and digital lectures seem to vary widely among students. However, students are exposed to different degrees of financial and health burdens. (Rüegg & Eggli, 2020). Research in the field of teacher education indicates that most students could organize themselves well, but they describe their learning processes as rather superficial. Thereby, the heterogeneity of the experience is high. A dichotomous comparison of online vs. presence or synchronous vs. asynchronous or the question of the optimal mixture does too little justice to the complexity of the design task. Thus, the increased control of learning processes via assignments to be completed in self-study is very presuppositional both regarding the learning and working strategies of the students as well as the didactic preparation by the lecturers (Zellweger & Kocher, in press).

Different actors look back on this special period from different perspectives. Interpretations of the "emergency remote teaching" experience and discussions about the "new normal" have begun. What (strategic) considerations are higher education institutions using to shape the digitization of teaching and learning post Corona? This project follows strategic actors a few steps on the way out of the crisis towards a new normal.

3. RESEARCH QUESTIONS AND METHODOLOGICAL APPROACH

Based on the preceding considerations, we derive the following research questions:

What is the role of higher education digital strategies in coping with the pandemic?

Which strategic developments regarding the digitization in education can be observed post-pandemic and how are they motivated?

Under what conditions does strategy work support the further development of university teaching?

With this project, the need for action is to be identified and discussed with stakeholders in the higher education system to further develop framework conditions (in terms of structures and processes) for future-oriented teaching in the context of digitization. The methodical approach is planned in two phases:

Phase 1 (06-09 / 2021): Semi-structured interviews

In the transition between the end of the spring semester and the beginning of the autumn semester 2021, 7 interviews were conducted with experts in higher education institutions in Germany and Switzerland who hold management positions for teaching and further education or are responsible for university wide digitization initiatives.

For the selection of the interviewees, it was crucial that the persons in their function are closely involved in the strategic development of the university and at the same time are well acquainted with the operational challenges. In addition, attention was paid to a variety of perspectives based on the profile of the university as well as the people.

The discussions were analyzed using the "content structuring qualitative method" according to Kuckartz (2018, p. 97ff which suggests a sequence of deductive and inductive coding. For the first deductive coding, 13 main categories were defined in the three areas of strategy, digitization, processes / roles. In the following, sub-categories are inductively developed and condensed on the material within the main categories.

Phase 2 (10-12 / 2021): reflection and consolidation in focus groups

In the second phase, the results of the analysis are discussed and deepened with the interview partners as well as other experts in focus groups (Schultz et al., 2012).

It is also planned to repeat the interviews in the period in January 2022 when the planning of the spring semester is ongoing in order to trace how the discourse has developed over time. Are there new goals, what are they? Have expectations been met? What are current discussions? Reflection on decision-making? The analysis of these discussions is again made available and deepened in focus groups.

4. PRELIMINARY RESULTS AND PERSPECTIVES

Studies show that the measures implemented in the short term during the pandemic enabled higher education institutions to continue operating (Karapanos, Pelz, Hawlitschek, & Wollersheim, 2021). It is assumed that these activities are not so much part of a profile-building strategy for higher education development, but rather focus on digitization itself. In many cases, therefore, established classroom formats are translated one-to-one into digital courses.

From the observation of the discussions at higher education institutions, it can be assumed that the measures for implementing digital teaching since the beginning of the pandemic have been less guided by strategies or aimed at a long-term planning horizon.

Initial results of the analysis of the interview data indicate that the abrupt switch to emergency remote teaching at universities with elaborate digitization strategies went relatively smoothly. They were able to rely on an already well-developed technical infrastructure. In addition, universities in which a strategic discourse on digitization in education had already started were able to build on existing discussions and use established exchange and support structures and expand them as required.

In all universities in the sample, when switching to emergency remote teaching, reported high agility and willingness to cooperate within their own institution as well as across universities. With the duration of the pandemic, however, it also becomes apparent that there is primarily a great learning effect in the use of digital media. Didactic innovations, which also go hand in hand with a change of attitude, occurred far less. Decisions regarding digitization in the context of teaching and further education were not made with regard to long-term strategic perspectives during the pandemic. Rather, it was about keeping teaching operations going.

Under the impressions of the special situation since the beginning of the pandemic, an increased willingness to change was recorded. Wanting to use this as potential for the further development of university teaching is a frequently expressed wish. On the other hand, there are concerns about a sudden breakdown in developments if the framework conditions change. The pandemic situation as well as political decisions have a direct influence on the structuring options of the actors at the universities. For example, the decision of various federal states to plan the autumn semester "on campus" deprives university management of arguments to lead teachers in the direction of future-oriented blended learning concepts.

In retrospect, the adaptability of the actors was formulated as the most impressive insight during the pandemic. However, the question arises as to how sustainably this radical experience can be translated into innovation in teaching and learing. In the further analysis, the focus should therefore primarily be on the question under which conditions a qualitative development can take place and which pedagogical, technological, organizational, socio-cultural and economic aspects are of particular importance (Seufert & Euler, 2003).

REFERENCES

Castañeda, L., & Selwyn, N., 2018. More than tools? Making sense of the ongoing digitizations of higher education. *International Journal of Educational Technology in Higher Education*, 15(1), 22. https://doi.org/10.1186/s41239-018-0109-y

Hodges, C.B. et al, 2020. The Difference Between Emergency Remote Teaching and Online Learning. *Educause Review:* https://er.educause.edu/articles/2020/3/the-difference-between-emergency-remote-teaching-and-online-learning

Karapanos, M., et al, 2021. Hochschullehre im Pandemiebetrieb: Wie Studierende in Sachsen das digitale Sommersemester erlebten. *MedienPädagogik: Zeitschrift für Theorie und Praxis der Medienbildung*, pp 40, 1-24.

Kerres, M. & Getto, B., 2015. Vom E-Learning Projekt zur nachhaltigen Hochschulentwicklung: Strategisches Alignment im Kernprozess „Studium & Lehre". In A. Mai (Hrsg.), *Hochschulwege 2015. Wie verändern Projekte die Hochschulen?* Dokumentation der Tagung in Weimar am 8.–9. März 2015. Weimar.

Kerres, M. & Getto, B., 2017. Akteurinnen/Akteure der Digitalisierung im Hochschulsystem: Modernisierung oder Profilierung? In: *Zeitschrift für Hochschulentwicklung* 12, pp. 123-142. Retrieved from: http://www.zfhe.at/index.php/zfhe/article/view/973

Kuckartz, U. (2018). *Qualitative Inhaltsanalyse*. (4 Aufl.). Weinheim: Beltz Juventa.

Mulders, M., & Krah, S., 2021. Digitales Lernen während der Covid-19-Pandemie aus Sicht von Studierenden der Erziehungswissenschaften: Handlungsempfehlungen für die Digitalisierung von Hochschullehre. *MedienPädagogik: Zeitschrift für Theorie und Praxis der Medienbildung*, 40, pp. 25-44.

Rüegg, R., & Eggli, A., 2020. *COVID-19-Studierendenbefragung. Bericht der Berner Fachhochschule zur «International COVID-19 Student Well-being Study»*. Retrieved from https://doi.org/10.5281/zenodo.4422660

Schulz, M., Mack, B. & Renn, O. (Hrsg.). (2012). *Fokusgruppen in der empirischen Sozialwissenschaft*. Wiesbaden: Springer.

Seufert, S., & Euler, D. (2003). *Nachhaltigkeit von e-learning Innovationen*. (SCIL Arbeitsbericht 2). Universität St. Gallen.

Zellweger, F., & Kocher, M. (in Press). Das Engagement von Lehramtsstudierenden im Distance Learning im Frühling *2020. MedienPädagogik: Zeitschrift für Theorie und Praxis der Medienbildung.*

DEVELOPING AN ONLINE CURRICULUM FOR AN INTERNATIONAL AND INTER-DISCIPLINARY MASTER PROGRAMME. A CASE REPORT OF A DAAD FUNDED PROJECT IN GERMANY

Ly Lutter[1], Sabrina A. L. Frohn[2], Mishael Gabrielle Pizana Cruz[2] and Tobias Thelen[1]
[1]*Center for Digital Teaching, Campus Management and Higher Education Didactics; Institute of Cognitive Science, Osnabrück University, Germany*
[2]*Institute of Cognitive Science, Osnabrück University, Germany*

ABSTRACT

This paper describes the methodology of the ongoing efforts to design and integrate an online curriculum as an additional track to an existing, well-established interdisciplinary master programme for international students studying remotely and asynchronously with on-site students. We aspire to integrate online teaching and learning into in-person lectures so that both online and on-site students profit from the joint educational experience. During the initial orientation, we conducted a field-based investigation to define the problem, analysed the context, and assessed needs of the involved stakeholders. Prominent outputs of this phase were a literature review, a SWOT analysis of the target setting, a synopsis of stakeholder needs and wishes, and course goals. This enabled us to devise communication strategies with the stakeholders, define learning objectives, and course transformation plans to feed the design of new learning scenarios combining elements of online teaching and learning (OTL) with traditional on-site teaching. These integrate into communication tools that build on mixed student teams of online and on-site students working collaboratively.

KEYWORDS

Curriculum Design, Educational Design, Virtual University, Distance Learning

1. INTRODUCTION

This project, funded by the German Academic Exchange Service (DAAD), aims to make German study programs more internationally competitive and attractive to previously excluded target groups. For integrating online teaching and learning into in-person educational practices, we plan to instantiate work forms, such as assignments or groupwork that utilize the benefits of the international and asynchronous setting. In particular, we aim to take advantage of the slow but reflective nature of written communication and the diverse academic backgrounds of students for facilitating cognitive presence and student engagement.

Conclusively, we are developing new learning scenarios in close collaboration and alignment with the instructors' requirements and their course goals. Firstly, we utilize communication tools such as chats and threaded discussions to facilitate interaction among course participants and instructors. Secondly, we build on mixed student teams of online and on-site students who work on joint assignments and receive mentoring and exercise peer counselling on study progress, study goals and career perspectives in our overall design of the online study programme.

The rationale for the different steps and perspectives that must be considered for sound curriculum development on a global level was provided by McKenney and Reeves (2012). In order to explain why and how the instructional design process should be undertaken on the course level, we designed backwards as proposed by Wiggins and McTighe (2008). First, we identified what students should understand and be able to accomplish according to instructors, the module handbook and course materials. Secondly, we then identified what the instructors would accept as evidence of student understanding and their ability to use their learning in new and authentic situations (Wiggins & McTighe, 2008). The targeted courses are centred around programming, mathematics and neuroscience, which are the most popular among international students.

All six courses are based on lecture recordings and slides provided by the course instructors and some feature student-generated summaries and study material as products of assignments from previous teaching cycles.

2. INITIAL ORIENTATION AND FIELD-BASED INVESTIGATION

The results of our field-based investigation (SWOT analysis of the target setting, a synopsis of the stakeholder needs and wishes) and the literature review for the curriculum design process culminate in a problem definition and long-range goal. This initial orientation issued the design requirements and propositions for transforming the first six courses that were traditionally taught in an in-person lecture format to hybrid courses. To that end, we met with the instructors and addressed the official project goals while gauging their attitudes, values, and interests. Moreover, in order to collect perceptions about current online teaching and learning, we interviewed the involved stakeholders from the institute which include the student body, the study programme coordinator, the subject-specific mentoring team, and the university vice president. Additionally, we conducted a policy synthesis of the existing module handbook and investigated general and subject-specific student evaluations of the previous online corona semester. Our endeavour was led by efforts to determine how instructors, students, and stakeholders within the university system experienced the integration of OTL and / or what they suspect as the causes for its' scarcity (McKenney & Reeves, 2012). Further, we placed high importance on elucidating the needs and wishes of the involved parties to digitalize the courses in alignment with the individual teaching style and teaching capacities as well as what students and instructors would desire for OTL (McKenney & Reeves, 2012). Based on these insights, we synthesized a problem definition and designed measures which promote self-directed learning (Ke, 2010) and the establishment of a community of inquiry (Rubin et al., 2013).

Currently, the (online) educational practice significantly lacks social and intellectual interaction among students, between students and instructors, and between the German and the international student group. The courses are based on unspoken expectations regarding prior knowledge and skills that are shaped/ formed by cultural norms and habits. For example, "basic math" implies German Abitur-level math skills, which is not clearly stated nor necessarily comparable for internationals. This points to a systemic problem for international students in learning and integrating into the community. Furthermore, instructors have difficulties assessing students' needs and detecting and correcting misconceptions in students' understanding. The instructors express that they do not know how to engage students. While there seems to be insufficient resources for designing and facilitating learning activities that foster higher-order-thinking, a discrepancy seems to exist between the desire to discuss with students and the time constraints of instructors. Many lectures lack scaffolds for student learning such as clear instructions, advice on how to work in groups, or how to approach tasks that support students to move in their zone of proximal development (Vytgosky, 1978). Further, students report that some assignments are very artificial and that they experience uncertainty and confusion as to what is expected of them. For example, there are instances when students do not know how to apply theory to coding assignments. Instructors are not satisfied with students' knowledge transfer and scientific skills, which was visible in the drop of exam results and student interactivity in the past corona-semester. Yet, students focus on learning for the test and not on learning for understanding because of the high amount of content, which is partially also due to students taking too many courses at once.

By analyzing our interview notes in a SWOT analysis, we identified the jurisdiction of change, which revealed a clear understanding of strengths (e.g. students like self-directed and group-based learning, all instructors seek new methods for social interaction with students), weaknesses (e.g. instructors' partial unawareness for the need for informal communication between instructors and students, leading to uncertainty about students learning journey and students becoming passive consumers of content), opportunities (e.g. technical facilities and educational methods are available) and threats (students must learn and be supported to adapt to online learning, cultural mismatch and (implicit) biases regarding international students within the context of the study programme) that mitigate/contribute to the problem or even might facilitate/hinder a solution. By these means, we were able to study the formal, perceived, and enacted curriculum, which facilitated hypotheses about the factors that determine the implementation and spread of the digital curriculum. Utilizing the different strategies and methods served a balanced portrayal of the situation, created a broader ownership for the project, enabled respondent triangulation (McKenney & Reeves, 2012), and shaped our literature review which we wrote simultaneously.

3. SCRUTINIZING SELF-DIRECTED LEARNING AND A COMMUNITY OF INQUIRY

We aim to integrate online teaching and learning within on-site educational practices of a higher education institution and establish a community among the whole student body. Therefore, we use a framework that offers guidance for: (1) Designing asynchronous online learning experiences where there is a poverty of social signals (tacit signs of approval, understanding, or puzzlement) and that address the need to assure new ways to communicate and interact (Berge, 2008); (2) using self-directed learning as a lens to address adult learning in higher education and asynchronous learning settings. This supports student success in distance learning and offers flexibility regarding time, pace, and location that learners need due to the partially asynchronous setting (Bailey & Card, 2009; Kebritchi et al., 2017).

We analysed the existing courses and teaching practices regarding the facilitation of self-directed learning to accommodate the needs of online adult students, as SDL is a prominent concept for adult learning and for assessing and facilitating online learning in remote teaching and learning circumstances (Bailey & Card, 2009; Ke, 2010; Martin et al., 2019). Knowles (1992) (Bailey & Card, 2009) defines self-directed learning as a process in which learners take responsibility for diagnosing their learning needs, establishing learning goals, implementing learning strategies, identifying the human and material resources for their learning, and evaluating their learning outcomes. Further, we analysed and redesigned the courses using the Community of Inquiry (CoI) framework because it integrates constructivist and self-directed learning paradigms and highlights the importance of an online learning community (Garrison et al., 1999). The CoI outlines the three elements teaching, social and cognitive presence. These elements and their overlaps provide "the structure to understand the dynamics of deep and meaningful online learning experiences" (Garrison et al., 2010, p. 32). Moreover, the CoI offers a structured approach to assess the enlivenment of each of the presences (Garrison et al., 2001; Garrison et al., 2010).

4. INTEGRATING ONLINE TEACHING AND LEARNING INTO CURRENT IN-PERSON TEACHING PRACTICES

The instructors emphasized the importance of student understanding, interaction and communication with and among students and scalability of assessment methods for the course transformation, so we are closely collaborating with the instructors to identify the (1) links between concepts and conclusions students should draw and remember after they have forgotten most of the details, (2) the prerequisite knowledge and skills to arrive at these conclusions and (3) subject matter that is worth being familiar with (Wiggins & McTighe, 2008). With this lens on the courses, we are currently developing thought-provoking, open-ended questions that require justification and raise additional questions (Wiggins & McTighe, 2008) to facilitate cognitive and behavioural engagement in written discussion forums.

Furthermore, all instructors addressed the importance of student understanding, interaction and communication with and among students and scalability of assessment methods. All lecturers sought new methods to facilitate student engagement and expressed a desire to communicate with the students in order to gauge what the students are doing or whether they understood the subject correctly. Hence, student behavioural, cognitive and affective engagement in online courses were stipulated as goals of the integration of the online into the in-person lecture (Bond et al., 2020; Galikyan & Admiraal, 2019), as well as communicative measures that acknowledge the new roles and responsibilities instructors and students have in these hybrid teaching formats (Bailey & Card, 2009; Berge, 2008; Galikyan & Admiraal, 2019; Kebritchi et al., 2017) and clear instructions to scaffold students' learning, especially during group work (Molenaar et al., 2014). We identified the informal hallway chatter and missing role models for academic approaches to scientific inquiries by instructors in in-presence lectures to be one of the most substantial differences for cognitive presence in online learning scenarios. In online scenarios, students are not exposed to the habitus and behaviour of scientists like they would be when being in the same room, such that this vacuum needs to be filled or compensated. The next paragraph describes the measures we designed to address the identified gaps between online and in-presence teaching formats.

4.1 Designing Measures to Promote Student Engagement and Self-Directed Learning in a Community of Inquiry

We instantiated instructor-monitored, low threshold communication with course spaces and topical channels (chatrooms) in an instant messaging client (Element) to facilitate co-construction of meaning in a learning community. In these channels, we highlight critical reflection and discourse. Links on top of the forum titled "How do I write a good post?" or "Do's & Don't's" guide students when using and leveraging the discussion forums for the greatest learning benefit. These discussion channels pose the infrastructure to interact and monitor the integration and resolution level of cognitive presence for instructors, which will be utilized to uncover and correct misconceptions of students. The purpose of instructional and educational measures is clearly communicated to students in a timely manner within the LMS as suggested by Van der Meij and Carroll (1995). Furthermore and for the first time, students will receive syllabi which synthesize all necessary information about the courses, as suggested by Galikyan and Admiraal (2019). To that end, we filtered out learning objectives from course material to address students' confusion. The learning objectives convey what is expected of students to focus on (Wunderlich & Szczyrba, 2016). These expectations are clearly communicated at the beginning of every unit in the LMS so that students can self-monitor their learning. Moreover, we synthesized the expectations of instructors, the instructional modality, teaching philosophy and assignment instructions which communicate evaluation criteria and clear objectives including checklists for submission in the course syllabi for every course. Further, micro lectures were generated from 90-minute lecture recordings which consider cognitive load theory (Jong, 2010; Star & Stylianides, 2013) and student engagement (keeping it brief and using a conversational style for the newly recorded videos). Additionally, we promote active learning by embedding the micro lectures into a meaningful context as suggested in a review by Brame (2016).

In order to move from a passive to a more active learning experience, we designed short activities that accompany these newly created micro lectures to facilitate cognitive engagement and made the micro lectures part of larger homework assignments aiming to increase the sensibility of the micro lectures (Brame, 2016; Hung et al., 2010). Aside from the technical and subject matter transformation of course content, we placed high importance on scaffolding the students' learning journey. We situated the different elements of the courses (micro lectures, activities, discussion prompts, discussion infrastructure, assignments, evaluation criteria) in a structured and self-explanatory fashion within the LMS, following minimalist design principles to address self-directed learning (Kebritchi et al., 2017; Van der Meij & Carroll, 1995). Considering the Community of Inquiry, these means targeted enhancing cognitive, social and teaching presence.

5. CONCLUSION

The current project describes the ongoing efforts to design and implement an online track from existing courses of an on-site study programme for international students. The first project cycle has demonstrated the importance of sensibly merging both analytical and creative perspectives. These perspectives allow us to understand the current situation in which the project resides and discover opportunities to leverage the project goals. The various endeavours require systematic, focused and open-minded activities at the same time which often are inseparable from each other. In our experience, well-prepared interviews and careful listening to both systematic issues as well as personal interests were most insightful and provided a fruitful basis for the ongoing collaboration. To that end, we intensively studied the material of the courses. Our team attitude to be sincerely and genuinely interested in the experiences and needs and wishes of the instructors as well as the online students, established the grounds for constructive discussions on how and why current teaching practices unfold as they do. We addressed the teaching experiences, scarce time and pedagogical knowledge of instructors by clear and transparent communication, i.e. informing instructors about frameworks we would use to understand and revise current teaching practices and communicated the links of these frameworks to their own requirements and the project goal. Student assistants who were onboarded after the initial orientation (who studied online in the past semesters in this study programme) confirmed the problem statement. This confirmation acknowledged the analysis to be a concise and accurate reflection of their impressions of the current situation of teaching and learning. According to the instructors, we were able to suggest new learning activities that address the course goals and adhere to their requirements of scalability and manageability such as group assignments which are revised based on peer review and clear evaluation criteria. Taken together, this feedback suggests that the educational transformation of courses to OTL requires a field-based investigation utilizing different methods for phrasing an accurate problem statement and a profound overview about current research on the themes that emerge from the project goals and the initial orientation. The literature review in particular not only serves understanding but also inspires the design of educational measures.

Given the very ambitious time plan of having to transform a whole master study programme within two years, it was a challenge to resist the urge to act without having understood the causes and goals. This required thorough communication about the educational design steps and trust in the team. Despite that, constant efforts had to be put into sensitively navigating between the instructors' enthusiasm to transform a course to completely being held online and their scarce availability. Whilst the course design was traditionally guided by textbook coverage, our backwards design approach was admittedly well-taken, but with a certain amount of discomfort given the effort it entails. Thus, we offered support in all tasks and condensed as much information as possible from the available material (presentation slides, lecture recordings and interviews) to arrive at course goals and learning objectives. Our team served not only as a help desk but also as institutional support for transforming the courses which we view as a critical success factor. Based on the courses' purposes and big ideas, we created demo versions of one unit that include contextualized blanks which illustrated what kind of information and actions were still necessary for the instructors to do. This approach was extremely successful because it inspired the instructors to think of their own courses with new eyes. The design of the demo courses facilitated to think from the student's perspective *because* we addressed the needs and wishes of the instructors to (1) improve student understanding and facilitate deep learning, (2) facilitate interaction and communication with students that allows instructors (3) to keep oversight over what students are up to and to (4) create scalable and reusable material. These experiences point to the need of striking a balance between project goals and the ideal situation on the one hand and matters of feasibility on the other. This balance necessitates compromising planning, designing, and implementing the feasibility of eight months' time. Hence, we opted to focus on the course design instead of the course facilitation in our first cycle of the transformation and developed simple guidelines which translate theoretical understanding and best practices of micro lectures, leaning objectives, or discussion prompts into hands-on manuals that are useful for subject matter experts when designing courses.

The generalisability of the insights from this project phase are subject to certain limitations. For instance, we cannot yet evaluate the efficacy of the taken measures to facilitate OTL in an international remote and on-site student group due to the early stage of the project. This, however, is part of the next project cycle and is already addressed by the instantiation of a continuous and low threshold feedback channel for students and instructors. Moreover, we plan to conduct formative and iterative evaluations throughout the coming test phase when the first online students enrol in courses. Another natural progression of this work would be to investigate the impact and usability of the guidelines for creating educational material that were created based on best practices and insights from research on online teaching and learning. Taken together, the endeavours of the current project kick off a shift in teaching and learning paradigms which require thorough institutional assistance and support for both instructors and students.

REFERENCES

Bailey, C. J., & Card, K. A. (2009). Effective pedagogical practices for online teaching: Perception of experienced instructors. *The Internet and Higher Education*, *12*(3-4), 152–155. https://doi.org/10.1016/j.iheduc.2009.08.002

Berge, Z. L. (2008). Changing instructor's roles in virtual worlds. *Quarterly Review of Distance Education*, *9*(4), 407–415.

Bond, M., Buntins, K., Bedenlier, S., Zawacki-Richter, O., & Kerres, M. (2020). Mapping research in student engagement and educational technology in higher education: a systematic evidence map. *International Journal of Educational Technology in Higher Education*, *17*(2), 1–30. https://doi.org/10.1186/s41239-019-0176-8

Brame, C. J. (2016). Effective Educational Videos: Principles and Guidelines for Maximizing Student Learning from Video Content. *CBE Life Sciences Education*, *15*(4). https://doi.org/10.1187/cbe.16-03-0125

Galikyan, I., & Admiraal, W. (2019). Students' engagement in asynchronous online discussion: The relationship between cognitive presence, learner prominence, and academic performance. *The Internet and Higher Education*, *43*, 1–9. https://doi.org/10.1016/j.iheduc.2019.100692

Garrison, D. R., Anderson, T., & Archer, W. (1999). Critical Inquiry in a Text-Based Environment: Computer Conferencing in Higher Education. *The Internet and Higher Education*, *2*(2-3), 87–105.

Garrison, D. R., Anderson, T., & Archer, W. (2001). Critical thinking, cognitive presence, and computer conferencing in distance education. *American Journal of Distance Education*, *15*(1), 7–23. https://doi.org/10.1080/08923640109527071

Garrison, D. R., Cleveland-Innes, M., & Fung, T. S. (2010). Exploring causal relationships among teaching, cognitive and social presence: Student perceptions of the community of inquiry framework. *The Internet and Higher Education*, *13*(1-2), 31–36. https://doi.org/10.1016/j.iheduc.2009.10.002

Hung, M.-L., Chou, C., Chen, C.-H., & Own, Z.-Y. (2010). Learner readiness for online learning: Scale development and student perceptions. *Computers & Education*, *55*(3), 1080–1090. https://doi.org/10.1016/j.compedu.2010.05.004

Jong, T. de (2010). Cognitive load theory, educational research, and instructional design: some food for thought. *Instructional Science*, *38*(2), 105–134. https://doi.org/10.1007/s11251-009-9110-0

Ke, F. (2010). Examining online teaching, cognitive, and social presence for adult students. *Computers & Education*, *55*(2), 808–820. https://doi.org/10.1016/j.compedu.2010.03.013

Kebritchi, M., Lipschuetz, A., & Santiague, L. (2017). Issues and Challenges for Teaching Successful Online Courses in Higher Education. *Journal of Educational Technology Systems*, *46*(1), 4–29. https://doi.org/10.1177/0047239516661713

Martin, F., Ritzhaupt, A., Kumar, S., & Budhrani, K. (2019). Award-winning faculty online teaching practices: Course design, assessment and evaluation, and facilitation. *The Internet and Higher Education*, *42*, 34–43. https://doi.org/10.1016/j.iheduc.2019.04.001

McKenney, S. E., & Reeves, T. C. (2012). *Conducting educational design research*. Routledge.

Molenaar, I., Sleegers, P., & van Boxtel, C. (2014). Metacognitive scaffolding during collaborative learning: A promising combination. *Metacognition and Learning*, *9*(3), 309–332. https://doi.org/10.1007/s11409-014-9118-y

Rubin, B., Fernandes, R., & Avgerinou, M. D. (2013). The effects of technology on the Community of Inquiry and satisfaction with online courses. *The Internet and Higher Education*, *17*, 48–57. https://doi.org/10.1016/j.iheduc.2012.09.006

Star, J. R., & Stylianides, G. J. (2013). Procedural and Conceptual Knowledge: Exploring the Gap Between Knowledge Type and Knowledge Quality. *Canadian Journal of Science, Mathematics and Technology Education*, *13*(2), 169–181. https://doi.org/10.1080/14926156.2013.784828

Van der Meij, H., & Carroll, J. M. (1995). Principles and Heuristics for Designing Minimalist Instruction. *Technical Communication*, *42*(2), 243–261. https://www.ingentaconnect.com/content/stc/tc/1995/00000042/00000002/art00007

Vytgosky, L. S. (Ed.). (1978). *Interaction Between Learning and Development.*

Wiggins, G. P., & McTighe, J. (2008). *Understanding by design* (1st ed,). Association for Supervision and Curriculum Development.

Wunderlich, A., & Szczyrba, B. (2016). *Learning-Outcomes 'lupenrein' formulieren.* Zentrum für Lehrentwicklung, TH Köln.

TOWARDS A WEB-BASED HIERARCHICAL GOAL SETTING INTERVENTION FOR HIGHER EDUCATION

Felix Weber, Jana Kernos, Mae Grenz and Jueun Lee
Osnabrück University, Germany

ABSTRACT

In this paper we present the current state of a digital goal-setting intervention for higher education, which is based on the concept of hierarchical goal systems (HGS). Findings from organizational psychology, motivational psychology and educational psychology related to goals, self-regulated learning and goal systems are covered as a theoretical background. Subsequently, hierarchical goal systems are introduced conceptually and the concrete implementation and the essential functions of the digital HGS intervention are presented. Next, the current state of the development process and four studies currently in progress are briefly summarized. The studies are designed to answer the following research questions: How can students be supported in the discovery of personally relevant educational goals? How can students be supported in the construction of hierarchical goal systems directed towards such personally relevant educational goals? The paper concludes with an outlook on the benefits between students and researchers in the upcoming field study with the digital goal setting intervention.

KEYWORDS

Hierarchical Goal Systems, Goal Hierarchies, Self-Regulated Learning, Goal Setting, Higher Education, Digital Assistants

1. INTRODUCTION

There are at least three reasons why goals are interesting objects of investigation in educational research. The first is that they can be understood as a concrete manifestation of motivation. Humans are more likely able to elaborate on their goals than on abstract motivational dispositions, while goals can shed light onto the motivational dispositions. A second reason why goals are of significant relevance in the context education is, that goal settings has been shown to affect a broad variety of variables relevant for learning, such as activity, academic performance, well-being and vitality (Locke and Latham, 2002, 2019; Morisano, 2013). A third reason is, that considering goals as "internal representations of desirable states" (Vancouver and Austin, 1996), almost every human (learning) behavior can be viewed as being goal-directed. Consequently goal change has the potential to lead to behavior change.

Classical goal setting research originating from organizational psychology showed that the right degree of challenge has remarkable effects on performance (Locke and Latham, 1990, 2002, 2019). The more challenging the goal, the higher is the performance until the threshold of subjective ability to is exceeded. Beyond this point, performance rapidly decreases. In the domain of higher education these findings are essential because students need to find personal goals with the right degree of challenge.

More recent findings have shown correlations between motivation and well-being. For instance Ryan and Deci have outline a taxonomy of motivation and self-regulation styles in their self-determination theory (Deci and Ryan,1985; Ryan and Deci, 2017). SDT distinguishes a continuum between amotivation, different stages of external motivation and intrinsic motivation. The process of internalization of goals in this model can be promoted by the personal importance, self-endorsement, self-congruence of the goal and personal interest in the goal. This indicates that guiding students in the development of personally meaningful goals can to an increase intrinsic motivation, which is beneficial for learning and well-being.

Self-regulated learning is a conceptualization of learning, which is theoretically supported by a variety of theoretical frameworks, ranging from operant, social cognitive to cognitive constructivist perspectives (Zimmerman, 1989). A core element of self-regulated learning is the active role learners play by regulating their behavior. Cyclic models of self-regulated learning assume iterative strategic loops (Figure 1) with phases of planning, acting and reflecting learning processes (Zimmerman, 1989, 1990). In such models, individual learning goals serve a foundation for planning and benchmarks for evaluation.

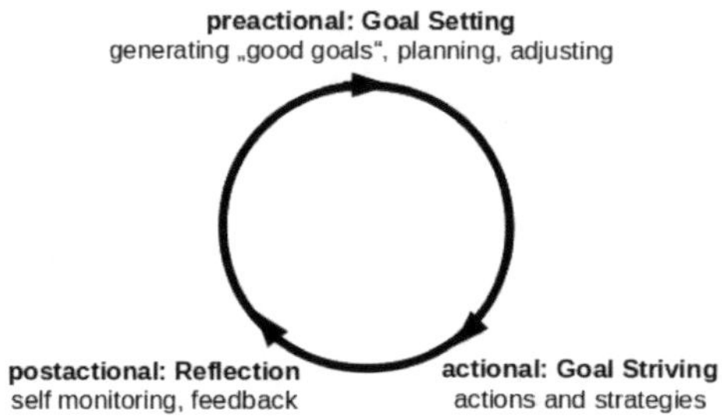

Figure 1. An iterative strategic loop is at the core of cyclic models of self-regulative learning. It can be assumed that learners in higher education experience phases and loops on various time levels and in parallel in various contexts

Goal clarification and related activities, such as elaboration and planning can lead to progress in terms of goal-achievement on a long-term perspective. Elaboration on goals and intensive writing about goals and ideal future can significantly increase academic performance (Morisano, 2008; Schippers et. al 2020). From these findings it can be concluded that students can benefit from intensive thinking, writing or digitally working on their personal educational goals. Hence, a digital assistant for guiding students through processes of goal setting, goal striving and reflecting about goal progress and goal achievement in higher education has the potential to accelerate individual academic progress.

2. HIERARCHICAL GOAL SETTING IN A DIGITAL STUDY ASSISTANT

In recent years there is a trend in goal setting research towards the study of goal systems and the relationships between goals (Kung & Scholer 2018, 2020). Goals with synergistic relationships can be modeled as coherent goal systems. Technically, hierarchical goal systems (HGS) are tree-shaped goal system, in which each goal has exactly one superordinate goal, except for the root goal. It has been shown that the structure of goal systems is a predictor for peoples' ability to choose the right means for goal pursuit and that a tree-shaped structure of goal systems increases tractability for humans (Bourgin et al., 2017). Hence, hierarchical representations seem to be compatible with mental models of goal systems.

Compared to other types of goal systems representations, such as sequential models and network models, hierarchical goal systems show at least three distinguishing properties concerning self-regulation. Firstly, every actionable goal contributes to a superordinate goal, which highlights its purpose and may increase motivation. Secondly, in the actional phase of goal-striving, action selection from the bottom layer is simple and a balance between guidance and free choice is given. Thirdly, in phases of reflection, goal progress can be evaluated based on quantity of achieved subgoals, and alternative actions and strategies can be dynamically added. The cost for these functional advantages is the effort of transforming the goal-related problem domain into a strict hierarchical schema. Participants in our studies have reported the translation to be especially challenging for subgoals contributing to more than one superordinate goal. Once a higher order goal and the problem domain has been modeled as HGS, goal pursuit is promoted by the former mechanisms.

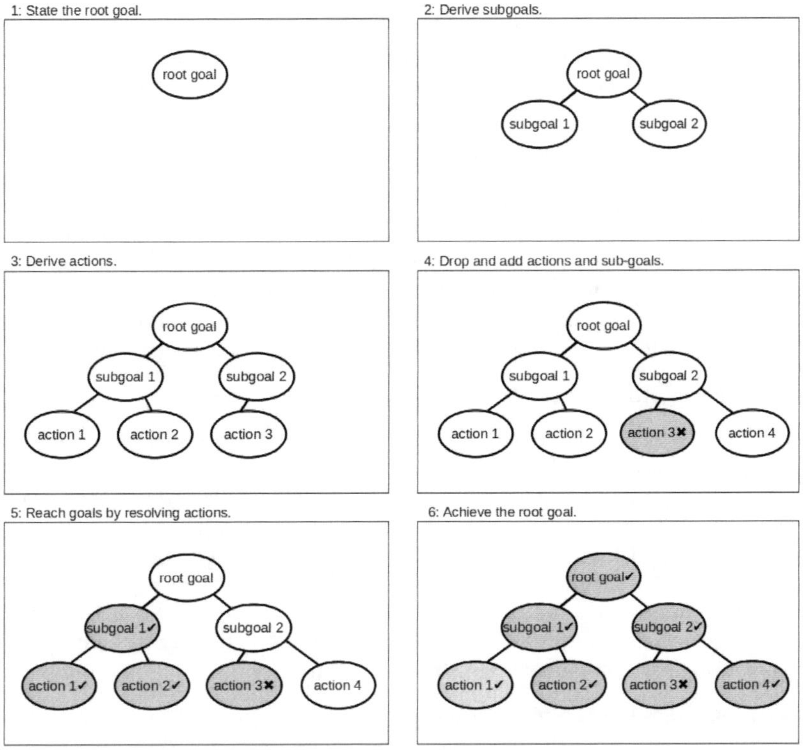

Figure 2. User interactions with a hierarchical goal system during its' life cycle

Our aim is to support students in the development of skills in self-organization and self-regulated learning. In their everyday life, university students learn on a concrete curricular level, but also on a meta-level of self-organization. They have to organize and prioritize tasks and plan and individualize their study paths. The current research prototype of a digital tool for hierarchical goal setting supports students by the following mechanisms:

- Students are encouraged or nudged to think about abstract personal goals and to define them. This functionality can lead to more motivation caused by meaningful educational goals.
- Connections between personally meaningful long-term goals to concrete tasks in everyday-life become transparent. This helps to activate and motivate for the concrete learning tasks ahead.
- The resulting personal educational root goals and maintained in the study assistant over time. This externalized memory supports goal stability and can increase attentional and volitional focus.
- Students are regularly nudged to think about new sub-goals, actions and strategies suitable to achieve personal root goals. This can lead to the refinement of suitable metacognitive strategies.
- Task selection and prioritization is done by picking tasks from the bottom layer of a hierarchical goal system. Simplified selection and prioritization reduces mental costs.
- Reflecting and evaluating goal progress, applied actions and strategies based on the goal system representation in the assistant leads to self-realization and learning on a metacognitive level.

Figure 2 illustrates how hierarchical goal systems can serve to bridge the gap between possibly abstract and distal root goals and concrete actions.

2.1 Current State of the Development Process

In a paper-pencil prestudy and a digital pilot study data was collected and analyzed exploratively. This helped us to identify two central challenges. The first is, that is a non-trivial task for students to spontaneously identify personal goals suitable as root goals. Consequently, we are developing and testing procedures that support students in discovering and developing personally relevant, distal educational goals. The second challenge is to develop an intuitive interface that makes it easy for students to construct hierarchical goal systems based on the root goals. To solve the second challenge, we have implemented four different types of hierarchical visualizations which are investigated regarding usability, user experience and personal preferences resulting from character traits. The following four studies are currently in progress.

2.1.1 Qualitative Usability and UX Think-aloud

In the first study, user experience and usability is optimized by testing the software with help of Think-Aloud Method (Albert & Tullis, 2008, p. 103). The TA-Method is supposed to provide detailed qualitative feedback in each step for each of four possible visual representations currently implemented in the software. Four subjects are randomly assigned to one visualization type, and instructed to verbalize the actions, and thoughts, during use the software. This method is supposed to shape the usability of the visual representation of the digital assistant and to provide insights about functional differences between visualizations.

2.1.2 Quantitative Usability and UX

In the second study, the four visual representations are examined with quantitative methods. Therefore, 48 students in four conditions go through a pseudo-randomized between-group experiment with a fixed scenario. In this study we shall compare their performance measuring the amount of time they spend on the task and the amount of clicks and errors they make. Additionally we want to measure self-reported efficiency, effectiveness and satisfaction with the help of System Usability Scale (Brooke, 1996) and After-Task Questionnaire (Lewis, 1991, Albert & Tullis, 2008, pp. 128-129). This study seeks to compare the success and satisfaction level of students using different visual implementations of the hierarchical goal system. With the help of received data we want to find out which visual representation is more suitable for the digital study assistant to design its interface in the most suitable and intuitive way.

2.1.3 Effects of OCEAN Personality Traits

In the third study, we aim to investigate the effects of OCEAN or Big Five personality traits (Goldberg, 1990; McCrae & Costa 1987) on the preference for a visualization type. Furthermore, participants are asked to evaluate the perceived complexity of the visualizations on a multi-item Likert scale and construct a personal hierarchical goal system with a randomly assigned visualization. The System Usability Scale (Brooke, 1996) is used to measure the usability of the intervention and a ranking of the visualizations by the participants allow to measure preferences for the visualizations types. This study explores a possible prediction of the preferred visualization type by the OCEAN personality traits. Since the web-based intervention is driven by personal goals, the visualization should ideally fit the individual preferences to allow for a more pleasant experience, increasing the motivation to continuously use the intervention.

2.1.4 Root Goal Elicitation with Priming

The fourth study uses priming to elicit goals with specific characteristics. Goals' self-concordance is not only a positive predictor of persistent effort in goal pursuit but also associated with increased happiness and goal attainment in the longer term (Sheldon, 2014). This study aims to investigate whether the priming of different motivations based on the self-determination continuum (intrinsic, identified, introjected, extrinsic motivation and amotivation) can influence the self-concordance of subsequently elicitated goals. In addition, it will be examined how the priming effect influences other goal characteristics such as goal specificity. This study hypothesizes that motivations that are intrinsically regulated are positively associated with higher goal concordance, thus students primed with stimuli related to intrinsic motivation select more self-concordant goals than those primed with stimuli related to extrinsic motivation or amotivation. In a within-subjects online experiment, participants will be assigned to each of the five conditions (intrinsic, identified, introjected, extrinsic motivation and amotivation) in pseudo-random order and asked to complete a writing task as priming stimulus. In a second task they are asked to formulate a personal academic goal. The goal characteristics questionnaire (Iwama et al., 2019) is used to measure the characteristics of resulting goals. The goal of this study is to gain insights how to build a priming task to elicit self-concordant goals as root goals for the hierarchical goal setting intervention.

3. OUTLOOK

The two most important intermediate goals of the outlined research are a) to build a hierarchical goal setting intervention that improves students' academic life and b) to implement a field study which allows the collection of hierarchical goal systems in a natural environment. To convince students to use the hierarchical goal setting intervention, we are working on an attractive interface with low interaction costs and high availability, embedded into the local learning management system. Goal characteristics will be measured and transparently displayed to students, enriched with background information. In this way students can benefit from scientific insights into human goal setting and goal pursuit and at the same time valuable data is generated which can promote scientific progress.

ACKNOWLEDGEMENT

The authors would like to express their very great appreciation to D.B., who did a great job implementing the software and took care of countless technical wishes of the authors to make all of the studies possible. Thank you!

REFERENCES

Albert, W., & Tullis, T. (2008). How to identify an issue. In *Measuring the User Experience: Collecting, Analyzing, and Presenting Usability Metrics* (Interactive Technologies) (1st ed., p. 103). Morgan Kaufmann.

Albert, W., & Tullis, T. (2008). Post-task ratings. In *Measuring the User Experience: Collecting, Analyzing, and Presenting Usability Metrics* (Interactive Technologies) (1st ed., pp. 128-129). Morgan Kaufmann.

Bourgin, D., Lieder, F., Reichman, D., Talmon, N., & Griffiths, T. L. (2017). The Structure of Goal Systems Predicts Human Performance. *Proceedigns of the 39th Annual Meeting of the Cognitive Science Society*, 1660–1665.

Brooke, J. (1996). SUS: A quick and dirty usability scale. In P. W. Jordan, B. Thomas, B. A. Weerdmeester, & I. L. McClelland (Eds.), *Usability evaluation in industry*. London: Taylor & Francis.

Cheung, E. (2004). Goal Setting as Motivational tool in Student's Self-regulated Learning. *Educational Research Quarterly*, *27*(3), 3–9.

Deci, E. L. and Ryan, R. M. (1985) *Intrinsic Motivation and Self-Determination in Human Behavior, Intrinsic Motivation and Self-Determination in Human Behavior*. doi: 10.1007/978-1-4899-2271-7.

Ryan, R. M., Deci, E. L. and (Eds.) (2017) *Self-Determination Theory: Basic Psychological Needs in Motivation, Development, and Wellness, Self-Determination Theory: Basic Psychological Needs in Motivation, Development, and Wellness*. Edited by R. M. Ryan and E. L. Deci. Guilford Press. doi: 10.1521/978.14625/28806.

Doran, G. T. (1981) 'There's a S.M.A.R.T way to write management's goals and objectives', *Management Review*, 70(11), pp. 35–36.

Ehrlich, C. (2012) 'Be careful what you wish for but also why you wish for it - Goal-striving reasons and subjective well-being', *Journal of Positive Psychology*, 7(6), pp. 493–503. doi: 10.1080/17439760.2012.721382.

Elliot, A. J. and Thrash, T. M. (2001) 'Achievement Goals and the Hierarchical Model of Achievement Motivation', *Educational Psychology Review*, 13(2), pp. 139–156.

Goldberg, L. R. (1990). Personality processes and individual differences - An Alternative " Description of Personality ": The Big-Five Factor Structure. *Journal of Personality and Social Psychology*, *59*(6), 1216–1229.

Iwama, G., Wirzberger, M. and Lieder, F. (2019) 'The Goal Characteristics (GC) questionnaire: A comprehensive measure for goals ' content , attainability , interestingness , and usefulness', (July). doi: 10.13140/RG.2.2.24237.84961.

Komarraju, M., Karau, S. J., Schmeck, R. R., & Avdic, A. (2011). The Big Five personality traits, learning styles, and academic achievement. *Personality and Individual Differences*, *51*(4), 472–477. https://doi.org/10.1016/j.paid.2011.04.019

Kung, F. Y. H. and Scholer, A. A. (2020) 'The pursuit of multiple goals', *Social and Personality Psychology Compass*, 14(1), pp. 1–14. doi: 10.1111/spc3.12509.

Lewis, J. R. (1991). Psychometric evaluation of an after-scenario questionnaire for computer usability studies: Thes ASQ. *SIGCHI Bulletin*, 23(1), 78-81.

Locke, E. A. and Latham, G. P. (2019) 'The development of goal setting theory: A half century retrospective.', *Motivation Science*, 5(2). doi: 10.1037/mot0000127.

Locke, E. A. and Latham, G. P. (1990) *A theory of goal setting and task performance*. Englewood Cliffs, NJ, USA: Prentice Hall.

Locke, E. A. and Latham, G. P. (2002) 'Building a practically useful theory of goal setting and task motivation: A 35-year odyssey', *American Psychologist*, 57(9), pp. 705–717. doi: 10.1037/0003-066X.57.9.705.

Louro, M. J., Pieters, R. and Zeelenberg, M. (2007) 'Dynamics of Multiple-Goal Pursuit', *Journal of Personality and Social Psychology*, 93(2). doi: 10.1037/0022-3514.93.2.174.

Neal, A., Ballard, T. and Vancouver, J. B. (2017) 'Dynamic Self-Regulation and Multiple-Goal Pursuit', *Annual Review of Organizational Psychology and Organizational Behavior*. doi: 10.1146/annurev-orgpsych-032516-113156.Louro, M. J., Pieters, R. and Zeelenberg, M. (2007) 'Dynamics of Multiple-Goal Pursuit', *Journal of Personality and Social Psychology*, 93(2). doi: 10.1037/0022-3514.93.2.174.

McCrae, R. R., & Costa, P. T. (1987). Validation of the Five-Factor Model of Personality Across Instruments and Observers. *Journal of Personality and Social Psychology*, *52*(1), 81–90. https://doi.org/10.1037/0022-3514.52.1.81

Morisano, D. (2013) 'Goal setting in the academic arena', in Locke, E. A. and Latham, G. P. (eds) *New developments in goal setting and task performance.* New York, NY: Routledge/Taylor & Francis Group, pp. 495–506. Available at: http://search.ebscohost.com/login.aspx?direct=true&db=psyh&AN=2013-00428-030&site=ehost-live.

Mora-Villalobos, C. R., Oreopoulos, P. and Petronijevic, U. (2017) 'Goal Setting, Academic Reminders, and College Success: a Large-Scale Field Experiment', *Uniagraria*, Volumen 5. Available at: http://www.nber.org/papers/w23738%0Ahttps://www.socialscienceregistry.org/trials/810%0Ahttp://www.nber.org/data-appendix/w23736.

Sheldon, K. M. (2014). Becoming oneself: The central role of self-concordant goal selection. *Personality and Social Psychology Review*, *18*(4), 349-365.

Schippers, M. C. *et al.* (2020) 'Writing about personal goals and plans regardless of goal type boosts academic performance', *Contemporary Educational Psychology*. Elsevier, 60(November 2019), p. 101823. doi: 10.1016/j.cedpsych.2019.101823.

Vancouver, J. B. and Austin, J. T. (1996) 'Goal constructs in psychology: Structure, process, and content.', *Psychological Bulletin*, 120(3), pp. 338–375.

Vansteenkiste, M. *et al.* (2004) 'Motivating Learning, Performance, and Persistence: The Synergistic Effects of Intrinsic Goal Contents and Autonomy-Supportive Contexts.', *Journal of Personality and Social Psychology*, 87(2), pp. 246–260. doi: 10.1037/0022-3514.87.2.246.

Weber, F. (2019) 'Goal Trees as Structuring Element in a Digital Data-Driven Study Assistant', in Sampson, D. G. et al. (eds) *16th International Conference on Cognition and Exploratory Learning in the Digital Age (CELDA 2019)*. Cagliari, Italy: IADIS Press, pp. 413–416.

Werner, K. M. *et al.* (2016) 'Some goals just feel easier: Self-concordance leads to goal progress through subjective ease, not effort', *Personality and Individual Differences*, 96. doi: 10.1016/j.paid.2016.03.002.

Zimmerman, B. J. (1989). *Models of Self-Regulated Learning and Academic Achievement* (pp. 1–25). https://doi.org/10.1007/978-1-4612-3618-4_1

Zimmerman, B. J. (1990). Self-regulating academic learning and achievement: The emergence of a social cognitive perspective. *Educational Psychology Review*, *2*(2), 173–201. http://www.jstor.org.libraryproxy.griffith.edu.au/stable/pdfplus/23359581.pdf

TOWARDS A CONCEPT FOR A HIDDEN OBJECT GAME WITH DYNAMIC DIFFICULTY ADJUSTMENT

Daniel Atorf[1], Sergius Dyck[1] and Jonas Steinbach[2]
[1]*Fraunhofer IOSB, Fraunhoferstr. 1, 76131 Karlsruhe, Germany*
[2]*Hochschule Worms, Erenburgerstraße 19, 67549 Worms, Germany*

ABSTRACT

This short paper elaborates on a work in progress concept for a hidden object game in the knowledge domain of remote sensing. Previous evaluations of the serious game Lost Earth 2307 revealed the need for shorter gameplay variants while still supporting the main learning objectives. It also affirmed the need to individually improve player immersion. To address this need, the short paper briefly depicts the method of the adaptivity cycle by Shute and Zapata and dynamic difficulty adjustment (DDA). The DDA is a popular method to adapt games and requires the finding of relevant difficulty levels and applying it in the game. The process of mapping and applying the difficulty in the game is called parametrization. This short paper shows a first concept of how to parameterize an adaptive game by a prototype implementation of an adaptive hidden object game. The short paper concludes with the results of a first informal test of the implementation and further steps.

KEYWORDS

Digital Game-Based Learning, Adaptive Game Design, Immersion, Flow

1. INTRODUCTION

The basic idea for this concept derived from the serious game Lost Earth 2307. It was developed for teaching on how to analyze aerial and satellite images and on how to formally describe the identified objects by using specific terms and write a report. This training domain is rather complex to teach, therefore individual training courses last several months and trainers have a high interest in keeping the students motivated over a long time. The game addressed this need by following the ideas of Digital Game Based learning (Prensky 2007) and Immersive Didactics (Bopp 2006). It was integrated into the course as an optional element in the informal learning phase where students had to intensify their knowledge through exercises.

Iterative evaluations during development and further on-site evaluations showed a need for streamlining the game design (Atorf et al. 2020). A main issue was the overall needed time to complete a mission. The initial type of task covered actions on each step of the image exploitation process cycle. This mapped exactly the exercises given to students for the informal learning phase in the afternoons. However, this kind of task required several hours to complete, thus there was not enough time for students to play "just another mission" in addition to the regular exercises. Therefore, missions in the game needed to evolve into smaller and more accessible tasks while keeping the major learning goals. In addition, there was a need to individually improve player immersion.

This short paper describes a work in progress concept and implementation for a hidden object game. This game genre promises to enable tasks which are quite close to actual image interpretation tasks, hence supporting original learning goals but providing a smaller and more fun task. The paper also describes the concept behind the parameterization of the game in order to enable a dynamic difficulty adjustment (DDA). The DDA addresses the individual improvement of player immersion. Finally, a first informal test of the concept is depicted and further steps are discussed.

2. METHOD

Analog to the original game Lost Earth 2307, the concept still follows the ideas of Digital Game Based Learning by Prensky and Immersive Didactics by Bopp. This means the game concept should support immersion or as Prensky states "*[...] the top two reasons people say they play interactive games [...] is because they are challenging and relaxing. This formulation seems very close to that magical state of motivation some refer to as flow.*" Immersion and flow act as a vehicle for facilitating positive user experience in order to maximize the impact of educational games (Kiili 2005).

Cairns et al define immersion in games as "*the engagement or involvement a person feels as a result of playing a digital gam*e" (Cairns et al. 2014). They describe three levels of immersion: engagement (player invests time and effort to play a game), engrossment (player pays a lot of attention to the game and is also emotionally involved) and total immersion (player "feels in the game"). According to Csikszentmihalyi, flow describes an "*automatic, effortless, yet highly focused state of consciousness*" (Csikszentmihalyi 1997). Cairns' Total Immersion can be compared to the state of flow (Kannegieser 2019). To sum up, a good serious game must enable player immersion and ideally create a state of flow.

To keep the user constantly in a state of immersion, thus constantly in the state of flow, the game must support some sort of adaptivity. Dynamic difficulty adjustment (DDA) is a possibility to keep the balance between challenge and skill (see Figure 1, left). The model of Shute & Zapata (see Figure 1, right) is suitable for the design of an adaptive system. The system monitors the user in a cycle and adapts itself to his needs (Shute and Zapata 2012). This adaptive cycle consists of four phases. In "Capture," a learner interacts with the system and all relevant data from the user interaction (e.g., scores, errors, engagement, etc.) are captured. In "Analyze", the data from the interaction is analyzed and fed to a learner model. The learner model describes the learner's knowledge of the respective learning domain. In "Select", new information and learning strategies relevant for the learner are selected based on the learner model, learning domain and learning goals. In "Present" the selected information is visualized and presented to the learner.

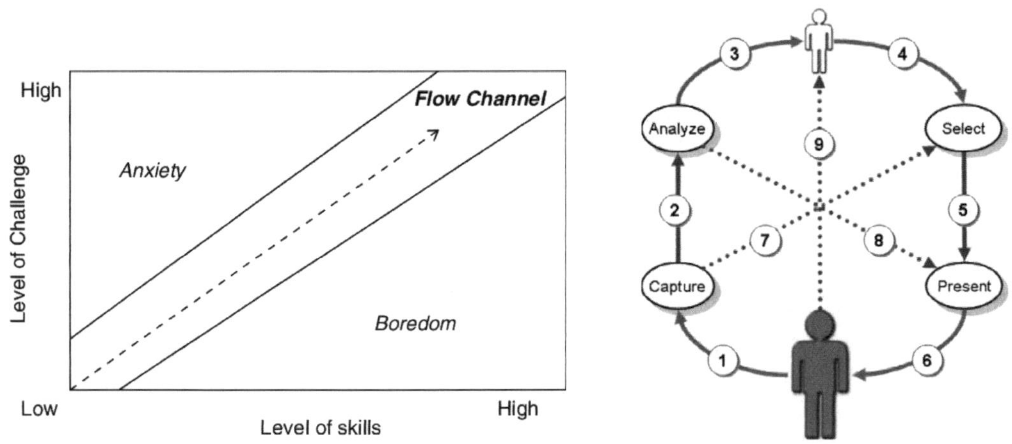

Figure 1. Left: Flow channel (Csikszentmihalyi 1997); Right: Adaptivity cycle (Shute & Zapata 2012)

For the concept of the game "Present" is especially relevant, as the game, which the user sees and plays, acts as the presenter. Hence, the game concept assumes a successful loop through the cycle and a corresponding response from the "Select" phase, the so-called Adaptivity Response (AR). The AR expresses the difficulty in a few scalar, normative parameters (Streicher 2020): Performance (current performance of the user), Assistance (whether and when the user should get help), and Skill (long-term performance of the user, i.e., how well the user has performed in e.g., exams). As said, "Present" includes the nature and structure of the game in relation to the learner model. For this concept, this includes a dynamic adaptation of difficulty (DDA) to the user, and accordingly, enabling parameterization of the game. The parametrization answers the question of "what to adapt", i.e. how the game has to be structured so that it can be adapted.

3. CONCEPT AND IMPLEMENTATION

The general game idea is based on the concept of a "Wimmelbilderbuch" or hidden objects. A classic example of hidden objects is the book series "Where's Wally?"(Handfort 1987) in which the main character named Wally has to be found on every page. In the field of computer games, there is the commercially successful genre of "hidden object games". Hidden object games are immersive and tell a story (Ioannidou 2018). Often the player is assigned to solve a given task. To do this, he has to move from one scene to the next and find various "hidden" objects within them. The essence of hidden object games is similar to the learning goal "Typenkunde" in image exploitation. An image analyst must not only recognize whether and where a relevant object can be seen on an image, but also what kind of object it actually is. This makes this type of interaction almost identical to that in hidden object games. And due to its immersive nature, they also meet requirements of DGBL.

The implemented game world for the hidden object game is based on a generated map. The current map section can be repositioned and zoomed in and out. The map shows vehicles to be found (target objects) and other objects (distractors) that resemble the target objects and/or are intended to distract the player. The player has to mark the target objects in a given time. Correctly marked objects are awarded points, incorrectly marked objects result in a penalty. The speed with which the objects were correctly marked has a positive effect on the total score. Figure 2 shows a screenshot of the game.

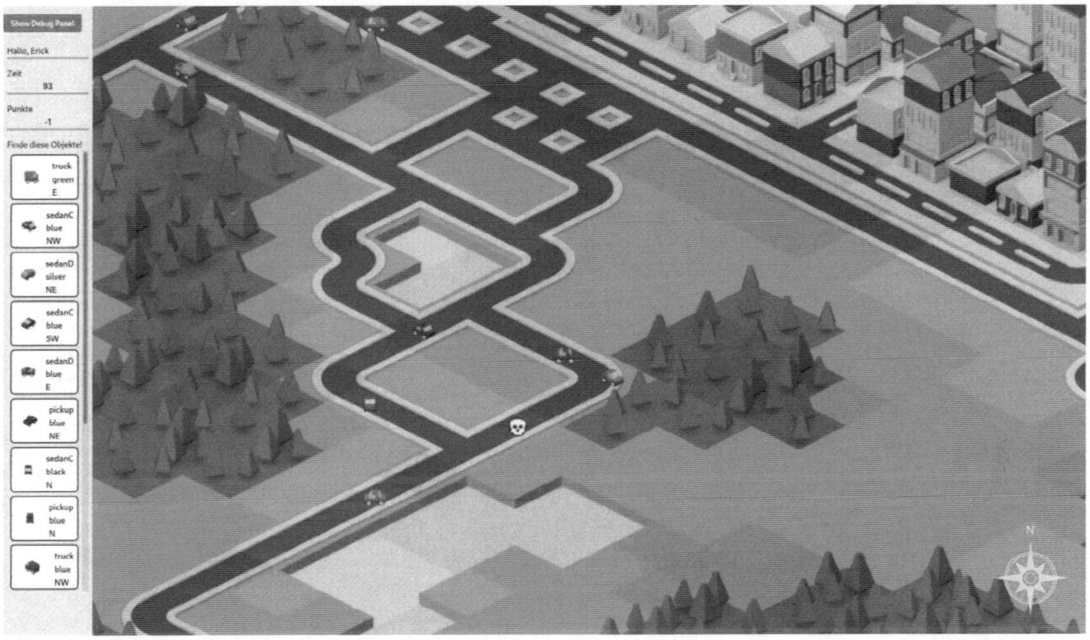

Figure 2. screenshot Hidden Object game (Left: list of objects, score, remaining time; Right: Scene)

With each new game, a new map is generated and the target objects as well as the distractors are repositioned. In addition to pure placement, options for customizing the target objects and distractors are also provided to enable training of "Typenkunde". Hence, the target objects are vehicles differing in shape, size, color and orientation, representing the characteristics mentioned by Lillesand (Lillesand et al 2015). The scene is procedurally generated using the tiling method and Perlin Noise to generate the landscape in the scene (Perlin 1985). During the game, other perturbations are added (e.g. day&night cycle). An adjustment of the difficulty level according to DDA is achieved by changing the map size, type of vehicles, number of vehicles to be found, number of distractors and the time available. To be more precise, there is a mapping on the adaptive response message parameters. The performance parameter controls the generation of the map, especially the size of the map and proportions of streets and cities. The assistance parameter controls the level of help and was realized in two variants: Highlighting of occasional target objects on the map (1) and displaying a thumbnail of the sought target objects in the list of objects to be found (2). The skill parameter controls target objects and distractors. It determines the number of different vehicle variants, the distribution of vehicles on the map, the number of vehicles and distractors, the game duration and the day&night cycle.

4. DISCUSSION & FURTHER STEPS

There is no universal guide for creating adaptive games, but the ideas of DGBL were applied by implementing a hidden object game. Following the model of Shute & Zapata the game adapts in the "Present" phase by implementing the adaptive response parameters, enabling DDA.

Five participants (3 image interpreters) went through a very first test of the game. A test followed two phases. In phase 1 participants played two complete rounds of the game as a 'Think Aloud Session', where participants were asked to verbalize what happens inside their head (Albert and Tullis 2013). The second game round in this phase was used to adjust the difficulty. Phase 2 was interviewing the respective participant. According to the think aloud sessions and the interviews, the vehicles used in the game are suitable for the application context. But the sprites used are too small and need to be improved (see Lillesand et al. 2015). The test users especially liked the number of distractor variants, describing them as "creative" and "promising". The concept showed that there is a great potential for creativity here, and that a great variety of distractors is possible. The use of time as an adaptable dimension to create stressful situations, seemed to be a promising approach and should be further explored in the next steps.

Overall the concept and the first prototype implementation seems promising. Further steps will include a formal evaluation with the target audience, especially focusing on fun and on learning goals.

REFERENCES

Albert, W., Tullis, T., 2013. *Measuring the user experience: collecting, analyzing, and presenting usability metrics*. Morgan Kaufmann, Waltham.

Atorf, A. et al. 2020. Towards A concept for streamlining game design of an existing serious game and preliminary evaluation. *In Proceedings of the IADIS International Conference WWW/Internet 2020*, pp. 155 – 160.

Bopp, M. 2006. Immersive Didaktik und Framingprozesse in Computerspielen. *In Neitzel, B. and Nohr, R.F. Das Spiel mit dem Medium. Partizipation-Immersion-Interaktion. Zur Teilhabe an den Medien von Kunst bis Computerspiel*, pp. 170-186, Schüren, Marburg.

Cairns, P. et al. 2014. Immersion in Digital Games: Review of Gaming Experience Research. *In Handbook of digital games 1*, p. 767.

Csikszentmihalyi, M. 1997. Flow and the Psychology of Discovery and Invention. *In Harper Perennial*, New York, p 39.

Handfort, M. 1987. *Where's Wally?* Walker Books.

Ioannidou. E. 2018. Neo-Victorian Hidden Object Games, Participatory Culture, and the Interaction Between Past and Present. *In Adaptation* 11.2, pp. 159–170.

Kannegieser, E. et al. 2019. Conducting an Experiment for Validating the Combined Model of Immersion and Flow. *In Proceedings of the 11th International Conference on Computer Supported Education*, Vol 2, pp. 252-259.

Kiili, K. 2005. Digital Game-Based Learning: Towards an Experiential Gaming Model. *In The Internet and Higher Education 8.1*. pp. 13–24.

Lillesand, T. et al. 2015. *Remote Sensing and Image Interpretation*. John Wiley & Sons.

Perlin, K. 1985. An Image Synthesizer. *In ACM Siggraph Computer Graphics 19.3*, pp. 287–296.

Prensky, M. 2007. *Digital Game-Based Learning*. Paragon House, St. Paul.

Shute, V.J. and Zapata-Rivera, D 2012. *Adaptive Educational Systems*. Cambridge University Press, pp. 7 -27.

Streicher, A. et al . 2019. Usage Simulation and Testing with xAPI for Adaptive E-Learning. *In: European Conference on Technology Enhanced Learning*. Springer, pp. 692–695.

THE ROLE OF AUTONOMOUS AGENTS IN TRAINING SCHOOL PSYCHOLOGY GRADUATE STUDENTS

Rogerio Eduardo da Silva and Elise N. Hendricker
University of Houston-Victoria
3007 N Ben Wilson st., Victoria-TX, USA

ABSTRACT

Graduate training in helping professions, such as psychology, requires knowledge, skills, and competency in discipline specific knowledge, as well as interpersonal skills. School psychologists are unique professionals trained to work with children, families, and school staff in public schools. The profession requires critical communication competencies across all domains of practice, yet training programs remain stagnant in ways to teach, measure, and evaluate these competencies in innovative ways. Interdisciplinary collaboration between computer science and school psychology holds great promise in remediating these concerns and advancing training using technology. Specifically, mixed reality and artificial intelligence tools, such as an autonomous training agent (ATA), where students can practice verbal and non-verbal communication strategies during clinical situations has the ability to provide deliberate practice for students in the classroom setting prior to working with real clients.

KEYWORDS

School Psychology, Mixed Reality, Autonomous Agents, Artificial Intelligence

1. INTRODUCTION

School psychologists are licensed professionals who provide psychological support in schools for children ages 3-21. They are uniquely trained to play a vital role in mental health promotion, prevention, and early intervention of social, emotional, and behavioral concerns. The National Association of School Psychologists [NASP] (2020) outlines graduate training standards of school psychology practices, along with ten domains of practice in which school psychologists should exhibit knowledge and competency. NASP (2020) also notes core beliefs drive school psychological practice, such as using effective strategies and skills to help children, demonstrating knowledge and skills effective for professional practice, and ensuring knowledge and skills reflect human diversity, cultural awareness, and social justice.

Across all the roles of the school psychologist, whether it be mental health assessment, consultation, intervention, or prevention, is the embedded organizational principle of professional communication (NASP, 2020). School psychologists must collaborate with a variety of stakeholders and exhibit strong communication skills to elicit appropriate information from children and families. They must effectively share results to make educational decisions, and display supportive, empathic communication with students and families to support their needs.

While these training domains and professional practices are outlined, graduate training programs in School Psychology are given latitude as to how these domains, knowledge, skills, and competencies are taught within their coursework. Research in the field has identified that communication competencies are critical to effective school psychology practice (Erchul et al., 2014), yet little has been done to identify how to teach these competencies (Newell & Newman, 2014). For example, when teaching graduate students how to effectively conduct a suicide risk assessment, an instructor may simulate the role of an adolescent to ensure the graduate student can display the proper knowledge, skills, and communication techniques. Graduate students may also be paired with one another to simulate real world experiences.

More recently, integrating technology into training experiences has been explored. Studies incorporating technology using a deliberate practice approach to improve school psychology graduate students' communication skills has shown great promise, while also building the self-efficacy of students within their professional interactions (Newman et al., 2021). Applications from computer science, specifically using autonomous agents and artificial intelligence, holds great promise in providing advanced training to prepare school psychology students for the plethora of skills they will need to be successful in their careers.

The goal of this project is to develop a mixed reality tool where a school psychology student should be able to interact, using natural language and gestures, with an autonomous training agent (ATA) specially trained to perform a specific role, acting as the client during a session.

2. DESIGNING AN AUTONOMOUS TRAINING AGENT

To design these autonomous training agents, we anticipate three levels of description will be necessary: embodiment, behavior, and interaction.

Embodiment has to do with describing how the agent will appear to the user, i.e., its physical appearance, movements that include facial expressions, lip synching, body posture, voice synthesis, etc. Behavior should focus on creating the decision-making process for the agent, i.e., to decide how to proper respond to the user's dialog and gestures while still playing a predefined role during the conversation. Interaction has to do with the technological framework to be used to provide such an interface that is easy to use (intuitive and natural).

The next sections describe our initial ideas for each one of these levels.

2.1 Embodied Conversational Agents

In computer science, *autonomous agents* can be understood as "*computational systems that inhabit some complex, dynamic environment, sense and act autonomously in this environment, and by doing so realize a set of goals or tasks for which they are designed*" (Maes, 1995). Although these agents can be applied to a variety of applications, we are interested in relying on these agents to create a virtual actor.

According to Iurgel and Marcos (2007), a virtual actor is "*an analogy to a real actor, which autonomously, and by its independent interpretation of the situation, can perform its role according to a given script, as part of a story*". Once more, according to the literature, virtual actors can be called by many different names depending on their characteristics, goals, and application: virtual humans, autonomous digital actors, or embodied conversational agents.

Embodied Conversational Agents (or ECA) (Cassell 2000) are characters capable of engaging in a face-to-face conversation autonomously deciding proper behaviors considering four main functions: emotional, personality, performative and conversational.

- Emotional function relates to the ability the agent should demonstrate of understanding human emotion (face, voice, speech intonation, etc.) and responding coherently.
- Personality function means the agent should demonstrate a unique pattern of thoughts, emotions, and behavior.
- Performative function represents the agent's ability to communicate believably with a human interlocutor verbally (words and intonation), non-verbally (gestures, gaze, posture), and para-verbally (sounds).
- Conversational function relates to being able to understand what is being said in a conversation. E.g., words, sentences, dialog structure, and semantics.

2.2 Producing Autonomous Behavior

There are basically three types of agents: reactive, deliberative, and hybrid. Reactive agents act by reflex, which means that they establish a direct correlation between input and output; deliberative agents act as if, for each input, the agent would be capable of some sort of analysis and planning before acting; hybrid agents process the characteristics of both reactive and deliberative agents.

One hypothesis we intend to explore during this project is the feasibility of implementing the ECA as an EBDI agent (Jiang et al, 2007; Thume and Silva, 2012). An EBDI agent (emotion-belief-desire-intention) is an example of hybrid agents that relies on two concurrent paths for deliberation:

- The primary emotions path (reactive layer) act as "filters", adjusting the priority of beliefs, allowing agents to accelerate the decision-making process.
- The secondary emotions path (deliberative layer) is used to refine this decision when time permits.

2.3 Mixed Reality Interface

To allow these autonomous training actors to provide a more vivid and productive learning experience to the student, the following aspects must be achieved:

1. They must look and move as realistically as possible.
2. They must behave as similar to human behavior as possible.
3. The interaction with them must be intuitive and natural, much like in a real scenario as possible.

For the first aspect, there are already tools available in the market to create and animate *digital humans*[1] that should provide a very realistic quality for the agent's embodiment. In terms of human behavior simulation, as mentioned in section 2.2, we are planning to explore EBDI agents as a means to convincingly mimic human behavior.

Regarding producing an intuitive and natural interface for the students to interact with the agents, our proposal is to develop a mixed reality interface.

Mixed reality is a blend of physical and digital words that allows users to interact with virtual and real-world objects simultaneously[2]. It results from the combination of users' actions, environment sensing (through camera, microphones, and other sensors), and computer-generated systems (virtual worlds) at the same time, thus enhancing the user's physical environment with virtual objects that are interactable in a similar fashion than other objects within the environment.

Figure 1. Example of mixed reality application using Microsoft Hololens
(Source: https://medium.com/hackernoon/the-dawn-of-mixed-reality-hololens-apps-9070a9800c26)

3. FINAL REMARKS

The proposed interdisciplinary project has clear advantages in advancing the training of school psychology graduate students. Communication skills, including verbal responses to clients, communication patterns, and understanding non-verbal behaviors, are often considered "soft skills" that are difficult to teach and practice, yet can play a large role in client outcomes in psychology disciplines. Advancing the use of technology to increase these skills can be beneficial in a number of helping fields (e.g., psychology, social work, and counseling) and other liberal arts and business disciplines (e.g., communication, marketing, and public relations).

[1] http://www.unrealengine.com/en-US/digital-humans
[2] https://docs.microsoft.com/en-us/windows/mixed-reality/discover/mixed-reality

REFERENCES

Erchul, W. P., Grissom, P. F., Getty, K. C., & Bennett, M. S. (2014). Researching interpersonal influence within school consultation: Social power base and relational communication perspectives. In W. P. Erchul & S. M. Sheridan (Eds.), Handbook of research in school consultation (2nd ed., pp. 349–385). Routledge. https://doi.org/10.4324/9781315759623-24

Iurgel, I. A., and Marcos, A. F. (2007). Employing personality-rich virtual persons—New tools required. Computers & Graphics 31, 6 (Dec.), 827–836.

Jiang, H., Vidal, J. M., and Huhns, M. N. (2007). EBDI: An architecture for emotional agents. In Proceedings of the Autonomous Agents and Multi-Agent Systems Conference, IEEE Computer Society.

Maes, P. (1995). Artificial life meets entertainment: Lifelike autonomous agents. Communications of the ACM, 38(11):108-114.

National Association of School Psychologists (2020). The Professional Standards of the National Association of School Psychologists. Author.

Newell, M., & Newman, D. S. (2014). Assessing the state of evidence in consultation training: A review and call to the field. In W. P. Erchul & S. M. Sheridan (Eds.), Handbook of research in school consultation (2nd ed., pp. 421–449). Routledge.

Newman, D. S., Gerrard, M. K., Villarreal, J. N., & Kaiser, L. T. (2021). Deliberate practice of consultation microskills: An exploratory study of training. Training and Education in Professional Psychology. http://dx.doi.org/10.1037/tep0000368

Thume, G. S., and Silva, R.E. (2012). An Extended EBDI Model Applied to Autonomous Digital Actors, In: Brazilian Symposium on Games and Digital Entertainment (SBGAMES), Brasilia-DF, Brazil.

A DIGITAL EDUCATIONAL GAME FOR PRACTICING OER EDITING

Lubna Ali[1,2], Vu Tuan Tran[2], Rene Roepke[1,2] and Ulrik Schroeder[1,2]
[1]Learning Technologies Research Group
[2]RWTH Aachen University
Aachen, Germany

ABSTRACT

The concept of Open Educational Resources (OER) was introduced to the world more than twenty years ago. Despite the fact that countless efforts have been made to promote the development of OER since then, the awareness of OER around the world is still considerably low. Many educators, who are familiar with the concept of OER, still hesitate to use OER in teaching and educational practices because they are concerned of violating copyright laws. This is mainly due to the lack of knowledge and practice in working with the OER. To disseminate the knowledge of OER, we have applied Game-based learning (GBL) and implemented a digital educational game that does not only help players practice editing and combining different OERs using suitable licenses but also motivates them to discover the world of OER by themselves. The game will be integrated within the introductory OER Workshops held at RWTH Aachen University. In this paper, we present the educational game and illustrate its main functionalities.

KEYWORDS

Open Educational Resources, Game-based Learning, Creative Commons, Educational Game, Licensing

1. INTRODUCTION

According to the United Nations Educational, Scientific, and Cultural Organization (UNESCO), the right to education is an international human right. Universal education is considered as one of the most important targets to be achieved besides providing people with food, clean water, and basic accommodation (UNESCO 2021). It is not only one of the most powerful tools for eradicating poverty but also the primary key to sustainable and peaceful development in the world. Nevertheless, according to the most recent reports on the website of UNESCO, there are still more than 262 million children and young people, who cannot go to school (UNESCO 2021). While their parents struggle to provide them with food and basic accommodation, they also cannot afford expensive textbooks and education. To help break out the cycle of poverty and lack of education, educational resources must be freely available to everyone. Based on this idea, the concept of Open Educational Resources (OER) was born.

OER are free learning materials that can be accessed by anyone (UNESCO 2021). They are presented in many forms such as documents, research papers, videos, audio files, images, slides, etc. Some of the most well-known platforms for distributing OER are YouTube, Wikimedia Commons, and MIT Open Course Ware. OER do not only benefit the users by delivering high-quality learning content without any cost but also the content creators (Caswell 2008). Although OER can be accessed free of charge, creators can still set the terms of use for their content by providing the OER with suitable licenses. In most cases, OER are licensed with Creative Commons (CC) licenses. CC licenses were introduced and are maintained by the non-profit organization Creative Commons, which helps people overcome legal difficulties in producing and using OER. Due to the human readability of the licenses, users can easily figure out what they are allowed to do and not.

In practice, people often mix different OER to create their own resources. Here, we consider two types of OER combinations: the *composition* and the *collage*. In the composition, each used OER has a clear and complete reference to its original source so that users can easily distinguish the different OERs used within the composition. Contradictory, collage is the kind of content, in which the resources are mixed and users can hardly determine the original resources.

While it is rather easy to combine OER if they have the same CC licenses, combining OER licensed under different licenses can be quite challenging. To support people in practicing the editing of OER, we have deployed a Game-based Learning (GBL) concept to develop an educational game that does not only convey the knowledge of OER but also motivates them to discover the world of OER themselves. In this paper, we will introduce the game and illustrate how it can be used within introductory OER workshops to support the participants in practicing and understanding the concept of OER Editing.

2. RELATED WORK

There are various tools that can be used when combining or editing different OERs. One of these tools is the Creative Commons Mixer (CC Mixer[1]), which is an online web service used for checking if a combination of different CC licenses is valid. Because the CC Mixer is just a fast-developed product for a hackathon, the usage of the CC Mixer is still very limited. For example, the CC Mixer assumes that all combinations are collages. Another tool that also supports users in properly licensing their creative work is the Creative Commons Chooser (CC Chooser[2]). CC Chooser is also an online tool that helps people choose the right CC license for their work. In general, CC Chooser has a friendlier User Interface (UI) than CC Mixer. However, CC Chooser was built for people who create the whole content on their own without using any available OER and want to publish their work with a CC license. This is quite dangerous because there is no clear hint on the website of CC Chooser reminding the user to pay attention to the licenses of external OER used.

Overall, existing tools that support the creation and editing of OER are either limited in functionality or do not provide support in combining existing OER using the correct licensing. Therefore, these tools are not suitable to present to people learning about OER and starting to create and edit OER. In addition, they fail to motivate and encourage people to explore the world of OER. In our attempt to provide a new tool supporting users to create and edit OER, we decided to apply Game-based Learning (GBL), as it helps users interact with learning environment and motivate people to explore and practice presented learning content. Indeed, the efficiency of GBL was verified by many experiments conducted in real life.

In (Rahmah 2019), Dr. Rahmah Fithriani at the Universitas Islam Negeri Sumatera Utara turned her grammar class into a playground, in which students learn English through various types of game namely *Guessing the Word*, *Board & Dice Game*, and *Run & Guess*. After the course, a survey was conducted to verify the efficiency of the game-based teaching method. The result was very positive. Before the course, more than 93% of the students said that they did not like learning grammar. After the course, all of them changed their opinion and said that they loved learning grammar. Before the course, less than 24% of students thought that grammar was necessary for communication. However, after the course, more than 96% of them agree that grammar was very helpful. Besides the aforementioned experiment, Mas-Machuca, M. et al. applied GBL in a Human Resources Management (HRM) course during the academic year of 2018/2019 at Universitat Internacional de Catalunya, Spain (Mas-Machuca 2019). Instead of purely teaching academic theory, they turned the course into a competition, in which students have to be active outside the classroom in order to win. After the course, a survey was conducted to evaluate the efficiency of the new approach. Results show that all the students prefer the game-based method to the traditional one. The authors claim that GBL not only helps them understand how the theory can be applied in real life but also strengthens the bond among students.

3. PROTOTYPE

One does not simply give the learners a game containing educational content and then expect increased motivation or significantly improved learning results. For that reason, we chose to follow the guidelines in (Plass 2015) to design a game that fits to the target audiences and the learning content. For simplicity, we chose to build a question-based game. The game consists of various multiple-choice questions about OER and CC license system.

[1] http://ccmixer.edu-sharing.org/, last accessed on 02.08.2021

[2] https://creativecommons.org/choose/?lang=de, last accessed on 02.08.2021

Regarding the narrative, we created a storyline that takes place in medieval time to distract players from the fact that they are learning about OER and immerse them into a thematic environment. In the story, as the best smiths in the realm, players are asked to forge a sword for the King. We choose this storyline because there are many similarities in the process of creating/editing OER to the process of forging a sword. For example, the process of mixing different material to create steel is very similar to the process of mixing different OER to create new OER.

Furthermore, to motivate the players to achieve the best in-game result, we built a leaderboard that honors the best players with the highest scores. The score of each level is calculated based on the performance of the player as well as the time they spend on the level. Regarding the learning content, the game is structured from easy to difficult.

In the first three levels, players are supported with practices. These practices are not only for preparing the players before jumping into the main storyline but also for reviewing the knowledge they learned in the OER workshops. In the main levels, players will have to apply their understanding of editing OER to overcome the challenge.

The target group of our game comes from various fields and is interested in editing or creating their own OER. We assume that most players already have basic knowledge about OER and the CC license system but do not have much practical experience with OER. Figure 1 shows a screenshot of the game interface.

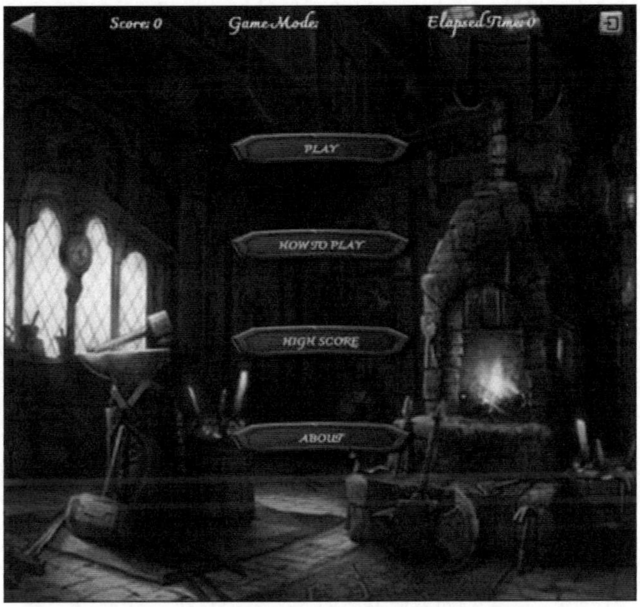

Figure 1. Screenshot of the game interface

Our game was developed as web-based game that can run in most modern browsers. The architecture behind the game consists of three main components: The frontend, the backend, and the database. The frontend is used to control and present the user interface. The backend serves as a bridge connecting the frontend and the database. The database is used to store the leaderboard information and user data.

4. USE CASE FOR EVALUATION

As a first testbed for our game, we consider the participants of an introductory workshop about OER organized by the Learning Technologies Research Group at RWTH Aachen University. The participants are either academic educators at the university or students in teacher education programs, who will become teachers in the schools after they graduate. The game will be introduced within the workshops as a tool to help the participants practice their knowledge about OER they have acquired in the workshop. The game is therefore utilized as a practical assignment. The workshop organizers will provide access and sufficient time to play the game (10 to 15 minutes). After playing the game, we plan to evaluate it by using a short survey. Players can then evaluate the functionality and user experience of the game. Open-ended questions allow for qualitative feedback regarding improvement ideas for the game. This way, we can explore how to extend our game for future workshops.

5. CONCLUSION AND FUTURE WORK

One of the barriers hindering the development of OER is the lack of knowledge about OER and, consequently, lack of practice in using OER. GBL is a concept that proposes the use of games in education. Through many studies, GBL has proven its advantages over traditional teaching methods. Besides conveying knowledge to the learners, GBL can increase their engagement in the learning process and encourage them to seek knowledge themselves.

Realizing the potential of GBL we have developed a digital educational game that supports players in practicing OER editing interactively during introductory OER workshops. The game was carefully designed, so that even people who do not have much experience with editing OER and the CC licensing system should be able to play and learn from the game without any problems. The game´s user interface was implemented to simplify the interaction between the players and the game as much as possible, so that the users do not need to read the instruction to know how to play the game. To motivate the players to strive for the best result, we added a leaderboard honoring the best players as an incentive system to the game. For further investigation and evaluation, we will gather feedback from the participants in upcoming OER workshops

Although the game has fulfilled our initial requirements of helping people practice OER editing, there is still plenty of room for extensions. To make the game more attractive, the storyline could be expanded or even a second one could be added. Another storyline would not only increase the complexity of the game, but also help players to understand OER better through providing more practice opportunities. Regarding the used game mechanics, our current game prototype is based on simple question mechanic. The interactions between the players and the game are very simple. The advantage of this simplicity is that the users do not need to read the instruction to know how to play. However, because of its simplicity, the players might get easily bored and lose interest. One suggestion for the improvement is to add more methods for players to interact with the game such as controllable avatars and different game mechanics.

Conclusively, we have developed a game that not only help players practice editing OER but also motivate them to discover the world of OER and CC licensing. Currently, we are planning to extend the game so that it can help people practice not only editing OER, but also the thematic fields of searching, using, and creating OER. Through this game, we have indirectly contributed to the promotion of the development of OER and advocated the right to education for everyone.

REFERENCES

Boyle, E. et al, 2016. *An update to the systematic literature review of empirical evidence of the impacts and outcomes of computer games and serious games*, Computers & Education 94, 178-192.

Caswell, T. et al, 2008. *Open Educational Resources: Enabling universal education*, International Review of Research in Open and Distance Learning Vol 9 No. 1.

Mas-Machuca, M. et al, 2019. *Implementation of Game-based Learning in Higher Education: an example in HR Management*, 5th International Conference on Higher Education Advances (HEAd'19), pp. 1043–1050.

Plass, J. et al. *Foundations of Game-Based Learning*, Educational Psychologist: Vol 50, No. 4, 258-283 (2015).

Rahmah, F, 2019. *Communicative game-based learning in EFL grammar class: Suggested activities and students' perception*, Journal of English Education and Linguistics Studies 5(2), 171–188.

UNESCO (2021). *Right to education*. Available at: https://en.unesco.org/themes/right-to-education, (Accessed: 30 June 2021).

UNESCO (2021). *Open Educational Resources (OER)*. Available at: https://en.unesco.org/themes/building-knowledge-societies/oer, (Accessed: 29 June 2021).

TEACHERS' PERCEPTIONS REGARDING THE USE OF INTERACTIVE WHITEBOARDS TO ENHANCE ELEMENTARY LITERACY DEVELOPMENT

Takashi Crum and John W. Hatcher III
New York City Department of Education, New York, New York 11201, USA
Southeastern Louisiana University SLU 10549, Hammond, LA. 70402, USA

ABSTRACT

This research study explored the effective use of interactive whiteboards to prepare students with basic literacy concepts to compete in a global economy. A single case study was employed to explore elementary teachers' adoption rates of interactive whiteboards (IWBs) to improve elementary literacy development. This qualitative narrative approach used observations, interviews, member-checking, and field notes to explore elementary teachers' perceptions related to professional development training for literacy instruction. The findings of this study revealed themes of integrated technology, instruction, elementary teacher perceptions, and elementary teacher's self-efficacy about using interactive whiteboards to improve elementary literacy development.

KEYWORDS

Elementary Literacy, Integrated Technology, Interactive Whiteboards (IWBs)

1. INTRODUCTION

In the United States of America, the inability to read and utilize print materials was viewed as an individual problem with implications for career opportunities, educational attainment, self-fulfillment, and participation in society (Lu, Ottenbreit-Leftwich, Ding, & Glazewski, 2017). According to the National Assessment of Adult Literacy, literacy was learned, while illiteracy was passed along from parents who could not read or write. The National Center for Education Statistics (2015) reported that one out of four children grow up not knowing how to read. Molin and Lantz-Andersson (2016) stated digital technologies for reading impacted what and how literacy instruction was provided to enhance student learning. Instructional resources such as digital technologies, interactive whiteboards (IWBs), and iPads were often used inefficiently; the literacy instruction students received rarely required them to read print. The National Assessment of Educational Progress (2011) reported that 33% of general education students and 68% of students with disabilities scored below the basic level on their grade level assignment. The efforts of the No Child Left Behind Act, prompted evidence-based literacy instruction in classrooms and transformed evidence-based literacy instruction into practical instructional standards that helped to develop the foundations of authentic learning in classroom environments (Sumak, Pusnik, Hericko, & Sorgo, 2017).

2. BODY OF PAPER

Low literacy rates among elementary students in the United States have been a grave concern regarding readiness for the 21st century global economy. Since the late 1990s, governments and schools have increased their investment to provide an effective technology infrastructure around the assumption that student achievement and elementary teachers' instructional practices would be enhanced. In addition, technology would alter education such that teaching, and learning would be more effective (Kearney, Schuck, Aubusson, & Burke, 2018). Given some elementary teachers' apprehension about technology integration, this study explored the low rates of elementary teachers' adoption of the interactive style technology to enhance elementary literacy development. The specific purpose and nature of this qualitative single case study was to explore elementary teachers' perceptions regarding the usage of interactive whiteboards in the classrooms of an inner-city school located in the Bronx, New York. The following questions guided the study:

- How do elementary teachers perceive the interactive whiteboard as a resource to improve literacy skills?
- How do elementary teachers perceive interactive whiteboards as a tool to enhance their teaching practices?
- How do elementary teachers perceive the interactive whiteboard as it relates to teachers' training and pre-literacy development in early elementary students?

The integration of the interactive whiteboard was grounded in the Technological Pedagogical and Content Knowledge framework (TPACK), which encompassed the complex nature of teaching and how the integration of technology compounded elementary teachers' ability to effectively teach (Koehler, Mishra, & Cain, 2013). The TPACK was an extension of Shulman's (1986) Pedagogical Content Knowledge (PCK) framework and included knowledge of technology (See Figure 1.). Researchers described TPACK as a complex structure that delineated elementary teachers' interrelated knowledge of instructional standards related to content, pedagogy, and technology, while further reporting that educators gained the knowledge needed to integrate technology into their pedagogical practices effectively (Koehler, Mishra, & Cain, 2013). Researchers conducted a cluster analysis using the TPACK framework and discovered how elementary teachers' TPACK development was used to teach technology, content knowledge, and pedagogy, which were required factors to effectively design, engage, and analyze curriculum and instruction with technology effectively (Koh & Chai, 2014).

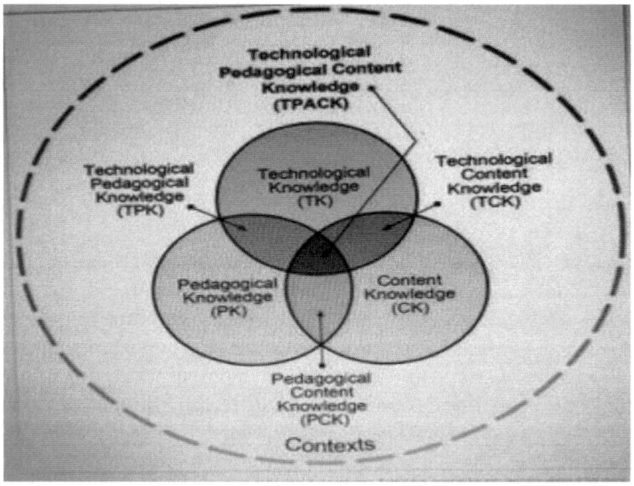

Figure 1. Three domains of elementary teachers' knowledge required to effectively teach and integrate technology Adapted from What is technological pedagogical content knowledge (TPACK)? by Koehler, M. J., Mishra, P., & Cain, W. (2013). *Journal of Education*, *193*(3), 13–19. Reproduced by permission of publisher, @ 2012 by tpack.org

2.1 Literacy Proficiency

In New York City public schools, there was a critical need for literacy education between 2009 and 2013. Approximately 26 percent of the student population could not speak English proficiently. Specifically, in the borough of the Bronx, 3% of the student population were not receiving literacy education (Zong & Batalova, 2015). The ability to assess, evaluate, and integrate information from a wide range of textual sources defined what it meant to be literacy proficient (Clarke, 2014). Literacy proficiency requires students to decode known and unknown vocabulary, comprehend print and digital print materials, and strong phonemic awareness knowledge. Critical literacy skill for struggling readers was phonological awareness which is an essential factor for reading instruction, fluency, and comprehension (Alhumsi & Affendi, 2014). Technology was redefining reading success for student literacy skills necessary to align with the changing model (Hutchison & Beschorner, 2015).

2.2 Technology Integration

Technology usage enhanced the efficiency of delivering content knowledge and it extended beyond the classroom environment yet, it did not explore interactive whiteboard technology's direct role in enhancing literacy learning and instruction. Keane, Keane, and Blicblau (2016) explored the issue regarding the gap between technology usage and academic achievement; the findings provided statistics that reflected how appropriate technology usage affects students' educational achievements. The integration of the IWBs opened a virtual environment to deliver and support learning activities within a group who were connected by common characteristics such as identity features, values, beliefs, interests, and goals (Farjon, Smits, & Voogt, 2019). However, according to Thoma, et. al. (2017), technology integration occurred infrequently or superficially in some classrooms and literacy instruction was dependent on technology integration to provide active learning and established a developmentally appropriate environment for problem-solving, supporting individual learning, and assessment and progress in students' learning. While the integration of the interactive whiteboard helped build a more visual and interactive learning environment conducive to teaching; elementary teachers' high involvement was related to significant student outcomes, but the actual role interactive whiteboard usage played in literacy achievement and instruction was not explored (McKnight, O'Malley, Ruzic, Horsley, Franey, & Bassett, 2016).

2.3 Elementary Teachers' Perception

Karaseva, Siibak, and Pruulmann-Vengerfeldt (2015) discovered that many people believe that technology played an integral part in student learning, but some elementary teachers believed otherwise. Transforming the learning environment relied on elementary teachers' perceptions, training, and selection of developmentally appropriate curriculum, software, and applications. The findings suggested that elementary teachers' redesign of technology integrated activities enhanced student learning and elementary teachers' experience of introducing technology, specifically interactive whiteboard technology for organization, professional development, and student achievement was identified (Karaseva, et al., 2015). Elementary teachers improved their teaching practice by accessing cutting edge learning resources and materials, adopted a student-centered approach to instruction, and enhanced communication between elementary teachers, students, and parents (Langub & Lokey-Vega, 2017).

3. METHODOLOGY

In this study, the researcher employed a single school narrative case study to describe elementary teachers' perceptions of the use of the interactive whiteboard as a tool to enhance the teaching and learning of elementary literacy skills. This qualitative methodology was appropriately designed to provide an interpretive analysis of elementary teachers' perspectives that gave voice to their lived experiences (Yin, 2016). A purposeful sample size was utilized of elementary teachers from kindergarten through 2nd grade at an inner-city public school in New York City. The goal of this study was to present the value of the interactive whiteboard for student learning and elementary teachers' perceptions related to professional development for literacy instruction. The New York City school district comprised 1,722 schools across five boroughs during this study. The participating school in this study was one of 98 schools in district 9 of the Bronx, New York. This inner-city elementary school educates students in grades Pre-K through fifth grade. The targeted population included elementary teachers with three or more years of teaching experience. The sample of participants in this study demonstrated four specific characteristics, (1) they were certified elementary teachers, (2) they had more than three years of teaching experience, (3) they taught grades kindergarten thru 2nd, and (4) they used technology in the classroom for at least one year. The sampling pool of participants consisted of 25 elementary teachers; 15 elementary teachers were general educators, five were intervention specialists, and five were special educators. A sample of 12 elementary teacher participants who met the criteria were sought to provide an adequate voice for elementary teachers' perceptions regarding the integration of IWBs as a tool to enhance literacy development.

The researcher was the primary instrument for data collection within a prescribed method for engaging participants, organizing data, and facilitating interviews. There were six sources of evidence and three principles of data collection for conducting this case study: direct observation, participant observation, documentation, archival records, interviews, and physical artifacts. The three principles of data collection used by the researcher were (a) use of multiple sources of data, (b) the creation of a case study database, and (c) the maintenance of a chain of evidence (Yin, 2016). Data were collected using a semi-structured interview protocol followed by 45-minute classroom observations. The interviews were bound by a field-tested interview protocol. The interview protocol was used to gather in-depth knowledge about elementary teachers' perceptions regarding the challenges they faced utilizing the interactive whiteboard to enhance literacy skills. To fortify credibility and transferability, data sources were triangulated using data collected during observation and coded on the observational guide to highlight how elementary teachers adopted the use of IWBs during literacy lessons, identified themes related to the research question(s), and denoted any occurrences related to elementary teachers' training. The 12 interviews were conducted in individual elementary teachers' classrooms afterschool at least one week before the classroom observations. A semi-structured interview protocol was used to ask questions and each interview was recorded using a digital recorder such as an iPad or iPhone. Data from each interview and field notes were processed by using unidentifiable code to protect participants' privacy. The data analysis was done manually. The conclusion of interview transcription, data analysis was printed out on a spreadsheet. The spreadsheet contained three columns pertaining to participants' identification number, the question, and the response. A basic content analysis methodology was applied to categorize the data and member checking occurred to validate the data (Saldana, 2015). Limitations of the study were relying on self-reported data as the main method of data collection and the population of teachers participating was small and consisted of 12 teachers; although attempts were made to include participants that were in many ways representative of the single school case. The themes derived from participant interviews and the classroom observations were grouped and discussed according to the research questions and applied to the following subsections: pedagogical beliefs, value beliefs, training, and support, and IWB usage for literacy instruction.

4. DISCUSSION

In this qualitative single case study approach, the questions were developed to gain insight relating to elementary teachers' perceptions of the interactive whiteboard as a tool for not only improving elementary teachers' pedagogy but reading literacy among their students. The findings of this study revealed themes of integrated technology, instruction, elementary teachers' perceptions, and elementary teachers' self-efficacy about using interactive whiteboards to improve elementary literacy development.

All participants agreed that integrating IWBs provided both whole class and small group interactive experience for visual, auditory, and kinesthetic learners. Thus, the instructional process unfolded gradually with elementary teachers' explicit instruction, guided practice, partner practice, and then independent practice. "*I create and write lessons, ELA specifically to teach phonemic awareness and decoding strategies as it presents students the opportunity to not only learn but be engaged and practice independently.*" Three participants stated that interactive whiteboards allowed them the opportunity to explore various teaching strategies and methods. "*IWB is essential because it provides another teaching voice to clarify students' misconceptions and reinforces a more engaging way for students to memorize taught concepts.*" Despite elementary teachers' comfort level, some elementary teachers readily incorporated IWBs for not only literacy instruction but all subjects to customize the instructional needs of students. "*I utilize it to display the information that you need students to learn, i.e., interactive websites, games, and just presenting/displaying the information whereas students can hear, see, and interact with the information.*" However, elementary teachers' overall perceptions regarding the interactive whiteboard as it related to elementary teacher training and pre-literacy development in early elementary students were mixed.

Elementary teachers' lack of training rendered IWBs usage ineffective for pre-literacy development because the IWBs usage was limited to engagement and motivation for students but not teaching and learning. "*Since technology is readily available, students have at home access thus their learning was not affected.*" Yet, "*my lack of confidence and experience renders IWBs usage ineffective.*" Some elementary teachers also believed that training or professional development should be consistently offered throughout the school year to effectively teach and enhance student learning in all subjects; consistency would build confidence in IWBs usage. "*I believe usage and impact would be more effective if training was consistent; inconsistent access and dilapidated machinery are a hindrance to IWBs usage and integration.*" Since elementary teachers were solely in control in their classrooms, their voices for training, support, and respect for their knowledge regarding teaching and learning were imperative to preparing 21st-century global citizens and eradicating low literacy rates.

It was discovered that elementary teachers' beliefs had the maximum impact on technology usage because elementary teachers controlled the presented content, the method of presentation, students' interaction, and the tools and resources needed for student learning. "*I believe IWBs are a valuable tool that have a high impact on teaching and learning; my students are highly motivated to learn, more attentive and focused and instruction is student-centered and self-directed.*" Overall, participants stated interactive whiteboard technology provided a motivational tool for students to be actively engaged learners, changed how participants thought about planning lessons, how to teach certain learning objectives, and provided another resource for lessons to be student-centered rather than teacher directed. This knowledge aligned with the theoretical framework, TPACK which provided the instructional standards educators needed and used to effectively plan and teach with technology, which impacted literacy instruction and learning.

5. CONCLUSION

The integration of technology into schools and classrooms in the 21st century has enhanced the teaching and learning process for both educators and students regarding elementary literacy development. This technological revolution was the introduction of the interactive whiteboards, which became a critical resource to enhance how elementary teachers taught and engaged their students to enhance elementary literacy skills. The perceptions of elementary teachers in this study found that the use of interactive whiteboards empowered students to take greater responsibility for the development of their learning and the use of interactive whiteboards was a critical tool to enhance elementary teachers' instructional delivery. Finally, the elementary teachers in this study perceived that when professional development was consistent and designed specifically to increase their self-efficacy with the use of interactive whiteboards value was added to their pedagogy. The relevant knowledge derived from this study may encourage other elementary teachers to embrace the difficult task of infusing technology into their elementary literacy lessons to improve students' literacy development. This study's findings offered insight for educators to overcome low literacy rates among early elementary students by recognizing the underutilization of the interactive whiteboard as a tool to improve students' literacy and other basic skills. The increase in the use of technology in the teaching and learning process is hopefully heading in a positive direction especially after the COVID-19 pandemic.

ACKNOWLEDGEMENT

We thank the New York City Department of Education and the administrative team for their consent to engage in this study. In addition, we acknowledge the single elementary school in the borough of the Bronx and our deepest gratitude for all the elementary teachers who provided their time, classrooms, professional perspective, their lived experiences regarding technology integration, and the benefits and limitations of the interactive whiteboard as a tool to enhance student achievement. We are also grateful to Koehler, M.J., Mishra, P., & Cain, W. (2013) for granting permission to use their TPACK framework.

REFERENCES

Alhumsi, M. H. & Affendi, A. (2014). Beginning readers have no prior experience with sound segmentation. *Journal of Education and Practice*, *5*(11), 32-41. Retrieved from www.iiste.org

Cakiroglu, O. (2015). Elementary teachers' views on the use of interactive whiteboards in secondary schools. *Eurasia Journal of Mathematics, Science & Technology Education, 11*(2), 251-259. Retrieved from www.ejmste.com

Clarke, L.W. (2014). Reader response 2.0: Using technology to support literacy growth. *New England Reading Association Journal*, *50*(1), 44-49. Retrieved from http://www.nereading.org

Farjon, D., Smits, A., & Voogt, J. (2019). Technology integration of pre-service elementary teachers explained by attitudes and beliefs, competency, access, and experience. *Computers & Education, 130*, 81-93. doi: 10.1016/j.compedu.2018.11.010

Hutchison, A. & Beschorner, B. (2015). Using the iPad as a tool to support literacy instruction. *Technology, Pedagogy and Education, 24*(4), 1-16. doi: 10.1080/1475939X.2014.918561

Karaseva, A., Siibak, A., & Pruulmann-Vengerfeldt, P. (2015). Relationships between elementary teachers' pedagogical beliefs, subject cultures, and mediation practices of students' use of digital technology. *Cyberpsychology: Journal of Psychosocial Research on Cyberspace, 9*(1). doi: 10.5817/CP.2015.1.6

Keane, T., Keane, W.F., & Blicblau, A.S. (2016). Beyond traditional literacy: learning and transformative practices using ICT. *Education and Information Technologies, 21*(4), 769-781. doi: 10.1007/s10639-014-9353-5

Kearney, D., Schuck, S., Aubusson, P., & Burke, P. (2018). Elementary teachers' technology adoption and practices: Lessons learned from the IWB phenomenon. *Elementary Teacher Development, 22*(4), 481-496. doi: 10.1080/13664530.2017.1363083

Koehler, M. J., Mishra, P., & Cain, W. (2013). What is technological pedagogical contentknowledge (TPACK)? *Journal of Education, 193*(3), 13–19. doi:10.1007/978-1-4614-3185-5_9

Koh, J.H.L. & Chai, C.S. (2014). Elementary teacher clusters and their perceptions of technological pedagogical content knowledge TPACK) development through ICT lesson design. *Computers & Education, 70*, 222-232. doi: 0.1016/j.compedu.2013.08.017

Langub. L. & Lokey-Vega, A. (2017). Rethinking instructional technology to improve pedagogy for digital literacy: A design case in a graduate early childhood education course. *Tech Trends, 61*(4), 322-330. doi: 10.1007/s11528-017-0185-1

Lu, Y., Ottenbreit-Leftwich, A.T., Ding, A., & Glazewski, K. (2017). Experienced iPad-using early childhood elementary teachers: Practices in the one-to-one iPad classroom. *Computers in the Schools, 34*(1-2), 9-23. doi: 10.1080/07380569.2017.1287543

McKnight, K., O'Malley, K., Ruzic, R., Horsley, M.K., Franey, J.J., & Bassett, K. (2016). Teaching in a digital age: How educators use technology to improve student learning. *Journal of Research on Technology in Education, 48*(3), 194-211. doi: 10.1080/15391523.2016.1175856

Molin, L. & Lantz-Andersson, A. (2016). Significant structuring resources in the reading practices of a digital classroom. *Journal of Information Technology Education: Research, 15*, 131-156. Retrieved from http://www.informingscience.org/Publications/3513

National Assessment of Educational Progress (NAEP). (2011). *Nation's Report Card: Reading* (NCES 2012-457). Washington, D.C.: U.S. Government Printing Office.

National Center for Educational Statistics (NCES). (2015). *The Condition of Education 2015*. (NCES 2015-144). Washington, D.C.: U.S. Government Printing Office.

Saldana, J. (2015). *The coding manual for qualitative researchers*. Thousand Oaks, CA: Sage Publications.

Sumak, B., Pusnik, M., Hericko, M., & Sorgo, A. (2017). Differences between prospective, existing, and former users of interactive whiteboards on external factors affecting their adoption, usage, and abandonment. *Computers in Human Behavior, 72*, 733-756. doi: 10.1016/j.chb.2016.09.006

Thoma, J., Hutchison, A., Johnson, D., Johnson, K., & Stromer, E. (2017). Planning for technology integration in a professional learning community. *The Reading elementary teacher, 71*(2), 167-175. doi: 10.1002/trtr.1604

Yin, R.K. (2016). *Qualitative research from start to finish*. New York, NY: The Guildford Press.

Zong, J. & Batalova, J. (2015). European Immigrants in the United States. Migration Policy Institute. Retrieved from www.migrationpolicy.org

PILOT STUDY OF THE RELATIONSHIP BETWEEN VOCABULARY ABILITY AND LEARNING PERFORMANCE FOR UNFAMILIAR KNOWLEDGE IN ONLINE VIDEO CLASSES

Kaori Tamura
Department of Information and Systems Engineering, Faculty of Information Engineering,
Fukuoka Institute of Technology
3-30-1 Wajiro-higashi, Higashi-ku, Fukuoka 811-0295, Japan

ABSTRACT

The COVID-19 pandemic has led to the introduction of online courses in higher education worldwide, including online video courses. In a video course, it is difficult to predict which students cannot follow a course that provides unfamiliar knowledge. Therefore, this pilot study investigated the relationship between learning performance of unfamiliar knowledge and Japanese vocabulary ability. A total of 59 college students participated in this pilot study. After their Japanese proficiency levels were measured by their grammatical and vocabulary abilities, they took a video course about the "Structure of Brain" (as an unfamiliar topic). The students took a short pre- and post-lecture knowledge test. The results of this study revealed that students with a high level of Japanese vocabulary ability showed higher learning performance for unfamiliar knowledge delivered via the video lecture. This pilot study contributes to predicting students' online learning performance based on student properties.

KEYWORDS

e-Learning, Video Course, Vocabulary, Prediction of Learning Performance

1. INTRODUCTION

In 2020, many universities were forced to provide online classes instead of conventional face-to-face classes due to the COVID-19 pandemic. Although the importance and effectiveness of remote education have been discussed in previous studies, most educational institutes provided conventional face-to-face classes before the pandemic. The pandemic forced instructors to make a sudden shift to online learning platforms. The use of a combination of online and face-to-face learning styles will be increasingly used even after the COVID-19 pandemic has subsided.

Lectures can be delivered remotely in several ways. Recorded video lectures enable students to learn flexibly, with no restrictions regarding time and place; however, they also have some drawbacks. For instructors, it is difficult to judge whether learners understood the content of the recorded video lectures because of a lack of simultaneous feedback and immediate interaction in the medium. When teaching new knowledge belonging to an unfamiliar field to learners, an instructor will fail to predict learners' understanding in recorded video lectures.

In this study, we aimed to explore the parameters of learners that helped predict their learning performance after watching a video lecture that provided unfamiliar knowledge. These parameters will enable the appropriate pacing of video course lectures despite the lack of simultaneous feedback from learners. In this study, we focused on learners' grammatical and vocabulary abilities of the language used for instruction, that is, Japanese. Existing studies have reported that learners' vocabulary is related to reading comprehension (Dickinson and McCabe, 2001; Ouellette, 2006), that can affect their knowledge acquisition. We hypothesized that grammatical and vocabulary abilities could be candidate parameters to predict learners' learning performance in video courses.

2. METHOD

All procedures of this study were performed in accordance with the guidelines of the ethics committee of Fukuoka Institute of Technology. A total of 59 undergraduate students of Fukuoka Institute of Technology participated in the study. They were students of the faculty of Information Engineering and took a class on "human biological system." All the participants provided informed consent in accordance with the Declaration of Helsinki. All the participants, excepting one student, were native Japanese speakers. Two participants declined to participate in the experiments after their written consent statements were obtained. One participant's responses were not considered in the final analysis because he was unable to complete his test responses within the stipulated time (over mean response time + 2SD). Finally, the data from 56 participants were analyzed.

The participants were asked to participate in two online experiments. Experiment 1 measured their Japanese language skills, and Experiment 2 measured their understanding and acquisition of unfamiliar knowledge delivered using an online video lecture. Their responses were collected using Microsoft Forms (Microsoft Corporation, Redmond, WA, USA).

2.1 Experiment 1: Japanese Language Skills

To measure the participants' Japanese language skills, we used the Grade I of the Japanese Language Examination (conducted by the Japanese Language Examination Committee), that is designed for all Japanese speakers, including native speakers. The Grade I of the examination is equivalent to the advanced level of business Japanese, with a pass rate of 22.3 % in 2020. In this experiment, we used 10 quizzes for measuring participants' vocabulary ability and 10 quizzes for measuring their grammatical ability; these quizzes were derived from the abovementioned examination. Each quiz contained multiple-choice questions, with a correct response to be chosen from four options.

2.2 Experiment 2: Video Lecture

The participants watched a lecture movie about the human brain anatomy, a part of the class on human biological system, and took a short pre- and post-lecture knowledge test. The questions in the tests were related to the content of the lecture movie. The length of the movie was approximately 15 min, and it consisted of slides about the learning content with the instructor's voiceover. The instructor did not reveal her face.

After watching the movie, the participants were also asked about their perceptions of cognitive load and situational interest (Wang, Antonenko and Dawson, 2020) (ranked from 1 to 7). Cognitive load is classified into overall load and three subtypes: intrinsic load, extraneous load, and germane load (Wang, Antonenko and Dawson, 2020). The overall load was assessed by the participants' self-report of the amount of mental effort invested in watching the video (Paas, 1992). The intrinsic load was measured by the students' ratings of content difficulty, and it has been assumed in this study that the intrinsic load was affected by the content and not by the instructional design (Cierniak, Scheiter and Gerjets, 2009). In this experiment, the intrinsic load was measured by the students' ratings for several difficult terminologies in the movie, texts in slides, auditory inputs (information from the narration). The extraneous load was measured by the students' ratings of how easy it was to learn from the online movie. The germane load was measured by the participants' self-reported level of concentration while watching the movie. Situational interest was measured by students' ratings for the statements "I am interested in the content" and "I am willing to learn new content related to the movie content".

3. RESULTS

3.1 Learning Performance after the Video Lecture

We confirmed the students' prior knowledge related to learning content and learning performance from the lecture movie. The rate of correct responses between the pre- and post-lecture knowledge test was compared.

The mean ± standard error (SEM) of the rate of correct responses pre-lecture was 0.24 ± 0.025, and that of post-lecture was 0.47 ± 0.033. A paired t-test showed a significant difference between pre- and post-lecture ($t(55) = -6.9$, $p < 0.001$) rates. The statistical results indicate that the rate of correct responses significantly increased after the students watched the movie lecture.

3.2 Japanese Language Ability and Learning Performance

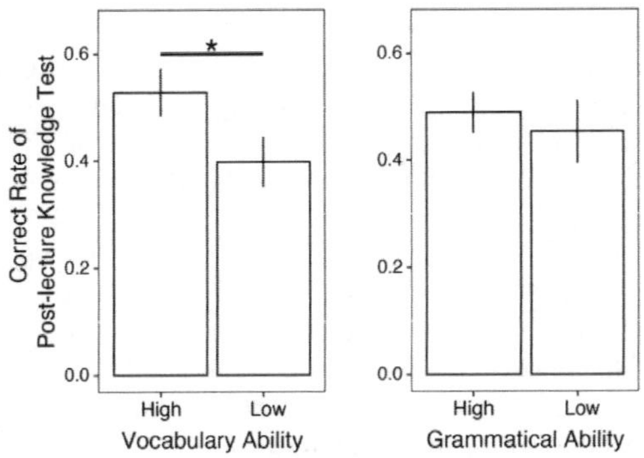

Figure 1. Mean and SEM of the correct rate of post-lecture knowledge test. The participants were divided by vocabulary ability scores (left) or grammatical ability scores (right) measured in Experiment 1 (*: $p < 0.05$)

We analyzed the relationship between the participants' Japanese language ability and post-lecture knowledge test scores (Fig. 1). Based on a balanced median split on the vocabulary ability scores as measured in Experiment 1, a high-vocabulary and a low-vocabulary ability group were formatted. The high-vocabulary ability group showed significantly higher scores on the post-lecture knowledge test than the low vocabulary ability group ($t(51) = 2.0$, $p = 0.047$).

Based on a balanced median split on the grammatical ability scores as measured in Experiment 1, a high-grammatical and low-grammatical ability group were formatted. For grammatical ability, there were no significant differences in the post-lecture knowledge test scores between the high and low grammatical ability groups ($t(40) = 0.50$, $p = 0.62$).

3.3 Learner Perceptions and Learning Performance

We analyzed the relationships between the participants' learning performance and perceptions. There was no significant correlation between the rate of correct responses post-lecture and the four types of cognitive load: overall load, intrinsic load, extraneous load, and germane load (Table 1). Regarding the situational interest, there was a significant but very weak correlation between the post-lecture learning performance and the ratings regarding the following statement: "I am willing to learn new content related to the movie content."

Table 1. Correlation coefficients between perception ratings and the rate of correct responses in the post-lecture test. All the correlation coefficients were calculated from several ratings and the rate of correct responses post-lecture. P-values indicated the significances of the correlation coefficients. Asterisk indicates significance level (*: $p < 0.05$)

Perception rating	Subtypes	Correlation coefficient	p-value
Overall load		0.13	0.35
Intrinsic loads	Difficulty in terminology	0.094	0.50
	The difficulty of texts in slides	0.13	0.36
	The difficulty of auditory inputs	0.012	0.93
Extraneous load		0.086	0.53
Germane load		0.23	0.083
Situational interest	Interested in the lecture	0.19	0.18
	Willing to learn more	0.28	0.041*

4. DISCUSSION

In this study, we aimed to investigate the relationship between undergraduate students' language abilities and learning performance of unfamiliar knowledge. From our results, we can suggest that vocabulary ability can affect students' learning performance of unfamiliar knowledge; however, we could not find any significant effect of grammatical ability on students' learning performance of unfamiliar knowledge.

The participants with higher scores in the Japanese vocabulary ability test showed a higher level of knowledge acquisition from the video lecture. Thus, vocabulary ability seems to relate to learning unfamiliar knowledge, although the vocabulary items asked in the Japanese language examination did not include terms related to the structure of the brain. We can assume that high vocabulary ability can support the acquisition of unfamiliar knowledge. The relationship between vocabulary skills and learning performance (Cain, Oakhill, & Lemmon, 2004) has been discussed previously; however, these studies investigated elementary and junior high school students. We suggest the possibility that vocabulary skills could affect undergraduate students' acquisition of knowledge from video courses.

The limitations of this study need to be discussed. In this study, we investigated only one topic, the "Structure of Brain," as it belonged to a knowledge field unfamiliar to the participants. To generalize the findings of this study, more learning contents should be assessed. We could not determine whether the scores reflected the test difficulty or the participants' low motivation for the experiment. For further investigation, it is necessary to assess participants' language proficiency levels with a lower grade of Japanese Language Examination. This study focused on learning with online video lectures, but there is a need to investigate the results of this study in other environments, including face-to-face lessons.

This pilot study showed a high probability that students with high vocabulary ability can learn new knowledge from online video courses efficiently. The results of this study will help instructors predict learners' performance in online education.

ACKNOWLEDGEMENT

This work was supported by a JSPS Grant-in-Aid for Early-Career Scientists (Grant Number 19K14319).

REFERENCES

Cain, K., Lemmon, K. and Oakhill, J. (2004) 'Individual differences in the inference of word meanings from context: The influence of reading comprehension, vocabulary knowledge, and memory capacity', *Journal of Educational Psychology*, 96(4), pp. 671–681. doi: 10.1037/0022-0663.96.4.671.

Cierniak, G., Scheiter, K. and Gerjets, P. (2009) 'Explaining the split-attention effect: Is the reduction of extraneous cognitive load accompanied by an increase in germane cognitive load?', *Computers in Human Behavior*. Pergamon, 25(2), pp. 315–324. doi: 10.1016/j.chb.2008.12.020.

Dickinson, D. K. and McCabe, A. (2001) 'Bringing it all together: The multiple origins, skills, and environmental supports of early literacy', *Learning Disabilities Research and Practice*, 16(4), pp. 186–202. doi: 10.1111/0938-8982.00019.

Ouellette, G. P. (2006) 'What's meaning got to do with it: The role of vocabulary in word reading and reading comprehension', *Journal of Educational Psychology*, 98(3), pp. 554–566. doi: 10.1037/0022-0663.98.3.554.

Paas, F. G. W. C. (1992) 'Training strategies for attaining transfer of problem-solving skill in statistics: A cognitive-load approach', *Journal of Educational Psychology*, 84(4), pp. 429–434. doi: 10.1037/0022-0663.84.4.429.

Wang, J., Antonenko, P. and Dawson, K. (2020) 'Does visual attention to the instructor in online video affect learning and learner perceptions? An eye-tracking analysis', Computers and Education. Elsevier Ltd, 146, p. 103779. doi: 10.1016/j.compedu.2019.103779

LEARNER INTERACTIONS AND BEHAVIORAL PATTERNS IN ENTERPRISE MOOCS

Marc Egloffstein[1], Muhittin Şahin[2], Max Bothe[3], Tobias Rohloff[3], Nathanael Schenk[4], Florian Schwerer[4] and Dirk Ifenthaler[5]
[1]University of Mannheim, Germany
[2]Ege University, Turkey and University of Mannheim, Germany
[3]Hasso Plattner Institute, Potsdam, Germany
[4]SAP SE, Walldorf, Germany
[5]University of Mannheim, Germany and Curtin University, Australia

ABSTRACT

This short paper investigates learner behavior in Enterprise MOOCs with the help of interaction patterns. By means of lag sequential analysis, data from 13 openSAP MOOCs from the topic areas business, design, and technology with a total number of N=72,668 active learners have been analyzed. Starting from consistent high-level behavioral patterns, a deeper analysis on the interaction level revealed variations between the course topic areas: Behavioral patterns in technology courses differ from business and design courses. Drawing upon these results, implications for future research are mapped out.

KEYWORDS

Enterprise MOOC, openSAP, Sequential Analysis, Behavioral Patterns, Learning Analytics

1. INTRODUCTION

MOOCs have become a viable alternative for corporate training and professional development (Egloffstein & Ifenthaler, 2017). A notable example of this is openSAP, an open learning platform related to the Tech/IT-sector. While many companies do not seize the full potential of MOOCs for training and development (Condé & Cisel, 2019) or lack adequate support (Hamori, 2019), openSAP implements so-called Enterprise MOOCs (Schwerer & Egloffstein, 2016) to convey knowledge about new technologies and business topics within the organization as well as to external stakeholders throughout the 'SAP universe' (Renz et al., 2019). Against the background of the common criticism of MOOCs in terms of instructional quality (Egloffstein et al., 2019) or completion rates (Reich & Ruipérez-Valiente, 2019), openSAP seeks to optimize its offering and to constantly improve the learning experience based on learning analytics (Khalil & Ebner, 2016).

This paper reports on the results of an initial study conducted as part of an academia-industry R&D partnership around openSAP. Focusing on learner behavior in different Enterprise MOOCs, the project aims to develop data-driven recommendations for learning design (Ifenthaler, 2017) and course facilitation. Following on from previous research (Rohloff et al., 2020), the study seeks to (a) identify typical behavioral patterns in openSAP Enterprise MOOCs and (b) determine whether such patterns differ between courses from different topic areas. This work-in-progress report extends existing high-level findings (Şahin et al., 2021) by analyzing learner behavior at the more granular level of system interactions.

2. METHOD

2.1 Sequential Analysis of Learning Behavior

As a well-established method of inferential statistics (Wald, 1973), sequential analysis can be employed for investigating behavior of learners in online learning systems (Şahin et al., 2020). It is a suitable approach when investigating behavior within an ongoing interaction (Bakeman & Gottman, 1997) and has been applied to various MOOC settings (e.g. Liu et al., 2021). Sequential relationships of observations and events with each other are also considered in sequential analysis (Bakeman & Gottman, 1997). Log-linear models, lag sequential methods, z-scores, and sequential pattern mining can be used to determine sequential patterns. In order to identify typical learning behaviors, transition probabilities are used to identify significant patterns (Bakeman & Gottman, 1997). The stochastic models provide the mathematical basis for precisely computing learning-dependent changes in online learning environments such as MOOCs. The Lag Sequential Analysis (LSA) process for this project consists of five distinctive steps: (1) develop event sequences, (2) map out transitional frequency matrices, (3) derive the transitional probability matrix, (4) calculate z-scores and carry out a test of significance, and (5) create a state transition diagram.

2.2 Sample, Data Collection, and Procedure

User events from 13 openSAP courses from the topic areas Business, Design and Technology have been analyzed with regard to patterns in learner behavior. The courses in the sample show variations in terms of length, effort, and design parameters like assessment configuration or additional instructional design elements (e.g., reflection prompts or coding exercises). The data used to conduct LSA consists of learners' interactions with the digital learning environment on the basis of traceable system states and events. In a preceding step of data preparation, the event data generated by platform interactions was coded based on the individuals. A total of 10,454,430 activities of N=72,668 professional and/or lifelong learners were analyzed. The sample reflects the characteristics of the overall population of openSAP learners, about two-thirds of whom are between 25 and 40 years old.

Following the overall structure of the openSAP MOOC platform, the learner events within a course were assigned to four main categories on a global level: learning (L), discussion (D), progress (P), and announcement (A). To gain deeper insights, we examined learners' sequential behavior patterns on the more granular level of system interactions. These interactions consist of 20 system events such as submitting assignments, downloading presentations, submitting surveys, visiting textual instructions, visiting videos, playing videos from category (L), posting comments, posting replies for category (D), visiting progress in category (P), and visit announcements in category (A).

In the first step of LSA, event sequences were created for each learner based on the interactions with the learning platform. An example of such a event sequence would be: LLLLDDLLLPDAALLLL. In the second step, transitional frequency matrices were created. Then, the transitional probability matrix was mapped out. Transitional probability is a conditional probability; events occur in different times and 'lag' is used to express these time differences (Şahin et al., 2020). In order to test the statistical significance of the transitions, z-scores were calculated, together with a Bonferroni adjustment to determine the z-score threshold. In the last step, a state transition diagram was generated for displaying the results.

3. RESULTS

3.1 Transitions Between Top Level Categories

Over all 13 courses in the sample, significant transitions between the four main categories could be traced. The respective state transition diagram for the high-level interactions is shown in Figure 1.

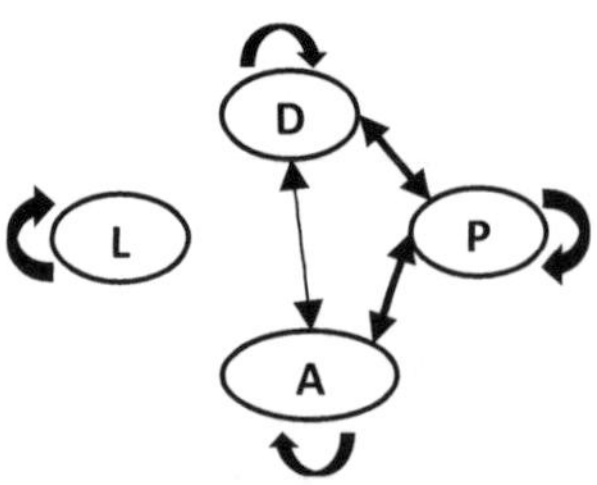

Figure 1. State Transition Diagram for the Overall Sample

The state transition diagram shows significant transitions between all the main categories except for the learning category. Looking at high-level interactions, the biggest category in terms of events captured is rather isolated.

With regard to the second research question, LSA was carried for each 'course bucket' (i.e., set of courses from one topic area) separately. As the learning category, again, remains isolated from the others, the data show a consistent pattern on this high level of analysis. Apart from that, behavioral patterns are similar but with some minor differences. For example, learners interact within the discussion category and then interact with the progress.

3.2 Transitions between Interaction Level Categories

There are twenty interaction categories and numerous transitions on the interaction level. An excerpt of the transition table for two interaction categories is presented in Table 1. Detailed information about these system interactions can be found in the appendix.

Table 1. Transitions on the Interaction Level

Interaction categories	Business	Design	Technology
Announcement (i1)	⇒ Announcement [BDT] ⇒ Discussion visit [BDT] ⇒ Progress [BDT] ⇒ Textual instructional visit [BDT] ⇒ Assignment submit [BT] ⇒ Textual discussion prompt visit [BT] ⇒ Final-exam submit ⇒ Survey submit	⇒ Announcement [BDT] ⇒ Discussion visit [BDT] ⇒ Progress [BDT] ⇒ Textual instructional visit [BDT] ⇒ Textual hands-on visit	⇒ Announcement [BDT] ⇒ Discussion visit [BDT] ⇒ Progress BDT ⇒ Textual instructional visit [BDT] ⇒ Assignment submit [BT] ⇒ Textual discussion prompt visit [BT]
Assignment submit (i2)	⇒ Assignment submit [BDT] ⇒ Progress [BDT] ⇒ Textual discussion prompt visit [BDT] ⇒ Textual instructional visit [BDT] ⇒ Textual download visit [BD] ⇒ Discussion visit ⇒ Survey submit	⇒ Assignment submit [BDT] ⇒ Progress [BDT] ⇒ Textual discussion prompt visit [BDT] ⇒ Textual instructional visit [BDT] ⇒ Textual download visit [BD] ⇒ Textual hands-on visit [DT]	⇒ Assignment submit [BDT] ⇒ Progress [BDT] ⇒ Textual discussion prompt visit [BDT] ⇒ Textual instructional visit [BDT] ⇒ Textual hands-on visit [DT] ⇒ Post create

Note. [BDT] joint transitions for Business, Design, and Technology; [BD] joint transitions for Business and Design; [BT] joint transitions for Business and Technology; [DT] joint transitions for Design and Technology

Results show that learners interacted with the announcements, discussions, progress, and textual instructions after visiting announcements in the courses from all three topic areas. Learners interacted with assignments and textual discussion prompts areas after visiting announcements in the Business and Technology courses. In addition to these, learners interacted with final-exams and surveys after visiting announcements in the Business courses. Looking at the assignment category, results show that learners interact with assignments, progress, textual discussion prompts, and textual instructions after visiting assignments in all three topic areas. Learners interacted with textual downloads after visiting assignments in the Business and Design courses. Learners visited textual hands-ons after visiting assignments in the Design and Technology courses.

Looking at the results of the LSA from a holistic perspective, both similarities and differences in students' sequential interaction preferences according to the course topic area become evident. Interactions of students in the Business and Technology areas seem rather similar.

From a closer perspective, sequential analysis shows that learners interact first with the assignments and then with the progress. Or, on the contrary, learners interact first with the progress and then with assignments. This result can be interpreted as learners submitting their task and then controlling their process/task or vice versa. Submissions of self-tests tend to induce video visits. This could be interpreted an indicator for a demand of additional knowledge about the respective topic. When learners download the video they also tend to download the audio and presentation. Learners can find information about the learning content and course elements when they visit the textual interactions. After visiting the textual instructions, learners interact with the announcements, submit surveys, and visit textual instructional prompts, textual downloads, textual instructions, and videos. This allows the interpretation that when learners discover the course details, they tend to visit the course elements and interact with these.

4. DISCUSSION

This work-in-progress study reported typical behavioral patterns in openSAP Enterprise MOOCs and possible variations between courses from different topic areas on the granular level of system interactions. Findings indicate that (1) there are consistent patterns, and (2) many characteristics of those patterns also apply when a differential perspective is adopted with respect to the topic areas. Among the top level categories, the learning category, which contains the majority of system interactions, remains isolated from the other categories. This might be due to a clear learner focus on working through the content and towards the assignments, while the announcement, progress, and discussion categories are more likely to be addressed at the beginning or the ending of a learning session. Moreover, announcements are also communicated via additional channels (e.g., via e-mail), and the learner progress is evident in the learning area, too. So if there is a need to better connect learning activities to collaborative (e.g., discussions) or meta-cognitive (e.g., announcements or progress visits) activities, cannot be decided at this stage yet.

The detailed analysis on the interaction level focused on the learning environment and its linear structure. The interactions are presented to the learners respectively, for example textual instructional visit, video visit, self-test, video visit, etc., textual download visit, and assignment submit. But when we examine the sequential transitions, learners do not prefer to interact with the remaining learning elements. Generally, one would expect learners to interact with a video and then with a self-test (Li et al., 2015). However, this is not observed in the interactions. Findings show that learners play the video without subsequent significant transitions to the other interactions afterwards. Thus, a more detailed analysis is needed. For example, video metrics such as play, pause, etc. could be taken into consideration here (Li et al, 2015).

To sum up the findings, we can conclude that if there is an access link in the pages, learners will interact with these materials sequentially. When we look at the results of LSA, both similarities and differences in students' sequential interaction preferences according to the topic areas become evident. Apparently, the interactions of students in courses from the Business and the Technology area are more similar. Within the scope of this research, LSA was conducted based on the system events. In addition, other metrics such as time spent could be included (Boroujeni & Dillenbourg, 2019), allowing for the discovery of more in-depth patterns and a deeper understanding of the learning process (Ifenthaler et al., 2018; Knight et al., 2017). After all, we expect to gain deeper insights into (successful) online-learning behavior in openSAP by combining LSA results with progress and performance data in the following steps of the research project.

REFERENCES

Bakeman, R., & Gottman, J. (1997). *Observing interaction: An introduction to sequential analysis* (2nd ed.). Cambridge University press.

Boroujeni, M., & Dillenbourg, P. (2019). Discovery and temporal analysis of MOOC study patterns. *Journal of Learning Analytics, 6*(1), 16–33. https://doi.org/10.18608/jla.2019.61.2

Condé, J., & Cisel, M. (2019). On the Use of MOOCs in Companies: A Panorama of Current Practices. In M. Calise, C. Delgado Kloos, J. Reich, J. Ruiperez-Valiente & M. Wirsing (Eds.), *Digital Education: At the MOOC Crossroads Where the Interests of Academia and Business Converge. LNCS Vol. 11475* (pp. 37-46). Springer. https://doi.org/10.1007/978-3-030-19875-6_5

Egloffstein, M., & Ifenthaler, D. (2017). Employee perspectives on MOOCs for workplace learning. *TechTrends*, *61*(1), 65–70. https://doi.org/10.1007/s11528-016-0127-3

Egloffstein, M., Koegler, K., & Ifenthaler, D. (2019). Instructional quality of business MOOCs: Indicators and initial findings. *Online Learning*, *23*(4), 85–105. https://doi.org/10.24059/olj.v23i4.2091

Hamori, M. (2019). MOOCs at work: what induces employer support for them? *The International Journal of Human Resource Management*. Advance online publication. https://doi.org/10.1080/09585192.2019.1616593

Ifenthaler, D. (2017). Learning analytics design. In L. Lin & J. M. Spector (Eds.), *The sciences of learning and instructional design. Constructive articulation between communities* (pp. 202–211). Routledge. https://doi.org/10.4324/9781315684444-13

Ifenthaler, D., Gibson, D. C., & Dobozy, E. (2018). Informing learning design through analytics: Applying network graph analysis. *Australasian Journal of Educational Technology*, *34*(2), 117–132. https://doi.org/10.14742/ajet.3767

Khalil, M., & Ebner, M. (2016). When Learning Analytics Meets MOOCs - a Review on iMooX Case Studies. In G. Fahrnberger, G. Eichler & C. Erfurth (Eds.*), Innovations for Community Services. 16th International Conference I4CS* (pp. 3-19). Springer. https://doi.org/10.1007/978-3-319-49466-1_1

Knight, S., Wise, A., & Chen, B. (2017). Time for Change: Why Learning Analytics Needs Temporal Analysis. *Journal of Learning Analytics*, *4*(3), 7–17. https://doi.org/10.18608/jla.2017.43.2

Li, N., Kidziński, Ł., Jermann, P., & Dillenbourg, P. (2015). MOOC video interaction patterns: What do they tell us? In G. Conole, T. Klobučar, C. Rensing, J. Konert & É. Lavoué (Eds.), *Design for teaching and learning in a networked world. LNCS Vol. 9307* (pp. 197–210). Springer. https://doi.org/10.1007/978-3-319-24258-3_15

Liu, B., Wu, Y., Xing, W., Cheng, G., & Guo, S. (2021). Exploring behavioural differences between certificate achievers and explorers in MOOCs. *Asia Pacific Journal of Education*. Advance online publication. https://doi.org/10.1080/02188791.2020.1868974

Reich, J., & Ruipérez-Valiente, J. A. (2019). The MOOC Pivot. *Science* 363(6423), 130-131. https://doi.org/10.1126/science.aav7958

Renz, J., Meinel, C., & Link, C. (2019). openSAP: Why Are Enterprise MOOCs Working? *International Journal of Advanced Corporate Learning, 12*(3), 59-69. https://doi.org/10.3991/ijac.v12i3.11262

Rohloff, T., Schwerer, F., Schenk, N., & Meinel, C. (2020). openSAP: Learner behavior and activity in self-paced enterprise MOOCs. *International Journal of Advanced Corporate Learning, 13*(2), 30-40. https://doi.org/10.3991/ijac.v13i2.16531

Şahin, M., Keskin, S., & Yurdugül H. (2020). Sequential Analysis of Online Learning Behaviors According to E-Learning Readiness. In P. Isaias, D. G. Sampson & D. Ifenthaler (Eds.), *Online Teaching and Learning in Higher Education* (pp. 117-131). Springer. https://doi.org/10.1007/978-3-030-48190-2_7

Şahin, M., Egloffstein, M., Bothe, M., Rohloff, T., Schenk, N., Schwerer, F., & Ifenthaler, D. (2021). Behavioral Patterns in Enterprise MOOCs at openSAP. In C. Meinel, T. Staubitz, S. Schweiger, C. Friedl, J. Kiers, M. Ebner, A. Lorenz, G. Ubachs, C. Mongenet, J. A. Ruipérez-Valiente & M. Cortes Mendez (Eds.), *EMOOCs 2021* (pp. 281-288). Universitätsverlag Potsdam. https://doi.org/10.25932/publishup-51030

Schwerer, F., & Egloffstein, M. (2016). Participation and Achievement in Enterprise MOOCs for Professional Learning. In D. G. Sampson, J. M. Spector, D. Ifenthaler & P. Isaias (Eds.), *Proceedings of the 13th International Conference on Cognition and Exploratory Learning in the Digital Age* (pp. 269-276). IADIS. https://eric.ed.gov/?id=ED571404

Wald, A. (1973). *Sequential Analysis*. Dover Publications.

APPENDIX

Table 2. Detailed Findings for System Interactions

			Business				Design				Technology		
	xm_1	leo2	pa1_tl	s4h15	sbw1	build1	cwr1	dafie1	sps3	ieux1	java1	mobile3	sps2
Presentation download	2458	10359	35241	40143	6385	N/A	N/A	N/A	6746	3162	42190	9591	N/A
Self-test submit	37904	182830	68825	677567	334268	157533	20033	N/A	187980	86824	769628	236563	N/A
Survey submit	3813	7599	3265	9656	4883	2917	902	1722	2180	7783	69592	2435	6104
Textual discussion prompt visit	1132	1586	18948	6352	3583	2229	2175	7382	N/A	2084	2080	1825	5006
Textual download visit	2945	10685	12674	29313	33502	17817	2390	10945	15977	6463	46856	20756	28464
Textual instruction visit	6463	39465	30197	109784	77573	45409	5671	26161	37503	15998	157994	53620	73956
Video download	1495	9087	5676	22433	25776	6661	895	2455	10375	4037	35116	7887	14027
Video play	32788	124835	130648	542470	310660	88075	19471	39447	79509	3468	682540	176273	282455
Video visit	17860	75571	60718	253581	192063	68235	9743	27118	78263	38091	414748	99033	35595
Textual hands on visit	N/A	N/A	N/A	N/A	N/A	5955	N/A	N/A	2067	N/A	46783	67145	15887
Assignment submit	10206	30564	35241	113114	97210	48249	6736	53445	47142	21643	91153	54869	232590
Audio download	292	859	881	2715	N/A	N/A	77	294	N/A	300	3667	727	N/A
Final exam submit	N/A	12697	8959	25323	N/A	7023	N/A	N/A	N/A	N/A	11806	8217	17644
Discussion visit	1574	4820	7432	21179	48738	7280	4804	11559	14743	N/A	76253	20926	N/A
Post comment	11	90	392	237	899	196	253	284	463	14	3842	1012	669
Post create	22	123	119	295	517	158	193	550	295	45	1604	498	532
Post reply	28	131	764	336	157	192	86	366	275	35	3169	599	810
Post visit	940	3964	9483	18027	58866	6351	4724	10473	14639	2116	109033	23278	15379
Visit progress	4824	17817	14840	61348	26461	16991	3598	11233	18779	9728	152482	21258	35929
Visit announcement	392	1287	1353	3130	199	1049	321	626	1254	760	4185	1441	1921

DESIGN THINKING ONLINE: APPROACHING CONSTRUCTIVE LEARNING IN FOOD SCIENCE

Marco Garcia-Vaquero
School of Agriculture and Food Science
University College Dublin, Belfield, Dublin 4, Ireland

ABSTRACT

This work aims to re-structure to an online environment and address the needs for integration of a module focused on the Science of Food Packaging delivered face-to-face. This was performed by identifying threshold concepts and applying the principles of constructive alignment when designing new learning activities and assessments adapted to an online environment for the module "Design Thinking for Food Packaging" within the framework of the Food Science Programme. Several complex threshold concepts were identified, as well as the need to integrate the contents of the module, while maintaining curriculum coherence and aligning learning activities and assessment strategies. The re-structured learning activities online included both asynchronous and synchronous activities delivered through the online platforms Brightspace and Zoom, respectively. Synchronous online learning via Zoom was designed as a problem based learning scenario to be solved by groups of learners using the design thinking methodology as scaffolding for problem solving. Asynchronous materials supported the synchronous learning, serving as the initial stepping stones for the learning and research of each group into the threshold concepts identified for this discipline. The assessment strategy focused on continuous assessment of individual and group learning and introduced the learners to the "reflective practice" via individual online learning journals. Future work is necessary to evaluate the learners' perception of the changes implemented when adapting the module to an online environment. The re-designed module online clearly aligns previous module's learning outcomes with the new learning activities and assessment strategies, facilitating the integration of knowledge while developing the interpersonal skills of the learners feeding-forward into their future professional practice as food scientists.

KEYWORDS

Constructive Alignment, Threshold, Integration, Design Thinking, Online learning, Food Science

1. INTRODUCTION

The module "Design Thinking for Food Packaging" aims to integrate the knowledge of key concepts of food packaging (material science and regulatory requirements in food packaging) with previous learning in the curriculum, such as food chemistry, product development and food technology. The original module was delivered face-to-face via lectures and tutorials as well as parallel guided problem solving activities in which the learners interact with industries, acting as consultants to solve their queries. This approach has certain innovative aspects related to the contact of the learners with real industries and active learning activities, however, the contents of the module were poorly integrated. Thereby, the aforementioned consultation work with industry was posed by each company to the groups and the problems identified by the learners rarely related to food packaging which is the main focus of the theoretical content covered during the module, resulting in two differentiated "works" within the module that caused fragmented learning and thus, did not allow a deeper learning and understanding of concepts relevant for their professional development. Similar problems of fragmented learning were also appreciated in modules related to Food Science and were addressed by re-designing the learning activities and aligning them with the learning objectives (Sjöö et al., 2010).

Moreover, due to Cov-19 restrictions to face-to-face delivery of the content, there was a need to limit the content delivered face-to-face and thus, the module had to be re-designed by exploring the use of alternative online tools and technologies, addressing correctly the original learning outcomes of the face-to-face module while ensuring a challenging and active learning experience that could be effective even if the restrictions due to Cov-19 crisis were eased. Moreover, the integration issues of the learning activities of the face-to-face module also needed to be addressed when re-designing the module by elucidating novel and interactive online learning activities and assessments more aligned with the proposed learning outcomes while maintaining the active learning or learning by doing approach of the original module design.

This work focuses on the modifications and novel aspects of the re-designed work of the module "Design Thinking for Food Packaging" to adapt it to an online environment, while addressing the need for integration of the previous content delivered face-to-face in the module. The identification of threshold concepts and the application of the principles of constructive alignment when designing new learning activities and assessment strategies adapted to an online environment are also described, as well as the implementation plan performed to ensure the current and future delivery of the learning objectives of this module within the framework of the Food Science Programme even after the Cov-19 crisis.

2. THRESHOLD CONCEPTS

A threshold concept as described by Meyer and Land (2003) is an "akin to a portal, opening up a new and previously inaccessible way of thinking about something. It represents a transformed way of understanding, or interpreting, or viewing something without which the learner cannot progress". Several threshold concepts were identified in the module:

(1) Food products and raw materials. Understanding the needs of multiple food products and how these needs may influence their packaging materials. Thereby, when packaging fresh vegetables (salad leaves or full lettuce with roots) the needs of packaging both products are different (Sandhya, 2010). Thus, understanding the food products and raw materials in the context of food packaging is a threshold in this module.

(2) Food packaging materials and regulations. The physical properties of different polymers and their chemistry may influence their use depending on the intended use of the food products (Arvanitoyannis and Kotsanopoulos, 2014, Vera et al., 2020). The understanding of the basic chemistry, physical properties of the materials together with the regulations available in the country is a threshold concept involving broad knowledge of multiple disciplines relevant for their professional activities in the future.

(3) Food processing and manufacturing. The use of one packaging material over another may have strong influence on the industrial machinery and processing of the product at industrial level with implications for the cost of the product and also the time the product may be preserved (shelf-life) (Sarker, 2020). This is a threshold concept involving previous knowledge of the learners related to food technology and deep thinking on the bigger picture and industrial implications of packaging.

(4) Consumer acceptability and market. Even when the packaging materials follow the regulations and they are good for the preservation of the food product, the acceptance of the food can be drastically affected by the materials of choice to package the product and may result in decreased sells. The understanding of this threshold requires also the integration with previous knowledge on food science and food sensory together with economic implications of the choices made.

As seen from the previous analysis of the module, the threshold concepts will bring together different aspects of the subject that previously did not appear to be related (Biggs, 2003) covering the new concepts of packaging and materials, but also previous knowledge of food chemistry, technology, sensory, consumer perception and basic economics. Thus, the comprehension of these threshold concepts may transform the internal view of the content of the module by the learner and influence their future professional practice.

3. CONSTRUCTIVE ALIGNMENT

The variety and complexity of the thresholds identified and the need to integrate the contents of the module, while maintaining the curriculum coherence and aligning the learning activities, assessment and learning outcomes will be key for the success of the module online. The principles of constructive alignment were applied when re-designing the learning activities and assessment strategy of this module to an online environment. Constructive alignment has been defined as an outcome-based approach in which the learning outcomes are defined before the teaching takes place and the teaching activities and assessments are designed to guide the learners to achieve them (Biggs, 2014). This theory is based on the principles of alignment between course objectives and assessment targets defined by instructional designers (Biggs, 1996) and previous teaching philosophies of constructivism. Constructivism focuses on developing teaching activities that create meaning or learning by doing defined by Tyler (2013) as "learning takes place through the active behavior of the learner: it is what he does that he learns, not what the teacher does". The alignment of the learning outcomes, learning activities, assessment and grading of the re-designed module online are summarized in Figure 1.

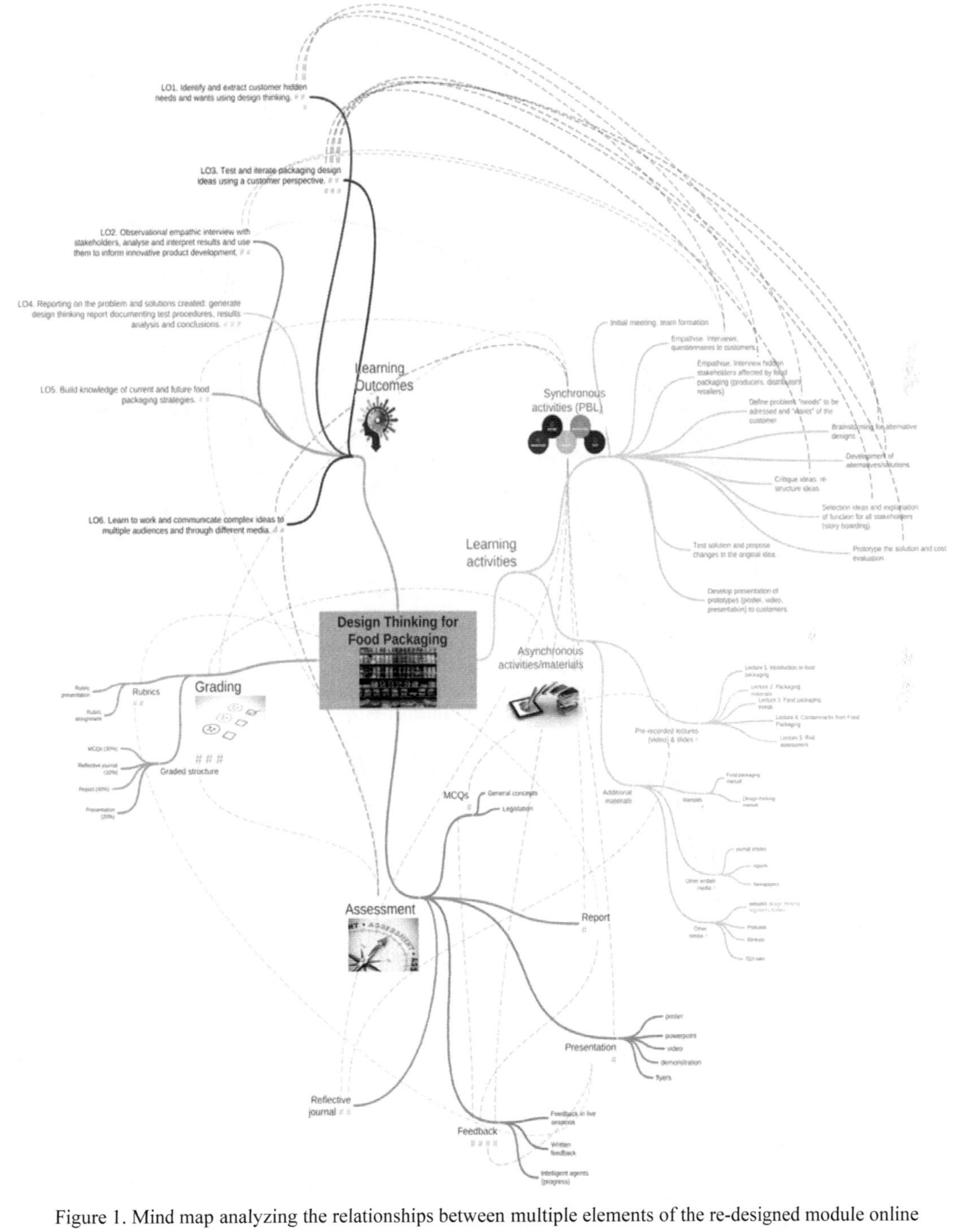

Figure 1. Mind map analyzing the relationships between multiple elements of the re-designed module online

4. IMPLEMENTATION PLAN

4.1 Online Learning Activities

4.1.1 Synchronous Learning Activities

The learners were divided into groups of 6-5 to work together as part of a "food consultant group" for a period of 10 weeks. The groups of learners were then adhered to 2 cohorts that were posed with 2 different problem based learning (PBL) scenarios related to the packaging of different food products. Moreover, the learners were also introduced to the methodology of design thinking, designed by Hasso Plattner Institute of Design at Stanford University (https://dschool.stanford.edu/), to solve the PBL. Design thinking is a methodology for creative problem solving aiming to maximize creativity and innovation in industry settings counteracting human biases that hinder creativity through strong emphasis on empathy with clients, end users and innovators, while addressing the challenges of costs-risks and employee buy-in (Liedtka, 2018). This methodology comprises five steps - empathize, define, ideate, prototype, test and assess (Hasso Plattner, Institute of Design at Standford) - and include specific activities within each step that will act as the main scaffoldings during the PBL process as represented in Figure 2.

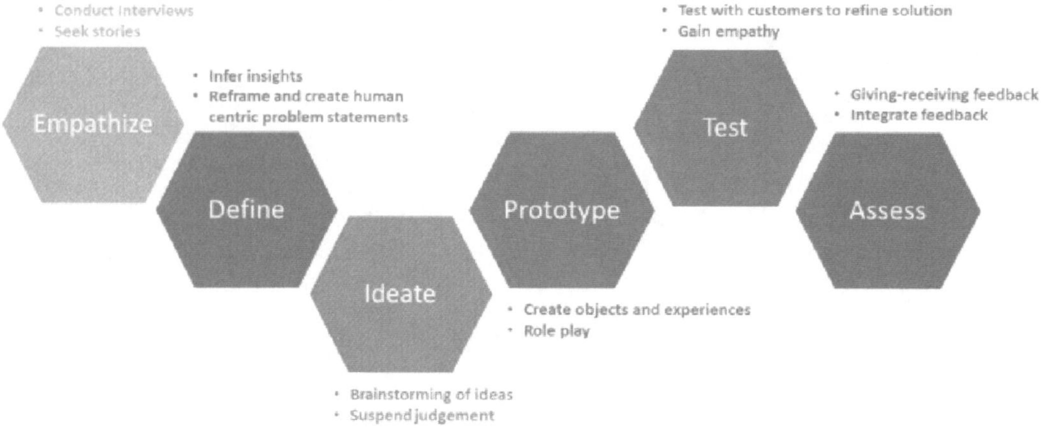

Figure 2. Design thinking methodology steps followed for problem solving. The content of this figure was modified from the Institute of design of Stanford University (https://engineering.stanford.edu/get-involved/give/hasso-plattner-institute-design, https://dschool.stanford.edu/)

The PBL process was guided through online sessions (synchronous learning) via Zoom and the group activities of the learners were facilitated via break-out rooms available in this online platform. The online activities facilitated the discussion and brainstorming of the groups and allowed the module coordinator to provide feedback on each group's performance towards achieving the main learning outcomes of each session. Moreover, the design thinking approach includes additional activities ("empathic interviews", questionnaires and formal interviews to stakeholders related to food packaging) involving "action learning", as the learners will have to engage with external stakeholders and gain insights to understand the problem further and propose better solutions and prototypes. This "action learning" required the development and practice of communication and interpersonal skills and an increased empathy with stakeholders affected by the food package (consumers, distributors, retailers and waste collectors). All these learning activities helped the learners to achieve a deeper understanding of the problem posed and to apply their knowledge into key thresholds identified in the discipline - food processing and manufacturing; consumer acceptability and market – while contributing also to identify areas for further research during their PBL - food products and raw materials, food packaging materials and regulations - in order to successfully design their packaging and solve the problems posed.

4.1.2 Asynchronous Learning Activities

The online synchronous learning activities were complemented with 6-8 hours of pre-recorded lectures (short videos, full lectures, slides and notes) and other additional learning resources (reading materials, videos, blogs, podcasts and web-sites/online publications of professional associations and regulatory bodies related to food packaging) shared with the learners during 10 weeks via the online platform of the module (Brightspace). The lectures and additional resources served as a theoretical guidance on new concepts related to the threshold concepts previously identified (1) food products and raw materials, (2) food packaging materials and regulations, (3) food processing and manufacturing and (4) consumer acceptability and market. These asynchronous learning activities and resources were relevant for the learners as they had to use them to advance in their packaging knowledge to develop potential solutions to the problems covered during the synchronous sessions. Thus, the asynchronous learning served as stepping stone towards a deeper understanding of key concepts that the learners will have to tailor and apply specifically to their PBL, researching further and exploring in depth their specific food products with different packaging needs during the synchronous sessions.

4.2 Assessment Strategy

The assessment strategy of the re-designed "Design Thinking for Food Packaging" online reflected both the individual and collective efforts towards achieving the learning outcomes of the module. Thus, the assessment strategy was aligned with the learning activities and learning objectives of the module and it was implemented as:

(1) Individual assessment: multiple choice questions (MCQs) and online learning journal. The new theoretical content of the module delivered through the asynchronous learning activities was evaluated by MCQs performed via the online platform of the module (Brightspace). This allowed an individual assessment of the progress of each learner on the theoretical contents of the module. Moreover, as part of their individual assessment, the learners were introduced to the "reflective practice" via an electronic learning journal. This journal included nine entries in which each learner reflected on their own individual learning journey by identifying key experiences, learning acquired as result of those experiences and how this learning will be applied in their future professional practice. This assignment also allowed an individual assessment of the learners' achievements in relation to their interpersonal skills as they reflected on different aspects of group work (i.e. problem solving, communication, time management, organization) and engagement with stakeholders through the proposed "action learning" activities (i.e. interviews to stakeholders with different cultural backgrounds and professional relationships established during this process).

(2) Group assessment: presentation session and portfolio of group work. The assessment of the group work was done in a presentation session (poster, video, PowerPoint) in which the learners presented to an audience the packaging prototype developed by the group as well as the details on how the packages work and the specific problem/s that the newly developed prototype solves. This presentation session was performed online via Zoom with invited speakers from multiple industries that posed questions to the groups on their work. Moreover, the learners also generated a full portfolio of work based on their project using several collaborative platforms (Dropbox or shared drive in Google). This portfolio followed the structure and steps of the PBL of each group and the additional research conducted in different aspects of their food packaging (i.e. regulatory/scientific aspects of packaging) that concluded with the design and presentation of the proposed prototype presented in the online session. This allowed the assessment of the application and further research performed by the learners, as well as their capacity to integrate the knowledge of all the key threshold concepts identified in the discipline to solve each of the problem based scenarios posed to the groups.

5. CONCLUSION

Future work is necessary to evaluate if the changes implemented in the module delivered online led to noticeable improvements in the learning experience and achievement of the learning outcomes proposed. The main tool to allow an objective evaluation of the module will be based on collecting feedback and pose specific questions related to the learning activities and assessment strategy, as well as perceived achievement of the learning outcomes, via an online questionnaire that could be compared with previous general feedback of the module evaluated by cohorts of learners evaluating the original module delivered face-to-face.

Overall, the re-structured module online clearly aligned the existing learning objectives with new learning activities and assessment strategy online, facilitating the integration of knowledge. The new synchronous learning activities online (solving PBL by the "design thinking" methodology) were strategically designed to facilitate the learners' further understanding of the asynchronous materials (lectures and readings) as well as to engage the learners into further research involving the main threshold concepts identified within this module - (1) Food products and raw materials; (2) Food packaging materials and regulations; (3) Food processing and manufacturing; (4) Consumer acceptability and market – enabling them to establish connections between multiple disciplines of the Food Science Programme and to apply this knowledge during problem solving activities, similarly to real scenarios and problems they will face in their future professional practice.

The interpersonal skills (communication, empathy and leadership skills) of the learners were further develop through "active learning" while engaging multiple stakeholders in relation to their future packaging solutions as part of the design thinking methodology used as scaffolding for solving the PBL. These valuable learning experiences within the re-designed "Design Thinking for Food Packaging" module will feed-forward into the professional and personal development of the learners at the beginning of their careers as food scientists working in a wide variety of industries, including food companies (i.e. food processors, quality and safety control, sensory experts) and other related businesses (i.e. regulatory agencies, food safety inspectors), in which the learners will have to engage with a wide range and variety of stakeholders in their professional capacities.

ACKNOWLEDGEMENT

Marco Garcia-Vaquero would like to thank América Martín Mezquita and Blanca Vaquero Martín for their constant support, wisdom and passion for education that was passed on to everyone around them. América Martín Mezquita "Study, learn and get educated! Money can come and go; Knowledge will always stay with you and it will help you forever".

REFERENCES

Arvanitoyannis, I. S. and Kotsanopoulos, K. V., 2014. Migration phenomenon in food packaging. Food–package interactions, mechanisms, types of migrants, testing and relative legislation—a review. *Food and Bioprocess Technology,* 7, 21-36.

Biggs, J., 1996. Enhancing teaching through constructive alignment. *Higher Education,* 32, 347-364.

Biggs, J., 2003. *Teaching for Quality Learning at University*. SRHE and Open University Press, Buckingham, United Kingdom.

Biggs, J., 2014. Constructive alignment in university teaching. *HERDSA Review of Higher Education* Vol. 1, pp. 5-2.

Hasso Plattner. *An Introduction to Design Thinking. Facilitator's Guide*. Institute of Design at Standford, USA.

https://dschool.stanford.edu/ (Accessed 19th November 2020).

https://engineering.stanford.edu/get-involved/give/hasso-plattner-institute-design (Accessed 19th November 2020).

Liedtka, J., 2018. Why Design Thinking Works. *Harvard Business Review*, September-October 2018 issue, pp. 72-79.

Meyer, J. and Land, R., 2003. *Threshold Concepts and Troublesome Knowledge 1 – Linkages to Ways of Thinking and Practising' in Improving Student Learning* – Ten Years On. C.Rust (Ed), OCSLD, Oxford, United Kingdom.

Sandhya, 2010. Modified atmosphere packaging of fresh produce: Current status and future needs. *LWT - Food Science and Technology,* 43, 381-392.

Sarker, D. K., 2020. *Packaging Technology and Engineering: Pharmaceutical, Medical and Food Applications*, John Wiley & Sons.

Sjöö, M., Rayner, M. and Ostman, E., 2010. *Concept Circuit Training: A new pedagogic approach for better teaching and learning*.

Tyler, R. W., 2013. *Basic principles of curriculum and instruction*, University of Chicago press.

Vera, P., Canellas, E. and Nerín, C., 2020. Compounds responsible for off-odors in several samples composed by polypropylene, polyethylene, paper and cardboard used as food packaging materials. *Food Chemistry,* 309, 125792.

SUSTAINABLE BLENDED TEACHING PRACTICES: LESSONS LEARNED FROM INSTRUCTOR PERSPECTIVES

Pavani Vemuri[1], Stephan Poelmans[1], Veerle van Rompaey[1], Yi-Shan Tsai[2], Mark Brown[3] and Dragan Gasevic[2]
[1]KU Leuven, 3000 Leuven, Belgium
[2]Monash University, 3800 Clayton, Australia
[3]Dublin City University, 9 Dublin, Ireland

ABSTRACT

The higher education (HE) sector has undergone drastic changes due to the preventive measures needed to cope with the Covid-19 pandemic since March 2020. As a result, most traditional classroom teaching had to move to synchronous or asynchronous online instruction. In the post-Covid-19 era, institutions will, at least partially, go back to teaching in person, and blended teaching (BT) practices will conceivably become the true norm. Although BT practices have been employed and researched extensively over the past two decades, a deeper or more extensive blending of courses will still be a major switch for many teachers and students. More than ever, it is vital for instructors not just to understand how to blend but also to understand the evolution of BT practices and the choices made to arrive at sustainable practices that positively impact the learning experience. In this article, the authors aim to elaborate on the contexts which stimulate or provide a catalyst for the use and subsequent growth of sustainable BT practices in HE. A mixed approach of inductive and deductive thematic analysis is used to analyze 26 interviews of instructors, considered either as pioneers or experienced BT adopters in six HE institutions across Europe (Belgium, Denmark, Finland, Ireland, Netherlands, UK). This preliminary analysis revealed that the identified over-arching themes, the drivers and enablers that promote BT, are dynamic in nature and vary in diverse contexts. This study can give insights into BT adoption and help instructors and institutions improve planning or (re)design of courses into successful and sustainable BT practices.

KEYWORDS

Blended Teaching Practices, Drivers, Enablers, Instructor Perspectives, Blended Education, Blended Learning

1. INTRODUCTION & MOTIVATION

Over the past decade, Blended Teaching (BT) has been considered as a significant educational trend (e.g., Dziuban, et al 2018; Dziuban, Shea & Moskal 2020). BT practices have been used to achieve different purposes. BT increases learning outside the traditional face-to-face classroom settings and can have a positive impact on student motivation, engagement (Ibrahim & Nat 2019) and learning performance (Lu et al. 2019). While a vast number of studies on the usefulness of blended learning (BL) already exist, discussions of BT approaches and their maturity and sustainability are quite rare.

There is still a need to better investigate the alignment of pedagogy and the use of educational technologies (Castro 2019) and understand the contexts in which BL can result in the best possible learning outcomes (Porter & Graham 2016). Ibrahim and Nat (2019) suggest a need for research in considering factors motivating instructors to integrate BL in their courses. While switching to BL in a HE setting, the literature describes numerous challenges: resistance to change, lack of sufficient pedagogical models or BL policies (Porter & Graham 2016), and lack of interest, time, or staff to engage in BT (Smith & Hill 2019).

More than ever, higher education (HE) institutions are exploring different BL formats. It is vital for instructors to understand how to blend and understand the possible choices to be made to arrive at sustainable BT practices. In this article, the authors aim to elaborate on the contexts which stimulate the use and subsequent growth of sustainable, successful, and mature BT practices in HE. In particular, we want to understand which enabler(s) and driver(s) can explain the instructor's choices for using BT approaches. The research questions can be stated as follows:

RQ1. Which enabler(s) and driver(s) influence an instructor's choice of using BT approaches?

RQ2. Do enabler(s) and driver(s) change with subsequent iterations of a course taught using BT approaches?

In order to do this, a mixed approach of inductive and deductive thematic analysis is used to extract information from interviews of instructors, teaching teams or course designers. This study can give insights into BT adoption and help instructors and institutions improve planning or (re)design of their respective courses into successful and sustainable BT practices.

2. LITERATURE

Blended learning is defined as "learning as a result of a deliberate, integrated combination of online and face-to-face learning activities. Instruction encompasses activities which the educators organize and implement deliberately, in order for learners to be able to achieve stated educational objectives" (van Valkenburg 2020). In recent years, a growing number of literature reviews, meta-analyses and empirical studies have been published on the following topics on and for the success of BT practices: BL design (e.g., Boelens, De Wever, Voet 2017); consequences and adoption of BL with student perceptions and attitudes; learning outcomes and completion rates; challenges for tutors and learners (e.g., Rasheed, Kamsin & Abdullah, 2020; Müller & Mildenberger 2021, etc.); focus on the implementation, adoption, and maturity of BL approaches internationally (such as Porter et al. 2016; Marshall, 2010; Goeman et al 2021); those that have considered such factors as motivations, drivers, enablers, and incentives (Laurillard 2014; Ibrahim & Nat 2019). Some studies discuss perceived barriers to successful integration of technology (Bingimlas 2009; Lawrence and Tar, 2018; Mercader and Gairin 2020). Other previous studies that conducted thematic analysis (Lam 2015; King & Cerrone Arnold 2012) either had limited scope or focused on impact and/or challenges in only one domain or discussed a small sample of practices not necessarily mature or sustainable.

There exists a gap in the literature in studying sustainable BT practices and the factors that lead instructors to adopt BT and persistently use and revisit their BT approaches (per each course run), enhancing the quality and maturity of their BT practices. Laurillard (2014) in her vision paper of BT, mentions several drivers and enablers and states 'updating educational drivers and enablers to keep pace with the digital world could be sustainable and progressive over the long term, and would make innovation affordable as a natural part of how institutions operate'. In our study, we look for evidence and dive deeper into the connections and the core issues that drive and enable instructors to adopt and continue using BT and in diverse educational contexts.

3. PROJECT AND METHODOLOGY

As a part of a European Erasmus+ project, to develop the European Maturity model for Blended EDucation (EMBED, https://embed.eadtu.eu/), the partners identified 32 diverse BT practices (at participating universities); both at course and program levels. They were sustainable either in using innovative design & tool of BE practice or had several iterations (maturity) of the BL course. A semi-structured questionnaire was used for the interviews which were recorded, transcribed and translated to English if necessary. To understand instructor perspectives, the current study focuses only on 26 course-level practices. The interviews were analyzed by thematic analysis (Braun, Clarke, 2006) using NVivo 12 to perform the coding. A coding scheme was developed using a mix of both inductive and deductive approaches (Fereday & Muir-Cochrane 2006) from an extensive literature review during the first year of the project and by coding the transcripts.

This was done in a 3-stage process: First, literature was shared between the coders to start analyzing the transcripts, which the three codes then coded. Each coder looked for insights in the transcripts and developed their own coding schema. Next, we merged the codes from the individual coding schemes with those deducted from the literature. To clarify and align the meaning of the codes, definitions were established and fine-tuned in several iterations resulted in a unified coding scheme. Lastly, to establish sufficient consensus between the coders, three interviews were coded by all the coders and the codes' definitions were finalized.

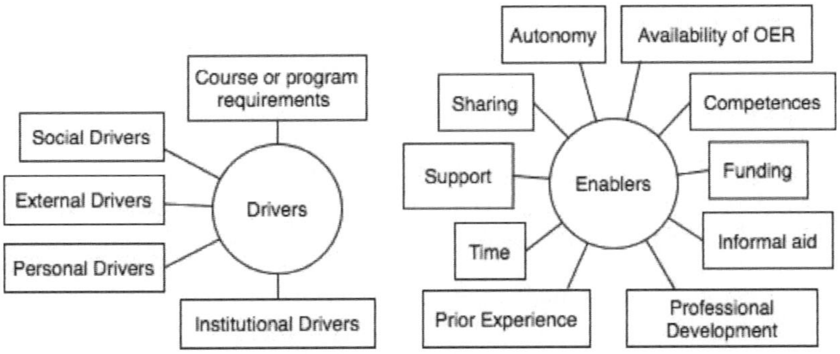

Figure 1. Partial thematic map with drivers and enablers

A thematic map was created for the final unified coding scheme containing 5 main themes: 1) Drivers, 2) Enablers, 3) Challenges and Constraints, 4) Impact of practices and 5) Lifecycle. Our initial analysis presented in this paper contains only the first 2 themes of which a partial thematic map is shown in Figure 1. The three coders applied the unified coding scheme to the 26 interviews divided into three parts.

4. PRELIMINARY RESULTS

To answer RQ1, we take a closer look at which drivers and enablers influenced the instructors in this section.

Drivers: Overall, all the instructors (but two) were strongly driven by (a blend of) personal drivers such as catering to students' needs and skills, enhancing learner experiences, or improving their own teaching experiences. A few instructors were also driven by educational research purposes, while others were driven by their interest in using technology and tools. The influence from peers or students also motivated some instructors to adopt BT. Others were driven by course and program requirements like short time frames or evening programs for working professionals. Institutions can also drive instructors to adopt BT by providing university strategies and policies and by offering incentives or opening calls for educational projects. Only two instructors were prompted by external drivers: one was triggered by a call for educational projects outside the university and another worked towards a professional standards framework by a HE regulatory body.

Enablers: Most of the instructors reported needing and receiving technological help, especially at the first run of their course using BT tools. There was a rather limited demand for pedagogical assistance. Some instructors were enabled by peers sharing resources (experiences or material) in structured or unstructured activities and getting help even informally from the academic community. Another major enabler was funding - in the form of grants, investments in MOOCs, staff scholarships, or paying for temporary personnel, etc. Professional development and Open Education Resources also enabled some BT practices. As interviewees typically had a high degree of autonomy over the mode of course delivery, only few mentioned this as an enabler.

Evolution of Drivers and Enablers: For several instructors, the drivers and enablers for a first run of a course were different from those for subsequent iterations of a course answering RQ2. Furthermore, depending on the lifecycle of the course, a code could be a driver or an enabler revealing a dynamic nature. For example, some viewed funding as a driver but for others, it was only an enabler.

5. DISCUSSION AND CONCLUSION

Preliminary analysis revealed the dynamic nature of drivers and enablers. A code could both be used as a driver or an enabler depending on the lifecycle (iteration) of the course, the competences of the instructors and diverse contexts. Moreover, drivers or enablers for an initial iteration of a course are constantly evolving in future runs. Further analysis is needed to understand their relationships and interactions, and the diverse contexts affecting them. Other findings include advice to work in didactic teams to implement BL, impacts of approaches, challenges and constraints faced for adoption or continued use and possible workarounds. A limitation of this study is that only instructor perspectives on BT are considered. While students' perspectives are just as important when discussing the impact of BT education, there were several limitations in collecting information from a representative sample of students across multiple disciplines, in different European universities. Future research could focus on students' perspectives and comparing them to those of the instructors'.

The pandemic undoubtedly was a forceful driver for instructors to teach online or adopting BT but it is important to understand differences in employing truly optimal and purposeful BT versus teaching traditional content (a)synchronously online or via hybrid methods. Institutions have also stepped up their response, increasing their support in several ways. In a post-pandemic context, due to student needs, institutions may demand more on-campus instruction, thereby inciting instructors to return to their previous ways of teaching without the use of online modes, and instructors may not be able to fully reap the benefits of their investments in online teaching during the pandemic. To this end, our research can give insights into BT adoption and provide HE institutions with necessary insights to promote and support the creation and continued use of successful, sustainable practices.

ACKNOWLEDGEMENT

The data for this research was collected as a part of the EMBED project. This research would not have been possible without the collaboration of the EMBED partners who each conducted four to six interviews in their respective universities. We would also like to express our sincere gratitude to the numerous interviewees for their time and the information and insights they shared. Finally, we thank the European Association of Distance Teaching Universities (EADTU) for chairing, and the EU for funding the project.

REFERENCES

Boelens, R., De Wever, B., & Voet, M. 2017. Four key challenges to the design of blended learning: a systematic literature review. *Educational Research Review*, Vol. *22*, pp 1–18.

Bingimlas, K., A., 2009. Barriers to successful Integration of ICT in teaching and learning environments: a review of the literature. *Eurasia Journal of Mathematics, Science and Tech Ed,* Vol. 5, No. 3, pp. 235-245.

Braun, V., Clarke, V., 2006. Using Thematic Analysis in Psychology. *Qualitative Research in Psychology*. Vol. 3, No.2, pp. 77–101.

Castro, R., 2019. Blended learning in higher education: Trends & capabilities. *Educ & Information Technology*, Vol. 24, No.4, pp.2523–2546.

Dziuban, C., et al, 2018. Blended learning: The new normal and emerging technologies. *International Journal of Educational Technology in Higher Education*, pp. 1–16.

Dziuban, C., Shea P., and Moskal, P., 2020. A Question of Blended Learning: Treatment Effect or Boundary Object? *Educause Review. Why IT matters to Higher Education.*

Fereday, J. and Muir-Cochrane, E., 2006. Demonstrating Rigor Using Thematic Analysis: A Hybrid Approach of Inductive and Deductive Coding and Theme Development. *International Journal of Qualitative Methods*, pp. 80–92.

Goeman, K., et al, 2021. Development of a Maturity Model for Blended Education: A Delphi Study. *International Journal on E-Learning,* Vol. 20, No.3, pp. 229-258.

Ibrahim, M.M., Nat, M., 2019. Blended learning motivation model for instructors in higher education institutions. *International Journal of Education Technology in Higher Education,* Vol. 16, No.12.

King, S. E., & Cerrone Arnold, K., 2012. Blended learning environments in higher education: A case study of how professors make it happen. *Mid-Western Educational Researcher*, Vol.*25, No.*1, pp. 44-59.

Lam, J. 2015. A Thematic Analysis of the Blended Learning Experiences of Undergraduate Students in Hong Kong. *CITE2014*, Hong Kong. Vol. 494, pp. 215-224.

Laurillard, D., 2014. Thinking about blended learning A paper for the Thinkers in Residence programme. pp. 1–26.

Lawrence, J., E., & Tar U., A., 2018. Factors that influence teachers' adoption and integration of ICT in teaching/learning process. *Educational Media International,* Vol. 55, No.1, 00 79-105.

Lu, O. H., et al, 2018. Applying learning analytics for the early prediction of Students' academic performance in blended learning. *Journal of Educational Technology & Society*, Vol. 21, No.2, pp 220–232.

Marshall, S., 2010. A Quality Framework for Continuous Improvement of E-Learning: The E-Learning Maturity Model. *Journal of Distance Education*, Vol. 24, No. 1, pp. 143-166.

Mercader & Gairin, 2020. University teachers' perception of barriers to the use of digital technologies: the importance of the academic discipline. *International Journal of Educational Technology in HE,* Vol 17, No. 4.

Müller, C., & Mildenberger, T, 2021. Facilitating flexible learning by replacing classroom time with an online learning environment: A systematic review of blended learning in higher education. *Educational Research Review,* Vol. 34.

Noetel, M., et Al, 2021. Video Improves Learning in Higher Education: A Syst Review. *Review of Educ Research* Vol. 91.

Porter, W. W., & Graham, C. R., 2016. Institutional drivers and barriers to faculty adoption of blended learning in higher education. *British Journal of Educational Technology,* Vol. 47, No. 4, pp. 748-762.

Rasheed, R. A., Kamsin, A., & Abdullah, N. A., 2020. Challenges in the online component of blended learning: A systematic review. *Computers and Education,* Vol. 144, 103701.

Smith, K., & Hill, J., 2019. Defining the nature of blended learning through its depiction in current research. *Higher Education Research & Development*, Vol. 38, pp. 383-397.

van Valkenburg, W.F. et al, 2020. European Maturity Model for Blended Education. Report published by *European Association of Distance Teaching Universities*.

PRELIMINARY FINDINGS OF A VIRTUAL REALITY APP FOR CHILDREN WITH SPECIAL NEEDS

Danijel Bjelic and Thomas Keller
ZHAW, Switzerland

ABSTRACT

Immersive Virtual Reality (VR) is slowly finding its way into classrooms as an alternative form of experience and action-oriented learning. Generally VR shows a value-added for topics that either are too far away to visit, too small to touch, to dangerous or expensive to manipulate or simply virtual. This range of application is potentially extended for children with special needs or complex disorders. One reason may be that our world is simply too complex for them and hence jeopardizes their health. But often people simply are too stressed to take some extra time to take care in the daily routine. Therefore, a value added for an immersive VR learning unit may simply be a realistic model of a public place like a train station where these children can exercise and practice their skills, e.g., finding places. Together with a foundation for children with special needs, their therapists and teachers, and five children a learning unit playing at a train station was evaluated as a pilot regarding usability and acceptance amongst all concerned stakeholders. Although only a very limited number of participants were involved the pilot application showed potential for further development in this very special context.

KEYWORDS

Virtual Reality, Children with Complex Disorders

1. INTRODUCTION

(Hattie et al., 2017) showed that digitization plays a major role in learning. It is also stated that digitization has an effect size of 0.57 for children with special needs. Any value above 0.4 is considered more effective than the effect of ordinary school attendance. VR as a digital form of experiential and action-oriented learning in (Swiss) elementary schools is currently still in its infancy. Commercially available learning units that can be conducted via fully immersive head-mounted displays are hardly available today. There is no established procedure model for creating a VR lesson and measuring the effect. However, usability tests at elementary schools have shown that the use of VR is considered promising by teachers. In addition, there is a high acceptance among the children. In field experiments three prototypically developed VR learning units were tested (Keller et al., 2018) (Keller et al., 2019).

The use of virtual environments for children with complex disabilities is as diverse as the field of complex disabilities itself and the people it serves. People with special needs often have problems with attention, language, spatial perception, memory, higher reasoning, and knowledge acquisition (Cai et al., 2017). Research on the use of virtual learning environments targets both cognition and behavior (Jeffs, 2010). Back in 2011, Parsons and Cobb published an article on the state-of-the-art of VR technologies for children with autism spectrum disorder. Newer studies were performed by (Bradley & Newbutt, 2018) and . In it, they state that there is unique potential for the use of the technology. However, the features of VR must be used in a way that best supports the learning process (Parsons & Cobb, 2011). In 2018, a Systematic Review based on empirical studies was conducted on the topic of autism and VR head-mounted displays. The conclusion stated that there is a contradiction in this area of research. This is because research around head-mounted displays proposes user immersion in a computer-generated environment that represents and reflects real-world features and activities, but rarely conducts real-world verification (Bradley & Newbutt, 2018). Thus, in this work, during the evaluation phase, this gap in previous research will be addressed and real-world verification will be conducted.

2. OBJECTIVE

The work is carried out in cooperation with a Foundation for children with special needs. The foundation describes itself as a learning and living space and, in addition to residential groups and a wide range of therapies, also offers a school. There, the children and young people are taught basic skills for different stages of life.

The aim of the research work is the development of a virtual reality learning unit especially for children with complex disabilities. Whereby the focus is on the improvement of independence and orientation in the real world. The learning unit is intended to provide supplementary support for traditional teaching. The main part of the work consists of the development and the preceding conception of a prototype for the use case around challenges at a train station. The aim here is to create a representation of the world that is as real as possible without overwhelming the children.

3. THE USE OF VIRTUAL REALITY FOR CHILDREN WITH SPECIAL NEEDS

Hollenweger & Bühler define complex disabilities as follows: "Complex disability involves an intelligence disorder (ICD-10: F70-F73) or a profound developmental disorder (ICD-10: F84) (*Classification of Diseases (ICD)*, n.d.). According to ICD-11, complex disability is newly understood as a neurodevelopmental disorder and defined as a "disorder of intellectual development" (Disorder of Intellectual Development, 6A00). This may occur in combination with other disorders (e.g., Autism Spectrum Disorder (ASD)), diseases (Fragile X Syndrome in relation to protein formation), or impairments in bodily functions (e.g., visual or auditory functions, movement-related functions)." (Hollenweger & Bühler, 2019)

VR learning units allow researchers and educators to study and assess student behavior while maintaining control over the stimuli generated. In doing so, there is the opportunity to adjust the complexity of a learning task and specifically measure learning performance (Bozgeyikli et al., 2017). In the future, the use of VR may complement or even replace traditional assessment tools and methods for diagnosis (*VrSocial*, 2018). There are numerous scientific papers that propose, demonstrate and validate the use of VR for children with special needs, very often in the scope of Autism Spectrum Disorder (ASD), e.g.,virtual travel training (Simões et al., 2018), social-emotional stories (Ghanouni et al., 2019). Most VR applications to date for children with complex disabilities are found in the areas of social skills, anxiety management, mobility, mathematics, science, or (sign) language. There are also combinations of these areas (Ip et al., 2018).

In a research on the selection and development characteristics of a virtual learning environment, navigation and interaction were investigated. It was found that navigation is one of the most difficult tasks for people with learning disabilities. Therefore, it was important that the input devices be compatible with the performance of the learning task (Lannen et al., 2002). Hands-on learning activities provided within a virtual learning environment are beneficial for individuals with learning disabilities to practice and acquire new skills (Cromby et al., 1996).

People with ASD often have difficulties with social interactions, verbal and nonverbal communication, and cognitive tasks, such as contextualization, impulse control, inhibitions, or other behaviors (WHO, n.d.). One study examined multimedia interfaces for users with high-functioning autism. It was found that richer multimedia learning interfaces do not add value to facilitate learning for people with autism. In fact, simple interfaces work best for these individuals (Grynszpan et al., 2008).

Various studies (Cobb, 2007), (Self et al., 2007), (Parsons, 2000), (Herrera et al., 2006) confirm that people with ASD can adapt skills they have acquired using virtual realities to the real world.

In a recent research from Ukraine, children with ASD were taught basic traffic rules as pedestrians using VR and machine learning (ML). The VR provides a game-like environment and a controllable avatar that represents the student. The ML portion of the system is responsible for adjusting the response of the environment based on the student's behavior. It was found that the children were more socialized after the learning session. However, it had to be noted that it also took explanations from the children' parents and caregivers for the understanding about certain situations to be achieved. (Horbova et al., 2020).

4. THE PROTOTYPE

The prototype includes a model of the Lucerne train station. Following Figure *1* gives an impression of the quality of the model. The prototype was developed with Unreal and has been tested and used with an HTC Vive.

Figure 1. An impression of the quality of the model of the train station Lucerne

Learning unit 1 starts in the basement of the Lucerne train station. In front of the user, there is a large light blue cylinder on the floor that activates the first task. If the student walks into this cylinder, the task of finding the toilets follows via the audio channel. If the student finds the toilets and steps into the next light blue cylinder, the task is acoustically confirmed as successfully completed and the next task is announced. The next task is to find the retailer Coop. In front of the Coop there is again a blue cylinder which, when it overlaps with the student, announces the next and last task of this learning unit. The last task is about finding the meeting point. This task is also no longer marked with a blue cylinder. Once the meeting point has been found, the session ends and the End level is started.

Learning unit 2 starts in front of the platforms. In front of the user is a large light blue cylinder which activates the first task. This tells the student to go to platform 10. In front of platform 10 is the next cylinder. The next cylinder confirms the completion of the first task and announces the next one. The student has to board the train at the right place. The task is completed when the student is in front of the first passenger door of the train at track 10. As in session 1, the session is ended and the End level is started.

5. THE FIELD EXPERIMENT

The field experiment included three phases:

• The first phase consisted of an excursion to a real train station. Most of the children would use this station if they were more independent. There, the children were successively given the same or similar tasks as subsequently in the learning units. In the process, they were filmed with a video camera.

- The second phase consisted of the application of the VR learning unit, which took place over two weeks. The children went through the tasks a total of five times.
- Finally, the third phase consisted of another field trip to a different train station to qualitatively observe the children's progress and to determine whether the VR learning units had an effect on the children' behavior in the real world. The children were again given the same or similar tasks as in the learning unit. They were also filmed with a video camera during the second visit.

A total of five children and their respective caregivers participated in the complete field experiment. Unfortunately, a larger number of children was not possible due to the current circumstances.

Generally it is claimed that the highest possible degree of immersion should be aimed for and that, optimally, all possible stimuli should be generated by the VR system. This is contrasted with the findings from studies of individuals with complex disabilities, which claim that too many stimuli are counterproductive. It was interesting to see that some of the children were severely overwhelmed with the mental challenge of being in a virtual world, seeing it, being a part of it, and at the same time paying attention to the auditory stimuli of the learning task. Omitting the headphones and using only one controller eliminated some VR-generated stimuli from the learning session. However, this allowed the children to cope better with the new situation.

It is unclear whether an increase in VR-generated stimuli would have been justifiable with longer engagement with the learning units. It would be helpful if different levels of stimulus generation could be parameterized. This would allow the learning unit to accommodate each student's current stimulus tolerance. The multiplayer approach could also provide interesting insights. For example, several children could enter a virtual environment together with their teachers and leave the announcement of the learning task to the teacher.

When selecting the use case, it has proven useful to follow the finding of Dalgarno and Lee (2010) and use VR where a real situation is difficult to depict and perform in the real world. Also relevant seems to be the verification of what is learned in the real world. Bradley and Newbutt (2018) criticized in their systematic review that often verification is not done. To be able to verify the impact of the learning units, the two visits to the train stations were particularly important. Learning is also a social process and children with complex disabilities in particular often struggle to show what they have learned or are underappreciated by society. Therefore, real-world verification is an important element in the approach.

6. CONCLUSION

The children enjoyed learning with the VR learning units and were highly motivated. Whether the motivation and enthusiasm of the children can be maintained over a longer period of time will be seen in the following months. All children would like to continue learning with a VR offering in the future. This was to be expected, as it was a positive change from traditional teaching. For many of the children, it was also their first exposure to a fully immersive VR system. A clear benefit for children is the controlled environment provided by VR. This allows unwanted situations to be avoided. The children can build up their skills in a protected setting without fear of the unexpected. Whether this leads to a negative effect in the long term, in the sense of a blunting against possible dangers, could not be recognized in this short duration.

The implementation of the learning units also aroused the interest of other teachers and supervisors who were not directly involved in the project. The few who had put on the headset were convinced of the technology's potential. Some were already talking about future use cases, such as traffic training. Others saw potential opportunities for other input devices and their use, such as eye tracking control, which is already in use in some cases for children with wheelchairs.

REFERENCES

Booth, A., Sutton, A., & Papaioannou, D. (2016). *Systematic Approaches to a Successful Literature Review*. SAGE.

Bozgeyikli, L., Raij, A., Katkoori, S., & Alqasemi, R. (2017). A survey on virtual reality for individuals with autism spectrum disorder: Design considerations. *IEEE Transactions on Learning Technologies*, *11*(2), 133–151.

Bradley, R., & Newbutt, N. (2018). *Autism and virtual reality head-mounted displays: A state of the art systematic review*. 16.

Cai, Y., Chiew, R., Nay, Z. T., Indhumathi, C., & Huang, L. (2017). Design and development of VR learning environments for children with ASD. *Interactive Learning Environments*, *25*(8), 1098–1109. https://doi.org/10.1080/10494820.2017.1282877

Classification of Diseases (ICD). (n.d.). Retrieved May 28, 2021, from https://www.who.int/standards/classifications/classification-of-diseases

Cobb, S. V. G. (2007). Virtual Environments Supporting Learning and Communication in Special Needs Education. *Topics in Language Disorders*, *27*(3), 211–225. https://doi.org/10.1097/01.TLD.0000285356.95426.3b

Cromby, Standen, & Brown. (1996). *The potentials of virtual environments in the education and training of people with learning disabilities*. https://doi.org/10.1046/j.1365-2788.1996.805805.x

Dalgarno, B., & Lee, M. J. W. (2010). *What are the learning affordances of 3-D virtual environments?* 17.

Ghanouni, P., Jarus, T., Zwicker, J. G., Lucyshyn, J., Mow, K., & Ledingham, A. (2019). Social Stories for Children with Autism Spectrum Disorder: Validating the Content of a Virtual Reality Program. *Journal of Autism and Developmental Disorders*, *49*(2), 660–668. https://doi.org/10.1007/s10803-018-3737-0

Grynszpan, O., Martin, J.-C., & Nadel, J. (2008). Multimedia interfaces for users with high functioning autism: An empirical investigation. *International Journal of Human-Computer Studies*, *66*(8), 628–639. https://doi.org/10.1016/j.ijhcs.2008.04.001

Hattie, J., Zierer, K., & Beywl, W. (2017). *Lernen Sichtbar Machen Für Lehrpersonen. Überarbeitete Deutschsprachige Ausgabe* (3. Unveränderte Auflage). Schneider Verlag Hohengehren GmbH.

Herrera, G., Jordan, R., & Veraa, L. (2006). *Abstract concept and imagination teaching through Virtual Reality in people with Autism Spectrum Disorders*. http://dx.doi.org/10.3233/TAD-2006-18403

Hevner, A., March, S. T., Park, J., & Ram, S. (2004). *Design science in information systems research. MIS Quarterly, 28 (1)*, 75–105.

Hollenweger & Bühler. (2019). *20190611_Anwendung des LP21 für SuS mit komplexen Behinderungen.pdf*. https://www.regionalkonferenzen.ch/sites/default/files/inline-files/20190611_Anwendung%20des%20LP21%20f%C3%BCr%20SuS%20mit%20komplexen%20Behinderungen.pdf

Horbova, M., Andrunyk, V., & Chyrun, L. (2020). *Virtual Reality Platform Using ML for Teaching Children with Special Needs*. 12.

Ip, H. H., Wong, S. W., Chan, D. F., Byrne, J., Li, C., Yuan, V. S., Lau, K. S., & Wong, J. Y. (2018). Enhance emotional and social adaptation skills for children with autism spectrum disorder: A virtual reality enabled approach. *Computers & Education*, *117*, 1–15.

Jeffs, T. L. (2010). *Virtual Reality and Special Needs*. 16.

Keller, T., Hagen, F., & Brucker-Kley, E. (2019). *A field study about the impact of a VR learning unit*. 307–314. https://digitalcollection.zhaw.ch/handle/11475/18788

Keller, T., Hebeisen, A., & Brucker-Kley, E. (2018). *Integration of Children with Special Needs In Mathematics Through Virtual Reality*. 8.

Kurz, B., & Kubek, D. (2021). *Kursbuch Wirkung Das Praxishandbuch für alle, die Gutes besser tun wollen*.

Lannen, T., Brown, D., & Powell, H. (2002). Control of virtual environments for young people with learning difficulties. *Disability and Rehabilitation*, *24*(11–12), 578–586. https://doi.org/10.1080/09638280110111342

New learning concepts for schools. (2021). https://neuelehrkonzepte.ch/?p=146

Parsons, S. (2000). Development of social skills amongst adults with Asperger's Syndrome using virtual environments. *Virtual Reality*, 9.

Parsons, S., & Cobb, S. (2011). *State-of-the-art of virtual reality technologies for children on the autism spectrum*. 13.

Self, T., Scudder, R. R., Weheba, G., & Crumrine, D. (2007). A Virtual Approach to Teaching Safety Skills to Children With Autism Spectrum Disorder. *Topics in Language Disorders*, *27*(3), 242–253. https://doi.org/10.1097/01.TLD.0000285358.33545.79

Simões, M., Bernardes, M., Barros, F., & Castelo-Branco, M. (2018). Virtual travel training for autism spectrum disorder: Proof-of-concept interventional study. *JMIR Serious Games*, *6*(1), e5.

Someren, M. W. van, Barnard, Y. F., & Sandberg, J. A. C. (1994). *The think aloud method: A practical guide to modelling cognitive processes*. Academic Press.

Stiftung Vivala. (2021, May 28). https://www.vivala.ch/

VrSocial. (2018). https://dl.acm.org/doi/abs/10.1145/3173574.3173778

WHO. (n.d.). *ICD-11—Mortality and Morbidity Statistics*. Retrieved May 1, 2021, from https://icd.who.int/browse11/l-m/en#/http%3a%2f%2fid.who.int%2ficd%2fentity%2f437815624

Wieczorrek, H. W., & Mertens, P. (2011). *Management von IT-Projekten*. Springer Berlin Heidelberg. https://doi.org/10.1007/978-3-642-16127-8

VROBOTATOR: A VIRTUAL ROBOT FACILITATOR OF SMALL GROUP DISCUSSIONS FOR K-12

Elinor Mizrahi, Noa Danzig and Goren Gordon[1]*
Curiosity Lab, Department of Industrial Engineering, Tel-Aviv University, Israel

ABSTRACT

The COVID-19 pandemic has stressed the importance of efficient and accommodating online educational experiences. In this contribution, we present work-in-progress on the development of a novel system for facilitation of small group online discussions using an avatar during video conferencing. Four groups of eighth and ninth grades' students interacted with the system, with and without avatar guidance. Our pilot study results show that students reported the avatar-guided learning to be more efficient, easier to follow, and inducing more engagement and active participation. Students also showed better understanding of the learned subject with the avatar guidance, as shown by the post-session questionnaires. This system shows promise in future online educational activities as a facilitator of discussions with K-12 students.

KEYWORDS

Virtual Agent, Group Activity, Video Conference, Facilitation

1. INTRODUCTION

Prior to the COVID-19 pandemic, online learning environments for K-12 have not been a mainstream methodology. However, the pandemic has revealed the importance, as well as the advantages and drawbacks of video conferencing technologies, as well as other social educational technologies.

In this short paper, we introduce a system we developed and started testing during the pandemic. The system aims to facilitate small online group discussions during video conferencing. It introduces an avatar, a virtual agent, that guides the students through a learning module as well as facilitates group discussions. The content for the learning modules was created by teachers using an LMS (Learning Management System) we designed for this purpose. The students interact with the system through a dedicated website, which embeds a Zoom live video chat, a virtual agent and an interactive content area.

In a pilot study, four groups interacted with the system. Each group completed two learning modules, one with the avatar guidance and one without guidance. Of the four groups, two groups of eight-grade students learned a science unit, and two groups of ninth-grade students learned a literature unit. Questionnaires assessing both the students' experience with the system and their understanding of the learned material were administered after completing each module. The system also computed speech detection and facial expression recognition in real-time.

Our preliminary results show that: (i) the students preferred the avatar-guided module on all scales, e.g. they reported they listened more to their group members and learned more; (ii) they learned better with the avatar guidance and ;(iii) they engaged more in the discussion and actively participated more with the avatar guidance.

This pilot study shows the promise of a new online system to promote students for better discussion skills and advancing their learning in an online environment, which is predicted to become more prevalent in the post COVID era.

[1] * Corr. Author: goren@gorengordon.com

2. RELATED WORK

Small group learning activities have been considered as a promising education format (Johnson and Johnson 2009). Small-group activities can enhance student thinking and learning of both formal (e.g., math) and informal (e.g., appropriate social skills, motivated student engagement) content and skills, e.g., (Elias and Schwab 2006; Webb 1995; Hadwin, Järvelä, and Miller 2018). Moreover, children who participated in structured group activities have been shown to be more willing to work with others on the assigned tasks and they provided more elaborate help and assistance to each other than their peers in the unstructured groups (Gillies 2004).

While on-line discussion forums have prospered in recent years (Chiu and Hew 2018; Pendry and Salvatore 2015; Yang et al. 2015), with artificial intelligence (AI) assisting in managing such forums (Goel and Joyner 2017), studies have shown that personal face-to-face interactions and discussions in small groups have their advantages (Chen and Chen 2015; Thomas and Thorpe 2019). The question of scaling-up group facilitation is, thus, of prominent importance. Acquiring observational data during group activities is important to better understand the group dynamics (Vriesema and McCaslin 2020), and is easier when the facilitator is a virtual agent with full information.

The appearance of virtual visual agents, avatars, has also initiated a wider usage of conversational and social aspects of interaction. While a face of a conversational agent has been shown to increase rapport and other participant-agent related measures (Shamekhi et al. 2018), it remains an open question of what *educational benefits* such an avatar presents.

3. METHODS

THE SYSTEM. The system includes two web applications composed of multiple sub-systems. The first web application is an LMS (Learning Management System), which allows teachers and instructional designers to create learning modules containing interactive content. A module is composed of blocks, each containing content sections that either appear on the screen, e.g. multiple-choice questions, reading material; or delivered orally by the avatar. A block also contains several options allowing to prompt a facilitated discussion following the content delivery.

The second web application, and the focus of this report, is the student-centered platform, with which the students interact. The application embeds (see Figure 1: left): (a) a robotic avatar from SitePal.com; (b) a frame with the Zoom web API, that enables gallery view to see all the group members in a live chat, and; (c) an interactive content panel, displaying the content created in the LMS.

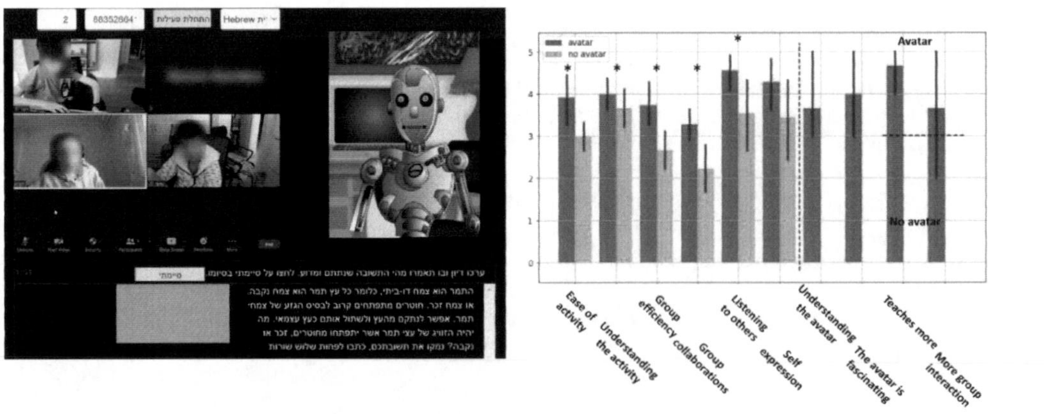

Figure 1. Left: A screenshot of the system, with (left) a Zoom API, (right) SitePal.com robotic avatar and (bottom) interactive content panel displaying a passage followed by an open-ended question, and a text-box for typing the answer. Right: Results of a 5-point semantic differential scale on various questions after the activity with and without the avatar. * $p<0.05$, Wilcoxon signed-ranked test

During a learning session, the students are individually presented with the interactive content created by the teacher in the LMS, followed by a group discussion facilitated by the avatar. A student can click on a "done" button in the interactive panel to inform the system a task is finished, so the learning session can continue to the next section.

The system is equipped with perceptual sensors (Figure 2:left). Using face-api.js, a client-side facial expression recognition system was activated, that enabled real-time and continuous analysis of facial expression such as happy and angry. A sound volume-meter was activated on the client-side, in order to detect speech in real-time.

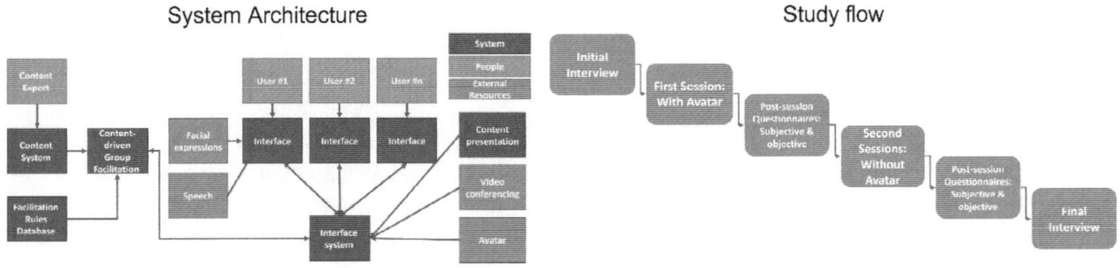

Figure 2. System architecture and study flow

The avatar was programmed with behaviors that reflect group facilitation best practices. An expert group facilitator aided in formalizing the appropriate system behaviors, e.g. giving feedback and dealing with objections, which were then programmed into the avatar. Each behavior was formulated as trigger/event pairs. For example, personal feedback was formulated as: trigger - whether the system was in a state after a question with a discussion, and whether there is a student who has not yet received positive feedback. If the condition is met, the action will be performed at the end of the question / discussion in the form of a single positive feedback to the student, out of the following types: correct answer ("great job, David, you have answered correctly"), correct and quick answer ("great job, David, you answered correctly and fast"), participation in a discussion or answering a question ("thank you, David, for contributing to the discussion"). Another example is the behavior to initiate the discussion, by addressing students. Therefore, the trigger, for example, is if all the students answered wrong answers and a discussion begins; and the action is that the facilitator addresses the student who spoke the least.

PARTICIPANTS. The study was conducted on eighth and ninth grades students, in a single middle school. Out of the eighth-grade participant pool, 20 participants (12 males, 8 females) were recruited, but due to technical difficulties such as slow internet connection and lack of camera and/or microphone, only 5 remained (3 males and 2 females). The participants were divided into 2 groups: (a) 3 participants (2 males and 1 female), (b) 2 participants (1 male and 1 female). The two groups each completed two learning modules in science (cell biology unit).

Out of the ninth-grade participant pool, 15 participants (11 males and 4 females) were recruited. Due to similar technical difficulties, 9 students were excluded. The participants were divided into 2 groups: (a) 3 participants (3 males), (b) 3 participants (2 males and 1 female.) The two groups each completed two learning modules in literature.

All participants' parents signed a consent form. The study was approved by the institutional IRB and the ministry of education.

CONDITIONS & MEASURES. Each group interacted with the system twice, completing two learning modules – one facilitated by the avatar and one non-facilitated.

While a learning module content stay the same whether the avatar is present or not, an avatar-facilitated learning experience includes oral instructions, direct address to group members and various types of feedback given by the avatar, in addition to written instructions on the interactive content panel. A non-facilitated learning experience includes written instructions only, and the avatar is not shown at all on the students' screen.

During the non-facilitated parts, we confirmed with each group that they indeed saw and understood the written instructions, e.g. start a discussion. However, we did not interfere or facilitate the discussion in any way.

The study was designed to have two types of measures: subjective, self-report; and objective, perceptual. After each activity, each student filled two types of online questionnaires: the first was composed of eight 5-point semantic differential scale questions regarding the activity and two rating questions on a scale of 1-5 comparing the avatar-facilitated experience to the non-facilitated experience, and the second was composed of four true/false questions based on the material covered in the learning module. Furthermore, the perceptual part of the system supplied information regarding when each student spoke and a continuous stream of facial expressions.

4. RESULTS

Questionnaires: Students reported (Figure 1: right) that the avatar-guided learning session was easier, induced a more efficient group interaction and collaboration, compared to the non-guided session. Furthermore, they reported to have listened more to their group members as well as expressing themselves more with the avatar guidance, compared to the non-guided session. Finally, the avatar was rated to be fascinating and easy to follow, and when asked to compare it directly to the non-guided session, students reported that the avatar-guided session induced more effective learning and more group interaction.

Learning: Students interacting with the avatar answered more material-related questions correctly, compared to the a learning session without the avatar, Figure 3: right-top.

Dynamics: An example of the continuous perceptual data can be seen in Figure 3: left, where the avatar's prompting was followed by more discussion, especially by the individual students it addressed.

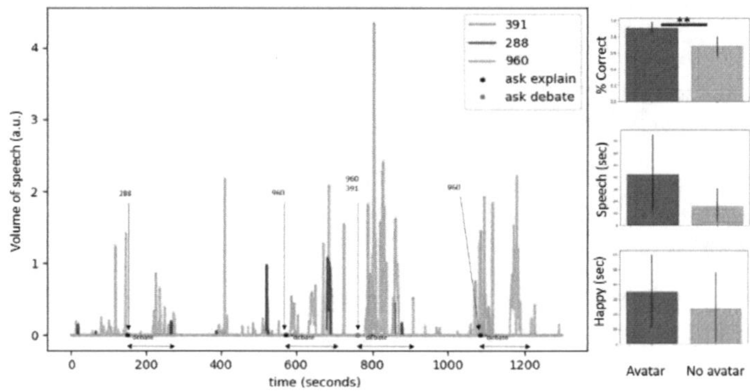

Figure 3. Left: Dynamics of interaction, as measured by the volume of speech per participant. The avatar's prompting is also presented. Right: mean over students per condition (error bars represent standard-deviation). Top: Percent of correct answer (out of eight true/false questions), four after an avatar-guided session and four after a non-guided session. Middle: cumulative time of speech. Bottom: Cumulative time of happy expression. ** $p<0.01$, Wilcoxon signed-ranked test

5. DISCUSSION AND CONCLUSIONS

This short paper introduces a work-in-progress of a novel system that facilitates small group on-line discussion using video conferencing and group-facilitation best practices. The pilot study had several major limitations: The first is the large number of technical difficulties, which resulted in massive loss of participants. The second is that the first session was avatar-guided while the second was non-guided, introducing a confound of order effects. Finally, the small number of participants does not enable conclusions regarding generalizations.

This study is, to the best of our knowledge, the first to have a fully autonomous virtual agent facilitating a small group discussion in school context, with curricular content. However, more studies, both in depth and in breadth, should be performed before any conclusions regarding the efficacy of the presented system can be determined. Nevertheless, the pilot study results show the promise of this novel system as a facilitator of more effective and engaging discussions and more learning in an environment that is becoming more prevalent in the formal educational system.

REFERENCES

Chen, Yang-Hsueh, and Pin-Ju Chen. 2015. "MOOC Study Group: Facilitation Strategies, Influential Factors, and Student Perceived Gains." *Computers & Education* 86 (August): 55–70. https://doi.org/10.1016/j.compedu.2015.03.008.

Chiu, Thomas K. F., and Timothy K. F. Hew. 2018. "Factors Influencing Peer Learning and Performance in MOOC Asynchronous Online Discussion Forum." *Australasian Journal of Educational Technology* 34(4): 16–28. https://doi.org/10.14742/ajet.3240.

Elias, Maurice J., and Yoni Schwab. 2006. "From Compliance to Responsibility: Social and Emotional Learning and Classroom Management." *Handbook of Classroom Management: Research, Practice, and Contemporary Issues*, 309–41.

Gillies, Robyn M. 2004. "The Effects of Cooperative Learning on Junior High School Students during Small Group Learning." *Learning and Instruction* 14 (2): 197–213. https://doi.org/10.1016/S0959-4752(03)00068-9.

Goel, Ashok K., and David A. Joyner. 2017. "Using AI to Teach AI: Lessons from an Online AI Class." *AI Magazine* 38 (2): 48–59. https://doi.org/10.1609/aimag.v38i2.2732.

Hadwin, Allyson, Sanna Järvelä, and Mariel Miller. 2018. "Self-Regulation, Co-Regulation, and Shared Regulation in Collaborative Learning Environments." In *Handbook of Self-Regulation of Learning and Performance, 2nd Ed*, 83–106. Educational Psychology Handbook Series. New York, NY, US: Routledge/Taylor & Francis Group.

Johnson, David W., and Roger T. Johnson. 2009. "An Educational Psychology Success Story: Social Interdependence Theory and Cooperative Learning:" *Educational Researcher*, June. https://doi.org/10.3102/0013189X09339057.

Pendry, Louise F., and Jessica Salvatore. 2015. "Individual and Social Benefits of Online Discussion Forums." *Computers in Human Behavior* 50 (September): 211–20. https://doi.org/10.1016/j.chb.2015.03.067.

Shamekhi, Ameneh, Q. Vera Liao, Dakuo Wang, Rachel K. E. Bellamy, and Thomas Erickson. 2018. "Face Value? Exploring the Effects of Embodiment for a Group Facilitation Agent." In *Proceedings of the 2018 CHI Conference on Human Factors in Computing Systems*, 1–13. CHI '18. New York, NY, USA: Association for Computing Machinery. https://doi.org/10.1145/3173574.3173965.

Thomas, Glyn, and Stephen Thorpe. 2019. "Enhancing the Facilitation of Online Groups in Higher Education: A Review of the Literature on Face-to-Face and Online Group-Facilitation." *Interactive Learning Environments* 27 (1): 62–71. https://doi.org/10.1080/10494820.2018.1451897.

Vriesema, Christine Calderon, and Mary McCaslin. 2020. "Experience and Meaning in Small-Group Contexts: Fusing Observational and Self-Report Data to Capture Self and Other Dynamics." *Frontline Learning Research* 8 (3): 126–39. https://doi.org/10.14786/flr.v8i3.493.

Webb, Noreen M. 1995. "Learning in Small Groups." *Interaction in Cooperative Groups: The Theoretical Anatomy of Group Learning*, 102.

Yang, Diyi, Miaomiao Wen, Iris Howley, Robert Kraut, and Carolyn Rose. 2015. "Exploring the Effect of Confusion in Discussion Forums of Massive Open Online Courses." In *Proceedings of the Second (2015) ACM Conference on Learning @ Scale*, 121–30. L@S '15. New York, NY, USA: ACM. https://doi.org/10.1145/2724660.2724677.

CREATING A MARKETPLACE OF IDEAS: EQUITY IN EDUCATION AND TECHNOLOGY DURING COVID-19

John W. Hatcher III and Takashi Crum
Southeastern Louisiana University SLU 10549, Hammond, LA. 70402, USA
New York City Department of Education, New York, New York 11201, USA

ABSTRACT

This research study explored the issue of equity in education and technology during the COVID-19 pandemic. A virtual forum was created that included a panel of educators from across the United States to discuss educational challenges related to equity and the use of technology during their transition from physical classrooms to the virtual classroom setting. This research was intended to provide insight into the perceptions of some educators regarding equity in education and technology as students received instruction from home and teachers engaged a variety of online platforms to deliver instruction. In this study an interview protocol was used to facilitate action research with a focus group of educators in the context of a two hour and twenty minute Zoom session that generated relevant responses from participants. Effective communication from school leaders with educational stakeholder groups emerged as a major theme among study participants.

KEYWORDS

Equity in Education, Technology, Accessibility, Accountability, COVID-19

1. INTRODUCTION

During the first quarter of 2020 the world was hit by the COVID-19 pandemic, which led to schools across the United States closing for weeks at a time. School districts struggled to provide clear guidance about when and how schools would reopen as the 2019-20 school year came to an abrupt end for many school communities. The COVID-19 virus continued to rage as school leaders were left with the questions of how to continue to meet the academic needs of students, the instructional needs of teachers, as well as, the overall safety needs of their school communities. Stakeholder groups had to explore the question of how to reopen schools. Many were forced to transition from face-to-face instruction to a variety of virtual platforms and hybrid models in order to deliver instruction based on local infection rates. This study explored some of the inequities within the U.S. system of education, which were highlighted by the pandemic and could result in relevant changes to how students, teachers, and schools engaged in the teaching and learning process. This study further explored the perspectives of educational practitioners through a virtual forum, while examining nuanced practices that intimately embedded technology into our current system of education. The significance of this research will provide educational stakeholders with practical insights into creating a more equitable system of education during and post the COVID-19 pandemic.

2. EQUITY IN EDUCATION DURING COVID-19

Equity in education has been a struggle in the United States of America since the days of the landmark cases of Plessy versus Ferguson (1896) and the infamous Brown versus Topeka Board of Education (1954). In 2015, President Barack Obama signed into law the Every Student Succeeds Act, which highlighted "...equity by upholding critical protections for America's disadvantaged and high-need students" (https://www.ed.gov/essa).

For the purposes of this study the investigators defined "equity," as the fair distribution of available resources based on the needs of students, teachers, schools, school districts, and states.

The overarching research question was, "What does equity in education and technology look like in schools during COVID-19?" The researchers hosted a two hour and twenty minute virtual forum entitled, "Creating a Marketplace of Ideas: Equity in Education and Technology during COVID-19." The forum included a panel of six educators from across the United States, who collectively had more than 150 years of experience as educational practitioners. The virtual forum was organized into three 40 minute segments and was facilitated by three distinct cohorts of graduate students in educational leadership. There were 49 participants in the virtual forum hosted on the Zoom platform, while an additional audience participated by asking questions and making comments as the event was streamed live via Facebook. The three segments of the virtual forum had the following subtopics:

- Accessibility to Instruction and Technology during COVID-19
- Accountability of Principals, Teachers, & Students during COVID-19
- School Leadership during the COVID-19 crisis

The virtual forum began with the research team presenting the overarching question for each panelist to introduce themselves and respond to the overarching research question. During the remainder of the forum participants engaged in a forum protocol of questions developed specifically to glean the perspectives of panelists related to the three subtopics of the forum. Each of the three segments of the forum ended with a five-minute period for audience participation in which other educators could pose follow-up questions to the panelists or share their perspective on the topic.

2.1 Accessibility to Instruction and Technology During COVID-19

Instructional equity became the focus of schools across the United States. The instructional platform offered in most school districts was remote with hybrid and face-to-face as secondary modes for instructional delivery. According to the Pew Research, analysis of 2015 American Community Survey Data, at least 15% of U.S. households with school age children did not have access to high-speed internet and many households were low income. Panelist #3 stated equity access starts with students' access to technology when schools network with local businesses since some offered cheaper and more affordable subscriptions for parents. While Panelist #2 believed it was the schools' responsibility to procure grants and corporate partnerships to ensure students did not fall further behind academically. Puckett and Rafalow (2020) stated unequal access to technology was the first level of the digital divide with many students still unprepared for technology based-learning. As a result, Panelist #1 incorporated the use of YouTube or Khan Academy as technological resources to illustrate complex concepts that provide visualizations and interactive learning for students to understand and apply their knowledge. Thus, policy and practice of using technological resources should be the focus for students to develop as scholars.

The practices utilized by Panelist #1 were examples of the lasting effects of COVID-19 pandemic on the future of education. Panelist #3 stated, "that technology is now the backbone of education, teachers are now being given more flexibility and control in how instruction is imparted to their students, while parents now have a better understanding of the school's function and standardized testing may become a thing of the past." As technology comes to the forefront of instruction, it should be integrated in partnership with all school stakeholders involved. According to Panelist #1, school budgets will shift from purchasing only textbooks to technology and software and teachers' roles will change, requiring credentials for virtual learning for both teachers and administrators. Accessibility to instruction and technology requires monitoring outcomes and accountability in the use of technology and achievement to identify gaps along all socio-economic levels (Puckett & Rafalow, 2020).

2.2 Accountability of Principals, Teachers, & Students during Covid-19

Domaleski (2020) stated accountability during COVID-19 specifically 2020 is entirely offline; the U.S. Department of Education issued waivers to all 50 states and provided an opportunity to explore significant improvement to accountability. Districts, schools, and teachers created new and innovative ways to ensure academic success for all students. According to Panelist #6, students have to learn therefore, teachers must be held accountable to teach and facilitate instruction. While Panelist #2 believed that without evaluations teachers assumed they received a free pass; however, teachers still needed to provide documentation of their communication with parents, students, while demonstrating the delivery of instruction.

According to Panelist #1, to support continuous student learning, school and district leaders should be held accountable for meeting the needs of all students by creating a contingency plan that provides computer hubs for the community. Panelist #2 stated, "school districts have a responsibility to ensure students' needs are met because they receive grants, established corporate partnerships, and local funding." Panelist #3 stated, "…teachers were given the authority not just to teach the script but engaging parents to work together to ensure students' success beyond standardized testing." Audience members in the backchannels commented that communication was key to understanding how accountability related to students receiving quality instruction. One audience member stated, "Schools established purposeful relationships with parents by communicating expectations and focused on what students were learning and not the time it took them to learn." Students were responsible for their attendance in whatever format instruction was delivered, while being actively engaged in the instructional activities designed and created by their teachers.

All stakeholders, districts, principals, teachers, students, and parents are responsible and are accountable for our evolving and increasingly digital communication in spite of COVID-19. Panelist #3 stated, "Schools are institutions in which society replicates itself and are changing how education and instruction occurs as a means to address (highlighted) COVID issues." According to Panelist #6, "as education shifts, the role of teachers and students shifts to include virtual learning credentials and tailoring the education to the student; preparing students to meet the demands of the 22nd Century."

2.3 School Leadership during the Covid-19 Crisis

Leadership researcher Paul Hersey (Schermerhorn, 1997) stated, "Successful leaders are those who can adapt their behavior to meet the demands of their own unique situation." Hersey went on to describe situational leadership as the interaction between the directions given by the leader, the amount of socio-emotional support the leader provides, and the preparedness of those charged with executing the task. The early months of the COVID-19 pandemic found school leaders challenged by a myriad of questions surrounding school safety, instructional delivery methods, technology resources, and professional development for teachers just to name a few. In order to address these challenges our panelists were presented with a series of questions developed to share experiences and insight about how to remain effective as a school leader during COVID-19.

Throughout this school leadership segment of the forum there was a major theme that emerged from participants' responses in support of communication as a critical aspect of the school leader's behaviors. One of the questions presented in this segment of the forum was, "How do administrators and teachers plan for the delivery of instruction for the 2020-21 school year? Participants communicated that multiple scenarios and plans were needed, while school leaders engaged all stakeholder groups. Panelist #4 suggested a town hall style meeting where plans and procedures were shared and stakeholders have the opportunity to give input and ask questions. Panelist #4 then emphasized, "All stakeholders in the school are (should be) involved in the decision making." Another question asked in this segment of the forum was, "How can we (school leaders) ensure that the messages we communicate are being received? Panelist #1 stated that, "Information and communication are key during this time (of COVID-19)." Panelist #1 shared that school leaders must establish a variety of communication channels, such as, email, text message, and social media platforms in order to disseminate information to all stakeholders, while also managing for any harmful mis-information. An additional question posed during this school leadership segment of the forum was, "How will an administrator advise teachers to compensate for the lack of in-person feedback when they may only see students' faces on a computer screen? Participant #6 expressed that communication must be ongoing and that it should be used as an accountability measure in which teachers are constantly assessing students' needs. This ongoing communication is also necessary for engaging with parents and other stakeholders.

The school leadership segment of the forum highlighted participants' perceptions of the need for effective and efficient communication skills and behaviors demonstrated by school leaders. Meaning clear directions, an awareness of student, teacher, and school needs. In addition, sufficient training to ensure the capacity of those who are expected to complete assigned tasks and standards are all-necessary for success. The relevant use of technology resources in the process of communication is also a critical component to ensure that school leaders maximize their communication efforts with all stakeholder groups.

3. METHODOLOGY

This action research endeavor is a snapshot of what has become a series of focus groups made up of educational stakeholder groups designed to combine experimental approaches with the work of educators for the purpose of advancing theory and practice (Putman & Rock, 2018). The researchers used a focus group of educators who were selected on a voluntary basis to share their perspectives on the topic of equity in education and technology during COVID-19 (Krueger, 1994). An interview protocol was developed with eight to ten questions for each of the three segments of the forum. These questions were developed to generate relevant responses and gather the perspectives of experienced educators from across the United States. The six panelist that made up the focus group were educational practitioners from a variety of states including New York, Virginia, Illinois, Alabama, and Louisiana. Follow-up questions could be asked by the other 40 plus educators who participated in the virtual forum during the five minute audience participation portion of each segment using the backchannel provided by the Zoom platform. The entire Zoom meeting was electronically recorded by the researchers and transcribed into a Word document. The transcripts were stored on electronic devices accessed by the researchers via secure passwords. The transcripts were analyzed as themes emerged and the researchers reviewed the recorded perspectives of the participants. A synthesized discussion of the themes that emerged follows in the next section.

4. DISCUSSION

What does equity in education and technology look like in schools during COVID-19? The COVID-19 pandemic illuminated inequities in education in regards to the accessibility and use of technology for marginalized students from across the United States. It was in the context of a forum that researchers and panelists explored equity in education related to accessibility of technology, accountability of stakeholder groups, and school leadership.

The forum panelists acknowledged some teachers struggled with converting from the physical face-to-face learning environment to the virtual learning environment, yet were able to be flexible and creative to provide a level of instructional rigor that enabled students to meet the established standards beyond standardized tests. The panelists emphasized that in light of the pandemic that traditional educational practices were changed by the instructional delivery methods, such as, remote, hybrid, and face-to-face. Equity in education as it relates to the accessibility of technology was found to be a major issue in some rural areas of the country such as in a variety of parishes in the state of Louisiana where broadband infrastructure was unavailable. In order to meet the demands of remote learning, the panelist agreed that school leaders needed to exhaust available resources, grants, and established partnerships to ensure that students receive high-speed internet services and technological devices including developmentally appropriate software. The expansion of the technological infrastructure across the United States would provide more equitable access to broadband services, thereby enhancing the potential for student success.

Equitable accountability for student progress during COVID-19 was the next area of focus for the virtual forum in regards to the responsibilities of principals, teachers, students, and parents. The panelists communicated that accountability needs to be the responsibility of school principals, teachers, parents, students, and community partners. While school principals were accountable for monitoring and evaluating teachers, they were equally responsible for ensuring resources were adequately distributed and utilized to support the delivery of rigorous instruction, and engaging community partners. Teachers were responsible for not only meeting students' instructional needs but their social emotional growth and parental engagement. Parental engagement was crucial to students meeting learning targets when clear expectations were communicated with parents and parents were fully trained on navigating devices, technological software, and platforms needed to support students' learning at home. Furthermore, student accountability was viewed from a task oriented lens that required students to not only attend class but be actively engaged in the learning environment in support of their learning. Students were required to have their cameras on, join breakout rooms, participate in small groups, engage in study lounges, while also completing tasks that provided teachers with the necessary assessment data. Community partners would provide available resources in support of the school's mission. The emerging theme for accountability aspect of the forum was an understanding that stakeholder groups are all in the learning process together and continuous communication is the foundation necessary to support academic achievement, as well as, meeting social and emotional needs.

The forum panelists emphasized the critical importance of effective and efficient communication by school leaders, which will support the improvement of equity in school communities. Many school leaders struggled with leading and managing their schools because of the uncertainties surrounding COVID-19; however, greater equity in education could be realized by broadening the information sharing processes utilized within school communities. The ability of school leaders to articulate a clear direction for their school improvement plans with detail, while actively listening to and considering the needs of their students, teachers, and other stakeholders will go a long way in increasing the perceptions of equity. It would be advantageous for school leaders to create, develop, and keep an updated effective and efficient communication plan that is well known throughout the school community by all stakeholder groups.

5. CONCLUSION

Educators across the United States of America will agree that equity in education is the order of the day for our current system of education. It is the responsibility of all stakeholders to ensure students are provided instruction that meets their needs and that parents, teachers, students, and school leaders are actively engaged partners in the education process. The forum highlighted that a shift in education to ensure equity begins with communication, resources, authentic teaching, and moving beyond standardized testing. Equity in education during COVID-19, requires that all students, teachers, parents, and school leaders have access to relevant technology and are held accountable for the academic progress of all students. School leaders must become master communicators as they lead schools, teachers, and academic achievement efforts. Through established communicative relationships between and among principals, teachers, parents, students, and other stakeholder groups, equity in education will be at the forefront of increased academic achievement for all students. The COVID-19 pandemic highlighted inequities in education that has prompted educational stakeholders to begin to reimagine an improved educational system in the United States.

ACKNOWLEDGEMENT

We would like to acknowledge the Southeastern Louisiana University EDL 702 graduate students, Dr. Helen Stiff-Williams professor at Regent University, Virginia Beach, Virginia, Dr. Mary Fasbender retired superintendent of Cedar Rapids , Iowa, Dr. Nan Adams professor at Southeastern Louisiana University, Hammond, Louisiana, Dr. Takashi Crum teacher at New York City Department of Education, New York, New York, Dr. Toussaint Williams educator in Huntsville, Alabama, and Dr. Travis Ford principal Amite High School in Amite, Louisiana. You all's time and commitment to promoting equity in education across our great country is both admirable and greatly appreciated. Thank you!

REFERENCES

Brown v. Board of Education, 347 U.S. 483 (1954). https://www.loc.gov/item/usrep347483/

Domaleski, C. (2020). "The Impact of COVID-19 on ESSA." Centerline (49), April 7, 2020, https://www.nciea.org/blog/essa/outlook-essa-school-accountability-after-covid-19

Krueger, R.A. (1994). Focus Groups: A practical guide for applied research. Thousand Oaks, CA: Sage Publications.

Pew Research Center (2021). As schools close due to the coronavirus, some U.S. students face a digital homework gap'. https://www.pewresearch.org/fact-tank/2020/03/16/

Plessy v. Ferguson, 163 U.S. 537 (1896). https://www.loc.gov/item/usrep163537/

Puckett, C. & Rafalow, M. (2020). COVID-19, Technology, and Implications of Educational Equity. *American Sociological Association, 48*(3). www.asanet.org

Putman, S.M. & Rock, T. (2018). Action Research: Using strategic inquiry to improve teaching and learning. Thousands Oaks, CA: Sage Publications.

Schermerhorn, J. R. (1997). Situational Leadership: Conversations with Paul Hersey. *Mid-American Journal of Business*, Vol. 12, No. 2

U.S. Department of Education, Every Student Succeeds Act (2015), (https://www.ed.gov/essa?src=policy)

Gap in pagination due to formatting issues.

Pages 365-366

ENHANCING EXECUTIVE FUNCTIONS IN PRESCHOOLERS: TECHNOLOGIES YES OR NOT?

Sabrina Panesi and Lucia Ferlino
Institute for Educational Technology of the CNR, Via de Marini, 6, Genoa, Italy

ABSTRACT

Training to improve executive functions in pre-schoolers is a hot topic since it's very important to enhance these cognitive abilities starting from a young age. Executive functions are associated with and predictive of other cognitive and social components. In literature, several researches support the idea that training with technological tools can provide more benefits, while others underline the importance of training with analogue materials. This paper highlights strengths and weaknesses of these two approaches and stimulates reflection on further research.

KEYWORDS

Executive Functions, Cognitive Training, Preschoolers, Educational Technologies

1. INTRODUCTION

Executive Functions (EFs) is an umbrella term that refers to a family of adaptive, goal-directed, top-down mental processes that are activated to focus and pay attention in those cases where an automatic response would be insufficient (e.g., Burgess & Simons, 2005). In adults, Miyake and colleagues (2000; 2012) argued that EFs is composed of partially dissociable components that share an underlying process. They focused on three core EFs components: *inhibition,* the ability to suppress task-irrelevant cognitive processing and ignore salient yet irrelevant features of the situation (Miyake et al., 2000), *shifting*, the ability to switch between different operations or levels of processing (Miyake et al., 2000), and *updating*, the ability to encode, hold and monitor incoming information in working memory replacing information that is no longer relevant with new information (Panesi & Morra, 2017). Furthermore, Miyake and colleagues (2000; 2012) suggested the possibility that all EFs rely to some extent on *working memory* (WM), i.e. the simultaneous maintenance and manipulation of information. Actually, if on the one hand there is an agreement about the structure of EFs in adults, on the other hand the structure of EFs and their development is widely debated in developmental research, in particular referring to pre-schoolers (Garon, Bryson, & Smith, 2008; Morra, Panesi, Traverso, & Usai, 2018; Panesi & Morra, 2020). Recent studies involving pre-schoolers with typical and atypical development found that EFs were associated with other cognitive abilities, such as representational systems (Panesi & Morra, 2018), and predictive of future academic outcomes (Allan & Lonigan, 2011), social cognition (Denham, Bassett, Zinsser, Wyatt et al., 2014), and self-regulation (Sokol, Muller, 2007). It is therefore fundamental to promote EFs with specific training, starting from a young age. For this reason, in literature, there is an increasing interest in investigating the effect of training to promote EFs in pre-schoolers, but while several researches claim that training with technologies can provide more benefits, others are in favour of training with analogue playful materials. The present paper has the aim to stimulate a reflection about these two lines of thought highlighting strengths and weaknesses of both (Figure 1).

2. ENHANCING EFs WITH TECHNOLOGIES IN PRESCHOOLERS

In the digital era, technologies are very motivating and familiar to digital natives, so they can represent a "powerful" tool to involve young children. In the context of cognitive training, the mostly used technological tools to enhance EFs in pre-schoolers are software (e.g., Thorrell et al., 2009), apps (e.g. Panesi, Freina

& Ferlino, 2020), and educational robotics (e.g. Di Lieto et al., 2020). Initially, technological tools, in particular software, were used to enhance EFs in a clinical context, to promote cognitive abilities in children with some deficit in EFs, and these interventions involved one child at a time, usually with a specific computer software. Recent research highlighted the importance to improve EFs in all children, also those with typical development, starting from preschool years and several approaches to training EFs in the educational context have been developed. Among these, some are based on the use of technologies, such as educational robotics (Di Lieto et al., 2020) or apps (Panesi, Ferlino & Podestà, 2020), with little groups of children with typical and atypical development, within the school environment. Interventions based on digital apps have the double advantage of allowing task difficulty to automatically adapt to the child's performance and permitting to focus on the specific EFs components. On the other hand, such applications are, for the most part, self-contained training applications: they are seldom generalizable to daily life activities and are resource consuming, involving individual exercises and extensive teacher training to be correctly deployed (e.g. Thorrell et al., 2009).

3. ENHANCING EFs WITHOUT TECHNOLOGIES IN PRESCHOOLERS

Training programs without technologies are based on low-cost paper-and-pencil activities and are more widespread in the educational context (e.g., Traverso et al., 2015). Unlike training with technologies, these are more generalizable and ecological to daily life activities. On the other hand, they also present some weaknesses. First, with these kind of training, the customization of activities is difficult, when not impossible. Furthermore, it is more difficult to focus on the specific EFs components. Finally, they are not in line with the pervasive drive for digitally-based school innovations.

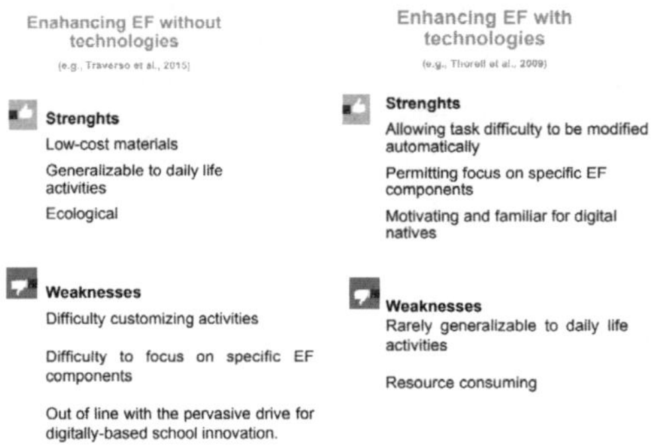

Figure 1. Training with and without technologies to enhance EFs: strengths and weaknesses

4. COMBINING TRAINING WITH AND WITHOUT TECHNOLOGIES

Integrating digital approaches with more traditional, low-tech activities could bring added advantages to foster the development of EFs in pre-schoolers. In literature, Röthlisberger and colleagues (2012) proposed mixed individual and group training based on different types of activities and games. Their intervention focused on the basic components of EFs and represents a good tradeoff between individualized computer-based interventions and large-group curricular interventions. In line with Röthlisberger and colleagues (2012), Panesi, Ferlino & Podestà (2019) present a training intervention designed to promote EFs in preschoolers with typical and atypical development within the educational context. The intervention combines the use of technology (through specific apps) along with analogical materials. These studies open to a new field of research and provide practical implications in both educational and clinical contexts, allowing teachers and clinicians to offer children both individualized and collective activities by exploiting the potential of interventions with analog and digital tools.

5. CONCLUSION

In sum, according to the literature analysis, both types of training have some strengths and some weaknesses. Therefore, in our opinion, further research is needed, aiming at the integration of digital approaches with the more traditional, low-tech activities, oriented to the definition of specific training paths, tailored to each child, taking into account their environment with the aim of fostering EFs in young digital natives.

ACKNOWLEDGEMENT

We would like to thank Laura Freina for reviewing the English of the manuscript.

REFERENCES

Allan, N., Lonigan, C., 2014. Exploring dimensionality of effortful control using hot and cool tasks in a sample of preschool children. *Journal of Experimental Child Psychology,* Vol. 122, pp. 33–47.

Denham, S.A., Bassett, H.H., Zinsser, K., Wyatt, T.M., 2014. How preschoolers' social–emotional learning predicts their early school success: Developing theory promoting, competency based assessments. *Infant and Child Development,* Vol 23, no. 4, pp. 426-454.

Di Lieto, M. C., Castro, E., Pecini, C., Inguaggiato, E., Cecchi, F., Dario, P., Cioni, G., Sgandurra, G., 2020. Improving Executive Functions at School in Children With Special Needs by Educational Robotics. *Frontiers in psychology*, 10, 2813.

Garon, N., Bryson, S. E., & Smith, I. M., 2008. Executive function in preschoolers: A review using an integrative framework. *Psychological Bulletin*, Vol. 134, No.1, pp. 31–60.

Miyake, A., & Friedman, N. P., 2012. The nature and organization of individual differences in executive functions: four general conclusions. *Current Directions in Psychological Science*, Vol.21, No.1, pp. 8-14.

Miyake, A., Friedman, N. P., Emerson, M.J., Witzki, A.H., Howerter A., Wager, T.D., 2000. The unity and diversity of executive functions and their contributions to complex "Frontal Lobe" tasks: a latent variable analysis. *Cognitive Psychology*, Vol.41, No. 1, pp. 49-100.

Morra, S., Panesi, S., Traverso, L., Usai, M. C., 2018. Which tasks measure what? Reflections on executive function development and a commentary on Podjarny, Kamawar, and Andrews (2017). *Journal of Experimental Child Psychology*. Vol. 167, pp. 246–258.

Panesi, S., Ferlino, L., Podestà, M., 2020. Apps and collective playful activities to foster executive functions in preschoolers following an inclusive approach: a case study. *Proceedings of EDULEARN20 12th annual International Conference on Education and New Learning Technologies.*

Panesi, S., Freina, L., Ferlino, L., 2020. A Kit of apps to improve and assess executive functions and working memory capacity in preschoolers. *17th International Conference on Cognition and Exploratory Learning in Digital Age (CELDA 2020)*, pp. 331-334

Panesi, S., Morra, S., 2017. La casetta magica. Uno strumento per indagare l'aggiornamento (updating) della memoria di lavoro in età prescolare [The magic house. A new measure of updating for preschoolers]. *Psicologia Clinica dello Sviluppo*, Vol. 21, No.3, pp.443-462.

Panesi, S., Morra, S., 2018. Relationships between the early development of drawing and language: The role of executive functions and working memory. *The Open Psychology Journal*, *11*(1).

Panesi, S., Morra, S., 2020. Executive functions and mental attentional capacity in preschoolers. *Journal of Cognition and Development*, Vol.21, No.1, pp. 72-91.

Röthlisberger, M. Neuenschwander, R. Cimeli, P. Michel, E., Roebers, C.M. (2012).Improving executive functions in 5-and 6-year-olds: Evaluation of a small group intervention in prekindergarten and kindergarten children. *Infant and Child Development*, Vol. 21, no.4, pp. 411-429

Sokol, B.W., Müller, U. 2007. The development of self-regulation: Toward the integration of cognition and emotion [Editorial]. *Cognitive Development*, Vol. 22, no. 4, pp. 401–405.

Thorell, L.B., Lindqvist, S. Bergman Nutley, S., Bohlin, G., & Klingberg, T., 2009. Training and transfer effects of executive functions in preschool children. *Developmental science*, Vol. 12, No.1, pp.106-113.

Traverso, L., Viterbori, P., & Usai, M. C., 2015. Improving executive function in childhood: evaluation of a training intervention for 5-year-old children. Frontiers in psychology, 6, 525.

SCHOOL EDUCATION IN A VIRTUAL SPACE: BETWEEN DAMAGE CONTROL, SCHOOL DEVELOPMENT AND INNOVATION

Annika Wilmers[1] and Bettina Waffner[2]
[1]Leibniz Institute for Research and Information in Education
Rostocker Str. 6, 60323 Frankfurt am Main, Germany
[2]University of Duisburg-Essen, Chair of Educational Technology and Knowledge Management
Universitätsstr. 2, 45117 Essen, Germany

ABSTRACT

This contribution presents current findings on the conditions of success and challenges to school-related learning with digital media. A particular focus is placed on teachers and school leaders, because these two groups take a key position in shaping education in a digital world. While we focus on examples taken from the German school context, we are nevertheless able to compare them with international research findings and to analyze similarities as well as disparities between different education systems.

KEYWORDS

Critical Review, School Development, Digitalization, Educational Technology

1. BODY OF PAPER

The Covid-19 pandemic has led to school closures in nearly all countries worldwide (Gouëdard, Pont, Viennet, 2020). Digital media have replaced classic school settings, to enable remote teaching as quickly as possible in this exceptional situation. This emergency remote teaching, however, distorts the perspective on potentials and tension fields of integrating digital media into teaching practice. The pandemic-related handling of digitizing in school education has thus entailed a risen awareness of potentials of virtual ways of contacting, providing learning resources, and submitting tasks. At the same time, this will not lead to an orientation and societal agreement on what schools might look like in a post-pandemic digital world. The characteristic feature will probably not be to expand distance learning. Rather, the understanding of education will change in a world that is permeated by digital technology and our actions are closely linked to digital technology. Education in the digital world will be less about mastering technology. It also points beyond the present to a future in which technology is not to be understood as a tool but rather as a (co-)actor (Kerres, 2021).

Against this background media integration can serve as a catalyst for school development (Sipilä, 2014) and it can mean long-term change reaching far beyond the current global crisis. For example, shifting learning to individual learning environments can also be discussed in terms of a chance for individual learning concepts (Burow, 2018; Zhao, 2020). The current debate in Germany rather focuses on existing deficits of digitizing and an acerbation of existing inequalities in education. Since the outbreak of the pandemic, respective political measures have thus targeted a removal of present deficiencies, such as is illustrated by an agreement on the loan of electronic devices to teachers (BMBF, 2021). At the school level, inequalities relate to differences in learning support due to technical and administrative conditions, teacher competencies and the existing degree of integration of digital media into the learning context (e.g. Bremm & Racherbäumer, 2021; LIfBi, 2020).

Against this background, we present current findings on the conditions of success and challenges to school-related learning with digital media. We can assume that we are facing a paradigm shift. Schools will have to understand (disruptive) change as an integral part of school development and create various possible solutions in the change process, resulting in multiple future scenarios (Rolff & Thünken, 2020). A particular focus is placed on teachers and school leaders, because these two groups take a key position in shaping education in a digital world.

The analysis is based on results from the project "Digitizing in education" (Digi-EBF) by the Federal Ministry of Education and Research. Subject to a series of reviews, the state of research on relevant actors as well as organizational and socio-political structures of the education system is assessed and analyzed together with content contexts of hybrid learning arrangements for five educational sectors. Methodologically, the project links up to critical review procedures. Critical reviews typically focus on identifying conceptual components of the included literature and often contribute to either existing models in the field or support the development of new models (Grant & Booth, 2009; Booth, Sutton & Papaioannou, 2016). The research synthesis enables an outline and discussion of current developments as well as identification of research needs and future directions. The following findings are based on two such critical reviews focusing on the school sector, for which a systematic and comprehensive literature search was conducted in selected German and international databases that were identified as highly relevant for digitization in education nationally and internationally such as FIS Bildung (largest German database for education research), ERIC, Web of Science - Social Citation Index, ERC and LearnTechLib. A total of 4936 studies was screened in a multistep process. As a result from the coding process 125 (from the years 2010-2019, review 1) respectively 56 (2016-2020, review 2) studies published in German and English were selected for an analysis and research synthesis (for a description of the method and lists of all included studies, see Wilmers, Anda, Keller & Rittberger, 2020 and Wilmers, Achenbach, Keller, 2021 in print).

When introducing digital media to teaching practice, this can be done in different ways. The scope ranges from use as a medium of presentation and substitute of classical analogue media, to support and modernize traditional lesson formats, and pedagogical instructional innovations that lead to more self-governed types of learning and knowledge acquisition due to cooperative learning. In this case, learning at school will change and pay tribute to an increasingly digitized, global world.

A focus of current research lies in the question which factors benefit an implementation of digital media in instructional practice. In this regard, little attention has so far been paid to the teachers' use of digital media and whether by the integration of such media, implications are evident for instructional formats and pedagogical practice. There is empirical evidence that digital media are already well established in the teachers' professional lives, as communication and presentation tools. However, this is rarely guided by (media)pedagogical goals, and digital media are rather regarded as tools than being an integral part of learning. This corresponds with the finding that most teachers take a rather positive stance regarding computers and smartboards. On the other hand, they are skeptical regarding the Worldwide Web or social networks, such as Twitter and Facebook as instruments reaching beyond the classroom. This seems to explain why moderate to sound technical-instrumental user competencies of teachers do exist, while a development and implementation of digitally based didactic pedagogical lesson formats is comparatively rare. These findings have far-reaching implications for school development in the digital world. They show that the digitalisation push by the Covid-19 pandemic (Kleinert, Bächmann, Schulz, Vicari & Ehlert, 2021) does not automatically lead to media integration that adapts teaching practices to the digital world. In order to create schools in the digital world, it is necessary to deal with pedagogical-didactic possibilities of using digital media in the classroom, further training for teachers, suitable technical equipment and leadership.

If and how digital media are used in instructional practice is highly dependent on individual teachers. In this regard, it is especially important to assess competencies and competence acquisition in terms of initial and further training. A focus on so-called "new digital competencies" that immediately emerge from handling technical devices disregards the fact that "digitizing permeates traditional teaching practice" (Kerres, 2020, p. 8). With respect to current research findings, we can thus observe a need for a shift from a technical to a pedagogical focus in the discussion of competencies. At the same time, the discussion remains at the point of identifying additional competencies that go beyond those of a subject and its instructional design.

In summary, five synthesis statements are identifiable: (1) the Digital is well established in professional teaching practice, in terms of communication and presentation tools. 2) Digitally based pedagogical instructional formats are rarely used. A successful integration of media requires teachers to have (3) personal traits such as an extrovert, intrinsically motivated personality, time resources, suitable technical equipment and administrative support. Teachers moreover need (4) methodological and technical, but also pedagogical-didactic competencies for media use in instructional practice as well as competencies to use the enhanced possibilities of communication and collaboration. The current research debate has discussed

(5) situated digitally supported long-term trainings on media technical foundations, accompanied by phases of reflection and coaching and an exchange among peers.

The mere availability of media does not present a sufficient condition of media integration into instructional practice. An improvement of teaching and learning practices can only be expected if besides technical and pedagogical-didactic support systems for teachers, teacher professionalization and a change of roles, the need is also recognized to adapt organizational procedures. These processes need to be interlinked and strategically located in a school development process that requires leadership. In this regard, a central position is assigned to school principals. They can initiate and govern school developmental processes and changes. Via their professional identity, they contribute to a vision how schools should be shaped in a digital world. They act within a system of different aspects such as school development, actors and conditions and they co-ordinate a complex interplay of top-down and bottom-up processes.

We can summarize that the rapid process of digital transformation requires a change of narrative linked to the school as a system. This is about understanding change and transformation as an integral part of school. Since educational reform at the beginning of the 19th Century that is linked to Wilhelm von Humboldt, the school system has been characterized by a high degree of stability. In the context of digitizing, change and transformation need to be shaped in a participative way and strategically implemented - and this needs to be integrated into school culture as a criterion of quality.

REFERENCES

Booth, A., Sutton, A. & Papaioannou, D., 2016. *Systematic Approaches to a Successful Literature Review*. SAGE, Los Angeles.

Bundesministerium für Bildung und Forschung (BMBF), 2021. *Zusatz-Verwaltungsvereinbarung „Leihgeräte für Lehrkräfte" zum Digitalpakt Schule 2019 bis 2024* vom 27. Januar 2021, Bundesanzeiger vom 18.02.2021. https://www.bmbf.de/foerderungen/bekanntmachung-3388.html

Burow, O., 2018. *Schulleitung in Zeiten von Globalisierung und Digitalisierung*. In Schule 2030plus. Back to the future - Gestalten Sie die Zukunft Ihrer Schule. Sonderausgabe für Carl-Link-Abonnenten.Carl Link, Kronach, pp. 71–83.

Gouëdard, P., Pont, B. & Viennet, R., 2020. *Education responses to Covid-19: Implementing a way forward*. OECD Working Paper No. 224. https://doi.org/10.1787/19939019.

Grant, M.J. & Booth, A., 2009. *A typology of reviews*. Health information and libraries journal, 26 (2), pp. 91–108. https://doi.org/10.1111/j.1471-1842.2009.00848.x

Kerres, M., 2020. *Bildung in der digitalen Welt: Über Wirkungsannahmen und die soziale Konstruktion des Digitalen*. MedienPädagogik. [preprint]. https://www.medienpaed.com/. https://doi.org/10.21240/mpaed/jb17/2020.04.24.X

Kerres, M. 2021. *Didaktik. Lernangebote gestalten*. Waxmann. Münster/New York (in press).

Kleinert, C., Bächmann, A.-C., Schulz, B., Vicari, B. & Ehlert, M., 2021. *Für wen brachte Corona einen Digitalisierungsschub? Veränderungen in der Nutzung digitaler Technologien während der COVID-19-Pandemie*. NEPS Corona & Bildung. Aktuelle Auswertungen des Nationalen Bildungspanels. Bericht Nr. 6. pp. 1-6. https://www.lifbi.de/Portals/13/Corona/NEPS_Corona-und-Bildung_Bericht_6-Digitalisierung.pdf?ver=yjR73zOPp4QhA6Q4U8eAvg%3d%3d

Leibniz-Institut für Bildungsverläufe (LIfBi)., 2020. *Corona-bedingte Schulschließungen - Und nun funktioniert alles digital…?* NEPS Corona & Bildung | Bericht Nr. 1, pp. 1–7. https://www.lifbi.de/Portals/13/Corona/NEPS_Corona-und-Bildung_Bericht_1-Schule.pdf.

Rolff, H.-G. & Thünken, U., 2020. *Digital gestütztes Lernen. Praxisbeispiele für eine zeitgemäße Schulentwicklung.*, Beltz, Weinheim.

Sipilä, K., 2014. *Educational Use of Information and Communications Technology: Teachers' Perspective. Technology, Pedagogy and Education*, 23(2), pp. 225–241. https://doi.org/10.1080/1475939X.2013.813407.

Wilmers, A., Anda, C., Keller, C. & Rittberger, M. (eds.)., 2020. *Bildung im digitalen Wandel. Die Bedeutung für das pädagogische Personal und für die Aus- und Fortbildung*. Waxmann Verlag, Münster. https://doi.org/10.31244/978383099199

Wilmers, A., Achenbach, M. & Keller, C. (eds)., 2021, in press. *Bildung im digitalen Wandel: Organisationsentwicklung in Bildungseinrichtungen*. Waxmann Verlag, Münster.

Zhao, Y., 2020. *COVID-19 as a catalyst for educational change*. Prospects, 49, pp. 29–33. https://doi.org./10.1007/s1125-020-09477-y

AUTHOR INDEX

International Association for Development of the Information Society (IADIS)
Rua Sao Sebastiao Da Pedreira
No. 100, 30, 1050-209
Lisbon, Portugal

ISBN 978-1-7138-3939-2

9 781713 839392

CURRAN ASSOCIATES INC.
proceedings.com

NAACL-HLT 2007/AMTA Workshop on Syntax and Structure in Statistical Translation

(SSST)

Held at NAACL-HLT 2007

Rochester, New York, USA
26 April 2007

ISBN: 978-1-61738-515-5